Lecture Notes in Computer Science 4494

Commenced Publication in 1973
Founding and Former Series Editors:
Gerhard Goos, Juris Hartmanis, and Jan van Leeuwen

Hai Jin   Omer F. Rana   Yi Pan
Viktor K. Prasanna (Eds.)

Algorithms
and Architectures
for Parallel Processing

7th International Conference, ICA3PP 2007
Hangzhou, China, June 11-14, 2007
Proceedings

 Springer

Volume Editors

Hai Jin
Huazhong University of Science and Technology
School of Computer Science and Technology, Wuhan, 430074, China
E-mail: hjin@hust.edu.cn

Omer F. Rana
Cardiff University
School of Computer eScience and Welsh Science Center
5 The Parade, Cardiff CF24 3AA, UK
E-mail: o.f.rana@cs.cardiff.ac.uk

Yi Pan
Georgia State University
Computer Science Department
34 Peachtree Street, Suite 1450, Atlanta, GA 30302-4110, USA
E-mail: pan@cs.gsu.edu

Viktor K. Prasanna
University of Southern California
Ming Hsieh Department of Electrical Engineering
Los Angeles, CA 90089-2562, USA
E-mail: prasanna@usc.edu

Library of Congress Control Number: Applied for

CR Subject Classification (1998): D, F.1-3, C, I.6

LNCS Sublibrary: SL 1 – Theoretical Computer Science and General Issues

ISSN   0302-9743
ISBN-10   3-540-72904-6 Springer Berlin Heidelberg New York
ISBN-13   978-3-540-72904-4 Springer Berlin Heidelberg New York

Springer is a part of Springer Science+Business Media

springer.com

© Springer-Verlag Berlin Heidelberg 2007
Printed in Germany

Typesetting: Camera-ready by author, data conversion by Scientific Publishing Services, Chennai, India
Printed on acid-free paper   SPIN: 12072903   06/3180   5 4 3 2 1 0

Preface

Parallel and distributed computing in the 1980s and 1990s had great influence on application development in science, engineering and business computing. The improvements in computation and communication capabilities have enabled the creation of demanding applications in critical domains such as the environment, health, aerospace, and other areas of science and technology. Similarly, new classes of applications are enabled by the availability of heterogeneous large-scale distributed systems which are becoming available nowadays (based on technologies such as grid and peer-to-peer systems). Parallel computing systems exploit a large diversity of computer architectures, from supercomputers, shared-memory or distributed-memory multi processors, to local networks and clusters of personal computers.

With the recent emergence of multi core architectures, parallel computing is now set to achieve "mainstream" status. Approaches that have been advocated by parallel computing researchers in the past are now being utilized in a number of software libraries and hardware systems that are available for everyday use. Parallel computing ideas have also come to dominate areas such as multi user gaming (especially in the development of gaming engines based on "cell" architectures) – often ignored by many "serious" researchers in the past, but which now are set to have a growing user base of tens of millions across the world. In recent years, focus has also shifted to support energy efficiency in computation, with some researchers proposing a new metric of performance based on Flops/Watt.

Another topic that has gained significant importance is work within distributed and wireless sensor networks – which provide the capability of data capture, along with actuation support in some instances. Grid computing has dominated much work being undertaken within parallel and distributed systems in recent years. The ability to group regional and national-scale resources to create computational infrastructure for grand-challenge problems has now been demonstrated effectively in Europe, the United States and in China. Grid computing research continues to play an active part in bringing together computational science and parallel computing communities.

ICA3PP is a premier conference series that brings together researchers and practitioners from academia, industry and governments around the world to advance the theories and technologies of parallel and distributed computing. Previous ICA3PP conferences have been successfully organized in Brisbane (1995), Singapore (1996), Melbourne (1997, 2005), Hong Kong (2000), and Beijing (2002).

ICA3PP 2007 featured a number of papers that address these themes, and selected papers for the conference also provide an insight into many emerging themes that have become important in parallel and distributed systems laboratories and groups around the world over recent years.

ICA3PP 2007 was hosted in one of the most beautiful cities in the world, in Hangzhou – the capital of Zhejiang province in China. Hangzhou is known for its natural beauty and provides an atmosphere fostering creativity. We believe the conference in this city will encourage dialogue and interaction between world leaders in parallel and high-performance computing, and encourage greater collaboration between the researchers who attended the conference.

In total, the conference received 176 papers from researchers and practitioners from 9 countries. Each paper was reviewed by at least three internationally renowned referees, and selection was based on originality, significance, correctness, relevance, and clarity of presentation. Some of the papers were subsequently further reviewed by the Program Chairs to assess quality and relevance. From the submissions received, 40 papers were selected. All of the selected papers are included in the proceedings. To encourage and promote the work presented at ICA3PP 2007, we are delighted to inform the authors that some of the papers will be accepted in special issues of *Parallel Computing, Computer Communication, Journal of Supercomputing, and IJHPCN.* All of these journals have played a prominent role in promoting the development and use of parallel and high-performance computing and networking.

We are also delighted to have been able to host well-known international scholars, Reiner Hartenstein from the Computer Science Department, Kaiserslautern University of Technology, Germany, and Hai Zhuge from the Institute of Computing Technology, Chinese Academic of Science, China, who delivered the keynote speeches.

We would like to take this opportunity to thank all the authors for their submissions to the conference. Many of them traveled a considerable distance to participate in the conference. We also thank the Program Committee members and additional reviewers for their efforts in reviewing the large number of papers. Thanks also go to the local conference organizers for their great support.

Last but not least, we would like to express our gratitude to all of the organizations that supported our efforts to bring the conference to fruition. We are grateful to Springer for publishing the proceedings this year. Special thanks go to Wanlei Zhou (from Deakin University, Australia) and Yi Pan (Georgia State University, USA). Their guidance, hard work and support made ICA3PP 2007 possible. We are also grateful to Michael Hobbs (Deakin University), who served as Co-chair in 2005 and provided support for this event.

March 2007   Hai Jin
                                                                              Omer Rana

Organization

The ICA3PP 07 conference was organized by the Cluster and Grid Computing Lab, Huazhong University of Science and Technology, and undertaken by Hangzhou Dianzi University. It was held in cooperation with *Lecture Notes in Computer Science* (LNCS) of Springer.

Executive Committee

Steering Chairs	Andrzej Goscinski, Deakin University, Australia
	Anke Xue, Hangzhou Dianzi University, China
	Wanlei Zhou, Deakin University, Australia
General Chairs	Yi Pan, Georgia State University, USA
	Viktor Prasanna, University of Southern California, USA
Program Chairs	Hai Jin, Huazhong University of Science and Technology, China
	Omer F. Rana, Cardiff University, UK
Local Organizing Chair	Jian Wan, Hangzhou Dianzi University, China

Program Committee

Jemal H. Abawajy	Deakin University, Australia
Joseph Arul	Fu Jen Catholic University, Taiwan
Mark Baker	University of Portsmouth, UK
Amol Bakshi	University of Southern California, USA
Amnon Barak	Hebrew University, Israel
Maarten Boasson	University of Amsterdam, The Netherlands
Arndt Bode	Technical University of Munich, Germany
Rajkumar Buyya	University of Melbourne, Australia
Jiannong Cao	Hong Kong Polytechnic University, Hong Kong
Jianer Chen	Texas A&M University, USA
Francis YL Chin	University of Hong Kong, Hong Kong
Toni Cortes	Universitat Politecnica de Catalunya, Spain
Jose Cunha	New University of Lisbon, Portugal
Robert Dew	Deakin University, Australia
Jack Dongarra	University of Tennessee, USA
Ding-zhu Du	University of Minnesota, USA
Michael John Hobbs	Deakin University, Australia
Bo Hong	Drexel University, USA
Shi-Jinn Horng	National Taiwan University of Science and Technology, Taiwan

Ali Hurson	Pennsylvania State University, USA
Ching-Hsien Hsu	Chung Hua University, Taiwan
Weijia Jia	City University of Hong Kong, Hong Kong
Xiaohua Jia	City University of Hong Kong, Hong Kong
Hong Jiang	University of Nebraska-Lincoln, USA
Peter Kacsuk	MTA SZTAKI Research Institute, Hungary
Krishna Kavi	The University of North Texas, USA
Zvi M. Kedem	New York University, USA
Wayne Kelly	Queensland University of Technology, Australia
Jacek Kitowski	AGH University of Science and Technology, Poland
Laurent Lefevre	INRIA, France
Keqin Li	State University of New York, USA
Kuan-Ching Li	Providence University, Taiwan
Yunhao Liu	Hong Kong University of Science and Technology, Hong Kong
Thomas Ludwig	University of Heidelberg, Germany
Dan Meng	Institute of Computing Technology, CAS, China
Teo Yong Meng	National University of Singapore, Singapore
Edgar Nett	University of Magdeburg, Germany
Jun Ni	University of Iowa, USA
George A. Papadopoulos	University of Cyprus, CYPRUS
Marcin Paprzycki	SWPS and IBS PAN, Poland
Weizhong Qiang	Huazhong University of Science and Technology, China
Rajeev Raje	Indiana University Purdue University at Indianapolis, USA
Michel Raynal	IRISA-IFSIC, France
Justin Rough	Deakin University, Australia
Srinivas Sampalli	Dalhousie University, Canada
Edwin H-M. Sha	University of Texas at Dallas, USA
Jackie Silcock	Deakin University, Australia
Chengzheng Sun	Nanyang Technological University, Singapore
Liansheng Tan	Central China Normal University, China
David Taniar	Monash University, Australia
G.Z.Terstyanszky	Westminster University, UK
Putchong Uthayopas	Kasetsart University, Thailand
Cho-Li Wang	University of Hong Kong, Hong Kong
Jie Wu	Florida Atlantic University, USA
Yue Wu	University of Electronic Science and Technology, China
Cheng-Zhong Xu	Wayne State University, USA
Jingling Xue	University of New South Wales, Australia
Chao-Tung Yang	Tunghai University, Taiwan
Laurence T. Yang	St. Francis Xavier University, Canada

Table of Contents

Keynote Speech

Invited Papers

Track 1: Parallel Algorithms

Track 2: Parallel Architecture

Track 3: Grid Computing

Track 4: Peer-to-Peer Technologies

Track 5: Advanced Network Technologies

Added

RSM-Based Gossip on P2P Network*

Hai Zhuge and Xiang Li

China Knowledge Grid Research Group, Key Lab of Intelligent Information Processing
Institute of Computing Technology, Chinese Academy of Sciences, 100080, Beijing, China
zhuge@ict.ac.cn, xiangli@kg.ict.ac.cn

Abstract. Classification is a kind of basic semantics that people often use to manage versatile contents in daily life. Resource Space Model (RSM) is a semantic model for sharing and managing various resources using normalized classification semantics. Gossip-based peer-to-peer (P2P) techniques are reliable and scalable protocols for information dissemination. Incorporating RSM with gossip-based techniques forms a new decentralized resource sharing mechanism with the improved performance of unstructured P2P systems. Theoretical analysis and experiments validate the feasibility of the mechanism. Such incorporation is a way to synergy normalization and autonomy in managing decentralized large-scale complex resources.

1 Introduction

P2P systems aim at decentralization, scalability, ad-hoc connectivity, reduced cost of ownership and anonymity [1]. Unstructured P2P networks allow peers to self-organize and resources to be randomly placed. Such networks have low maintenance cost and are robust against accidental failures. Simulating the propagation of contagious diseases, gossip mechanisms have attractive scalability, reliability and degradation properties in realizing information dissemination in large networks [2]. Every node that receives a message randomly selects a certain number of nodes from its neighbors to multicast the message. They scale well since the load of nodes grows logarithmically compared with the number of nodes in the network. The performance of the gossip mechanisms can be improved in semantic space by designing appropriate mapping from the network into semantic space [12]. Ontology has been used to improve structured P2P systems [10]. Classification is a kind of basic semantics that people often use to effectively manage versatile contents in daily life.

A Resource Space Model RSM is a semantic model for effectively sharing and managing various Web resources (information, knowledge and services) based on normalized classification semantics [11]. Incorporating resource space with gossip mechanisms is a way to improve the performance of P2P network.

---

* Keynote at the 7th International Conference on Algorithms and Architectures for Parallel Processing (ICA3PP'07). This work is supported by the National Basic Research Program of China (973 Semantic Grid Project, Grant No. 2003CB317001), the International Cooperation Program of Ministry of Science and Technology of China (Grant No. 2006DFA11970), and the EU 6th Framework Program GREDIA (Grant No. IST-FP6-034363).

H. Jin et al. (Eds.): ICA3PP 2007, LNCS 4494, pp. 1–12, 2007.

2 Incorporating RSM with P2P

An *n*-dimensional Resource Space represents *n* kinds of partition on a set of resources. A Resource Space can be mapped onto a partition tree (e.g., Fig. 1(a) can be mapped onto Fig. 1(b)). The classification semantics of a partition tree can be used to improve the performance of a P2P system because a peer could get the satisfied answer with high probability by interacting more frequently with the peers of the same community sharing common interests. Peers also need to communicate with peers of other communities.

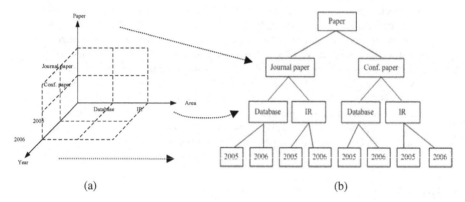

(a)   (b)

Fig. 1. (a) A 3-dimensional resource space. (b) The partition tree corresponding to Fig. 1 (a).

Each leaf corresponds to peers in the same category. The tree is a rather stable commonsense, and the whole system could use only a part of it. The communities in leaves of the partition could change with joining and departing of peers.

As shown in Fig. 2, peers can be classified into communities corresponding to the leaves of the semantic partition tree. Each peer maintains neighbors in a hierarchical structure. The number of layers of the hierarchical structure a peer maintains depends on the depth the peer lies in the partition tree. Taking a peer p in the bottom-left community of the partition tree for example, it should maintain four layers of its neighbors, denoted as View(i) where $0 \leq i \leq 3$. View(i) is a set/list containing the neighbors' information (address etc.) that shares the nearest common ancestor at ith level with p. p's View(3) maintains the information of some peers within the same community, while p's View(2) maintains the information of its neighbors having the nearest common ancestor at level 2, and so on.

When a peer sends a query, it will make a decision on which level(s) in its view should be selected to forward the query (category of the level are relevant to the query). Then, neighbor(s) at that level will be selected to forward the query. When a query reaches a community, a gossip-based mechanism will be adopted to disseminate the message. The peer that receives and could answer the query sends back the corresponding resources.

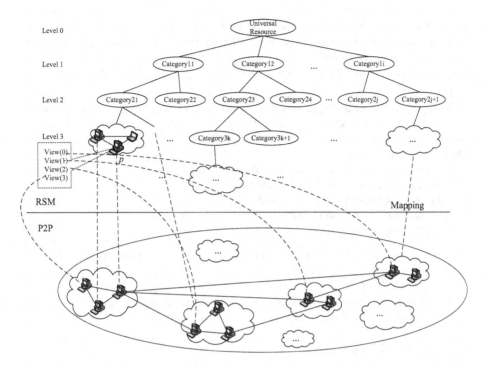

Fig. 2. Incorporating one resource space with a P2P network

3 The Construction Mechanism

It is reasonable to assume that all peers share a consistent knowledge of partition. A partition hierarchy could be known by informing the newly joined peer of the partition ontology.

The similarity between the peer and the category is measured by $\cos\theta =$ $A{\cdot}B/(\|A\|{\cdot}\|B\|)$, where A and B are term vectors of the new peer and the category respectively [3]. The category with the maximum similarity value is chosen as the category that the joined peer belongs to.

The static partition of the resource space can bring important advantage to P2P systems. When a new peer joins, it just needs to contact one peer which will feed back the partition information on the resource space. Using the partition information, the peer determines which category it belongs to. If some resource indices included in the peer belong to the other categories, the indices are reissued to other peers that are in charge of those resource categories. Using the information the first-contacted peer provided, the peer contacts the peers in the categories it belongs to and update its neighbors' information.

In the partition tree, the universe resource is assigned *Level0*. Then, the universe space is first divided into a set of categories (in Fig. 1(b), it consists of *Journal paper* and *Conf. paper*), which constitute *Level1*. The categories in *Level1* are further partitioned into categories constituting *Level2*, and so forth. Along with the peers joining the system, the leaf categories produced in the aforementioned mechanism can be further partitioned dynamically into different levels. The dynamic partition of leaves can be realized through a group size limit gl. When the size exceeds the limit, the group is partitioned into two parts with size $\lfloor gl/2 \rfloor$ and $\lceil gl/2 \rceil$ respectively.

The dynamic partition of the space works well with the skewed data distribution such as power-law distribution found in many circumstance. Meanwhile, the static characteristics of the resource space partition improve the scalability of P2P system that peers join and depart autonomously and frequently, and reduce the cost of update when peers join or depart.

The disseminated message contains the content and some assistant information: (1) the type of the message, which could be *join*, *leave*, *issuing*, or *query*; (2) time to live (*TTL*) of the message, which is used in *join*, *issuing* and *query* messages; and, (3) a list of identifiers of the peers that have received the message.

The following are definitions used for easier discussion:

(1) *fanout* — the number of neighbors one peer selects to disseminate when it receives a message;
(2) *TTL* (Time To Live) — the iterative rounds for a message to disseminate;
(3) *outView(i)* — the neighbors that peer i can send messages to; and,
(4) *inView(i)* — the neighbors that peer i can receive messages from.

3.1 Resource Issuing Process

When a resource index is issued by one peer, the peer r first decides the category the resource belongs to by utilizing the partition information of the resource space. A limit l restricting the whole steps of the process should be set. Along with each hop the message has transferred, l will be reduced by one. Then the peer forms an *issuing* message which includes the resource index, and sends the message to one of the peers in that category through its level views. When a peer receives the message, it first decides whether to add the index to its maintaining repository in consideration of its capacity. If the capacity will exceed its upper limit, then it randomly selects one neighbor from its proper level view and disseminates the *issuing* message. The issuing process will proceed until the resource index is accepted or l reaches zero. When l is zero, peer r also joins the community to manage the resources.

3.2 Peer Join Process

When one peer is going to join the system, it first connects to one of the contacted peers. With the information of the resource space fed back from the contacted peer, the newly joined peer decides its category with reference to the categories of its major resources. If there is more than one community in the category, the contacted peer randomly chooses a community. Then, the contacted peer forms a *join* message including the joining peer's information, and forwards the message to one of the peers in that community utilizing its level views.

During the process, a limit sl restricting the whole steps of dissemination should be set. Along with each hop the message transferred, sl will be reduced by one. When the peer receives the message, it first decides whether to add the peer to its view with reference to its view size. If this causes the overflow of the view size, it will forward the *join* message to one randomly selected neighbor in the community until the peer is accepted or *sl* is zero. If the joining peer is still not accepted by one peer when *sl* reaches zero, the community is regarded as full and a new community should be created in the same resource space position as the full community. The joining peer forms its level views by exchanging information with peers in the same category.

The newly joined peer maintains the index information of its major resources and issues the resource indices not belonging to its resource space position to the system adopting the aforementioned resource issuing mechanism.

To further break the existing community into approximately equal size, a simple mechanism could be adopted: peers initiate a random interaction when they have not decided which community they belong to. If the contacted peer is undecided also, the two peers make choice for different communities. Otherwise, the peer chooses the different community from the contacted peer.

3.3 Peer Departure Process

When peer r wants to depart the system, the following method is used to keep the peers in r's *inView* and those in its *outView* connected. For each peer (take peer s for example) in its *outView*, peer r selects one of the peer ID (q for example) from its *inView* randomly, then forms a *failure* message including q and forwards it to s. When s receives the message, it will substitute r's ID(r) with q in its *inView*, then forwards a message with r and q. When q receives the message, it will update r with q in its *outView*. So the withdrawal behavior of a pivot peer will not lead to the partition of the whole network.

When a peer crashes without notifying other peers, the peers can detect this situation by interchanging their states periodically [8]. After a certain period elapsed, if no response is returned from one of its neighbors, the peer deems it as being crashed and removes it from corresponding view.

If one existing community is small, it is necessary to merge communities in the same parent category: If a community p wants to hand off its index, it should find its siblings first. If the siblings of the community p are also leaves of the partition tree and the number of its siblings is one (q, for example), then simply coalesce p and q, make their direct parent a leaf, and assign community q to that leaf. In this way, the indices of p and q merge into a single index that is assigned to community q. If the number of its siblings is larger than one, then pick up one leaf that has the least load and hand off the index to the picked community.

If the siblings of the community p are not the leaves of the partition tree, perform the depth-first search in the sub-tree of the partition tree rooted at one of its siblings such as q until the leaves of the sub-tree are reached. Merge the two communities r and p into one.

3.4 Query Processing Process

When sending a query, the peer first compares the query with its index on resources, and then adopts different mechanisms to gossip queries making use of neighbor lists at different levels. In most applications, the resources a peer possesses reflect its interests, and the queries from the peer would be similar to its interests with high probability. In this situation, the query could be answered in the community the query-initiator belongs to, and only the neighbor list at the lowest level is needed for the query processing. While the query fits perfectly with other level, it will be routed to that appropriate category, and a gossip process initiates there. When the query corresponds to more than one level, then a certain number of gossip processes take place in parallel in the corresponding categories. The top-k correlative categories can be selected to make trade-off between the whole network cost and the acceptable results.

Haming distance is a suitable distance measure for multidimensional non-ordered discrete data space [7], which can be regarded as the correlative metric between query and the categories. Hamming distance $dist(a_1, a_2)$ between vectors a_1 and a_2 in an discrete data space is the number of dimensions on which the corresponding components of a_1 and a_2 are different. The distance between a vector $a=(a_1, a_2, \ldots, a_d)$ and a discrete rectangle $S=S_1*S_2*\ldots*S_d$ can be defined as:

$$dist(a, S) = \sum_{i=1}^{d} f(a_i, S_i), \text{ where } f(a_i, S_i) = \begin{cases} 0 & a_i \in S_i \\ 1 & otherwise \end{cases}.$$

4   Performance Analysis

4.1   Reliability

Suppose the number of peers in the system is n, and the resource space partitions the peers into m categories. For the purpose of simplicity, group members are assumed to be evenly distributed, that is, the sizes of categories are equal to n/m approximately. And, the assumption will be relaxed in the experiments. We use the following notations for further discussion.

(1) s—the source peer of one message;
(2) ε—the probability of message loss during the gossip process.
(3) τ—the probability of a peer crash during the gossip process.
(4) A—the event that there is a directed path from s to all peers in the category s belongs to.
(5) B—the event that there is at least one link directed from s to other categories.
(6) $P(C)$—the probability that the event C happens.

Gossip style protocols are reliable in a probabilistic sense. By adopting the analysis in [4], the probability of a given peer receiving the disseminated message will be $1-(1/n^{fanout})(1 + o(1))$. And if the message loss is considered, the probability will be $1-(1/n^{(1-\varepsilon) fanout})(1+o(1))$.

We can disseminate the message in three different mechanisms:

(1)   Using the partition tree, the original source peer could make a decision and pick up one level in its views. Thereafter one peer in the view at this level is randomly selected, and a gossip process is initiated with the selected peer being the source. In this precondition: P(every peer in the selected category will receive the message)$= P(A) \cdot P(B) = (1-(1/(n/m)^{(1-\varepsilon) fanout})(1+o(1))) \cdot (1-\varepsilon) \cdot (1-\tau)$.

Applications could make the messages communicate reliably through protocols like TCP, and in this way, ε would approach zero. In addition, n, being a large number in P2P systems, leads the protocol to be reliable.

(2) The original source peer randomly selects one peer from each of its views, and disseminates the message to them, (the number of levels will be m at most). The selected peers launch the gossip process in its group in parallel. And under the condition: P(every peer in the system will receive the message)= $P^m(A) \cdot P(B)=$ $(1-(1/(n/m)^{(1-\varepsilon)fanout})(1+o(1)))^m \cdot (1-\varepsilon) \cdot (1-\tau)$.

In the selecting process, if sending message to the selected peer is failed, another peer could be selected randomly in the view at the same level. In this way, the bad influence of m in the previous equation will be further reduced to guarantee the reliability of the mechanism.

(3) The original source peer selects peers in different level view with different probabilities. And then the selected peers will receive the message and disseminate it in their communities. Therefore, P(every peer in the selected communities will receive the message) $= P^l(A) \cdot P(B)$, where l is the number of communities being selected and $1 \leq l \leq m$. Consequently, $P^m(A) \cdot P(B) \leq P^l(A) \cdot P(B) \leq P(A) \cdot P(B)$, and the gossip process adopting the mechanism will be reliable.

4.2 Hop Count Expectation

With reference to [6], the total rounds $TTL(n, fanout)$ in the gossip-style system, necessary to infect an entire group of size n obeys: $TTL(n, fanout) = \log n \cdot (1/fanout+1/\log(fanout)) + c + o(1)$, where c is a constant. There exists a tradeoff between $fanout$ and TTL in the network of n peers. Therefore in our systems, all peers are partitioned into different categories by one resource space. Assume the sizes of categories are equal approximately, i.e., n / m, the round of message dissemination in the sub-partitions will be: $TTL(n / m, fanout)$. Considering the category selecting process, the hop count of message dissemination in the whole system will be: $TTL_1(n, fanout) = 1 + TTL(n / m, fanout) = \log(n/m) \cdot (1/fanout+1/\log(fanout)) + c_1 + o(1)$, where c_1 is a constant.

5 Experimental Evaluation

Experiments are carried out on the topologies using flat gossip mechanism and using our semantic partitioning mechanisms. The experiments are carried out on two kinds of directed networks of 1000 nodes: random networks and random power-law networks. Each experiment with different parameters ($fanout$ and TTL) is repeated 100 times on each network we generated, and the initial node is randomly selected for each time. The average value of these 100 results is used to illustrate the feasibility.

Considering the graph of n nodes where the edge between each pair of nodes is present with probability $[\log(n) + c + o(1)] / n$. In the prerequisite, the probability that the graph is connected goes to $exp(- exp(- c))$, where c is a constant. And the target could be reached by defining the appropriate $View$ sizes of nodes. For the networks constructed this way, there is a sharp threshold in the required $fanout$ at $\log (n)$ [4].

Therefore, the gossip systems with size n will have promising effect when the *fanout* value is set to be around log (n). Two performance metrics are: (1) comparisons between average network load, and (2) the number of nodes that do not receive the message using different mechanisms.

5.1 Random Networks

Experiments are done on the directed graphs with 1000 nodes. An epidemic algorithm must make a tradeoff between scalability and reliability: larger views reduce the probability that nodes are isolated or that the network is partitioned, while smaller views help the network obtain better scalability. For the random networks, the number of neighbors of each node at lowest level is 10 in our experiments on average. And the view sizes of other levels are rather smaller, in the simulation, it is 2. The community size is 100 in the experiment.

5.2 Random Power-Law Networks

Many large networks like the hyperlink network follow the power law distribution of node degrees [5]. The degree distribution is $p_k = Ak^{-\tau}$, where $A^{-1} = \sum_{k=2}^{k_{max}} k^{-\tau}$, k is the degree, k_{max} is the maximum degree, and $\tau > 0$ is the exponent of the distribution [9]. Researches have shown that only when the virus accumulates to certain critical threshold, it will be prevalent. And, when the virus is working on the networks that follow the power-law distributions, the critical threshold does not exist. The virus does not need to accumulate to certain limitation, and it could propagate quickly through hubs of the network.

The reason of considering power-law networks is that some unstructured P2P networks are characterized by random power-law and heavy tailed degree distributions. To keep the nodes connected, we adjust degree from 15 to 100 following the aforementioned distribution with $\tau = 2.0$ in constructing random power law networks. For each link, the start node and the end node are selected randomly, and as a result, the random power-law graph is constructed with average 14 neighbors in the lowest level. The view sizes of other levels are rather smaller, and its size is 2. The community size is 100 in the experiment

The simulation results from gossip networks without considering semantic partitions are denoted as *FlatGossip*, while the results making use of semantic partitions are denoted as *RSMGossip*. In the partition-based gossip mechanisms, different number of gossip levels could be chosen according to the comparison between the query and the category the query initiating peer is in. If the query strictly belongs to one category, then routing the query to other categories will not bring any benefit. And in this situation, the results are denoted by *RSMGossip1*. When the query corresponds to several categories, it should be routed to all the categories to obtain the complete results. For example, the query is going to be answered in 3 or 5 categories, and the results are denoted by *RSMGossip3* and *RSMGossip5*.

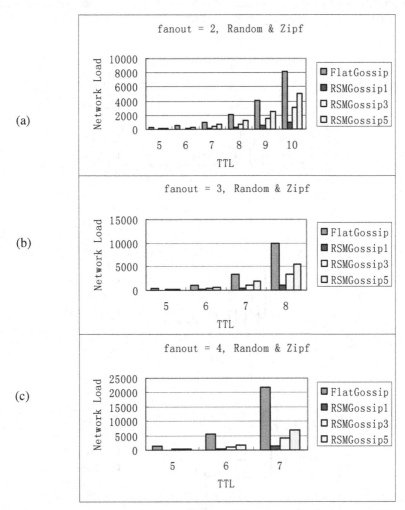

Fig. 3. Comparisons of the network load among different mechanisms in the 1000 node networks. (a). *fanout* = 2. (b). *fanout* = 3. (c). *fanout* = 4.

Both on the random networks and the random power-law networks, if the networks have the equal size and the gossip mechanisms have the same parameters (*fanout* and *TTL*), the network load will be the same. Fig. 3 shows average network load according to different parameters. The horizontal axis denotes the parameter *TTL*, and the vertical axis denotes the average network load during 100 times operation. As Fig. 3(a) presents, we set the *fanout* value as 2 uniformly and range *TTL* from 5 to 10. Fig. 3(b) and Fig. 3(c) are obtained in the similar way by using different parameters' values. We can see from the figures that the network loads are reduced sharply when adopting the partition-based gossip mechanisms. Taking *fanout* = 3 for example, when *TTL* approaches 8, about 88.9%, 66.7% and 44.5% network loads are reduced by *RSMGossip1*, *RSMGossip3* and *RSMGossip5* respectively comparing to the flat gossip mechanism, which justifies our approaches.

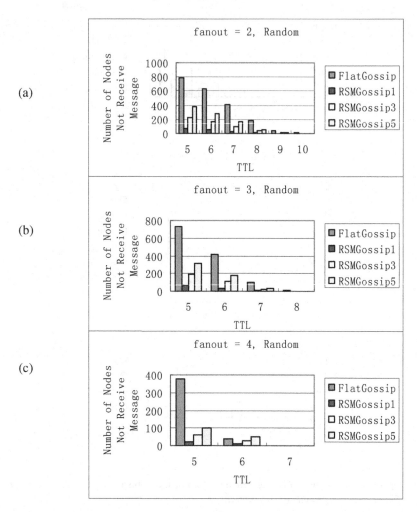

Fig. 4. Comparisons of the number of nodes that do not receive messages in the 1000-node randomly connected networks. (a). *fanout* = 2. (b). *fanout* = 3. (c). *fanout* = 4.

During message dissemination, the number of nodes that do not receive the disseminated messages is an important issue we concern. Compared with the previous algorithms, the number of nodes that do not receive messages decreases evidently after adopting the proposed mechanisms as presented in Fig. 4. Taking *fanout* = 3 for example, when *TTL* approaches 6, about 36.44, 109.32 and 182.2 number of nodes, which should receive the disseminated message, has not received it when making use of *RSMGossip1*, *RSMGossip3* and *RSMGossip5* mechanisms separately. Meanwhile it is 416.57 for the flat gossip mechanism. Though it is partly because the range is decreased for the partition-based mechanism, the performance is improved considerably, which justifies the rationale of the semantic partitioning mechanism.

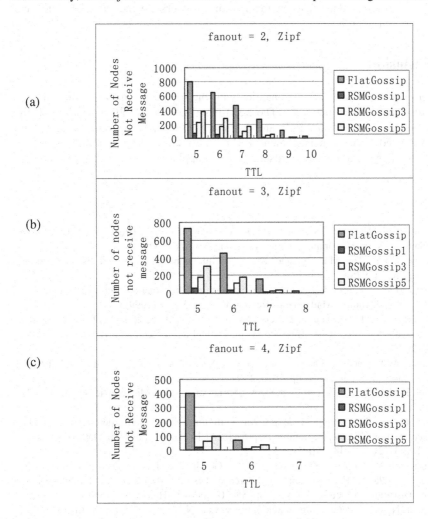

Fig. 5. Comparisons of the number of nodes that do not receive messages in the 1000-node random power-law networks. (a). *fanout* = 2. (b). *fanout* = 3. (c). *fanout* = 4.

For the random power-law networks, the results about the number of nodes that do not receive messages are presented in Fig. 5. We can see the similar phenomena as those done on the random networks: the number of nodes that do not receive messages is also reduced sharply comparing with the partition-based gossip mechanisms to the flat gossip. Taking *fanout* = 3 for example, when *TTL* approaches 6, averagely about 35.77, 107.31 and 178.85 number of nodes do not receive the disseminated message when making use of *RSMGossip1*, *RSMGossip3* and *RSMGossip5* mechanisms respectively. Meanwhile for the flat gossip mechanism it is

455.13. The results are better than those on the random networks for the partition-based mechanisms, while the flat gossip mechanism performs worse on the random power-law networks than that on the random networks, which also declares the necessary of our approaches.

6 Conclusion

Incorporating the classification semantics with the gossip mechanisms can improve the performance of P2P network. The RSM-based gossip on P2P network owns the advantages of both RSM and P2P, and can synergy the normalization and autonomy in decentralized resource management. RSM's normalization theory, integrity theory and operation language can support semantic-rich applications over P2P networks.

References

1. Androutsellis-Theotokis, S., Spinellis, D.: A Survey of Peer-to-Peer Content Distribution Technologies. ACM Computing Surveys 36(4), 335–371 (2004)
2. Bailey, N.T.J.: The Mathematical Theory of Infectious Diseases and Its Applications. Hafner Press (1975)
3. Berry, M.W., et al.: Matrices, Vector Spaces, and Information Retrieval. Society for Industrial and Applied Mathematics Review 41(2), 335–362 (1999)
4. Kermarrec, A.M., Massoulié, L., Ganesh, A.J.: Probabilistic Reliable Dissemination in Large-scale Systems. IEEE Transactions on Parallel and Distributed Systems 14(3), 248–258 (2003)
5. Leland, W.E., et al.: On the Self-similar Nature of Ethernet Traffic. IEEE/ACM Transactions on Networking, pp. 1–15 (1994)
6. Pittel, B.: On Spreading a Rumor. SIAM Journal of Applied Mathematics 47(1), 213–223 (1987)
7. Qian, G., et al.: Dynamic Indexing for Multidimensional Non-ordered Discrete Data Spaces Using a Data-partitioning Approach. ACM Transactions on Database Systems (TODS) 31(2), 439–484 (2006)
8. Renesse, R.V., Minsky, Y., Hayden, M.: A Gossip-style Failure Detection Service. In: Middleware98: IFIP international Conference, Distributed Systems and Platforms and Open Distributed Processing. LNCS, pp. 55–70. Springer, Heidelberg (1998)
9. Sarshar, N., et al.: Percolation Search in Power Law Networks: Making Unstructured Peer-to-Peer Networks Scalable. In: Proceedings of the 4th International Conference on Peer-to-Peer Computing, pp. 2–9 (2004)
10. Schlosser, M., et al.: A Scalable and Ontology-Based P2P Infrastructure for Semantic Web Services. In: Proceedings of the 2nd Int'l Conf. Peer-to-Peer Computing (2002)
11. Zhuge, H.: The Knowledge Grid. World Scientific Publishing Co., Singapore (2004)
12. Zhuge, H., Li, X.: Peer-to-Peer in Metric Space and Semantic Space. IEEE Transactions on Knowledge and Data Engineering, 19(6) 759-771 (2007)

AnyServer: Ubiquitous Real-Time Multimedia Communication System

Weijia Jia

Department of Computer Science
City University of Hong Kong, Hong Kong SAR, China
itjia@cityu.edu.hk
www.anyserver.org

Abstract. Ubiquitous communications require wireless networking and infrastructure network support. The first step is to look at how the different available technologies will integrate and work with each other. One of the next steps is to seek solutions for connecting "ubiquitous devices" to such "integrated and heterogeneous networks". These two steps together form the evolutionary approach towards ubiquitous communications. This paper introduces our currently implemented ubiquitous transmission system for "ubiquitous devices/terminals/handset", called AnyServer with Intelligent Multi-mode Nodes (IMN) for 3G/GSM/WiFi/Internet. AnyServer is an intelligent platform to provide the IMNs with smooth QoS connections/ communications, synchronization and roaming over the heterogeneous networks which is open, scalable, and complaint with IEEE/IETF standards. AnyServr enables IMNs to setup/maintain the real-time video/audio connections among the networks, facing the mobility in the heterogeneous networks.

Keywords: Ubiquitous Real-Time Multimedia Communication System, Heterogeneous VoIP.

1 Introduction

Ubiquitous communication will be one of the paradigms for the next decades to harness various networks to connect/integrate with each other. Platform for ubiquitous communication is a hot topic commonly used by network designers, developers and vender to depict their vision of future communications networks and platform. The ubiquitous communication is a multidisciplinary research and development. Any Server is intended to enable the heterogeneous networks to be integrated for the real-time multimedia communications such as video calls or conference. Compared with the pure Internet, there are several obstacles that make end-to-end wired and wireless multimedia transmission difficult to achieve:

(1) Low capability and limited resource of terminals: Wireless terminals typically have a small display supporting quite slow processor and limited size of memory etc. However, the multimedia applications usually require high graphic processing capability, large size of memory space and also a big screen to display videos. Obviously, wireless terminals can only support limited multimedia applications.

H. Jin et al. (Eds.): ICA3PP 2007, LNCS 4494, pp. 13–24, 2007.

(2) Diversity of networks and terminals interoperability: Network can apply various transmission protocol and media codec standards. Wireless terminals often support only a limited set of data formats due to their low capability and limited resource. When two different wireless terminals communicate with each other, their supported data formats may not be compatible and the communication cannot succeed. Even if some data from one terminal could be converted into the format supported by the receiver, such conversion often costs much and is not practical or acceptable to resource-limited wireless terminals.

(3) Low bandwidth of wireless networks: Wireless devices may use different transcoding across telecommunication such as 3G/GSM and wireless networks such as WiFi. On the other hand, they are usually of low capabilities, multimedia streams created by wireless devices can not be compressed much and need high bit rate for real-time transmission. Therefore, it is challenge to develop some real-time multimedia communication applications such as audiovisual conversation and videoconferencing.

(4) Fluctuated bandwidth and block of wireless connections: Multimedia data transmission, especially real-time transmission, requires steady high bit rate and is intolerant of package delay. On the contrary, wireless networks have fluctuated bandwidth and high probability of traffic congestion. Usually, the transmission time of multimedia data in a session is quite long, but the blackout of wireless connection may cause frequent reconnection and data retransmission.

The AnyServer architecture is shown in Fig. 1. To our best knowledge, there is no similar system as that of AnyServer which can integrate 3G-WiFi-GSM and Internet for real-time multimedia transmissions.

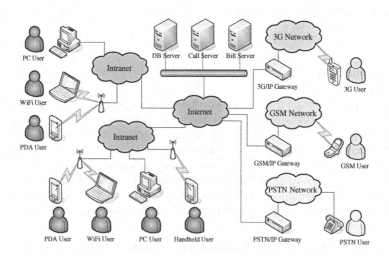

Fig. 1. AnyServer platform architecture

AnyServer has provided various types of services to many kinds of client devices using SIP with the following objectives:

- To ensure the data can be delivered smoothly between Internet and mobile telecom networks.
- To provide integration for both Internet network and mobile telecom network, so that the heterogeneous mobile devices can interoperate with seamless communication and content can be displayed uniformly in devices of receivers.
- To serve as a service broker and provider to provide sets of services and common interfaces to clients on behalf of third party service providers through different network connection protocols. Detailed implementation includes the following tasks

The paper is structured as follows: Section 2 presents the 3G-324M multimedia transmission protocols stack and its design and implementation for mobile wireless video/audio communications. We intend to make the IMNs be interconnected and to support video/audio transmission through 3G and WiFi (WLAN) infrastructures. Section 3 discusses the session initiation protocol (SIP) based multi-mode soft-switching package for 3G and internet transmission: Implementation of the multi-mode transmissions for circuit switching and packet switching protocols based on SIP sessions. Section 4 illustrates the Soft-Switching package for server and networking functions. The functions will be implemented through Call Server, Media gateway, Signaling gateway, and Home/Visitor Location Registration (HLR/VLR) servers. Adaptive Soft-Switching Package to support IMNs routing and roaming in the heterogeneous 3G/GSM/WiFi/Internet are given in Section 5. Related works are discussed in Section 6 and we conclude in the final section.

2 3G-324M Multimedia Transmission Protocols Stack

3G-324M is a standard made by ITU-T for low bit rate multimedia communication for packet-switching, while H.245 and H.223 are two main parts under 3G-324M and have given specific descriptions about the procedures of message transformation and data transmission multiplexing. Thus 3G-324M is an "umbrella standard" in respect with other standards which specify mandatory and optional video and audio codecs, the messages to be used for call set-up, control and tear-down (H.245) and the way that audio, video, control and other data are multiplexed and demultiplexed (H.223). 3G-324M terminals offering audio communication will support G.731.1 audio codec. Video communication offered in 3G-324M terminals will support H.263 and H.261 video codecs. 3G-324M terminals offering multimedia data conferencing should also support T.120 protocol. In addition, other video and audio codecs and data protocols can optionally be used via negotiation through exchange of the H.245 control messages.

The section focuses on the efficient re-design and implementation of complete 3G-324M protocol stack, including multiplexing protocols H.245 and H.223, ARM and H.263 for mobile wireless video communication. Our implementations aim to support the video call with the capability of transmitting/receiving video/audio streams simultaneously. The 3G-324M protocol stack is shown in Fig. 2.

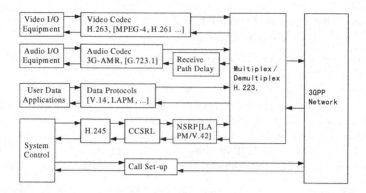

Fig. 2. 3G-324M protocol stack

2.1 3G-324 M Protocol Stack Implementation

The 3G-324M protocol stack is optimized through event-driven approach, single-step direct message transformation and multiplex table serialization. We first illustrate the overall operations of 3G-324M protocol and then discuss our approaches in dealing with message transformation in H.245 and data transmission multiplexing in H.223.

In 3G-324M implementation, the performance and quality of service are critical to the success of execution of entire system. Specifically, we implemented (1) Event-driven approach for the overall information exchange in facing hundreds of messages/states; (2) Single-step direct message transformation for the optimization of tree-structured message processing; and (3) Serialization of nested multiplex table entries in multiplexing processing. Our implementation of 3G-324M has been tested in a realistic heterogeneous 3G/WIFi communication environment for transmission of real-time video, audio and data. The major components of 3G-324M protocol stack, including H.245 and H.223 were implemented as the classes. 324M class performs the negotiation about video/audio settings etc., with the remote terminal through H.245 class, and handles the video/audio data exchange through H.223 class. The H.223 and H.245 classes also keep a pointer to each other so that the H.245 class can send or receive control messages through H.223. The H.223 can then retrieve the parameters about various settings from H.245 and the implementations of H.245 and H.223 are detailed as follows:

H.245 defines a general message type MultimediaSystemControlMessage (MSCM) and four major types of special messages in MSCM as request, response, command and indication. A request message incurs a specific action and requires an immediate response. A response message responds to a request message and a command message requires an action but no explicit response. An indication message contains information that does not require action or response. Messages with various types are transformed into MSCM format for uniform processing.

In H.245, *Signaling Entity* (SE object) is referred to as a procedure that is responsible for special functions in reacting events such as incoming streams of audio and video. It is designed as a state machine and changes the current state upon reaction to an event. With the SE class design, H.245 object hierarchy is packaged in the H245 class. It has a member variable of H245_MESSAGE which provides message definitions and operations. Member variable (X691) will be used for PER encoding/decoding and nine variables derived from H245_SE, each stands for one signaling entity in H.245. There is also a pointer referring to upper layer protocol of H.324 stack.

H.223 provides the sending/receiving interface for 3G-324M. In the point-to-point conversations, H.223 objects invoke the send/receive functions and buffer incoming data for multiplexing/demultiplexing and sending/receiving of video/audio. Our implementation will focus on H.223 efficiency with (de)multiplexing and multi-thread handling mechanisms.

Multiplex table processing--According to H.223 standard, there should be four different kinds of streams from the upper layer: (1) the control information between two IMNs via H.245; (2) information from data applications for real-time audio-graphics conferencing; (3) audio stream encoded by audio codecs defined in 3G-324M, such as Adaptive Multi-Rate (AMR) codec; (4) video stream encoded by video codecs defined in 3G-324M, such as H.263 and MPEG-2. Every information stream is identified as a logical channel with a unique Logical Channel Number (LCN). The multiplex table entry specifying a LCN and the corresponding data length will describe how a data packet is multiplexed. The data structure of multiplex table entry, called multiplex descriptor, takes the form of an element list. Each element in the list represents a slot of data from a specific information source. The multiplex descriptor uses a nested form for complicated multiplex patterns which may introduce the performance penalty. We consider that each element in the element list can be extended to a sub-element-list, which also contains other elements. Thus, when the structure is complicated with many sub-lists in the descriptor, the processing overhead may be high as recursive function calls have to handle the nested lists, this may result in low processing performance. To tackle with the problem, we applied a serialization approach to process the multiplex table, which will transform the 'nested' structure of a multiplex descriptor by flattening it into serialized linear lists. Using these serialized linear lists can save much processing time during the multiplexing process and introduces less overhead for the modification of the multiplex descriptors.

Multiple send/receiving--We applied the decomposition approach to the original H.223 design by dividing H.223 class into two separate parts: H223_Sender assumes the responsibilities of multiplexing and sending the outcoming streams; meanwhile, H223_Receiver handles the task of receiving the incoming streams and performs the demultiplexing for the incoming media streams. Both H223_Sender and H223_Receiver provide convenient sending or receiving interfaces. In order to handle the multiple media streams in a multi-point conference, a new MultiH223 class will be implemented to keep two separate linked lists as H223_Senders and H223_Receivers. Thus a real-time multipoint conference may be extended with the function to allocate/release the resources [29].

2.2 WiFi and 3G-324M Transmission Protocol

Our implementations use both WiFi infrastructure and ad-hoc modes for the connections of IMNs and AnyServer. In the ad-hoc mode, through the MAC layer of WiFi, the ad-hoc mode comprises a group of IMNs communicating with the same transmission range. Scheduling of transmission is the responsibility of MAC layer. The key factor of implementation of WiFi and 3G-324M transmission lays in the transcoding between 3G circuit switching and WiFi packet switching. We have applied the following protocol to handle such transmissions:

1. AnyServer collects the encoded data in chunks, e.g., every 20 msec in a chunk.

2. Both video/audio chunks along with RTP protocol header form a packet, which is encapsulated into a UDP segment.

3. RTP header indicates type of audio encoding in each packet sender can change encoding during a call session.

4. RTP header also contains sequence numbers and timestamps.

However, RTP does not provide any mechanism to ensure timely delivery of data or provide other quality of service guarantees. RTP encapsulation can be seen at the IMN node and not seen by the intermediate node. Any intermediate node providing the best-effort service does not make any special effort to ensure that RTP packets arrive at the destination in a timely matter. We have incorporated with RTCP/H.245 for the QoS control for the transmission of multimedia packets.

3 SIP based Multi-mode Soft-Switching Package

This section discusses the implementation of the multi-mode transmissions into AnyServer (through Media-gateway) including circuit switching and packet switching protocols between Session Initiation Protocol (SIP) and 3G-324M. SIP is an application layer signaling protocol which is used for managing multimedia sessions among different parties. Recently, Voice over IP community has adopted SIP as its protocol of choice for signaling. SIP is an RFC standard (RFC 3261), the body responsible for administering and developing the mechanisms that comprise the Internet. SIP is still evolving and being extended as technology matures and SIP products are socialized in the marketplace. Little work is done to enable end-to-end QoS multimedia transmission of heterogeneous wired and wireless networks using SIP.

In SIP, a session can be a simple two-way telephone call or collaborative multimedia conference sessions. The ability to establish these sessions means that a host of innovative services become possible for IP Centrex services such as video conferencing. SIP is an application layer signaling protocol standardized by IETF (Internet Engineering Task Force), which is used for managing multimedia sessions among different parties. The principle role of SIP is to set up sessions or associations between two or more IMNs. SIP does not transport data. On the other hand, sessions initiated with SIP can be used to exchange the various types of media data using appropriate protocols such as RTP, RSTP and so on. It can carry out bi-directional authentication and capability negotiation. SIP is simple and extensible. It accepts complementary information inserted as SIP payload for other applications. Currently, SIP is able to set up a call carrying the information of detailed multimedia session using protocols as Session Description Protocol (SDP). The implementations of SIP are described following based on AnyServer architecture.

3.1 SIP Based Transmission Selection Protocol

We have implemented novel adaptive protocol for selecting the most suitable communication protocol for IMN devices adaptively during connection without any interruption and disconnection. Besides, the protocols are required for call setup signaling and collecting the information of all communication parties required in protocol selection process. SIP is a control protocol for establishing media sessions. The addresses for the sessions to be established are carried in the body of the application layer message. It has two types of messages: *request* and *response*. SIP messages carry the descriptions of media sessions in their payload/header using SDP. Some additional mechanism is needed for payload modification.

To achieve SIP based end-to-end multimedia transmissions, SIP is not only used for call setup signaling, but also carries information for session making in adaptive protocol selection mechanism. SIP carries an SDP packet describing an audio or video session, indicating supported communication protocols, end terminals capabilities, QoS requirements of applications and session ID which is used for user identification of multi-parties communications in video-conferencing. Based on soft-switching to be described in next section, AnyServer can adapt the best suitable protocol intelligently in a connection. Data buffering service is also provided such that the media data flows must transmit between IMNs at their best acceptable QoS level without any interruption and disconnection, regardless the types of devices, platforms and protocols.

3.2 Agent-Based Connection Protocol

SIP based end-to-end multimedia transmission system can integrate IP tele-communication and wireless networks and provide applications such as video conferencing. Four main parts of SIP, called User Agent in client device, SIP Proxy Server, Database Server and Agent Server, enable the heterogeneous wireless devices to communicate with each other through Internet access services. We here only discuss User Agent and Agent Server.

User agent (UA) is a protocol stack working on terminals and helps terminals to communicate with servers. It provides services to the upper-layer protocols and applications through collecting device profile, sending them to the server and converting user's commands and application signaling into formats that can be read by servers and also translates server response for applications. UA is also responsible for the communication control, data transmission among terminals and servers, and user profile management. User profile maintained by and stored in the center server can be accessed and edited by owners through user agent. Instead of creating a new kind of description language, we also applied XML for representing user profiles, as well as the device profile. Device profile is used to describe the technical specifications and capabilities of the device such as multimedia processing and network transmission capability. Device profile must be in a universal format so that the servers are able to recognize all kinds of devices and provide appropriate services to them. As user profile, device profile is also given as an XML formatted file listing device specifications and capabilities. In user agents, communication control using SIP covers session initialization, sending device profile, exchange of control and indication information. It enables terminals to communicate with servers. Database server stores the information of all SIP proxy servers and provides services similar to DNS. On the other hand, Agent server provides many categories of services to terminals. Its data buffering service prevents transmitters from retransferring the lost data due to network congestion or disconnection. Its data transcoding service helps the heterogeneous IMNs to communicate with each other seamlessly and efficiently.

4 Integrated Network Routing, Roaming and Mobility

WiFi becomes popular for the wireless networks and the applications of WiFi for easy and cheaper communications which has been widely deployed. Since many 3G users will site in the office, to use WiFi for the communication can be promising. We believe that in the near future, roaming in 3G and WiFi/Internet could be the major bottleneck for the VoIP applications. Our focus is on the platform design and implementations for end-to-end communications between the terminals and to map SS7 to SLR correctly through Call Server so that the call of WiFi terminals can be smoothly transferred to 3G transmissions. To support soft-switching between packet and circuit switching among 3G/GSM/WiFi networks for routing and mobility, the protocols outlined below (for details, refer to www.anysrver.org) are currently under the development:

1. Multi-mode of 3G & GSM & WiFi for wireless Access: In 3G mode, the IMN acts as exactly a 3G IMN set, with standard 3G TDMA air interfaces support. In GSM mode, IMN acts as a GSM IMN set exactly, with standard GSM TDMA air interfaces whereas in the WiFi mode, the IMN acts as a SIP UA (or a SIP soft IMN).
2. IMNs WiFi network calls 3G IMN: When an IMN in WiFi calls a 3G IMN, it must check the called network type and then select the corresponding multimedia transmission protocols and then the call can be set up.
3. IMNs for WiFi and GSM: The communications between WiFi and GSM are similar to that between 3G and WiFi. Our implementation allows the both IMNs to negotiate the same codes (such as H.263/MPEG-4 for video codec) during the multimedia transmission capability exchanges.
4. IMN roaming between 3G and WiFi: For the 3G terminals that roam in the WiFi, AnyServer uses Info Synch and HLR/VLR Adaptor to enable the communications between WiFi and 3G. The roaming interface is to be established in AnyServer platform based on 3G and WiFi standards.
5. IMN Registration through WiFi Networks: For WiFi-IMN, the WiFi layer authentication procedure is achieved through WiFi gateway.
6. AnyServer enables WiFi Registered IMN to roam into 3G networks: When IMN enters 3G networks, it is able to hear the broadcast message from 3G base station (BS) and then it registers the BS through VLR. After the registration, AnyServer can make the IMNs location update.

5 Related Work

The use of the Internet in such applications demands for a highly reliable and secure system [25]. The discussions of the demand for ubiquitous communications necessitate the development of wireless communication systems, which are able to offer high bandwidths for different types of traffic are given in [9]. As the Internet evolves into a ubiquitous communication infrastructure and provides various services including telephony, it will be expected to meet the quality standards achieved in the public switched telephone network [17]. Some of the key problems that may be encountered when designing a broadband multiple access system with bandwidth on the order of tens or even hundreds of megahertz are identified in [18]. Personal communications services (PCS) key objective is to provide ubiquitous communication services. The success of PCS will depend on the network resources to ensure the quality-of-service required by service subscribers [26].

Ad hoc wireless networks represent a new communication paradigm and could be an important means of providing ubiquitous communication in the future [10]. Internet based mobile ad hoc network (IMANET) is an emerging technique that combines a wired network (e.g. Internet) and a mobile ad hoc network (manet) for developing a ubiquitous communication infrastructure [11]. Ad-hoc networking has been of increasing interest in recent years. It encapsulates the ultimate notion of ubiquitous communications with the absence of reliance on any existing network infrastructure. [14]. A new architecture, heterogeneous wireless network (HWN) and a dynamic adaptive routing protocol (DARP) for HWN have been presented [15] to support ubiquitous communication with integration of the cellular network with the ad hoc network.

Mobility management plays a central role in providing ubiquitous communications services in future wireless mobile networks [4]. Location tracking in wireless networks is essential for ubiquitous communication service. Since a user may move freely, the network has to keep track of the location of the mobile terminal to deliver messages or calls [13]. The vision of ubiquitous and continuous communications for a mobile user entails several emerging mobility types, which pose new requirements, for location management. An integrated approach for advanced location management is presented in [27].

As the Internet evolves into a ubiquitous communication infrastructure and provides various services including telephony, it has to stand up to the toll quality standards set by traditional telephone companies [21]. It is well known that company Intranets are growing into ubiquitous communications media for everything. As a consequence, network traffic is notoriously dynamic, and unpredictable [22]. In order to standardize communication interfaces for the electronics assembly industry, the IPC/CAMX standards have been developed. CAMX proposes standard messages defined in XML that are exchanged through Web-based message oriented middleware [5]. An ever-growing number of Internet-connected devices is accessible to a multitude of users. Being a ubiquitous communication means, the Internet could allow any user to reach and command any device connected to the network [16]. Broadband

and mobile/wireless networks will remove various bottlenecks which block the way to the ubiquitous communication [23]. The details of the evolutionary steps towards ubiquitous communications with prime focus on security are discussed in [3]. Security demands that all devices in a pervasive system must be able to authenticate each other and then communicate [6].

Many visions of the future include people immersed in an environment surrounded by sensors and intelligent devices, which use smart infrastructures to improve the quality of life and safety in emergency situations [1]. The work presented in [7] represents two strands of the work of the ambient system team at NMRC to produce ultraminiature sensor modules. The miniaturization of computing devices and the need for ubiquitous communication has augmented the demand for pervasive computing. Security demands that all devices in a pervasive system must be able to authenticate each other [20]. Reference [12] proposes a software interface model to be used for quickly constructing peer-to-peer (P2P) application systems, in which a lot of devices such as sensors, processing chips and wearable computers will be connected. A continuous-wave (CW) millimetre-wave (MMW) was generated by using optical signal propagating nonlinear materials for MMW wireless communications and ubiquitous communications systems [2]. In RFID-tags of ubiquitous communication systems, meander line antennas are appeared as promising small antennas as shown in [6]. UbiCom program (developed at TU Delft) [28] aims at carrying out research needed for specifying and developing platform systems for mobile multimedia communications with focus on (i) real-time communication and processing; (ii) architectural issues and performance optimization for heterogeneous communications.

6 Conclusion

AnyServer is a comprehensive system consisting of hundreds and thousands of lines of codes in compliance with ITU/IETF/IEEE standards. The standards are also contains thousands of pages. The Alpha version of AnyServer system has been released to some ISPs for testing and we are currently implementing the real-application system for public and business partners. All the forge of the huge of work and efforts comes from the motivation that the IMN should become both hard as well as the soft clients anywhere anytime to enable millions of users with ubiquitous real-time communications anywhere anytime. For further information of AnyServer, interested readers are referred to www.anyserver.org.

Acknowledgment

The work described is supported by Innovation and Technology Fund (ITF), Innovation and Technology Commission, SAR Hong Kong under no. (CityU) and (ITF) 9440048 (GHP/052/05).

References

1. Nojeong, H., Varshney, P.K.: Energy-Efficient Deployment of Intelligent Mobile Sensor Networks. IEEE Transactions on Systems, Man. and Cybernetics, Part A. 35(1), 78–92 (2005)
2. Park, K.H.: Generation of CW MMW Using Optical Signal Propagating Nonlinear Materials for Wireless Communications and Ubiquitous Communications Systems. Electronics Letters 41(10), 599–601 (2005)
3. Prasad, A.R., Schoo, P., Wang, H.: An Evolutionary Approach Towards Ubiquitous Communications: a Security Perspective. 2004 International Symposium on Applications and the Internet Workshops, pp. 689–695 (2004)
4. Fang, Y.: Movement-based Mobility Management and Trade off Analysis for Wireless Mobile Networks. IEEE Transactions on Computers 52(6), 791–803 (2003)
5. Delamer, I.M., Lastra, J.L.M., Tuokko, R.: Ubiquitous Communication Systems for the Electronics Production Industry: Extending the CAMX Framework. INDIN '04. 2004 2nd IEEE International Conference on Industrial Informatics, pp. 463–468 (2004)
6. Pirzada, A.A., McDonald, C.: Secure Pervasive Computing without a Trusted Third Party. In: Proceedings The IEEE/ACS International Conference on Pervasive Services, pp. 240 (2004)
7. Michishita, N., Yamada, Y., Nakakura, N.: Miniaturization of a Small Meander Line Antenna by Loading a High /spl epsiv/r Material. In: Proceedings 5th International Symposium on Multi-Dimensional Mobile Communications, vol. 2, pp. 651–654 (2004)
8. Barton, J., Majeed, B., Dwane, K., Delaney, K., Bellis, S., Rodgers, K., O'Mathuna, S.C.: Development and Characterisation of Ultra Thin Autonomous Modules for Ambient System Applications Using 3D Packaging Techniques. In: Proceedings Electronic Components and Technology, vol.1, pp. 635–641 (2004)
9. Capar, F., Martoyo, I., Weiss, T., Jondral, F.: Analysis of Coexistence Strategies for Cellular and Wireless Local Area Networks. IEEE 58th Vehicular Technology Conference 3, 1812–1816 (2003)
10. Ferrari, G., Tonguz, O.K.: MAC Protocols and Transport Capacity in Ad Hoc Wireless Networks: Aloha versus PR-CSMA. IEEE Military Communications Conference 2, 1311–1318 (2003)
11. Lim, S., Lee, W.-C., Cao, G., Das, C.R.: A Novel Caching Scheme for Internet based Mobile Ad Hoc Networks. In: Proceedings of 12th International Conference on Computer Communications and Networks, pp. 38–43 (2003)
12. Yamada, M., Ono, R., Kikuma, K., Sunaga, H.: A Study on P2P Platforms for Rapid Application Development. The 9th Asia.-Pacific Conference on Communications 1, 368–372 (2003)
13. Choi, W-J., Tekinay, S.: Distance-based Location Update Scheme with Isotropic Random User Motion with Drift. IEEE 55th VTC Spring 3, 1111–1115 (2002)
14. Doyle, L.E., Kokaram, A.C., O'Mahony, D.: Error-Resilience in Multimedia Applications over Ad-Hoc Networks. In: Proceedings of 2001 IEEE International Conference on Acoustics, Speech, and Signal Processing, vol. 3, pp. 1457–1460 (2001)
15. Wu, E.H-K., Huang, Y-Z., Chiang, J-H.: Dynamic Adaptive Routing for Heterogeneous Wireless Network. IEEE GLOBECOM '01 6, 3608–3612 (2001)
16. Oboe, R.: Web-Interfaced, Force-Reflecting Teleoperation Systems. IEEE Transactions on Industrial Electronics 48(6), 1257–1265 (2001)

17. Markopoulou, A.P., Tobagi, F.A., Karam, M.J.: Assessing the Quality of Voice Communications over Internet Backbones. IEEE/ACM Transactions on Networking 11(5), 747–760 (2003)
18. Yang, L.-L., Hanzo, L.: Multicarrier DS-CDMA: a Multiple Access Scheme for Ubiquitous Broadband Wireless Communications. IEEE Communications Magazine 41(10), 116–124 (2003)
19. Oboe, R.: Force-Reflecting Teleoperation over the Internet: the JBIT Project. In: Proceedings of the IEEE 91(3), 449–462 (2003)
20. Pirzada, A.A., McDonald, C.: Secure Pervasive Computing without a Trusted Third Party. IEEE/ACS International Conference on Pervasive Services, pp. 240–240 (2004)
21. Markopoulou, A.P., Tobagi, F.A., Karam, M.J.: Assessment of VoIP Quality over Internet Backbones.In: Proceedings INFOCOM 2002, vol. 1, pp. 50–159 (2002)
22. Kampichler, W., Goeschka, K.M.: Plain End-to-End Measurement for Local Area Network Voice Transmission Feasibility. In: Proceedings 9th International Symposium on Modeling, Analysis and Simulation of Computer and Telecommunication Systems, pp. 235–240 (2001)
23. Arakawa, Y.: Network Device Technologies for Ubiquitous IT in the 21st Century. International Microprocesses and Nanotechnology Conference, vol. 4 (2001)
24. Kampichler, W., Goeschka, K.M.: Measuring Voice Readiness of Local Area Networks. IEEE GLOBECOM '01 4, 2501–2505 (2001)
25. Mink, S., Pahlke, F., Schafer, G., Schiller, J.: FATIMA: a Firewall-Aware Transparent Internet Mobility Architecture. In: Proceedings 5th IEEE Symposium on Computers and Communications, pp. 172–179 (2000)
26. Serrano, L., Orozco-Barbosa, L., Quiroz, E.: Implementation Issues and Performance Evaluation of Intelligent Network Services in PCS Networks. IEEE ICC '99 1, 625–629 (1999)
27. Wang, Q., Abu-Rgheff, M.A.: Integrated Mobile IP and SIP Approach for Advanced Location Management. 4th International Conference 3G Mobile Communication Technologies, pp. 205–209 (2003)
28. http://www.ubicom.tudelft.nl/
29. Jia, W., Tso, F., Zhang, L.: Efficient 3G-324M Protocol Implementation for Low Bit Rate Multi-Point Video Conferencing. Journal of Networks, vol. 1(5), Academy Publisher, (September/ October 2006)

Performance Analysis of Interconnection Networks Under Bursty and Batch Arrival Traffic

Yulei Wu, Geyong Min, and Lan Wang

Department of Computing, School of Informatics, University of Bradford,
Bradford, BD7 1DP, U.K.
{Y.L.Wu,G.Min,L.Wang9}@brad.ac.uk

Abstract. Analytical models for adaptive routing in multicomputer interconnection networks with the traditional non-bursty Poisson traffic have been widely reported in the literature. However, traffic loads generated by many real-world parallel applications may exhibit bursty and batch arrival properties, which can significantly affect network performance. This paper develops a new and concise analytical model for hypercubic networks in the presence of bursty and batch arrival traffic modelled by the Compound Poisson Process (CPP) with geometrically distributed batch sizes. The computation complexity of the model is independent of network size. The analytical results are validated through comparison to those obtained from the simulation experiments. The model is used to evaluate the effects of the bursty traffic with batch arrivals on the performance of interconnection networks.

Keywords: Parallel Processing, Multicomputers, Interconnection Networks, Virtual Channels, Compound Poisson Process.

1 Introduction

The interconnection network is one of the most critical architectural components in parallel computers as any interaction between the processors ultimately depends on its effectiveness. Hypercube has become the important message-passing architecture for multicomputers due to its attractive properties, such as regularity, symmetry, low diameter, recursive structure and high connectivity to deal with fault-tolerance [1], [4]. An n-dimensional hypercube consists of $N = 2^n$ nodes with 2 nodes per dimension. Each node consists of a processing element (PE) and a router. The router has $(n+1)$ input and $(n+1)$ output channels. Each node is connected to its n neighboring nodes through n input and n output channels. The remaining channels are used by the PE to inject/eject messages to/from the network respectively. The router contains flit buffers for input virtual channels, where a virtual channel shares the bandwidth of the physical channel with other virtual channels in a time-multiplexed fashion [3]. The input and output channels are connected by a $(n+1)V$-way crossbar switch, V being the number of virtual channels, which can simultaneously connect multiple input to multiple output channels.

H. Jin et al. (Eds.): ICA3PP 2007, LNCS 4494, pp. 25–36, 2007.

Switching technique determines when and how switches are configured and buffers are reserved. Wormhole switching [1] has been widely adopted in multicomputers mainly because it requires low buffer space. An advantage of wormhole switching is that it makes message latency almost insensitive to the distance between source and destination in the absence of blocking in the network. In wormhole switch, a message is divided into elementary units, called flits, each of a few bytes for transmission and flow control. The header flit, containing routing information, governs routing through the network and the remaining data flits follow in a pipelined fashion. When the header is blocked, the remaining flits are blocked in situ.

In deterministic routing [1], messages with the same source and destination addresses always take the same network route. Consequently, they cannot use alternative paths that may avoid blocking. Fully adaptive routing has been proposed to overcome this limitation by enabling messages to explore all available paths in the network [1], [2], [5]. Duato's adaptive routing algorithm requires only one extra virtual channel per physical channel compared to deterministic routing to ensure deadlock-freedom [1], [2]. This algorithm divides the virtual channels into two classes: a and b. At each routing step, a message can adaptively visit any available virtual channel from Class a. If all the virtual channels belonging to Class a are busy it crosses a virtual channel from Class b using deterministic routing. The virtual channels of Class b define a complete virtual deadlock-free subnetwork, which acts like a "drain" for the subnetwork built from the virtual channels of Class a [2].

Analytical models are cost-effective and versatile tools that can be used for testing and evaluating system performance under different design alternatives. One of the most significant advantages of the analytical model is that it can be used to obtain performance results for large systems, which is hard to analyse through simulation. Many analytical performance models for hypercube networks have been widely reported in the literature [3], [5], [7], [12], [15], [16]. However, most existing models have been analysed under the assumption that traffic follows the traditional non-bursty Poisson arrival process or have not taken the batch arrival properties of traffic into account. However, traffic loads generated by many real-world parallel applications may exhibit bursty and batch arrival characteristics, which can significantly affect network performance [6], [14], [17]. In order to investigate the performance behaviour of multicomputer networks under different design alternatives and working conditions, this paper develops a new and concise analytical model for hypercubic interconnection networks in the presence of bursty traffic with batch arrival process.

This model adopts the Compound Poisson Process (CPP) with geometrically distributed batch sizes or, equivalently, Generalised Exponential (GE) distributed inter-arrival time [8] to capture the properties of the bursty and batch arrival traffic. We use GE/G/1 queueing theory [10] to calculate the message waiting time and GE/G/1/V queueing theory [18] with finite buffer to computer the average degree of virtual channel multiplexing. The model requires only a constant number of steps to compute message latency, regardless of the network size. The validity of the model is demonstrated by comparing analytical results to those obtained through simulation of the actual system. The proposed model is then used to assess network performance in the presence of the bursty and batch arrival traffic.

The rest of the paper is organised as follows. Section 2 presents the model for bursty and batch arrival traffic. Section 3 derives the analytical model. The results obtained from the constructed model are validated in Section 4. Section 5 uses the analytical model to carry out network performance analysis. Finally, Section 6 concludes this study.

2 Bursty and Batch Arrival Traffic

This section briefly presents the Generalised Exponential (GE) distribution for modelling bursty and batch arrival network traffic. Let X denote a random variable represented by a GE distribution with mean, $1/\lambda$, and squared coefficient of variation (SCV), C^2. The cumulative distribution function, $F(t)$, of X can be given by [8], [9]:

$$F(t) = P(X \le t) = 1 - \tau e^{-\tau\lambda t}, \quad t \ge 0 . \tag{1}$$

where

$$\tau = \frac{2}{C^2 + 1} . \tag{2}$$

For $C^2 > 1$, the GE distribution can be interpreted as a bulk-type distribution [11] with an underlying counting process equivalent to a Compound Poisson Process (CPP) which has the mean batch inter-arrival time $1/\sigma$ with $\sigma = \tau\lambda = \dfrac{2\lambda}{C^2 + 1}$, and geometrically distributed batch sizes with mean, $1/\tau$, and SCV, $1 - \tau$.

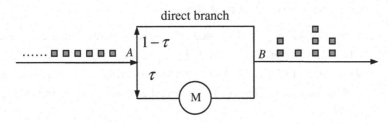

Fig. 1. The GE distribution with parameters λ and C^2

The arrival process of the random variable with a GE distribution is depicted in Fig. 1. Assume that there are always packets waiting at Point A to enter into the system. Each packet has to select either the up-branch (i.e., direct branch) or the down-branch (i.e., exponential branch) in order to reach the departing Point B. The selection criterion per packet constitutes a Bernoulli trial process. Specifically, a packet chooses the down-branch with probability, τ, and then receives an exponential service with mean time $1/\sigma$. The packet can also choose the up-branch with probability, $1-\tau$, and reaches Point B directly without service. The bulk of packets consist of a head which comes from the exponential branch together with a number of successive packets arriving through the direct branch before the appearance of a new packet coming from the exponential branch. The GE distribution is versatile, owning a simple form of cumulative distribution function and possessing pseudo-memoryless properties which make the solution of many queueing systems and networks with GE distribution analytically tractable [8], since it allows the use of many attractive properties of the exponential distribution.

3   The Analytical Model

The model is based on the following assumptions [3], [5], [7], [12], [15], [16]:

a) The arrivals of traffic generated by each source node follow a GE distribution denoted by $GE_s(\lambda_s, C_s^2)$ with the mean arrival rate, λ_s, and SCV, C_s^2.

b) Message destinations are uniformly distributed across the network nodes.

c) Message length is M flits, each requiring one-cycle transmission time to cross a physical channel.

d) The local queue in the source node has infinite buffer capacity.

e) Messages are routed adaptively through the network according to Duato's routing algorithm [2]. In this algorithm, V ($V \geq 2$) virtual channels are used per physical channel. Class a contains $(V-1)$ virtual channels, which are crossed adaptively, and Class b contains one virtual channel, which is crossed in an increasing order of dimensions.

The mean message latency is composed of the mean waiting time at the source node, W_s, and the mean latency experienced by messages to cross the network, $\overline{T}$. In order to model the effect of virtual channel multiplexing, the mean message latency has to be scaled by the average degree, $\overline{V}$, of virtual channel multiplexing. Therefore, we can write [16]

$$Latency = (W_s + \overline{T})\overline{V} \ . \tag{3}$$

3.1 Mean Network Latency ($\overline{T}$)

Under the uniform traffic pattern, messages generated by each node have equal probability to destine to any of the $(N-1)$ remaining nodes in an n-dimensional hypercubic network. The destination of an i-hop message (i.e. a message traversing

i ($1 \leq i \leq n$) channels to cross the network) can be any of the $\binom{n}{i}$ nodes that are i hops away from its source. Therefore, the average message distance, $\overline{D}$, is given by

$$\overline{D} = \frac{\sum_{i=1}^{n} i \binom{n}{i}}{N-1} = \frac{n}{2} \frac{N}{N-1} . \tag{4}$$

The mean network latency, $\overline{T}$, includes the actual message transmission time and the waiting time at the network channels along the message route and can be written as [16]

$$\overline{T} = M + \overline{D} + \sum_{j=1}^{\overline{D}} Pb_j W_c . \tag{5}$$

where M is the message length, W_c is the mean waiting time at network channels and Pb_j is the blocking probability experienced by a message at the jth ($1 \leq j \leq \overline{D}$) hop channel.

A message is blocked at a network channel when all adaptive virtual channels of the remaining dimensions to be visited, and also the adaptive and deterministic virtual channels of the lowest dimension still to be crossed are busy [2]. Let P_a denote the probability that all adaptive virtual channels at a network channel are busy, and $P_{a\&d}$ is the probability that all adaptive and also deterministic virtual channels are busy. The blocking probability, Pb_j, at the jth hop channel can be expressed by

$$Pb_j = P_a^{\overline{D}-j} P_{a\&d} . \tag{6}$$

Let P_V denote the probability that V virtual channels at a given physical channel are busy (P_V is determined below). The probabilities P_a and $P_{a\&d}$ are given by [12]

$$P_a = P_V + \frac{P_{V-1}}{C_V^{V-1}} . \tag{7}$$

$$P_{a\&d} = P_V . \tag{8}$$

Adaptive routing allows messages to cross any channel to advance towards its destination, resulting in a balanced traffic load on all channels under uniform traffic pattern. Therefore, the arrival process at the network channels exhibits similar statistical behaviour. Eq. (4) reveals that the average message distance, $\overline{D}$, is always less than the network dimension, n. This means that the traffic at a given network channel is a fraction of the traffic generated by a source node. This fraction, h, can be estimated by [13]

$$h = \frac{N\overline{D}}{Nn} = \frac{N}{2(N-1)} \; . \tag{9}$$

Let $GE_c(\lambda_c, C_c^2)$ model the traffic arriving at a network channel. Using the principle of splitting a GE distribution, λ_c and C_c^2 are given by [9]

$$\lambda_c = h\lambda_s \; . \tag{10}$$

$$C_c^2 = 1 - h + hC_s^2 \; . \tag{11}$$

In the event of blocking, a message has to wait for the deterministic virtual channel at the lowest dimension still to be visited [2]. To determine the mean waiting time, W_c, for a message to acquire the virtual channel at the lowest dimension, a physical channel is treated as a GE/G/1 queueing system with the arrival process modelled by $GE_c(\lambda_c, C_c^2)$. With adaptive routing and the uniform traffic pattern, the mean service time at each channel is identical and is equal to the mean network latency, $\overline{T}$. The waiting time, W_c, can be expressed by [10]

$$W_c = \frac{\overline{T}}{2}\left(1 + \frac{C_c^2 + \rho_c C_x^2}{1 - \rho_c}\right) - \overline{T} \; . \tag{12}$$

where the server utilisation $\rho_c = \lambda_c \overline{T}$ and SCV of the service time $C_x^2 = \frac{\delta_x^2}{\overline{T}^2}$. Since the minimum service time at a channel is equal to the message length, M, the variance of the service time distribution can be approximated as [5]

$$\delta_x^2 = (\overline{T} - M)^2 \; . \tag{13}$$

Therefore, the mean waiting time seen by a message at a given channel can be rewritten as

$$W_c = \frac{\overline{T}}{2}\left(1 + \frac{C_c^2 + \rho_c \frac{(\overline{T}-M)^2}{\overline{T}^2}}{1 - \rho_c}\right) - \overline{T} \; . \tag{14}$$

3.2   Waiting Time at the Source Node (W_s)

Messages generated by a source node follows a GE_s distribution and can enter the network through any of the V virtual channels with the equal probability $1/V$. To determine the mean waiting time, W_s, at the source node, the local queue is modeled as a GE/G/1 queueing system. The derivation of W_s is similar to that used to calculate the mean waiting time. Let $GE_v(\lambda_v, C_v^2)$ denote the traffic arriving at an injection virtual channel in the source node. GE_v can be obtained by splitting $GE_s(\lambda_s, C_s^2)$ with the splitting probability $1/V$, and the corresponding parameters λ_v and C_v^2 can be given by [9]

$$\lambda_v = \frac{1}{V} \lambda_s . \tag{15}$$

$$C_v^2 = 1 - \frac{1}{V} + \frac{1}{V} C_s^2 . \tag{16}$$

Therefore, the mean waiting time, W_s, at the source node can be expressed as

$$W_s = \frac{\overline{T}}{2} \left(1 + \frac{C_v^2 + \rho_v \frac{(\overline{T} - M)^2}{\overline{T}^2}}{1 - \rho_v} \right) - \overline{T} . \tag{17}$$

$$\rho_v = \lambda_v \overline{T} \tag{18}$$

3.3 Average Degree of Virtual Channels Multiplexing $(\overline{V})$

The probability, P_v, that v $(0 \le v \le V)$ virtual channels at a given physical channel are busy can be determined using the probability that there are v packets in a GE/G/1/V finite queueing system where the system capacity is V, the arrival process is modelled by $GE_c(\lambda_c, C_c^2)$ and the service time is equal to the network latency. Thus, P_v is given by [18]

$$P_v = \begin{cases} \dfrac{1 - \rho_c}{1 - \rho_c \alpha^V} & v = 0 \\[4mm] P_0 \dfrac{2\rho_c}{1 + C_c^2} \alpha^{v-1} & 1 \le v \le V \end{cases} . \tag{19}$$

$$\alpha = 1 - \frac{2(1 - \rho_c)}{1 + C_c^2} . \tag{20}$$

In virtual channel flow control, multiple virtual channels share the bandwidth of a physical channel in a time-multiplexed manner. The average degree of multiplexing of virtual channels that takes place at a given physical channel is given by [3]

$$\overline{V} = \frac{\displaystyle\sum_{i=0}^{V} i^2 P_i}{\displaystyle\sum_{i=0}^{V} i P_i} . \tag{21}$$

4 Validation of the Model

The analytical model has been validated through a discrete-event simulator, operating at the flit level. Each simulation experiment was run until the network reached the steady state. The network cycle time in the simulator is defined as the transmission time of a single flit to cross from one node to the next. Messages generated by each source node are based on a Compound Poisson Process (CPP) with geometrically distributed batch sizes or, equivalently, a Generalised Exponential (GE) distributed inter-arrival time. Message destinations are uniformly distributed across the network.

To validate the model, numerous simulation experiments have been performed for several combinations of network sizes, message lengths, number of virtual channels per physical channel and different GE_s input traffic. However, for the sake of specific illustration, latency results are presented for the following cases only:

- Network size is $N = 2^6$ and 2^8 nodes.
- Message length $M = 16$ and 64 flits.
- Number of virtual channels $V = 2$ and 6 per physical channel.
- Exponential branch selection probability $\tau = 0.67$, 0.8, and 1, representing different degree of burstiness and batch sizes.

Figs. 2 and 3 depict the results of message latency predicted by the above constructed model plotted against those provided by the simulator as a function of generated traffic into the 6- and 8-dimensional hypercubes, respectively. In these two figures, the x-axis denotes the traffic rate, λ_s, while y-axis represents the mean message latency. Generally speaking, these figures reveal that the mean message latency obtained from the analytical model has a reasonable degree of accuracy in the steady state region, and its tractability makes it a practical and cost-effective evaluation tool to gain insight into the behaviour of interconnection networks under bursty and batch arrival traffic.

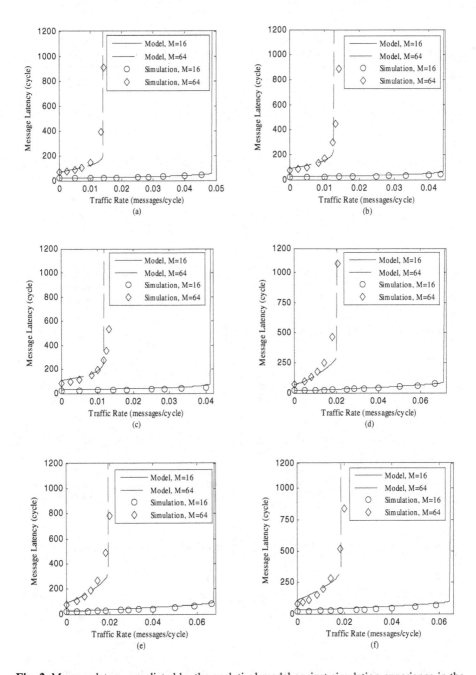

Fig. 2. Message latency predicted by the analytical model against simulation experience in the 6-dimensional hypercube: (a) $V = 2$, $\tau = 1$, (b) $V = 2$, $\tau = 0.8$, (c) $V = 2$, $\tau = 0.67$, (d) $V = 6$, $\tau = 1$, (e) $V = 6$, $\tau = 0.8$, and (f) $V = 6$, $\tau = 0.67$

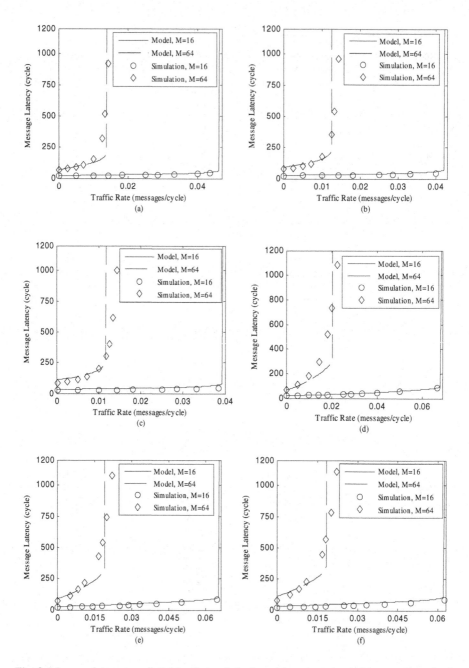

Fig. 3. Message latency predicted by the analytical model against simulation experience in the 8-dimensional hypercube: (a) $V = 2$, $\tau = 1$, (b) $V = 2$, $\tau = 0.8$, (c) $V = 2$, $\tau = 0.67$, (d) $V = 6$, $\tau = 1$, (e) $V = 6$, $\tau = 0.8$, and (f) $V = 6$, $\tau = 0.67$

5 Performance Analysis

In this section, we use the derived analytical model to investigate the impact of bursty and batch arrival traffic with various batch sizes on the performance of hypercubic networks. For the purpose of illustration, the performance results are shown for 6-dimensional networks with the message length $M = 16$ and 64 flits, and the batch size $= 1/\tau$ where $\tau = 1, 0.8$, and 0.6, respectively.

As can be seen from Table 1, the decrease in τ (i.e. increasing the batch size) degrades the network performance as the message latency increases. Moreover, the longer messages experience higher latency than the shorter messages as the batch size increases. Thus, the traffic loads with a smaller value of τ exhibit higher burstiness than that with a larger value of τ, even if they have the same traffic rate. For instance, when the traffic rate is 0.025 and message length is 16, the message latency increases 30% and 80% as the value of τ drops from 1 to 0.8 and 0.6, respectively.

Table 1. Comparison of message latency with different batch sizes and various message length in the 6-dimensional hypercube with $V = 6$

Traffic Rate (λ_s)	Analytical Message Latency					
	$\tau = 1$		$\tau = 0.8$		$\tau = 0.6$	
	$M = 16$	$M = 64$	$M = 16$	$M = 64$	$M = 16$	$M = 64$
0.00125	19.5	73.47	25.41	95.17	35.97	133.56
0.001667	19.67	75.77	25.62	97.89	36.21	136.8
0.0025	20.02	80.6	26.03	103.57	36.71	143.48
0.005	21.1	97.22	27.3	122.72	38.25	165.1
0.01	23.44	141.68	30.06	170.51	41.49	214.8

6 Conclusion

Analytical models are cost-effective and versatile tools that can be used for investigating system performance under different design alternatives and various working conditions. Existing analytical performance models for interconnection networks have been developed under the assumption that traffic follows the traditional non-bursty Poisson arrival process or have not considered the batch arrivals. In order to obtain a detailed understanding of the performance behaviour of multicomputer networks, this paper has proposed a new analytical model for hypercubic interconnection networks under bursty and batch arrival traffic which is modelled by the Compound Poisson Process (CPP) with geometrically distributed batch sizes or, equivalently, a Generalised Exponential (GE) distributed inter-arrival time. Extensive simulation experiments have been used to validate the analytical results of message latency. The model has been used to investigate the effects of bursty and batch arrival traffic and demonstrated that such a traffic pattern can significantly degrade network performance.

References

1. Duato, J., Yalamanchili, S., Ni, L.: Interconnection Networks: An Engineering Approach, IEEE Computer Society Press, Silver Spring, MD (1997)
2. Duato, J.: A New Theory of Deadlock-Free Adaptive Routing in Wormhole Routing Networks. IEEE Trans. Parallel & Distributed Systems 4(12), 1320–1331 (1993)
3. Dally, W.J.: Virtual Channel Flow Control. IEEE Trans. Parallel and Distributed Systems 3(2), 194–205 (1992)
4. Dally, W.J., Towles, B.P.: Principles and Practices of Interconnection Network. Morgan Kaufmann, Seattle, Washington (2003)
5. Draper, J.T., Ghosh, J.: A Comprehensive Analytical Model for Wormhole Routing in Multicomputer Systems. Journal of Parallel & Distributed Computing 32(2), 202–214 (1994)
6. Dinda, P.A., Garcia, B., Leung, K.S.: The Measured Network Traffic of Compiler Parallelized Programs, pp. 175–184, IEEE Computer Society Press, Silver Spring, MD (2001)
7. Kim, J., Das, C.R.: Hypercube Communication Delay with Wormhole Routing, IEEE Trans. Computers 43(7), 806–814 (1994)
8. Kouvatsos, D.D.: Entropy Maximisation and Queueing Network Models. Annals of Operations Research 48(1), 63–126 (1994)
9. Kouvatsos, D.D., Awan, I.U.: Entropy Maximisation and Open Queueing Networks with Priorities and Blocking. Performance Evaluation 51(2-4), 191–227 (2003)
10. Kouvatsos, D.D., Assi, S., Ould-khaoua, M.: Performance Modelling of Wormhole-Routed Hypercubes with Bursty Traffic and Finite Buffers. Int. Journal of Simulation, Practics, Systems, Science & Technology 6(3-4), 69–81 (2005)
11. Kleinrock, L.: Queueing Systems, vol. 1. John Wiley, New York (1975)
12. Loucif, S., Ould-Khaoua, M., Mackenzie, L.M.: Modelling Fully-Adaptive Routing in Hypercubes. Telecommunication Systems 13(1), 111–118 (2000)
13. Min, G., Ould-Khaoua, M.: Message Latency in Hypercubic Computer Networks with the Bursty Traffic Pattern. Computers and Electrical Engineering 30(3), 207–222 (2004)
14. Min, G., Ould-Khaoua, M.: A Performance Model for Wormhole-Switched Interconnection Networks under Self-Similar Traffic. IEEE Trans, Computers 53(5), 601–613 (2004)
15. Ould-Khaoua, M., Sarbazi-Azad, H.: An Analytical Model of Adaptive Wormhole Routing in Hypercubes in the Presence of Hot Spot Traffic. IEEE Trans, Parallel and Distributed Systems 12(3), 283–292 (2001)
16. Ould-Khaoua, M.: A Performance Model for Duato's Fully Adaptive Routing Algorithm in k-Ary n-Cubes. IEEE Trans, Computers 48(12), 1297-1304 (1999)
17. Silla, F., Malumbres, M.P., Duato, J., Dai, D., Panda, D.K.: Impact of Adaptivity on the Behavior of Networks of Workstations under Bursty Traffic, pp. 88–95, IEEE Computer Society Press, Silver Spring, MD (1998)
18. Wu, J.: Maximum Entropy Analysis of Open Queueing Networks with Group Arrivals. Journal of the Operational Research Society 43(11), 1063–1078 (1992)

Protocols for Traffic Safety Using Wireless Sensor Network

Yi Lai, Yuan Zheng, and Jiannong Cao

Internet and Mobile Computing Lab, Department of Computing, the Hong Kong
Polytechnic University, Hung Hom, Kowloon, Hong Kong
{csylai,csyuazheng,csjcao}@comp.polyu.edu.hk

Abstract. Wireless Sensor Networks (WSNs) have attracted wide interests
from both academic and industrial communities due to their diversity of
applications. In this paper, we describe the design and implementation of
energy-efficient protocols that can be used to improve traffic safety using WSN.
Based on these protocols, we implement an intelligent traffic management
system. Low-cost wireless sensor nodes are deployed on the roadbed and work
collaboratively to detect potential collisions on the road. Experiments have been
performed on this system and the results demonstrate the effectiveness of our
protocols.

Keywords: Wireless Sensor Networks (WSNs), Intelligent Transportation,
Pervasive Computing.

1 Introduction and Related Works

Recent development in wireless communication and electronics has made it possible
to create low-cost, low-power wireless sensor nodes. Each sensor node usually
contains a wireless transceiver, a micro processing unit and a number of sensors. The
sensor nodes can collect data and do some simple processing locally, and can
communicate with each other to form an ad hoc wireless sensor network (WSN) [1].
A WSN is usually self-organized and self-maintained without any human intervene-
tion. Wireless sensor networks have been used in various application areas such as
smart building [2], wild environment monitoring [3], battle surveillance [1] and
healthcare [4].

With the rapid world-wide increase of motorization, the need for intelligent traffic
management service is expected to grow quickly in the near future. There are quite a
lot of studies on sensing technologies in the field of Intelligent Transportation
Systems (ITS). Inductive loop has been used in many countries to detect traffic flow
[5]. However, inductive loop is usually quite large and the road needs to be torn up
during installation so the traffic flow is usually disrupted. Inductive loop is also prone
to breakage as a result of other construction. Therefore, it may not be convenient
during deployment. Some countries use ultrasonic sensors [17] [18] but ultrasonic
sensors are very sensitive to the weather.

Most commercial traffic management systems are made using video cameras.
Human operators sitting in a control room watch images from the cameras, identify

H. Jin et al. (Eds.): ICA3PP 2007, LNCS 4494, pp. 37–48, 2007.

incidents, and assign speed rankings to various roads. This technology does not require any hardware to be placed in the road. However, the need for human operators makes it cost-effective only for the most-traveled roads [4].

More recently, there are growing interests in using automated vision-based approaches such as [6] and [7]. However, automated machine vision is still an active research topic and still faces to a lot of challenges such as shadows and reflection of light. More importantly, all of the above mentioned technologies rely on wired communication and power supply so are difficult to deploy.

There are already some works that try to make use of WSN such as those reported in [8] and [10]. However, these works have different focuses. [8] is mainly concerned with hardware design while [10] is mainly concerned with high level algorithms for controlling the traffic lights based on the information collected from sensors. Unfortunately, none of the works has discussed how to design and implement practical protocols and systems based on WSN in order to improve existing traffic systems.

The problem of collision detection has also been discussed in some works such as [6] and [19]. However, these works are based on the above-mentioned technologies such as automatic machine vision so they also have the problems in terms of deployment as described earlier.

In this paper, we describe the design and implementation of protocols used by the sensor nodes for improving the traffic safety. Taking the advantages of the small, robust, easily manageable and inexpensive wireless sensor nodes [8], our system is able to provide an economic yet efficient solution to improving traffic safety upon the current transportation system. The wireless sensor nodes are deployed on the road and collaborate with each by exchanging collected data and local decisions. We propose protocols for the sensor nodes to determine their logical positions relative to each other and work together to detect potential collisions. In order to save energy, most of the sensor nodes are put into the sleep mode whenever possible. By using Berkeley MicaZ [9] sensor nodes, we implement a prototype of such a system and perform some experiments on it.

The remaining part of this paper is organized as follows. Section 2 briefly reviews the related work. Section 3 provides an overview of the system components and describes the system model. Section 4 describes the logic positioning protocol. Section 5 describes the traffic safety protocol which is able to let the sensor nodes work collaboratively to detect potential collisions. Section 6 presents the experimental and simulation results. Finally, Section 7 concludes the paper and discusses our future work.

3 System Design and Model

We have designed a WSN-based intelligent traffic management system, which consists of two major components. The first component is called TrafficDetection which includes the local operations and protocols that run on the wireless sensor nodes. The second component is called TrafficView which is mainly for the visualization and data management. Figure 1 shows a high level view of the traffic management system.

TrafficView is installed at the sink and is responsible for displaying and managing the data collected by the WSN. The essential WSN protocols proposed in this paper

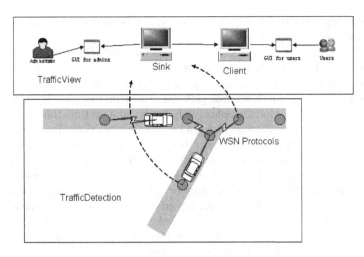

Fig. 1. Overview of traffic management system

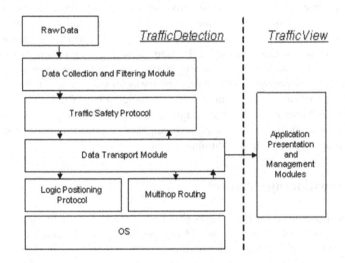

Fig. 2. Software architecture of TrafficDetection

are part of the TrafficDetection component. The architecture of TrafficDetection component and its relationship with TrafficView is shown in Figure 2.

TrafficDetection consists of several modules. The Data Collection and Filtering Module is mainly responsible for collecting raw data and filter the unwanted noise on each sensor node. The processed information will be used as input to the traffic safety protocol for the system to make necessary decision if there is any potential collision. The Data Transport Module is responsible for delivering the data with certain success rate. The routing module is used by the Transport Module to send some of the interesting data and transmit to the sink where the TrafficView application will visualize and manage the data. The logic positioning protocol helps individual sensor node find its logic position and its neighbors' positions so that each sensor node can know which sensor nodes it need to cooperate with.

The current design of the protocols is based on the following system model. There are $S = \{s_1, s_2, ... s_n\}$ sensor nodes in the wireless sensor network to be deployed to the roads. We assume that there are $R = \{r_1, r_2, ... r_m\}$ roads in the system where $n \geq m$. Each road is a straight, unidirectional path with one-lane that allows a single car to pass at a time. In reality, more complex roads can be built up from this kind of simple road. Each sensor node s_i belongs to a road r_j and their relationship can be uniquely expressed as $s_i = (r_j, k)$ where k denotes that s_i is the k_{th} sensor node on the road r_j. The deployment of the sensor nodes do not need to be very dense. In real world, the distance between two neighboring sensor nodes on the same road is at least 10 meters.

Each sensor node has two modes, sleep or active. During the sleep mode, sensor nodes only have their radio transceivers turned on so that they can receive wake-up messages. When a sensor node receives a wake-up message, it switches to active mode and tries to sample the data in a very high frequency so as to detect a high speed vehicle. Energy consumption in active mode is much higher than in sleep mode [16].

All of the sensor nodes on the same road are deployed in such a way that the distance between each of the two consecutive sensor nodes is fixed. There are a small number of special sensor nodes called landmarks. Each landmark sensor node is located at the beginning of a road. The responsibility of the landmark sensor nodes is to let other sensor nodes automatically find their logic positions based on our protocol. Compared with ordinary sensor nodes, landmark sensor nodes are more powerful in terms of energy. Some of the landmarks stay active at all the time so that they can be the first one to detect an incoming vehicle on their roads.

In order to achieve more reliable communication, on the same road, each sensor node only communicates with its closest neighbor. Contacting with other sensor nodes is achieved by multi-hop communications.

4 Logic Positioning Protocol

The major responsibility for the logic positioning protocol is to help each sensor node find its logic position along the road. More specifically, each sensor node needs to find out its own 'k' value in the relationship $s_i = (r_j, k)$ which has been defined in our system model. In addition to its own 'k', each sensor node needs to find out the 'k' values for some other sensor nodes with which it will cooperate. The traffic safety protocol needs this information in order to forward wake-up messages to the correct sensor node so that the speed of the vehicles can be measured and collisions can be detected. Figure 3 shows a very simple example of how the traffic safety protocol works.

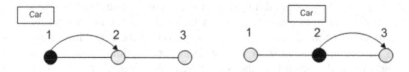

Fig. 3. Basic idea of the traffic safety protocol

When a car has reached sensor node 1, that sensor node will record the time stamp and transmit it to the sensor node 2. Upon receiving the time stamp, sensor node 2 will become active. When the car passes by, it will record another time stamp. With these 2 time stamps, the sensor nodes can estimate the speed of the car and detect potential collisions. Therefore, in order to make this system work, each sensor node needs to know its logic position and its neighbors. The logic positioning protocol makes use of a small number of landmarks and let the sensor nodes find their logic positions in a distributed fashion.

The protocol assigns each sensor node a unique coordinate which can be used to identify its logic position. The coordinate is composed of two parts: 'block number' and 'position'. 'Block number' is the minimum number of hops for the sensor node to reach the landmark. 'Position' is the relative position for a sensor node within a block. As shown in Figure 4, the coordinate has the following properties:

- The smaller the 'block number', the closer to the landmark.
- If two coordinate have the same 'block number', then the larger the 'position', the closer to the landmark.

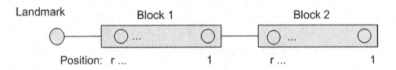

Fig. 4. Coordinates for the sensor nodes

The logic positioning protocol is composed of two phases. In the first phase, each sensor node is assigned a unique coordinate. The protocol can be most clearly illustrated by dividing it into 3 steps:

1. Landmark broadcasts a HELLO message, all of the receiver will be assigned block number 1 automatically:

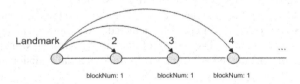

Fig. 5. Logic positioning protocol - step 1

2. Each sensor node in block 1 will broadcast an ASSIGNMENT message. The receivers of those messages will be assigned block number 2 if it hasn't been assigned any block number yet. Because of the different distances from block 1, each sensor node in block 2 will receive different number of messages. The number of messages received is assigned as the 'position' for each of the sensor node in block 2.

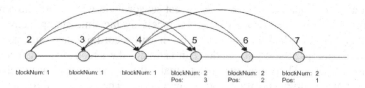

Fig. 6. Logic positioning protocol - step 2

3. Repeat step 2 until each sensor node is assigned a coordinate. The sensor nodes in block 2 will broadcast an ASSIGNMENT message. Sensor nodes in block 1 and block 3 will receive the broadcast messages and they can determine their position by counting the number of messages they have received.

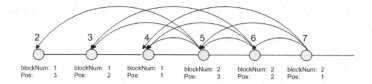

Fig. 7. Logic positioning protocol - step 3

In the second phase, after each sensor node is assigned a unique coordinate in order, the sensor nodes simply need to exchange their coordinates with their neighbors and their logic positions can be easily determined based on the neighbors' coordinates.

5 Traffic Safety Protocol

The traffic safety protocol is used to detect potential collision on the road and send warning messages. Basically, there are three types of collisions. The first type occurs on the same lane where the vehicles hit with each other on the tail or head as shown in Figure 8. This type of collision could be detected if each sensor node keeps a record of the last passed vehicle. The speed of the newly arrived vehicle can then be compared with the last passed vehicle so as to find potential collisions.

Fig. 8. Collision on the same lane

The second type of collision occurs when the vehicles are trying to switch lane as shown in Figure 9. This type of collision can be viewed as an extension to the first application scenario. Now the sensor nodes on different roads will need to work together. In order to detect such kind of collision, when a vehicle passes by a sensor node, that sensor node will need to send wake-up messages not only to the sensor nodes on the same road, but also sensor nodes on the neighboring road.

Fig. 9. Collision during lane switching

The third type of collision occurs in the intersections when vehicles are driving too fast near the intersection, as shown in Figure 10. This kind of collision can also be viewed as an extension to the first scenario because when the sensor node near the intersection detects a vehicle, it simply wakes up other sensor nodes near the intersection in order to detect collision.

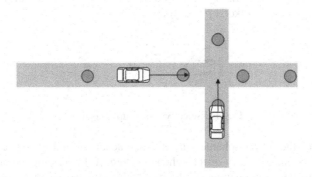

Fig. 10. Collision in the intersection

In order to detect potential collisions, the sensor nodes first need to measure the speed of the vehicles. For the first type of collisions, assume that there are two vehicles with speeds v_1 and v_2, respectively. The time interval between the arrivals of the two vehicles is t. The distance between two consecutive sensor nodes is d. As a result, in order to avoid collision within distance d, which is the coverage of each sensor node, we should have: $v_2 < d/t + v_1$. Potential collision in the second case can also be estimated by speed v_1 and v_2, time interval t, and distance d. In order to avoid collision, a vehicle is allowed to switch lane only when $v_2 < d/t + v_1$ is satisfied. Collision in the intersection can be estimated in a similar manner. Suppose the speeds of the two vehicles are v_1 and v_2. The distance between the sensor node at the road end and the intersection is d'. Then, the formula $|v_1/d' - v_2/d'|$ should be smaller than a threshold which ensures the safety of both vehicles.

Since all sensor nodes are battery-powered and usually it is very difficult to re-charge the battery, energy should be taken into consideration when designing such the protocol. As mentioned above, the sensor nodes need to measure the speed of the vehicle so that they can detect potential collisions. Therefore, each sensor node should be active when a vehicle passes it. During the rest of the time, they should be kept in sleep mode. Here, we propose a couple of schemes that can be combined to achieve a good trade-off between accuracy and energy efficiency.

1. *Always-on*: This is the simplest scheme where all of the sensor nodes are active at all the time.
2. *Random wake-up*: all the sensor nodes just wake up randomly.
3. *Normal wake-up*: When a sensor node detects a vehicle, it will wake up the next sensor node that is going to be reached by the vehicle.
4. *Normal wake-up + random wake-up*: in addition to the previous scheme, each sensor node will also wake up randomly in case some of the wake-up messages are lost.
5. *Selective wake-up*: this scheme is similar to normal wake-up. Sensor nodes are woken up in turns depending on the safety of the vehicles and the energy of the sensor nodes. For instance, as shown in the Figure 11, when a vehicle reaches sensor 2, sensor 2 will forward the wake-up message either directly to sensor 3 or through 2 hops to sensor 4 depending on the speed of the vehicle. If the vehicle is moving fast and safely, sensor 2 may directly wake up sensor 4 and skip sensor 3. In this way, in terms of sensor 3 and sensor 4, only one of them needs to be woken up at a time.

Fig. 11. Selective wake-up scheme

We compare the above schemes in terms of accuracy and energy consumption. First, we analyze the accuracy of the schemes. Here, A denotes the average accuracy for each scheme and accuracy means the probability of a sensor node being in active mode when a vehicle passes it. Let $\bar{n}$ denotes the one-hop transmission error rate. n is a parameter which denotes the number of sensor nodes on a road. P_w is the wake-up probability.

Always-on: in this scheme, since the sensor nodes are turned on at all the time, the accuracy is nearly 100% for every collision scenario described above.

Random wake-up: in this scheme, the accuracy equals the wake-up probability: $A=P_w$

Normal wake-up: in this scheme, each sensor node will not be active until it receives a wake-up message from the previous sensor node. As a result, the sensor nodes that are farther away from the beginning of the road tend to have poorer accuracy. This is because once the wake-up message fails to be delivered to a certain sensor node, all of the sensor nodes following that particular sensor node will not be able to wake up and detect the vehicle.

$$A = \frac{1 + (1-\rho) + (1-\rho)^2 + (1-\rho)^3 + ... + (1-\rho)^{n-1}}{n} = \frac{1 - (1-\rho)^n}{n\rho}$$

Normal wake-up + random wake-up: this scheme is the combination of normal wake-up and random wake-up. We may analyze its accuracy from the first sensor node on the road. The accuracy of the first sensor node is:

$$A_1 = P_w + (1 - P_w)(1 - \rho)$$

With the same approach, we can get accuracy for other sensor nodes as well. Finally, we can get:

$$A = \frac{A_1 + A_2 + ... + A_n}{n} = P_w + \frac{P_w(n - \frac{1-q^n}{1-q})}{n(1-q)} + \frac{1-q^n}{(1-q)n},$$

where $q = (1 - P_w)(1 - \rho)$

Selective wake-up: it has the similar results as normal wake-up here because this scheme simply let some of the sensor nodes work in terms.

Second, we analyze the average energy consumption, E, for each scheme. Here energy consumption is defined as the ratio between the amount of time spent in active mode and total amount of time. We define that in each time unit T, m vehicles pass through a particular sensor node randomly.

Always-on: in this scheme, the sensor nodes are always in active mode so the energy consumption is 100%.

Random wake-up: in this scheme, the energy consumption is simply the wake-up probability: P_w

Normal wake-up: First, let e be the average energy consumption for a sensor node in T time unit during which there are m cars passing by. Therefore, the average energy consumption for this scheme is:

$$E = Ae = \frac{1-(1-\rho)^n}{n\rho} e$$

Normal wakeup with self-wakeup: this scheme can be regarded as a combination of both normal wakeup and random wake-up:

$$E = Ae + P_w = \frac{1-(1-\rho)^n}{n\rho} e + P_w$$

Selective wakeup: this scheme consumes only half the energy as the normal wake-up scheme because sensor nodes are working in turns.

As we can see from the above analysis, the average accuracy for normal wake-up scheme is largely related to the total number of sensor nodes on the road. The sensor nodes far away from the beginning of the road will have poor accuracy so they should use random wake-up to make up for the poor accuracy. Currently, we set P_w to be *1-k*(1-ñ)* with a max value of *0.5*. Selective wake-up is a good scheme for highway because sensor nodes don't need to wake up so often due to the high speed of the vehicles.

Based on the analysis in the previous section, we design an algorithm for the sensor nodes to select the scheme best suit to the current condition. The pseudo code of the algorithm is shown below:

```
Set scheme=normal wake-up; random=0

If (k>3)

Random=(1-k*(1-•))>0.5?(1-k*(1-ρ)):0.5;

If (getAverageSpeed ()>80)
Scheme=selective wake-up;
```

6 Performance Evaluation

The protocols have been implemented by using the NesC [12] programming language on the MicaZ [9] platform equipped with the TinyOS [11] operating system. All the sensor nodes are clock-synchronized with the ETA protocol [15].

We have conducted real experiments in our campus car park to measure the speed of the vehicles with our protocol. The sensors that have been used are light sensors. As shown in Figure 12, the raw data obtained by the sensor contains a lot of noises. Therefore, we develop a simple data filtering algorithm that can be used to filter the raw data. The basic idea of the filtering algorithm is that a change in the sensory data is identified only when the newly changed value has lasted for a while.

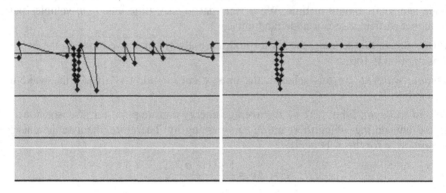

Fig. 12. Raw data (left) and filtered data (right)

Using the data filtering algorithm, we measure the speed of the vehicle. In the campus car park, the sensor nodes are deployed rather densely (around 7 meters between 2 consecutive sensor nodes). We let the vehicle move at different speeds from 10km/hour to 25km/hour. Our normal wake-up scheme is already good enough to measure the approximate speed.

To further demonstrate the effectiveness of our protocols in different application scenarios, we set up a testbed with some toy cars and a few self-made 'roads' as shown in Figure 13. The toy cars have been tailored so that they can move automatically and communicate with the sensor nodes under the roads. In our testbed, we have simulated a few application scenarios, including collision detection on the highway, collision detection in the intersection, traffic light controlling and automatic

Fig. 13. Testbed for highway (left), intersection (middle), carpark (right)

In addition to the field experiment, we have also conducted some simulations. The 'logic positioning protocol' has been simulated in TOSSIM [13]. As shown in Figure 14, in the simulation environment, the sensor nodes are able to correctly find their correct coordinates with our protocol.

Fig. 14. Logic positioning protocol in TOSSIM

7 Conclusion and Future Works

In this paper, we have described how to design and implement WSN protocols to improve safety and efficiency upon the existing transportation system. Based on the protocols, we have implemented and tested an intelligent traffic management system. We believe that WSN can be a very promising technology to be used in future ITS. We will improve our existing work in the following aspects:

1. We will continue to test our system in outdoor environments.
2. We will establish an information disseminating platform for this system to publish the interesting and helpful information to the drivers.
3. Combine the work with on-going projects like intelligent parking system [14] to provide more and better services.

References

1. Akyildiz, I., Su, W., Sankarasubramaniam, Y., Cayirci, E.: A survey on sensor networks. In IEEE Communication Magazine 40(8), 102–114 (2002)
2. Lynch, J.P., Lo, K.: A Summary Review of Wireless Sensors and Sensor Networks for Structural Health Monitoring Shock and Vibration Digest, Sage Publications, vol. 38(2), pp. 91–128 (2005)
3. Mainwaring, A., Culler, D., Polastre, J., Szewczyk, R., Anderson, J.: Wireless sensor networks for habitat monitoring. In: ACM international workshop on Wireless sensor networks and applications? (September 2002)

4. Lo, B., Thiemjarus, S., King, R., Yang, G.: Body Sensor Network-A Wireless Sensor Platform for Pervasive Healthcare Monitoring. The 3rd International Conference on Pervasive Computing (2005)
5. Klein, L.A.: Traffic parameter measurement technology evaluation. In: Proceedings of the IEEE-IEE Vehicle Navigation and Information Systems Conference, pp. 529–533 (1993)
6. Atev, S., Arumugam, H., Masoud, O., Janardan, R., Papanikolopoulos, N.P.: A vision-based approach to collision prediction at traffic intersections. IEEE Transactions on Intelligent Transportation Systems. vol. 6(4) (2005)
7. Kumar, P., Ranganath, S., Weimi, H., Sengupta, K.: Framework for real-time behavior interpretation from traffic video. IEEE Transactions on Intelligent Transportation Systems, vol. 6(4) (2005)
8. http://www.media.mit.edu/resenv/vehicles.html
9. http://www.xbow.com/
10. Wenjie, C., Lifeng, C., Zhanglong, C., Shiliang, T.: A realtime dynamic traffic control system based on wireless sensor network. International Conference Workshops on Parallel Processing, pp. 258–264 (June 2005)
11. TinyOS website: http://www.tinyos.net/
12. Gay, D., Levis, P., von Behren, R., Welsh, M., Brewer, E., Culler, D.: The nesC Language: A Holistic Approach to Network Embedded Systems. In: Proceedings of the ACM SIGPLAN 2003 Conference on Programming Language Design and Implementation (2003)
13. Levis, P., Lee, N., Welsh, M., Culler, D.: TOSSIM: Accurate and Scalable Simulation of Entire TinyOS Applications. In: Proceedings of the First ACM Conference on Embedded Networked Sensor Systems (SenSys 2003) (2003)
14. Tang, V.W.S., Zheng, Y., Cao, J.: An Intelligent Car Park Management System based on Wireless Sensor Networks, In: Proc. 1st International Symposium on Pervasive Computing and Applications (SPCA-2006), Urumchi, Xinjiang, China (August 3–5 2006)
15. Kusy, B., Dutta, P., Levis, P., Maroti, M., Ledeczi, A., Culler, D.: Elapsed time on arrival: a simple and versatile primitive for canonical time synchronisation services. International Journal of Ad Hoc and Ubiquitous Computing, vol. 1(4) (2006)
16. He, T., Krishnamurthy, S., Stankovic, J.A., Abdelzaher, T., Luo, L., Stoleru, R., Yan, T., Gu, L., Hui, J., Krogh, B.: Energy-efficient surveillance system using wireless sensor networks. In: Proceedings of the 2nd international conference on Mobile systems, applications, and services (2004)
17. Matsuo, T., Kaneko, Y., Matano, M.: Introduction of intelligent vehicle detection sensors. In: Proceedings of 1999 IEEE/IEEJ/JSAI International Conference on Intelligent Transportation Systems, pp. 709–713 (1999)
18. Sakamoto, K., Takimoto, H.: Comparative study for performance level between two types of vehicle detector: comprehensive results. In: Proceedings of 1999 IEEE/IEEJ/JSAI International Conference on Intelligent Transportation Systems, pp. 1008–1012 (1999)
19. Trivedi, M.M., Gandhi, T., McCall, J.: Looking-In and Looking-Out of a Vehicle: Computer-Vision-Based Enhanced Vehicle Safety. IEEE Transactions on Intelligent Transportation Systems, vol. 8(1) (2007)

A Lazy EDF Interrupt Scheduling Algorithm for Multiprocessor in Parallel Computing Environment

Peng Liu[1], Guojun Dai[1], Tingting Fu[2], Hong Zeng[1], and Xiang Zhang[1]

[1] Institute of Computer Application Technology, Hangzhou Dianzi University, Hangzhou,
PRC, 310018
perryliu@hz.cn, daigj@hdu.edu.cn
[2] Institute of Graphics and Image, Hangzhou Dianzi University, Hangzhou, PRC, 310018
ftt@hdu.edu.cn

Abstract. Many approaches have been proposed to improve efficiency of interrupt handling, most of which aim at single processor systems. Traditional model of interrupt management has been used for several decades in parallel computing environment. It can work well in most occasions, even in real-time environments. But it is often incapable to incorporate reliability and the temporal predictability demanded on hard real-time systems. Many solutions, such as In-line interrupt handling and Predictable interrupt management, all have special applying fields. In this paper we propose an algorithm that could schedule interrupts in terms of their deadlines for multiprocessor systems. Hard priorities of IRQs are still left to hardware, we only manager those who can get noticed by the kernel. Each interrupt will be scheduled only before its first execution according to their arrival time and deadlines so that it is called lazy Earliest-Deadline-First algorithm. The scheme tries to make as many as possible ISRs finish their work within the time limit. Finally we did some experiments using task simulation, which proved there was a big improvement in interrupts management.

Keywords: Multiprocessor, Interrupt scheduling, Parallel computing, Real-time system, Lazy EDF.

1 Introduction

Most parallel computing systems include a lot of external devices such as sensors, displayers, network interfaces or disks, requiring real-time guarantees in many cases during its operation. The interrupt mechanism is a very important interface between the kernel and peripherals which communicate the system with its external environment. Multiprocessor architecture like SMB is very common in parallel computing environments. Many of these systems perform control activities demanding constrained timing restrictions. One problem peculiar to multiprocessors is what to do with I/O interrupt requests (those interrupts which may be processed in parallel with current operations, as opposed to processor-related interrupts which are handled in series with the user routine). Several schemes now in use are: 1) send the

H. Jin et al. (Eds.): ICA3PP 2007, LNCS 4494, pp. 49–59, 2007.
© Springer-Verlag Berlin Heidelberg 2007

interrupt to the processor which initiated the I/O action originally, 2) have one processor declared as the one and only processor to handle I/O interrupts, 3) provide hardware registers whose contents define which interrupts go to what processors [15]. The method discussed in this paper involves making all processors in the system eligible for interruption by any I/O interrupt. This system embodies totally equivalent processors, plus separate and independent I/O controllers, all sharing a common memory, as shown in fig. 1. But if there are too many interrupt sources, which will cause the number of expired ISRs getting too large, the performance of the system will still become very bad. It will also cause potential system instability or inconsistency. As seen in fig. 2, I_1, I_2, I_3 are three interrupt routines which priorities meet $PI_1 < PI_2 < PI_3$. Their trigger time and endurance time can be seen in table 1. I_1 is preempted by I_2 even if it is about to finish its work. And I_2 is preempted by I_3 twice in succession. So I_1 completes its work at moment 15. Because its endurance time is 3 its work has been made no sense. I_2 has been overtime as well. In other words, about 10 units are wasted. You can imagine what a low performance it is. Disabling the preemption of an interrupt service routine would solve part of the problem. But it will bring more system latency and potentially prevent high level ISRs from being executed.

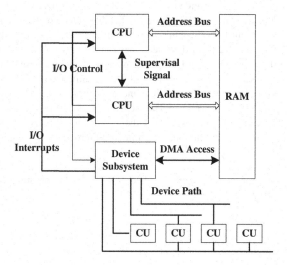

Fig. 1. The configuration of SMP system

Table 1. Four ISRs Invoked in the System

IRQ Number	Arrival T	Service T	Max. alive T	Priority
I_1	1	3	3	PI_1
I_2	3	7	10	PI_2
I_3	8	2	4	PI_3
I_3	11	2	4	PI_3

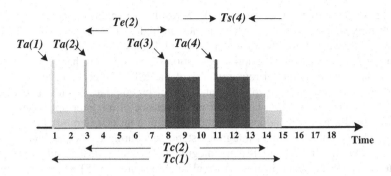

Fig. 2. Time out due to nested ISRs

In this paper, we propose a novel interrupt management method with the following contributes:

- The proposal of a Lazy EDF scheduling scheme for the management of interrupts in multiprocessor systems.
- The analysis and evaluation of the EDF scheme from the CPU's utilization point of view and the response time to external events.
- The implementation and experiment based on task simulation.

The rest of the work is arranged in following order. Section 2 discusses some related work. In section 3, the EDF algorithm and the model of the interrupt activity management are described. In section 4, we bring forward a way to evaluate our approach using task simulation. Section 5 describes the performance getting from the experiment. The final section covers the conclusion and future work.

2 Related Work

Many research works have bee carried out to propose alternatives which will enhance real-time capability, efficiency and robustness of the traditional interrupt model for real-time applications. The indiscriminate use of ISRs is considered as one of the most common errors in real-time programming in [6]. Some real-time operating systems tend to disable most external interrupts, except for those that come from the timer. They treat all peripherals by polling [7]. Real-time capability of these systems is very terrible though they avoid the non-determinism associated to interrupts. They keep CPU busy waiting in I/O operations. In [15], a method of assigning external interrupts to processors in a multiprocessor system is described. Features of a multilevel priority interrupt system are incorporated into a hardware component called the Interrupt Directory. The directory selects the most appropriate processor for serving the interruption at the time the event occurs. The "appropriateness" for interruption is based on the priority level of a processor's current task.

Integration among the different types of asynchronous activities, e.g., mixed priorities of task, process and interrupts, is address in some research papers. A method where interrupts are treated as threads is proposed in [8]. The goal of the scheme is to increase the scalability of the system in multiprocessor architectures oriented to operating systems of network servers. As a result, the interrupt threads still use a separate rank of priority levels which is not unified to the one of tasks. In [9] an approach is presented for the efficient reuse of legacy device drivers in real-time systems. It enforces a non-preemptive execution of the interrupt handlers in order to preserve the internal temporal requirements of the ISRs. Three main features of the method include: high priority of the hander, non preemptive execution, bandwidth reservation for the application tasks, and independence of the interrupt service policy from the scheduling policy adopted for the application tasks. Literature [14] proposes a schedulability analysis which integrates static scheduling techniques and response time computation. In [3] and [4] an integrated scheme of tasks and interrupts to provide predictable execution times to real-time systems. In [5] an in-line interrupt handling scheme is proposed. It can reduce the two sources of performance loss caused by the traditional method of handling interrupts, avoid the re-fetching and re-executing of instructions, and allow for user instructions and handler instructions to execute in parallel. Unlike our interrupt management model, none of the previous research works utilize an EDF scheduling mechanism to solve the problem of massive interrupts overtime caused by nested interrupts. The advantage of our scheme with respect to these proposals is that our scheme could distinctly decrease the quantity of overtime ISRs in a lot of cases.

3   Model and Mechanism

3.1   Lazy EDF Algorithm

Earliest-Deadline-First algorithm is a dynamic scheduling scheme. Priorities of tasks are dynamic according to their start-time and deadline. Those whose deadline is nearest to the current time have higher priorities. The difficulty of the algorithm lies in that how to sort tasks in terms of their distance to deadline. Tasks sequence can not be arranged because the time is various when processing. So that priorities should be calculated again after end of a task. The last step of scheduling is to choose a ready task which has highest priority. Typical EDF Algorithm has following properties for a task:

- Deadline d_i
- Execution time C_i
- The earliest possible start time of the task: s_i^{min}
- The latest possible start time of the task: s_i^{max}

Our scheme is a Lazy EDF algorithm which sorts interrupt service routines according to three factors: hard priority, arrival time and deadline. Only when higher ISRs have spare time to allow lower ISRs to finish their work scheduling will happen. Otherwise higher ISRs will preempt lower ones even though they may be overtime. Furthermore every ISR will be scheduled at most once for the sake of simplicity. This is why the algorithm is called lazy EDF algorithm. Most ISRs require a very short execution time so that a complex strategy and reduplicate scheduling will lead to lower efficiency. Just like a stack, once an ISR is scheduled to run as if it is put into "stack". Others may preempt it as put into "stack" above it. Only when it is the top item of the "stack" can it be performed again. In our scheme following properties are considered:

- Processor availability A(i)
- Maximum alive time (deadline) $T_b(i)$
- Arrival time $T_a(i)$
- Service time $T_s(i)$
- Execution time $T_e(i)$
- Nested time $T_n(i)$
- Hard Priority PI(i)
- Global available time at moment t on processor j: $U_j(t)$

Processor availability A(i) represents usability of processor i to the incoming interrupt. Maximum alive time means how long the ISR could stay in the system to finish his work before the deadline. Arrival time denotes when the interrupt is triggered. Service time means how long it would take for an ISR to complete a mission. Execution time indicates how long the ISR has taken to do its work. Nested time represent the period that the ISR is preempted by others. So we have:

$$U(t) = Min((U(t-1) - T_s(i)), (T_b(i) - T_s(i))) \qquad (1)$$

$$T_e(i) <= T_s(i) \qquad (2)$$

An interrupt j can be scheduled only and only if:

$$T_b(j) - T_s(j) >= T_s(i) - T_e(i) \qquad (3)$$

3.2 Schedulability Analysis of the Scheme

In traditional systems only tasks could be scheduled. Some systems also treat interrupts as tasks or threads [9] and schedule them with typical approaches. Some systems have an integrated mechanism which schedules interrupts and tasks in a mixed way [3][4].

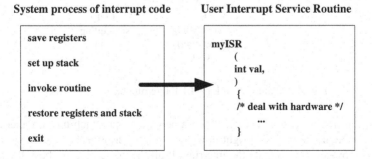

Fig. 3. An typical execution process of interrupts

A typical execution process of an interrupt service routine in an operating system could be described as shown in fig. 3. In our scheme because interrupts will be scheduled only once they needn't a structure like PCB to keep context. The real performers, user ISRs, could be extracted from wrapped interrupt execution sequence with entering and exiting code. Then they could be treated as an ordinary function and be invoked anytime. It can be inserted into, gotten from and deleted from lists.

3.3 Architecture and Implementation of the Lazy EDF interrupt Handling Algorithm

The Lazy EDF interrupt handling scheme maintains three important data structures: interrupt idle list (IIL), interrupt wait list (IWL) and execution time list (ETL). There are many initialized empty nodes in the interrupt idle list. For easy to be compatible with most existing systems we do not prefer a task and interrupt mixed scheduling scheme. In the proposed algorithm, an interrupt service routine should always take priority over a task. If a new incoming interrupt needs to be postponed a node will be taken from the IIL, filled with related parameters and inserted into IWL. Every processor in the system could access these data structure. The system records time information of ISRs by means of ETL.

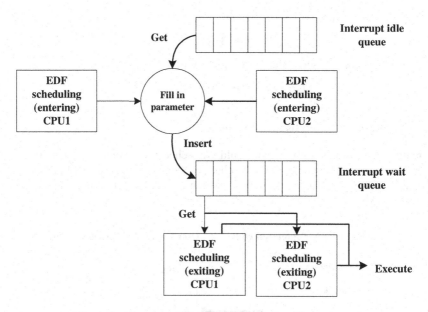

Fig. 4. Architecture of Lazy EDF interrupt handling scheme

Fig. 4 illustrates the architecture. When a new interrupt which has a higher priority comes in it should be executed right now according to priority. Firstly the system will find an idle processor to handle the interrupt. If all the processors are busy the one that is running tasks of lower relative priority will be interrupted. On that processor if current global available time is enough for the interrupt it will be executed directly. Otherwise if the interrupt has a farther deadline it will be put into IWL to wait for accomplishment of the previous interrupt. This makes both two interrupts can finish their work in time. If the current one has a nearer deadline it will be scheduled to run immediately, leaving the previous one overtime regardlessly. At the time an ISR is exiting it will check IWL and fetch the first eligible ISR to run. Other eligible processors are allowed to get waiting interrupts in IWL to execute. When running interrupts on different processors need to access share resources SPINLOCK is a very powerful method.

We encapsulate the scheduling code and user ISR into a code segment called realIntISR and use it to replace user ISR. It includes entering scheduling logic and exiting scheduling and is transparent to users.

The implemented algorithm can be described as:

```
IF found an idle processor;
  Assign it with the interrupt;
ELSE found a processor running low PRI task
  Assign it with the interrupt;

Entering scheduling
IF (!INT_CONTEXT()) /* not preempt other interrupt */
{
  U(t-1) = T_b(i);
  U(t) = T_b(i);
}
IF(U(t) >= T_s(i))
{
  U(t-1) = U(t);
  U(t) = Min((U(t) - T_s(i)), (T_b(i) - T_s(i)));
  Allow preemption, execute user ISR;
}
ELSE IF ((T_b(i) - T_s(i)) > (Ts(i-1) - Te(i-1)))
  Put it into the IWL;
ELSE
  Execute the user ISR;

Exiting scheduling:
U(t) = U(t-1) - Ts(i-1);
i    Get next node j from IWL, IF it is NULL goto step
iv;
ii   IF((Te(j) + Tn(j)) > Tb(j))
       timeout, just delete the node;
     ELSE
       renew time;
     IF(U(t)>= Ts(j))
       goto step iii;
     ELSE
       repeat step i;
iii execute userISR of node j, delete node j;
       renew time;
       repeat step i;
iv   Goto first node of IWL
v    Get next node k from IWL, IF it is NULL, end
vi   IF k could not wait, execute its user ISR, renew
time;
     ELSE repeat step v
```

4 Task Simulation

For the sake of easy to control and measure, we decide to use task simulation to evaluate our algorithm on VxWorks. VxWorks is an embedded real-time operating system which has a large number of users because of high performance kernel and reliability. It has been widely used in communication, military, aviation, and other fields requiring hard real-time. It adopts the structure of micro-kernel, supports multiprocessors, and has abundant network protocols and a good compatibility. In consequence, we propose an alternate strategy which manages interrupts using Lazy EDF scheduling and try to adopt it on VxWorks. Here we have three tasks to simulate three interrupts I_1, I_2 and I_3 respectively. They are K_1, K_2 and K_3 where their priorities have relationship as follows:

$$PK_3 > PK_2 > PK_1$$

Their parameters are set as shown in table 2:

Table 2. Parameters of three tasks

	Arrival T	Service T	Max. alive T	Priority
K_1	1s	3s	3s	PK_1
K_2	3s	7s	10s	PK_2
K_3	8s	2s	4s	PK_3
K_3	11s	2s	4s	PK_3

We first create three tasks synchronously. Then put them into sleep until their pre-set trigger time is matched, i.e., put K_2 to sleep for 3 seconds. The function of the task is very simple: just print message "intX is executing" onto the screen every second. Procedure in each task can be described as follows:

– Put itself into sleep for Ta(x) seconds;
– Nested interrupt count increase by 1;
– Insert a new time node into TIMERNODE;
– Get execution time of the current preempted ISR;
– Interrupt entering scheduling;
– If NON_SCH is returned, execute ISR function directly;
– Delete time node;
– Execute eoi function;
– If NON_SCH, execute Interrupt exiting scheduling;
– Nested interrupt count decrease by 1.

After testing of the task simulation, none-EDF interrupt handling which is used by the conventional system bring a result like what is shown in fig. 2. Obviously our scheme improves the efficiency of the system for a large scale. It can be seen from the figure, I_1 (simulated by K_1) is preempted by I_2, then by I_3 and I_4. So its real execution time is 14s though it only needs 3s to complete its job. Overtime makes its work meaningless. I_2 is overtime as well. The performance of the system is really bad. In improved system, EOI will be sent after scheduling immediately for not to prevent same level interrupt from entering. We augment time scale to second to see the result clearly so that a timer which has a precision of ms could be utilized. In real interrupt system, an accuracy timer about ns is needed. *RDTSC* instruction could get very precise time which could be machine clock rate in the X86 system.

A more intuitionistic chart is fig. 5, the total time consumed by three simulated task is not changed compared with original system. But all three interrupts finish their work in time while two of them fail in the conventional system.

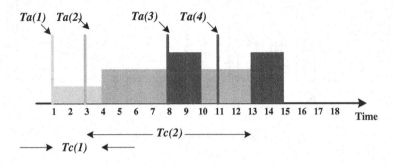

Fig. 5. Task simulation result using Lazy EDF algorithm

5 Performance

Performance of the algorithm is tested also using task simulation. The target machine is an IBM compatible PC with a Pentium CPU of 100MHz and RAM of 64MB, running an operating system - VxWorks. For time considering we set the time level to ms grade. In each ISR, execution timer is recorded. If it is overtime a global count will be increased. We set 5 tasks which have service time and other parameters as shown in table 3. We keep those tasks running for a fixed period on the original and improved systems respectively. The result can be seen in fig. 6. The left chart shows new algorithm can do more interrupts than traditional algorithm. The right chart shows new algorithm has less overtime interrupts than traditional algorithm. In conclusion, our scheme can improve the performance about 30% in situation that there are a good many interrupts and most of them have limited execution time while some of them could wait for execution for some time.

The overhead of our algorithm lies in the time measurements of two features: the interrupt latency and the context switch time. Due to the scheme introduced additional codes the interrupt latency will slightly increase. The interrupt response time is variational due to different scheduling situation. It is around 10us in a Pentium 100MHz/64M RAM PC system. The performance of the system maybe decreases when a lot of interrupts have very short service time and maximum alive time. At that time, a little increase to interrupt latency will lead to a vicious circle. Context-switch time will be affected as well.

Table 3. Parameters of five tasks

IRQ Number	1	2	3	4	5
Service time	990ms	150ms	1.9ms	1.8ms	1ms
Lifecycle(Deadline)	4800ms	600ms	6ms	6ms	4.2ms
Interrupt Frequency	12/60s	60/60s	3000/60s	3000/60s	4200/60s

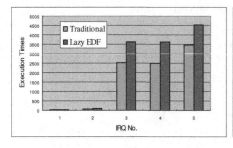 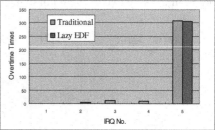

Fig. 6. Performance contrast

6   Conclusion

Most embedded and parallel systems have many interrupt sources and these interrupts will occur asynchronously. When there are too many nested interrupts those in low level are likely to run out of time which leads to failure of their work. In this paper we presented a Lazy Earliest-Deadline-First handling scheme to provide schedulability to interrupt management of the parallel system. Its algorithm and architecture were discussed. A simulation using tasks was presented. Result of performance test which was carried out based on that simulation was given. It was proved that using Lazy EDF scheduling could greatly reduce interrupt failure caused by nested interrupts and enhance robustness of the real-time system.

We tested our algorithm on a single processor PC using task simulation. We plan to deploy the scheme into real multiprocessor system, and do experiments using I/O IRQs. We are to produce those IRQs by signal generators. New features like mixed scheduling of interrupt and task is planed to be added. An over-head analysis will be given in detail in the next paper.

References

1. Kevin, J., Donald, L.S.: Accounting for Interrupt Handling Costs in Dynamic Priority Task Systems. In: Proceedings of Real-Time Systems Symposium, pp. 212–221 (1993)
2. Ayman, F., Pravin, V., Jean, W.: Analysis of Interrupt Handling Schemes in Real-time Systems. In: Proceedings of the 8th Annual International Phoenix Conference on Computers and Communications, pp. 260–263 (1989)

3. Luis E, L-d-F., Pedro, M-A., de Dionisio, N.: Predictable Interrupt Scheduling with Low Overhead for Real-Time Kernels. In: Proceedings of the 12th IEEE International Conference on Embedded and Real-Time Computing systems and Applications, pp. 385–394 (2006)
4. Luis E, L-d-F., Pedro, M-A., de Dionisio, N.: Predictable Interrupt Management for Real Time Kernels over Conventional PC Hardware. In: Proceedings of IEEE Real-Time and Applications Symposium, pp. 14–23 (2006)
5. Aamer, J., Bruce, J.: In-Line Interrupt Handling and Lock-Up Free Translation Lookaside Buffers (TLBs). IEEE Transaction on Computers 55, 559–574 (2006)
6. Stewart, D.B: Twenty-Five-Most Commons Mistakes with Real-Time Software Development. In: Proceedings of Embedded Systems Conference (1999)
7. Hermann, K., et al.: Distributed Fault-Tolerant Real-Time Systems: the MARS Approach. IEEE Micro 9(1), 25–40 (1989)
8. Steve, K., Joe, E.: Interrupts as Threads. ACM SIGOPS Operating Systems Review 29(2), 21–26 (1995)
9. Tullio, F., et al.: Non-Preemptive Interrupt Scheduling for Safe Reuse of Legacy Drivers in Real-time systems. In: Proceedings of the 17th EuroMicro Conference on Real-Time Systems, pp. 98–105 (2005)
10. Hoai, H., et al.: Computing the Minimum EDF Feasible Deadline in Periodic Systems. In: Proceedings of the 12th International Conference on Embedded and Real-Time Computing Systems and Applications, pp. 125–134 (2006)
11. Cecilia, E.: Clairvoyant Non-Preemptive EDF Scheduling. In: Proceedings of the 18th EuroMicro Conference on Real-Time Systems, pp. 23–32 (2006)
12. Theodore, P.B.: An Analysis of EDF Schedulability on a Multiprocessor. IEEE Transaction on Parallel and Distributed System 16(8), 760–768 (2005)
13. Zhi, Q., Jong-Moon, C.: A Statistical Framework for EDF Scheduling. IEEE Communications Letters 7(10), 493–495 (2003)
14. Sanstrom, K., Erikssn, C., Fohler, G.: Handling Interrupts with Static Scheduling in an Automotive Vehicle Control Systems. In: Proceedings of 5 International Conference on Real-Time computing Systems and Applications, pp. 158–165 (1998)
15. Gountanis, R.J, Viss, N.L: A ethod of Processor Selection for Interrupt Handling in a Multiprocessor System. In: Proceedings of the IEEE, vol. 54(12) pp. 1812–1819 (1966)

Efficient Representations of Row-Sorted 1-Variant Matrices for Parallel String Applications[*]

Carlos Eduardo Rodrigues Alves[1], Edson Norberto Cáceres[2], and Siang Wun Song[3]

[1] Universidade São Judas Tadeu, Brazil
prof.carlos_r_alves@usjt.br
[2] Universidade Federal de Mato Grosso do Sul, Brazil
edson@dct.ufms.br
[3] Universidade de São Paulo, Brazil
song@ime.usp.br

Abstract. We investigate the efficient storage of row-sorted 1-variant $(m + 1) \times (n + 1)$ matrices, $m > n$, that have the following properties: the rows are sorted in strictly increasing order and the set of elements of each row differs only by one single element from the set of elements of the next row. It has been shown that row-sorted 1-variant matrices are important in several parallel string comparison applications. Due to the large amount of redundancy in the row elements, we investigate efficient data structures to store such matrices. In this paper we propose a representation that stores a row-sorted 1-variant matrix in $O(m \log m)$ space and access time of $O(\log m)$ and can be constructed in $O(m \log m)$ time. We thus seek a representation that constitutes a nice balance between access time, representation construction time, and space requirement.

Keywords: row-sorted 1-variant matrices, data structure, parallel algorithms, longest common subsequence, all-substring longest common subsequence.

1 Introduction

One important issue in the design of parallel algorithms is the choice of adequate data structures. The amount of space used to store the necessary data, as well as the access time of the data are two important measures. The space requirement is particularly important if data structures are to be transmitted among processors, since it would then affect also the overall execution time of the parallel algorithm. On the other hand, it is not sufficient to have a space efficient data structure that does not provide quick access time. Often there is no single data structure that minimizes both measures and a solution of compromise is often necessary.

---

[*] Partially supported by FAPESP Proc. No. 2004/08928-3, CNPq Proc. No. 55.0094/05-9, 30.5362/06-2, 30.2942/04-1, 62.0123/04-4, 48.5460/06-8 and FUNDECT 41/100.115/2006.

We discuss one such situation that arises in the design of efficient coarse-grained parallel algorithms to find the LCS (longest common subsequence) of two given strings composed by symbols of a given alphabet. Given two strings, obtention of the longest subsequence common to both strings is an important problem with applications in DNA sequence comparison, data compression, pattern matching, etc. [10]. The LCS is a new string, of the longest possible length, that can be obtained from the given strings by removing symbols from them such that the resulting strings become the same. For example, given the input strings *helloworld* and *hollywood* a longest common subsequence is *hllwod*, of length 6. Another solution is *hllood*. So there may be more than one answer. Usually we are interested in obtaining the length of the LCS.

The LCS problem, as other related problems such as the string editing problem [7], can be modeled as a *grid directed acyclic graph* and solved by the dynamic programming approach [4]. In the parallel solution derived from a technique from Lu and Lin [9], each processor needs to deal with an $(m+1) \times (n+1)$ matrix, called a row-sorted 1-variant matrix, whose elements satisfy some interesting properties, that we show in this section. In the next section, for the sake of completeness and to make this paper as self-contained as possible, we give a brief description of how this matrix is derived from the directed acyclic graph that models the LCS problem.

We now show the properties of a row-sorted 1-variant matrix M of $m+1$ rows and $n+1$ columns, with $m > n$. The elements of M are integers or contain the special value ∞, with the following properties. (Figure 1 shows an example row-sorted 1-variant matrix M.)

$M(i,j)$	0	1	2	3	4	5	6	7	8
0	0	1	2	3	4	5	6	8	9
1	1	2	3	4	5	6	8	9	∞
2	2	3	4	5	6	8	9	13	∞
3	3	4	5	6	8	9	11	13	∞
4	4	5	6	8	9	11	13	∞	∞
5	5	6	7	8	9	11	13	∞	∞
6	6	7	8	9	11	13	∞	∞	∞
7	7	8	9	11	13	∞	∞	∞	∞
8	8	9	10	11	13	∞	∞	∞	∞
9	9	10	11	12	13	∞	∞	∞	∞
10	10	11	12	13	∞	∞	∞	∞	∞
11	11	12	13	∞	∞	∞	∞	∞	∞
12	12	13	∞	∞	∞	∞	∞	∞	∞
13	13	∞	∞	∞	∞	∞	∞	∞	∞

Fig. 1. M is an example row-sorted 1-variant matrix with $m = 13$ and $n = 8$

1. All the rows are sorted in strict increasing order, that is, except the special ∞ value, there are no repeated numbers in each row.
2. For $0 \leq i < m$, all the elements in row i, except the first element, are also present in row $i+1$.

3. For $0 < i \leq m$, all the elements present in row $i + 1$, with the exception of one element (that may be any element), are also present in row i.
4. All the integer elements have value from 0 to m. When a row has less than $n+$ 1 integer elements, it is completed with special ∞ symbols at the rightmost positions.

We say that such matrices are *row-sorted* (because of property 1) and *1-variant* because of properties 2 and 3, in the sense that the set of elements of one row differs only in one single element with the set of elements of the next row.

2   The Role of Row-Sorted 1-Variant Matrices in the LCS Problem

In this section we discuss the LCS problem and one related problem called the ALCS problem (defined below). Then we give a brief description of how row-sorted 1-variant matrices arise during the design of parallel algorithms for these problems. Details can be found in [2,4]. The reader can skip this section without affecting understanding of this paper. Its purpose, however, is to motivate the reader on the importance of efficient storage schemes for row-sorted 1-variant matrices.

Consider a string of symbols from a finite alphabet. A *substring* of a string is any contiguous fragment of the given string. A *subsequence* of a string is obtained by deleting zero or more symbols from the original string. A subsequence can thus have noncontiguous symbols of a string. Given two strings X and Y, the *longest common subsequence* (LCS) problem finds the length of the longest subsequence that is common to both strings. The *all-substring longest common subsequence* (ALCS) problem finds the lengths of the longest common subsequences between X and *any* substring of Y.

2.1   The Grid Directed Acyclic Graph G

Both the LCS and ALCS problems can be solved through a grid directed acyclic graph G. Consider two strings X and Y of lengths m and n, respectively. As an example, consider $X = $ baabcbca and $Y = $ baabcabcabaca. The grid directed acyclic graph G has $(m+1) \times (n+1)$ vertices (see Figure 2). We number the rows and columns starting from 0. All the vertical and horizontal edges have weight 0. The edge from vertex $(i - 1, j - 1)$ to vertex (i, j) has weight 1 if $x_i = y_j$. If $x_i \neq y_j$, this edge has weight 0 and can be ignored.

To simplify the presentation, from now on we will use G to denote the grid directed acyclic graph. The LCS algorithm finds the length of the best path between the upper left corner and the lower right corner of G. The more general ALCS algorithm finds the lengths of the best paths between all pairs of vertices with the first vertex on the upper row of G and the second vertex on the lower row.

The vertices of the *top row* of G will be denoted by $T(i)$, and those of the *bottom row* of G by $B(i)$, $0 \leq i \leq n$. Given a string Y of length n with symbols

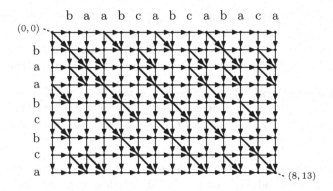

Fig. 2. Graph G for the ALCS problem, with $X = $ baabcbca and $Y = $ baabcabcabaca. The darker diagonal edges have weight 1 and the other edges weight 0.

y_1 to y_n, denote by Y_i^j the substring of Y consisting of symbols y_i to y_j. Define the *cost* or *total weight* of a path between two vertices as follows.

Definition 1 (Matrix C). *For $0 \leq i \leq j \leq n$, $C(i,j)$ is the cost or total weight of the best path between vertices $T(i)$ and $B(j)$, representing the length of the longest common subsequence between X and the substring Y_{i+1}^j. If $i \geq j$ (Y_{i+1}^j is empty or nonexistent), then $C(i,j) = 0$.*

Values of $C(i,j)$ are shown in Figure 3. For example, $C(0,9) = 8$. This means the length of the longest common subsequence between $X = $ baabcbca and $Y_1^9 = $ baabcabca is 8. However, note that $C(0,10)$ is also 8. That is, if we take one more symbol of Y, the length of the longest common subsequence is still the same. This leads to the next definition of M that deals with this leftmost position (in the example, 9 and not 10) to achieve a fixed length value (in the example, 8).

$C(i,j)$	0	1	2	3	4	5	6	7	8	9	10	11	12	13
0	0	1	2	3	4	5	6	6	7	8	8	8	8	8
1	0	0	1	2	3	4	5	5	6	7	7	7	7	7
2	0	0	0	1	2	3	4	4	5	6	6	6	6	7
3	0	0	0	0	1	2	3	3	4	5	5	6	6	7
4	0	0	0	0	0	1	2	2	3	4	4	5	5	6
5	0	0	0	0	0	0	1	2	3	4	4	5	5	6
6	0	0	0	0	0	0	0	1	2	3	3	4	4	5
7	0	0	0	0	0	0	0	0	1	2	2	3	3	4
8	0	0	0	0	0	0	0	0	0	1	2	3	3	4
9	0	0	0	0	0	0	0	0	0	0	1	2	3	4
10	0	0	0	0	0	0	0	0	0	0	0	1	2	3
11	0	0	0	0	0	0	0	0	0	0	0	0	1	2
12	0	0	0	0	0	0	0	0	0	0	0	0	0	1
13	0	0	0	0	0	0	0	0	0	0	0	0	0	0

Fig. 3. C corresponding to G of Figure 2

The values of $C(i,j)$ have the following property. For a fixed i, the values of $C(i,j)$ with $0 \leq j \leq n$ form a nondecreasing sequence that can be given implicitly by only those values of j for which $C(i,j) > C(i,j-1)$. This fact has been used in the PRAM algorithm presented in[9] motivates the following definition.

Definition 2 (Matrix M). *Consider G for the ALCS problem for the strings X and Y. For $0 \leq i \leq n$, $M(i,0) = i$ and for $1 \leq k \leq m$, $M(i,k)$ indicates the value of j such that $C(i,j) = k$ and $C(i,j-1) = k-1$. If there is no such a value, then $M(i,k) = \infty$.*

Implicit in this definition is the fact that $C(i,j) \leq m$. For convenience, we define M as a matrix with indices starting from 0. We denote by M_i the row i of M, that is, the row vector formed by $M(i,0), M(i,1), \ldots, M(i,m)$. As an example, we again consider G of Figure 2. The values of M are shown in Figure 4.

$M(i,k)$	0	1	2	3	4	5	6	7	8
0	0	1	2	3	4	5	6	8	9
1	1	2	3	4	5	6	8	9	∞
2	2	3	4	5	6	8	9	13	∞
3	3	4	5	6	8	9	11	13	∞
4	4	5	6	8	9	11	13	∞	∞
5	5	6	7	8	9	11	13	∞	∞
6	6	7	8	9	11	13	∞	∞	∞
7	7	8	9	11	13	∞	∞	∞	∞
8	8	9	10	11	13	∞	∞	∞	∞
9	9	10	11	12	13	∞	∞	∞	∞
10	10	11	12	13	∞	∞	∞	∞	∞
11	11	12	13	∞	∞	∞	∞	∞	∞
12	12	13	∞	∞	∞	∞	∞	∞	∞
13	13	∞	∞	∞	∞	∞	∞	∞	∞

Fig. 4. M corresponding to the graph G of Figure 2

To understand the M matrix, consider $M(i,k)$. Index i is the starting index of the Y string at the top row of G. The value k is the desired length of the common subsequence between X and the string Y starting at i. Consider G of Figure 2. If we start from position i of the top row and proceed to the bottom row at the position given by $M(i,k)$ then we can get a path of total weight k. Actually $M(i,k)$ gives the leftmost position that gives the total weight k. Let us illustrate this with an example. Since the length of string X is 8, the maximum value we can expect for k is therefore 8. Let us consider $M(0,8) = 9$. This means the following: in the graph G of Figure 2, start from the index 0 of the top row and take edges at either of the three directions: by taking the diagonal we get a weight 1 while by taking the horizontal or vertical edges we get weight 0. Now if we wish to have a total weight of 8, then the leftmost position at the bottom row will be 9. Thus we have $M(0, 8) = 9$. If we make i greater than 0 then we compare X with the string Y starting at position i.

Matrix M has the following nice property [9]. For $0 \leq i \leq n-1$, row M_{i+1} can be obtained from row M_i by removing the first element ($M_i(0) = i$) and inserting just one new element. It can be shown that matrix M has all the properties of a row-sorted 1-variant matrix. The parallel ALCS algorithm deals directly with M and thus it is crucial that it has a compact representation for M and at the same time provides quick access time. To the end, in the next sections, we explore the similarity between rows of the M matrix and thereby reduce the amount of space in the representation by eliminating redundancy. Another issue to have a compact representation is that it reduces the communication time when this data structure needs to be communicated among processors.

3   Two Inadequate Representations

3.1   The Naïve Representation

A row-sorted 1-variant matrix M with $m+1$ rows and $n+1$ columns can be stored in a naïve and straightforward way in a two-dimensional $(m+1) \times (n+1)$ array, using thus $O(mn)$ space. In the comparison of biological sequences (e.g. DNA or protein sequences), m and n can be very large and thus this storage scheme is not adequate. The waste in space is obvious since the similarity between consecutive rows is not taken into consideration. Some improvement can be achieved by using linked lists or arrays with varying row lengths. The improvement, however, is small.

3.2   The Linear-Space Representation

An obvious way that takes advantage of the fact that consecutive rows of M are similar is as follows. Denote by M_i row i of M. Then M can be represented by just its first row M_0 and a vector V, indexed from 1 to m, that indicates the new elements inserted in each row of M. With M_0 and V, the original matrix M can be reconstructed by simply reconstructing rows M_1 through M_{m-1}. In other words, for $0 \leq i < m$, row M_{i+1} is obtained from row M_i by excluding its first element and including a new element given by $V(i+1)$.

An additional property of the matrix M in the LCS problem is that *all* the elements between 0 and m should appear. This allows the reconstruction of M by using only the vector V, without the row M_0, since this row is given by the numbers not present in V. Whether using this additional property or not, the representation of M is only of $O(m)$, a drastic reduction in space. This modest space requirement makes it suitable to be transmitted among processors. However, there is a serious problem in this representation in that it does not provide quick access to elements of the matrix M. Given indices i and j it is desirable to obtain $M(i, j)$ in constant time. Thus, once a processor receives V it has to reconstruct the entire matrix M.

k	1	2	3	4	5	6	7	8	9	10	11	12	13
$V(k)$	∞	13	11	∞	7	∞	∞	10	12	∞	∞	∞	∞

Fig. 5. V corresponding to the graph G of Figure 2

4   A Constant Access Time Representation

The straightforward 2-D array representation of M allows constant access time with the high cost of $O(mn)$ space. In this section we present a representation of M that allows constant access time and uses $O(m\sqrt{n})$ space.

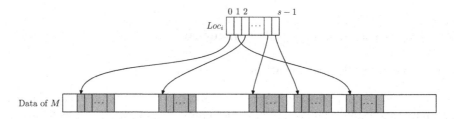

Fig. 6. One row of M stored in memory in pieces. Loc_i denotes row i of the auxiliary array Loc.

The elements of a single row of M are stored in the memory in pieces of size $s = \lceil \sqrt{n} \rceil$. To access any piece of any row of M, we use an auxiliary $m \times s$ array called Loc that takes $O(m\sqrt{n})$ space. $Loc(i, j)$ indicates the address of the jth piece of row M_i. Thus it is possible to access any element of M in an indirect way. For example, to locate $M(i, k)$, we first find the piece in which this element is located. This is easily done by inspecting the value of k. We then locate this piece by using Loc_i and finally locate the desired element in the piece located. All this can be done in $O(1)$ time. Figure 6 illustrates the use of Loc.

The total space requirement of this representation is only $O(m\sqrt{n})$ because pieces of distinct rows can be overlapped in the memory, whereby taking advantage of the similarity among the rows. For this to be feasible, we need to pay special attention during the construction of the representation of M. More precisely, when two adjacent rows M_i and M_{i+1} are divided into pieces, the comparison of pieces of index i and j can give the following results:

- The two pieces are equal. This occurs in the final pieces of the two rows. In this case, since matrix M is used only for queries, we can save space in memory by using the same piece for both rows. In other words, we make $Loc(i + 1, j) = Loc(i, j)$.
- The two pieces are different, because the data inserted in row $i + 1$, that is $V(i+1)$, appears in piece j. In this case, it is necessary to create a new space for the piece j of row $i + 1$.

- The piece of row $i + 1$ is identical to that of row i, with the exception of a shift to the left: the first element of the piece of row i is not present and the last piece of row $i + 1$ is new. We can share the space of the piece of row i, by making $Loc(i + 1, j) = Loc(i, j) + 1$, that solves the problem of skipping the first element of row i. To add a new element at the end of the piece of row $i + 1$, we copy this element in the space immediately after the piece of row i.

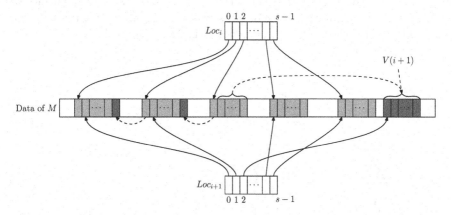

Fig. 7. Overlapping of the representation of rows M_i and M_{i+1} in memory. The dark color indicates data that are used only in the representation of M_{i+1}. The dash arrows indicate copy of data.

The last case requires the existence of some empty space right after the memory space used to store a certain piece. To guarantee this, every time a memory area is allocated to store a new piece (that is, when it is not possible to use the data of a previous row), we allocate actually a space of size $2s$, by using only the first s first positions for the data of the piece and leaving the next s positions empty. This allows the inclusion of up to s new elements on the right of this piece. When this space is exhausted, a new piece of size $2s$ must be allocated. Figure 7 illustrates how two rows of M can share space. A complete description of this structure, including an analysis of the space used and the time for the construction, is given in [1].

5   An $O(\log m)$ Access Time Representation

The storage scheme of the previous section is adequate to be used for parallel algorithms in terms of access time. There are, however, situations in which a reduced storage requirement is also very important, in addition to the access time. An intermediate data structure to satisfy both requirements is given in this section. It requires $O(m \log m)$ space, which is less than the $O(m\sqrt{n})$ space of the previous section. However, the access time is $O(\log m)$, as opposed to the constant time of the previous data representation.

5.1   Row Representation

Each row of the matrix M is represented by a complete binary tree with 2^k leaf nodes, $2^k \leq m + 1 < 2^{k+1}$. Number the leaf nodes from 0 to 2^k from left to right. Each leaf node represents a number from 0 to 2^k that may or may not be present in the matrix row.

Each tree node contains an integer. Row i of M, or M_i, is represented as follows. The leaf node j contains 1 if j is present in M_i or if $j < i$. If $j \geq i$ and j does not belong to M_i, then the leaf node j contains 0. Each internal node of the tree contains the sum of of its two sons. Figure 8 illustrates the tree representation for row 2 of the example matrix M of Figure 1.

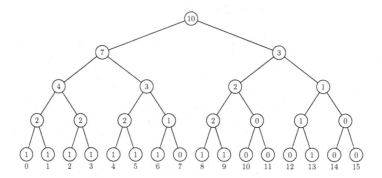

Fig. 8. Representation of row 2 of the example matrix M

With this representation, the following queries can be done in $O(\log m)$ time.

- Verifying if a number k is present on row M_i: it suffices to go down from the root node of tree M_i to the leaf node corresponding to the number k and check if its value is 0 or 1.
- Counting the number of elements of M_i less or equal to a certain number k: as above, do a traversal from the root to the leaf node corresponding to the number k and do a counting, starting with the count 0 at the root and, each time the traversal proceeds to a right son of a certain node, add the value of the left son to the count. When reaching the leaf node, add the value of the leaf node and subtract i from the count. This operation is useful in the context of the LCS problem.
- Querying the element $M(i, j)$: do the counting as above, but instead of going from the root towards a specific leaf node, use the count to direct the descent. The objective is to reach the end with a count equal to $j - i$. This is similar to a search in a binary search tree [8].

The space to store a single row of M is $O(m)$. If all the rows were represented in a straightforward way, without considering the similarities among the rows, then the total space would be $O(m^2)$. We show in the following how to take advantage of the row similarities so that their representation can be overlapped.

5.2 Representation of the Entire Matrix

Given two consecutive rows M_i and M_{i+1} of M, the only difference in the leaf nodes of their tree representations is the one that indicates the inclusion of element $V(i + 1)$, by changing the value of the leaf node $V(i + 1)$ from 0 to 1. The exclusion of the first element of $V(i)$ does not need to be represented in the leaf nodes, since the leaf node i will be ignored in the accesses to the row M_{i+1}. Furthermore, the tree representations of the two rows will differ in the values of the nodes between the leaf node $V(i + 1)$ and the root.

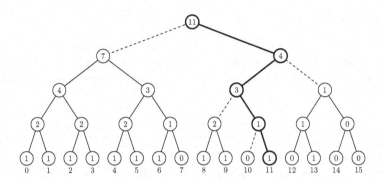

Fig. 9. Representation of row 3 of the example matrix M. The nodes joined by darker lines were created specifically for row 3, the other nodes were already used in row 2. The dash lines join the new and old nodes.

In this way, we can construct the representation of M_{i+1} by sharing the entire tree of M_i, with the exception of the nodes on the path from the root to the leaf node $V(i + 1)$. The additional space required is only $O(\log m)$ and the construction takes $O(\log m)$ time. Figure 9 shows the representation of row 3 of the example matrix M of Figure 1.

The complete structure takes $O(m \log m)$ space and can be constructed in $O(m \log m)$ time. It is an acyclic directed graph, with the roots of the several trees as origins (sources) and the leaf nodes as destinations (sinks).

This new scheme constitutes a trade-off between space requirement, access time, and construction time.

6 Related Work

In [11] Tiskin considers the sequential ALCS algorithm proposed by Alves et al. [5,3] and proposes a sequential algorithm to solve the *all semi-local longest common subsequence problem*, which is a generalization of the ALCS problem. In addition to computing the lengths of the longest common subsequence (LCS) between one given string and all the substrings of the other given string, it also computes the lengths of the LCS of all prefixes of one string with all the suffixes of the other string. His sequential algorithm is also based on the row-sorted 1-variant matrix M. He defines a characteristic matrix which is basically an extended M by considering an extended grid directed acyclic graph and defining the region outside the original grid directed acyclic graph G in such a way that the more general semi-local LCS problem can be solved in an elegant way. He proposes an $O(m + n)$ space representation for this characteristic matrix. Compared to Tiskin's proposal, the data structure proposed in this paper is simpler. We should observe, however, that Tiskin solves a more general problem.

7   Conclusion

In this paper we present three data structures to represent a certain class of matrices called the row-sorted 1-variant matrices. Fig. 10 summarizes the results of this paper, indicating the representation, the space requirement and the access time.

Representation	Data structure	Space requirement	Access time
Naïve	2-D array	$O(mn)$	$O(1)$
Linear space	Row M_0 and V	$O(m)$	$O(m)$
Constant time	Loc and each row in $\sqrt{n}$ pieces	$O(m\sqrt{n})$	$O(1)$
Log time	Binary tree	$O(m \log m)$	$O(\log m)$

Fig. 10. Comparison of the storage representations of $(m + 1) \times (n + 1)$ row-sorted 1-variant matrix M

The three storage structures present different space and access time characteristics. Row-sorted 1-variant matrices appear under the context of parallel algorithms design for string processing applications, e.g. the obtention of the LCS (longest common subsequence) of two strings and related problems [4]. For this problem, each of the three data structures plays an important role: the linear representation, using the row M_0 and a vector V, is used in the communication among processors; the constant access time representation is used in local computations in the processors, and the binary tree representation as a compromise between both the space and access time requirements. Another string processing problem that can use the proposed binary tree representation is the string alignment problem with non-overlapping inversions [6]. This data structure is shown to be adequate and constitutes a nice balance between access time, representation construction time, and space requirement.

It may seem that the results presented here do not appear to be general and apply strictly to the mentioned string processing problems. They nevertheless illustrate the necessity to choose adequate data structures in the design of efficient parallel algorithms. It is crucial to take advantage of the characteristics of the data used, regarding e.g. redundancy and symmetries, and thereby choosing a storage scheme that is more suitable for the parallel application.

References

1. Alves, C.E.R.: Coarse-Grained Parallel Algorithms for String Alignment Problems (in Portuguese). PhD thesis, Department of Computer Science - University of São Paulo (2002)
2. Alves, C.E.R., Cáceres, E.N., Song, S.W.: Sequential and parallel algorithms for the all-substrings longest common subsequence problem. Technical report, Universidade de São Paulo (April 2003)
3. Alves, C.E.R., Cáceres, E.N., Song, S.W.: An all-substrings common subsequence algorithm. 2nd Brazilian Symposium on Graphs, Algorithms and Combinatorics. Electronic Notes in Discrete Mathematics 19, 133–139 (2005)
4. Alves, C.E.R., Cáceres, E.N., Song, S.W.: A coarse-grained parallel algorithm for the all-substrings longest common subsequence problem. Algorithmica 45(3), 301–335 (2006)
5. Alves, C.E.R., Cáceres, E.N., Song, S.W.: An all-substrings common subsequence algorithm. Discrete Applied Mathematics (To Appear) (2007)
6. Alves, C.E.R., Lago, A.P., Vellozo, A.P.: Alignment with non-overlapping inversions in $O(n^3 \log n)$ time. 2nd Brazilian Symposium on Graphs, Algorithms and Combinatorics. Electronic Notes in Discrete Mathematics 19, 365–371 (2005)
7. Apostolico, A., Atallah, M.J., Larmore, L.L., Macfaddin, S.: Efficient parallel algorithms for string editing and related problems. SIAM J. Comput. 5(19), 968–988 (1990)
8. Cormen, T.H., Leiserson, C.E., Rivest, R.L.: Introduction to Algorithms. The MIT Press, Cambridge, MA (1989)
9. Lu, M., Lin, H.: Parallel algorithms for the longest common subsequence problem. IEEE Transactions on Parallel and Distributed Systems 5(8), 835–848 (1994)
10. Pevzner, P.A.: Computational Molecular Biology - An Algorithmic Approach. The MIT Press, Cambridge, MA (2000)
11. Tiskin, A.: All semi-local longest common subsequences in subquadratic time. In: Grigoriev, D., Harrison, J., Hirsch, E.A. (eds.) CSR 2006. LNCS, vol. 3967, pp. 352–363. Springer, Heidelberg (2006)

PHC: A Rapid Parallel Hierarchical Cubing Algorithm on High Dimensional OLAP*

Kongfa Hu[1], Ling Chen[1], and Yixin Chen[2]

[1] Department of Computer Science and Engineering, Yangzhou University, 225009, China
[2] Department of Computer Science and Engineering, Washington University, 63130, USA
kfhu05@126.com

Abstract. Data cube has been playing an essential role in OLAP (online analytical processing). The pre-computation of data cubes is critical for improving the response time of OLAP systems. However, as the size of data cube grows, the time it takes to perform this pre-computation becomes a significant performance bottleneck. In a high dimensional OLAP, it might not be practical to build all these cuboids and their indices. In this paper, we propose a parallel hierarchical cubing algorithm, based on an extension of the previous minimal cubing approach. The algorithm has two components: decomposition of the cube space based on multiple dimension attributes, and an efficient OLAP query engine based on a prefix bitmap encoding of the indices. This method partitions the high dimensional data cube into low dimensional cube segments. Such an approach permits a significant reduction of CPU and I/O overhead for many queries by restricting the number of cube segments to be processed for both the fact table and bitmap indices. The proposed data allocation and processing model support parallel I/O and parallel processing, as well as load balancing for disks and processors. Experimental results show that the proposed parallel hierarchical cubing method is significantly more efficient than other existing cubing methods.

Keywords: data cube, parallel hierarchical cubing algorithm (PHC), high dimensional OLAP.

1 Introduction

Data warehouses integrate massive amounts of data from multiple sources and are primarily used for decision support purposes. They have to process complex analytical queries for different access forms such as OLAP (on-line analytical processing), data mining, etc. OLAP refers to the technologies that allow users to efficiently retrieve data from the data warehouse for decision support purposes [1]. A lot of research has been done in order to improve the OLAP query performance and to

* The research in the paper is supported by the National Natural Science Foundation of China under Grant No. 60673060; the National Facilities and Information Infrastructure for Science and Technology of China under Grant No. 2004DKA20310; the National Tenth-Five High Technology Key Project of China under Grant No. 2003BA614A; the Natural Science Foundation of Jiangsu Province under Grant No. BK2005047 and BK2005046; the 'Qing Lan' Project Foundation of Jiangsu Province of China.

H. Jin et al. (Eds.): ICA3PP 2007, LNCS 4494, pp. 72–82, 2007.

provide fast response times for queries on large data warehouses. Efficient indexing [2], materialization [3] and data cubing [4] are common techniques to speed up the OLAP query processing. Many efficient cube computation algorithms have been proposed recently, such as BUC [5], H-cubing [6], Quotient cubing [7], and Star-cubing [8]. However, in the large data warehouse applications, such as bioinformatics, the data usually has high dimensionality with more than 100 dimensions. Since data cube grows exponentially with the number of dimensions, it is generally too costly in both computation time and storage space to materialize a full high-dimensional data cube. For example, a data cube of 100 dimensions, each with 100 distinct values, may contain as many as 101^{100} cells. If we consider the dimension hierarchies, the aggregate cell will increase even more tremendously. Although condensed cube [9], dwarf cube [10], or star cubes [8] can delay the explosion, it does not solve the fundamental problem [11]. The minimal cubing approach from Li and Han [11] can alleviate this problem, but does not consider the dimension hierarchies and cannot efficiently handle OLAP queries. In this paper, we develop a feasible parallel hierarchical cubing algorithm (PHC) that supports dimension hierarchies for high-dimensional data cubes and answers OLAP queries efficiently. The algorithm decomposes a multi-dimensional hierarchical data cube into smaller cube segments. This proposed data allocation and processing model supports parallel I/O and parallel processing as well as load balancing for disks and processors. This proposed cubing algorithm is an efficient and scalable parallel processing algorithm for cube computation.

2 Shell Parallel Prefix Cube Segmentation

2.1 Cube Segmentation

We proposed a decomposition scheme that partitions a high dimensional data cube into low dimensional shell cube segments with support for dimensional hierarchies.

In the data warehouse, a cube C is formally defined as the following (n+m)-tuple: $C=(D_1,...,D_n, M_1, ...,M_m)$ where D_i, for $1<= i <=n$, is a dimension and M_j, for $1<= j <=m$, is a measure. Each dimension D_i containing the hierarchical attributes $\{ L_1^i, L_2^i, \cdots, L_h^i \}$ (L_1^i being the most aggregated level and L_h^i the most detailed one), where L_j^i is the level j dimension hierarchy of the dimension D_i.

To illustrate the method, a tiny warehouse, Table 1, is used as a running example.

Table 1. A Sample Warehouse with Two Measure Values

TID	DimProduct			dimRegion			dimTime			Measure	
	Class	Item	Product	Country	Province	City	Year	Month	Day	Count	Num
1	Class1	Item1	Exploder	China	Jiangsu	Nanjing	1998	1	1	1	20
2	Class1	Item1	Exploder	China	Jiangsu	Nanjing	1998	1	2	1	60
3	Class1	Item1	Exploder	China	Jiangsu	Yangzhou	1998	1	2	1	40
4	Class1	Item1	Exploder	China	Jiangsu	Yangzhou	1998	1	3	1	20
...	...	...	...	...	...	...	...	...	...	...	...
367	Class1	Item1	Exploder	China	Jiangsu	Nanjing	1999	1	2	1	60
...	...	...	...	...	...	...	...	...	...	...	...

In Table 1, the original cube PRT have three dimensions, such as (P,R,T). From the RPT Cube, we would compute eight cuboids: {(P,R,T),(P,R,All),(P,All,T), (All,R,T), (P,All,All), (All,R,All), (All,All,T), (All,All,All)}. For a cube of d dimensions, it will create 2^d cuboids. If we consider the dimension hierarchies of each dimension, the cube will create $\prod_{i=1}^{d}(h_i+1)$ cuboids (where h_i is the number of hierarchy levels of dimension D_i). For example, the RPT cube in Table 1 has three dimensions: *DimProduct,DimRegion* and *DimTime*. The *DimProduct* dimension has three hierarchies as (*Class,Item,Product*), the *DimRegion* dimension has three hierarchies as (*Country,Province,City*), and the *DimTime* dimension has three hierarchies as (*Year,Month,Day*).Thus,this cube will generate $\prod_{i=1}^{d}(h_i+1)=(3+1)*(3+1)*(3+1)=64$ cuboids such as {(*Product,City,Day*), (*Product,City,Month*), (*Product,City,Year*), (*Product,City,All*) ,..., (*All,All,All*)}.

There is a substantial I/O overhead for accessing a fully materialized data cube. Cuboids are stored on disk in some fixed order, and that order might be incompatible with a particular query. Processing such queries may need a scan of the entire corresponding cuboids. One could avoid reading the entire cube if there are multi-dimensional indices constructed on all cuboids. But in a high-dimensional warehouse with many cuboids, it may not be practical to build all these indices. Furthermore, reading via an index implies random access for each row in the cuboids, which could turn out to be more expensive than a sequential scan of the raw data.

A partial solution, which has been implemented in some commercial data warehouse systems, is to compute a thin shell cube. For example, one might compute all cuboids with 3 dimensions or less in a 30-dimensional data cube. There are two disadvantages to this approach. First, it still needs to compute $C_{30}^3 + C_{30}^2 + C_{30}^1 = 4525$ cuboids, and it needs compute $2^h * C_{30}^3 + C_{30}^2 + C_{30}^1 = 2^3*4525=36200$ cuboids while we consider each dimension has h=3 levels dimension hierarchies.

In this paper, we propose to partition all the dimensions of the high-dimensional cube into independent groups, called Cube segments. For example, for a warehouse of 30 dimensions, D_1, D_2,...,D_{30}, we first partition the 30 dimensions into 10 Cube segments of size 3: (D_1,D_2,D_3), (D_4,D_5,D_6),...,(D_{28},D_{29},D_{30}).For each cube segment, we compute its full data cube. For example, in Cube segment(D_1,D_2,D_3),we compute eight cuboids:{(D_1,D_2,D_3), $(D_1,D_2,All),(D_1,All,D_3),(All,D_2,D_3),(D_1,All,All),$ (All,D_2,All),(All,All,D_3), (All,All,All)}. If we consider each dimension of the cube (D_1,D_2,D_3) has three hierarchies as $D_1(L_1^1,L_2^1,L_3^1),D_2(L_1^2,L_2^2,L_3^2),D_3(L_1^3,L_2^3,L_3^3)$,we compute 64 cuboids:{$(L_3^1,L_3^2,L_3^3),(L_3^1,L_3^2,L_2^3)$,...,(All,All,All)}.

For a base cube of 30 dimensions, there are only 8×10 = 80 cuboids to be computed according to the above shell segment partition, while we consider the each dimension has three hierarchies there are 64×10 = 640 cuboids to be computed. And comparing this to 4525 cuboids for the cube shell of size 3 and 4525×8=36200 cuboids while we consider each dimension has h=3 levels dimension hierarchies, the saving is significant.

2.2 Bitmap Indexing and Its Prefix Encoding

To index the data, we employ a bitmap join index called dimension hierarchical encoding on the higher-cardinality dimensions *dimProduct, dimRegion* and *dimTime*. This is illustrated in Table 4 for the *dimTime* dimension where we use separate bit sub-patterns to encode *Years, Months within Years, Days within Months* etc. We only need 12 bits to identify a particular *TimeID* so that the index only consists of 12 bits instead of 1,860 bits needed for simple bitmaps. Therefore, to locate all fact rows of a specific time, we need to evaluate only 12 bitmaps (which we will access in parallel). The encoded bitmap indices on *dimProduct* and *dimRegion* need 16 and 16 bitmaps, respectively.

For each dimension D_i, each hierarchy level L_j^i is encoded as $B^{L_j^i}$:dom(L_j^i)$\rightarrow$\{<b_{k-1}... b_i...b_0>|$b_i \in$ \{0,1\},i=0,...,k-1\}.The dimension hierarchical encoding B^{D_i} of each member on the dimension D_i is defined as follows.

$$B^{D_i} = (...((B^{L_1^i} <<Bit_{L_2^i} |B^{L_2^i})<<Bit_{L_3^i} |B^{L_3^i})...)<<Bit_{L_h^i} |B^{L_h^i}$$

Where k is the bit number of the hierarchy level L_j^i on the dimension D_i . k can be computed by k =$Bit L_j^i = \lceil \log_2 m \rceil$, where m= max($| L_j^i |$) is the max number of the distinct member of the hierarchy L_j^i . $B^{L_j^i}$ is the encoding of the level of every hierarchy on the dimension D_i and $Bit L_j^i$ is the bit number of the $B^{L_j^i}$.

We can create the *DimTime, dimRegion* and *dimProduct* dimension hierarchy encoding shown in Table 2, Table 3 and Table 4.

Table 2. *DimTime* dimension hierarchy encoding

TimeID	Year	Month	Day	B^{TimeID}
	yyy	mmmm	ddddd	yyymmmmddddd
1	98	Jan	1	001000100001
2	98	Jan	2	001000100010
3	98	Jan	3	001000100011
...	...	...	...	...
367	99	Jan	1	010000100011
...	...	...	...	...

Table 3. The *dimRegion* Dimension Hierarchy Encoding

RegionID	Country	Province	City	$B^{RegionID}$
	uuuuuuuu	vvvvv	cccc	uuuuuuuuvvvvvcccc
1	China	Jiangsu	Nanjing	0000001000010001
2	China	Jiangsu	Yangzhou	0000001000010010
...	...	...	...	...

Table 4. The *dimProduct* Dimension Hierarchy Encoding

ProductID	Class	Item	Product	$B^{ProductID}$
	gggg	aaaa	pppppppp	ggggaaaapppppppp
1	Class1	Item1	Exploder	0001000100000001
2	Class1	Item1	Exploder	0001000100000010
...	...	...	...	...

In Table 1, the dimension *DimTime* has three hierarchy levels {*Year,Month,Day*}. The Bit_{Year} of the hierarchy level *Year* is $Bit_{Year} = \lceil \log_2 \max(|Year|) \rceil = \lceil \log_2 5 \rceil = 3$ *bit*. The Bit_{Month} of the hierarchy level *Month* is $Bit_{Month} = \lceil \log_2 \max(|month|) \rceil = \lceil \log_2 12 \rceil = 4$ *bit*. The Bit_{Day} of the hierarchy level *Day* is $Bit_{Day} = \lceil \log_2 \max(|day|) \rceil = \lceil \log_2 31 \rceil = 5$ *bit*. The Bit_{Time} of the dimension *DimTime* is $Bit_{Time} = Bit_{Year} + Bit_{Month} + Bit_{Day} = 12$ *bit*. It is smaller than the integer encoding.

The dimension hierarchical encoding of the member "1999.Jan.2" on the dimension *DimTime* is 010000100010. It consists of $B^{Year=1999}B^{Month=1}B^{Day=2}$ and is computed by $B^{1999.Jan.2} = (B^{Year=1999} << Bit_{Month} | B^{Month=1}) << Bit_{Day} | B^{Day=2} = (010<<4|0001)<<5|00010 = 010000100010$.

By using the prefix bitmap encoding for dimensional hierarchies, we can register a list of tuples IDs (tids) associated with the dimension members for each dimension. For example, the TID list associated with the *dimProduct*, *dimRegion* and *dimTime* dimension are shown in Table5, Table 6 and Table 7.

To compute a data cube for this warehouse with the measure avg(), we need to have a tid-list for each cell: {tid_1,..., tid_n}. Because each tid is uniquely associated with a particular set of measure values, all future computations just need to fetch the measure values associated with the tuples in the list. Table 8 shows what exactly should be kept, which is substantially smaller than the warehouse itself.

Table 5. *dimProduct* dimension TID

$B^{ProductID}$	TID List
0001000100000001	1-2-3-4-367
...	...

Table 6. *dimRegion* dimension TID

$B^{RegionID}$	TID List
0000001000010001	1-2-367
0000001000010010	3-4
...	...

Table 7. *dimTime* dimension TID

B^{TimeID}	TID List
001000100001	1
001000100010	2-3
001000100011	4
...	...
010000100001	367

Table 8. TID-measure array of Table 2

tid	Cnt	Num
1	1	20
2	1	60
3	1	40
4	1	20
...	...	...
367	1	60
...	...	...

3 Parallel Hierarchical Cubing Algorithm

3.1 Parallel Hierarchical Cubing Algorithm

The data cube can be distributed across a set of parallel computers or Grid hosts by parallel constructing the Cube segments. Therefore, for the end-user and other potential applications, we consider this data cube as one large virtual cube, which is distributed across a set of parallel computers or Grid hosts, which manage the creation, updates and querying of the associated cube portions. To develop appropriate scheduling mechanisms for these management tasks, we consider that the virtual cube is split into several smaller parts, called Cube segments. But a Cube segment could furthermore also be split into smaller segments and so on, till we achieve the level of chunks. They can then be assigned to parallel computers or Grid hosts, having sequential or parallel computing power, which are responsible for their management. The algorithm for shell prefix cube segment parallel computation can be summarized as follows.

```
Algorithm 1. Parallel computation of shell cube segments
{/*Input: A base cuboid BC of n dimensions:(D₁; ...
;Dₙ).
   Output: (1) A set of Cube segment partitions {P₁;...,
   Pₖ} and their corresponding (local)  Cube segments
   {CS₁; ... ; CSₖ}, where Pᵢ represents some set of
   dimension(s) and P₁∪...∪ Pₖ are all the n
   dimensions, and (2) an ID measure array if the
   measure is not tuple-count such as {sum, avg}.*/
   partition the set of dimensions :(D₁; ... ;Dₙ) into a
      set of k Cube segments {P₁;..., Pₖ};
   scan base cuboid BC once and do the  following with
      parallel processing
         {insert each <tid, measure> into ID-measure
         array;
            for each attribute value aᵢ of each dimension Dᵢ
               build an dimension hierarchy encoding index
               entry: <B: TID list>;}
   parallel processing all segment partition Pᵢ as follows
         build a local  Cube segments CSᵢ by intersecting
            their corresponding tid-lists and computing
            their measures;
}
```

We can parallel construct the high dimensional cube with the Cube segments parallel construction. The system architecture of these shell Cube segment parallel construction is shown in Figure 1.

The Cube *Constructor* reads one tuple after the other, passes over the items to the index warehouse, retrieves its global index and then passes the (raw) measure and its associated global index to the data cube structure. The *Querying Cube operator* is some kind of highly sophisticated, recursively nested loops for aggregation of measures. Because the number of computational operations of nested aggregation depends on the size of the dimensions and thereby on the order in which dimensions are aggregated, the engine uses a kind of query plan optimization to select dimensions in a "good" way. The procedure of dimension selection is done by traversing a tree which in literature usually is called the cube lattice(see Figure 2) . The task of aggregation is realized sequentially by loading one chunk after the other and aggregating them one by one.

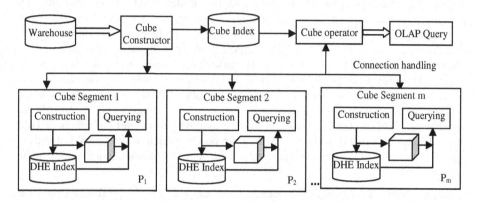

Fig. 1. The System Architecture of Parallel Construction of Shell Cube Segments

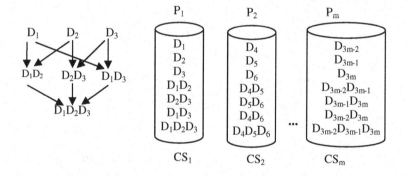

Fig. 2. Cube Segment Parallel Construction and CS₁ Cube Lattice

3.2   Efficient OLAP Query

Based on the bitmap indexing, we can efficiently retrieve the matching hierarchy levels of each dimension, evaluate the set of query ranges for each dimension, and improve the efficiency of OLAP queries. A key property of our encoding is that it is a prefix indexing scheme that allows one to quickly retrieve a path prefix for each dimension.

The path prefix of the member d_k^i of the hierarchy level L_j^i is defined as

$$DMPrefixpath\ DTree, d_k^i) = \cup_{j=i}^1 DMPrefixpath\ (DTree, Parent\ (d_k^j)) = \{\ Ancesto$$

$r(d_k^i)\}$, where $Ancestor\ (d_k^i)$ is the all *ancestors* of the member d_k^i according to its dimension hierarchy tree. The encoding prefix of the member d_k^i is defined as

$$Bprefix (B^{d_k^i}, L_{m-1}^i) = B^{d_k^i} >> \sum_{l=m}^{j} (Bit\ L_l^i), \text{ where } m=\{1, ...j\}.$$

Example 2. In the above example, the path prefix of the member "1999.Jan.2" on the dimension *DimTime* is *DMPrefixpath(DTimeTree*, 1999.Jan.2)={1999.Jan, 1999}. Its encoding prefix on the hierarchy *Month* is $BPrefix(B^{1999.Jan.2}, Month) = B^{1999.Jan} = B^{1999.Jan.2} >> Bit_{Day} = 010000100010 >> 5 = 0100001$. Its encoding prefix on the hierarchy *Year* is $BPrefix(B^{1999.Jan.2}, Year) = B^{1999} = B^{1999.Jan.2} >> (Bit_{Day} + Bit_{Month}) = 010000100010 >> (5+4) = 010$.

By using the path prefix, we can register the dimension hierarchy encoding and its TID list for every dimension hierarchy level. For example, the dimension hierarchy encoding and its TID list associated with the dimension hierarchies *Month* and *Province* are shown in Table 9 and Table 10.

Table 9. *Month* hierarchy encoding *Prefix* AND its TID

B^{TimeID}	$Bprefix(B^{TimeID}, Month)$	TID List
001000100001		
001000100010	0010001	1-2-3-4
001000100011		
...	...	...

Table 10. *Province* hierarchy encoding *Prefix* AND its TID

$B^{RegionID}$	$Bprefix(B^{RegionID}, Province)$	TID List
0000001000010001	000000100001	1-2-3-4-367
0000001000010010		
...	...	...

For each shell Cube segment, we compute the complete data cube by intersecting the TID-lists in the dimension and its hierarchies in a bottom-up depths-first order in the cuboid lattice (as seen in [8]). For example, to compute the cell {0001000100000001, 0000001000010001, 0010001 }, we intersect the TID lists of $B^{ProductID}$ =0001000100000001, $B^{RegionID}$ =0000001000010001, and $Bprefix(B^{TimeID}, Month) = 0010001$ to get a new list of {1,2}. Cuboid (Product,City,Month) and Cuboid (Product,Province,Month) are shown in Table 11 and Table 12.

Table 11. Cuboid (Product,City,Month)

Cell			Intersection	TID List	Measure	
$B^{ProductID}$	$B^{RegionID}$	$Bprefix(B^{TimeID}, Month)$			Cnt	Num
0001000100000001	0000001000010001	0010001	1-2-3-4-367∩1-2-367∩1-2-3-4	1-2	2	80
0001000100000001	0000001000010001	0100001	1-2-3-4-367∩1-2-367∩367	367	1	60
0001000100000001	0000001000010010	0010001	1-2-3-4-367∩3-4∩1-2-3-4	3-4	2	60
0001000100000001	0000001000010010	0100001	1-2-3-4-367∩3-4∩367	Φ	0	0
...	...	...	...	...	...	...

Table 12. Cuboid (Product,Province,Month)

Cell			Intersection	TID	Measure	
$B^{ProductID}$	$Bprefix(B^{RegionID}$,Province)	$Bprefix(B^{TimeID}$,Month)		List	Cnt	Num
0001000100000001	000000100001	0010001	1-2-3-4-367∩1-2-3-4-367∩1-2-3-4	1-2-3-4	4	140
0001000100000001	000000100001	0100001	1-2-3-4-367∩1-2-3-4-367∩367	367	1	60
...	...	...	...	...	...	...

4 Performance Study

In this section, we perform a thorough analysis of these costs. In our experimentation we generated a large number of synthetic data sets which in terms of the following parameters: d— number of dimensions, h_i — number of hierarchy levels of dimension D_i, m— maximum number of distinct members of the hierarchy L^i_j, T— number of tuples , f — size of the shell cube segment.The entire shell Cube segment will create $\sum_{i=1}^{f} C_f^i * d / f = (2^f * d/f)$ cuboids and needs $O(T* \sum_{i=1}^{f} C_f^i * d / f) = O(T* (2^f * d/f))$ storage space, while the partial cube will create $\sum_{i=1}^{f} C_d^i$ cuboids needs $O(T* \sum_{i=1}^{f} C_d^i)$ storage space, and the full cube will create 2^d cuboids and needs $O(|T|*2^d)$ storage space. If we consider each dimension has h hierarchies, our parallel hierarchical cubing (PHC) method will create $\prod_{i=1}^{f}(h_i +1) * d / f = ((h+1)^f * d/f)$ cuboids, while the minimal cubing method will create $\sum_{i=1}^{f} C_f^i (\sum_{j=1}^{h_i} C_{h_i}^j) * d / f = (2^{f+h} * d/f)$ cuboids. Our parallel hierarchical cubing (PHC) method needs O $(T*((h+1)^f * d/f)* \lceil \log_2 m \rceil /8)$ storage space, while the minimal cubing method needs $O(T*(2^{f+h} * d/f)* \lceil \log_{10} m \rceil)$ storage space.

The performance results of parallel hierarchical cubing (PHC) and the minimal cubing are reported from Figure 3 to Figure 6. Figure 3 shows the storage size of the two methods on the cube had $T=10^6$ tuples and h =1 level hierarchy and with shell fragment size f=3, and the storage size of the two methods on the cube had h=3 levels hierarchies is shown in the Figure 4[From the result of the minimal cubing of Li's and Han's [11], the shell fragment size f is between 2 and 4 is a reasonable range. So we mostly consider the shell fragment size is f=3.]. Figure 5 shows the average I/O page access for online query of the two methods on the cube had different levels of hierarchy and with shell fragment size f=3 and $T=10^6$ tuples. Figure 6 shows the time needed to compute the shell Cube segments with fragment size f=3.

The analytical results show the method of Cube segments has more efficient than other cube such as partial cube and full cube. The Figure 3 - Figure 6 show the performance of the parallel hierarchical cubing (PHC) method is more efficient than the other existed leading cubing algorithms such as minimal cubing.

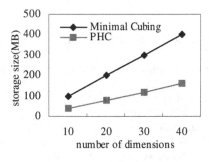

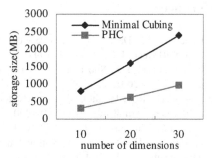

Fig. 3. Storage Size of Shell Segment h=1   **Fig. 4.** Sorage Size of Shell Segment h=3

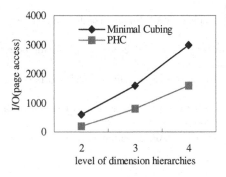

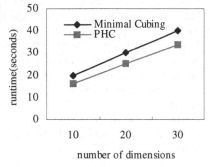

Fig. 5. Average I/Os with f=3   **Fig. 6.** Cube segments computation

5 Conclusions

Data cube has been playing an essential role in fast OLAP in many multi-dimensional data warehouses. The pre-computation of data cubes is critical to improving the response time of OLAP systems. But in a high-dimensional OLAP (such as the applications of bioinformatics and statistical analysis, etc.), it might not be practical to build all these cuboids and their indices. We have proposed a novel approach for OLAP in high-dimensional datasets with a moderate number of tuples. It partitions a high dimensional cube into a set of disjoint low dimensional cubes (i.e., shell cube segments). Using a prefix bitmap indexing and pre-aggregated results, OLAP queries are computed online by dynamically constructing the cuboids from these cube segments. We have experimentally compared the proposed parallel hierarchical cubing method with the other existing cubing algorithms such as partial cubing and minimal cubing. The analytical and experimental results show that the proposed PHC algorithm is significantly more efficient in time and space than the other leading cubing methods on large data warehouses.

References

1. Chauduri, S., Dayal, U.: An overview of data warehousing and OLAP technology. SIGMOD Record 26(1), 65–74 (1997)
2. Wu, K., Otoo, E.J., Shoshani, A.: A performance comparison of bitmap indexes. CIKM pp. 559–561 (2001)
3. Mistry, H., Roy, P., Sudarshan, S.: Materialized view selection and maintenance using multi-query optimization. SIGMOD(2001), pp. 307–318 (2001)
4. Gray, J., Chaudhuri, S., Bosworth, A., Layman, A., Reichart, D., Venkatrao, M., Pellow, F., Pirahesh, H.: Datacube: A relational aggregation operator generalizing group-by, cross-tab and subtotals. Data Mining and Knowledge Discovery 1, pp. 29–54 (2001)
5. Beyer, K., Ramakrishnan, R.: Bottom-up computation of sparse and iceberg cubes. ACM SIGMOD, pp. 359–370 (1999)
6. Han, J., Pei, J., Dong, G., Wang, K.: Efficient computation of iceberg cubes with complex measures. ACM SIGMOD, pp.1–12 (2001)
7. Lakshmanan, L.V.S., Pei, J., Han, J.: Quotient cubes: how to summarize the semantics of a data cube. VLDB, pp. 778–789 (2002)
8. Xin, D., Han, J., Li, X., Wah, B.W.: Star-cubing:computing iceberg cubes by top-down and bottom-up integration.VLDB, pp. 476–487 (2003)
9. Sismanis, Y., Deligiannakis, A., Kotidis, Y., Roussopoulos, N.: Hierarchical dwarfs for the rollup cube.VLDB, pp. 540–551 (2004)
10. Lakshmanan, L. V. S., Pei, J., and Zhao, Y.: QC-trees: An efficient summary structure for semantic OLAP. ACM SIGMOD, pp. 64–75 (2003)
11. Li, X., Han, J., Gonzalez, H.: High-dimensional OLAP: A minimal cubing approach. VLDB, pp. 528–539 (2004)

A Time and Interaction Model for Open Distributed Timing Computation*

Limin Shen[1], Shangping Ren[2], Feng Li[1], and Yunfeng Mu[1]

[1] Department of Computer Science and Technology, Yanshan University
Qinhuangdao, Hebei 066004, China
shenllmm@sina.com, ysu_lifeng@126.com, yfm@ysu.edu.cn
[2] Department of Computer Science, Illinois Institute of Technology
Chicago, IL 60616, USA
ren@iit.edu

Abstract. A time and interaction coordination model is presented to address the dynamic changes of interaction topology and real-time constraints among autonomous entities in open distributed timing computation. Driven by events, the model distinguishes between three kinds of entities: time coordinators, interaction coordinators and computation entities, which are separated from traditional autonomous entities based on the separation of concerns. A time coordinator is responsible for controlling real-time behaviors; an interaction coordinator is to coordinate interaction and reconfigure interconnection topology among computation entities; a computation entity is only responsible for performing pure computation. An implementation framework is additionally suggested based on Java Message Service and EJB technology. Finally, an application to a vehicle navigation system is presented, including several traffic control centers, a GPS and a navigator. It illustrates how the model and the framework can be used to achieve both the interaction topology and the timing constraints.

Keywords: distributed timing computation, coordination model, real-time, separation of concerns, message, event.

1 Introduction

In open distributed computation environment such as Internet, the system may demand to add or reduce autonomous and mobile components or entities meanwhile the entities may enter or leave the system. These frequent changes make distributed computation system more dynamic, uncertain, and real-time requirements more difficult satisfy. Hence, a significant challenge in designing distributed real-time computation system is to design coordination mechanisms that allow the satisfaction of real-time behaviors while allowing a dynamic interconnection topology. However, past research in this area has often concentrated on either supporting coordination with real time constraints or supporting dynamic interconnection topology alone. Few

* Supported by the State Scholarship Foundation, China (Grant No.2003813003).

H. Jin et al. (Eds.): ICA3PP 2007, LNCS 4494, pp. 83–94, 2007.

researches have aimed at providing a model for discussing and expressing the real-time and the reconfiguration as well as their relationship.

While open systems embed computation and interaction logics, traditional program paradigms have usually been computation-centric, where interaction logic and timing constraints are intertwined with pure computational functionalities, where application-specific coordination logic is hard coded in the components. Hence, it becomes increasingly expensive to change functionality, timing constraints and interconnection topology.

To overcome the shortcomings above, we present a time and interaction coordination model, in which the three categories of entities: time coordinators, interaction coordinators, and computation entities, are separated from traditional entities based on the separation of concerns. A time coordinator is responsible for controlling real-time behaviors and imposing the desired timing constraints on computation entities; an interaction coordinator is used to build communication connections and reconfigure interconnection topology among computation entities as needed; and finally computation entities accomplish the pure function of the system. Because computation entities are freed from interaction and timing concerns, and the coordinators are restricted to accomplish coordination behaviors, they can be modeled and designed independently. The model not only simplifies the design of open distributed computing applications, but also upholds the reusability, dynamic adaptability and reconfiguration of both computational entities and coordinators.

The rest of the paper is organized as follows: section 2 discusses related work. Section 3 discusses the model in detail. Section 4 gives an implementation framework by using the Java Message Service and the EJB technology. Section 5 illustrates an application of the model through a vehicle navigation example. At the end, section 6 concludes the paper and presents future research work.

2 Related Work

The software coordination is the process of building interconnection among autonomous entities, controlling and constraining their interaction activities, and making them work harmoniously. A coordination model materializes software coordination technology, which is the glue that binds a group of separate activities together and provides a framework for expressing interaction among coordinated entities [8].

"Separation of concerns" has long been recognized as an important principle for handling software complexity [2], [11] since 1970's. Coordination models and its languages have been classified as in two major categories [8], data-driven and control-driven. A data-driven model provides a shared data space and a set of primitives for the computation components to manipulate data in the space that is content-addressable; while in the control-driven models, coordination components that are usually completely separated from the computation. In data-driven models, at least stylistically and linguistically, there exists a mixture of coordination and computation codes.

Data-driven models are exemplified by Linda [1],[3], in which tuple spaces work as passive information storage and active entities determine which messages can be put into or picked up. The activity in a data-driven application tends to center around a substantial body of shared data; the application is essentially concerned with what happens to the data. However, the data-driven coordination is not able to control data flow because ability to control data flow is distributed inside entities.

The control-driven model addresses some of the shortcomings in the data-driven model. As an example in [6],[9], Papadopoulos and Arbab (1998) presented the IWIM model and corresponding language MANIFOLD where the application's activity is centered on the explicit control flow between the activities that consume input data, and subsequently produce, remember, and transform this data.

In aspects of real-time coordination, [5], [7] and [10] gave approaches dependent on underlying system architecture or real-time languages to impose real-time constraints. They did not discuss real-time, interaction issues and their relations at the same time.

3   A Time and Interaction Coordination Model

3.1   Separation of Concerns

Open real-time distributed systems, such as onboard navigation systems, traffic control systems and control systems in airplanes, have three main characteristics. They are: (1) dynamic, the communication topology among autonomous entities within a system that changes frequently; (2) real-time aware, there are some timing constraints imposed on some behaviors; (3) functional, the systems are designed to execute tasks and achieve goals. Based on the "separation of concern" principle, the concerns in these three aspects can be designed to be orthogonal to each other, and they are specified and modelled independently as time coordinators, interaction coordinators and computation entities. A Time and Interaction Coordination (TIC) Model is induced shown as Fig. 1. During running time, these entities are combined together by coordinators without introducing new functionalities into computation entities.

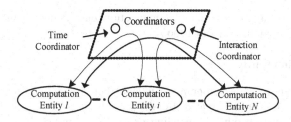

Fig. 1. Separation of computation and coordination in model TIC

3.2   Event-Driven Coordination and Message Connection

In the TIC model, inspired by the control-driven approach, there are two types of communication media: messages and events. Messages are only generated by computation entities, which transmit computation information through message channels built by the interaction coordinators point-to-point and asynchronous communication. Events can yield at computation entities or coordinators and they transmit control information to tell what is happening in the event source, which are broadcast and almost instant. Different from the events in MANIFOLD, the TIC model's events can carry simple parameters. In principle, any active entity in the environment can pick up a broadcast event and react to that event asynchronously, but in practice an observer is only interested in a subset of events. The events at higher level should not be of interest to the entities at lower level.

There is also an event mechanism for information exchange. When an observer at the current state observes an occurrence of some specific event, the event triggers the observer to enter another state and perform some actions. Once an event has been raised, its source generally continues with its activities, while the event occurrence propagates through the environment independently and is observed by other entities according to each observer's own sense of priorities.

The real-time behaviors in some sense are reactions to events that can always be done in bounded time, even if not instantaneously. The event driven mechanism can provides a bounded-time response for real-time requirement. The time coordinators control time relationships by yielding timing event, meanwhile the interaction coordinators react to timing events, and dynamically redirect messages connection between computation entities to satisfy system's temporal requirement.

3.3 Elementary Framework of the Model

The main characteristics of the TIC model are as follows:

- Coordinated entities are computation entities of the distributed application;
- Coordination media are messages connections and events;
- Coordination laws are defined through the semantics of the interactions and timing constraints in the coordination media;
- Coordination is event-oriented in the sense that the coordinators observe the occurrence of events and execute some actions based on defined conditions, i.e., ECA (Event-Condition-Action).
- Coordinators are transparent to computation entities meanwhile computation entities are transparent to each other too.

3.4 Computation Entity

A computation entity is an autonomous, independent and active object dedicated to specific computation task, treated by the coordinators as black boxes. It can communicate with each other by sending or receiving messages through using the primitives send and receive. It is not necessary for a computation entity to know the source or the destination of a communication, so communication is anonymous. Its only other communication with its environment is by means of raising its events, but it does not concern the external events. Its state changes are dependent on the messages received. It does not concern coordinator's events and states. Hence, coordinators are completely transparent to computation entities. Such a computation entity can be moved to any other environment and as long as it gets suitable messages. It will produce the required output messages without knowing who has sent it messages, who will make use of its output messages, or who are its coordinators.

The entity encapsulates system's functional behaviors and possesses two message queues and a control thread. Its behaviors are composed of a set of states and a set of methods that manipulate messages at the states. Only messages may trigger their activities and state changes. The computation entities are asynchronous, and unprocessed messages are buffered in their queues.

A computation entity has a unique name and uses the following primitive operations:

- *Send(MessageType, message)* sends a message;
- *Receive(MessageType, message)* receives a message;
- *Raise(event-name, $V_1,...,V_k$)* yields a specific event with parameters $V_1,...,V_k$ to show what has happened in the computation entity.

3.5 Interaction Coordinator

An interaction coordinator is a non-functional active entity in that it does not contribute to the system's functional behaviors. However, it has states and knowledge about a set of existing computation entities' name and interfaces. The functionalities of interaction coordinator are to build up interconnection among computation entities and route messages from senders to receivers based on the coordinator's states. Hence, interaction coordinators determine the system's interconnection topology, support and manage dynamic reconfiguration.

A coordinator waits for observing an occurrence of some specific event at the current state, which triggers it to enter another state and perform some actions. Typical actions in an interaction coordinator consist of setting up or breaking off connections between computation entities. It then remains in that state until it observes the occurrence of other event that causes the preemption of the current state in favour of a new one corresponding to that event.

An interaction coordinator uses following primitives operations:

- *Event(event-name)* observes a specific event which may trigger some actions.
- *Connect(ce_1, ce_2)* dynamically sets up a message connection between computation entities ce_1 and ce_2;
- *Disconnect(ce_1, ce_2)* dynamically breaks off a message connection among computation entities;
- *Raise(event-name, $V_1,...,V_k$)* yields a specific event with parameters $V_1,...,V_k$ to show what has happened in the coordinator;
- *Wait-event()* is waiting for the occurrence of events.

3.6 Time Coordinator

A time coordinator defines temporal behaviors and timing constraints. Similar to interaction coordinators, a time coordinator does not participate in computation. The functionalities of time coordinator are to impose or dismiss timing constraints based on the coordinator's states, events, and defined rules. A time coordinator has its states and uses the primitive operations: *Event, Raise, Wait-event, Impose* and *Dismiss*. The primitive *Event, Raise and Wait-event* are the same as those in interaction coordinators.

- *Impose(E_1, E_2, Bounded-Time, Timeout-Event)* imposes a timing constrain *Bounded-Time* on a event pattern(E_1, E_2), which means if E_2 does not occur in period of *Bounded-Time* after E_1, an event *Timeout-Event* will happen and the timing constraint is dismissed at the same time.
- *Dismiss(E_1, E_2, Bounded-time)* dismisses the constraint on the pattern (E_1, E_2).

3.7 Use of Primitives

The primitive operations *Event, Raise* and *Wait-event* can be used commonly in the coordinators and computation entities. The usage of *Connect* is different from *Impose*. *Impose* only imposes a timing constraint on individual event pattern once whereas *connect* builds up a long term of connection until *disconnect* execution. The primitive in a statement is usually triggered by a specific event and guarded by a Boolean expression of coordinator's states and associated constraints.

4   Implementation of Model

4.1   The Implementation Framework of Model

The model is implemented based on JMS (Java Message Service) [4] and EJB(Enterprise Java Bean)[12]. JMS is a Java API that allows applications to create, send, receive and read messages. An enterprise bean is a server-side component that can encapsulate the business logic of an application. There are the three types of enterprise beans, namely, session bean, entity bean and message-driven bean.

The implementation framework is composed of JMS client, JMS server and EJB server (Fig.2). JMS server provides communication facility for JMS client, and EJB server manages the coordinators dynamically.

The JMS client functionality is to create a connection with JMS server, create message receiver and sender objects, send and receive messages, execute a computation entity.

A JMS server is a communication plateform among entities, which can provide service of asynchronous or synchronous message communication and event broadcast based on the point-to-point and the publish/subscribe mode, and create, delete and control a message queue.

An EJB server is the environment of executing and managing EJB components, which is used for deploying time coordinators and interaction coordinators. EJB2.0 introduces a message-driven bean that allows J2EE applications to process messages or events asynchronously. When a message or an event arrives, the EJB server invokes the coordinator's onMessage method to process the message or the event.

Based on JMS and EJB technology, our framework can simply implement message transmission and event broadcast mechanism, which is available and realistic. It not only satisfys the need of implementing model but also does not require the special architecture and language.

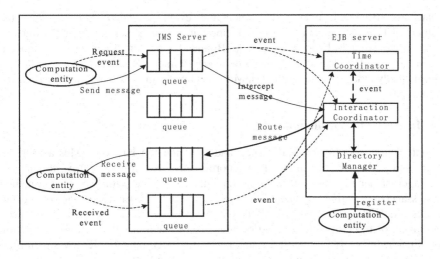

Fig. 2. Implementation framework of model

4.2 Computation Entity

A computation entity is a JMS client. It contains two very importance objects, the sender(sendQueue) and receiver(receiveQueue), which are created by using JMS API during the computation entity initializtion. The sender(sendQueue) and receiver (receiveQueue) simplify the implementation of sending and receiving messages in computation entities because they encapsulate a set of JMS connection and communication. The parameters sendQueue and receiveQueue are queue's name defined by the developer; the sender's method send(message) can send a message to sendQueue; the receiver's method receive(message) can receive a message from receiveQueue. The primitive operations send and receive are implemented easily by the sender and receiver objects. They can be also used to broadcast an event, so we can use them to implement the primitive *raise* too.

4.3 Time Coordinator

A time coordinator is implemented and designed based on message-driven Bean and JMS. The interfaces of the MessageListener, MessageDrivenBean, TimerService and TimeObject provide the timing and event operations for the time coordinator. MessageDrivenBean's method ejbCreate() is used to look for the connection factory and the message queues in the JMS server, and establish connections between them and the time coordinator. The TimerService's interface provides a method createTimer(Bound-time, null) to create a timer for a event. The MessageListener interface provides a method onMessage(), similar to an event listener. When an event arrives, the EJB server invokes the time coordinator's onMessage() to process the event. The onMessage() contains the primitive operations: *Impose* and *Dismiss*. An impose() will impose a timing constraints on event pattern (E_1, E_2). The impose() is implemented as follow: based on the observed even E_1, a timer with a timing constraint Bounded-Time is created for the event E_1 by using the method createTimer(Bounded-Time□null); when the event Bounded-Time reaches, the method ejbTimeout(timer) can carry out time-out actions, generally raising a time-out event; if the event E_2 happens before the Bounded-Time, the timer will be removed. When an entity broadcasts an event to its interface, the EJB server receives the event automatically, and then the method onMessage() performs some actions based on the event type.

4.4 Interaction Coordinator

An interaction coordinator is designed and implemented based on Message-driven Bean and JMS. In the interaction coordinator, only MessageDrivenBean and MessageListener interfaces need to be implemented. Three primitives in the method onMessage() are defined: connect, disconnect and route. When a message or an event arrives, the EJB server firstly sends it to onMessage(), which executes the connect, disconnect or route operation based on the type of event and the state of interaction coordinator. In connect(ce_1, ce_2), ce_1 and ce_2 represent computation entity's identifier. Connect(ce_1, ce_2) uses ce_1 and ce_2 to look up their detail information in the directory manager, and then saves these information into a connection table. The method route() re-routes the message to a receiver based on the connection. When the interaction coordinator observes a message sent by the computation entity, it looks up the receiver in the connection table, and then it calls the method messageSender (Messagetype, message, type, queueName) to send the message to the receiver's queue.

5 An Application

5.1 Description of Example

A vehicle navigation system is aided by a GPS (Global Position System) and traffic control centers. Given a destination, the GPS system is able to navigate the vehicle to the destination. There may be different optimization goals for the vehicle in deciding the path to the destination, such as shortest or fastest path, etc. Taking road, traffic or environment condition into account, the shortest path or the regular highway path may not be the quickest path. Therefore, the vehicle needs frequently communicate with the traffic control center to get the current road and traffic information in detail. Different control center controls different regions. As the vehicle moves on, it needs to communicate with different control centers to get accurate and up to date information. Furthermore, as the vehicle should not stop in the middle of the road for too long waiting for information arrival, after a limited time, if no information from the traffic center is received, it must make a decision based only on the GPS information to decide path. This example unveils two important characteristics of this type of applications: (1) there are real-time constraints applied upon the autonomous entities; (2) the communication topology among the autonomous entities, such as a vehicle navigator, a GPS and traffic control centers, changes dynamically.

5.2 Application of Model

Assuming that there are several control centers that the vehicle needs to contact, and at each decision point, the car is allowed for 20 seconds to wait for receiving information from a traffic center before it uses the GPS. Furthermore, the control center needs to be checked every 5 minutes to confirm whether it needs to be changed to another one based on current location and destination.

With the TIC model, the navigation system is composed of five parts: a navigator, serveral traffic control centers, a GPS, a time coordinator and an interaction coordinator. The navigator is a decision-maker, which only makes decisions based on its current state and information delivered to it. The traffic control center only provides traffic information service. The time coordinator imposes some timing constraints on the messages to the navigator by specific event patterns. The interaction coordinator sets up or breaks off connection and routes message among the navigator, the traffic control centers, and the GPS. The navigator, the GPS and the traffic control center are computation entities. The navigator, the time coordinator, the interaction coordinator are deployed in the car. The high level description of the time coordinator and the interaction coordinator is given in Fig.3 and Fig.4. The interconnection and timing constraints rules are stored in their rule inventory, which facilitates modification or update of the rules.

```
Time-Coordinator() {
    ......
    // event-in: Information-requested, Information-received, Traffic-Center
    //event-out: Time-Coordinator-initial, Received-timeout, Traffic-Center-Timeout
    // state 0
    EVENT:      event("Time-Coordinator-initial")
                impose("Information-requested", "Information-received", 20, "Received-timeout");
                wait-event()
    //State 1
    EVENT:      event ("Received-timeout")
    ACTION:     impose("Information-requested", "Information-received", 20, "received-timeout");
                wait-event()
    //State 2
    EVENT:      event("Information-received") ;
    ACTION:     dismiss ("Information -requested", "Information-received", 20, "received-timeout");
                impose("Information -request", "Information-received", 20, "Received-timeout");
                wait-event()
    //State 3
    EVENT:      event("Traffic-Center")
    ACTION:     dismiss( "Traffic-Center", "Traffic-Center", 5*60, "Traffic-Center-Timeout");
                impose ("Traffic-Center", "Traffic-Center", 5*60, "Traffic-Center-Timeout");
                wait-event()
    //State 4
    EVENT:      event("Traffic-Center-Timeout")
    ACTION:     impose ("Traffic-Center", "Traffic-Center", 5*60, "Traffic-Center-Timeout");
                wait-event()
                }
```

Fig. 3. Description of time coordinator

```
Interaction-Coordinator() {
       ......
    // Event-in: Information-requested, Information-received, Received-timeout, Received-timeout,
    //          Traffic-Center-Timeout
    // Event-out: Traffic-Center, Interaction-Coordinator-initial
//State 0
    EVENT:      event("Interaction-Coordinator-initial")
    ACTION:     connection=" ";    T_Center=" ";
                    ......
                wait-event()
//State 1
    EVENT:      event("Information-requested")
    ACTION:     location= Information-requested.loc; destination=Information-requested.des;
                T_Center1= Find-Traffic-Center(location, destination )
                if T_Center1<>" "{
                    if connection= =" Traffic-Center" and T_Center1<> T_Center
                        disconnect(Navigator,T_Center);
                    if connection= ="GPS"
                        disconnect(Navigator, GPS);
                    connect(Navigator,T_Center1);
                    connection="Traffic-Center";
                    T-Center= T-Center1;
                    raise("Traffic-Center")
                }
                if T_Center1==" and connection= =" "{
                    connect(Navigator,GPS); connection="GPS";
                    T-Center= " "
                }
            wait-event()
//State 2
    EVENT:      event("Received-timeout")
    CONDITION:  if connection== "Traffic-Center"{
    ACTION:         disconnect( T-Center, Navigator);
                    connect( Navigator, GPS);
                    connection="GPS";
                    T_Center=" "
                }
                wait-event()
    }
// State 3
    EVENT:      Event("Traffic-Center-Timeout")
    ACTION:     T_Center1= Find-Traffic-Center(location, destination )
                If   T_Center1<>" "{
                    if connection= =" Traffic-Center"and T_Center1<>T_Center
                        disconnect(Navigator,T_Center);
                    if connection= ="GPS"
                        disconnect(Navigator, GPS);
                    connect(Navigator,T_Center1);
                    connection="Traffic-Center";
                    T-Center= T-Center1;
                    raise("Traffic-Center")
                }
                wait-event()
    }
```

Fig. 4. Description of interaction coordinator

When the car driver requests traffic information to the navigator, the navigator triggers an event "information-requested", and sends a requested message. When the time coordinator intercepts the event information-requested, and imposes a 20 seconds constraint on the event pattern (*Information-requested, Information-received*). When the navigator is successfully connected with a traffic control center, the interaction coordinator will raise the event *traffic-center* to show a connection has been established between a control center and the navigator meanwhile the time coordinator also imposes 5 minutes constraint on the event pattern (*Traffic-Centre, Traffic-Centre*). When the interaction coordinator observes the event *Information-requested* or *Traffic-Center-Timeout*it uses find-traffic-center service to find an appropriate traffic center based on current location and destination of the car. If it finds an appropriate traffic center, it will connect it with the navigator. Otherwise, it will connect the navigator with GPS. Before imposed timing constraints on event pattern, if the constraint has been imposed on the event pattern, the previous timing constraint has to be dismissed. Two types of timing actions, receiving traffic information and updating traffic center, are achieved by timing the event patterns (*Information-requested, Information-received*) and (*Traffic-Center,Traffic-Center*).

6 Conclusion

We have described a time and interaction coordination model for open distributed real-time computation. Additionally, an implementation framework based on JMS and EJB as well as a vehicle navigation application are shown. This approach has the following benefits. Firstly, the implementation of the model doesn't adhere to special architectures or real-time programming languages, so that it provides a better framework for developing distributed applications. Secondly, the time coordinator, the interaction coordinator and the computation entities are defined as orthogonal dimensions, so they can be modeled and designed independently, which simplifies the design and implementation of open distributed real-time applications, and increases their reusability and flexibility. Thirdly, the time coordinators can dynamically impose or release timing constraints, and the interaction coordinators can dynamically reconfigure the interaction topology among computation entities, which leads to the dynamic adaptability of interaction topology and timing constraints among computation entities. Therefore, the model and the framework are suitable for developing such soft real-time distributed computing systems with general technologies.

This is our initial investigation on design and implementation of the model. There is still a lot of work to be done in the future as follows: the performance analysis, the formalized description, and the exploration of other implementation approaches.

References

1. Carriero, N., Gelernter, D.: Linda in context. Communications of the ACM 32(4), 444–458 (1989)
2. Dijkstra, E.: A Discipline of Programming. Prentice Hall, Englewood Cliffs (1976)
3. Gelernter, D.: Generative communication in Linda. ACM Transactions on Programming Languages and Systems, pp. 80–112 (1985)

4. Heppner, M., Burrbidge, R.: Java Message Service API Tutorial and Reference. Tsinghua University Press, Beijing (2002)
5. Limniotes, T.M.C., Papadopoulos, G.A.: Event-driven coordination of real-time components. Distributed Computing Systems Workshops, 2002. In: Proceedings, pp. 589–594 (2002)
6. Papadopoulos, G.A., Arbab,F.: Modelling Activities in Information Systems Using the Coordination Language MANIFOLD. In: Proceedings of the 1998 ACM symposium on Applied Computing, pp. 185–193 (1998)
7. Papadopoulos, G.A., Arbab, F.: Coordination of systems with real-time properties in manifold [A]. In: COMPSAC'96. Proceedings of 20th International Computer Software and Applications Conference, pp. 50–55. IEEE Press, New York (1996)
8. Papadopoulos, G.A., Arbab, F.: Coordination models and languages. Advances in Computers 46, 329–400 (1998)
9. Papathomas, M., Blair, G.S., Coulson, G.: A Model for Active Object Coordination and Its Use for Distributed Multimedia Applications. LNCS, pp. 162–175. Springer, Heidelberg (1995)
10. Ren, S., Agha, G.A.: RTsynchronizer: Language Support for Real-Time Specifications in Distributed Systems. ACM SIGPLAN Workshop on Languages, Compilers and Tools for Real-Time Systems, La Jolla, California (1995)
11. Ren, S., Shen, L., Tsai, J.: Reconfigurable coordination model for dynamic autonomous real-time systems. In: The IEEE International Conference on Sensor Networks, Ubiquitous, and Trustworthy Computing, pp. 60–67. IEEE, New York (2006)
12. Roman, E., Sriganesh, R.P.: Mastering Enterprise JavaBeans. Publishing House of Electronic Industry, Beijing (2005)
13. Wills, L., Kennan, S.: An open platform for reconfigurable control. IEEE Control Systems Magazine 21(3), 49–60 (2001)

Efficient Linkable Ring Signatures and Threshold Signatures from Linear Feedback Shift Register

Xiangxue Li[1,3], Dong Zheng[2,4], and Kefei Chen[2,4]

[1] School of Information Security Engineering, Shanghai JiaoTong University
xxli@sjtu.edu.cn
[2] Department of Computer Science and Engineering, Shanghai JiaoTong University
[3] State Key Laboratory of Information Security(Institute of Software of Chinese
Academy of Sciences), China
[4] National Laboratory for Modern Communications, Chengdu 610041

Abstract. For many practical usages or resource-limited environments, it is often desirable to speed up the cryptographic systems without any security lost. Linkable ring signature is a kind of signatures which can simultaneously provide the properties of anonymity, spontaneity as well as linkability. Threshold signature is a useful tool for decentralizing the power to sign a message by distributed computing. The paper presents linkable ring signatures and threshold signatures using n-th order characteristic sequences generated by a linear feedback shift register (LFSR). Our schemes enjoy the following attractive features: (i) main computation operations are performed in $GF(q)$; and (ii) security properties rely on the difficulty of solving the state based discrete logarithm problem(S-DLP) and on state based decisional Diffie-Hellman(S-DDH) assumption. Since the complexity of breaking S-DLP(S-DDHP, *resp.*) is computationally equivalent to that of solving traditional DLP(DDHP, *resp.*) in $GF(q^n)$, the proposed schemes successfully enhance the security of the system and meanwhile maintain low computational costs. All these make our schemes more flexible.

Keywords: characteristic sequence, linear feedback shift-register, linkable ring signature, threshold signature.

1 Introduction

For many practical applications or resource-limited environments, it is often desirable to speed up the cryptosystems without any security lost. Indeed, this is a very challenging task for researchers in order to meet the requirements of various security strategies. At least three issues are involved in this aspect, *i.e.*, communication overhead, computational costs and security level.

On the one hand, short digital signatures with appended messages are needed in low-bandwidth communication environments or those scenarios where a human is asked to manually key in the signature[2]. Thus, it is sometimes desirable to minimize the total length of the original messages and the resulting signatures. For example, small messages including time, date and identifiers are signed in certified email services and time stamping services. In wireless environments, it is even

H. Jin et al. (Eds.): ICA3PP 2007, LNCS 4494, pp. 95–106, 2007.

more significant to reduce communication overhead due to bandwidth limitation. The finite field based public-key cryptosystems, such as ElGamal, DSS, *etc*, require that sizes of the underlying field must be chosen large enough to strengthen their securities. For applications where bandwidth is limited, this is undesirable.

On the other hand, we always hope that the security level of the employing system be as high as possible and the computational costs as low as possible. All measurements are welcome to enhance the security of the system, and meanwhile to maintain low computational costs.

Ring signature attracts significant attention since its invention[15]. In a ring signature scheme, a user selects a set U(called a ring) of possible signers including himself. A possible signer is anyone with a public key of PKI. The user can then sign a message using his private key and the public keys of all the members in the ring U. The resulting signature can be verified to be generated by someone in the ring, but the identity of the actual signer will not be revealed, hence the signature provides for the signer the property of anonymity which cannot be revoked. To date, numerous ring signature schemes have been proposed [18,19]. Further, we need in some cases that ring signatures have the specific property-**Linkability:** Any one can tell if two ring signatures are generated by using the same private key. In other words, linkability means two signatures by the same actual signer can be identified as such, but the signer remains anonymous. Linkable ring signature scheme($\mathcal{LRSS}$ for short)[10] is really essential (i) to detect double-voting in an e-voting system; and (ii) to conduct an anonymous and voluntary questionnaires among the employee of a company with the requirement that only legitimate members can submit the questionnaires, and at the same time, each member cannot submit more than one questionnaire; etc.

Threshold signature[1,3,4] is a useful tool for decentralizing the power to sign a message by distributed computing. More concretely, the idea behind the (t, n)-threshold cryptography approach is to distribute secret information (*i.e.*, a secret key) and computation (*i.e.*, signature generation or decryption) between n parties in order to remove single point of failure. The goal is to allow any subset of more than t (a threshold) parties to jointly reconstruct a secret and perform the computation while preserving security even in the presence of an active adversary which can corrupt up to $t - 1$ parties. In threshold signature schemes the secret key is distributed among n parties with the help of a trusted dealer or without it by running an interactive protocol among all parties. To sign a message m any subset of more than t parties can use their shares of the secret and execute an interactive signature generation protocol, which outputs a signature of m that can be verified by anybody using the unique fixed public key. Security notion for threshold signature schemes($\mathcal{TSS}$ for short) requires that no PPT adversary that corrupts any $t - 1$ parties can learn any information about the secret key or can forge a valid signature on a new message of its choice.

Recently, several cryptosystems have been proposed to shorten the representation of the elements in the finite field[5,8,12,16] by representing them with the coefficients of their minimal polynomials. Indeed, these schemes are very successful in reducing the key size and speeding up the computation. For instance,

Niederreiter[12] designed encryption and key agreement schemes based on general n-th order linear feedback shift register (LFSR) sequences. Giuliani and Gong[5] proposed a general class of LFSR-based key agreement and signature schemes based on n-th order characteristic sequences. The contributions in these work are twofold: on the one hand, these schemes have the advantage that they do not require as much bandwidth as their counterparts based on finite fields; on the other hand, they aren't accompanied by formal security analysis. Cryptographic primitives or protocols without a rigorous proof cannot be regarded as secure in practice. There are many schemes that are originally thought as secure being successfully cryptanalyzed, which clearly indicates the need of formal security assurance. With provable security, we are confident in using cryptographic applications to replace the traditional way in physical world.

In current work, we will propose, based on n-th characteristic sequences generated by an LFSR, a linkable ring signature scheme($\mathcal{LLRSS}$ for short) and a threshold signature scheme($\mathcal{LTSS}$ for short). Our schemes provide at least the following attractive features:

i. security properties rely on the state based discrete logarithm assumption and state based decisional Diffie-Hellman assumption as defined in the coming section;

ii. most computation operations are performed in $GF(q)$. In fact, besides hash evaluations and addition/multiplications in Z_P, only multiplications of elements in $GF(q)$ are involved in our scheme. This particularly produces a fast system.

Due to the fact that state based discrete logarithm problem is proved to be equivalent to traditional DLP in $GF(q^n)$ [17] and that the complexity of breaking S-DDH assumption is computationally equivalent to that of solving traditional decisional Diffie-Hellman problem in $GF(q^n)$[5], the proposed schemes successfully enhance the securities of the systems, at the same time, with low computational costs. In other words, to get a system equivalent to one based on the multiplication group $GF(q^n)$, there is no need to compute any exponentiation in $GF(q^n)$.

Organization. The rest of the paper is organized as follows. We first introduce some conceptions related to n-th characteristic sequences in Section 2, then present the LFSR-based linkable ring signature scheme $\mathcal{LLRSS}$, its advantages and its security analysis in Section 3. Section 4 is devoted to the threshold signature scheme $\mathcal{LTSS}$ based on n-th characteristic sequences. Finally, concluding remarks are made in Section 5.

Notations. Throughout this paper, let Z_P denote the set $\{0, 1, 2, \cdots, P-1\}$, and Z_P^* denote $Z_P \backslash \{0\}$. By $\in_R S$, it means choosing a random element from the set S with a uniform distribution. For an algorithm $\mathcal{A}$, we use $x \leftarrow \mathcal{A}$ to denote that $\mathcal{A}$ is executed on some specified input and its output is assigned to the variable x; if $\mathcal{A}$ is a probabilistic algorithm, we write $x \xleftarrow{R} \mathcal{A}$. Finally, throughout this paper, we often equate a user with his identity, his public key or his secret key without risks of confusion according to the context.

Negligible Function. We say a function $f : \mathbb{N} \rightarrow \mathbb{R}$ is *negligible* if for every constant $c \geq 0$, there exists an integer k_c such that $f(k) < k^{-c}$ for all $k > k_c$.

2   Preliminaries

2.1   LFSR Sequences

Let q be a prime or a power of prime, $f(x) = x^n + a_1 x^{n-1} + a_2 x^{n-2} + \ldots + a_n, (a_i \in GF(q))$ be an irreducible polynomial over $GF(q)$ with α a root of order P in the extension $GF(q^n)$. A sequence $s = \{s_k\}$ over $GF(q)$ is said to be an LFSR sequence generated by $f(x)$ if $s_{k+n} = a_1 s_{k+n-1} + a_2 s_{k+n-2} + \ldots + a_n s_k (k \geq 0)$.

We denote $\bar{s}_i = (s_i, s_{i+1}, \ldots, s_{i+n-1})$ the i-th state of the LFSR sequence. If an initial state of s is given by $s_k = tr(\alpha^k), k = 0, 1, \ldots, n-1$, where $tr(\cdot)$ is the trace map from $GF(q^n)$ to $GF(q)$, then s is called an n-th order characteristic sequence. It is well-known that the period of the n-th characteristic sequence s is equal to the order of α. Let P be the period of s, we may define $s_k = s_{P+k}$ for all $k \leq 0$, thus we can consider the sequence s with indices running over all integers. Set $A_k = (s_k, s_{2k}, \ldots, s_{rk})$, where r is defined by

$$r = \begin{cases} n-1 & \text{for general } q \text{ and } n, \\ n/2 & \text{if } q = p^2, \text{and } n \text{ is even}, \\ (n-1)/2 & \text{if } q = p^2 \text{ and } n \text{ is odd}. \end{cases} \quad (1)$$

Vector $A_k = (s_k, s_{2k}, \ldots, s_{rk})$ needs smaller bits for representation than that in the ordinary case(for mare details, see [5]).

2.2   LFSR-Based Complexity Problems

We start this part by recalling several main sequence operations, *i.e.*, SO1, SO2 and SO3, which will be repetitively employed in our schemes. Both SO1 and SO2 can be performed efficiently by the existing algorithms [5], and SO3 can be viewed to be derived from SO1 and SO2 [9]. The following sequence operations can be jointly used to design *smart* and *efficient* cryptographic primitives, including our constructions as depicted in Section 3 and 4.

- Sequence Operation 1(SO1): Given $A_k(k$ is unknown) and an integer l, where $0 \leq k, l < P$, to compute A_{kl}.
- Sequence Operation 2(SO2): Given states $\bar{s}_k(k$ is unknown) and $\bar{s}_l(l$ is unknown) for some $0 \leq k, l < P$, to compute $\bar{s}_{k+l}$.
- Sequence Operation 3(SO3): Given $\bar{s}_k(k$ is unknown), and an integer l, where $0 \leq k, l < P$, to compute $\bar{s}_{kl}$.

We proceed to recall the definitions of state based discrete logarithm problem (S-DLP) and of stated based decisional Diffie-Hellman problem(S-DDHP) on which the securities of our schemes are based.

Definition 1. *The problem **S-DLP** is, given $(q, n, P, \bar{s}_1, \bar{s}_k)$, to compute k. For a probabilistic polynomial-time (PPT) adversary $\mathcal{A}$, we define his **advantage** against the S-DLP as $Adv_{\mathcal{A}}^{S-DLP} := Pr[\mathcal{A}(\bar{s}_1, \bar{s}_k) = k]$, where the probability is taken over the random coins consumed by $\mathcal{A}$.*

*We say that the (t, ϵ)-**S-DL assumption** holds, if no t-time adversary $\mathcal{A}$ has advantage at least ϵ in solving the S-DLP.*

Definition 2. *The problem **S-DDHP** is, given $(q, n, P, \bar{s}_1, \bar{s}_u, \bar{s}_v, \bar{s}_w)$, to decide wether $w = uv$ holds. For a PPT adversary $\mathcal{A}$, we define his **advantage** against the S-DDHP as*

$$Adv_{\mathcal{A}}^{S-DDHP} := |Pr\left[\mathcal{A}(\bar{s}_1, \bar{s}_u, \bar{s}_v, \bar{s}_{uv}) = 1\right] - Pr\left[\mathcal{A}(\bar{s}_1, \bar{s}_u, \bar{s}_v, \bar{s}_w) = 1\right]|, \quad (2)$$

where the probability is taken over the random coins consumed by $\mathcal{A}$.

*We say that the (t, ϵ)-**S-DDH assumption** holds, if no t-time adversary $\mathcal{A}$ has advantage at least ϵ in solving the S-DDHP.*

It is known that the state based discrete logarithm problem as defined above is computationally equivalent to the traditional DLP in $GF(q^n)$, and that the complexity of breaking state based decisional Diffie-Hellman problem is equivalent to that of solving decisional Diffie-Hellman problem in the field $GF(q^n)$[5,17]. Refer to [6] for more details about the theory of LFSR sequences.

3   Efficient Linkable Ring Signatures from Linear Feedback Shift Register

3.1   Framework of Linkable Ring Signatures

We first give an overview for the $\mathcal{LRSS}$ model. On the one hand, as original ring signatures, $\mathcal{LRSS}$ contains the system initialization algorithm Setup, users' key generation algorithm KeyGen, signature generation algorithm Sign and signature verification algorithm Verify. On the other hand, $\mathcal{LRSS}$ has a special algorithm called Link from which any verifier can decide whether two given ring signatures are generated by using the same secret key.

Definition 3. *A linkable ring signature scheme $\mathcal{LRSS}$ consists of a tuple of five polynomial-time algorithms:*

Setup: *a probabilistic algorithm, taking as input the security parameter 1^λ, returns a public common parameter param. We write param $\xleftarrow{R}$ Setup(λ).*

KeyGen: *a probabilistic key generation algorithm, taking as input the system parameter param and a user's identity $ID \in \{0,1\}^*$, returns the public/secret key pair (PK, SK) for the user. We write $(PK, SK) \xleftarrow{R}$ KeyGen(param, ID);*

Sign: *a probabilistic signing algorithm, taking as input the system parameter param, a message m and the secret key SK_i of the actual signer with identity ID_i, and the public keys $PK_1, ..., PK_n$ of the ring, returns a pair (m, σ) composed of the original message and the resulting signature σ. We write $(m, \sigma) \xleftarrow{R}$ Sign(param, $SK_i, PK_1, ..., PK_n, m$);*

Verify: *a deterministic verification algorithm, taking as input the system parameter param, a candidate signature σ on the original message m and the public keys $PK_1, ..., PK_n$ of the ring, returns 1 if (m, σ) is a valid signature, and 0 otherwise. We write (1 or 0) $\xleftarrow{R}$ Verify(param, $PK_1, ..., PK_n, m, \sigma$);*

Link: *the algorithm takes as inputs two valid signatures σ_1 and σ_2, and returns either 1 for linked or 0 for unlinked. We write $(0 \ or \ 1) \xleftarrow{R} \mathsf{Link}(\sigma_1, \sigma_2)$.*

3.2 The Proposed $\mathcal{LLRSS}$

Previously, linear feedback shift register(LFSR) is prevalently used to generate pseudo-random sequences which are essential in stream cipher [6]. In [7], Gong and Harn studied over a finite field the 3-rd order LFSR sequences whose cryptographic properties are employed to construct public-key distribution scheme and RSA-type encryption algorithm. Recently, Giulian and Gong [5] proposed an ElGamal-like LFSR-based signature scheme without formal security proof. Provable security is an important research area in cryptography. Cryptographic primitives or protocols without a rigorous proof cannot be regarded as secure in practice. There are many schemes that are originally thought as secure being successfully cryptanalyzed, which clearly indicates the need of formal security assurance. With provable security, we are confident in using cryptographic applications to replace the traditional way in physical world.

Current section will construct an LFSR-based linkable ring signature scheme $\mathcal{LLRSS}$ which is useful for the scenarios where linkability and unconditioned anonymity are simultaneously required. Its advantages over existing $\mathcal{LRSS}$s will also be analyzed. Our $\mathcal{LLRSS}$ consists of the following five algorithms:

Setup: Set $\mathbb{M}$ as the message space and $\mathbb{S}$ the state space $\mathbb{S} = \{\bar{s}_k : \forall k \in \mathbb{Z}\}$.
Given a security parameter λ, this algorithm generates the system parameter $param = \{q, n, \bar{s}_1, P, H_1, H_2\}$ where $H_2 : \{0,1\}^* \to \mathbb{S}$ is a hash function and $H_1 : \{0,1\}^* \to Z_P$ is a collision resistent hash function which will be viewed as random oracles in the security analysis process.

KeyGen: given an identity ID, the algorithm works as below:
  1. Randomly pick $\omega \in_R Z_P^*$;
  2. Compute $\bar{s}_\omega$ by using SO3 from $\bar{s}_1$ and ω;
  3. Make the value $\bar{s}_\omega$ public as the user ID's public key PK;
  4. Transfer ω to the user as his secret key SK via a secure channel .
Assume that there are n members in the ring $L = \{ID_1, ID_2, ..., ID_n\}$, and the corresponding public keys are $PK_1 = \bar{s}_{\omega_1}, PK_2 = \bar{s}_{\omega_2}, ..., PK_n = \bar{s}_{\omega_n}$.

Sign: given a message $m \in \mathbb{M}$, the signer with secret key $\omega_\tau (1 \le \tau \le n)$ produces the signature on m as follows:
  - Compute $\bar{s}_h = H_2(L)$ and $\bar{s}_{h\omega_\tau}$;
  - Choose $k, c_i(i = 1, ..., n, i \ne \tau) \in_R Z_P^*$ and compute $\bar{s}_k$;
  - Compute $U = \bar{s}_{k + \sum_{i=1, i \ne \tau}^n c_i \omega_i}$;
  - Compute $V = \bar{s}_{kh + h\omega_\tau \sum_{i=1, i \ne \tau}^n c_i}$;
  - Set $c_\tau = H_1(L, \bar{s}_{h\omega_\tau}, m, U, V) - \sum_{i=1, i \ne \tau}^n c_i$ and $\sigma = k - c_\tau \omega_\tau$;
  - Output $(\bar{s}_{h\omega_\tau}, \sigma, c_1, ..., c_n)$ as the ring signature on the message m.

Verify: given a purported ring signature $(\bar{s}_{h\omega_\tau}, \sigma, c_1, ..., c_n)$ of the ring L on a message m, a verifier can check its validity via the following process.
  - Compute $\bar{s}_h = H_2(L)$;
  - Compute $U = \bar{s}_{\sigma + (c_1\omega_1 + ... + c_n\omega_n)}$ and $V = \bar{s}_{h\sigma + h\omega_\tau(c_1 + ... + c_n)}$;

- Accept the signature iff. the following equality holds: $c_1 + ... + c_n = H_1(L, \bar{s}_{h\omega_\tau}, m, U, V)$.

Link: given two valid ring signatures $(\bar{s}'_{h\omega_\tau}, \sigma', c'_1, ..., c'_n)$ and $(\bar{s}_{h\omega_\tau}, \sigma, c_1, ..., c_n)$ generated by the same ring L, any receiver can check whether the equality $\bar{s}'_{h\omega_\tau} = \bar{s}_{h\omega_\tau}$ holds: if yes, then the algorithm returns 1 for linked and the receiver can claim that the two signatures are produced by the same signer in the ring L; otherwise, return 0 for unlinked.

This ends the description of our proposed $\mathcal{LLRSS}$. The consistency of the scheme can be easily validated via the three sequence operations as defined in Section 2.

3.3 Security Analysis

For the security analysis for linkable ring signatures, there are three aspects we should consider. Firstly, we need to examine the scheme's resistance to forgery[11]. Let $L = \{ID_1, ID_2, ..., ID_n\}$ be a set of users, whose public keys are generated by KeyGen with fresh coin flips. We consider the following oracles which together model the abilities of an adversary:

- $\mathcal{SO}(\cdot, \cdot)$: a *signing oracle*, upon receiving a tuple $\langle L, m \rangle$ containing a ring $L(|L| = n)$ and a message m, returns a ring signature of L;
- $\mathcal{H}_1(\cdot), \mathcal{H}_2(\cdot)$: *random oracles*, upon receiving some query, return an uniformly chosen random element from the appropriate range with consistency.

Definition 4. *Let Π be an $\mathcal{LRSS}$. For a PPT adversary $\mathcal{A}$, we define his **advantage** as*

$$Adv^{\Pi}_{\mathcal{A},\mathcal{UF}}(\lambda) := Pr \begin{bmatrix} param \xleftarrow{R} Setup(\lambda); (PK_i, SK_i) \xleftarrow{R} KeyGen(param, \\ ID_i); U \leftarrow \{ID_1, ID_2, ...\}; (L^*, m^*, \sigma^*) \leftarrow \\ \mathcal{A}^{\mathcal{SO}}(param, U) : Verify(param, L^*, m^*, \sigma^*) = 1 \end{bmatrix} \quad (3)$$

where it is mandated that (L^*, m^*, σ^*) is not one of the outputs of oracle $\mathcal{SO}$.

We say that Π is existentially unforgeable against adaptively chosen message(and chosen public key) attack if for any PPT adversary $\mathcal{A}$, $Adv^{\Pi}_{\mathcal{A},\mathcal{UF}}(k)$ is negligible.

Due to the particular structure of the resulting ring signature, using the generic technique rewind simulation[11,13,14], our scheme $\mathcal{LLRSS}$ can be shown to be existentially unforgeable against adaptive chosen message and chosen public-key attacks by reducing to state based discrete logarithm problem. For space limitation, we do not hire outright the formal security reduction for the scheme $\mathcal{LLRSS}$. For brevity, however, we adopt a *very short but informal* proof that is much easier to understand.

Theorem 1. *Assume that H_1, H_2 are cryptographic hash functions. If a valid signature of our proposed scheme $\mathcal{LLRSS}$ can be generated without the knowledge of the secret keys of the members in the ring L, then the S-DLP problem can be solved in polynomial time.*

Proof. Suppose that without the knowledge of the secret keys of the members in the ring $L^* = \{ID_1, ID_2, ..., ID_n\}$, an adversary $\mathcal{A}$ can successfully construct on the message m^* a valid signature $(\bar{s}^*, \sigma^*, c_1^*, c_2^*, ..., c_n^*)$ which can pass the verification algorithm $c_1^* + ... + c_n^* = H_1(L^*, \bar{s}^*, m^*, U^*, V^*)$ where U^* and V^* are determined by $(L^*, \bar{s}^*, \sigma^*, c_1^*, c_2^*, ..., c_n^*)$ and the public keys $\bar{s}_{\omega_1}, \bar{s}_{\omega_2}, ..., \bar{s}_{\omega_n}$. Herein, H_1, H_2 are hash functions whose outputs can be viewed as random elements. To achieve his goal, $\mathcal{A}$ may have the following three ways.

Firstly, $\mathcal{A}$ may first randomly choose σ^*, and $c_1^*, ..., c_n^*$, then try to obtain $\bar{s}^*$ directly from the equation $\sum_{i=1}^{n} c_i^* = H_1(L^*, \bar{s}^*, m^*, U^*, V^*)$. Since H_1 is a collision-resistent hash function, $\mathcal{A}$ faces the difficulty of finding the pre-image of H_1. Thus the adversary $\mathcal{A}$ cannot produce a valid ring signature by this way.

Secondly, $\mathcal{A}$ may first pick a random state $\bar{s}^*$ and random $c_1^*, ..., c_n^*$, therefore he can compute $\sum_{i=1}^{n} c_i^*$, and try to compute the pre-image of $\sum_{i=1}^{n} c_i^*$. Even if he can do so, to get a valid σ^*, he has to solve the discrete logarithm of V^* which is part of the pre-image. Thus, in this case $\mathcal{A}$ faces the difficulties of solving S-DLP as well as the hardness of cryptographic hash functions.

Lastly, $\mathcal{A}$ may choose σ^*, and $n - 1$ c_i^*s(say, $c_1^*, ..., c_{n-1}^*$) and a random state $\bar{s}^*$, and try to determine the last c_n^*. Clearly this is not easier than in the second case.

Putting all together, the soundness of the conclusion follows. □

Secondly, anonymity, *i.e.*, signer ambiguity, must be ensured. Generally speaking, anonymity says that given a signature with respect to a ring L of n members, an adversary should not be able to identify the identity of the actual signer with probability significantly greater than $\frac{1}{n-t}$ when t private keys of the ring are known. In a valid signature $(\bar{s}_{h\omega_\tau}, \sigma, c_1, ..., c_n)$ of scheme $\mathcal{LLRSS}$, c_is($i \neq \tau$) are random, c_τ is determined by the output of H_1, and σ by a random number k. Thus, $\mathcal{LLRSS}$ intuitively provides the property of anonymity. Indeed, $\mathcal{LLRSS}$ can be shown to be signer anonymous provided that S-DDH assumption holds[11].

The notion of linkability allows anyone to determine whether two signatures have been issued by the same member in the ring. As for the linkability of the scheme $\mathcal{LLRSS}$, we achieve it via the value $\bar{s}_{h\omega_\tau}$ where $\bar{s}_h = H_2(L)$. If anyone who gains the secret ω_τ produces a valid ring signature that passes the verification algorithm, then the first part of the signature must have the form $\bar{s}_{h\omega_\tau}$. This in turn means that $\mathcal{LLRSS}$ satisfies the linkability property under the S-DL assumption.

3.4 Advantage Concern

For practical usages, it is often desirable to speed up the cryptographic systems without any security lost. Our scheme explores LFSR mechanism to speed up the system computation, and meanwhile to maintain its security level.

On the one hand, from the construction of the proposed signatures, one can see that besides some evaluations of hash functions and simple modular addition/multiplication (modular P), to produce a valid signature only requires the sequence operations SO2 and SO3 which are only involved in multiplication and square evaluation in $GF(q)$. There do not exist any exponentiation computation in $GF(q^n)$. This particularly produces a fast system.

On the other hand, as showed in the above section, the securities of the scheme $\mathcal{LLRSS}$ rely on the state based discrete logarithm problem and state based decisional Diffie-Hellman problem. Since the complexity of breaking S-DL assumption is computationally equivalent to that of solving traditional discrete logarithm problem in $GF(q^n)$, and S-DDH problem is as hard as decisional Diffie-Hellman problem in finite field $GF(q^n)$, the proposed scheme successfully enhances the security of the system, at the same time, with low computational costs.

To sum up, we manage to obtain our goal, $i.e.$, to get a system equivalent to one based on the multiplication group $GF(q^n)$, there is no need to compute any exponentiation in $GF(q^n)$. These attractive features makes our scheme highly adapt to practical applications.

4   LFSR-Based Threshold Signature Scheme

Threshold signature is a useful tool for decentralizing the power to sign a message. More concretely, the idea behind the (t, n)-threshold cryptography approach[3,4] is to distribute secret information ($i.e.$, a secret key) and computation ($i.e.$, signature generation or decryption) between n parties in order to remove single point of failure. Generally, the participants in a threshold signature scheme are the set of n players $\{P_1, ..., P_n\}$ connected by a broadcast channel as well as by secure point-to-point channels[1].

Definition 5. *The set of values $(x_1, ..., x_n)$ is said to be a (t, n)-threshold secret sharing of the value x if any $k < t$ values from this set does not reveal any information about x and there exists an efficient algorithm which takes as input any t values from this set and outputs s. We write $(x_1, ..., x_n) \xrightarrow{(t,n)} x$.*

Definition 6. *A (t, n)-threshold signature scheme $\mathcal{TSS} = (TK, TS, V)$ consists of the following three algorithms:*

TK: *a randomized distributed threshold key generation algorithm run by the players $P_1, ..., P_n$, taking system parameter param as input, returns the public key y, and the private output of each player P_i is a value x_i such that $(x_1, ..., x_n) \xrightarrow{(t,n)} x$, where (x, y) are matching secret/public key;*

TS: *a (possibly) randomized threshold signature generation algorithm TS run by t out of n players, taking as input a message m, the player's private input x_i and system parameters outputs the player's signature share σ_i. All signature shares are then combined into an integrated signature σ on the message m. We write $(m, \sigma) \leftarrow TS(param, x_{i_1}, x_{i_2}, ..., x_{i_t}, m);$*

V: *a deterministic verification algorithm, taking as input the system parameter param, a candidate signature (m, σ) on the original message m and the public key y, returns 1 if (m, σ) is a valid signature, and 0 otherwise. We write $(1\ or\ 0) \leftarrow V(param, m, \sigma, y).$*

Consistency requires that $\forall\ m \in \mathbb{M}$, $\mathsf{V}(param, m, \sigma, y) = 1$ holds, where $\mathbb{M}$ denotes the message space and $(m, \sigma) = \mathsf{TS}(param, x_{i_1}, x_{i_2}, ..., x_{i_t}, m)$ (y and x are the matching public/secret keys, and $(x_1, ..., x_n) \xrightarrow{(t,n)} x$).

Combining the concepts threshold signature and linear feedback shift register to realize "LFSR-based threshold signature" is the focus of current section. Our $\mathcal{LTSS}$ enjoys the attractive features as aforementioned in previous section and consists of the following four algorithms Setup, KeyGen, Threshold signature generation, and Signature verification.

Setup: Given the security parameter 1^λ, the algorithm Setup generates the domain parameters: $\{q, n, P, \bar{s}_1\}$. Moreover, to produce a threshold signature on an arbitrary message m, one cryptographic hash function $H : \{0,1\}^* \longrightarrow Z_P^*$ is also required.

KeyGen: There are three kinds of entities: the dealer, the n members who can cooperatively generate valid threshold signatures, and the verifier, in our scheme. Let the n members in the group be $\{U_1, U_2, ..., U_n\}$, $\omega(0 < \omega < P)$ be the private key of the whole group, $\bar{s}_\omega$ the matching public key of the whole group. The dealer determines a polynomial $f(x) = \omega + d_1 x + ... + d_{t-1} x^{t-1}$, where $d_i(i = 1, ..., t-1)$ are random integers in Z_P.

The secret key for U_i is computed as $\omega_i = f(i)$ which is then securely delivered to U_i(for $i = 1, ..., n$). The corresponding public key for U_i is $\bar{s}_{\omega_i}$.

Threshold signature generation: Without loss of generality, let $S = \{U_1, U_2, ..., U_t\}$ be the set of t signers who want to cooperatively generate a threshold signature on behalf of the whole group on the message m. Each signer $U_i(i = 1, ..., t)$ acts as follows. If all these steps are performed successfully, the receiver will obtain a valid threshold signature (r, σ).

1. Compute $e_i = c_i \omega_i \bmod P$, where $c_i = \prod\limits_{U_j \in S - U_i} \frac{j}{j-i}$ is the Lagrange coefficient;

2. Pick randomly a number k_i ($0 \le k_i < P$);

3. Compute $\bar{s}_{k_i}$ from $\bar{s}_1$ and k_i using SO3;

4. Broadcast $\bar{s}_{k_i}$ to all other signers;

5. Compute $\bar{s}_{\sum\limits_{i=1}^{t} k_i}$ from $\bar{s}_{k_i}(i = 1, ..., t)$ using SO2 after receiving all $\bar{s}_{k_i}$'s from other co-signers;

6. Set

$$r = H(\bar{s}_{\sum\limits_{i=1}^{t} k_i}, m), \qquad \sigma_i = k_i - r e_i; \qquad (4)$$

7. Broadcast σ_i to all other co-signers;

8. Validate $\sigma_j(j = 1, ..., t, j \neq i)$ by the equality $\bar{s}_{k_j} = \bar{s}_{\sigma_j + r c_j \omega_j}$, where $\bar{s}_{\sigma_j + r c_j \omega_j}$ can be computed from $\bar{s}_1, \sigma_j, \bar{s}_{\omega_j}$, and $r c_j$ using SO2 and SO3; If the verification for some σ_j does not hold, U_j is requested to resubmit a value again. When all σ_j's are valid, proceed to the next step;

9. Compute $\sigma = \sum\limits_{j=1}^{t} \sigma_j$;

10. Output (r, σ) as the threshold signature on the message m.

Signature verification: Upon receiving a signature (r, σ) on the message m from the group $\{U_1, ..., U_n\}$ with public key $\bar{s}_\omega$, any verifier can perform the following tasks to check its validity.

1. Compute $\bar{s}_{\sigma+r\omega}$ from $\bar{s}_1$, σ, r, and $\bar{s}_\omega$ using SO2 and SO3;
2. Check whether the following equation holds:

$$r = H(\bar{s}_{\sigma+r\omega}, m). \tag{5}$$

If yes, accept the signature (r, σ); reject otherwise.

This ends the description of our $\mathcal{LTSS}$. From the secret sharing process and the signature generation algorithm, we can note that no polynomial-time adversary that corrupts any $t - 1$ parties can learn any information about the secret key or can forge a valid signature on a new message of its choice.

5   Conclusion

For efficient applications, especially in resource-limited environments, it is desirable to speed up the cryptographic systems without any security lost. n-th order characteristic sequences generated by a linear feedback shift register can be used to reduce the key sizes and bandwidth in public-key cryptographic systems. In this paper, we presented linkable ring signatures and threshold signatures from an LFSR. Their advantages are twofold: (i) main computation operations are performed in $GF(q)$; and (ii) security properties of the schemes are equivalent to those of systems based on the multiplication group $GF(q^n)$. The appealing features make our schemes more flexible and highly adaptable to practical applications in the sense that they together enhance the security of the system and meanwhile maintain low computational costs.

Acknowledgements

The authors would like to thank anonymous referees for their insightful comments and invaluable suggestions for improvement of the paper. This work is partially supported by NSFC(No. 60573030, 60673076) and NLMCSFC (No.51436040 405JW0304).

References

1. Boldyreva, A.: Threshold signatures, multisignatures and blind signatures based on the Gap-Diffie-Hellman group signature scheme. In: Proceedings of the 6th International Workshop on Practice and Theory in Public Key Cryptography (PKC 2003) Miami, FL, USA, pp. 31–46 (2003)
2. Boneh, D., Lynn, B., Shacham, H.: Short signatures from the weil pairing. In: Boyd, C. (ed.) ASIACRYPT 2001. LNCS, vol. 2248, pp. 514–532. Springer, Heidelberg (2001)

3. Desmedt, Y., Frankel, Y.: Threshold cryptosystems. In: Brassard, G. (ed.) CRYPTO 1989. LNCS, vol. 435, pp. 307–315. Springer, Heidelberg (1990)
4. Desmedt, Y.: Threshold cryptography. European Transactions on Telecommunications 5(4), 449–457 (1994)
5. Giuliani, K., Gong, G.: New LFSR-based cryptosystems and the trace discrete logrithm problem (Trace-DLP). In: Helleseth, T., Sarwate, D., Song, H.-Y., Yang, K. (eds.) SETA 2004. LNCS, vol. 3486, pp. 298–312. Springer, Heidelberg (2005)
6. Golomb, S.: Shift register sequences. Laguna Hills, CA, Aegean Park (1982)
7. Gong, G., Harn, L.: Public-key cryptosystems based on cubic finite field extensions. IEEE Transaction on Information Theory 24, 2601–2605 (1998)
8. Lenstra, A., Verheul, E.: The XTR public key system. In: Bellare, M. (ed.) CRYPTO 2000. LNCS, vol. 1880, pp. 1–19. Springer, Heidelberg (2000)
9. Li, X., Zheng, D., Chen, K.: LFSR-based signatures with message recovery. Intenational Journal of Network Security 4(3), 266–270 (2007)
10. Liu, J., Wei, V., Wong, D.: Linkable spontaneous anonymous group signature for ad hoc groups. In: Wang, H., Pieprzyk, J., Varadharajan, V. (eds.) ACISP 2004. LNCS, vol. 3108, Springer, Heidelberg (2004)
11. Liu, J., Wong, D.: Linkable Ring Signatures: Security Models and New Schemes. In: Proceedings of the International Conference on Computational Science and Its Applications (ICCSA 2005), Singapore, pp. 614–623 (2005)
12. Niederreiter, H.: Finite Fields and cryptology. Finite Fields, Coding Theory, and Advances in Communications and Computing, pp. 359–373, M. Dekker, New York (1993)
13. Ohta, K., Okamoto, T.: On concrete security treatment of signatures derived from identification. In: Krawczyk, H. (ed.) CRYPTO 1998. LNCS, vol. 1462, pp. 354–369. Springer, Heidelberg (1998)
14. Pointcheval, D., Stern, J.: Security arguments for digital signatures and blind signatures. Journal of Cryptology 13(3), 361–396 (2000)
15. Rivest, R., Shamir, A., Tauman, Y.: How to leak a secret. In: Boyd, C. (ed.) ASIACRYPT 2001. LNCS, vol. 2248, Springer, Heidelberg (2001)
16. Smith, P., Skinner, C.: A public-key cryptosystem and a digital signature system based on the Lucas function analogue to discrete logarithms. In: Safavi-Naini, R., Pieprzyk, J.P. (eds.) ASIACRYPT 1994. LNCS, vol. 917, Springer, Heidelberg (1995)
17. Tan, C., Yi, X., Siew, C.: On the n-th order shift register based discrete logrithm. IEICE Trans. Fundamentals, E86-A, pp. 1213–1216 (2003)
18. Wei, V.: A bilinear spontaneous anonymous threshold signature for ad hoc groups. Cryptology ePrint Archive, Report 2004/039, available at: http://eprint.iacr.org/
19. Zhang, F., Kim, K.: ID-Based blind signature and ring signature from pairings. In: Zheng, Y. (ed.) ASIACRYPT 2002. LNCS, vol. 2501, pp. 415–432. Springer, Heidelberg (2002)

An Implementation of Parallel Eigenvalue Computation Using Dual-Level Hybrid Parallelism[*]

Yonghua Zhao[1,2,3], Xuebin Chi[1], and Qiang Cheng[1]

[1] Supercomputing Center, Computer Network Information Center,
Chinese Academy of Sciences, 100080, Beijing, China
{yhzhao,chi,swall}@sccas.cn
http://www.sccas.cn
[2] Institute of Software, Chinese Academy of Sciences, 100080, Beijing, China
[3] Department of Computer Science, Dezhou University, 253000, Dezhou, China

Abstract. This paper describes a hybrid two-level parallel method with MPI/OpenMP for computing the eigenvalues of dense symmetric matrices on cluster of SMP's environments. The eigenvalue computation is Based on both the Householder tridiagonalization method and a divide-and-conquer algorithm of tridiagonal eigenproblem. In hybrid parallel design, We take a coarse-grain approach to OpenMP shared-memory parallelization, which keeps BLAS-3 operations in tridiagonalization. Moreover, dynamic work sharing is used in the divide-and-conquer algorithm of tridiagonal eigenproblem. So the amount of synchronization has also been reduced, and these could have an effect on the load balance. In addition, we analyze the communication overhead between hybrid MPI/ OpenMP and pure MPI. An experimental analysis on the Deepcomp6800 shows the hybrid algorithm performs good scalability.

Keywords: MPI/OpenMP, hybrid parallel algorithm, parallel solver, matrix eigenvalue.

1 Introduction

A great deal of effort has been spent for building efficient parallel symmetric eigensolver for distributed systems. Routines for this problem have been developed as part of a number of numerical libraries. Among these the best known are the Scale Linear Algebra Package (ScaLAPCK)[5], Parallel Eigensolver (PeIGS)[18], the Parallel Research on Invariant Subspace Methods (PRISM) project[17], Parallel Engineering and Scientific Subroutine Library (PESSL)[16], and the Parallel Linear Algebra Package (PLAPACK)[19]. All of these packages attempt to achieve portability by embracing the Message-Passing Interface(MPI) and The Basic Linear Algebra Subprogram (BLAS).

---

[*] This work was partially supported by the National Natural Science Foundation of China (No.60533020, No.60373060, No.60673064), 973 Program(2005CB321702).

H. Jin et al. (Eds.): ICA3PP 2007, LNCS 4494, pp. 107–119, 2007.

Today most systems in High Performance Computing are clusters with multi-level memory hierarchy and different communication bandwidth. These include SMP clusters and emerging clusters with multicore processors. These systems mix two memory model: each node uses a shared memory and the communication between nodes uses a "message-passing" hardware. The challenge presented to application developers by such parallel system architectures is that they exhibit a hierarchical parallelism with complex non-uniform memory access data storage. As a consequence, the hybrid programming paradigm combining the message passing and a shared-memory parallelism has become popular in the past few years.

The hybrid model has already been applied in many applications, ranging from costal wave analysis[1,6] to atmospheric research [7], to molecular dynamics analysis[3]. Usually, programmers resort to MPI for the message passing communication, using OpenMP as a interface for writing multi-threaded application. The adoption of this model is facilitated by both the architectural developments of modern super-computers and the characteristics of a wide range of applications [4,2].

In this paper we focus on how to accommodate and exploit particular features of Cluster of SMP's environments in order to improve the performance of eigensolvers of symmetric matrices. Based on the Householder parallel blocking algorithm and a divide-and-conquer algorithm of tridiagonal eigenproblem, we present a hybrid MPI/OpenMP parallel implementation for the eigenvalues of symmetric matrices on the cluster of SMP architectures. We take into account two different implementations of the problem: one based on MPI and the other one based on a hybrid parallel paradigm with MPI/OpenMP. In hybrid MPI/OpenMP parallel, in order to keep BLAS-3 matrix-matrix operations in tridiagonalization, we take a coarse grain OpenMP approach to parallel implementation within SMP node. This achieves the completed load balance between threads within a node. In solving the eigenproblem of a tridiagonal symmetric matrix, we adopt a OpenMP dynamic scheduling to improve the load balance in the original pure message passing algorithm[10].

This paper is organized as follows: the second section gives the Householder transformation and a blocking Algorithm of the tridiagonalization. The third section discusses the parallel algorithm in MPI and MPI/OpenMP hybrid. The fourth section is about The tridiagonal eigenproblem. The fifth section analyzes the performances of hybrid parallel eigensolver. We give some conclusions in the last section.

2   The Householder Transformation and a Blocking Algorithm of the Tridiagonalization

Basic operations utilized by the reduction to tridiagonal form are the computation and application of Householder transformations.

Theorem 1. *Given a vector $z \in R^n$, we can find a vector $u \in R^n$ and a scalar $\beta \in R$ such that (See [9])*

$$(I - \beta uu^T)z = (z_1, \cdots, z_{k-1}, \sigma_k, 0, \cdots, 0)^T \tag{1}$$

where $\sigma_k = sign(z_k)\|z_{k+1:n}\|_2$.

The scalar $\beta \equiv 2/\|u\|_2^2$ and the reflector vector $u \equiv (0, \cdots, 0, z_k + \sigma_k, z_{j+1}, z_n)^T$ are a pair of quantities which satisfy the above theorem. The reflection $(I - \beta uu^T)z$ in Theorem 1 is called Householder transformation. We present $(I - \beta uu^T)$ by H. This reflection does not effect the elements $z_1, \cdots, z_k$.

Given a symmetric matrix A, we can compute $H_j(j = 1, 2, \cdots, n - 2)$ such that

$$T = H_{n-2} \cdots H_1 A H_1 \cdots H_{n-2}$$

is a tridiagonal symmetric matrix. And applying a both-sided Householder transformation to A, we can get

$$(I - \beta uu^T)A(I - \beta uu^T) = A - uw^T - wu^T \tag{2}$$

where $w = v - \dfrac{\beta}{2}(v^T u)u, v = \beta Au$. The right side of the equation 2 is called rank-2 modification of A.

In RISC based processors, it is known that blocking algorithms are more efficient than a non-blocking algorithm. The basic principle of the blocking algorithm is to accumulate a certain number of the vectors u and w into a block update. If we reserve b pairs of vectors u, w, then we can gather b rank-2 modifications of A to be a rank-$2b$ modification using the BLAS-3 operation. Here, we suppose the matrix is divided into column panels with width b, then the operations of the blocking algorithm include $\lceil n/p \rceil$ column panel reduce steps, and an out-panel matrix modification follows each panel reduction.

Fig. 1 provides a schematic of the column panel reduction. During the column panel reduction, the Householder transformation is performed to the part in a column panel, and reserve vectors w and u produced during the transformation to form $n \times b$ matrices W and U that are used to modify the rest parts A_{22} of the matrix. The updating of A_{22} is performed by running the rank-$2b$ modification

$$A_{22} = A_{22} - UW^T - WU^T$$

after panel operations complete. Subsequently, the same procedure is applied to the new modified submatrix A_{22} until the column panel is not existed.

The delayed modification of A_{22} makes the producing of vector v more complicated because the elements stored in matrix A_{22} are not updated in time during the panel transformation. So when solving w, the computation $v = \beta Au$ needs to be replaced by

$$v = \beta \left(Au - UW^T u - WU^T u\right)$$

where $UW^T u$ and $WU^T u$ correspond to out-panel corrections of A.

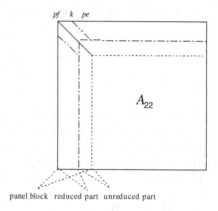

<figure>Fig. 1. A column panel reduction</figure>

3   Parallel Tridiagonalization Algorithm on SMP Cluster

Because SMP cluster owns distributed memory on cluster system and shared memory on SMP system simultaneously, the corresponding hybrid parallel algorithm can be decomposed into cluster level algorithm and node level algorithm. When designing cluster level algorithm, we look the whole SMP cluster system as a distributed memory system composed of nodes, while the algorithm adopts message passing parallelism. But different from that a process runs on only one processor in pure MPI algorithm, a process is mapped onto a node in cluster level algorithm. Node level algorithm can be also called SMP algorithm, which converts the computation task assigned to each node in cluster level algorithm into an efficient multi-thread parallel algorithm within a node.

In SMP clusters, inter-node communication costs are a magnitude higher than accessing local memory. Thus, algorithmic design must attempt to minimize inter-node communication. This is a similar optimization criterion as for designing pure message-passing algorithms. Hence, a successful strategy is to first design an efficient message-passing algorithm, and then adapt the algorithm to the hybrid-programming model[4, 16].

The node level algorithm in this paper is based on OpenMP multi-thread parallelism. The simplest OpenMP parallelism is the loop-nested parallelization using the work sharing construct in OpenMP. This kind of parallelism is also called fine-grain OpenMP parallelism. Another OpenMP parallelism is coarse-grain parallelism. In coarse-grain parallelism, OpenMP adopts SPMD programming model in that a thread is similar to a MPI process. Thread function declaration depends on library routines omp_get_num_threads() and omp_get_thread_num(), which respectively return the number of threads in a parallel region and the sequence number id of the running thread (all the threads are numbered from 0, the thread numbered 0 is the master thread). The program calls these two routines at the beginning of the parallel region, then assigns the thread functions according to their values. Different threads can perform either the same or different operations, so that the data parallel and task parallel are implemented.

3.1 The Mapping of Data to Nodes

We will assume that our SMP clusters consists of N_{node} nodes , and there are r symmetric processors per node. Notice that each CPU has its own on-chip cache (L_1) and a large off-chip level two(L_2). In practice, SMP configurations range between 2 and 36 CPU modules attached to a shared bus and main memory.

In cluster level algorithm, the matrix is first distributed onto N_{node} nodes in block-cyclic column distribution. We will use the following mapping of matrices to nodes: Given $A \in R^{n \times 2}$ and panel width $b \geq 1$, assume for simplicity that $n = r * b$ and partition

$$A^{(k)} = (A_1^{(k)} A_2^{(k)} \cdots A_r^{(k)}) \tag{3}$$

where $A_j^{(k)} \in R^{n \times b}$ is a panel of width b. The panel-wrapped storage scheme assigns $A_j^{(k)}$ to node $Node_{(j-1)mode N_{node}}$. i.e., $A_{i+1}, A_{i+N_{node}+1}, \cdots$ are assigned to $Node_i$. If $b=1$, the result is the familiar column-wrapped storage scheme.

3.2 The Cluster Level Algorithm of Matrix Tridiagonalization

We now describe the parallel implementation of the blocked reduction to tridiognal form in the cluster level. We will use panel-wrapped storage above, and supposed that the symmetric matrix has been distributed onto SMP nodes, where the panel width corresponds to b. For the cluster level parallel blocking algorithm of tridiagonalization, first performing parallel reduction in panel within node, which requires producing a vector w of W and a vector u of U at each reduction step, where u is produced by a node and broadcasted to other nodes. While computing vector w, vector $z = \beta(AU - UW^T u - WU^T u)$ can be solved together by all nodes in parallel. So U must be distributed in order to be able to perform the update $z = \beta(AU - UW^T u - WU^T u)$.

Because the updates of matrix elements in the column panel and out of the column panel are not synchronized, we have to ascertain the element subscripts realigned. Let the columns set of the unprocessed part of A in the current node be LS, then the computed part of Au in the current node is $A_{k+1:n,LS}$. For the update operations $UW^T u$ and $WU^T u$ on the out-panel elements of A, the corresponding operations in the node are $U(W^T)_{LS\cap(pe+1:n)}u_{LS\cap(pe+1:n)}$ and $W(U^T)_{LS\cap(pe+1:n)}u_{LS\cap(pe+1:n)}$ respectively, where pe is the first column number of the column panel processed by the current node. By these computations, each process on nodes can solve the local part of the vector z in parallel. A global reduction sum operation is performed subsequently, and then each node owns a full copy of z.

Processed by the above steps, vectors z and u have been owned by each SMP node, then operation $w = z - (\alpha z^T u/2)u$ can be performed within each local node. Subsequently, modification of the panel is finished by each node in parallel. After reduction in the panel, the modifications of out-panel parts are implemented by each process on node that perform rank-$2b$ modification of the local matrix, the distribution of modified matrix keeps unchanged on node. Algorithm 1 shows the cluster-level parallel blocking algorithm of tridiagonaliztion.

Algorithm 1. Cluster level parallel blocking algorithm

(* P_{myid} owns column set LS of matrix A, and $V, W, X, Y \in R^{n \times b}$*)
$nb = \lceil (n-2)/b \rceil$
for $j = 1 : nb$
  (* first and last column in the panel block *)
  $pf = (i-1) \times b + 1 \qquad pe = \min(pf + b - 1, n - 2)$
  $W = [\phi] \qquad U = [\phi]$
  for $k = pf : pe$ (* parallel translation in the panel block *)
    if ($\lfloor k/nb \rfloor$ mod $N_{node} = myid$)
    generate u, β and broadcast β and u to all nodes
    else
      $root\_id = \lfloor k/nb \rfloor$ mod N_{node}
      receive β and u from node $root\_id$
    endif
    $\Lambda = \{pe+1 : n\} \qquad \Pi = \Lambda \cap LS$
    $PS = \{1 : k - pf\} \qquad CS = \{k + 1 : n\}$
    local matrix-vector production: $Z_{CS} = A_{CS,LS} u_{LS}$
    (* correct for out of date entries of A *)
    $X_{PS} = U_{\Pi,PS}^T u_\Pi \qquad Y_{PS} = W_{\Pi,PS}^T u_\Pi$
    $Z_{CS} = Z_{CS} - (W_{CS,PS} X_{PS} + U_{CS,PS} Y_{PS})$
    Sum among all nodes yielding z
    local computing:$w = z - (\sigma z^T u/2)u$
    $W = [W|w] \qquad U = [U|u] \qquad \omega = (k + 1 : pe) \cap LS$
    (* update remainder of panel block *)
    $A_{CS,\omega} = A_{CS,\omega} - u_{CS} w_\omega^T - w_{CS} u_\omega^T$
    if ($k \in LS$) then $LS = LS - k$
  endfor
  (* rank-$2b$ update of the submatrix A_{22} *)
  $PB = 1 : pe - pf + 1$
  $A_{\Lambda,LS} = A_{\Lambda,LS} - W_{\Lambda,PB} U_{LS,PB}^T - U_{\Lambda,PB} W_{LS,PB}^T$
endfor

The size of algorithm block in Algorithm 1 is not restricted by the size of storage block. This makes operation of each column panel performed by more processors. thereby it is easy to achieve better load balancing and scalability.

3.3   Combining Coarse Grain Shared-Memory Parallelization and MPI Parallelization

Fig. 2 provides a schematic of the hybrid parallel tridiaganolization. In the cluster level multiple MPI processes are employed. In the node level, within each MPI process with multiple OpenMP threads conduct the computations within the node in parallel. Data exchanges between nodes employ MPI message passing. within each process, access to shared objects of multiple threads within each node are coordinated by OpenMP synchronization.

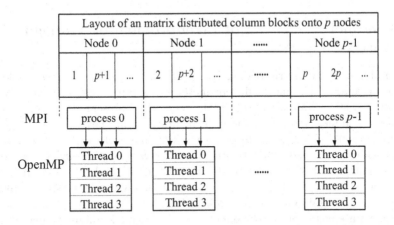

Fig. 2. Hybrid parallel model of reducing into tridiagonal form

As shown in Fig. 2, in hybrid MPI+OpenMP parallel algorithm, computation task assigned to each node is mapped to an efficient SMP algorithm. This can be simply performed by OpenMP *PARALLEL DO* directive. This approach is also called fine-grain OpenMP parallelism. However, the OpenMP directive will destroy matrix-matrix operations in blocking algorithm. To keep the high performance of BLAS-3 operation within the node, coarse-grain SPMD OpenMP parallelism must be adopted. This also avoids overhead associated with frequent thread creations and destructions inherent in fine grain method.

OpenMP parallel occurs in the row regions determined by sets $CS = k + 1 : n$ and $\Lambda = pe + 1 : n$. It is implemented by sharing computation occurred in the two regions among all OpenMP threads. During tridiagonalization, these two regions keep changing continually. So as to the boundaries formed by dividing region among threads will be computed at each step of column panel reductions. Because of using OpenMP coarse-grain parallelism, each thread can ascertain this region according to its own thread ID and the number of threads within the node. This partitioning construction of region among threads makes each thread can operate continuous matrix elements and vectors in shared memory space, which keeps BLAS-3 operations in MPI+OpenMP hybrid parallel algorithm. Moreover, task of MPI process on node is assigned among threads dynamically during reductions, which ensures the complete load balancing among threads.

In hybrid parallel model, message passing between nodes are launched by one thread within process through MPI call. Comparing to pure MPI program on SMP clusters, the advantage of this model is that the nodal messages are assembled into a single large message and thus reduces network latency overhead.

Moreover, because of great decrease of the number of processes in hybrid parallelism, the number of communication times decreases, which correspondingly decreases the communication overhead. And comparing to the pure MPI algorithm, cyclic column blocks are distributed among nodes more equally, which makes the load balancing of hybrid parallel algorithm better.

4   Tparallel Algorithm of Eigenproblem of Tridiagonal Matrix on SMP Cluster

Eigenproblem of symmetric tridiagonal matrix is the kernel of eigenproblem of symmetric matrix. The most efficient method of solving this problem is divide-and -conquer (D&C) algorithm[11]. Many researchers presented different parallel divide-and-conquer algorithms and implementations on shard memory multiprocessor, hypercubic MPC and cluster of workstations[12,14,15,13]. Based on the rank-2 modification D&C MPI algorithm put forward by C.Treffz [20], we give a multi-granulariy hybrid parallel divide and conquer method. This hybrid parallel algorithm combines two kinds of metods: MPI+fine-grain OpenMP parallelism and MPI+coarsegrain OpenMP parallism[10].

Thinking about the eigenproblem of $n \times n$ tridiagonal symmetric matrix T on r-way SMP nodes. For convenience, set $n = 2^m$, number of nodes $n_{node} = 2^d$, $r = 2^k$, so the number of processors $P = 2^{d+k}$.

4.1   Cluster-Level Algorithm of Eigenproblem of Tridiagonal Matrix

A main target of parallel algorithm design is to maximize computation time of every process. Accordingly, we first design an efficient cluster-level algorithm of eigenproblem of tridiagonal matrix . Supposed that nonzero elements of the tridiagonal symmetric matrix have been distributed onto SMP nodes, cluster-level D&C algorithm is given in algorithm 2.

Algorithm 2. Cluster level parallel of D&C
    Let $t = m - d$;
    Each node Obtains a local tridiagonal submatirx of size 2^t;
    (I) Locally compute the eigenvalues of the tridiagonal submatirx;
    for j=1 to k do
        $master\_proc$=int($(myid/2^j)2^j$);
        if ($master\_proc$ .eq. $myid$)
            gather eigenvalues from other nodes in the same group;
            merge and sort 2^{t+j} received eigenvalues;
            distributes them evenly among nodes $myid, \cdots, myid+ 2^j$-1;
        else
            Send 2^t approximated eigenvalues to process $master\_proc$;
            Receive 2^t approximated eigenvalues from processor $master\_proc$ process;
        endif
        (II) use Laguerres iteration to find 2^t eigenvalues corresponding
            to tridiagonal submatirx of size 2^{t+j};
    endfor

4.2   Eigenproblem of Tridiagonal Matrix Hybrid Parallelism

In the MPI/OpenMP hybrid paradigm, each SMP node runs a multi-thread MPI process. In algorithm 2, multithread parallelisms within node are presented at operation (I) and operation (II), so task (I) and task (II) can be finished by the threads within node. The former multithread Multi-thread paralleliza-tion in task (I) is similar to MPI process parallelism. It includes the submatrix division and solving among threads on the same node, approximated eigenval-ues exchange among threads and solving approximated eigenvalues of combined submatrices by Laguerres iterations. This can employ coarse grain SPMD OpenMP model. In coarse-grain parallelism, because the threads within a node share memory, when the matrix is distributed among these threads, array re-gion of every thread need to be calculated to get the mapping from array region to thread. Broadcast and scatter operations of the eigenvalues during combin-ing are implemented via data duplication rather than message passing, avoiding communication overhead.

OpenMP parallelism of task (II) solves the approximated eigenvaules of com-bined submatrices on nodes. In a process, solving the eigenvalues of the sub-matrix by Laguerres iteration is a loop operation. It can be simply performed by OpenMP PARALLEL DO directive. Under the default scheduling method (*static*), OpenMP directives evenly assign the approximate eigenvalues compu-tations in the loop among all threads within a node (processors on a node). Because the numbers of Laguerres iterations on different approximated threads may be different, this can lead to load imbalance. In order to improve load bal-ancing and reduce synchronization overhead, we use dynamic scheduling method, schedule(*dynamic*, *chunk_size*), among threads.

4.3   Communication Overhead Analysis

In the D&C hybrid parallel algorithm of eigenproblem of tridiagonal matrix, message passings appear out of OpenMP parallel regions and are implemented by master thread on each node. And the number of iterations of outer loop j determine the number of message passing. Here, the number of iterations of outer loop j equals to $\log_2[number of processes]$.

For a cluster with r-way SMP nodes, the number of processes of hybrid par-allel algorithm equals to the number of nodes, namely n_nodes. And the num-ber of processes of MPI parallel algorithm equals to the number of processors. $n\_node * r$. So the number of iterations of j in hybrid parallel algorithm is only $\frac{1}{log_2 r}$ of the number of iterations in MPI parallel algorithm. This decreases the number of communication between processes and reduces communication over-head. Another overhead of hybrid parallel algorithm is thread synchronization, which appears after each OpenMP directive. Because the number of synchro-nizations in above hybrid parallel algorithm only equals to logarithm of the number of SMP nodes, $log_2^{n\_nodes}$, which reduces the number of synchroniza-tions. Synchronization overhead come from here affects algorithm performance a little.

5   Result and Discussion

We have implemented our parallel eigensolver on the DeepComp 6800 at Super-computing Center, Chinese Academy of Sciences, and evaluated its performance. DeepComp 6800 is a cluster of SMP's environments. It consists of 265 nodes; each node owns 4-way Intel Itanium II 1.3 GHz processors, 8 GB or 16 GB memory; all the nodes are interconnected by QsNet with bandwidth of 300 MB/s and latency of 7 μs. The operating system is Redhat Linux Advanced Server 64-bit 2.1, the MPI library is QsNet optimized MPICH 1.2.4. All the test programs are compiled by Intel C compiler 64-bit 7.1 with the option "-O3".

For eigenproblem of symmetric matrix, we give two different implementations: pure MPI version and hybrid MPI+OpenMP version, which mainly test the performances and the scalabilities of MPI and MPI+OpenMP.

5.1   The Frank Matrix

To evaluate performance and to check the program, we calculated all eigenvalues for the following Frank matrix:

$$A = (a_{ij})_{n \times n}, \quad a_{ij} = n - \max(i, j) + 1.$$

Its eigenvalues are known to be

$$\lambda_k = \frac{1}{2(1 + \cos((2k - 1)\pi/(2n + 1)))}, \quad k = 1, 2, \ldots, n.$$

5.2   Performance for Calculating All Eigenvalues

We measured the execution time of all eigenvalues of a symmetric matrix. The order of test matrix is 8000, while the number of processors is the product of the number of MPI processes and the number of OpenMP threads per process. In our test, we use 64 nodes, and number of OpenMP threads per process is varied among 1, 2 and 4. Therefore there are 3 type solutions in total: the pure MPI program, in which the number of processors equals to the number of MPI processes that is varied form 4 to 256 (4, 8, 16, 32, 64, 128, and 256); and the MPI/OpenMP hybrid program with 2 threads, in which the number of MPI processes is varied from 2 to 128 (2, 4, 8, 16, 32 64, and 128); and the MPI/OpenMP program with 4 threads, in which the number of MPI processes is varied from 1 to 64 (1, 2, 4, 8, 16, 32 and 64).

The table 1 illustrates the wall clock running time versus the total number of nodes for two programming paradigms, including the pure MPI and the MPI/OpenMP hybrid. The table shows that the pure MPI is the slowest one, the MPI/OpenMP hybrid with 2 threads is slightly faster than the pure MPI, the MPI/OpenMP hybrid with 4 threads is the fastest one. The MPI/OpenMP hybrid with 4 threads is about 15%–35% faster than the pure MPI, and it is

Table 1. Running times of the pure MPI and the MPI+OpenMP hybrid programs

Num. of Nodes	Running time(s)		
	MPI+OpenMP (4 threads)	MPI+OpenMP (2 threads)	Pure MPI
1	79.27	82.62	90.65
2	39.83	42.36	46.61
4	21.55	22.94	25.54
6	13.34	15.10	16.87
16	8.08	10.30	10.9
32	4.88	5.56	6.85
64	3.79	4.36	5.81

Table 2. Speedups of the pure MPI and the MPI+OpenMP hybrid programs

Num. of Nodes	Speedup		
	MPI+OpenMP (4 threads)	MPI+OpenMP (2 threads)	Pure MPI
1	1	1	1
2	1.97	1.95	1.94
4	3.63	3.60	3.55
8	5.87	5.47	5.37
16	9.69	8.02	8.32
32	16.04	14.87	13.23
64	20.64	18.95	15.60

5%–15% faster than the MPI/OpenMP Hybrid with 2 threads. The relative speed gaps between them are getting larger with the increase of the number of nodes.

The table 2 shows the speedups. The computation of speedups uses the formula by Liu et al that is suitable to SMP cluster[21]:

$$S_{node} = \frac{T_p(1\_node)}{T_p(n\_node)}$$

where $T_p(1\_node)$ is the running time by using single node, $T_p(n_node)$ is the running time by using n nodes.

As shown in the table, the pure MPI has the worst speedup; and the MPI/ OpenMP hybrid with 4 threads performs the best in speedup; the speedup of the MPI/OpenMP hybrid with 2 threads is still in the middle. These show that MPI+OpenMP parallelism has better load balancing and better scalability than MPI parallelism.

OpenMP reduces the communication overhead within the same node which is one of the reasons that make the MPI/OpenMP hybrid programs achieve better performance. Moreover, the coarse-grain parallelism in OpenMP can help getting better load balance, which is another reason for the performance increase.

6   Conclusion

On a cluster of SMP's, the MPI/OpenMP hybrid paradigm outperforms the MPI paradigm in solving the eigenvalues of a symmetric dense matrix. Generally, coarse-grain hybrid parallelism and dynamic work sharing schedule can get better performance than fine-grain hybrid pallelism and static schedule, because it may promote load balance in some applications and reduce the amount of synchronization. However, serious consideration must be given to the nature of codes and the characteristics of an application before embarking on a hybrid parallelization implementation.

References

1. Bova, S.W., Breshears, C., Cuicchi, C., Demirbilek, Z., Gabb, H.A.: Dual-level parallel analysis of harbor wave response using MPI and OpenMP. Int. J. Perform Comput. Appl. 14, 49–64 (2000)
2. Rabense, R., Wellein, G.: Communication and optimization aspects of parallel programming models on hybrid architecture. International Journal of High performance Computing Applications 17(1), 49–62 (2003)
3. Dong, S., Karniadakis, G.E.: Dual_level parallelism for high-order CFD methods. Parallell Computing 30, 1–20 (2004)
4. Cappello, F., Etiemble, D.: MPI versus MPI+OpenMP on IBM SP for the NAS benchmarks. In: Proceedings of the 2000 ACM/IEEE conference on Supercomputing, Dallas, Texas, USA (2000)
5. Blackford, L.S., Choi, J., Cleary, A., D'Azevedo, E., Demmel, J., Dhillon, I.S., et al.: ScaLAPACK Users's Guide. SIAM, USA (1997)
6. Luong, P., Breshears, C.P., Ly, L.N.: Coastal ocean modeling of the U.S. west coast with multiblock grid and dual-level parallelism. In: Supercomputing 2001: High Performance Networking and Computing (SC2001)
7. Loft, R.D., Thomas, S.J., Dennis, J.M.: Terascale spectral element dynamical core for atmospheric general circulation models. Supercomputing 2001: High Performance Networking and Computing (SC2001)
8. Hendrickson, B., Jessup, E., Smith, C.: Toward an efficent parallel eigensolver for dense symmetric matrices. SIAM J.Sci. Compute. 20(3), 1132–1154 (1999)
9. Demmel, J.: In: Applied Numerical Linear Algebra, SIAM, USA (1997)
10. Zhao, Y., Chen, J., Chi, X.B.: Solving the symmetric tridiagonal eigenproblem using MPI/OpenMP hybrid parallelization. Lecture Notes for Computer Science, vol. 3756 pp. 164–173 (2005)
11. Cuppen, J.J.M.: A divide and conquer method for symmetric tridiagonal eigenproblem. Numer. Mathematik. 2(36), 177–195 (1981)
12. Sameh, A., Kuck, D.: A parallel QR algorithm for symmetric tridiagonal matrices. IEEE tans. Comput. C-26, 81–91 (1977)
13. LI, T.Y., Zeng, Z.: Lagurre's iteration in solving the symmetric tridiagonal eigenproblem. SIAM J. Scientific Comput. 15, 1145–1173 (1994)
14. Gu, M., Eisenstat, S.C.: A divide-and conquer algorithm for symmetric tridiagonal eigenproblem. SIAM J. Mat. Anal. Appl. 16(1), 172–191 (1995)
15. Dhillon, I.S., Parlett, B.N.: Multiple representations compute orthogonal eigenvertors of symmetric tridiagonal matrices. Lin. Alg. Appl. 387, 1–28 (2004)

16. http://www.hpcx.ac.uk/support/documentation/IBMdocuments/a2272734.pdf
17. Philadelphia, 1997 Bischof, C. Gerorge, W. Huss-Lederman, S. Sun, X., Tsao, A., Turnbull, T.: Prism software (1997) http://www.mcs.anl.gov/Projects/PRISM/lib/software.html
18. Alpatov, P., Baker, G., Edwards, C., Gunnels, J., Morrow, G., Overfelt, J., van de Gejin, R., Wu, Y.-J.J.: PLAPACK: Parallel linear algebra package - design overview. In: Processing of SC97 (1997)
19. Fann, G., Littlefield, R.: Performance of a fully parallel dense real symmetric eigensolver in quantum chemistry applications. In: Proceedings of the Sixth SIAM Conference on Parallel Processing for Scientific Computation. SIAM (1994)
20. Treffz, C., Huanf, C.C.: A scalable eigenvalue solver for symmetric tridiagonal matrices. Parallel Computing 21, 1213–1240 (1995)
21. Liu, W., Zheng, W.M., Zheng, X.W.: The concept of node-oriented speedup on SMP cluster. Computer engineering and design, vol. 21(5) (October 2000)

An Improved Algorithm for Alhusaini's Algorithm in Heterogeneous Distributed Systems

Jianwei Liao and Jianqiao Yu

College of Computer and Information Science,Southwest University of China
Beibei, Chongqing, P.R. China, 400715
liaotoad@163.com

Abstract. In most of mapping Algorithms for application in HDC, the Alhusaini's method is one of the most important Algorithms. However, we find there are some weaknesses in Alhusaini's method though the experiments and analysis. So, we propose a two-phase algorithm called 2-phases dynamic resource co-allocation algorithm (2PDRCA) based on Alhusaini's method. The first phase only generates the data that will be used in the second phase. The second phase will selected a set of independent tasks and allocate according to the weight of each task in our method. The simulation results show that the method is effective, and solves the problem such as Low efficiency of Alhusaini's method in communication intension application.

Keywords: Alhusaini's Algorithm, Improved Algorithm, Dynamic Resource Mapping, Weighted Compatibility Graph, Heterogeneous Distributed Systems.

1 Introduction

Different kinds of resources interconnected with a high-speed network provide a computing platform, called Heterogeneous Distributed Computing (HDC) system [7]. The mapping problem is defined as the problem of assigning application tasks to suitable resource and ordering task execution in time to optimize a specific object function. Many algorithms are proposed for mapping applications in HDC system [10]. Most of the previous algorithms focus on computing resources only.

We consider the problem of mapping a set of applications to a HDC system where application tasks require concurrent access to multiple resources of different types. In general, this problem is the resource co-allocation problem. In this research area, Alhusaini is a pioneer, and he proposed two methods for resource co-allocation problem [7], [8]. Both of them are two phase algorithms. In a communication intensive application, Alhusaini's method will suffer a disadvantage, that is, schedule length increases quickly caused by the communication cost.

In order to overcome the disadvantage in Alhusaini's method, we also proposed a two phase's algorithm that is called the 2-phases dynamic resource co-allocation

H. Jin et al. (Eds.): ICA3PP 2007, LNCS 4494, pp. 120–130, 2007.
© Springer-Verlag Berlin Heidelberg 2007

algorithm (2PDRCA). In the first phase, we will only generate the data that will be used in the second phase. The main allocation mechanism is in the second phase. We successfully overcome the disadvantage in Alhusaini's method and propose an effective and efficient algorithm for resource co-allocation problem.

2   Related Works and Fundamental Background

2.1   Alhusaini's Method

Alhusaini [8] proposed an algorithm by releasing a resource rk if the task that holds the resource r_k in run time won't use it again. Thus, this algorithm is except for the run-time adaptation phase.

The run-adaptation phase is used while a mapping event is happened, where a mapping event can be repeated at fixed time intervals, every time a task finishes, or every time a resource become available. Each process of mapping event is processed as follows. A sub set of tasks, S, that can be executed now is selected starting from the first waiting task based in the scheduling order of the scheduling plan that produce at compiler-time mapping phase. All tasks in S are considered for execution one-by-one in their scheduling order in the schedule plan. For each task Ti, it will first find the best machine mb that gives the shortest finish time for Ti at this mapping event. Then it uses a comparison condition to decide a machine to task Ti. Based on this comparison, it decides if we would execute Ti on machine mb or mj that has been assigned to Ti in compiler time mapping phase as specified in schedule plan at this mapping event. The comparison condition (migration condition) is:

$$\text{Exec}\,(Ti, m_b) \ \leq \text{Exec}\,(Ti, m_j) + \varDelta \text{Exec}\,(Ti, m_j) \tag{1}$$

where $\varDelta$ is a value between 0% and 100%. It will execute Ti on machine mb if the condition is true.

To begin with, we know that Alhusaini's method with early resource releasing will allocate a machine mj $\in$M in our system to each task Ti in DAG at compiler time.

For each task Ti, it will find a best machine mb which has the earliest finish time among all machines. Next, it uses a migration condition to decide whether the task Ti need to be migrated to machine mb or not while machine mb and machine mj are different. This may result in one situation that task Ti will not be allocated to machine mb because the migration condition doesn't satisfy. We can easily find that when the heterogeneity is getting larger, the migration condition is more difficult to be satisfied.

Furthermore, if task Ti doesn't be allocated to machine mb, the finish time of task Ti will not be the earliest. This is the first disadvantage of Alhusaini's migration mechanism. For example, Fig. 1 (b) is the estimated execution time of task T2 on each machine. We assume that mj and mb are m2 and m1, respectively. Testing the migration condition by the estimated execution times of

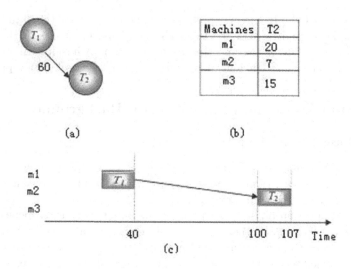

Machines	T2
m1	20
m2	7
m3	15

(a)   (b)

(c)

Fig. 1. (a) Part of DAG (b) estimated execution time of task T2 on each machine (c) part of schedule plan

task T2 on machines m2 and m1, we can find that the migration condition will be false.

In the migration condition, we can find the migration condition don't consider the communication cost between task Ti and its immediate predecessors. This will result in the situation that the schedule length increases quickly caused by the communication cost especially for the communication intensive applications. For example, in Fig. 1, we assume that there are three machines and the Task T1 is allocated to machine m1 in the run time. Fig. 1(a) is part of the DAG for a communication intensive application and Fig. 1(b) is the estimated execution time of task T2 on each machine. Moreover, we assume that the task T2 is allocated to machine m2 in the compiler time phase. We will consider how to allocate the task T2 in run-time adaptation phase now. First, it will find a best machine which is m1 now because the estimated earliest finish time of task T2 on machine m1 is the shortest that is calculated by Formula 1. Then, when we test the migration condition, we find that the migration condition is false even if the value, Δ, is 100%. Therefore in Fig. 1(c), the task T2 will be allocated to machine m2 and completes at time unit 107. We can find that if task T2 was allocated to machine m1, the finish time of task T2 will be 60. In a communication intensive application, the schedule length will increase quickly caused by migration condition fail.

2.2   Application Model

We consider a heterogeneous computing system with m compute resources (machines), $M = m_1, m_2, \ldots, m_m$, and a set of r non-compute resources (resource), $R = r_1, r_2, \ldots, r_r$. A machine can be a HPC platform, a workstation, a personal

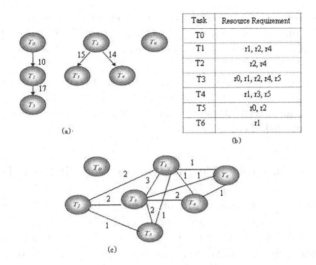

Task	Resource Requirement
T0	
T1	r1, r2, r4
T2	r2, r4
T3	r0, r1, r2, r4, r5
T4	r1, r3, r5
T5	r0, r2
T6	r1

Fig. 2. (a) Two DAGs (b) resource requirement of tasks (c) weighted compatibility graph

computer, etc. A non-compute resource can be a data repository, an input/output device, etc. Resources are interconnected by the network. And, we define the DAG which is often used to represent the parallel program. We assume that a parallel program is composed of n tasks $T1, T2, \ldots, Tn$ in which there is a partial order. The partial order $Ti < Tj$ implies that Tj can not start execution until Ti finishes due to the data dependency between them.

Definition 1. A parallel program can be represented by a Directed Acyclic Graph (DAG) G = (T, E, C, R), where
   T={T1, T2...Tn} is a finite set of tasks;
   E is a set of edges which is between the tasks in T and each edge e(i, j) represents the data dependency between task Ti and task Tj;
   C is the function from E to integer in which c_{ij} represents the communication cost from task Ti to task Tj.
   R is a function from T to a set of resources in our system. When a task Ti is executed, it needs a set of resources, denoted as R(Ti).

Definition 2. Two tasks Ti and Tj are incompatible if and only if R (Ti) ∩R(Tj)≠ ϕ.
   Incompatible tasks cannot be executed concurrently even if they have no precedence constrains among them. This is the resource sharing constrain. Therefore, tasks may be unable to run concurrently for precedence constrains or resource sharing constrain. We use the compatibility graph defined below to capture the implied resource sharing constrains among tasks that may belong to the same or different application.

Definition 3. Given a set of tasks and the resource requirement of each tasks, the Weighted Compatibility Graph (WCG) W = (T, E, C), Fig. 2 shows an example of WCG:

T is the set of all tasks

E is a set of edges which is between the tasks in T; edge e (i, j) exists if task Ti and task Tj use some resources in common

C is a function form E to integer in which c_{ij} represents the number of common resources between task Ti and Tj.

3   2-Phases Resource Co-allocation Algorithm (2PDRCA)

In Alhusaini's method, the major part of the algorithm focuses on the allocation mechanism in compiler-time mapping phase. But we have no any information about when a task Ti will release e a resource r_k ∈R (Ti) before task Ti completes in compiler time. And, we don't know what resources will be available at any significant time unit. So, all tasks are assumed that they won't release any resource before they complete in compiler time. We will dynamic select a set of tasks to be allocated depending on the number of common resources and the data dependency between tasks which are unscheduled.

We will describe the basic principle of 2-Phases Dynamic Resource Co-allocation Algorithm (2PDRCA) for resource co-allocation problem in this section. 2PDRCA also has two dynamic phases: one is called the compiler time phase and the other is run time allocation phase.

3.1   Compiler Time Phase

In the compiler time phase, we only produce the data that will be used in run time allocation phase. There are only two steps in this phase. Step one is to construct the Weighted Compatible Graph (WCG), step two is to mark all task that need non-compute resource or not. Table 1 show of pseudo code of this phase:

Table 1. Part of pseudo code of the compiler time phase

```
Compiler time phase
Input: DAGs and their resource requirement
Output: WCG
Begin
1. Construct the weighted compatible graph for the DAGs
2. Mark all tasks that do not require any non-compute resource
End
```

3.2   Run Time Allocation Phase

The run time allocation phase is the major part of the algorithm focuses on the allocation mechanism. Table 2 shows of pseudo code of this phase.

Table 2. Part of pseudo code of run time allocation phase

Run time allocation phase
Begin
1. Let WCG be the weighted compatible graph generated in the compiler time phase
2. Counter = 0
3. While (counter ¡ total number of tasks) do:
4. At each mapping event do:
5. If (some non-compute resources are released in this mapping event)
6. Adjust WCG
7. Put all ready state tasks into the set *READY*
8. Extract all tasks that are marked at compiler time from *READY* and put them into set *M*
9. Construct set *C* from *READY*
10. Find a maximal independent set *S* from *READY* such that $C \subseteq S$
11. Reinsert all tasks from *M* into *S*
12. While (*S* is not empty) do:
13. If (*C* is not empty) do:
14. Pick the highest weight task t from *C*
15. Remove t from *C* and *S*
16. Else do:
17. Pick a task t from *S* and Remove t from *S*
18. Find a machine *mj* that has earliest finish time to t
19. Allocate $R(t)$ to t
20. Execute t on machine *mj*
21. Counter++
22. End(while)
23. End(while)
24. End

One of the steps in run time allocation phase is to select a maximal independent set S. But the time complexity of selecting a maximal independent set is really great. The time complexity is $O(2C^C R)$, where C is the number of tasks in the independent set not included the critical task vc, and R is the total number of non-compute resources. Therefore, in order not to increase the overhead in run time, we have to add some processes to restrict the integer C. There are two kinds of situations that we describe below.

First, if a task Ti doesn't require any non-compute resource and is in the ready state, it must be selected into the maximal independent set S. The reason is that task Ti will not suffer any resource sharing constrain between other tasks that is in ready state, too. Therefore, it can concurrently execute with other tasks that is also in the ready state. We can mark these tasks that do not require any non-compute resource in the compiler time and extract them before selecting the maximal independent set S. Then, we will reinsert them to the maximal independent set S after selecting the maximal independent set.

Second, for the selecting of maximal independent set, we select a set of critical tasks such that the integer C is less than k, where k is the number such that $2^k k$

is less than the total number of tasks. While we select more critical tasks, there is more non-compute resources will be reserve for them. So, there are more tasks that in the ready state suffer resource sharing constrain to critical tasks. We can remove them before selecting a maximal independent set. This process will have the time complexity of selecting maximal independent set to be O(NR), where N is the total number of tasks.

In run time allocation phase, there are some other processes at each mapping event. To ensure precedence constrain to be satisfied, we gather all tasks that are in the ready state to be set READY. Before we select a maximal independent set from READY, we must extract all tasks that is marked in compiler time phase. This will be helpful for us to restrict the time complexity of selecting a maximal set from READY.

As we mention above, we will reinsert them to the maximal independent set. We will select a set of tasks to be critical tasks according to the weight of each task. A task that has the greatest weight in the set READY will be selected first. There are two reasons for a task Ti to have the greatest weight in READY. Selecting a set of critical tasks will also help us reduce the time complexity of selecting maximal independent set.

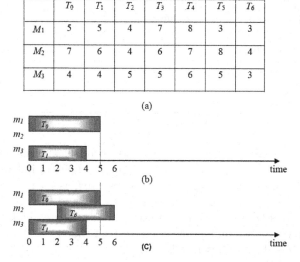

	T_0	T_1	T_2	T_3	T_4	T_5	T_6
M_1	5	5	4	7	8	3	3
M_2	7	6	4	6	7	8	4
M_3	4	4	5	5	6	5	3

(a)

(b)

(C)

Fig. 3. (a) The estimated computation cost of tasks in Fig. 2(a) (b) the result of first mapping event (c) the result after second mapping event at time unit 2

After deciding the critical tasks, we will select a maximal independent set S that included the critical tasks from READY to be allocated. For the allocation mechanism, we use the highest weight first for the critical tasks in S and the other tasks are random. We use a simple allocation mechanism and consider two situations to reduce the time complexity of selecting maximal independent set in our algorithm. This will help us reduce the overhead in run time. If the overhead is increase quickly in run time, the schedule length will also increase. When we want to allocate a task Ti to a suitable machine, we use the earliest finish time of task Ti on each machine to decide which machine is suitable. In Fig. 3, we show an example for the first mapping event of tasks in Fig. 3 (a) is their estimated execution time on each machine.

These two tasks will be put in the set READY that is task T0 and task T1. Because task T0 doesn't require any non-compute resource, it will be extracted before the selecting of maximal independent set. The result of first mapping event is shown in Fig. 3 (b). We assumed that task T1 would release resource r1 at time unit 2. The result after this mapping event is in Fig. 3 (c).

3.3 Discussion

We use the earliest finish time of a task Ti on each machine to choose a machine m_j that will make the task Ti completes earlier and allocate task Ti to machine m_j. This will help us avoid the schedule length increasing quickly in a communication intensive application. We will illustrate the effect of migration condition through the simulation Compiler time Run time Alhusaini's method $O(2N^N R)$ $O(N^2 R)$, and 2PDRCA cost $O(N^2 R)$ $O(N^2 R)$.

Table 3. Time complexity of Alhusaini's method and 2PDRCA result

	Compiler Time Phase	Run Time Allocation Phase
Alhusaini Method	$O(2N^N R)$	$O(N^2 R)$
2PDRCA	$O(N^2 R)$	$O(N^2 R)$

In Alhusaini's method, when the heterogeneity is getting bigger and bigger, the migration condition would be false frequently. It would be harder to allocate a task Ti to the best machine m_b. In 2PDRCA, we directly allocate a task Ti to a machine m_j in run time. Therefore, we can avoid the disadvantage of migration condition mechanism. Table 3 is the time complexity of Alhusaini's method and 2PDRCA. In the compiler time mapping phase of Alhusaini's method, the time complexity of selecting a maximal independent set is $O(2N^N R)$, where N is the total number of tasks and R is the total number of resources. The run time adaptation phase of Alhusaini's method, the time complexity is $O(N^2 R)$. In 2PDRCA, the time complexity of compiler time phase is focus on constructing the WCG. The time complexity of run time allocation phase in 2PDRCA is $O(N^2 R)$ [11].

4   Simulations and Performance Evaluation

In this section, we will evaluate the performance of 2PDRCA comparing with the Alhusaini's method. Firstly, we give some definitions, as we define in definition 1, the parallel program with n tasks can be represented as DAG with n tasks. In our simulation, we use following several parameters:

Number of tasks in the graph, (TASK).

Communication to computation ratio (CCR).

It is the ratio of the average communication cost to the average computation cost.

Range percentage of computation cost on machines, (HETERGENEITY).

A high percentage value causes a significant different in a task's computation cost among the machines and a low percentage indicates that the expected computation cost of a task is almost equal on any given machines in the system.

Number of machines in the system, (MACHINE).

We define the Schedule Length Ration (SLR) as the average schedule length of 2PDRCA divides by the average schedule length of Alhusaini's method. If the SLR is larger than 1.0 means the Alhusaini's method has the smaller schedule length. On the contrary, if the SLR is smaller than 1.0 means 2PDRCA has smaller schedule length.

We can observe the effect of CCR {0.1, 0.5, 1, 5, 10} with changing the TASK {100, 150, 200} and HETEROGENEITY {0.2, 1, 1.5} from Fig. 4 respectively. As the CCR increases, the SLR decreases quickly. So, in a communication intensive application, Alhusaini's method will have larger schedule length than 2PDRCA.

In a communication intensive application, an efficient method to reduce the communication cost between tasks will enormously shorten the schedule length. But, the migration condition in Alhusaini's method, only computation cost will be used to decide to re-assign a task to its best machine or not in run time. Therefore, the schedule length will increase quickly caused by the communication cost.

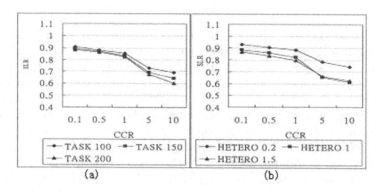

Fig. 4. (a) The simulation result of effect of CCR with changing TASK (b) The simulation result of effect of CCR with changing HETEROGENEITY

In the Fig. 5, we will illustrate the effect of HETEROGENEITY on SLR. Through these two experiments, we have found effect of HETEROGENEITY with changing CCR that the SLR decreases as the HETEROGENEITY increases.

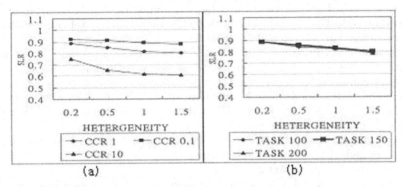

Fig. 5. (a) The simulation result of effect of HETEROGENEITY with changing CCR (b) The simulation result of effect of HETEROGENEITY with changing TASK

5   Conclusion

This paper proposed the 2-phases dynamic resource co-allocation algorithm; it has the following main advantages compared with Alhusaini's method. The simulation results show that 2PDRCA effectively shortens the schedule length comparing with Alhusaini's method. Especially in communication intensive application, we get better performance; the time complexity of run time phases in Alhusaini's method and 2PDRCA are in common. Both of them are $O(N^2R)$, where N is the total number of tasks and R is the total number of non-compute resources. But in compiler time phase, the time complexity of Alhusaini's method is $O(2^NNR)$ greater than 2PDRCA's time complexity which is $O(N^2R)$.

We can take the consideration of different parameters such as network topology, and system latency into the 2PDRCA. And, may expand our assumptions to consider usage of multiple compute resources and advance resource reservations.

References

1. Wang, L.Z., Cai, W.T., Lee, B.S., et al.: Resource co-allocation for parallel task s in computational grids[C]. In: Proceedings of the International Workshop on Challenges of Large Application s in Distributed Environments, pp. 88–95. IEEE Computer Society Press, Los Alamitos (2003)
2. Yang, J., Bai, Y., Qiu, Y.: A decentralized resource allocation policy in minigrid[J]. Future Generation Computer Systems (2006)
3. Rehn, C.: Dynamic mapping of cooperating tasks to nodes in a distributed system [J]. Future Generation Computer Systems, pp. 35–45 (2006)
4. Sanyal, S., Jain, A., Das, S.K., et al.: A hierarchical and distributed approach for mapping large applications to heterogeneous grids using genetic algorithms[C]. In: Proceedings of the IEEE International Conference on Cluster Computing, Hong Kong, pp. 496–499. IEEE Computer Society, Washington (2003)
5. Azzedin, F., Maheswaran, M., Arnason, N.: A synchronous co-allocation mechanism for grid computing systems [J]. Cluster Computing 7(1), 39–49 (2004)

6. Liao, J., Cai, H., et al.: Design and Implementation of Grid Monitoring System based on GMA[C], The sixth International Conference on Parallel and Distributed Computing, Applications and Technologies, pp. 94–96 (2005)
7. Alhusaini, A.H., Prasanna, V.K., Raghavendra, C.S.: A framework for mapping with resource co-allocation in heterogeneous computing system[C], 9th Heterogeneous Computing Workshop, pp. 273–286 (2000)
8. Alhusaini, A.H., Prasanna, V.K., Raghavendra, C.S.: Run-Time Adaptation for Grid environments[C]. In: Proceedings 15th International Parallel and Distributed Processing Symposium, pp. 864–874 (2001)
9. Topcuoglu, H., Hariri, S., Wu, M.-Y.: Performance-effective and low-complexity task scheduling for heterogeneous computing [J]. IEEE Trans. On. Parallel and Distributed System 13, 260–274 (2002)
10. Casanova, H.: Simgrid-A toolkit for the simulation of application scheduling[C]. In: Proceedings of the 1st IEEE international Symposium on Cluster Computing and the Grid (2001)
11. Hui-xian, L.I., Chun-tian, C.: A parallel method of resources co-allocation in grid system [J]. Journal of Dalian University of Technology 45, 272–276 (2005)
12. Topcuoglu, H., Hariri, S., Wu, M.-Y.: Performance-effective and low-complexity task scheduling for heterogeneous computing. IEEE Trans. On Parallel and Distributed System 13, 260–274 (2002)

Fuzzy-Grey Prediction Based Dynamic Failure Detector for Distributed Systems

Dong Tian[1,2], Shuyu Chen[2], and Taiping Mao[1]

[1] GuiZhou Electronic Computer Software Development Center, GuiZhou, China
[2] College of Computer Science, ChongQing University, ChongQing, China
{tiandong,sychen}@cqu.edu.cn, mtp@mail.gzst.gov.cn

Abstract. Fuzzy logic and grey theory, combined with adaptive heartbeat mechanism, are integrated to implement an adaptive failure detector for distributed systems. A GM(1,1) unified-dimensional new message model, which only needs a small volume of sample data, is used to predict heartbeat arrival time dynamically. Since prediction error is inevitable, a two-input (residual ratio and message loss rate), one-output (compensation value) fuzzy controller is designed to learn how to compensate for the output from the grey model, and the roughly determined fuzzy rule base is tuned by a reward-punishment learning principle. Experimental results show the availability and validity of the failure detector in detail.

1 Introduction

Failure detector is an essential component for building reliable distributed systems, and many ground-breaking advances have been made on failure detectors [8]. Moreover, with the emerging of large-scale, dynamic, asynchronous distributed systems, adaptive failure detectors which can adapt to changing network conditions have drawn much attention of literature, and some truly adaptive algorithms have been presented, such as [5-8].

The idea of adaptive failure detection is that a monitored process p periodically sends a heartbeat message ("*I'm alive!*"). A process q begins to suspect p if it fails to receive a heartbeat from p after some timeout. Adaptive failure detection protocols change the value of the timeout dynamically, according to the network conditions measured in the recent past [9]. Doing so, adaptive protocols are able to cope adequately with changing networking conditions, and hence they are particularly appropriate for common networking environment, or the Internet. In particular, they are able to maintain a good compromise between how fast they detect actual failures, and how well they avoid wrong suspicions.

Nevertheless, existing adaptive failure detectors (e.g.[5-8]) almost employ statistical methods to predict heartbeat arrival time dynamically, which need a large volume of sample data and require the sample data present in normal distribution, making them unsuitable for highly dynamic distributed systems. Moreover, they either ignore the problem of message loss (e.g., [6], [10]) or assume the loss of consecutive messages is uncorrelated [5]. In contrast, experiments [8] have shown that message losses are

H. Jin et al. (Eds.): ICA3PP 2007, LNCS 4494, pp. 131–141, 2007.

strongly correlated and tend to occur in bursts of various length, which is consistent with observations made by Keidar [11], as well as many people in the networking research community.

In this paper, we present a novel implementation of adaptive failure detector. It follows the adaptive heartbeat strategy, but employs a quite different method, that is, combined grey prediction algorithm with an adaptive fuzzy controller to modify the timeout dynamically according to network conditions. By use of an improved grey prediction method, we can predict the next heartbeat arrival time promptly through a small volume of sample data, and do no assumption on the distribution of sample data. Furthermore, with respect to both prediction error and message loss factors, a two-input/one-output fuzzy controller has been designed to generate a compensation value for the predicted one. Then, we can acquire a more accurate prediction result. Furthermore, experimental results demonstrate the validity and availability of our method.

The remainder of the paper is structured as follows. Section 2 describes the system model and presents the whole architecture of our failure detector. In Section 3, we give the improved grey prediction algorithm. Section 4 presents the adaptive fuzzy controller in detail. In Section 5, experimental results show the validity and availability of our failure detector. Finally, the paper is concluded in Section 6.

2 Architecture Overview

In this section, we first describe the system model of distributed systems. Then, present the architecture of our failure detector in detail.

2.1 System Model

Similar to the model of Chen *et al.* [5], we consider a simple asynchronous model consisting of two processes p and q. The processes are subject to crash failures only and, crashes are permanent. The processes are connected by two unidirectional channels that cannot create, duplicate, or garble messages. The channels are fair-lossy which means that, if a process, say p, sends an infinite number of messages to process q and q is correct, then q eventually receives an infinite number of message from p. In practice, a fair-lossy channel can be implemented by some best-effort lossy communication service, such as UDP.

In addition, processes have access to some local physical clock giving them the ability to measure time. We assume nothing regarding the synchronization of these clocks.

In the remainder of the paper, we consider the situation where process q monitors process p.

2.2 Architecture of Failure Detector

As is shown in Fig. 1, the implementation of failure detector on the receiving side can be decomposed into three basic parts as follows.

1. *Prediction layer*. An adaptive grey predictor is constructed using GM(1,1) unified-dimensional new message model (see in section 3). Upon receiving a new heartbeat message, the adaptive grey predictor calculates the next heartbeat message arrival time, generates both predict value and residual ratio.
2. *Compensation layer*. In order to decrease the predict error, this layer employs a two-input/one-output adaptive fuzzy controller (see in section 4) to generate a compensation value adaptively, the two-input are residual ratio and the message loss rate in specific period, the output is a compensation value.
3. *Execution layer*. The final prediction value is equal to the predicted value pluses the compensation one. Then, actions are executed as a response to triggered failures based on the execution layer whether or not receiving the next heartbeat within prediction time. This is normally done within applications.

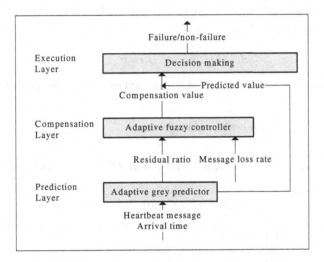

Fig. 1. The architecture of failure detector

3 Prediction Layer

Existing adaptive failure detectors (e.g. [5-8]) almost employ statistical methods, which need a large volume of sample data and require the sample data present in normal distribution. If the samples are distributed at random, the prediction values may become unstable and make the system predict inaccurately.

To avoid the above limitations, we explore grey theory [3] to predict heartbeat arrival time dynamically, and the GM(1,1) [4] *unified-dimensional new message model* is employed. The algorithm is depicted as algorithm 1:

Algorithm 1:
Step1: Get current time sequence.
Collecting the small number of the just passed heartbeat arrival time as prediction samples to form current time sequence, which denote by:

$$t^{(0)} = (t^{(0)}(1), t^{(0)}(2), t^{(0)}(3), \cdots, t^{(0)}(n)) \tag{1}$$

where n: the number of samples.

Step 2: Do accumulated generating operation (AGO) formation of $t^{(0)}$.

Defined $t^{(1)}$ as:

$$t^{(1)} = (t^{(1)}(1), t^{(1)}(2), t^{(1)}(3), \cdots, t^{(1)}(n)) \tag{2}$$

where $t^{(1)}(1) = t^{(0)}(1)$, and $t^{(1)}(k) = \sum_{m=1}^{k} t^{(0)}(m) \quad k = 2, 3, \cdots, n \tag{3}$

Step 3: Form GM (1, 1) model.

From the AGO sequence $t^{(1)}$, we can form a GM (1, 1) model, which corresponds to the following first-order difference equation:

$$dt^{(1)}(k)/dk + at^{(1)}(k) = b \tag{4}$$

Therefore, the solution of Eq.(4) can be obtained using the least square method. That is:

$$\hat{t}^{(1)}(k) = (t^{(0)}(1) - \tfrac{\hat{b}}{\hat{a}}) \times e^{-\hat{a}(k-1)} + \tfrac{\hat{b}}{\hat{a}} \tag{5}$$

where $$[\hat{a}, \hat{b}]^T = (B^T B)^{-1} B^T T_n \tag{6}$$

and $$B = \begin{bmatrix} -0.5(t^{(1)}(1) + t^{(1)}(2)), & 1 \\ -0.5(t^{(1)}(1) + t^{(1)}(2)), & 1 \\ \cdots & \cdots \\ -0.5(t^{(1)}(n-1) + t^{(1)}(n)), & 1 \end{bmatrix} \tag{7}$$

$$T_n = [t^{(0)}(2), t^{(0)}(3), t^{(0)}(4), \cdots, t^{(0)}(n)]^T \tag{8}$$

We obtained $\hat{t}^{(1)}$ from Eq.(5). Let $\hat{t}^{(0)}$ be the fitted and predicted series,

$$\hat{t}^{(0)} = (\hat{t}^{(0)}(1), \hat{t}^{(0)}(2), \hat{t}^{(0)}(3), \cdots, \hat{t}^{(0)}(n)) \text{ , where } \hat{t}^{(0)}(1) = t^{(0)}(1) \tag{9}$$

Step 4: Obtain the next heartbeat arrival time

Applying the inverse accumulated generating operation (IAGO), we then have

$$\hat{t}^{(0)}(k) = (t^{(0)}(1) - \frac{\hat{b}}{\hat{a}}) \times (1 - e^{\hat{a}}) \times e^{-\hat{a}(k-1)} \tag{10}$$

where $\hat{t}^{(0)}(n+1)$ is the next heartbeat arrival time.

Step 5: Form new prediction model.
Upon receiving the $(n+1)$th heartbeat, the monitoring process p reads the process clock and stores the heartbeat rank and arrival time into a sliding window (thus discarding the oldest heartbeat), and form new prediction model as follows.

$$t_{new}^{(0)} = \{t^{(0)}(2), t^{(0)}(3), \cdots, t^{(0)}(n), t^{(0)}(n+1)\} \tag{11}$$

Then, repeat steps 2- 4 to predict the (n+2)th heartbeat arrival time, and so on.

Step 6: Residual checking
A residual checking method is used to compare the predicted data with actual data after the predicted value are derived from GM(1,1) unified-dimensional new message model, shown in Eq.(12), and the residual ratio combined with message loss rate in specific period are used to the adaptive fuzzy controller to generate the compensation value.

$$e_t(k) = \frac{t^{(0)}(k) - \hat{t}^{(0)}(k)}{t^{(0)}(k)}, \ k=1, 2, 3, \cdots, n \tag{12}$$

4 Compensation Layer

Since prediction error is inevitable, and message loss rate is strongly correlated to the performance of failure detector [8][11]. Then, in order to make our failure detector more accurate, an adaptive fuzzy controller is designed to compensate the prediction error and message loss.

The basic components of the adaptive fuzzy controller include: (1) the fuzzification algorithm used for defining the linguistic variables in the fuzzy control rules; (2) the fuzzy control rules used for characterizing the control strategies of the expert; (3) a self-learning mechanism that adjusts the fuzzy rules adaptively; (4) the defuzzification algorithms used for getting crisp output from the fuzzy output set. More detailed descriptions of fuzzy sets and their operations can be found in [1]. In this paper, we use a simplified fuzzy reasoning method where triangular-shaped membership functions and the real values (singletons) are used for characterizing these linguistic values of the antecedent part and the consequent part respectively, and adjusts the fuzzy rules according to a reward-punishment principle. They are briefly described in the following.

4.1 Fuzzification Algorithm

The basic structure of the proposed adaptive fuzzy controller has two inputs and one output. The two inputs derive are *residual ratio* $e_t(k)$ and the *message loss rate* in specific time period (signed as $l_M(t)$, calculated by Eq.(13)). The single output is a compensation value, and this value plus the predicted one generated by prediction layer is the final predicted value of next heartbeat arrival time.

$$l_M(t) = \frac{M-N}{M} \times 100\% \tag{13}$$

where M is the heartbeat sending number by q, N is the heartbeat receiving number by p.

The fuzzification algorithm for $e_t(k)$ and $l_M(t)$ is shown in Fig.2(a), where the symmetric triangular-shaped membership functions are used, the fuzzification algorithm for $c(k)$ (compensation value) is shown in Fig.3(b), and the real number are used. "NL", "NM", "NS", "ZO", "PS", "PM" and "PL" stand for "Negative-large", "Negative-medium", "Negative-small", "Zero", "Positive-small" and "Positive-medium", "Positive-large", respectively.

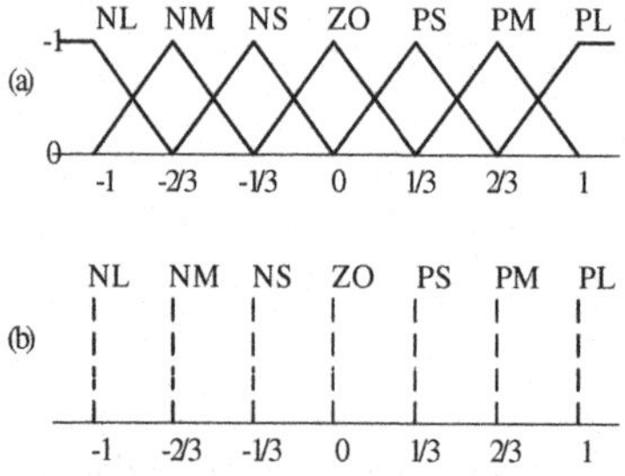

Table 1. Rules used in the fuzzy controller

Fig. 2. Membership functions of fuzzy

		e(k)						
		NL	NM	NS	ZO	PS	PM	PL
l(t)	NL	NL	NL	NL	NL	NM	NS	ZO
	NM	NL	NM	NM	NM	NS	ZO	PS
	NS	NL	NM	NM	NS	ZO	PS	PM
	ZO	NL	NM	NS	ZO	PS	PM	PL
	PS	NM	NS	ZO	PS	PM	PL	PL
	PM	NS	ZO	PS	PM	PL	PL	PL
	PL	ZO	PS	PM	PL	PL	PL	PL

4.2 Fuzzy Control Rules

The fuzzy controller is constructed by a rule base of individual control rules which are conditional linguistic statements of relationship between inputs and outputs. The set of control rules can be expressed as follows:

Rule R_{ij}: If e is E_i and l is L_j, then c is C_{ij}

Where e, l and c are linguistic variables and E_i, L_j, C_{ij} are linguistic values with membership functions $E_i: Ce \rightarrow [0,1]$, $L_j: Cl \rightarrow [0,1]$ and $C_{ij}: Cc \rightarrow [0,1]$ corresponding to the universe discourse of E_i, L_j and C_{ij} respectively. The membership functions of the above fuzzy sets are depicted in Fig.3, where the universe of discourse of each input is normalized in the interval [-1,1]. It is known that the control rules have an important effect on the control performance. The rules may be determined according to the step response of the system under study [2]. In this paper, the used control rules are given in Table 1.

4.3 Fuzzy Rule Self-learning Procedure

To provide the fuzzy controller with on-line and self-learning ability, the C_{ij} of each fuzzy rule is adjusted during the classification process based on the reward-punishment learning principle. When the selected fuzzy rule is able to correctly generate compensation value, C_{ij} is increased:

$$C_{ij}^{new} = C_{ij}^{old} + \delta_1 C_{ij}^{old} \qquad (14)$$

In Eq.(14) δ_1 is a positive learning factor for increasing C and $\delta_1 C_{ij}^{old}$ is the reward for the correct classification.

On the contrary, if the selected fuzzy rule fails to correctly generate compensation value, C is reduced:

$$C_{ij}^{new} = C_{ij}^{old} + \delta_2 C_{ij}^{old} \qquad (15)$$

As is shown in Eq.(15), δ_2 is a negative learning factor for decreasing C and $\delta_2 C_{ij}^{old}$ is the punishment for misclassification.

In our approach, a fuzzy rule base becomes more adaptive and flexible for different types of classification after implementing the above procedures.

4.4 Defuzzification Algorithm

If we sum all the output fuzzy sets to form the resultant output set, the defuzzification algorithm is used to convert it into a scalar output. In general, there are many methods to carry out this procedure. In this paper, the used defuzzification algorithm is the weighted average method. That is, when the input $e_t(k)$ and $l_M(t)$ are input to the fuzzy controller, the scaled control output $c(t)$ is obtained by the following equation:

$$c(t) = \frac{\sum_{i=1}^{49} w_i \Box y_i}{\sum_{i=1}^{49} w_i} \qquad (16)$$

where

$$w_i = E_i(e(k)) \Box L_i(l(t)) \qquad (17)$$

is the truth value of the antecedent part in the ith rule and y_i is the real value of the consequent part in the ith rule.

5   Experimental Results

We have analyzed the behavior of our failure detector between Internet and CERNET (Chinese Education and Research Net) in Chongqing city for a total duration of three weekdays. First, we describe the environment in which the experiments have been conducted. Second, we record heartbeat samples and calculate message loss rate. Third, we construct the adaptive fuzzy controller according to selected heartbeat samples and message loss rate. At last, we compare our failure detector to that of Chen's [5].

5.1 Experimental Setup

Analog to [7-9], our experiments involved two computers, with one locates in ChongQing University (CERNET), and the other locates outside of ChongQing University (Internet). All messages are transmitted with UDP protocol. Neither machine failed during the experiment.

The sending host locates outside of ChongQing University, the IP address is 221.5.183.108. It is equipped with a Celeron IV processor at (1.7GHz) and the memory is 256 MB, the operating system is Red Hat Linux 9 (kernel 2.4.20).

While the receiving host is locates in ChongQing University. It is equipped with a Pentium IV processor at 2.4 GHz and the memory is 512MB, the operating system is also Red Hat Linux 9 (kernel 2.4.20).

5.2 Experimental Results

The experiment was done in three phases. First, we record heartbeat arrivals using the experimental setup described above. Secondly, we calculate the message loss rate $l_M(t)$ for every one minute. Then, select 1000 heartbeat arrival time samples to construct fuzzy controller. At last, we have used simulation to replay the recorded traces with different failure detector implementations. The details are depicted as follows.

Phase 1: Recording heartbeat arrivals
The experiment lasts for three weekdays, during which heartbeat message is generated every 400ms. Fig.3 depicts the curves of the mean heartbeat sending interval and arrival interval from 10am to 4pm in the three days. We can know that message delay is a bit high, the highest message delay is 2428ms, and the lowest, 989ms. We think this is result from the transmit speed between CERNET and Internet is slowly.

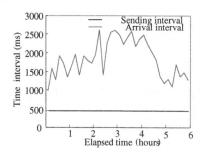 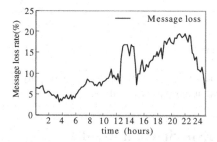

Fig. 3. Figure of message delay   **Fig. 4.** Figure of message loss rate

Fig.4 shows the mean message loss rate of the first two days. We can see that the message loss rate is also a bit high, in bursting hours, the message loss rate is almost nearly 20%. We think this is also result from the low transmit speed between CERNET and Internet is slowly.

Phase 2: Construct fuzzy controller
Experiment 1: *establishing fuzzy rule base*
According to the fuzzification algorithm in section 4, a total of 1000 momentary residual ratio and message loss rate points were selected to fed each of the 7x7 fuzzy rule base to generate compensation values. In our approach, each training sample contains three states, that is, residual ratio of predicted value, message loss rate in specific time period, and compensation value.

Experiment 2: *determining positive/negative learning factors*
After establishing the fuzzy rule base, we need to determine positive learning factor δ_1 and negative learning factor δ_2 (Eqs. (14) and (15)). The absolute value of δ can range from 0 to 1. A pair of likely values (based on experience) is selected and applied to the fuzzy rule base. The 1000 training samples were randomized as to order and, in this form, given the designation "test samples". The test samples were then input to the fuzzy rule base with a given δ-pair. This process yields the data of Table 2. It shows that the 7x7 (49 fuzzy rules) base with $\delta_1 = 0.01$ and $\delta_2 = -0.13$ yields a high correct-compensation percentage, i.e. 99.7%.

Table 2. Correctclass classifiction for different learning factors

δ_1	δ_2	7x7 fuzzy subsets(%)
0.001	-0.001	94.3
0.001	-0.15	99.2
0.005	-0.15	99.2
0.01	-0.005	91.7
0.01	-0.01	92.8
0.01	-0.1	99.4
0.01	-0.13	99.7
0.01	-0.14	99.6
0.01	-0.15	99.5
0.05	-0.15	98.8
0.1	-0.15	95.8
0.15	-0.01	88.1
0.15	-0.15	90.8

Phase 3: Simulating failure detectors
Experiment 1: *determine the size of prediction sample space.*
We set the size of sample space from 20 samples to 500 samples, and measured the accuracy obtained by the failure detector running during 10am and 4pm.

As is shown in Fig. 5, the experiment confirms that the mistake rate of our failure detector improves as the sample size increases. But the curve seems to flatten slightly when the size is more than 200, meaning that increasing it further yields only little improvement.

Experiment 2: *comparison with Chen's failure detector*
In order to validate the prediction accuracy of our failure detector, we compare it with a well-know adaptive detector, that of Chen *et al.* [5].

For the two failure detectors, we set the size of sample space as 300. The result is shown as in Fig. 6, we can see that the prediction value of the two methods is almost same, which means that our method is valid and available.

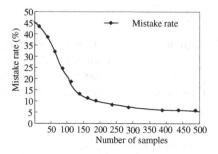
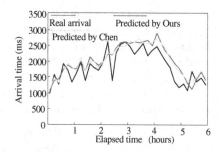

Fig. 5. Effect of sample space

Fig. 6. Accuracy comparison between two methods

6 Conclusion and Future Work

Failure detection is a fundamental building block for ensuring fault tolerance in distributed systems. In this paper, combining adaptive heartbeat mechanism with fuzzy grey prediction algorithm, we present a novel implementation of adaptive failure detector. That is, using grey prediction algorithm with a fuzzy controller to modify the timeout dynamically according to network conditions. In doing so, we only need a small number of sample data, and do no assumption on the distribution of sample data. Moreover, by using the residual ratio of predicted value and message loss rate in specific period as input variations of the fuzzy rule-based controller, we can acquire the confidence of failure/non-failure of distributed systems. At last, experimental results demonstrate the validity and availability of our method in detail. In the near future, we will implement a failure detection middleware based on the algorithms present in this paper.

Acknowledgment

This work is supported by Chinese National Sustentation Programs for Science and Technology Development, under contact No.2006BAF01A15, and GuiZhou Provincial Programs for Science and Technology Development, under contract No.2006(3025). Many thanks to Gang Yang for providing experimental program, as well as Jing Li, Changze Wu, Xiaobo Ji for many discussion.

References

[1] Sugeno, M.: An introductory survey of fuzzy control. Inform. Sci. 36, 59–83 (1985)
[2] Zimmermann, H.Z.: Fuzzy set theory and its applications, 2nd edn. Kluwer Academic Publishers, Dordrecht (1991)
[3] Deng, J.: Control problems of grey system. Systems Control Lett. 5, 288–294 (1982)
[4] Deng, J. L.: Grey Prediction and Decision, Huazhong University of Science and Technology, (in Chinese) (1986)

[5] Chen, W., Toueg, S., Aguilera, M.K.: On the quality of service of failure detectors. IEEE Transactions on Computers 51(2), 13–32 (2002)

[6] Bertier, M., Marin, O., Sens, P.: Implementation and performance evaluation of an adaptable failure detector. In: Proc. IEEE Intl. Conf. On Dependable Systems and Networks (DSN'02), pp. 354–363 (June 2002)

[7] Hayashibara, N., Défago, X., Yared, R., Katayama, T.: The φ accrual failure detector, In: Proc. 23nd IEEE Intl. Symp. On Reliable Distributed Systems (SRDS'04), pp. 66–78 (October 2004)

[8] Hayashibara, N., Défago, X., Katayama, T.: Flexible failure detection with κ-fd. Research Report IS-RR-2004-006, Japan Advanced Institute of Science and Technology, Ishikawa, Japan (February 2004)

[9] Hayashibara, N., Défago, X., Katayama, T.: Implementation and performance analysis of the φ-failure detector. Research Report IS-RR-2003-013, Japan Advanced Institute of Science and Technology, Ishikawa, Japan (October 2003)

[10] Hayashibara, N., Défago, X., Katayama, T.: Two-ways adaptive failure detection with the φ-failure detector. In: Proc. Workshop on Adaptive Distributed Systems (WADiS'03), pp. 22–27, Sorrento, Italy (October 2003)

[11] Kaidar, I., Sussman, J., Marzullo, K., Dolev, D.: Moshe: A group membership service for WANs. ACM Trans. Comput. Systems 20(2), 1–48 (2002)

A Two-Level Directory Organization Solution for CC-NUMA Systems

Guoteng Pan, Qiang Dou, and Lunguo Xie

School of Computer,
National University of Defense Technology,
Changsha, 410073, Hunan, P.R. China
gtpan@nudt.edu.cn

Abstract. Currently, directory-based cache coherence protocols are widely adopted in DSM systems. However, with the scaling of system size, directory-based protocols are also confronted with the problem of scalability. With the analysis of factors that affect the scalability of directory protocols, we propose a two-level directory organization solution based on directory cache in this paper. Simulation result shows that this directory organization can efficiently reduce storage space occupied by directory information to enable good scalability for the implementation of the protocol, with the performance of the system being considered.

1 Introduction

CC-NUMA systems are hardware implementations of distributed shared memory systems (DSM), such as SGI origin 3000[1] and HP Superdome [2]. As cache is distributed to nodes with processors, new problem is incurred when reducing the average access time and requirements of memory bandwidth, which is the problem of cache coherence: how to keep multiple copies of the same data block residing in different caches and memory consistent. The problem of cache coherence not only decides the correctness of the system, but also has a significant impact on system performance. Many cache coherence protocols have been put forward to address this problem.

It is key to track the state of shared data block in implementing cache coherence protocols. According to the technologies adopted in state tracking, there exist two kinds of protocols currently: snooping protocols [3, 4] and directory-based protocols. The former is based on broadcast mechanism provided by system bus. All the processors are inter-connected by shared bus. When any processor tries to write data, it must get the control of the bus, and then put the address of the to-be-invalidate data block on it. The other processors are snooping the bus all through, detecting whether the data block corresponding to the address resides in their caches. If it resides, the corresponding data block will be evicted. Snooping protocols are suitable for small size systems, but for the limitations from bus scalability, shared bus will become a bottleneck for performance with the scaling of system size. For better scalability compared to snooping protocols, directory-based cache coherence protocols [5-7] are

H. Jin et al. (Eds.): ICA3PP 2007, LNCS 4494, pp. 142–152, 2007.

usually adopted in CC-NUMA systems. But with the expansion of system size, directory-based protocols are also confronted with the problem of scalability.

Generally speaking, the factors that affecting the scalability of directory-based cache coherence protocols mainly include:

− Overheads in directory storage

In CC-NUMA systems, the copies of one data block might exist in the caches of multiple processors. To precisely record the shared information of each data block, directory is often organized in bit vector. The main drawback of this method is that storage space occupied by directory will increase with the expansion of system scale. Therefore, directory organization is an important factor that affects the scalability of directory-based protocols.

− Latency in accessing directory

The access modes of directory generally include read-modify-write. If the latency in accessing directory is large, system performance will be greatly impacted. But if directory is implemented in high-speed storage, the performance of read-modify-write will be improved, and the impact of this latency on system performance will be reduced.

− Overheads in processing cache coherence for data access

According to cache coherence protocols, the process of a data access request will generally involve multiple nodes and the multiple messages passing between these nodes. Especially when invalidate message is needed to send to all the shared copies or intervention request is needed to send by third parties, message communications will be even more on the network. The scale of interconnected network and the communication latency between nodes will increase with the expansion of system scale. Therefore, overheads in processing cache coherence for data access will increase with the expansion of system scale, which also greatly impacts the scalability of CC-NUMA systems.

Targeting the above three factors that impact the scalability of directory-based protocols, a directory-cache based two-level directory organization solution is proposed in this paper, which combines bit vector mode and limited pointers mode. By means of decreasing directory width and height, overheads in directory storage, latency in accessing directory and overheads in processing cache coherence are all reduced.

The rest of this paper is organized as follows: in section 2, related work is presented; in section 3, the directory-cache based two-level directory organization is introduced and analyzed; in section 4, simulation and evaluation are given; and finally in section 5, the whole paper is concluded.

2 Related Work

In directory-based cache coherence protocols, directory is responsible for the maintenance of cache block's shared information, and directory organization defines the storage structure and the characteristics of the stored information. The choice of directory organization will affect overheads in directory storage, impact system performance, and is important to the scalability of directory-based protocols. By far, the widely-adopted directory organization in commodity systems and academic fields mainly include: bit vector directory, limited pointers directory, chained directory and hybrid directory.

Bit vector directory is also called full-map directory [8], and each directory item has an N-bit vector, where N is the number of processors in system. And each bit within the N-bit vector corresponds to a processor, to denote whether there is a copy of the corresponding memory block in this processor's cache. The advantage of bit vector directory is that, the shared information of memory block is complete, and the invalidate messages can be correctly sent to the corresponding nodes according to the record of bit vector. As the storage space required for bit vector directory is in direct ratio to the number of processors in system, N, when N is large, storage overheads in implementing directory-based protocols will also be large.

Limited pointers directory [9] can decrease overheads in directory storage. It uses limited number of pointers (for example, m) to point to the processors that own copies of the data block, and each pointer needs log_2N bits, where N denotes the number of processors in system. To show the advantage of limited pointers directory, the precondition is the number of copies of the same data block in different caches should be smaller than some constant m ($m<<N$). Under this condition, storage overhead in limited pointers directory is far smaller than that in bit vector directory. However, when the number of copies is bigger than m (the pointer overflows), special operations must be taken. The usual method adopted is randomly selecting a pointer, sending *invalidate* message to the node it points, and invalidating the corresponding copy, which will result in serious impact on system performance.

From the aspect of information storage, bit vector directory and limited pointers directory are both memory-based, that is, all the information relating to shared data block are stored in home node's memory, by means of which information of all nodes can be obtained. The other storing manners are cache based, that is, directory information of shared data block does not reside in home node, but distributes to caches, and chained directory is such kind of cache-based directory.

In chained directory[10], all the caches owning the same copy of a data block is linked by chains, whose head pointer resides in the data block's home node. When one data block is buffered in some cache, the corresponding cache will be chained to the chain pointed by the data block's head pointer. When some data block is invalidated or replaced in some cache, the corresponding cache will be deleted from the chain pointed by the data block's head pointer. But if the shared status of some data block is expected to obtain, the whole cache directory chain has to be gone through, which makes chained directory protocols rather complex.

Different with the single directory organization method in multi-processor systems introduced above, SGI's Origin 3000 combines bit vector, coarse grain vector and limited pointers methods on the basis of bit vector directory, which provides a more flexible mixed directory organization. This system fully exploits the advantages of bit vector directory and coarse grain directory. For systems with node number exceeding 64, Oct (octant) field is introduced to avoid imprecise shared information in a large amount of shared information (when the number of shared processors is no larger than 128, they will fall into the same octant. The adoption of coarse grain vector enables the system to maximally support 512 nodes. Compared to bit vector directory, mixed directory can spare large storage; and compared to coarse grain vector directory, some imprecise shared information is avoided and network communication is reduced. The efficiency of directory storage is improved and the impact on system performance is reduced when the capacity of directory storage remains the same. The disadvantage of this method is that extra hardware is required in determining shared status (includes shared amount, whether falling into the same octant, and etc), so as to choose a suitable form to denote it. Besides, when directory state or shared status has been changed, special hardware will be needed for conversion between the three directory formats. These disadvantages increase hardware overheads and impact system performance.

Chang from Texas A&M University proposed a tree-based cache coherence protocol [11], which adopts hybrid directory organization combining limited pointer directory and chained directory. By utilizing a limited number of pointers in the directory, the proposed scheme connects the nodes caching a shared block in a tree fashion. In addition to the low communication overhead, the proposed scheme also contains the advantages of the existing bit-map and tree-based linked list protocols, namely, scalable memory requirement and logarithmic invalidation latency.

Acacio from Spain also proposed a hybrid directory organization solution [12, 13], which combines bit vector directory and limited pointer directory. With similar performance with bit vector, directory storage overheads are largely reduced. But these two levels of directories are put in memory, though directory storage overheads are reduced, access latency is not efficiently reduced.

3 Directory-Cache Based Two-Level Directory Scheme

3.1 Directory Architecture

In the last section, we have analyzed the pros and cons of various approaches to directory organization. Based on the analysis, we propose a directory-cache based two-level directory organization scheme. In this scheme, every node contains two types of directories:

- First level directory (directory cache): organized as bit vector. The directory contained only a part of all directory items, namely those of the current most active data blocks. The first level directory is actually the cache of the second level directory, hence called directory cache.
- Second level directory: organized as limited pointers. Every data block in the node memory has a corresponding item in the directory.

In order to reduce memory overhead, the two-level directory organization scheme is so designed that the height of the directory is decreased in the first level directory, and the width of the directory is decreased in the second level directory. Figure 1 shows the architecture of the two-level directory. The "Choose and Convert" logic in the right part of the figure functions as follows. When the tag comparator outputs a "1", it selects the N-bit vector from the first level directory and outputs it. When the tag comparator outputs a "0", it selects the limited pointers directory item containing M pointers from the second level directory, transforms the item to an N-bit vector, and outputs the vector.

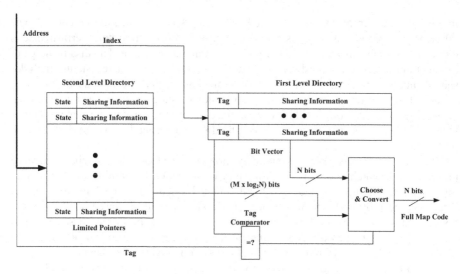

Fig. 1. Architecture of the two-level directory

3.2 Implementation

The first level directory is a bit-vector directory. It is organized as a cache, and implemented with a high-speed storage. As Figure 1 shows, the directory cache adopts the direct map rules. Each item in the directory cache consists of two parts: tag and sharing information. Tag indicates whether the corresponding memory block of the directory item is hit in the cache. Sharing information indicates the sharing state of the corresponding memory block. Because the general mode of accessing directory memory is "read-modify-write", the write-back policy is employed, which writes back to the second level directory when some item in the first level directory is replaced. Note that with the "read-modify-write" access mode, miss just occurs at read, while write always hits.

The second level directory is organized as a limited pointers directory. Every data block in the node memory has a corresponding directory item in the directory. The structure of directory items in the second level directory is similar to that in the first level directory. Each item consists of two parts: state and sharing information, which respectively indicates the state of the directory item and the sharing information of the node which has the copy of the data block.

In the following, we will introduce the process of accessing to the two-level directory.

When a processor takes a read or write operation to a memory block, the home node of the memory block first accesses the two-level directory. The address of the visited directory consists of two parts: *index* in the low-bits, and *tag* in the high-bits. The index part is used to access the first level directory, i.e. the directory cache. The access to the second level directory uses the whole address as an index. The visits to the two levels are executed at the same time. We will present the execution process in terms of cache read hit, read miss, write hit and write miss.

– Directory cache read hit

If the tag of an item indexed in the directory cache equals to the tag in the access address at read, the Tag comparator in Figure 1 outputs a "1". Then the Choose & Convert logic selects an N-bit vector from the directory cache and outputs it.

– Directory cache read miss

If the tag of an item indexed in the directory cache does not equal to the tag in the access address, then the Tag comparator in Figure 1 outputs a "0". In such case, the corresponding directory item will be replaced. The detailed process of the replacement is as follows.

a) The Choose & Convert logic obtains a limited pointer directory item from the second level directory. It transforms the item into an N-bit vector and outputs the vector.

b) The directory cache item to be replaced is selected. The directory cache adopts the write-back policy. Therefore the write-back to the second level directory is needed when an item is replaced. In such case, the write-back address is "high-bit Tag" (the *Tag* of the directory item obtained by the *Index*) + "low-bit Index" (*Index* of the access *Address*). When the corresponding directory item in the first level directory needs to write back to the second level directory, the first thing to do is directory transformation, i.e. to transform the N-bit vector item to a limited pointers item. Then the item can be written to the second level directory. In the transformation, number of the sharing nodes indicated by the N-bit vector may be greater than M, namely directory item overflow happens. The method to resolve it is to randomly select some sharing nodes and send them invalidate messages to invalid the corresponding copies so that the number of sharing nodes becomes M.

Then, following step a), the N-bit vector output by the Choose & Convert logic is put at the corresponding position of the replaced item in the first level directory.

– Directory cache write hit

As mentioned above, the common mode of accessing directory memory is "read-modify-write", thus miss usually happens at read. The corresponding write of a read miss always hit the directory cache. Since the directory cache adopts the write back policy, only write to the corresponding position in the first level directory is needed. It is unnecessary to operate the second level directory.

– Directory cache write miss

It will not happen.

3.3 Analysis on the Scalability

In this section, we analyze the scalability of the directory-cache two-level directory organization scheme from the perspectives of performance and memory overhead.

First, consider the memory overhead of the two-level directory organization scheme. The first level directory uses bit vector to keep the sharing information of the date block. With this manner, the width of directory items is wide. But the memory overhead is not high due to the limited number of directory items. In the second level directory, it is a one-to-one relation between the items and the data blocks in the memory. In order to reduce the memory overhead, we employ an imprecise manner, i.e. limited pointers directory, to keep the sharing information of data blocks. On all accounts, integration of the two levels effectively reduces the memory space cost by directory information, which facilitates a satisfying scalability of the protocol implementation.

Second, consider the performance of the two-level directory organization scheme. The directory items of current most used data always exist in the bit-vector directory. This enables low delay in access. Moreover, since the sharing information is represented in a precise manner, accesses do not affect the system performance. Directory items of current seldom-used data exist in the second level directory. Usage probability of such data blocks is small, so the sharing information stored with the imprecise manner has limited negative effects on the system performance. In the proposed organization scheme, when the first level bit-vector directory (directory cache) has a high hit ratio, the performance of the two-level directory is close to, even better than, that of individual bit-vector directory. This is because the high speed storage used in our first level directory that has a much better access delay than low speed storage used in ordinary bit-vector directories. Hit ratio of the directory cache is decided by a number of factors, including the size of the bit-vector directory, replacement policy and the temporal locality of the specific application.

In summary, the proposed directory-cache based two-level directory organization benefits both memory overhead and performance. On one hand, it effectively reduces the memory space cost by directory information, which improves the scalability of the protocol implementation. On the other hand, it avoids decreasing the system performance. During the protocol execution, the probability of sending invalidate messages using imprecise share information is made as low as possible so as to reduce negative effect on system performance. Besides, using high speed cache as the first level directory decreases actual visits to the directory memory, so that the cost of cache coherence is considerably reduced.

4 Performance Evaluation

The above section has analyzed the memory overhead of the directory-cache based two-level directory organization. In comparison with limited pointers directory, the proposed scheme needs a little more memory overhead. In this section, we build the system model of the proposed scheme, simulate and evaluate its performance.

4.1 Simulation Environment

We used a modified RSIM simulator as the simulation tool. RSIM was developed in the RICE University [14]. We selected 6 representative test programs to investigate the performance benefits of the two-level directory organization. These test programs are SOR and QS from RSIM, WATER from SPLASH (Stanford Parallel Applications for Shared Memory) benchmark suite and FFT, LU, RADIX from SPLASH-2 benchmark suite. Table 1 shows the setting of the main parameters of the simulator in our simulation.

Table 1. Simulation parameters

Parameters of processor	
Processor frequency	300MHz
Instruction issue width	4
Parameters of Cache	
Cache block size	64B
First level cache	16KB, direct map
Hit time	1 cycle
Second level cache	64KB, 4-way set associative
Hit time	5 cycles
Parameters of memory	
Delay of access memory	18 cycles
Interleaving	4
Parameters of bus	
Bus cycle	3 cycles
Bus width	32B
Parameters of network	
Topology	2D mesh
Router cycle	2 cycles
Flit size	8B
Parameters of the two-level directory	
First level directory (directory cache) hit time	8 cycles
Second level directory hit time	20 cycles

In the simulation, each item in the limited pointers directory of the second level directory contains 8 pointers. When the number of processors in the simulated system is large, the execution time is quite long. Therefore we simulated only the situations of 16 processors, 32 processors, and 64 processors. We executed 6 parallel test applications in the simulation. The setting of the input parameters of the applications is shown in Table 2.

Table 2. Applications Workload

Applications	Input size
SOR	128×64, 8 iterations
QS	16384 integers
FFT	65536 points
LU	256×256, block 8
RADIX	52488 keys, 1024 radix
WATER	512 molecules

4.2 Simulation Results

The chart in Figure 2 shows the effects of the two-level directory on execution time of the applications. The first level directory (directory cache) is a direct map cache with the size of 64 KB. The X-coordinate of Figure 2 denotes the number of processors in the system. The Y-coordinate denotes the improvement extent of test applications' performance when using the directory-cache based two-level directory organization scheme.

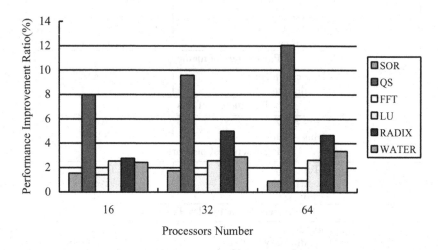

Fig. 2. Effects of the two-level directory on execution time of the applications

As shown in Figure 2, when the two-level directory organization scheme is used, the execution time of QS is greatly improved. The improvement rises with the increase of number of processors in the system. Concerning RADIX and WATER, although the using of the proposed two-level directory does not affect their execution time as much as on QS, the performance of them are improved to some extent, and the improvement also rises with the increase of processors. Concerning SOR, FFT and LU, directory cache does not greatly improve the system performance. The improvement extent falls with the increase of processors.

The applications' performance improves because during the system execution, the corresponding directory information of current most used data exists in the directory cache, which expedites the access of directory information. The extent of the improvement on a specific application lies on the hit ratio on the directory cache during the execution of the applications. As shown in Figure 2, for most applications, the improvement extent becomes more notable with the increase of processors. This is because that each application has certain work set. The work set on each node decreases when the number of processors increase. The hit ratio of the corresponding accesses to directory cache is improved, thus the improvement extent of performance rises.

5 Conclusion

In this paper, we analyzed the factors that affect the scalability of directory protocols and compared the currently typical types of directory organization schemes. Based on the analysis on the pro and cons of the various schemes, we proposed a two-level directory organization scheme. The proposal has considered the aspects of both memory overhead and system performance. On one hand, the use of this directory architecture effectively reduces the memory space cost by directory information, which improves the scalability of the protocol implementation. On the other hand, it does not decrease the system performance. During the protocol execution, the probability of sending invalidate messages using imprecise sharing information is made as low as possible so as to reduce the negative effects on the system performance.

Acknowledgement

This paper is supported by the National High-Tech 863 Project of China under grant No. 2002AA104510.

References

1. SGI. http://www.sgi.com/products/servers/origin/3000/overview.html
2. Gostin, G., Collard, J.-F., Collins, K.: The architecture of the HP Superdome shared-memory multiprocessor. In: Proceedings of the 19th annual international conference on Supercomputing. Cambridge, Massachusetts, pp. 239–245 (2005)
3. Hlayhel, W., Collet, J., Fesquet, L.: Implementing Snoop-Coherence Protocol for Future SMP Architectures. In: Amestoy, P.R., Berger, P., Daydé, M., Duff, I.S., Frayssé, V., Giraud, L., Ruiz, D. (eds.) Euro-Par 1999. LNCS, vol. 1685, Springer, Heidelberg (1999)
4. Bilir, E.E., et al.: Multicast snooping: a new coherence method using a multicastaddress network. In: Proceedings of the 26th International Symposium on Computer Architecture. Atlanta, GA, USA, pp. 294–304 (1999)
5. Laudon, J., Lenoski, D.: The SGI Origin: a ccNUMA highly scalable server. In: Proceedings of the 24th annual international symposium on Computer architecture. Denver, Colorado, USA, pp. 241–251 (1997)
6. Grbic, A.: Assessment of Cache Coherence Protocols in Shared-memory Multiprocessors: [Phd dissertation]. University of Toronto, Toronto, Canada (2003)
7. Gharachorloo, K., et al.: Architecture and design of AlphaServer GS320. In: Proceedings of the 9th international conference on Architectural support for programming languages and operating systems, Cambridge, Massachusetts, USA, pp.13–24 (2000)
8. Li, T., John, L.K.: ADir_pNB: A Cost-Effective Way to Implement Full Map Directory-Based Cache Coherence Protocols. IEEE Transactions on Computers 50(9), 921–934 (2001)
9. Chaiken, D., Kubiatowicz, J., Agarwal, A.: LimitLESS directories: A scalable cache coherence scheme. In: Proceedings of the fourth international conference on Architectural support for programming languages and operating systems. Santa Clara, California, USA, pp. 224–234 (1991)

10. Thapar, M., Delagi, B., Flynn, M.J.: Linked List Cache Coherence for Scalable Shared Memory Multiprocessors. In: Proceedings of International Parallel Processing Symposium, pp. 34–43 (1993)
11. Chang, Y., Bhuyan, L.N.: An Efficient Tree Cache Coherence Protocol for Distributed Shared Memory Multiprocessors. IEEE Transactions on Computers 48(3), 352–360 (1999)
12. Acacio, M.E., et al.: A Two-Level Directory Architecture for Highly Scalable cc-NUMA Multiprocessors. IEEE Transactions on Parallel and Distributed Systems 16(1), 67–79 (2005)
13. Acacio, M.E., et al.: A New Scalable Directory Architecture for Large-Scale Multiprocessors. In: Proceedings of the 7th International Symposium on High-Performance Computer Architecture. Monterrey, Mexico, pp. 97–106 (2001)
14. Hughes, C.J., et al.: RSIM: Simulating Shared-Memory Multiprocessors with ILP Processors. IEEE Computer 35(2), 40–49 (2002)

A Framework of Software Component Adaptation

Xiong Xie and Weishi Zhang

Department of Computer Science and Technology, Dalian Maritime University,
Dalian 116026, P.R. China
xxyj@newmail.dlmu.edu.cn, teesiv@dlmu.edu.cn

Abstract. Software component adaptation is a difficult problem to be solved in component-based software development. In this paper, we focus on a framework of component adaptation in which several adaptations are involved. The framework is described as a finite automaton which has only one initial state and only one final state. Using formal and informal methods we describe the precondition, the post-condition and the process of different component adaptation which are involved in the whole adaptation process. There may be several mismatches between the component and the requirement of application. For executing adaptation successfully the system involves a plan which can save all adaptation types with order. At last future work and limitation of the framework are discussed.

Keywords: Component adaptation, Component-based software engineering, Finite automaton.

1 Introduction

Software component adaptation is a difficult problem in component-based software engineering (CBSE). The developers would like to make use of the available components which have high quality and reliability to build applications according to the normal formal of the large-scale software development in CBSE. However, the differences between the names, parameters and their types of component and the requirement of application or the matter that the requirement of application is satisfied partly by the retrieved component is often unavoidable. Many kinds of differences (we call them as mismatch hence) can be occurred between the components used to build applications and the requirement of application, such as the component signature mismatch, the component function mismatch, the component behavior mismatch and the quality of server (QoS) of components, and so on. The component is a black-box entity and the developer can not know the inner source codes and the logic structure of the program. How to adapt a component which has a partly mismatch to the user's requirement in a process of software component adaptation according to the interface description of the component and the user's requirement? Component adaptation is an efficient way to solve this problem. Component adaptation includes signature adaptation, function adaptation, behavior adaptation and quality of service (QoS) adaptation. Recently, there has been a significant number of research works addressing software component adaptation issues [1, 2, 3, 4, 5, 6, 7, 8, 12]. In most situations, the

H. Jin et al. (Eds.): ICA3PP 2007, LNCS 4494, pp. 153–164, 2007.
© Springer-Verlag Berlin Heidelberg 2007

retrieved component can have several mismatches with the requirement application. If only one kind of mismatches can be solved from the beginning to the end of the component adaptation process, the adaptation process must be called time after time. The efficiency of the component adaptation is low and all mismatches occurred by the same component can not be solved entirely by the component adaptation system. In this paper, a framework of component adaptation process is proposed which can help the system to adapt all mismatches between the component and the requirement of application in a process.

The rest of this paper is organized as follows. In section 2, a component adaptation framework is designed firstly using finite automaton specification which has an adaptation plan helpful to finish the whole adaptation process. Then the precondition and the post-condition of different component adaptation are described in formal specification in section 3. And the adaptation plan is described in this section. The quality of the framework is assessed and a solution avoiding the deadlock is proposed in section 4. In section 5, we draw up the future work and the main limitations of the framework. At last section 6 gives the conclusion of our work.

2   The Framework Description

The component which is retrieved to satisfy the requirement of application can be an input parameter of the system and a new component which satisfies the requirement of application can be the output parameter of the system. The framework is described as a finite automaton in Figure 1.

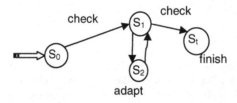

Fig. 1. The framework of component adaptation process

The framework includes four states and three actions. The input parameters of the framework can be not only a component and the requirement of application but also two components. We can select one situation as the input parameter according to the problem.

2.1   The Description of States

1)   State S_0

State S_0 is the initial state of the framework and the content in it is the input of the system. The content is described as a tuple $(Component, user\_require)$, where **Component** is the component which is passed into the component adaptation system and adapted to satisfy the requirement of application described as **user_require**. If the content of state S_0 satisfies the precondition of action **check,** the system will implement the action **check**. Otherwise, the system will stop.

2)   State S_1

The results of the action **check** will be saved in the state S_1. So the state S_1 denotes the adaptation types which will be passed to the action **adapt** and the conclusion which will be passed to the action **finish**. The conclusion has two meanings. One is that the component has no mismatch with the requirement and another is that the component can not satisfy the requirement after a sequence of adaptations. Because a component can has many mismatches with the requirement, the action **check** will has many results which will be saved in the sate S_1. We can describe the content of state S_1 as follow:

$$S_1 = \sum_{i=1}^{n} Adapt\_type_i \mid (null \mid \Phi),$$ (1)

Where, n is the number of mismatches checked by the action **check**, $Adapt\_type_i$ denotes a kind of component adaptation which is any element of the set $\{signature\_mismatch, function\_mismatch, Qos\_mismatch\}$ and   *null* denotes the first conclusion. The symbol Φ denotes the second conclusion. The system will has a plan according the content of the state S_1. All kinds of adaptation strategies are order in the plan. Then the system will pass the plan to the action **adapt**. The action **adapt** will finish all adaptations listed in the plan. So the action **adapt** is a complex sub system which must has a controller to select the right adaptation strategy to adapt the component which is the input of the action **check**.

3)   State S_2

State S_2 denotes the component has been adapted by the system and the adapted component satisfies the requirement much more. The content of State S_2 is the adapted component which comes from the action **adapt** and the requirement which comes from the system, which is described as a tuple $(Component', user\_require)$. If the content of state S_2 satisfies the precondition of action **check,** the system will implement the action **check**. Otherwise, the system will stop.

4)   State S_t

State S_t is the final state of the framework and the content in it is the output of the system. It includes two situations: one is success that the component satisfies the requirement of application after a sequence of adaptations and another is un-success that the component can not satisfies the requirement of application after a sequence of adaptations or that the adapted component not only can not satisfy the requirement of application but also can not be adapted any more. The content of the state S_t is described as a tuple $(Component' | \Phi)$. $Component'$ denotes a success and Φ denotes the un-success.

2.2 The Description of Actions

All actions are described as a tuple $(action, precondition, post - condition)$ described in Figure 2, where action denotes the execution of the action, the precondition denotes the conditions which must be satisfied to execute the action, the post-condition denotes the result of the action which has an affect to the system.

Fig. 2. The graphics of the action

1)   Action *check*

Action ***check*** is check mechanism to find the mismatch type according the component specification and the requirement of application. The result of action ***check*** will be saved in the state S_1. The check mechanism has been proposed in other work and it is not the emphases in this paper. The precondition of action ***check*** which will be executed is a tuple: $(Component, user\_require)$. The post-condition of action ***check*** is described as $\sum_{i=1}^{n} Adapt\_type_i | (null | \Phi)$, where n is the number of mismatches checked by the action ***check***, $Adapt\_type_i$ denotes a kind of component adaptation which can any element of the set $\{signature\_mismatch, function\_mismatch, Qos\_mismatch\}$ and the expression $null | \Phi$ denotes the conclusion. The execution process is described as $check = check(component, user\_require, S_1)$. The system can have all mismatches between the *component* and *the requirement of application* by the action ***check*** and the system saves the results in the state S_1.

2)   Action *adapt*

Action adapt is a component adaptation process according the content of the state S_1. There will be several types of component adaptation occurred, such as component signature adaptation (including component name adaptation, component parameter adaptation), component function adaptation, component behavior adaptation and component QoS adaptation. The system will select a type of component adaptation from the adaptation plan to adapt the component. The adapted component will be saved in the state S_2. The details are in section 3.

3)   Action *finish*

Action *finish* is a finish process of component adaptation which will pass a component satisfying the requirement of application to the system or tell the system that the component can not is used to fulfill the requirement of application even if the component is adapted by several types of adaptation. The precondition of the action *finish* which is executed is $S_1.content = null \vee S_1.content = \Phi$. The attribute $S_1.content$ denotes the content of the state S_1 that is also the result of the action *check*. The expression $S_1.content = null$ denotes the conclusion that the component satisfies fully the requirement of application and the expression $S_1.content = \Phi$ denotes the conclusion that the adapted component can not satisfy the requirement of application and can not continue to adapt it. The post-condition of the action *finish* is the expression $(Component' | \Phi)$ which is saved in the state S_t. The execution process is described as $finish = tell(user, component' | \Phi)$ which mean the system tells the user or the application the result of the whole component adaptation process.

2.3   The Restriction of the Framework

The framework has only one initial state and only one final state. From the initial state to the final state means that a component adaptation process is finished. The states S_0、S_1 and S_2 are the precondition of the corresponding actions respectively and the states S_1、S_2 and S_t are the post-condition of the corresponding actions respectively.

3   The Description of Action Adapt

Action *adapt* is a complex sub system which deals with several different adaptations. The flow chart of action *adapt* is given in Figure 3.

The content of the state S_1 determines the adaptation process of a component. For executing the adaptation successfully, the system will order all adaptation types according to the priority of different adaptation. We call it as the adaptation plan. The plan is the result of one action *check*. The system will maintain the plan after adaptation. The priority of different adaptation is constant described as follow:

Signature adaptation>function adaptation>behavior adaptation>QoS adaptation.

The priority of component signature adaptation is higher than the priority of component function adaptation, etc. The plan is described as follow:

$$PLAN(plan, \{action_1 > action_2 > ...\}),$$

Where, $plan = \{action_1, action_2, ...\}$，$action_i$ denotes the adaptation type. The second parameter lists the priorities of all adaptation types in state S_1.

The controller selects the right adaptation type to adapt the component according the priority of different adaptation which is defined as a constant. The execution of action adapt will stop when the adaptation plan is null and the adapted component will be saved in the state S_2. The algorithm of the controller is given in Figure 4. The adaptation type which has the highest priority will be returned by the algorithm as the selected adaptation by system to adapt the component. If the content of the plan is null, the symbol null will be returned to mean that all adaptations checked by the latest action check have been executed. There are two functions Head and Tail in the algorithm of the controller. The function Head is used to find the first element of the plan and the function Tail is used to find the tail of the plan. The tail of the plan is composed by the all elements of the plan without the first elements. The symbol n is the number of the elements of the plan. The symbol plan is the adaptation plan. The expression $|plan|$ is the number of the elements of the plan. The symbol Φ is a set which has no element. The functions Head and Tail are defined as equation (2) and (3) respectively.

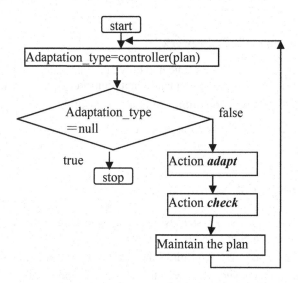

Fig. 3. The execution flow chart of action *adapt*

$$Head(plan) = \begin{cases} a_1 & if \quad plan = (a_1, a_2, \cdots a_n) \\ null & if \quad plan = \Phi \end{cases}, \tag{2}$$

$$Tail(plan) = \begin{cases} (a_2, \cdots, a_n) & if \quad plan = (a_1, a_2, \cdots a_n) \quad and \quad |plan| > 1 \\ \Phi & if \quad plan = \Phi \end{cases}, \tag{3}$$

The precondition of the action adapt is described as follow expression:

$$S_1.content \in \{signature\_mismatch, function\_mismatch, Qos\_mismatch\}.$$

The post-condition of the action adapt is a tuple $(Component', user\_require)$. Component' is the adapted component and user_require is the requirement of application. Every type of adaptation has the same the post-condition. We will not describe the post-condition any more.

```
Function Choose ( plan ) :  Adapt type
   //the controller of the action adapt
   //the input is the adaptation plan
   //the output  is  the  adaptation  type  with  the
//highest priority
       Adapt_type = Head ( plan );
       plan = Tail ( plan );
       return ( Adapt_type );
End Function Choose
```

Fig. 4. The controller of the action *adapt*

3.1   Component Signature Adaptation

Action *check* has checked the correspondence interfaces between the component and the requirement before the execution of the action *adapt*.

The precondition is described as follow: $S_1.content = signature\_mismatch$, Where,

$$signature\_mismatch = name\_mismatch \lor parameter\_mismatch. \qquad (4)$$

Name_mismatch denotes there is only a mismatch between the interface name of the component and the interface name of the requirement. Parameter_mismatch denotes there is parameter mismatch between the correspondence interfaces which implement the same functions and have the same interface names. There are three types of parameter mismatch. The number of interface parameters provided by the component is more than the number of the expected interface parameters. The number of interface parameters provided by the component is less than the number of the expected interface parameters. The order of interface parameters provided by the component does not match the expected interface. Action check can check different mismatch. The execution expression of signature adaptation is described as follow expression: $action(condition, Name\_match, Parameter\_match)$.

The first parameter of the expression is a judge condition which is described as $check.post-condition = name\_mismatch?$. If the logical of the condition is true then the adaptation of the second parameter of the expression is executed else the adaptation of the third parameter of the expression is executed. Name_match denotes the name adaptation of the component and Parameter_match denotes the parameter adaptation of the component.

The execution expression of the component name adaptation is described as follow:

$$Name\_match = replace(user.\text{int } erface.name, C.\text{int } erface.name, C'). \qquad (5)$$

The second part of the expression will be replaced by the first part of the expression and C' is the adapted component.

The execution expression of the component parameter adaptation is described as follow:

$$Para\_match = replace(user.\mathrm{int}\,erface.para, C.\mathrm{int}\,erface.para, Infor, C'),\qquad(6)$$

Where, the third part **infor** is a set which specifies the parameter mismatch between the component interface and the requirement interface. The content of **infor** comes from the action **check**. The system will produce a new interface in the component and the old interface will be called in the new interface. C' is the adapted component with the new interface.

3.2 Component Function Adaptation

There are two kinds of component function adaptation. One is that the requirement of application is a part of the function of the component. Another is that the function of the component is a part of the requirement of application. If the first mismatch is occurred we can cut out the unwanted part from the component. If the second mismatch is occurred we must decompose the requirement to two sub problem. One problem can be satisfied by the component and another problem must be passed to the system. The system will retrieve a new component from the base to satisfy the small problem and then compose the two components to a new component which can satisfy the first requirement. The composed component deals with the information which will be transferred form one to another. There are three kinds of function adaptation strategies: sequential architecture, alternative architecture and parallel architecture. Figure 5 shows the three strategies. Each component has its function which does not mean that there is no relation between them. In most situations, there are not only structure relations but also behavior relations between two components. If the implement of the behavior of the component has a positive affect to the other component we call it as positive behavior relation between two components. There is a positive behavior relation the two components which will be composed by the sequential architecture because a component needs the resource or the server of another component. If the implement of the behavior of the component balks the implement of another component we call it as negative behavior relation. The system will select the right adaptation architecture according to the relation between the two components so that the negative behavior relation between them will be reduced.

The precondition is described as follow: $S_1.content = function\_mismatch$.

The execution expression is described as follow: $C' = C\{[+C_{sub}]\,|\,[-C_{red}]\}$, Where,

$$C_{sub} = user\_requiremetn - Component,$$
$$C_{red} = Component - user\_requirement.\qquad(7)$$

The symbol $\{\cdots\}$ shows the content in it can be repeated time after time, the symbol $[\cdots]$ shows the content in it is optional parameters, the symbol $\cdots\,|\,\cdots$ shows the result of the expression may be the left part or the right part.

Here we only think about the strategy to compose two components. There are two components involve in the adaptation: Component1 and Component2. Every component may be the other adaptation architecture and three adaptation architectures may compose arbitrarily.

1). Sequential Architecture

Figure 5 (a) describes the sequential architecture. The output of the first component will be the input of the second component when they are composed in the adaptation architecture. The input condition of the requirement of application must satisfy the input condition of the first component. The output of the requirement of application is a subset of the output of the second component. The precondition is as follow:

$$(user\_require.input \subset Component_1.input)$$
$$\wedge\,(Component_1.output \in Component_2.input)$$
$$\wedge\,(user\_require.output \subset Component_2.output)$$

The execution expression is described as follow:

$$C' = Component_1 + Component_2, \tag{8}$$

Where, the symbol '+' denotes the sequential adaptation, the output of the left component of the symbol '+' is the input of the right component of the symbol '+'. The first component is executed firstly and then the second component is executed.

2). Parallel Architecture

Figure 5 (c) describes the parallel architecture. The executions of the two components must be finished at one point when they are composed in the parallel architecture and the union of their outputs can satisfy the requirement. They are isolated and there does not interfere with each other. The input of the requirement is a subset of the union of two components' input. The precondition is as follow:

$$(user\_require.input \subset (Component_1.input \cup Component_2.input))$$
$$\wedge\,(user\_require.output \subset (Component_1.output \cup Component_2.output)).$$

The execution expression is described as follow:

$$C' = Component_1 \parallel Component_2, \tag{9}$$

Where, the symbol '‖' denotes the parallel adaptation.

3). Alternative Architecture

Figure 5 (b) describes the alternative architecture. The function of every component both can satisfies the requirement at the specifically condition, but their input condition is a subset of the input condition of the requirement that is to say that the input condition of every component need more restrictions than the requirement. The input condition of the requirement is a subset of the union of their input condition. If the input condition of the left component satisfies the input condition of the requirement the system will select it to execute else the right one. The precondition is described as follow:

$$(user\_require.input \subset (Component_1.input \cup Component_2.input))$$

$$\wedge (Component_1.input \subset user\_require.input)$$

$$\wedge (Component_2.input \subset user\_require.input)$$

$$\wedge (Component_1.output \subset user\_require.output)$$

$$\wedge (Component_2.output \subset user\_require.output)$$

The execution expression is described as follow:

$$C' = Component_1 \mid Component_2 , \tag{10}$$

Where, the symbol 'I' denotes the alternative adaptation.

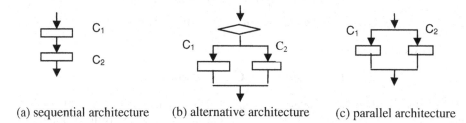

(a) sequential architecture   (b) alternative architecture   (c) parallel architecture

Fig. 5. Three architecture of component function adaptation

3.3   Component QoS Adaptation

The QoS of component includes mainly: usability, maintainability, performance, the time, memory used, and so on. Usually the adaptation will downgrade most of the QoS attributes in order to reach function interoperability. The QoS attributes impact the validity of the adaptation algorithm and decide whether a component needs to be adapted. Many works in the literature of component adaptation deal with the component QoS adaptation [9, 10, 11]. In this paper, the QoS adaptation means how to calculate the QoS of the adapted component according to the QoS of the initial component. This is our next work.

4   The Quality of the Framework

There is an adaptation plan to save all adaptation checked by the action check in the framework and a controller is proposed to select a right adaptation type to adapt the component so that the adaptation process can be finished successfully without waiting for the other resource and omitting an adaptation type. A component satisfying the requirement of application will be given by the system. But there are limitations in the framework. For example in Figure 6 (a), a deadlock will be produced in the parallel architecture or the alternative architecture. The condition c will be false after the execution of the component S_3, but if the precondition of the component S_2 needs the condition c is true and this time the component S_1 has been finished. So the component S_2 will wait for the precondition is true for ever. Thus there will not a successful parallel adaptation or a successful alternative adaptation. How to avoid the deadlock? We propose two different ideas. One is in Figure 6 (b) and the other is in Figure 6 (c). We can place the component S_3 on the front of the component S_1 or on the back of the component S_2.

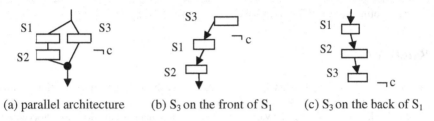

(a) parallel architecture   (b) S_3 on the front of S_1 (c) S_3 on the back of S_1

Fig. 6. The deadlock of parallel architecture or alternative architecture

5 Future Work and Limitation of Our Work

Now, there does not existing a standard for component adaptation. As shown, there is a big research effort being put in the field of automatic and dynamic component adaptation. Not many efforts have been devoted to concern the framework of component adaptation. Based on our previous work, some interesting issues still open which deserve future research.

Tool support: The whole idea is based on tools (the checking algorithm, component adaptation algorithm, etc.) which must be implemented and tested.

The algorithm to predict the QoS of component: How much the different adaptation makes a impact on the QoS of the adapted component? How to calculate the QoS of the adapted component according to the QoS of the existing component? All of these are still open issues.

Formal Method: Now, a complex problem is divided into several sub-problems, all of the sub-problems can be solved by existing adaptable components. A valid method of component adaptation can help to prove the correctness and the validity of component adaptation process in theory. There does not existing an objective or subjective standard to assess the component adaptation framework.

Whether the plan needs maintain after the adaptation: the system environment may be changed by the execution of the adaptation. If the plan is maintained after an adaptation the system will get a better adaptation process. The performance of the system will be deceased if the plan is maintained.

6 Conclusion

In this paper, a framework of component adaptation is proposed in which several adaptations are involved. The precondition, the post-condition and the execution process of different adaptation are described in formal specification. There may be several mismatches between the component and the requirement of application. For executing adaptation successfully the system involves a plan which can save all adaptation types with order.

Acknowledgements. This research is partially supported by the National Natural Science Foundation of China under Grant No. 60573087.

References

1. Bracciali, A., Brogi, A., Canal, C.: A formal approach to component adaptation. Journal of Systems and Software 74(1), 45–54 (2005)
2. Penix, J., Alexander, P.: Toward Automated Component Adaptation. In: Proceedings of the 9th International Conference on Software Engineering & Knowledge Engineering (SEKE-97), Madrid, Spain, pp. 535–542 (1997)
3. Radenski, A.: Anomaly-free component adaptation with class overriding. The. Journal of Systems and Software 71, 37–48 (2004)
4. Brogi, A., Canal, C., Pimentel, E.: Soft component adaptation. In: Electronic Notes in Theoretical Computer Science (ENTCS). vol. 85(3) (2003)
5. Brogi, A.: Systematic Component Adaptation. In: Proceedings of Workshop on Formal Methods and Component Interaction (FMCI'02), Málaga, Spain, pp. 340–351 (2002)
6. Bracciali, A., Brogi, A., Canal, C.: Adapting components with mismatching behaviors. In: Bishop, J. (ed.) CD 2002. LNCS, vol. 2370, pp. 185–199. Springer, Heidelberg (2002)
7. Canal, C.: On the dynamic adaptation of component behaviour. In: Proceedings of the First International Workshop on Coordination and Adaptation Techniques for Software Entities (WCAT'04), Oslo, Norway, pp. 81–88 (2004)
8. Kniesel, G.: Type-Safe Delegation for Run-Time Component Adaptation. In: Proceedings of the 13th European Conference on Object-Oriented Programming, Lisbon, Portugal, pp. 351–366 (1999)
9. Becker, S., Reussner, R.H.: The Impact of Software Component Adaptors on Quality of Service Properties. In: Proceedings of the First international workshop on coordination and adaptation techniques for software entities (WCAT04), Oslo, Norway, pp. 25–30 (2004)
10. Reussner, R., Mayer, J., Stafford, J.A., Overhage, S., Becker, S., Schroeder, P.J. (eds.): QoSA 2005 and SOQUA 2005. LNCS, vol. 3712, pp. 227–241. Springer, Heidelberg (2005)
11. Becker, S.: Using Generated Design Patterns to Support QoS Prediction of Software Component Adaptation. In: Proceedings of the 2nd International Workshop on Coordination and Adaptation Issues for Software Entities (WCAT'05), Glasgow, Scotland, pp. 9–16 (2005)
12. Canal, C., Poizat, P., Salaun, G.: Adaptation of Component Behaviour using Synchronous Vectors. Technical Report ITI–05–10, Universidad de Malaga (December 2005)

A Parallel Infrastructure on Dynamic EPIC SMT

Qingying Deng, Minxuan Zhang, and Jiang Jiang

College of Computer, National University of Defense
Technology, Changsha 410073, Hunan, P.R. China
freesunnybird@gmail.com
mxzhang@nudt.edu.cn
jiang_jiang@nudt.edu.cn

Abstract. There are only three real "dimensions" to processor performance increases beyond Moore's law: clock frequency, superscalar instruction issue, and multiprocessing. The first two have been pushed to their logical limits and we must focus on multiprocessing. SMT (simultaneous multithreading) [1] and CMP(chip multiprocessing)[2] are two architectural approaches to exploit thread-level parallelism using available on-chip resources. SMT processors execute instructions from different threads in the same cycle, which has the unique ability to exploit ILP(instruction-level parallelism) and TLP(thread-level parallelism) simultaneously. EPIC(explicitly parallel instruction computing) emphasizes importance of the synergy between compiler and hardware. In this paper, we present our efforts to design and implement a parallel environment, which includes an optimizing, portable parallel compiler OpenUH and SMT architecture EDSMT based on IA-64. The performance is evaluated using the NAS parallel benchmarks[1].

1 Introduction

The combination of limited instruction parallelism suitable for superscalar issue, practical limits to pipelining, and a "power ceiling" limited by practical cooling limitations has limited future speed increases within conventional processor cores to the basic Moore's law improvement rate of the underlying transistors. Processor designers must find new ways to effectively utilize the increasing transistor budgets in high-end silicon chips to improve performance in ways that minimize both additional power usage and design complexity. And it is also useful to examine the problem from the point of view of different performance requirements.

SMT and CMP are two architectural approaches to exploit TLP using available on-chip resources. SMT allows instructions from multiple threads to share several critical processor resources, thus increasing their utilization. The advantage of SMT is area-efficient throughput [3]. CMP, on the other hand, improve

---

[1] This work was supported by "63" project No. 2002AA110020, Chinese NSF No. 60376018, No. 60273069 and No. 90207011.

system throughput by replicating processor cores on a single die. As both these paradigms are targeted toward multithreaded workloads, comparing their efficiency in terms of performance, power, and thermal metrics has drawn the attention of several researchers [4][5][6].

Programmers must switch to more parallel programming models in order to exploit multi processors effectively, if they desire improved single-program performance. Because there are only three real "imensions" to processor performance increases beyond Moore's law: clock frequency, superscalar instruction issue, and multiprocessing. The first two have been pushed to their logical limits and now we must embrace multiprocessing, even if it means that programmers will be forced to change to a parallel programming model to achieve the highest possible performance. High performance multi-core processors are becoming an industry reality. Although multi-cores are suited for multithreaded and multi-programmed workloads, many applications are still mono-thread and multi-core performance with a single thread workload is still an important issue.

DSMT (Dynamic SMT)[7] integrates dynamic threads extracting and threads switching mechanism into SMT architecture, which further improves the ability to exploit TLP parallelism. Based on the software-hardware cooperation, EPIC can effectively exploit ILP with relatively low hardware complexity. A new microarchitecture called EDSMT was proposed to expand EPIC with simultaneous multithreading execution.

As a result, in order to have a deep research on parallel compilation SMT and CMP architecture, and hardware-software cooperation, construct a basic platform is very important. We studied EDSMT Microarchitecture and developed its simulator EDSMTSIM, which adopted the trace-driven simulation methodology. Key components of this simulator, such as pipeline, branch prediction, memory subsystem and dependency control, were carefully designed. We also use OpenUH(based on Pro64 and OpenMP) developed by University of Houston to construct our parallel compiler with some modifications.

We introduce our parallel compile environment in section 2. In section 3 we present our EDSMT architecture and EDSMTSIM simulator. In section 4 shows the simulation results. Conclusions and future work are given in section 5.

2   Parallel Compilation Structure

The goal of parallel compilation is narrow the gap between the peak speed of HPC and the actual performance which end user can get. Multi-source Multi-target, Multilevel, and Multigrid became the trend of parallel compilation[8], OpenUH is one of that kind.

OpenUH is available as stand-alone software or with the Eclipse integrated development environment. It is based on SGI's open source Pro64 compiler, which targets the IA-64 Linux platform. OpenUH merges work from the two major branches of Open64 (ORC and Pathscale) to exploit all upgrades and bug fixes. It is a portable OpenMP compiler, which translates OpenMP 2.5 directives in conjunction with C, C++, and FORTRAN 77/90 (and some FORTRAN 95).

It has a full set of optimization modules, including an interprocedural analysis (IPA) module, a loop nest optimizer (LNO), and global optimizer. A variety of state-of-the-art analysis and transformations are available, sometimes at multiple levels[9].

2.1   OpenMP

OpenMP is a programming standard that comes another step closer to the "code once, compile everywhere" ideal. Developed with shared memory architectures in mind, the basis of OpenMP is a set of standard compiler directives that enable Fortran (and eventually C) programmers to easily express shared-memory parallelism. OpenMP has no directives that specify data layout amongst processors since in an SMP system each processor can access memory of any other processor. The OpenMP compiler directives provide programmers with a powerful set of high-level parallel constructs and an extended parallel programming model, both of which meet a wide range of application-programming requirements.

The standard allows for code parallelism to range from fine loop-level code to coarse-grain parallelism within the full application. Much like HPF(High Performance Fortran), OpenMP lowers the entrance barrier to parallel computing by simplifying the porting of existing applications. This contrasts with MPI(Message Passing Interface), which requires extensive rewrites of existing applications. OpenMP also provides programmers with the flexibility to parallelize an application incrementally.

Nowadays OpenMP has gained wide popularity as an API for parallel programming on shared memory and distributed shared memory platforms. Despite its broad availability, there remains a need for a portable, robust, open source, optimizing OpenMP compiler for C/C++/Fortran90, especially for teaching and research, e.g. into its use on new target architectures, such as SMPs with chip multithreading, as well as learning how to translate for clusters of SMPs. Many compilers support OpenMP today, including such proprietary products as the Intel Linux compiler suite, Sun One Studio, and SGI MIPSpro compilers. However, their source code is mostly inaccessible to researchers and they cannot be used to gain an understanding of OpenMP compiler technology or to explore possible improvements to it. Several open source research compilers (Omni OpenMP compiler [10], OdinMP/CCp [11], and PCOMP [12]) are available. But none of them translates all of the source languages that OpenMP supports, and one of them is a partial implementation only.

2.2   Background on OpenUH

OpenUH, a portable OpenMP compiler based on the Open64 compiler infrastructure with a unique hybrid design that combines a state-of-the-art optimizing infrastructure with a source-to-source approach. It is a portable, robust, open source and optimizing OpenMP compiler for C/C++/Fortran 90 , includes numerous analysis and optimization components, and is a complete implementation of OpenMP 2.5.

Open64 was open sourced by Silicon Graphics Inc. from its SGI Pro64 compiler targeting MIPS and Itanium processors. It is now mostly maintained by Intel under the name Open Research Compiler (ORC) [13], which targets Itanium platforms. There also have several other branches of Open64(e.g. the Berkeley UPC compiler[14]).

Open64 is a well-written, modularized, robust, state-of-the-art compiler with support for C/C++ and Fortran 77/90. The major modules of Open64 are the multiple language frontends, the interprocedural analyzer (IPA) and the middle end/back end, which is further subdivided into the loop nest optimizer (LNO), global optimizer (WOPT), and code generator (CG).

The tree-based intermediate representations (IR) called WHIRL are classified as being Very High, High, Mid, Low, and Very Low levels, respectively. Most compiler optimizations are implemented on a specific level of WHIRL. For example, IPA and LNO are applied to High level WHIRL, while WOPT operates on Mid level WHIRL.

Two internal WHIRL tools were embedded in Open64 to support the compiler developer: one was whirlb2a, used to convert whirl binary dump files into ASCII format, and the other was whirl2c/whirl2f, to translate Very High and High level WHIRL IR back to C or Fortran source code. However, the resulting output code was not compilable.

The original Open64 included an incomplete implementation of the OpenMP1.0 specification, inherited from SGI's Pro64 compiler. Its legacy OpenMP code was able to handle Fortran 77/90 code with some OpenMP features until the linking phase. The C/C++ frontend of Open64 was taken from GCC 2.96 and thus could not parse OpenMP directives. Meanwhile, there was no corresponding OpenMP runtime library released with Open64. It was also lack of code generators for machines other than Itaniums.

The ORC-OpenMP compiler(one of the branches of Open64) from Tsinghua University, extended Open64's C frontend to parse OpenMP constructs and provided a tentative runtime library. The Open64.UH(another of the branches of Open64) compiler focused on the pre-translation and OpenMP translation phases. A merge of these two efforts has resulted in the OpenUH compiler and associated Tsinghua runtime library.

2.3   Overview of OpenUH

The OpenUH compiler uses the Open64.UH compiler which designed a hybrid compiler with object code generation on Itaniums and source-to-source OpenMP translation on other platforms, exploits improvements to Open64 from several sources and relies on an enhanced version of the Tsinghua runtime library to support the translation process. It recreats compilable source code right before the code generation phase to preserve most optimizations on all platforms.

The OpenUH consists of the frontends, optimization modules, OpenMP transformation module, a portable OpenMP runtime library, a code generator and IR-to-source tools. Fig. 1 shows the structure. Most of these modules are derived from the corresponding original Open64 module. It is a complete compiler for Itanium platforms, for which object code is produced, and may be used as a source-to-source compiler for non-Itanium machines using the IR-to-source tools.

The OpenMP program is parsed by the appropriate extended language frontend and translated into WHIRL IR with OpenMP pragmas. Then the interprocedural analyzer (IPA), is enabled if desired to carry out interprocedural alias analysis, array section analysis, inlining, dead function and variable elimination, interprocedural constant propagation and more. After that, the loop nest optimizer (LNO) will perform many standard loop analyses and optimizations, such as dependence analysis, register/cache blocking (tiling), loop fission and fusion, unrolling, automatic prefetching, and array padding. The transformation of OpenMP, which lowers WHIRL with OpenMP pragmas into WHIRL representing multithreaded code with OpenMP runtime library calls, is performed after LNO. Subsequently the global scalar optimizer (WOPT) is invoked. It transforms WHIRL into an SSA form for more efficient analysis and optimizations and converts the SSA form back to WHIRL after the work has been done. In WOPT phase , a lot of standard compiler passes out including control flow analysis (computing dominance, detecting loops in the flowgraph), data flow analysis, alias classification and pointer analysis, dead code elimination, copy propagation, partial redundancy elimination and strength reduction are carried.

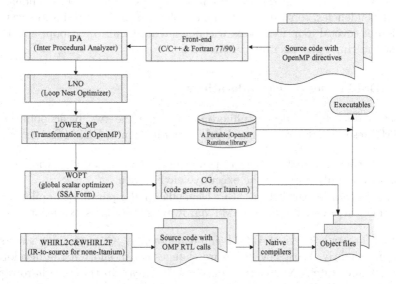

Fig. 1. OpenUH infrastructure

The CG(code generation) phase depends on the target machine: for Itanium platforms, CG in Open64 can be directly used to generate object files. For a non-Itanium platform, the whirl2c or whirl2f translator will be invoked instead; in this case, code represented by Mid WHIRL is translated back to compilable, multithreaded C or Fortran code with OpenMP runtime calls. To complete the translation by compiling the output from OpenUH into object files a native C or Fortran compiler must be invoked on the target platform.

The last phase is the linking of object files with the portable OpenMP runtime library and final generation of executables for the target machine.

3   Microarchitecture of EDSMT

SMT processors improve performance by allowing running instructions from several threads simultaneously at a single cycle. Co-scheduled threads share some resources, such as issue queues, physical registers, and functional units.

EPIC architectures developed by HP and Intel allow the compiler to express program instruction level parallelism directly to the hardware to deal with increasing memory latencies and penalties. Specifically, the Itanium architecture deploys a number of EPIC techniques which enable the compiler to represent control speculation, data dependence speculation, and predication to enhance performance. These techniques have individually been shown to be very effective in dealing with memory penalties. In addition to these techniques, the Itanium architecture provides a virtual register stack to reduce the penalty of memory accesses associated with procedure calls and to leverage the performance advantages of a large register file. Predication converts control dependencies to data dependencies, software pipelining enables the compiler to interleave the execution of several loop iterations without having to unroll a loop, and Branch Prediction Hints give accurate predication.

3.1   DSMT Design Considerations

DSMT and EPIC[15] design philosophy became the two basic points of our EDSMT research. There are two levels of parallelism in EDSMT.

- (1) Vertical parallelism-ILP: Depends on the Pro64 compiler, while EDSMT hardware only provides the executive environment.
- (2) Horizontal parallelism-TLP: Depends on the parallel compiler and dynamic thread extractor, EDSMT hardware supports its execution.

There are two kinds of DSMT implementations. One modifies superscalar structure slightly. With few hardware changes,it can shorten the development time (SMT in Intel's Xeon added only 5% die area). In this case hardware designer only need to focus on construction of a high speed superscalar processor and appliance of the multithreading switching and dynamic thread extraction. Threads share the hardware except fetch, context switch, instruction retirement, TraceCache, and speculation multithreading control. The other changes hardware a lot in order to dissociate the thread's instruction window and simplify the fetch and retire stage in the pipeline. Each thread has its own instruction window , decoder, register file and retirement logic to issue instructions at the same time. We choose the latter.

3.2   EPIC in Itanium

The microarchitecture of Itanium[16] which used EPIC as its design philosophy is another important base of our EDSMT design. Compiler can expose, enhance, and exploit parallelism in a program and make it explicit to the hardware, while hardware provides run-time information for compiler to develop static ILP and executive logic for the compiler hints(such as instruction templates, branch hints, and cache hints) .That's the concept behind explicit parallelism: instructions arrive at the processor explicitly ordered by the compiler. The compiler organizes the code for an entire program and makes the ordering explicit so the processor can execute instructions in the most efficient manner.

By adopting EPIC, instruction window exploited by software is much larger than by hardware, parallelism can be achieved; because the parallelism is mainly developed by compiler, the hardware design was simplified which can save a lot of resources,and the chip speed can also be improved.

Fig. 2 shows the conceptual view of EPIC hardware.Instructions in Itanium are issued in order , executed out-of-order and submitted in order. This mechanism can simplify the collision detection logic, and make fully use of function units(fully pipelined). Accurate interruption is also supported.

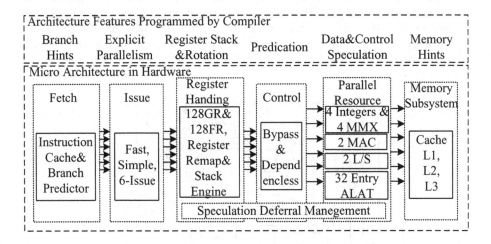

Fig. 2. Conceptual view of EPIC hardware

3.3   EDSMT Design

Based on DSMT and EPIC, EDSMT should make fully use of the resources in Itanium, but a few modifications must be considered.

(1)Software-Hardware Cooperation: ILP is completely exploited by compiler, while executive hardware was simply designed. TLP is developed staticly by compiler, in addition, the hardware provides run-time information to compiler and receives commands inserted by compiler to dynamic spawn new threads. Besides the thread creation command, branch , prefetch and store hints should also be provided.

(2) Instruction Dispatch: For selecting instructions from several independent threads and context switching, Itanium structure must be changed a lot. The easiest way is picking two threads from several waiting threads, then dispatching a bundle from each of the selected threads. The choosing policy affects performance directly and the instruction window should be carefully designed.

(3)Instruction Sequencing Considerations: As instructions from different threads issued at the same time, we shouldn't worry about their dependencies. Within a instruction group in a single thread, when RAW and WAW dependencies are guaranteed by compiler, Itanium's in-order issue logic assures the WAR dependency. The design of dependency logic is relatively simple.

(4) Dynamic Thread Speculation: Two-level self-adaptation prediction algorism which is similar to Itanium's branch prediction mechanism, can be used in dynamic thread speculation. At the same time, value prediction and instruction reuse can also be adopted with the help of compiler. Buffers need to be added for recovery from misprediction.

(5)Predication: Predication is the conditional execution of an instruction based on a qualifying predicate. A qualifying predicate is a predicate register whose value determines whether the processor commits the results computed by an instruction. We can use two groups of instructions with different predicate values as speculation threads, then choose the right one according to the value of predicate registers.

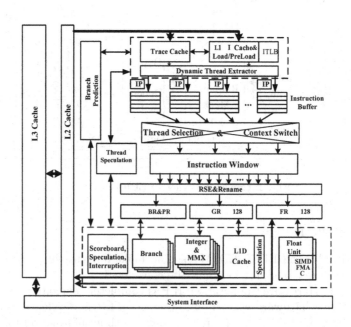

Fig. 3. Microarchitecture of EDSMT

(6)Other Issues: Register Rename and Register Stack Engine in Itanium can support Multithreading with a few changes, in addition, chip communication interface and bandwidth should be carefully designed for Multithreading applications.

Fig. 3 shows the Microarchitecture of EDSMT. Instruction bundles from different threads dispatched by the dispatch logic which works as the Multithreading scheduler. It is carefully designed to reduce dependency and get more parallelism.

3.4   EDSMTSIM Design

Simulator is important in architecture design. As EDSMT is a new Microarchitecture, We developed a simulator–EDSMTSIM for our research.

EDSMTSIM is a trace-driven microprocessor simulator which adopts some technologies in the Multithreading simulator-SMTSIM. In order to reduce complexity, the actual execution of instructions is separated from the pipeline control, that means the pipeline only processes dependency detection, branch, and exception, while actual execution is emulated by specific module which can be called by the pipeline. Instruction is executed right after the fetch stage, then we record its control information(trace) and modify the CPU states. Following the instruction trace, in the backend of the pipeline stages, activities such as dependency control, cache miss, branch misprediction, and modification of the scoreboard are simulated in a way of counting pipeline stall cycles.

Fig. 4 depicts the structure of EDSMTSIM. IU, FU, MU, and BU represent Integer Unit, Float Unit, Memory Unit and Branch Unit respectively. It has 11 Function Units including 4 IU, 3 FU, 3 BU, and 2 MU. Every thread has its own PC, RSB, Register Files and Instruction Bundle Queue. Instruction Cache, Data Cache, BHT and Function Units are shared by all the threads. Pipeline is divided to 8 stages as Itanium structure.

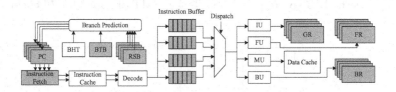

Fig. 4. EDSMTSIM Structure

4   Simulation Results

We used the popular NAS parallel benchmark (NPB) [17] to compare the performance. The target architectures are EDSMT on IA-64 and SMT on Alpha, while EDSMTSIM and SMTSIM worked as simulators respectively. Baseline configurations of our simulators are shown in Table 1.

Table 1. Baseline configuration of simulator

Parameter	SMTSIM	EDSMTSIM
Fetch Width	8 instructions per cycle	2 bundles ,6 instructions per cycle
Basic Fetch Policy	ICOUNT2.8	ICOUNT2.2
Instruction Queues	32 int, 32 fp, 32 load/store	16 for each separated Queues
Functional Units	6 int, 3 fp, 4 load/store	2 IU, 4 MU, 2 FU, 3 BU
Physical Registers	384 int, 384 fp	128 GR, 128 FR, 64 PR, 8 BR per thread
L1I cache, L1D cache	64KB, 2-way, 64-bytes lines, 1 cycle access	16KB, 4-way, 64-bytes lines, 1 cycle access
L2 cache	512KB, 2-way, 64-bytes lines, 10 cycles latency	256KB, 8-way, 64-bytes lines, 10 cycles latency
L3 cache	None	3MB, 12-way, 64-bytes lines, 50 cycles latency
Main Memory Latency	100 cycles	100 cycles

At first, We will show the speedup of our compiler over the open source Omni 1.6 compiler. A subset of the latest NPB 3.2 was compiled using the Class A data set for each of the compilers. The compiler option -O2 was used and the codes were run on EDSMTSIM with 4 threads. Fig. 5 shows the IPC improvement of OpenUH over Omni for seven benchmarks. Despite its reliance on a runtime system designed for portability rather than highest performance on a given platform, OpenUH even achieved better performance than Omni except for the EP benchmark . The average speedup is 2.055.The result of this test confirms that the OpenUH compiler can be used as a serious research OpenMP compiler on Itanium platforms.

For the portability and effectiveness of preserved optimizations using the source-to-source approach , We compiled NPB 2.3 OpenMP/C using OpenUH as frontend compiler for our test machines. The native GCC compiler on each machine is used as a backend compiler to compile the multithreaded code and link the object files with the portable OpenMP runtime library. All versions were executed with dataset A on four threads and compiler option -O2 was used. Fig. 6 shows the IPC speedup of EDSMT over SMT of Alpha for 7 benchmarks.

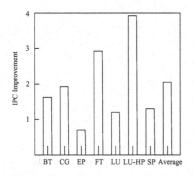

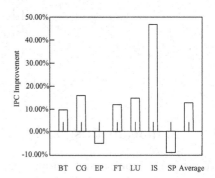

Fig. 5. IPC speedup of OpenUH over Omni using NPB3.2

Fig. 6. IPC speedup of EDSMT over SMT of Alpha using NPB2.3 OpenMP/C

We can see EDSMT outperform SMT of Alpha except for EP and SP. The average speedup is 12.48%, which means the EDSMT is a very hopeful architecture for the parallel applications.

5   Conclusions and Future Work

Throughput computing is the first and most pressing area where SMT and CMP are having an impact. This is because they can improve power/performance results right out of the box, without any software changes, thanks to the large numbers of independent threads that are available in these already multithreaded applications. In the near future, SMT and CMP should also have an impact in the more common area of latency-critical computations. Although it is necessary to parallelize most latency-critical software into multiple parallel threads of execution to really take advantage of a chip multiprocessor, SMT and CMP make this process easier than with conventional multiprocessors, because of their short interprocessor communication latencies.

The transition to SMT and CMP is inevitable[18] because past efforts to speed up processor architectures with techniques that do not modify the basic von Neumann computing model, such as pipelining and superscalar issue, are encountering hard limits. As a result, the microprocessor industry is leading the way to multicore architectures; however, the full benefit of these architectures will not be harnessed until the software industry fully embraces parallel programming.

We proposed a parallel infrastructure, including an optimizing, portable parallel compiler OpenUH and SMT architecture EDSMT based on IA-64. NAS parallel benchmarks were used as our benchmarks, which features offer numerous opportunities to explore further enhancements to OpenMP and to study its performance on existing and new architectures. The experiment results also demonstrate that our infrastructure is a very good choice for parallel compiler and architecture research, especially for the structure of EPIC which combined compiler and architecture tightly. In the future, we will focus on the specific technology optimizations such as register allocation and RSE constitution, fetch policy, resource organization and allocation, cache structure, thread scheduling and so on. Meanwhile, we are considering a compact EDSMT to construct homogeneous and heterogeneous CMP systems.

References

1. Tullsen, D., Eggers, S., Levy, H.: Simultaneous Multithreading: Maximizing On-Chip Parallelism. In: The 22rd Annual International Symposium on Computer Architecture (ISCA) pp. 392–403 (1995)
2. Olukotun, K., Nayfeh, B.A., Hammond, L., Wilson, K., Chang, K.: The Case for a Single-Chip Multiprocessor. SIGOPS Oper. Syst. Rev. 30(5), 2–11 (1996)
3. Li, Y., Brooks, D., Hu, Z., Skadron, K., Bose, P.: Understanding the Energy Efficiency of Simultaneous Multithreading. In: The 2004 International Symposium on Low Power Electronics and Design, pp. 44–49 (2004)

4. Sasanka, R., Adve, S.V., Chen, Y.-K., Debes, E.: The Energy Efficiency of CMP vs. SMT for Multimedia Workloads. In: The 18th Annual International Conference on Supercomputing, pp. 196–206 (2004)
5. Kaxiras, S., Narlikar, G., Berenbaum, A.D., Hu, Z.: Comparing Power Consumption of an SMT and a CMP DSP for Mobile Phone Workloads. In: The 2001 International Conference on Compilers, Architecture,and Synthesis for Embedded Systems, pp. 211–220 (2001)
6. Li, Y., Skadron, K., Hu, Z., Brooks, D.: Performance, Energy, and Thermal Considerations for SMT and CMP Architectures. In: The Eleventh IEEE International Symposium on High Performance Computer Architecture (HPCA) pp. 71–82 (2005)
7. Akkary, H., Driscoll, M.A.: A dynamic multithreading processor. In: The 31st annual ACM/IEEE international symposium on Microarchitecture, pp. 226–236 (1998)
8. Jianhua, Y.W.H.: Actuality and Trend of Parallel Language and Compilatio. Computer Engineering, pp. 97–98 (December 2004)
9. OpenUH: An Optimizing, Portable OpenMP Compiler (2006), http://www2.cs.uh.edu/~copper/pubs.html
10. Sato, M., Satoh, S., Kusano, K., Tanaka, Y.: Design of OpenMP compiler for an SMP cluster. In: the 1st European Workshop on OpenMP(EWOMP'99) pp. 32–39 (1999)
11. Brunschen, C., Brorsson, M.: OdinMP/CCp - a portable implementation of OpenMP for C. Concurrency - Practice and Experience 12, 1193–1203 (2000)
12. Min, S.J., Kim, S.W., Voss, M., Lee, S.I., Eigenmann, R.: Portable compilers for OpenMP. In: WOMPAT 2001, pp. 11–19. Springer, Heidelberg (2001)
13. Open research compiler for itanium processor family (2005), http://ipforc.sourceforge.net/
14. Chen, W.Y.: Building a source-to-source UPC-to-C translator. Master's thesis, University of California at Berkeley (2005)
15. Schlansker, M.S., Rau, B.R.: EPIC:Explicitly Parallel Instruction Computing[J]. IEEEComputer 32(2), 37–45 (2000)
16. Itanium Processor Microarchitecture Reference:for Software Optimization 05 (2002), http://www.developer.intel.com/design/ia64/itanium.htm
17. Jin, H., Frumkin, M., Yan, J.: The OpenMP implementation of NAS parallel benchmarks and its performance. Technical Report NAS-99-011, NASA Ames Research Center (1999)
18. olukotun, K., Hammond, L.: The Future of Microprocessors. QUEUE 3(7), 27–34 (September 2005)

The Thread Migration Mechanism of DSM-PEPE⋆

Federico Meza[1] and Cristian Ruz[2]

[1] Depto. de Ciencia de la Computación, Universidad de Talca
Camino Los Niches Km. 1, Curicó – Chile
`fmeza@utalca.cl`
[2] Escuela de Ingeniería Informática, Universidad Diego Portales
Ejército 441, Santiago – Chile
`cruz@inf.udp.cl`

Abstract. In this paper we present the thread migration mechanism of DSM-PEPE, a multithreaded distributed shared memory system. DSM systems like DSM-PEPE provide a parallel environment to harness the available computing power of computer networks. DSM systems offer a virtual shared memory space on top of a distributed-memory multicomputer, featuring the scalability and low cost of a multicomputer, and the ease of programming of a shared-memory multiprocessor.

DSM systems rely on data migration to make data available to running threads. The thread migration mechanism of DSM-PEPE was designed as an alternative to this data migration paradigm. Threads are allowed to migrate from one node to another, as needed by the computation. We show by experimentation the feasibility of the thread migration mechanism of DSM-PEPE as an alternative to improve application perfomance by enhancing spatial locality.

Keywords: Thread migration, distributed shared memory, multithreading, spatial locality.

1 Introduction

A large portion of the execution time of distributed applications is devoted to access remote data. Multithreading in a distributed system helps to reduce the impact of the latency produced by message exchange, by overlapping communication and computation [1]. While waiting for a long-latency operation, the processor allows the progress of threads other than the one being blocked.

Thread migration has been proposed as a mechanism to improve performance by enhancing data locality [2,3]. The main idea is to move threads closer to the data they need, that is, to gather at the same processor those threads using the data stored in that location, instead of moving the data to the processors where the threads are running. However, there is a tradeoff between the mechanisms used to increase data locality and load balance. The former aims to reduce

---

⋆ Federico Meza was supported by Fondecyt under grant 2990074.

H. Jin et al. (Eds.): ICA3PP 2007, LNCS 4494, pp. 177–187, 2007.

interprocessor communication while the latter attempts to increase utilization of the processors and hence the level of parallelism. If there are no restrictions, a system would exhibit high data locality at the cost of poor utilization of the processors.

In this paper we present the thread migration mechanism of DSM-PEPE, a DSM system with support for multithreading at the user-level. We show the potential of thread migration as an alternative to data migration to improve application performance by exploiting data locality. In particular, we present a series of experiments using an application with an access pattern that exhibits some degree of spatial locality. The application that uses our thread migration mechanism performed better than the original parallel application used for comparison and showed more regular speedup patterns.

The rest of the document is structured as follows. Section 2 deals with the main issues involved in the implementation of multithreading and thread migration. In Section 3, the thread migration mechanism of DSM-PEPE is presented. Details about the experiments are covered in Section 4. Section 5 summarizes other works related to thread migration. Finally, Section 6 presents some concluding remarks and future lines of research.

2   Multithreading and Thread Migration Issues

Multithreading can be implemented at kernel level or at user level. In the former, system calls are issued for thread creation and context switches. The kernel is highly involved in thread management; thus, this approach lacks portability. User-level threads are more portable and easier to manage; the context switch has a lower cost because the operating system is not aware of the threads. However, when a user-level thread is blocked, it could block the entire process, reducing the benefits of the use of multithreading. Some mechanism must be implemented to avoid this drawback.

Thread migration involves the suspension of a thread at some point of its execution. While suspended, it is copied or moved to another processor, and resumed at the new location at the same point where its execution was suspended. The resumed thread must not be aware of the migration being carried out. To migrate a thread, all data defining the thread state must be copied, that is, its stack and the values stored in the processor registers.

Special attention must be given to the migration of the thread stack. It can contain local variables, activation registers, and pointers that could refer to memory addresses inside or outside the stack. If the stack is relocated at a different address in the destination processor, pointers to stack addresses would be outdated. Also, pointers to memory addresses that are not part of the DSM space would point to invalid addresses in the target processor.

We are interested in thread migration in hardware homogeneous systems. Migration in heterogeneous environments introduces additional issues that must be considered and that are beyond the scope of this work.

3   DSM-PEPE Thread Migration Mechanism

Threads in DSM-PEPE are provided through a user-level library. A kernel timer is used to implement preemption and avoid blocking the entire process when a thread becomes blocked. The library runs on several processor arquitectures and operating systems. In particular, DSM-PEPE runs on top of MS-Windows and GNU/Linux, both on the Intel family of processors. Applications in DSM-PEPE follow a SPMD –Single Program Multiple Data– model [4].

A data structure called `thread` is used to store the information required to administer the threads. First, the library stores in this structure information about registers (*e.g.*, the stack pointer), administration data (*e.g.*, the thread *id*) and a pointer to the function that the thread is executing. Next, a fixed-size thread stack is stored, followed by the arguments passed to the thread function. Figure 1 shows the fields of the structure.

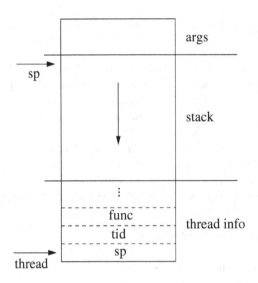

Fig. 1. DSM-PEPE thread structure

In DSM-PEPE, a function from the API allows an application-level thread to migrate to a different location by providing the *thread id* and the target *processor id*. Migration is prohibited to threads holding system resources, like files or locks, to ease resource management. In order to ensure coherence when the thread moves to another location, thread data must be stored in the DSM space or in thread local variables which reside in the thread stack.

The migration mechanism is supported by the concept of replicated threads. Each application-level thread is replicated at each processor when created. However, the thread is activated only at the forking processor while it remains suspended at the rest of the processors. In this way, we guarantee that the thread stack is located at the same address at each processor, avoiding the problem of outdated references to variables within the stack during a migration. Besides the *ready* queue, containing the threads that are currently waiting for the processor to be assigned, a *suspended* queue is used for the threads that are about to migrate and the thread replicas that wait for a migration to come in. Figure 2 shows how a thread running at a processor is migrated to another location. Thread t1 at P1 is migrated to P2 where it resumes execution on the suspended replicated thread that was created at P2 when t1 was originally forked. The thread that was running t1 on P1 now became suspended.

Fig. 2. Thread suspension and activation during a migration

Migration is accomplished by sending a message containing the `thread` structure to the target processor. The size of this message will depend on the size of the stack assigned to the thread during creation. Usually the thread stack will be 1 KB long, but in special circumstances a larger stack will be needed. This is the case of the application shown in Section 4 where we store a large data structure –up to 32 KB– in the stack of each thread. Upon reception of a migration message, the system on the target processor copies the received structure to the suspended replicated thread. This is accomplished by copying the stack to the same address where it was located at the originating processor.

4   Experiments and Results

In order to evaluate the effectiveness of the thread migration mechanism to improve performance by exploiting data locality, we ran a series of experiments with an application whose memory access pattern exhibits certain degree of spatial locality.

The application selected is 2D N-body, a simulation of the evolution of a system of n bodies or particles interacting under the influence of gravitational forces on a two-dimensional space. The force exerted on each body arises due to its interaction with all the other bodies in the system. Thus, at each step, $n - 1$ forces must be computed for each of the N particles. The computation needed grows as n^2. This application is refered to as *Sequential N-body*.

Parallelization was accomplished by distributing computation among 4 processors. Processor $P0$ initializes an array on distributed shared memory containing the mass, initial coordinates and initial velocity for all particles in the system. At each step, each processor is responsible for the computation of the new coordinates and velocity of $\frac{1}{4}$ of the total particles. To do this, the processor must read mass and coordinates data for all the particles in the system. The DSM system provides each process with data updated on other processors using the sequential consistency protocol. Barriers are used to synchronize progress. To reduce the false sharing induced by storing shared and not-shared data on the same array, a second array is used to store velocities and force accumulators. Hence, the array on DSM actually stores only truly-shared data: mass and coordinates. This application is refered to as *Parallel N-body*.

Thread migration was introduced in order to exploit data locality. At each step, each processor updates data for its own particles and reads data from other particles stored on the remaining processors. Local versus remote data exhibits a $\frac{1}{4}$ ratio at each processor. Hence, instead of making data from each processor to be updated by the consistency protocol on the remaining processors, each processor sends a migratory thread to accomplish computation at the processor where the data is stored. Threads store in their stacks the accumulators needed by computation, which are moved transparently as the threads migrate. This application is refered to as *Migratory Threads N-body*.

Four different problem sizes were used in the experiments: $2^{14} = 16384$, $2^{15} = 32768$, $2^{16} = 65536$, and $2^{17} = 131072$ particles. Each application was run to complete 1, 2, and 4 steps of computation, in order to lessen the overhead produced by the initial data distribution during the first iteration.

The testbed is composed of 4 computers with the same configuration: Intel Pentium IV processors running at 3 GHz, 256 MB RAM, 16 KB L1 cache, 2 MB L2 cache. The network link is an Ethernet switched at 100 Mbps. The operating system is GNU/Linux, kernel 2.6.15-23 (Ubuntu 6.06 LTS).

Figure 3 shows execution time of the sequential application as problem size increases. It can be seen that execution time grows as n^2. Figure 4 compares execution time for the three applications using the largest problem size: 2^{17}

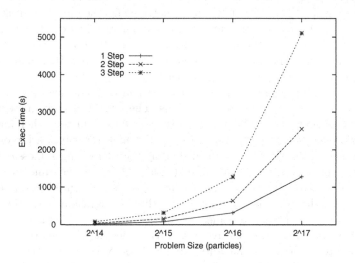

Fig. 3. Sequential N-body: Execution time grows as n^2

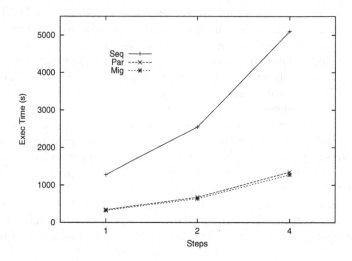

Fig. 4. Parallel and Migratory-Threads outperform Sequential N-body with speedups 3.77 and 3.99, respectively

particles. Both the parallel and the migratory-threads applications outperform the sequential application. The speedup for the parallel program was 3.77, while for the migratory-threads program it was 3.99. Results for the remaining problem sizes show the same behavior.

Figure 5 shows the speedups for both, the parallel and the migratory-threads based applications, for 1, 2 and 4 computation steps. Speedups for the application using thread migration are clearly higher and show a regular trend, improving as the number of computational steps increases. This is due to the ad-hoc migration strategy used to solve the problem that improves data locality, reducing the number of page faults and the total data exchanged. When a thread migrates to another processor it carries its acummulators and uses only local data to perform computation. Results for the largest data set are better due to the higher level of parallelism with respect to the amount of data exchanged, that is, larger data sets involve coarser computation granularity.

The parallel application involves a large number of small-size messages, most of them due to memory consistency actions. The largest of these messages is a 4 KB message sent as a reply to a remote page fault. On the other hand, the migratory application involves less messages but half of them of a large size.

Table 1 shows the time involved in sending and delivering a message of different sizes, as measured in our testbed. Table 2 shows the time involved in migrating a thread using two different stack sizes, as measured in our testbed. It can be seen that the time involved in a thread migration is sligthly higher than the time needed to send a message of the same size. This is the expected behavior because the migration involves copying the stack in the originating and destination processors and some additional actions. Nevertheless, as consistency

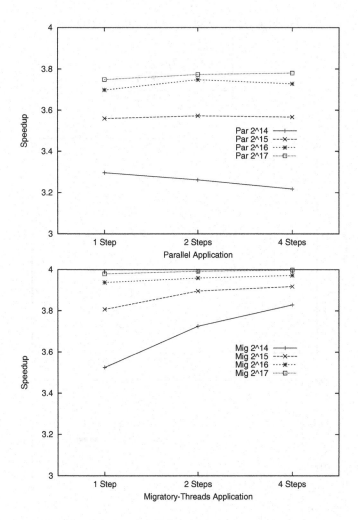

Fig. 5. Speedup for the Parallel and Migratory-Threads Applications

Table 1. Time involved in message transmission

Size (KB)	Time (μsecs)
≈ 0	66
4	514
32	2971

actions involve more than a single message (for example, to invalidate remote copies), it could be expected that an application that relies on migration to avoid page faults performs better and sends fewer messages.

Table 2. Time involved in thread migration

Stack size (KB)	Time (μsecs)
4	547
32	3445

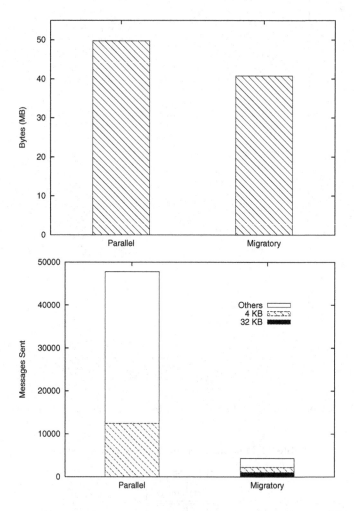

Fig. 6. Messages and data exchanged when computing 4 steps for 2^{17} particles

For the largest problem size -2^{17} particles– and 4 steps of computation, the parallel application exchaged 47790 messages for a total of 49, 75 MB, while the migratory application exchanged only 4302 messages for a total of 40, 78 MB. Of the total messages exchanged in the parallel application, 26% are page-fault replies –4 KB– while the remaining 74% are short messages, mostly related to

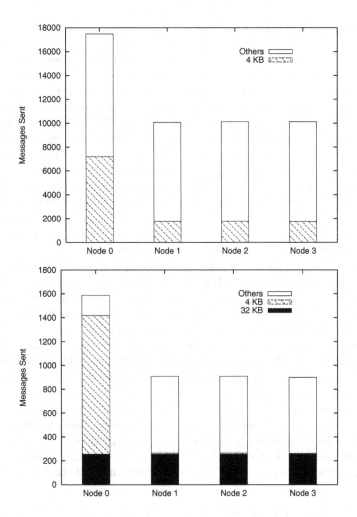

Fig. 7. Messages sent by each processor when computing 4 steps for 2^{17} particles

consistency and synchronization. In the migratory application, 24% of the total messages exchanged corresponds to large migration messages –32 KB– while 28% are page-fault replies –4 KB– and 48% are short messages. This comparison can be seen in Figure 6. Although the migratory application sends larger messages, caused by the large stack defined for the threads, the parallel application sends more cumulative data, mostly due to the large number of page faults involved.

Figure 7 compares the number of messages sent by each processor, when computing 4 steps of computation for the largest problem size. Because at the beginning of computation all data is stored at processor 0, a large amount of work is accomplished by that processor during the first step, in order to distribute data among the other processors. Afterwards the workload is uniformly distributed among all processors.

5   Related Work

Three different strategies to deal with the problem of addresses stored in the stack are found in the literature. The first approach is used in systems that rely on programming language and compiler support to obtain information about the pointers in order to update them during a migration. In this category are systems like Emerald [5], Arachne [6], and Nomadic Threads [3,7,8]. Emerald is an object-based system for the construction of distributed programs whose objects can move freely among processors. The compiler supports the translation of pointers during migration. Arachne provides thread migration across heterogeneous platforms by extending the C++ programming language. Nomadic Threads are compiler-generated fine-grain threads that migrate between processors to access data. They are supported by a runtime system that manages data and thread migrations. The approach followed by these systems lacks portability, because of their strong dependency on the compiler.

The second approach is to identify and update pointers stored in the stack at execution time, as it is done in Ariadne [9]. This is a user-level thread library. When a thread is migrated, its stack is inspectioned to identify and update outdated pointers. However, there is no guarantee that all pointers will be identified.

The third approach is the one used in DSM-PEPE, and in systems like Millipede [10], Nomad [11], and Amber [12]. Millipede is a DSM system for MS-Windows that implements multithreading at the kernel level and thread migration. Nomad is a light-weight thread migration system that delays the sending of the complete stack. Amber is an object-oriented DSM system implementing thread migration. Object location is handled explicitly by the application and the system requires a large address space to be available. Data outside the stack, being referenced by pointers in the stack, are not migrated.

There are also mixed approaches, like MigThread [13,14,15], that use preprocessing and run-time support to deal with the migration of the threads stacks.

6   Concluding Remarks

Distributed-memory applications implementing parallelism by data distribution among the processors usually benefits from a better cache utilization. This could be the case of the application used in this work and can explain the high speedups achieved.

The migratory application performs better than the parallel application, although the difference of speedups is not strong in relative terms. This can be explained because the parallel application was optimized to reduce the false sharing within the shared data structure. Also, the escence of the chosen problem involves a large number of pages that must be updated while the thread is migrating, causing a large stack to be moved along with each migration. In the future we will perform experimentation with other applications that may benefit from the enhanced data locality that thread migration can provide.

References

1. Thitikamol, K., Keleher, P.: Per-Node Multithreading and Remote Latency. IEEE Transactions on Computers 47, 414–426 (1998)
2. Thitikamol, K., Keleher, P.: Thread migration and communication minimization in DSM systems (invited paper). Proceedings of the IEEE 87, 487–497 (1999)
3. Jenks, S., Gaudiot, J.L.: An evaluation of thread migration for exploiting distributed array locality. In: (HPCS'02). Proceedings of the 16th Annual International Symposium on High Performance Computing Systems and Applications, IEEE Computer Society, Washington, DC (2002)
4. Meza, et al.: On the Design and Implementation of a Portable DSM System for Low-Cost Multicomputers. In: Kumar, V., Gavrilova, M., Tan, C.J.K., L'Ecuyer, P. (eds.) ICCSA 2003. LNCS, vol. 2667, pp. 967–976. Springer, Heidelberg (2003)
5. Jul, et al.: Fine-Grained Mobility in the Emerald System. ACM Transactions on Computer Systems 6, 109–133 (1988)
6. Dimitrov, B., Rego, V.: Arachne: A Portable Threads System Supporting Migrant Threads on Heterogeneous Network Farms. IEEE Transactions on Parallel and Distributed Systems 9, 459–469 (1998)
7. Jenks, S., Gaudiot, J.L.: A multithreaded runtime system with thread migration for distributed memory parallel computing. In: Proceedings of High Performance Computing Symposium (2003)
8. Jenks, S.: Multithreading and thread migration using mpi and myrinet. In: Proceedings of the Parallel and Distributed Computing and Systems (PDCS'04) (2004)
9. Mascarenhas, E., Rego, V.: Ariadne: Architecture of a Portable Threads System Supporting Thread Migration. Software – Practice and Experience 26, 327–356 (1996)
10. Itzkovitz, et al.: Thread Migration and its Applications in Distributed Shared Memory Systems. Journal of Systems and Software 42, 71–87 (1998)
11. Milton, S.: Thread Migration in Distributed Memory Multicomputers. Technical Report TR-CS-98-01, Dept of Comp Sci & Comp Sciences Lab, Australia National University, Canberra 0200 ACT, Australia (1998)
12. Chase, et al.: The Amber System: Parallel Programming on a Network of Multiprocessors. In: Proceedings of the 12th ACM Symposium on Operating Systems Principles, Litchfield Park AZ USA, pp. 147–158 (1989)
13. Jiang, H., Chaudhary, V.: MigThread: Thread Migration in DSM Systems. In: Proceedings of the ICPP Workshop on Compile/Runtime Techniques for Parallel Computing (2002)
14. Jiang, H., Chaudhary, V.: Compile/Run-time Support for Thread Migration. In: 16th International Parallel and Distributed Processing Symposium, Fort Lauderdale, Florida (2002)
15. Jiang, H., Chaudhary, V.: On Improving Thread Migration: Safety and Performance. In: Sahni, S.K., Prasanna, V.K., Shukla, U. (eds.) HiPC 2002. LNCS, vol. 2552, pp. 474–484. Springer, Heidelberg (2002)

EH*RS: A High-Availability Scalable Distributed Data Structure

Xueping Ren and Xianghua Xu

Institute of Software and Intelligent Technology, Hangzhou Dianzi University,
Hanghzhou, China, 310018
rxp123@hdu.edu.cn

Abstract. EH*RS is a new high-availability Scalable Distributed Data Structure (SDDS). The file structure and the search performance of EH*RS are basically these of EH*. It gets high availability based on record group and Reed-Salomon erasure correcting coding. EH*RS remains all data available despite the unavailability of any $k \geq 1$ servers by storing the additional information: the parity information. The value of k transparently grows with the file, to prevent the reliability decline. The storage overhead for the high-availability is small. The example shows that EH*RS file performs as expected. Finally, the scheme of EH*RS provides new perspectives to data-intensive applications (DBMSs), including the emerging ones of grids and of P2P computing.

1 Introduction

Multicomputers (shared–nothing configurations of computers connected by a high-speed link) allow for high aggregate performance. These systems gained in popularity with the emergence of grid computing and P2P applications. They provide high performance, and need new data structures that scale well with the number of components [1]. Scalable Distributed Data Structures (SDDS) aim to fulfill this need [2, 3]. The SDDS addressing scheme has no centralized components. This allows for operation speeds independent of the file size. They provide for hash, range or m-d partitioned files of records identified by a primary or by multiple keys.

Among the best-known SDDS schemes is the LH* scheme [2, 4, 5]. In 1993, W. Litwin et al. introduced LH*[8], an efficient, extensible, distributed variant of the Linear Hashing [7] data structure. LH* creates scalable, distributed, hash-partitioned files. In 2000, W. Litwin et al. [9] introduced LH*RS to get k-availability based on LH* using Reed-Solomon Codes and record group.

But LH* has some drawbacks. Splits must be ordered for the clients, since the splits are required to follow the bucket numbering order within each level. Determining when a bucket can be split is not an autonomous decision that can be made by the affected server. The ordering of splits is imposed on the buckets to support the directoryless character. This restriction is inherent in LH* because of the need for all buckets to be determined from one of two bucket location functions. For this reason a centralized split coordinator participates in the bucket split operation.

H. Jin et al. (Eds.): ICA3PP 2007, LNCS 4494, pp. 188–197, 2007.

Split coordinator can create a hot-spot [11]. Also, the bucket that is not allowed to immediately split must handle overflow locally. Further, since all the buckets on a level must split before the next level can start to be split; this causes premature splitting of non-full buckets. Because of those drawback of LH*, LH* RS has its corresponding shortcomings.

In 1997, V. Hilford et al. [11] introduced EH*, a distributed variant of the Extendible Hashing of Fagin et al. [12]. The directory data structure was replaced by a different data structure. This new data structure, called Cache Tables, eliminates the multiple directory entries that point to the same bucket. And there isn't an obvious drawback in EH*. So we will design the new scheme based on EH*.

At times, an EH* server can become unavailable. It may fail as the result of a software or hardware failure. It may also stop the service for good or an unacceptably long time, a frequent case in P2P applications. Either way, access to data becomes impossible. The situation may not be acceptable for an application, limiting the utility of the EH* scheme.

We say that it is *k-available*, if all data remain available despite the unavailability of any k servers. The information-theoretical minimum storage overhead for k-availability of m data servers is k/m. For files on a few servers, 1-availability usually suffices. Some proposals use mirroring to achieve 1-availability [13, 14]. Two schemes use only XORing to provide 1-availability [15, 16]. LH*g [10] and EH*g [20] use record group to achieve 1-availability. For largely scaling files, we need the *scalable availability*, adjusting k to the file size [17].

Below, we present an efficient scalable availability scheme we called EH* RS. It structures the EH* data buckets into groups of size m, providing each with $K \geq 1$ parity buckets. The values of m and of K are file parameters that can be adjusted dynamically. We call K the *intended availability level*. A group is typically K-available. Some can be $(K-1)$-available with respect to the current K if the file just increased it by one. The new level diffuses to the groups progressively with the splits. Changes to K value are transparent for the application.

Our current parity calculus is also an erasure correction scheme, using Reed-Solomon (RS)[19] coding just like LH*RS. Besides, our high-availability features are transparent to the application and do not affect the speed of searches and scans in EH*RS file. These perform as well as in an EH* file with the same data records and bucket size.

A great quantity of Major DBMSs could benefit from the new capabilities of EH*RS, such as DB2 and Oracle. The scalability of the files should also serve the emerging needs of data grids and of P2P applications. In particular, a number of new applications target there files larger than anything operationally workable till now, e.g., the Sky Server project to cite just one,[6] [18][21].

Below, we describe the general structure of an EH*RS file and how to scale the file's availability in Section 2. Section 3 presents the parity coding. We explain how to recover the data records in the EH*RS file in Section 4. Section 5 shows one example of EH*RS scheme. We present performance analysis in section 6. Section 7 concludes the study and proposes directions for the future work.

2 EH*RS

2.1 File Structure

EH*RS provides high availability based on the EH* scheme. EH* is a distributed variant of the Extendible Hashing data structure. An EH*RS file stores data records in data buckets, numbered 0,1,2... and parity records in separate parity buckets. And like EH*, EH*RS locates right buckets using cache table. They are kept by the clients and servers. These Cache Tables may become obsolete, but will never give incorrect information.

Data records contain the application data. A data bucket has the capacity of b >> 1 primary records. Additional records cause the splitting. The application interacts with the data records as in an EH* file. Parity records only provide the high availability and are invisible to the application. Figure 1a shows the structure of the EH*RS file with 2-available.

We store the data and parity buckets at the EH*RS server nodes. There is basically one bucket per server. The clients address the servers for data search or storage over the network.

An EH*RS operation is in normal mode as long as it does not encounter an unavailability. Otherwise it turns into degraded mode. We presume the normal mode unless otherwise stated. We first describe the storage and addressing of data records and the structure of parity records. And then we introduce file's scalable availability.

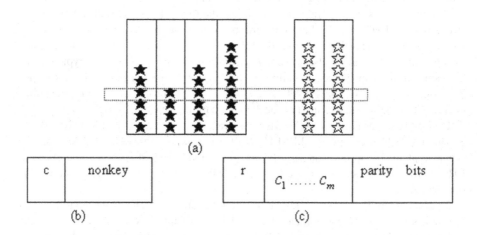

Fig. 1. EH*RS file: (a) 2-available bucket group, (b) data records and (c) parity records

2.1.1 Data Records

Structure of data records in an EH*RS file is not the same as in an EH*g file. A data record is also identified by its key c and has some non-key part. But there is not the group key and rank for each data record. As for the generic EH*, the correct bucket for data record in an EH*RS file is given by cache tables. Cache Tables have the characteristic that several levels of the file H (global depth of the file) coexist. We call this range of levels MinLevel and MaxLevel (PminLevel and PmaxLevel for parity files).Given a record R_i with the key c_i the pseudokey c_i' is generated. The meaning of these two levels is that Cache Tables are searched by using H from (MinLevel)-suffix bits of c_i' up to (MaxLevel)-suffix bits of c_i'. More details of the address computations can be found in [11]. Figure 1b shows the structure of data records.

2.1.2 Parity Records

The EH*RS data file gets the high-availability by storing the parity records in parity buckets at separate servers. The parity records let the application to get the values of data records stored on any unavailable servers, up to $k \geqslant 1$.We call k the availability level and the file k-available. The k value adjusts dynamically to the file size (Section 2.2).

EH*RS parity records is transparent to the application. It consists of bucket groups and record groups. All but perhaps the last bucket group contains the same size m (a power of 2). Bucket a belongs to the group numbered g = a **div** m, where **div** denotes integer division. Every data record in a bucket gets a unique *rank* r = 1, 2.... when it enters the bucket because of an insert, split, or merge. The last bucket group can contain less than m buckets. Every bucket group is provided with $k \geq 1$ parity buckets (p_0 ...... p_{k-1}), where the parity records for the group are stored. The value of k is the same for every record group in a bucket group.

Figure 1b shows the structure of a parity record. Field r contains the rank and serves as the key. The second Field contains m placeholders c_1, c_2 ...... c_m for the keys of the data records in the group. If a data record with rank r and key c exists in the *ith* -bucket of the group, then $c_i = c$ otherwise c_i is null. All k parity records in a record group have the same value in the first and second field. The last field is the *parity* field P, different for each parity record of a group. It calculates from the data records and the number of the parity buckets using Reed Solomon Codes.

We can recover any unavailable $s \leqslant k$ data records in the bucket group from any of $s \leqslant k$ parity records and the remaining $m-s$ data records. These properties are our basis for the k-availability.

2.2 Scalable Availability

The cost of storing and manipulating parity records in EH*RS file is almost more than it in EH*g [20] and increases with k. The storage overhead is at least k/m. We also need the access to all the k parity records whenever we insert, update, or delete a data record. However, we only need access one parity record in EH*g file at the same occasion. And the former provides k-availability; the latter provide 1-availability.

We maintain availability level k as a file parameter. Initially, k = 1. When the file size reaches some extent B_k, the availability level k increases by one for every group. One choice is $B_1 = m$, $B_i = (2^{f-1})^{i-1} m$, where $i > 1$ and $i < $ k-1, assumed

$m = 2^f$. That is, when the bucket group numbered g exceeds 1, 2^{f-1}, $(2^{f-1})^2$, $(2^{f-1})^3$ ....., the current availability level k increases by one for every group.

For the sake of the example, we choose $m = 4$ (f=2). Figure 2 illustrates the expansion of an EH*RS file. Parity buckets are represented shaded and on the right of the data file, right to the last, bucket of the group they serve. The file is created with data bucket 0 and one parity bucket, Figure 2a. The first insert creates the first parity record, calculated from the data record and from $m-1$ dummy records. The data record and the parity record receive rank 1. The file is 1-available. When new records are inserted into data bucket 0, new parity records are generated. Each new data and parity record gets the next rank. When data bucket 0 reaches its capacity of b records, $b \gg 1$, it splits based on the cache table. During the split, both the remaining and the relocated records receive new consecutive ranks starting with $r = 1$. Figure 2b shows the parity data records are recalculated, since the rank r has different data records. The splits append new data buckets 2, 3. Finally, a split creates data bucket $m+1$. This starts the second bucket group and its first parity bucket.

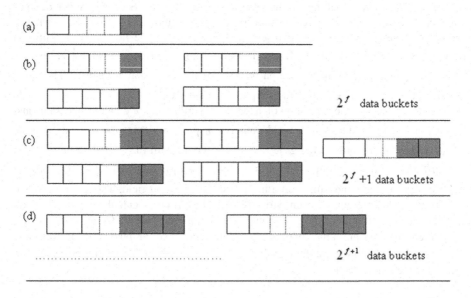

Fig. 2. Scalable availability of EH*RS file. (a) Initial file, (b) Max. 1-available file, (c) Beginning 2-availability and (d) 3-availability.

3 Parity Coding

We will provide in this section basic concepts and characteristics which are necessary for the understanding of parity coding.

EH*RS parity calculus uses the linear RS codes, which presents itself originally in the year of 1977[19]. These are originally error correcting codes, and they are maximal distance separating (MDS) codes among most efficient. We use them as erasure correcting codes recovering unknown data values. We give a brief review of the theory of Galois Fields at the basis of the RS codes. We use terms from [19].

A Galois Field $GF(N)$ is a set with N elements and the arithmetic operations of addition, subtraction, multiplication, and division. The addition and the subtraction of two elements are the same and equal to their Exclusive-Or (XOR). We have accelerated encoding and decoding, by using the logarithmic parity and decoding matrices (just like LH*RS). If $p^i = g$, $i = \log_p(g)$ and $g = anti\log_p(i)$. For every two elements g and $h, \in GF(2^f)$:

$$g \cdot h = anti\log_p(\log_p(g) + \log_p(h))$$
$$g / h = anti\log_p(\log_p(g) - \log_p(h))$$

For the sake of example, we give one Galois Field (2^4). Table 1 shows the field elements of $GF(2^4)$. It is generated by a primitive polynomial $\alpha^4 + \alpha + 1 = 0$. (More details can be found in [9] [19]).

Next, we focus on the parity coding. We use n for the maximal segment size, m for the record group size, and k for the number of parity buckets. Thus, $n = m + k$, and the group is k-available.

Table 1. Log table in GF (2^f)

String	A polynomial	int	Logarithm	String	A polynomial	int	Logarithm
0000	0	0	$-\infty$	1101	$1+\alpha+\alpha^3$	13	7
1000	1	8	0	1010	$1+\alpha^2$	10	8
0100	α	4	1	0101	$\alpha+\alpha^3$	5	9
0010	α^2	2	2	1110	$1+\alpha+\alpha^2$	14	10
0001	α^3	1	3	0111	$\alpha+\alpha^2+\alpha^3$	7	11
1100	$1+\alpha$	12	4	1111	$1+\alpha+\alpha^2+\alpha^3$	15	12
0110	$\alpha+\alpha^2$	6	5	1011	$1+\alpha^2+\alpha^3$	11	13
0011	$\alpha^2+\alpha^3$	3	6	1001	$1+\alpha^3$	9	14

For the sake of presentation, we assume that all parity records are generated at the same time. Similarly, we assume that all data records in the record group are inserted into the file simultaneously. The coding calculus is distributed in the EH*RS scheme. We are given m data records, each of which is a string of symbols. We calculate now the first symbol in all the parity records simultaneously. Subsequent symbols are calculated in precisely the same manner. First, we form the vector $\mathbf{a}$ = $(a_1, a_2, a_3, \ldots\ldots, a_m)$ where a_i is the symbol from the ith record in the group. We collect the first symbol in all records (data and parity) in the vector $\mathbf{u}$ = $(a_1, a_2, \ldots\ldots, a_m, a_{m+1} \ldots, a_n)$, to which we refer as a *code word*. $\mathbf{u} = \mathbf{a}\,\mathbf{G}$, $\mathbf{G}$ is a *generator matrix* of the linear (systematic) RS-code; $\mathbf{G}$ has m rows and n columns. $\mathbf{G}$ = I|P, where matrix $\mathbf{I}$ is an m x m identity matrix. Only the columns of the *parity* matrix $\mathbf{P}$ operationally contribute to the k parity symbols. Each parity symbol within ith parity record is produced by the vector multiplication of $\mathbf{a}$ by the ith column of $\mathbf{P}$. The entire record corresponds to the iteration of this multiplication over all the data symbols.

Details about how to generate Matrix $\mathbf{G}$ can be found in [9] [19].Different values of k lead to different elements in $\mathbf{P}$, despite same n. Each parity bucket contains only one column $\mathbf{p}$. This suffices as the parity symbol is the result of the product of $\mathbf{u}$ with the column $\mathbf{p}$.

4 Record Recovery

Assume that EH*RS finds at most k data or parity records of a record segment to be unavailable. We collect any m available records of the segment. Also, we get the m x m matrix $\mathbf{H}$ from the corresponding columns of $\mathbf{G}$. In virtue of the Vander monde matrix, any m x m submatrix of $\mathbf{G}$ is invertible. Using for example Gaussian elimination, we compute H^{-1}. Collect the symbols with the same offset from the m records into a vector $\mathbf{b}$. By definition, $\mathbf{a}.\mathbf{H} = \mathbf{b}$ implying $\mathbf{b}.\ H^{-1} = \mathbf{a}$. Hence, multiply $\mathbf{b}$ by H^{-1} to recover the missing symbols with the same offset. Using the same H^{-1}, iterate through the entire available records, to produce all missing records.

5 Example

In this section, an example is used to illustrate the EH*RS scheme. There is no space here to go into detail on all these methods, but deserve a mention and the bibliography will point to detailed references for those wishing this level of detail. The following example is constructed only for the purpose of explaining the EH*RS scheme discussed.

For the sake of simplicity, we continue with *GF* (16). The maximal segment size supported by *GF* (16) is $n = 17$. We set the bucket group size to $m = 4$. Our file availability level can scale to 13-availability.And we get a generator matrix G to be

$$G = \begin{pmatrix} 1 & 0 & 0 & 0 & 8 & F & 1 & 7 & 7 & 9 & 3 & C & 2 & A & E & 7 & 7 \\ 0 & 1 & 0 & 0 & F & 8 & 7 & 1 & 9 & 7 & C & 3 & A & 2 & 7 & E & 7 \\ 0 & 0 & 1 & 0 & 1 & 7 & 8 & F & 3 & C & 7 & 9 & E & 7 & 2 & A & 7 \\ 0 & 0 & 0 & 1 & 7 & 1 & F & 8 & C & 3 & 9 & 7 & 7 & E & A & 2 & 7 \end{pmatrix}$$

Assume the following four data records: "The file is...", "Jack went ...", "They are ...", "But this method   ". The bit strings in *GF* corresponding to the ASCII encoding for our four records are (in hexadecimal notation): "54 68 65 20 66 69 6c 65....", "4A 61 63 6B 20 77 65 6E....", "54 68 65 79 20 61 72 65....", "42 75 74 20 74 68 69 73....". To calculate the first symbols in each parity record we form the vector **a[1]** = (5,4,5,4) and multiply it by **G**. The product is vector **u[1]** = (5,4,5,4,D,D,0,F,D,1,1,1, 1,1,1,1,0). For the second symbol in each parity bucket, we form the vector **a[2]** = (4,A,4,2) and multiply by **G** to obtain code word **u[2]** = (4,A,4,2,0,6,A,B,2,5, B,3,9, D,5,8,B).u[1][5] = (5,4,5,4)*(8,F,1,7) =5*8 +4*F +5*1 + 4*7 = E+ 9+5+F = D. After those records insert, EH*RS file shown in table 2.

Table 2. Example of EH*RS with 2 parity buckets

Data Bucket 1	Data Bucket 2	Data Bucket 3	Data Bucket 4	Parity Bucket 1	Parity Bucket 2
54 68 65 20 66 69 6c 65.....	4A 61 63 6B 20 77 65 6E....	54 68 65 79 20 61 72 65....	42 75 74 20 74 68 69 73....	D0 13 16 E5 C4 93.........	D6 AB A8 3F 3B 4E.........

Assume that first two data records above became unavailable, i.e., then the third and fourth data record, and the first and second parity records are available. We form **H** from the columns 3 to 6 and compute H^{-1} as follows:

$$\mathbf{H} = \begin{bmatrix} 0 & 0 & 8 & F \\ 0 & 0 & F & 8 \\ 1 & 0 & 1 & 7 \\ 0 & 1 & 7 & 1 \end{bmatrix} \qquad H^{-1} = \begin{bmatrix} 0 & 0 & 1 & 0 \\ 0 & 0 & 0 & 1 \\ 8 & F & 1 & 7 \\ F & 8 & 7 & 1 \end{bmatrix}$$

The first vector **b** formed from the first symbols of the remaining records is **b** = (5, 4, D, D). Hence, **b**× H^{-1} = (5, 4, 5, 4). The next symbols lead to **b** = (4, 2, 0, 6) and **b**× H^{-1} = (4, A, 4, 2) etc. The first coordinates of **b** vectors provide the first missing data record "54...", and the second coordinates the second data record "4A..."

6 Performance Analysis

In this section, we analyze the new file's performance. Besides parity encoding and decoding time, the cost for high availability in EH*RS file is the storage and access time overhead.

Each bucket group carries k parity buckets, so the file storage overhead is at least k/m. The additional storage overhead is for RS calculus specific data at each parity bucket server. One needs stable storage basically only for the *m*-element single column of **P**, and for the 2^f elements of the log multiplication table. So it is almost negligible. The storage overhead is almost minimal for any *k*-available file.

Considering network speed and topology, we measure access performance with the number of messages. In normal mode, the performance of key search is that of EH* and an insert, update or delete carries the overhead of k messages to parity buckets. In degrade mode, successful key search and insert needs the record recovery time. An update or delete needs more time to recover the unavailable bucket. And the record and bucket recovery time depends on the bucket group size (m) and is independent of the file size (M). So the costs are either independent of M, or increase basically through the necessary increase to k.

7 Conclusion and Future Works

EH*RS scheme is the extension of EH*g in the availability. EH*g file has 1- availability and EH*RS file has k- availability. We use the Reed-Solomon Codes to provide scalable, distributed and high availability files, needed by modern applications. In section 5, the example clearly demonstrates that the profile of the EH*RS scheme. And it shows that EH*RS file seems to perform as expected.

In the paper, we provide the basic scheme of EH*RS in the previous sections. On account of space, we don't give the details about how to insert, delete and update one data records. We treat the update as the usual operation, and the inserts and deletes as special cases in the implementation. At present, we are developing the prototype to implement and evaluate the proposed scheme.

Future research could extend our results in two ways. First, we should analyze the variants deeper. Second, it would be interesting to compare our scheme with LH*RS scheme in the performance, storage and availability.

References

1. Special Issue on High-Performance Computing. Comm. Of ACM (1997)
2. Litwin, W., Neimat, M.-A., Schneider, D.: Linear Hashing for Distributed Files. ACM-SIGMOD International Conference on Management of Data (1993)
3. SDDS-bibliography.http://192.134.119.81/SDDS-bibliograhie.html
4. Litwin, W., Neimat, M.-A., Schneider, D.: LH* - A Scalable Distributed Data Structure. ACM Trans. On Database Systems (1996)
5. Karlson, J., Litwin, W., Risch, T.: LH*LH: A Scalable High Performance Data Structure for Switched Multicomputers. In: Karlson, J., Litwin, W., Risch, T. (eds.) Extending Database Technology, EDBT96, Springer Verlag, Heidelberg (1996)
6. Litwin, W., Moussa, R., Schwarz, T.: LH*RS – A Highly-Available Scalable Distributed Data Structure, vol.30(3). ACM Transaction on Database Systems (TODS) (2005)
7. Litwin, W.: Linear hashing: A new tool for file and table addressing. In: Proc. of VLDB, pp. 212–223 (1980)
8. Litwin, W., Neimat, M.-A., Schneider, D.: LH*: Linear Hashing for distributed files. In: ACM-SIGMOD Intl. Conference on Management of Data, pp. 327–336 (1997)
9. Litwin, W., Schwarz, T.: LH*RS: A High-Availability Scalable Distributed Data Structure using Reed Solomon Codes. ACM-SIGMOD International Conference on Management of Data (2000)
10. Litwin, W., Risch, T.: LH*g: a High-availability Scalable Distributed Data Structure through Record Grouping. Res. Rep. CERIA, U. Dauphine & U. Linkoping (1997)

11. Hilford, V., Bastani, F.B., Cukie, B.: EH*—Extenhible Hashing in a Bistributed Environment, pp. 217–222. IEEE, New York (1997)

12. Fagin, R., Nievergelt, J., Pippenger, N., Strong, H.R.: Extendible Hashing - A Fast Access Method for Dynamic Files. In: ACM Transactions on Database Systems, pp. 315–344 (1979)

13. Litwin, W., Neimat, M.-A.: High-Availability LH* Schemes with Mirroring. In: Intl. Conf. on Coop. Inf. Systems (COOPIS), IEEE Press, Orlando (1996)

14. Breitbart, Y., Vingralek, R.: Distributed and Scalable B+ tree Data Structures. Workshop on Distr. Data and Struct., Carleton Scientific (publ.) (1998)

15. Litwin, W., Neimat, M.-A., Levy, G., Ndiaye, S., Seck, T.: LH*S : a high-availability and high-security Scalable Distributed Data Structure. IEEE-Res. Issues in Data Eng. (RIDE-97) (1997)

16. Lindberg, R.: A Java Implementation of a Highly Available Scalable and Distributed Data Structure LH*g. Master Th. LiTH-IDA-Ex-97/65. U. Linkoping (1997)

17. Litwin, W., Menon J., Risch, T.: LH* with Scalable Availability. IBM Almaden Res. Rep. RJ 10121 (91937) (1998)

18. Gray, J., et al.: Data Mining of SDDS SkyServer Database. Intl. Workshop on Distributed Data Structures, (WDAS 2002) Carleton Scientific (2002)

19. Macwilliams, F.J., Sloane, N.J.A.: The Theory of Error Correcting Codes. Elsevier, North Holland, Amsterdam (1977)

20. Xueping, R.: EH*: A High-Available Scalable Distributed Data Structure. Computer engineering and Science, China (2005)

21. Schwarz, Th., S. J., Manasse, M.: Report on the 7th workshop on Distributed Data and Structures (WDAS 2006) vol. 35(2). ACM SIGMOD Record (2006)

Optimizing Stream Organization to Improve the Performance of Scientific Computing Applications on the Stream Processor

Ying Zhang, Gen Li, Xuejun Yang, and Kun Zeng

Institute of Computer, National University of Defense Technology, Changsha 410073, China
{zhangying,ligen,yangxuejun,zengkun}@nudt.edu.cn

Abstract. It is very important to organize streams well to make stream programs take advantage of the parallel computing and memory system of the stream processor effectively, especially for scientific stream programs. In this paper, after analyzing typical scientific programs, we present and characterize two methods to optimize the stream organization: stream reusing and stream transpose. Several representative scientific stream programs with and without our optimization are performed on a stream typical processor simulator. Simulation results show that these methods can improve scientific stream program performance greatly.

Keywords: Scientific computing, stream programming model, stream processor, cluster, SIMD, parallel computing, stream reusing, stream transpose, inter-cluster communication.

1 Introduction

Scientific computing has been an important and major part of research and industry, which makes feature of massive data, dense computation, and high degree of data level parallel. Now conventional architecture (as shown in Figure1) has been not able to meet the demands of scientific computing [1][2]. In all state-of-the-art architectures, the stream processor(as shown in figure 2)[3] draws scientific researchers' attentions for its processing computation-intensive applications effectively[4-8].

Both the organization of ALUs and the memory system of the stream processor are different from those of conventional architecture. There are N clusters controlled by a single controller to work in SIMD mode, and every cluster consists of M ALUs (in the stream processor prototype Imagine[9][10] developed by Stanford University, N = 8 and M = 6). As a result, plenty of ALUs can process intensive computations of scientific computing applications effectively and clusters working in an SIMD mode can exploit the high data parallelism sufficiently. At the same time, the stream processor has three level memory hierarchies – local register files (LRF) near ALUs, global stream register files (SRF) and streaming memory system, and the bandwidth ratios between three level memory hierarchies are generated according to the statistics

H. Jin et al. (Eds.): ICA3PP 2007, LNCS 4494, pp. 198–209, 2007.

of several stream applications, which can exploit the parallelism and locality of scientific computing applications fully.

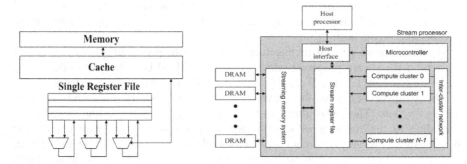

Fig. 1. Simplified diagram of a conventional processor

Fig. 2. Block diagram of a stream processor

Stream programming model exposes a lot of architecture details to programmers, such as the use of SRF, chip-off memory, and clusters. Although this provides a consistent structure that is specialized for stream applications, it improves the hardness to programme [11]. As a result, it is important to write stream programs which can take advantage of the stream processor effectively.

Compared with other applications, scientific computing applications have much more data, more complex data access methods and more strong data dependence. All these make scientific stream programs constrained by memory access or inter-cluster communications, such as swim stream programs developed by Du and Wang yielding a speedup of 0.53 over advanced x-86 architecture processor[7][8]. So it is very important to optimize the stream organization to make scientific computing stream programs take advantage of the characteristics of the stream processor architecture well.

In the paper, we present two optimization methods, stream reusing and stream transpose, according to the analysis of characteristics of scientific computing applications. And we give the steps how to use our methods to optimize stream organization. Then we perform several representative scientific stream programs with and without our optimization on Isim which is a cycle-accurate stream processor simulator supplied by Stanford University. Simulation results show that the optimization methods of stream reusing and stream transpose can improve scientific stream program performance efficiently.

2 Stream Processor

The stream processor architecture is developed to speed up stream applications with intensive computations. The stream programming model divides a application into a stream-level program that specifies the high-level structure of the application and one or more kernels that define each processing step[13][14][15]. Each kernel is a function that operates on streams[12], sequences of records.

2.1 Stream Processor Architecture

Generally, the stream processor act as a coprocessor of convention processor. Kernels responsible for processing streams run on the stream processor, while stream-level program responsible for organizing streams, calling kernels and processing output streams runs on the host.

Figure 2 shows general architecture of the stream processor[12]. There are N clusters in the stream processor which consists of M ALUs. Microcontroller issues VLIW instructions to these N clusters and control them to work in SIMD mode.

The stream processor has three level memory hierarchies: LRF, SRF and streaming memory system. The bandwidth ratio of three-level memory hierarchies is generated according to the statistics of several stream applications, which can exploit the parallelism and locality of stream applications fully. The ratio is 1:13:218 in Imagine. The memory system can exploit locality of stream applications from three aspects [16]: LRF exploits data locality in kernels, SRF exploits producer-consumer and producer-producer locality between kernels, and streaming memory system exploits global locality.

Figure 3 shows a data stream flows across three level memory hierarchies during the execution of a stream program. First, the data stream is loaded from chip-off memory into SRF and distributed into corresponding buffer. Then it is loaded from SRF to LRF to supply operands to a kernel. During the execution of this kernel, all records of the stream are stored in LRF. After the kernel is finished, the stream is stored back to SRF. If there is producer-consumer locality between this kernel and its later kernel, the stream is saved in SRF. Otherwise, it is stored back to chip-off memory.

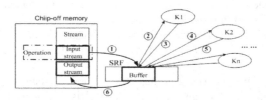

Fig. 3. Stream flowing across the memory system

2.2 Stream Programming Model

Corresponding with stream processor architecture, stream programming model has two levels: kernel-level and stream-level[14][15]. A kernel is a computation intensive function that operates on sequences of records called streams. Each kernel takes streams of records as input and produces streams of records as output. Kernels are written using a C-like language called KernelC. The stream program declares the streams and defines the high-level control- and data-flow between kernels. Stream programs are written using a programming language extension called StreamC intermixed with C++.

Stream programming model exposes three level parallelism of stream architecture to programmers: Instruction-Level Parallelism (ILP), Data-Level Parallelism (DLP) and Task-Level Parallelism (TLP).

3 Optimizing the Organization of Data Streams

In the stream programming model, the stream program declares the streams and defines the high-level control- and data-flow between kernels. So it is the responsibility of programmers to organize data streams. Organizing scientific stream programs' streams well to make them take advantage of the parallel computing and memory system well can improve stream program performance efficiently. We present two optimization methods — stream reusing and stream transpose — to optimize the organization of data streams. Then we take code in figure 4 from stream program MVM as example to depict our methods, where NXD equals to NX+2. In our experiments we let NX and NY equal to 832.

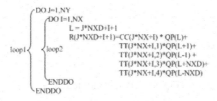

Fig. 4. Example code

3.1 Stream Reusing

Stream reusing is defined as that between loop iterations of a stream-level program, input or output streams of kernels in the former iteration can be used as input streams of kernels in the latter iteration. If input streams are reused, we call it input stream reusing. Otherwise, we call it output stream reusing. The essential of stream reusing optimization is to enhance the locality of SRF. Correspondingly, input stream reusing can enhance the producer-producer locality of SRF while output stream reusing can enhance the producer-consumer locality of SRF.

3.1.1 Analyzing the Stream Application

Figure 5 shows the data trace of QP(L), QP(L+NXD) and QP(L-NXD) participating in loop2 of figure 4. QP(1668,2499) is QP(L+NXD) of loop2 when J=1, QP(L) of loop2 when J=2, and QP(L-NXD) of loop2 when J=3. So, stream QP can be reused between different iterations of loop1. If QP(1668,2499) is organized as a stream, it will be in SRF after loop2 with J=1 finishes. When loop2 with J=2 or J=3 running, it doesn't get stream QP(1668,2499) from chip-off memory but SRF.

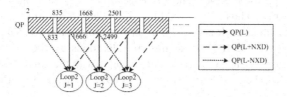

Fig. 5. Data trace of QP(L), QP(L+NXD) and QP(L-NXD)

3.1.2 Stream Reusing Optimization Organizes Data Stream

Figure 6 shows a generalized perfect nest of D loops. The body of the loop nest reads elements of the m-dimensional array A twice. If in the Pth level loop the data trace of one array A read references with $I_P=i$ is the same to that of the other array A read references with $I_P=i+1$ and different to that of the other array A read references with $I_P=i$, such as the data trace of array QP in loop2 in figure 4, the two array A read references can be optimized by input stream reusing. Then we give the step of using input stream reusing method to optimize stream organization.

```
DO I₁ = L₁, U₁
  DO I₂ = L₂, U₂
  ... ...
    DO I_D = L_D, U_D
I1    ... = A(F₁(I₁,...I_D),..., F_M(I₁,...I_D))
I2    ... = A(G₁(I₁,...I_D),..., G_M(I₁,...I_D))
    ENDDO
  ... ...
  ENDO
ENDDO
```

Fig. 6. A D-level nested loop

Step A. Organize different array A references in the innermost D-P loops as stream A1 and A2 according their data traces.

Step B. Organize all operations on array A in the innermost D-P loops as a kernel.

Step C. Organize all operations in the outmost P loops as stream-level program.

When the nest with $I_P=i$ of loop P in stream-level program operates on stream A1 and A2, one of them has been loaded into SRF by the former nest, which means that the kernel doesn't get it from chip-off memory but SRF. From the feature of the stream processor architecture, we can know the time to access chip-off memory is much larger than that to access SRF, so the method of stream reusing can improve stream program performance greatly.

The steps to use output stream reusing are analogous to steps above.

In stream program MVM unoptimized, we organize different array QP read in loop1 as three data streams according their data trace ,and. organize operations in loop1 as a kernel The length of each data stream is 832*832. When running, the stream program must load these three streams into SRF, the total length of which is 692224*3, nearly three times of that of array QP.

By the stream reusing method above, we organize different array QP read references in loop2 as three data streams according their own data trace, organize operations in loop2 as a kernel, and organize operations in loop1 except loop2 as stream-level program. Thus there would be 832*3 data streams in the stream program loop1, and the length of each is 832. So in stream program loop1, data stream QP(L), QP(L+NXD) and QP(L-NXD) of neighboring iterations can be reused. As a result, the stream program only need load 832 data streams with the length of 832 from chip-off memory to SRF, the total length of which is 692224, nearly 1/3 of that of program unoptimized.

3.1.3 Extended Applications

Figure 7 lists some typical applications in FORTRAN code that are available to be optimized by stream reusing and corresponding process. Code in figure 7(a), 7(b) and 7(c) are representative codes operating on 2-dimension array, while code in figure 7(d) and 7(e) are representative codes operating on 1-dimension array. Note that there are a lot of scientific computing applications that are available to be optimized by stream reusing, as long as they have analogous array reference trace as following code.

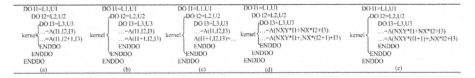

Fig. 7. Applications that can be optimized by stream reusing

3.2 Stream Transpose

Stream transpose involves transposing the distribution of a stream in buffers of SRF in order to make records distributed among successive clusters be distributed on the same cluster.

There are many buffers in SRF, and every buffer is connected with a functional unit to provide data for it, including clusters. Figure 8 shows the distribution of stream QP of loop2 in figure 4 among the buffers, assuming that the number of clusters is 8, buffer0 connects with Cluster0, buffer1 connects with Cluster1, and so on. Note that records are interleaved among buffers, which means QP(L), QP(L+1) and QP(L-1) participating in calculations of loop2 are distributed among sequential clusters.

If adjacent records from the same array participate in the same calculations, such as QP(L), QP(L+1) and QP(L-1) of loop2 in figure 4, we can streamize such applications as follow:

- Organizing the array as one stream. Correspondingly, we organize QP(L), QP(L+1) and QP(L-1) as one stream QP'(L). When $cluster_i$ executes operations of loop2, it must communicate with $cluster_{i+1}$ and $cluster_{i-1}$ to gather necessary records on other clusters. Because clusters work in SIMD mode and thus inter-cluster communications make them stall waiting for collecting data. Consequently, inter-cluster communications become the bottleneck of program performance. We call this inter-cluster communication implementation.
- Organizing different array references in the loop as multiple streams according their data traces. Correspondingly, we organize QP(L), QP(L+1) and QP(L-1) as three data stream according their data traces. Because there are a lot of chip-off memory traffics and the record set of every stream is almost the same, this method makes memory access become the bottleneck of the stream program. We call this multi-stream implementation.

By stream transpose optimization, we organize all records covered by the array references as one stream, and distribute adjacent records on the same cluster. So optimized stream programs will have as few inter-communications as multi-stream implementation and the same amount of memory traffics as inter-communication implementation.

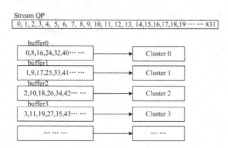

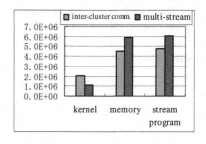

Fig. 8. Distribution of a data stream among buffers connecting with clusters

Fig. 9. Run time of memory, kernel and stream program MVM with these two implementations(cycles)

3.2.1 Analyzing the Stream Application

Figure 9 shows the active time of memory system, kernel and stream program MVM with inter-cluster communication and multi-stream implementation. From the figure, we can see that inter-cluster communication implementation has less memory access overhead, but more kernel execution time and multi-stream implementation is just the contrary.

3.2.2 Stream Transpose Optimization Organizes Data Stream

Stream transpose optimization involves transposing the distribution of a stream among clusters making use of the feature of derived streams. Then, the steps of stream transpose are given below.

Step A. If the stream program organizes adjacent records from the same array participating in the same computations as one stream, we can do the next step directly. Otherwise, we must join the streams of the same array first, which means organizing the whole array as a stream.

Step B. Derive a new stream with the streams to be transposed by letting the length of a record equal to $Length_{stream}/N_{cluster}$ and letting the stride equal to $Length_{stream}/N_{cluster}$, where $Length_{stream}$ represents the length of the stream to be transposed, and $N_{cluster}$ represents the number of clusters of the stream processor.

After the process above, the first "record" of the derived stream is distributed in buffer0, which means records from 0 to $Length_{stream}/N_{cluster}$ - 1 of the original stream are distributed in buffer0, and so on.

Correspondingly, we use this method to transpose stream QP by letting the length of a record equal 104 and letting the stride equal 104. The distribution of stream transposed among buffers is showed in figure 10. QP(L), QP(L+1) and QP(L-1) participating in calculations of loop2 will be distributed in the same buffer.

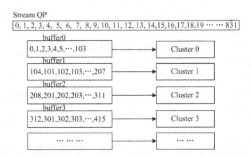

Fig. 10. Distribution of data stream in buffers of SRF after transposed

3.2.3 Extended Applications

Figure 11 lists some typical applications in FORTRAN code that are available to be optimized by stream transpose. Figure 11(a) lists representative codes operating on 2-dimension array, while figure 11(b) lists representative codes operating on 1-dimension array. Note that there are a lot of scientific computing applications that are available to be optimized by stream transpose, as long as they have analogous array reference trace as following code.

```
DO I1=L1,U1                    DO I1=L1,U1
  DO I2=L2,U2                    DO I2=L2,U2
    DO I3=L3,U3                    DO I3=L3,U3
    ...=A(I1,I2,I3);               ...=A(NXY*I1+NX*I2+I3);
    ...=A(I1,I2,I3+1);             ...=A(NXY*I1+,NX*I2+I3+1);
    ENDDO                         ENDDO
  ENDDO                          ENDDO
ENDDO                          ENDDO
      (a)                            (b)
```

Fig. 11. Applications that can be optimized by stream transpose

4 Experimental Results and Analysis

In our experiments, we use ISim cycle-accurate stream processor simulator supplied by Stanford University[12][13] to get the performance of stream programs unoptimized and optimized.

Several representative scientific stream programs are optimized by our optimization methods. QMRCGSTAB algorithm is a subspace method to solve large nonsymmetric linear systems[17]. MVM is a subroutine of a hydrodynamics application and computes band matrix multiplication. Laplace calculates two-dimension central difference. First_difference is the 14th Livermore loop. All applications above are used widely in scientific computing, and the performance of these scientific stream programs is constrained by memory access.

4.1 Stream Reusing

Table 1 illustrates the effects of the stream reusing method on stream program performance. Figure 12 lists the influence of stream reusing method to chip-off memory traffics. Simulation results show that stream reusing optimization can enhance the SRF locality and consequently the stream program performance efficiently. This method can cut down chip-off memory traffics proportionably, which is very important to stream programs constrained by memory access. Because applications in our experiment are optimized all by input stream reusing, load memory traffics are cut down obviously while there is no effect on store memory traffics. However, this method is not fit for First_difference application.

Table 1. Comparison of without and with stream reusing (cycles)

	QMRCGSTAB	MVM	Laplace(256)	First_difference(1024)
Without	74412079924	7619785	365565	4867
With	66113790568	6044064	267904	N/A
Speedup	**1.126**	**1.261**	**1.365**	**N/A**

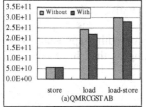 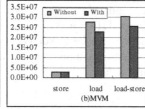 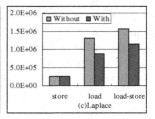

Fig. 12. Influence of stream reusing to memory traffics(B)

4.2 Stream Transpose

Figure 13 shows the comparison of stream program run time with different implementations. Figure 14 illustrates the speedup yielded by stream transpose over multi-stream and over inter-cluster communication implementation. Table 2 lists chip-off memory traffics and the number of inter-cluster communications of different implementation. From the results, we can know that: compared with multi-stream implementation, stream transpose can cut down the memory traffics proportionably and thus improve stream program performance greatly; compared with inter-cluster communication implementation, stream transpose can decrease the number of inter-cluster communications and thus improve stream program performance greatly; the memory traffics of stream programs optimized by stream transpose equal nearly to those of stream programs with inter-cluster communication implementation and the number of inter-cluster communications of the former equal nearly to that of stream programs with multi-stream implementation, i.e., stream programs optimized by stream transpose have both less memory traffics and less inter-cluster communications. However, the difference of memory traffics between stream transpose and inter-cluster communication implementation is generated by the amount of kernel code and that of data transferring from host to the stream processor.

For stream program QMRCGSTAB which is a large scientific computing application, there are only a few streams that can be optimized by stream transpose and consequently the speedup yielded by it is the smallest. For stream program First_difference, it is a small application kernel and there is only two array references that can be optimized by stream transpose, so its speedup is slower. For all stream applications, the data parallel address architecture of Isim simulator doesn't support the memory access pattern used by stream programs optimized by stream transpose efficiently. If we optimize the memory architecture according to [20] corresponding-ly, the performance increase gained by stream transpose will be much larger.

Figure 15 shows First_difference stream program's run time of different implementations with the increase of the stream length. From the figure, we can observe that with the increase of stream scale, compared with the other two implementations, stream transpose can get better and better performance.

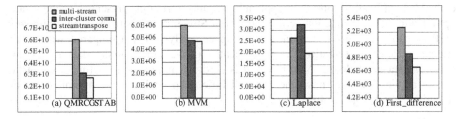

Fig. 13. Comparison with different implementations (cycles)

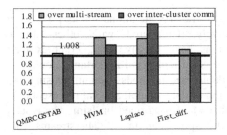

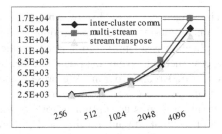

Fig. 14. Speedup yielded by stream transpose over the other two implementations

Fig. 15. Effects of the increase of stream scale,on first_difference stream program run time with different implementations (cycles)

Table 2. Comparison of chip-off memory traffics(MB) and the number of inter-cluster communications with different implementations

	QMRCGSTAB		MVM		Laplace (256)		First_difference	
	Traffics	Comm.	Traffics	Comm.	Traffics	Comm.	Traffics	Comm.
multi-stream	2.78E+08	0	2.5655E+04	0	1.1399E+3	256	17248	0
inter-cluster comm.	2.51E+08	8.0128E+9	2.0272E+04	3.2064E+6	6.4799E+2	2.6216E+6	14304	7176
stream transpose	2.53E+08	0	2.0639E+04	0	6.4061E+2	256	13280	0

5 Related Work

Imagine stream processor supports software pipeline and Strip-mining to optimize stream programs[13][14][15]. Software-pipelining involves dividing a loop into stages and overlapping execution of one stage of one iteration with execution of another stage of another iteration. Software-pipelining can be used to hide the memory access time of a sequential memory access, a memory access that must occur between a pair of sequential kernels. Software pipelining can hide the latency for this memory access by overlapping execution of a kernel from another stage with the sequential memory access. Strip-mining involves processing a large input stream in smaller batches so that the intermediate streams produced while processing a batch will all fit in the SRF. Stream reusing and stream transpose we present can be used together with the methods above, so that we could get better performance.

Now optimizations of stream applications are most oriented to media applications, embedded applications and DSP applications. Janis Sermulins presents a cache aware optimization of embedded stream programs in StreamIt[18]. Sitij Agrawal optimizes DSP stream programs using linear state space analysis[19]. Compared with other stream applications, scientific stream applications have more complex data access and stronger data dependence. As a result, it is hard and important to optimize scientific stream applications. By now, there is still little deep study on the optimizations of scientific stream applications.

6   Conclusion

The stream processor has drawn scientific researchers' attentions for its processing computation-intensive applications effectively. Compared with other stream applications, scientific computing applications have massive data, complex data access method, strong data dependence. So it is difficulty and important to optimize scientific stream program. We present and depict two methods – stream reusing and stream transpose – to optimize the organization of data stream. Several representative stream programs are optimized by our methods and performed on Isim. The results validates that stream reusing and stream transpose can make data streams take advantage of the stream processor well, and thus improve the stream program performance greatly.

Acknowledgments. We gratefully thank the Stanford Imagine team for the use of their compilers and simulators and their generous help. We also acknowledge the reviewers for their insightful comments. This work is supported by the National High Technology Development 863 Program of China under Grant No. 2004AA1Z2210.

References

1. Wulf, W.A., McKee, S.A.: Hitting the memory wall: implications of the obvious. Computer Architecture News. 23(1), 20–24 (1995)
2. Burger, D., Goodman, J., Kagi, A.: Memory bandwidth limitations of future microprocessors. In: Proceedings of the 23rd International Symposium on Computer Architecture, Philadelphia, PA, pp. 78–89 (1996)
3. Amarasinghe, W.S.: Stream Architectures. In: PACT 2003 (September 27, 2003)
4. Merrimac – Stanford Streaming Supercomputer Project, Stanford University, http://merrimac.stanford.edu

5. Dally, W. J., Hanrahan, P., et al.: Merrimac: Supercomputing with Streams, SC2003, Phoenix, Arizona (November 2003)
6. Erez, M., Ahn, J.H., et al.: Merrimac - Supercomputing with Streams. In: Proceedings of the, SIGGRAPH GP^2 Workshop on General Purpose Computing on Graphics Processors, Los Angeles, California (June 2004)
7. Guibin, W., Yuhua, T., et al.: Application and Study of Scientific Computing on Stream Processor, Advances on Computer Architecture (ACA'06), Chengdu, China (August 2006)
8. Jing, D., Xuejun, Y., et al.: Implementation and Evaluation of Scientific Computing Programs on Imagine, Advances on Computer Architecture (ACA'06), Chengdu, China (August 2006)
9. The Imagine Project, Stanford University, http://cva.stanford.edu/imagine
10. Kapasi, U. J., Dally, W. J., et al.: The Imagine Stream Processor, Processings of the 2002 International Conference on Computer Design (2002)
11. Johnsson, O., Stenemo, M., ul-Abdin, Z.: Programming and Implementation of Streaming Applications. Master's thesis, Computer and Electrical Engineering Halmstad University (2005)
12. Rixner, M.: Stream Processor Architecture. Kluwer Academic Publishers, Boston (2001)
13. Mattson, P.: A Programming System for the Imagine Media Processor. Dept. of Electrical Engineering. Ph.D. thesis, Stanford University (2002)
14. Mattson, P., et al.: Imagine Programming System Developer's Guide (2004)
15. Das, A., Mattson, P., et al.: Imagine Programming System User's Guide 2.0. (June 2004)
16. Kapasi, U. J., Rixner, S., et al.: Programmable Stream Processor, IEEE Computer (August 2003)
17. A Quasi-Minimal Residual Variant Of The Bi-Cgstab Algorithm For Nonsymmetric Systems Chan, T. F., Gallopoulos, E., Simoncini, V., Szeto,T., Tong, C.H.: SIAM Journal on Scientific Computing (1994)
18. Sermulins, J., Thies, W., et al.: Cache Aware Optimization of Stream Programs, LCTES 2005, Chicago, IL (June 2005)
19. Agrawal, S., Thies, W., et al.: Optimizing Stream Programs Using Linear State Space Analysis, CASES 2005, San Francisco, CA (September 2005)
20. Ahn, J. H., Dally, W.J.: Data Parallel Address Architecture, IEEE Computer Architecture Letters, vol.5(1) (2006)

A Parallel Architecture for Motion Estimation and DCT Computation in MPEG-2 Encoder

Jian Huang and Hao Li

Department of Computer Science and Engineering
University of North Texas
P.O. Box 311366, Denton, Texas 76203
{jh0274,hli}@unt.edu

Abstract. This paper presents a parallel architecture that can simultaneously perform block-matching motion estimation (ME) and discrete cosine transform (DCT). Because DCT and ME are both processed block by block, it is preferable to put them in one module for resource sharing. Simulation results performed using Simulink demonstrate that the parallel fashioned architecture improves the performance in terms of running time by 18.6% compared to the conventional sequential fashioned architecture.

1 Introduction

MPEG-2 is an audio/video digital compression standard developed by Moving Picture Experts Group (MPEG) in 1994 [1]. Now it is widely used in high definition television (HDTV), DVD, and three dimensional television. In these applications, quality, performance and power are important issues. A typical MPEG-2 encoder structure is shown in Fig. 1. Motion estimation (ME) and discrete cosine transformation (DCT) are the most computational expensive modules of the encoder system [2][3]. Motion estimation is used to reduce inter-frame temporal redundancy, i.e., generating motion vectors by comparing current frame with reference frame. On the other hand, DCT is used to reduce intra-frame spatial redundancy by transferring data from spatial domain to frequency domain. After DCT coefficients are computed, most energy will be concentrated into low frequency coefficients, and many other high frequency coefficients will be close to zero. Compression is achieved by discarding these near zero coefficients. Besides DCT, quantization (Q), variable length coding (VLC), and buffer control (BUF) unit are also included in a typical encoder system. The inverse quantization (IQ) and inverse DCT (IDCT) are used to reconstruct the reference frame, which will be used in motion compensated predictor and motion estimation unit.

In MPEG-2 encoder, both motion estimation and DCT are processed block by block. The difference is that motion estimation is done in 16×16 blocks and DCT is done in 8×8 blocks. We propose a new architecture to process them simultaneously in order to improve performance.

H. Jin et al. (Eds.): ICA3PP 2007, LNCS 4494, pp. 210–221, 2007.
© Springer-Verlag Berlin Heidelberg 2007

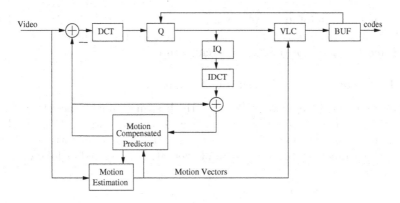

Fig. 1. Typical encoder structure for MPEG2 [1]

2   Related Work

There are various motion estimation algorithms available in literature. For example, full search [4], three-step search [5], four-step search [6], alternating pixel-decimation search [7] and so on. Among them, full search is the most accurate and often used as the benchmark [4]. However, it is inefficient in running time. To reduce computational complexity, several fast algorithms have been proposed. For example, three step search uses a center biased searching point and a half way stop technique [5]. And alternating pixel-decimation search subsamples pixel blocks by a factor of 4 [7]. In DCT algorithms, Chen's algorithm [8] and Lee's algorithm [9] both require 32 multiplications and 32 additions in DCT operation. Loeffler's algorithm requires only 11 multiplications and 29 additions [10].

Systolic array based architecture is commonly used in VLSI implementation for motion estimation due to its simplicity and regularity [11]. Yang *et al* proposed a general systolic architecture for motion estimation [4]. Similarly systolic based architectures have been proposed in [12] [13] intended for full search block matching algorithm. Distributed arithmetic (DA) based architecture is a popular candidate for VLSI implementation of DCT module [14].

We notice that motion estimation and DCT in MPEG-2 are both block processed. Thus, we would like to perform these two operations parallelly and design a common architecture sharing hardware resources. By doing so, we can achieve better performance, area and power efficiency. This paper is the first step in our research to develop realtime MPEG-2 codec. we propose a system level architecture which performs motion estimation and DCT simultaneously. The simulation results show that our proposed architecture indeed outperforms the conventional architecture.

3   Algorithm

In this section, we briefly present motion estimation and DCT algorithms used in our architecture. Full search block matching algorithm (FSBM) is the most popular one because of its simplicity and accuracy [13] [15]. Chen's algorithm is one of the most frequently referred algorithm for DCT [8]. Therefore, we choose FSBM and Chen's algorithm in our architecture.

3.1   Full Search Block Matching Algorithm

FSBM performs exhaustive search to find the best matching of the reference area within the search area. As shown in Fig. 2, we set search range (-7, 7), block size 16×16, and the search area 31×31. We use sum of absolute distortion (SAD) as our matching function. SAD in our implementation is defined as follows:

$$SAD_{(x,y)}(u,v) = \sum_{i=0}^{15} \sum_{j=0}^{15} |F_c(x+i, y+j)$$

$$-F_r(x+i+u, y+j+v)| \tag{1}$$

where F_c is the current frame, F_r is the reference frame, (x, y) is the upper left position of current frame, and (u, v) is the displacement in search area. Displacement (u, v) of the minimum SAD in the search area is known as motion vector. The objective of motion estimation is to generate motion vectors (mv) for the current frame.

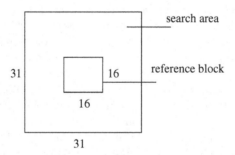

Fig. 2. Block matching algorithm

3.2   DCT Algorithm

In order to reduce the time complexity of 2D-DCT computation, we divide the 2-D DCT into two 1D-DCT, as shown in Fig. 3. We first perform one dimensional DCT row by row and save the results in a transpose memory. Then, one dimensional DCT is performed column by column on the results stored in the transposed memory. The outputs obtained from the second 1D-DCT are the coefficients of the 2D-DCT.

It is evident that the 1D-DCT is the key module to be designed. An eight point 1D-DCT is computed as:

$$F_i = \frac{1}{2} R_i \sum_{k=0}^{7} \left\{ \cos\left(\frac{(2k+1)i\pi}{16}\right) \right\} \{f(k)\} \tag{2}$$

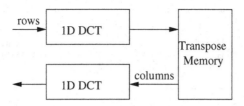

Fig. 3. Decomposition of 2D-DCT [14]

where R_i equals $(\frac{1}{\sqrt{2}})$ if i is 0; otherwise R_i equals 1. By using Equation (2) directly, the implementation of 8-point 1D-DCT would require 64 multiplications and 56 additions. Instead, we choose Chen's algorithm to reduce the number of operations. Chen's algorithm can be summarized as follows[8]:

$$\begin{pmatrix} F(0) \\ F(2) \\ F(4) \\ F(6) \end{pmatrix} = \frac{1}{2} \begin{pmatrix} A & A & A & A \\ B & C & -C & -B \\ A & -A & -A & A \\ C & -B & B & -C \end{pmatrix} \begin{pmatrix} f(0) + f(7) \\ f(1) + f(6) \\ f(2) + f(5) \\ f(3) + f(4) \end{pmatrix}$$

$$\begin{pmatrix} F(1) \\ F(3) \\ F(5) \\ F(7) \end{pmatrix} = \frac{1}{2} \begin{pmatrix} D & E & F & G \\ E & -G & -D & -F \\ F & -D & G & E \\ G & -F & E & -D \end{pmatrix} \begin{pmatrix} f(0) - f(7) \\ f(1) - f(6) \\ f(2) - f(5) \\ f(3) - f(4) \end{pmatrix}$$

where $A = \cos\frac{\pi}{4}, B = \cos\frac{\pi}{8}, C = \sin\frac{\pi}{8}, D = \cos\frac{\pi}{16}, E = \cos\frac{3\pi}{16}, F = \sin\frac{3\pi}{16}$ and $G = \sin\frac{\pi}{16}$. This method effectively reduces the number of multiplications to 32 and reduces the number additions to 32.

4 System Level Architecture

The system level architecture for motion estimation and DCT computation is shown in Fig. 4. It consists of address generator and data mapper, on-chip buffers for current frame and search area, and computational core. Address generator and data mapper unit is the bridge between external memory and on-chip buffer. It generates address for fetching data on external memory to on-chip current block buffer or search area buffer.

The system level architecture of computation core for motion estimation and DCT computation is shown in Fig. 5. It reads in 16×16 block of current frame and reference frame, and performs motion estimation for current block. After computing the motion vector of the current block, it computes prediction error. Finally, DCT computation is performed on the prediction error. Because DCT is computed in an 8×8 block, we put four DCT modules together to perform DCT parallelly. Unlike conventional approach, our design will process motion estimation and DCT simultaneously to provide motion vectors and DCT coefficients. In the following subsections, we will discuss the details of these units.

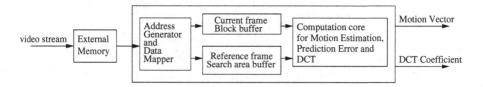

Fig. 4. System level representation of our proposed simultaneous architecture that performs motion estimation and DCT computation

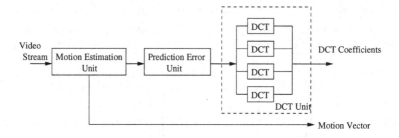

Fig. 5. System level architecture of the new computation core

4.1   Motion Estimation

Block level architecture diagram for motion estimation is shown in Fig. 6. Appropriate blocks from current frame (P) and reference frame (I) are selected for SAD computation using address generated by address generator. SAD computation includes subtracter, absolute, column sum and row sum. The SAD results are stored in matrix. Comparator selects the minimum SAD from the matrix. The coordinates of the minimum SAD are the motion vector for current block.

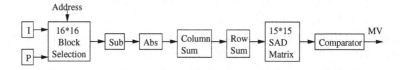

Fig. 6. Block level architecture diagram for motion estimation

4.2   Prediction Error

Block level architecture diagram for prediction error computation is shown in Fig. 7. Firstly, macroblocks from current frame (P) and reference frame (I) are selected using motion vector and address generated by address generator, Then subtraction is performed on these two blocks. Finally, the prediction error is assigned to proper position in the output matrix. Output matrix for prediction error has the same dimension as that of the input frame.

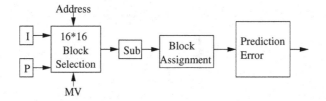

Fig. 7. Block level architecture diagram for prediction error

4.3 DCT

Block level architecture diagram for 2D-DCT is illustrated in Fig. 8. First, 1D-DCT is performed on each row of selected blocks of prediction error and results are stored in transpose memory. Then, 1D-DCT is performed on each column of the block in the transpose memory. Each 1D-DCT consists of 4 adders, 4 subtracters and 2 matrix multiplier. Matrix multiplier is also called multiply accumulator (MAC).

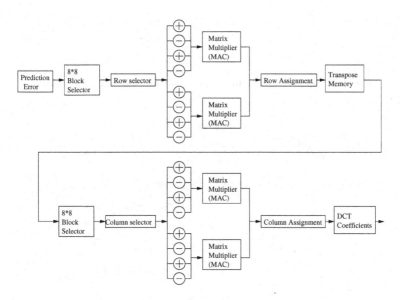

Fig. 8. Block level architecture diagram for 2D-DCT

5 Design and Implementation of Individual Modules in the Architecture

The module level diagram of the proposed architecture generated using Matlab/Simulink is shown in Fig. 9. It is composed of address generator and data mapper, address generator 1, address generator 2, motion estimation, prediction

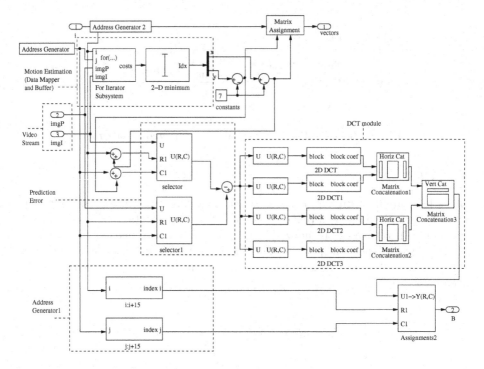

Fig. 9. Proposed simultaneous architecture diagram in Simulink

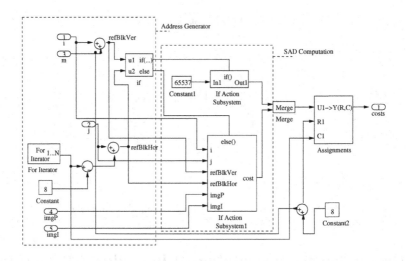

Fig. 10. Level 1 of motion estimation module

error computation and DCT module. Address generator generates the address for current block. Motion estimation module includes address generator, data mapper and buffer. Address generator 1 and address generator 2 are used to

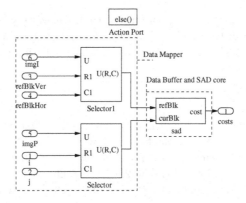

Fig. 11. Level 2 of motion estimation module

generate matrix of motion vectors and prediction error for the reconstruction part. Motion estimation, prediction error and DCT module forms the computation core. Then we output the motion vectors and DCT coefficients of prediction error. IDCT and motion compensation is performed in the reconstruction part. Finally, we get reconstructed video for verification.

5.1 Motion Estimation Module

Fig. 10 and Fig. 11 show two levels of the hierarchical design of motion estimation module. Level 1 includes address generator for the reference block and SAD computation. Level 2 includes data mapper, data buffer and SAD core.

5.2 Prediction Error Module

The prediction error module computes the reference block coordinates using motion vectors and current block coordinates. Then it selects corresponding

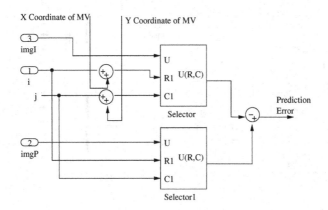

Fig. 12. Design of prediction error

reference block and current block for subtraction. The output of the subtraction is prediction error between these two blocks. Finally, prediction error is passed to DCT module. Fig. 12 shows the design module of prediction error computation.

5.3   DCT Module

An 8×8 2D-DCT is performed on the prediction error. First it divides prediction error block into four 8×8 sub-blocks, as shown in Fig. 13. Then 2D-DCT is performed on each sub-blocks. These four sub-blocks are finally converted to one block to generate the final output. The 2D-DCT is composed of two consecutive 1D-DCT modules. Fig. 14 shows the design of 1D-DCT computation core.

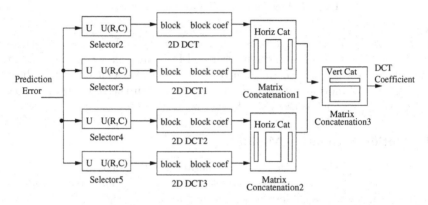

Fig. 13. Top level of 2D-DCT

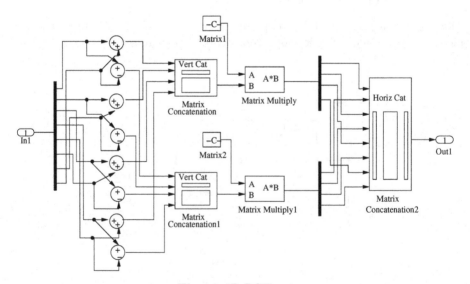

Fig. 14. 1D-DCT core

6   Simulation and Results

We have implemented and verified our proposed architecture that can perform both motion estimation and DCT simultaneously using Simulink. The input to our implementation is a 128×128 video stream in AVI format. We first perform motion estimation, prediction error computation and DCT. Motion vectors and bit-stream of prediction error are generated by ME block and DCT block, respectively. Then we perform IDCT on the bit-stream of prediction error. Next, motion compensation is executed using motion vectors and prediction error to reconstruct the video sequence and verify the correctness. We use four DCT units parallelly in the computational core to improve the performance. One motion estimation example is illustrated in Fig. 15. The motion vectors are generated by comparing the the reference frame and current frame.

Table 1 shows the comparison of our proposed architecture and the conventional architecture. In Our proposed architecture, DCT and ME work in a parallel fashion. On the other hand, in the conventional architecture, DCT and ME work in a sequential fashion. We use Simulink's Profiler tool to analyze their performance. Two systems are setup with the same simulation configuration. We set start time as 0s and stop time as 0.5s.The simulation results show that

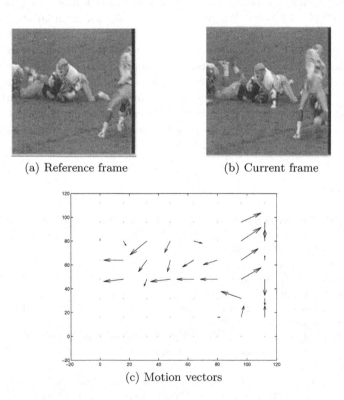

(a) Reference frame   (b) Current frame

(c) Motion vectors

Fig. 15. Motion estimation of football video

Table 1. Performance Comparison of Football video stream

	Football	
	Serial	Parallel
Total recorded time	92.84s	75.69s
# Block Methods	240	321
# Internal Methods	7	6
# Nonvirtual Subsystem	16	19
Clock precision	30ns	30ns
Clock Speed	300MHz	300MHz

our architecture improves the running time by 18.6% on average compared to the conventional architecture.

7 Conclusion

In this work, we have presented a parallel architecture of motion estimation and DCT in MPEG-2 encoder. We propose to put motion estimation, prediction error computation, and DCT into one computation core. By doing so, address generator and data mapper can be shared by these three modules. In addition, we use four 2D-DCT units to expedite the computation process. We have implemented the proposed architecture as well as the conventional architecture in Simulink. The simulation results justify that our proposed architecture reduces the running time by 18.6% compared with the conventional architecture for DCT and ME. In our future research, we plan to explore this idea to other standards, such as MPEG-4, H.264/AVC, and VC-1.

References

1. Haskell, B.: An introduction to MPEG-2. Chapman & Hall (1996)
2. Ahemd, N., Natarajan, T., Rao, K.R.: Discrete cosine transform. IEEE Trans. Computers C-23, 90–93 (1974)
3. Guttag, K., Gove, R.J., Van Aken, J.R.: A single chip multiprocessor for multimedia: The mvp. IEEE Computer Graphics and Applications, pp. 53–64 (1992)
4. Shengqi, Y., Wayne, W., Vijaykrishnan, N.: Power and Performance Analysis of Motion Estimation Based on Hardware and Software Realizations. IEEE Transactions on Computers 54, 714–726 (2005)
5. Li, R., Zeng, B., Liou, M.L.: A New Three-Step Search Algorithm for Block Motion Estimation. IEEE Transactions on Circuit and System for Video Technology 4, 438–442 (1994)
6. Po, L.M., Ma, W.C.: A Novel Four-Step Search Algorithm for Fast Block Motion Estimation. IEEE Transactions on Circuit and System for Video Technology 6, 313–317 (1996)

7. Liu, B., Zaccarin, A.: New Fast Algorithms for the Estimation of Block Motion Vectors. IEEE Transactions on Circuit and System for Video Technology 3, 148–157 (1993)
8. Chen, W., Smith, C.H., Fralick, S.: A fast computation algorithm for the discrete cosine transform. IEEE Transactions on communications 25, 1004–1009 (1977)
9. Lee, Y.P., et al.: A cost effective architecture for 8*8 two-dimensional DCT/IDCT using direct method. IEEE Transactions on Circuit and system for video technology 7, 459–467 (1997)
10. Loeffler, C., Lightenberg, A., Moschytz, G.S.: Practical fast 1-D DCT algorithm with 11 multiplications. In: Proceedings of ICASSP, vol. 2, pp. 988–991 (1989)
11. Kung, S.Y.: VLSI Array Processors. Prentice-Hall, Englewood Cliffs (1998)
12. Nam, S.H., Baek, J.S., Lee, M.K.: Flexible VLSI architecture of full search motion estimation for video applications. IEEE Transactions on Consumer Electronics 40, 176–184 (1994)
13. Eric, C., Sethuraman, P.: Motion Estimation Architecture for Video Compression. IEEE Transactions on Consumer Electronics 39, 292–297 (1993)
14. Jiang, M., Luo, Y., Fu, Y.L., Yang, B., Zhao, B.Y.: A low power 1D-DCT Processor for MPEG-targeted Real-time Applications. International Symposium on Communications and Information Technologies, pp. 682–687 (2004)
15. Nam, J., Choi, T.S.: A Fast Full-Search Motion-Estimation Algorithm Using Representative Pixels and Adaptive Matching Scan. IEEE Transactions on Circuits and Systems for Video Technology 10, 1040–1048 (2000)

EOP: An Efficient Object Placement and Location Algorithm for OBS Cluster[*]

Changsheng Xie, Xu Li, Qinqi Wei, and Qiang Cao

Huazhong University of Science and Technology
Wuhan National Laboratory for Optoelectronics, Wuhan, Hubei, China 430074
csxie@263.net, lixu_cn@163.com

Abstract. A new generation storage system which called Object-Based Storage system (OBS) is emerging as the foundation for building massively parallel storage system. In the OBS, data files are usually stripped into multiple objects across OBS's nodes to improve the system I/O throughput. A fundamental problem that confronts OBS is to efficiently place and locate objects in the dynamically changing environment. In this paper, we develop EOP: an efficient algorithm based on dynamic interval mapping method for object placement and lookup services. The algorithm provides immediately rebalance data objects distribution with the nodes' addition, deletion and capability weight changing. Results from theoretical analysis, simulation experiments demonstrate the effectiveness of our EOP algorithm.

Keywords: OBS, object placement, interval mapping, hash function.

1 Introduction

Combining the benefits of the conventional storage systems such as network- attached storage (NAS) and storage area networks (SAN) architectures, object-based storage is emerging as the next generation network storage system [1]. Unlike conventional block storage where the storage system must track all of the attributes for each block in the system, the object in OBS manages its particular piece of data by maintaining its own attributes to communicate with the storage system.

Widely research efforts have been devoted toward improving the performance of OBS. By distributing the objects across many devices, OBS have the potential to provide high capacity, throughput, reliability, availability and scalability [2]. Object striping has become one useful performance enhancing techniques for OBS. In the design of OBS, some key issues those need to be resolved are efficient object placement, location, and keeping objects distribution balanced in the dynamically changing storage resource environment.

In a large-scale OBS cluster, storage nodes may be added or temporarily unreachable due to network or node failure. When some nodes are added or removed,

---

[*] This research is supported by National 973 Great Research Project of P.R. China under grant No. 2004CB318203 and National Natural Science Foundation under grant No. 60603074 and No. 60603075.

H. Jin et al. (Eds.): ICA3PP 2007, LNCS 4494, pp. 222–230, 2007.
© Springer-Verlag Berlin Heidelberg 2007

objects may need to be redistributed from some nodes to the others to maintain the overall balance of the storage load. Also it is required that such relocations are executed with minimal data movement.

To address these essential OBS issues, we develop EOP: an efficient algorithm which is based on the concept of interval mapping for providing object placement and lookup services in OBS. EOP does well in both distributing data evenly and minimizing data movement when storage nodes are changed. Moreover, this algorithm is adaptable for multiple nodes' addition, nodes deletion and capability weight modification.

The rest of this paper is organized as follows. Section 2 provides a literature review of related works. Section 3 presents the details of our EOP algorithm and its theoretical analysis is given in Section 4. Our evaluation and measurement results are present in Section 5. We summarize this paper and propose future work in Section 6.

2   Related Work

Several data placement algorithms have been studied in distributed storage systems. Litwin, et al. have developed many variations on Linear Hashing (LH*) [3], LH* splits buckets in half, so that on average, half of the objects on a split disk will be moved to a new empty disk. The deficiency of LH* is the "hot spot" of disk and network activity between the splitting node and the recipient may lead system load imbalance.

Choy, et al. [4] describes algorithms for distributing data over disks which move an optimal number of objects when disks are added, but Choy does not support disk removal. OceanStore [5] and tapestry [6] adopt Bloom filters to support the object placement and lookup services. The weakness of Bloom filters is that the memory and bandwidth overhead could still turn out to be too high for a large-scale OBS cluster.

Chord [7] uses a variant of consistent hashing to assign keys to Chord nodes. It has two weaknesses: First is the locations of objects are not controllable to balance storage usages on different nodes; Second is each node in Chord need maintain information approximate O(log N) other nodes where N is the total number of nodes, and requires lookups via O(log N) messages to other nodes. RUSH [8] develops a decentralized algorithm for placing and locating replicated objects in a distributed storage system. But the RUSH family of algorithms is more efficient for object replication management than the object lookup service in OBS.

A new adaptive object placement algorithm is researched in [2], which can learn the parameters of the workloads under the real-time environment with the changing workloads. The Bit-Window based algorithm is developed by Renuga et al. [9]. However, in the worse case when an addition of a node needs the bit window size to expand, near 50% of the objects need to be migrated. But the disadvantage has been improved in EOP by use the dynamic interval mapping method.

LIU and ZHOU [10] propose a data object placement algorithm based on dynamic interval mapping, which is optimal in both distributing data evenly and minimizing data movement when storage nodes is changed. It is perhaps the closest method to our EOP algorithm. However, it does not support concurrent multiple nodes addition, deletion and weight change.

3 The EOP Algorithm

Like the Lustre file system [11] and Panasas [12], each object of the OBS has its exclusive object ID (the bit width of Lustre ID is 64bits and Panasas ID is 96bits). To ensure the object distributed evenly, we translate all the objects IDs into n-bit identifiers by using a consistent fast hash function Tiger [13]. We call these identifiers as object keys, and the n-bit object key can be denoted as: $k_{n-1}k_{n-2}...k_i...k_2k_1k_0$.

We define interval [0, 1) as the whole distribution space. Initially, inside a given set, the interval is divided into several subintervals with different length according to the weight of each storage node. Then we create a blank subinterval set for each node and insert such subinterval into the corresponding set. After that, there is a unique mapping relationship between a node index and its corresponding interval set. When the nodes number or some weights of nodes are altered, the intervals within the corresponding sets are divided into smaller intervals and then they are reassembled among these sets. For convenience, we sort these subintervals by the order of their starting numbers and form a table for subinterval sets.

3.1 Subinterval Set Initialization

Define N as the initial number of nodes with index from 0 to N-1, the weight of node i is w_i. For any j, let:

$$r_j = \sum_{i=0}^{j} w_i / \sum_{i=0}^{N-1} w_i \qquad (1)$$

for $0 \leq j \leq N\text{-}1$, and define $r_{-1} = 0$, then we get real numbers r_j where $0= r_{-1}<r_0<r_1<r_2<...<r_{N-1} = 1$. As shown in Figure 1, the jth subinterval is $b_{j0} = [r_{j-1}, r_j)$. We form the initial subinterval sets table as $ST_0 = \{s_0,...,s_j,...,s_{N-1}\}$, where $s_j =\{b_{j0}\}$. And the matched node index equals to the index of subinterval set.

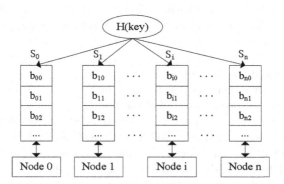

Fig. 1. Dynamic interval mapping method

Suppose currently the ith subinterval sets table is $ST_i = \{s_0,...,s_k,...,s_{N-1}\}$, where $s_j = \{b_{j0},b_{j1},...\}$ $(0\leq j\leq N\text{-}1)$. To construct the (i+1)th subinterval sets table we should consider three different cases in the following sections.

3.2 Multiple Nodes Joining

When m (m $\geq$ 1) nodes join the OBS which having N nodes already, the weights of them are presented as w_N, w_{N+1},...,w_{N+m-1}. For each previous subinterval set s_j ($0 \leq j \leq N-1$), a search is carried on to all available subinterval b_{j0}, b_{j1}..., until getting a subinterval subset B_j (When need, dividing one large subinterval into two parts) with the sum of all subinterval length:

$$\sum_{b_j \in B_j} |b_j| = w_j / \sum_{i=0}^{N+m-1} w_i \tag{2}$$

Reserve these intervals in the jth subinterval set, and migrate the remainder subintervals to the newly added nodes' subinterval set. For any newly added node i ($1 \leq i \leq m$) with the weight w_{N+i-1}, the new subinterval set is generated and the sum of the subinterval length is changed into:

$$\sum_{b_{N+i-1} \in B_{N+i-1}} |b_{N+i-1}| = w_{N+i-1} / \sum_{i=0}^{N+m-1} w_i . \tag{3}$$

Thus we update the subinterval set table as $ST_{i+1} = \{s_0,...,s_k,...,s_{N-1},s_N,...,s_{N+m-1}\}$, where $s_j = \{b_{j0}, b_{j1},...\}$ ($0 \leq j \leq N+m-1$).

3.3 Multiple Nodes Deletion

When m ($1 \leq m < N$) nodes depart from OBS cluster which having N nodes previously. The nodes are divided into two sets, one is reserve subset N_r and the other is apart subset N_a. For any node i in N_a, its weight is presented as w_i. We incorporate all subintervals of apart nodes into an aggregate subinterval set S_d, and the sum of all these subintervals length is:

$$|S_d| = \sum_{s_i \in S_d} |s_i| \tag{4}$$

For any reserved subinterval set s_j in N_r, we send a search in S_d until getting a subinterval subset B_j (dividing one large subinterval into two when need) with the total length of subintervals:

$$\sum_{b_j \in S_d} |b_j| = |S_d| * w_j / \sum_{i=0, i \in N_r}^{N-1} w_i \tag{5}$$

Then the obtained B_j is incorporated into s_j.

After all reserved subinterval sets are updated, the m nodes are deleted from subinterval sets and $ST_{i+1} = \{s_0,...,s_k,...,s_{N-m-1}\}$, where $s_j = \{b_{j0}, b_{j1},...B_j\}$ ($0 \leq j \leq N-m-1$).

3.4 Node Weight Adjustment

Since the capability of each member node is variable, our algorithm should take the weight changing into account. Here we suppose the weight of some nodes has changed, let the new weight of the ith node as w_i' $(0 \leq i \leq N-1)$, and the subinterval subset length difference is:

$$s_{di} = w_i' / \sum_{i=0}^{N-1} w_i' - w_i / \sum_{i=0}^{N-1} w_i \qquad (6)$$

For any subinterval set s_j which $s_{di} < 0$, a search is carried out to all available subinterval $b_{j0}, b_{j1}...$, in s_j, until getting a subinterval subset B_j (when required, dividing one large subinterval into two parts) with the sum of all subinterval length:

$$\sum_{b_j \in B_j} |b_j| = w_i' / \sum_{i=0}^{N-1} w_i' \qquad (7)$$

Reserve these intervals in the jth subinterval set, and incorporate the remainder subintervals into a temporary subinterval set s_t.

On the other hand, for any subinterval set s_j which $s_{di} > 0$, also a search is issued to all available subinterval $b_{j0}, b_{j1}...$, in S_t, until getting a subinterval subset B_j (dividing one large subinterval into two when required) with the sum of all subinterval length:

$$\sum_{b_j \in B_j} |b_j| = s_{di} \qquad (8)$$

Then these subintervals are migrated to s_j.

After these steps are done, the subintervals are distributed uniformly according to the up to date weight again. Thus we update the subinterval set table as $ST_{i+1} = \{s_0,...,s_k,...,s_{N-1}, s_N,...,s_{N-1}\}$, where $s_j = \{b_{j0}, b_{j1},...\}$ $(0 \leq j \leq N-1)$.

3.5 Object Placement and Lookup

As mentioned above, we generate the objects' keys using the Tiger hash function. The object keys are 192 bits long and numerous object keys in large-scale OBS are uniformly distributed in the interval $[0, 2^{192})$. Given an object key, let the key divided by 2^{192}, then we will get a real number X within the interval $[0, 1)$. We search in the subinterval sets table and can find X belonging to which subinterval with the matched node index, then place the object into the corresponding node.

The object lookup operation in the EOP algorithm is similar to the object placement. For a given object key, we determine its node index using the placement method. Then the corresponding node's IP address is obtained from the table which is maintained at metadata server.

4 Theoretical Analysis

Lemma 1. The number of objects placed in a node is proportional to the total length of subintervals contained in the corresponding subinterval set.

Theorem 1. The number of objects placed in any node is proportional to its capacity weight.

We omit the proofs of lemma 1 and theorem 1 here which can be found in [10].

Theorem 2. When nodes are changed, the number of objects migrated is the minimum.

Proof. By Lemma 1, we just need to prove that the total length of subintervals migrated is the minimum. Consider the following three cases.

(a) Adding nodes. By Theorem 1, the number of objects placed in any node is proportional to its capacity, then the minimum total length of subintervals migrated to new added nodes is $\sum_{k=N-1}^{N+m-1} w_k / \sum_{i=0}^{N+m-1} w_i$. The total length of subintervals migrated is:

$$\sum_{j=0}^{N-1}(w_j / \sum_{i=0}^{N-1} w_i) - \sum_{j=0}^{N-1} (w_j / \sum_{i=0}^{N+m-1} w_i) = 1 - \sum_{j=0}^{N-1} (w_j / \sum_{i=0}^{N+m-1} w_i) = \sum_{k=N-1}^{N+m-1} w_k / \sum_{i=0}^{N+m-1} w_i$$

(b) Removing nodes. The subintervals migrated are contained in an aggregate set S_d, and the sum of all these subintervals length is $|S_d| = \sum_{s_i \in S_d} |s_i|$, that is just the minimum.

(c) Node Weight adjustment. As the whole mapping interval space is fixed in $[0, 1)$, some subinterval's lengthen must result in some others' shorten. The minimum migration for each subinterval is equal to its length variation. For a subinterval set s_j, the length of s_i is $w_i / \sum_{i=0}^{N-1} w_i$ and the new s_i' is $w_i' / \sum_{i=0}^{N-1} w_i'$, so the difference which needs minimum migration is $s_{di} = s_i' - s_i$. If $s_{di} < 0$, it means this node's subinterval set length need to be decreased and if $s_{di} > 0$ its length need to be increased. The total decreased length is $|L_d| = |\sum_{s_{di}<0} s_{di}|$ and the total increased length is $|L_i| = |\sum_{s_{di}>0} s_{di}|$. The difference between decreased and increased length is:

$$|L_d| - |L_i| = |\sum_{s_{di}<0} s_{di}| - |\sum_{s_{di}>0} s_{di}|$$

$$= \sum_{s_{di}<0} (w_i / \sum_{i=0}^{N-1} w_i - w_i' / \sum_{i=0}^{N-1} w_i') - \sum_{s_{di}>0} (w_i' / \sum_{i=0}^{N-1} w_i' - w_i / \sum_{i=0}^{N-1} w_i)$$

$$= \sum_{i=0}^{N-1} (w_i / \sum_{i=0}^{N-1} w_i) - \sum_{i=0}^{N-1} (w_i' / \sum_{i=0}^{N-1} w_i') = 1 - 1 = 0.$$

This shows that our migration operation runs only among the lengthened and shortened subintervals, but total subintervals length migration just equal to L_d and L_i.

5 Performance Study

In this section, we present a simulation experiment to evaluate the performance of EOP algorithm. The simulation system comprises ten nodes at the beginning, and their capability weight is assigned initially as 6, 2, 1, 3, 6, 7, 5, 9, 2, and 4, respectively. We consider 1,000,000 objects for placement. To exam the performance of RSC synthetically, three independent experiment groups are designed as following:

5.1 Node Placement

Figure 2 shows how these objects distribute among the ten variable weight nodes. It can be observed that the objects are distributed across these nodes according to their capability weight. The difference between the theoretic distribution and simulation result is no more than 0.12%.

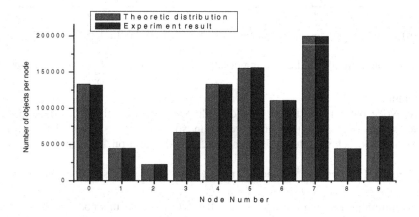

Fig. 2. Object Placement in a 10-node OBS cluster

5.2 Node Addition and Deletion

Figure 3(a) plots the redistribution of data objects in the system where some nodes are added. In this case, we add three nodes into the system with capability weight 10, 3, and 8, separately. Figure 3(b) shows the objects are distributed across the system where some nodes are removed from the original system. This time we remove the second, fourth, sixth and seventh node with capability weight 2, 3, 7 and 5, separately.

From both figure 3(a) and 3(b), we can see that the objects are always redistributed among the storage nodes according to their capability weights. The difference between the theoretic distribution and simulation result is less than 0.11% and 0.21% respectively. Data objects are migrated throughout all storage nodes in parallel after adding or removing cluster nodes, which will result in a minimum amount of replacement of data objects as possible.

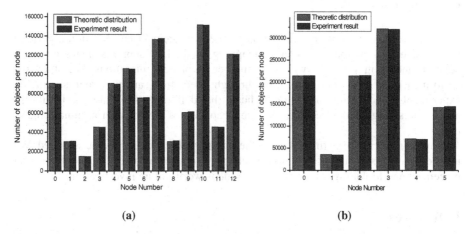

(a)   (b)

Fig. 3. (a) The redistribution of data objects after adding three nodes. **(b)** The redistribution of data objects after removing four nodes.

5.3 Node Weight Adjusting

We change the original configuration in 5.1 and set the weight of ten nodes as 3, 4, 2, 5, 4, 6, 8, 9, 1, and 4 respectively. From figure 4 we can observe that as the weight of each node changes, the distribution of objects also changes and still abides by the rule that the number of objects placed in any node is proportional to its capacity weight. This time the difference between the theoretic distribution and simulation result is less than 0.14%.

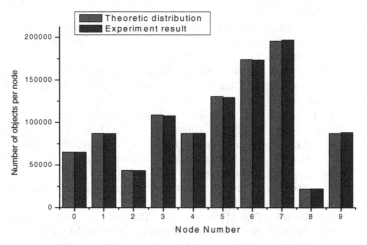

Fig. 4. The redistribution of data objects after nodes weight adjusting

6 Conclusion

In this paper, we present an efficient data objects placement and location algorithm based on hash function and interval mapping method. It supports nodes addition, deletion and weight change with low number of objects migrations. We study the performance of the EOP algorithm through theoretical analysis and simulation experiments. The simulation results indicate that data objects are always distributed across the storage nodes according to their capabilities weight with minimal objects migration.

However, after several times update, the subinterval sets must become scattered. We need develop a subinterval collation mechanism to improve the efficiency of object placement and lookup services. Thus this issue is worth future investigation.

References

[1] Mesnier, M., Ganger, G.R., et al.: Object-based Storage. IEEE Communications Magazine 41(8), 84–91 (2003)

[2] Feng, D., Qin, L.: Adaptive Object Placement in Object-Based Storage Systems with Minimal Blocking Probability. In: Proceedings of the 20th International Conference on Advanced Information Networking and Applications, AINA'06 (2006)

[3] Litwin, W., Neimat, M.A., Schneider, D.A.: LH*—A scalable, distributed data structure. ACM Trans. on Database Systems, pp. 480–525 (1996)

[4] Choy, D. M., Fagin, R., Stockmeyer, L.: Efficiently extendible mappings for balanced data distribution. Algorithmica, pp. 215–232 (1996)

[5] Kubiatowicz, D.B., et al.: OceanStore: An architecture for global-scale persistent storage. In: Proc. of the International Conference on Architectural Support for Programming Languages and Operating Systems, ACM Press, New York (2000)

[6] Tapestry: An infrastructure for fault-tolerant wide-area location and routing. Technical Report, UCB/CSD- 01-1141, Berkeley Computer Science Division, University of California (2001)

[7] Stoica, I., Morris, R., Karger, D., Kaashoek, F., Balakrishnan, H.: Chord: A scalable peer-to-peer lookup service for internet applications. In: Proceedings of the 2001 ACM SIGCOMM Conference, pp. 149–160 (2001)

[8] Honicky, R.J., Miller, E.: Replication Under Scalable Hashing: A Family of Algorithms for Scalable. In: Proceedings of the 18th International Parallel & Distributed Processing Symposium (2004)

[9] Kanagavelu, R., Leong, Y. K.: A Bit-Window based Algorithm for Balanced and Efficient Object Placement and Lookup in Large-scale Object Based Storage Cluster, IEEE Conference on Mass Storage Systems and Technologies, MSST2006 (2006)

[10] Zhong, L., Xing-Ming, Z.: A Data Object Placement Algorithm Based on Dynamic Interval Mapping. Journal of Software, pp. 1886–1893 (2005)

[11] Braam, P.J.: The Lustre Storage Architecture.: Cluster File Systems, Inc. (2003) http://www. lustre.org/docs/lustre. pdf

[12] Nagle, D., Serenyi, D., Matthews, A.: The Panasas Active Scale Storage Cluster-Delivering Scalable High Bandwidth Storage, IEEE SC2004 (2004)

[13] Anderson, R., Biham, E.: Tiger: A Fast New Hash Function. In: Gollmann, D. (ed.) Fast Software Encryption 3. LNCS, vol. 1039, Springer, Heidelberg (1996)

Data Interoperation Between ChinaGrid and SRB*

Muzhou Xiong, Hai Jin, and Song Wu

Service Computing Technology and System Lab
Cluster and Grid Computing Lab
School of Computer Science and Technology
Huazhong University of Science and Technology, Wuhan, 430074, China
hjin@hust.edu.cn

Abstract. Separated grid systems are becoming the new information islands when more and more grid systems are deployed. Grid interoperation is a direction to solve that problem. This paper introduces the implementation of data interoperation between ChinaGrid and SRB. The data interoperation between them is divided into two parts: data access from SRB to ChinaGrid and from ChinaGrid to SRB. Also this paper considers the issues about performance optimization. We get a satisfied experiment result through the optimization measures.

1 Introduction

Grid technologies [1, 2, 3] enable efficient resource sharing in collaborative distributed environments. We see hundreds of scientists in areas such as gravitational-wave physics [4], high-energy physics [5], astronomy [6] and many others coming together and sharing a variety of resources within collaboration in pursuit of common goals. These resources are geographically distributed and encompass people, scientific instruments, computer and network resources, applications and data. However, the new problem is whether grid technologies are the best way to solve those problems. Another side of that problem is whether grid technologies are the ultimate way to resource and data sharing. Obviously, the answer is negative, although grid computing can well solve the problem of resource and data sharing.

In fact grid computing lacks common standards to unify all the grid platforms and grid projects. The details of grid projects are much different although Globus [7, 8] may be the de facto standard of grid computing. Most of the grid projects are case-oriented, which means that it can handle only some applications in limited areas. Then the grid projects can be considered as new information islands because most of them are not able to communicate with the others. Also there is no collaboration among them. So we conclude that grid projects need interoperation. With interoperation, users under a grid platform can access resources and data in other grid platforms; and also a workflow may communicate with the other one in another grid environment. Through interoperation, grid platforms can be unified into a larger grid platform,

---

* This paper is supported by National Science Foundation of China under grant 90412010 and 60673174.

H. Jin et al. (Eds.): ICA3PP 2007, LNCS 4494, pp. 231–241, 2007.

which arrives at the objective of grid computing, eliminating the information island and making all the heterogeneous resources work collaboratively. In this paper, we focus on data interoperation in grid environment.

For data interoperation in grid environment, it is necessary to consider the difference of the metadata format, data transfer mechanism, and data management mechanism. Fortunately, there are two main trends for data management in grid environment, SRB (*Storage Resource Broker*) [9] and SRM (*Storage Resource Management*) [10]. The project of GIN (*Grid Interoperation Now*) [13] is proposed at GGF16 and GIN-Data is a part of that project. GIN-Data divides the grid data management into two islands, SRB-island and SRM-island. The first step is to integrate every island each and then it integrates both of them. After that, users can transparently access data in different grids, without considering the issues of security, access mode, metadata format, and transfer protocol.

The scenario mentioned above sounds good. Users could use heterogeneous data resource under different grid platforms after single login into a grid platform. But the problem comes. The largest one is about performance. In multi-grid environment the performance of data access may greatly drop, because of the increased network cost and additional cost in access operation. The network cost can be decreased by some mechanisms in a single grid platform, such as replica, layered data storing strategy. But in a multi-grid environment, those mechanisms become complicated. It is difficult to unify all those mechanisms. In other words, the mechanism of performance optimization in a single grid platform should be modified to meet the requirements of multi-grid environment. Or the traditional performance optimization should work under the new optimization mechanism. The other problem is about response time. The cost sometimes may be insufferable which largely reduces the data transfer speed.

This paper introduces how to implement data interoperation between ChinaGrid and SRB, which is a part of the project of GIN-data. The SRB supports shared collections that can be distributed across multiple organizations and heterogeneous storage systems. Also SRB provides a hierarchical logical namespace to manage the organization of data. Data management is one of the core components in ChinaGrid [14]. It manages heterogeneous storage resources and data in grid environment. When a user sends a request to data manager for storing a set of data, data manager selects a proper storage resource to store the data set and in the meaning while, it also records the relevant metadata. When a user wants to fetch a set of data, data manager will find the relevant metadata according to the data identifier and return a best replica.

Although the mechanisms of the two systems are similar, the implementation methods are quite different. In order to attain the goal of data interoperation between the two grid systems, this paper divides data interoperation into two aspects: one is to implement the access from SRB to ChinaGrid; and the other is the issue about the access from ChinaGrid to SRB. Both of these two aspects change the two systems as little as possible and the end user of the two systems need not change anything about the operation custom.

This paper also considers the issues about performance optimization. As analyzed in the above paragraph, too simple implementation may lead disastrous and unacceptable results. The reason that causes sharp performance decrease mainly exists in the following two aspects: one is the increased network cost; and the other is about the additional service cost among different grid systems. This paper solves the performance problem from above two aspects.

The rest of this paper is organized as the following: the next section is about related work. Section 3 introduces the data interoperation design between SRB and ChinaGrid. Section 4 is about the performance optimization. Section 5 is performance evaluation. This paper is concluded in section 6.

2 Related Work

Grid Interoperability Project (GRIP) [11, 12], funded partly by the European Union (EU), is to realize the interoperation of Globus and UNICORE and to work towards standards for interoperation in the Global Grid Forum. The objectives of the project include: 1) to develop software to facilitate the interoperation of UNICORE and Globus combining the unique strength of each system; 2) to build and demonstrate bio-molecular and meteorological inter-grid applications; and 3) to contribute and influence international grid standards. Together, the three objectives will lead to proliferation of grids, global support for e-Science, faster advances in grid development through sharing of solutions, and wider acceptance of grid technology by industry based on proven standards.

GIN-Data [15], part of the GIN project, is exploring interoperability between grid data management infrastructures with an initial focus on: 1) point to point movement of data between storage in different grids; and 2) usage of managed resources and their more sophisticated APIs (e.g. SRM, SRB). GIN-Data divides the grid data management into two islands, SRB-island and SRM-island. The first step is to integrate every island each and then it integrates the two islands. The design principle of data management in ChinaGrid is much like that of SRB, so it stands on the island of SRB. This paper is about the issues of the design of the data interoperation between SRB and data management of ChinaGrid. Also it contains the performance tuning.

3 Data Interoperation Design

SRB presents the user with a single file hierarchy for data distributed across multiple storage systems. It has features to support the management, collaboration, controlled sharing, publication, replication, transfer, and preservation of distributed data. ChinaGrid also implements those functions, and the implementation mechanism is much like that of SRB. With a set of hierarchical metadata servers, ChinaGrid manages metadata for all data stored in ChinaGrid system in a centralized way. The structure of ChinaGrid data management is composed by a set of connected metadata servers at the top layer, and storage resources at the second layer which stores all the data in ChinaGrid. Although the implementation principle is similar, the detail is much different. Also it is required that the data interoperation design should not change anything about the main part of both SRB and ChinaGrid.

In order to attain the goal of data interoperation between ChinaGrid and SRB, we design the solution from two directions: access from SRB to ChinaGrid and from ChinaGrid to SRB. After adding a middle-layer constructer, the goal of transparent data interoperation between the two systems attains. The rest of this section describes the implement of data interoperation from such two directions.

3.1   Data Access from SRB to ChinaGrid

The function of SRB zone is provided. A single SRB zone can work well in wide area network environment, which collects a set of storage resources to establish a larger storage system. What's more, multiple zones can work collaboratively to compose a huge storage system. In the multi-zone SRB environment, it can intrinsically make all the SRB systems work collaboratively, guaranteeing the SRB software version, file transfer protocol, authentication and authorization mechanisms unified.

The implementation of data access from SRB to ChinaGrid is not as simple as the data interoperation among SRB systems, although their design principles are very similar. SRB supports many types of storage devices as its resource type, such as Linux file system, DB2. For each storage type, it provides a corresponding driver which manages real storage device for SRB. Linux file system is one of the supported storage resource types in SRB. The data interoperation design with the access from SRB to ChinaGrid utilizes that feature. In our design, we implement a special ChinaGrid data client, which is in charge of interacting with ChinaGrid server and returning results to SRB users. This special data client is implemented as a Linux kernel module, enhancing the VFS with mounting capabilities of ChinaGrid data management volume. It can mount data management component of ChinaGrid in Linux file system. The implementation is shown in Fig 1.

Through that we register the data space of ChinaGrid into SRB data space. After the operation of mounting, SRB considers this file system as a storage resource and registers the relevant metadata into SRB system, which forms a SRB zone. The problem of interoperation between SRB and ChinaGrid changed to the interoperation between one SRB zone and the other.

In our implementation, we do not change anything about SRB and ChinaGrid. We transparently implement the data interoperation with the access direction from SRB to ChinaGrid.

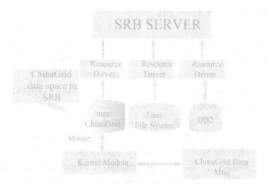

Fig. 1. ChinaGrid data space in SRB data space

3.2   Data Access from ChinaGrid to SRB

ChinaGrid is WSRF [16] compatible and all the interfaces to outside world are WSRF services. There exist three WSRF services for data management component of

ChinaGrid, which are *UserSpaceService*, *FileTransferService*, and *StorageResource-Service*. All the functions provided by ChinaGrid data management are operated through them, such as file transfer, file search. SRB provides a Java API, Jargon [18], for the access to SRB from outside world. For the access from ChinaGrid to SRB, middle-layer software is added into the ChinaGrid software building, where Jargon is embedded. There is no change about the main part of ChinaGrid.

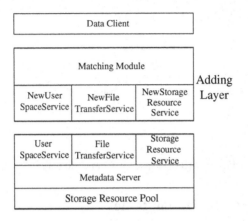

Fig. 2. Implementation of data interoperation from ChinaGrid to SRB

Fig. 2 describes how to implement the data interoperation for the access from ChinaGrid to SRB. The components of ChinaGrid data management is at the bottom of Fig. 2, including metadata servers and the storage resource pool. At the top of Fig. 2, the data client for end users accesses data resource in ChinaGrid. The middle layer of the software building is the added component which formerly does not exist in ChinaGrid software building. Three new WSRF services are in the adding layer. The functions of the new services are literally like that of ChinaGrid data management interface services. The Jargon APIs of SRB are embedded in the new three services.

Access to ChinaGrid is forwarded to the lower layer services, and access to SRB is performed through the Jargon APIs. So the new services can also handle the requests both to ChinaGrid and SRB, and they take over the task of the services in the bottom layer actually. Before the system initialized, the system registers the SRB data space into ChinaGrid data space. For example, a new subdirectory is added in the root of the data space, which is named with *SRBDataSpace*, as shown in Fig 3. So the view of SRB data space can be seen in ChinaGrid data space.

All the access requests from clients firstly arrive at the *Matching Module* at the top of the middle-layer, with the responsibility of judging which system the request accesses. The mechanism the matching module forwarding the request to which system is as the following: if it requests the data in the *SRBDataSpace* directory, it will access the SRB system; otherwise it will access data in ChinaGrid system. If it accesses ChinaGrid, the corresponding service of ChinaGrid data management is called; and if it is to SRB, the corresponding service in the middle-layer calls the Jargon API embedded in the middle-layer services which accesses SRB system and return the corresponding information. The middle layer attains the goal of data interoperation from

ChinaGrid to SRB. In order to synchronize the SRB data space in ChinaGrid, comparison may be performed periodically between the metadata of SRB data space in ChinaGrid and SRB. If they are different, new metadata will be registered into ChinaGrid. There is no modification in ChinaGrid and SRB, also the data space of the two systems are unified in ChinaGrid data space through the above methods.

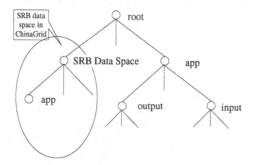

Fig. 3. SRB data space in ChinaGrid data space

4 Performance Optimization Issues

As analyzed in the first section, the performance of data interoperation between ChinaGrid and SRB will be sharply decreased according to the methods in the above section. The reasons which cause the performance decrease mainly exist at the following two aspects: one is the additional WSRF service cost; and the other is about the larger network cost than that in a single system. In this section, we propose two strategies to improve the performance about such two aspects respectively.

4.1 Service Cost Decrease

To reduce the service cost will decrease the response time. There are two types of operations in data interoperation, which are data operation and metadata operation. Both operations are accomplished through WRSF service, but the service cost has different effect on them. For data operation, data transfer is involved, so the service cost is much smaller than that of operation cost. For that reason, our strategy does not consider the type of data operation. For metadata operation, it is intolerant if the service cost is too large, because the cost of metadata operation is small and the service cost becomes the main part of the total cost.

In order to decrease the service cost, some static service instances are initialized before the system starts. The service initialization is the main cost of the entire service cost, so the initialized instances can decrease the total cost. Each instance can only handle one request at one time, and it may become the bottleneck if there are no enough service instances.

We consider the data interoperation system as a queuing system, where the server in the queuing system is the static service instance and the request from foreign system is the customer. Suppose that the request arrival ratio is λ in the time interval T_M = $[T-t, T]$, which means that the number of request arriving at the system is λ per second during T_M. The total cost of the operation, T_q, is divided into two parts: one is service time, represented as T_s, and the other is waiting time, represented as T_w. The total cost, represented as T_q, is the sum of T_s and T_w: $T_q = T_s + T_w$.

The service time is the cost the static instance spending to accomplish requested function. Given a value of λ, the service time, T_s is determined in the system for the type of metadata operation. The request may have to wait until one of the instances is idle. T_w refers to that duration. However, if the static instance, or the server in the queuing system, is not enough, T_w increases. That also makes T_q increases. In our design, the number of service instance, N, is a dynamic value. N changes according to the value of λ.

With a given N, the server utilization ratio, ρ, can be represented in formula 1 [17]. The server utilization ratio, ρ, describes the server's busy rate. We make a threshold for ρ, which is 70%, by default. In the following section, it gives the reason why we choose that value as the default threshold. When the value of ρ is larger than 70%, the number of service instance, N, is also increased. That operation decreases the value of ρ and makes it smaller than 70%. Through dynamically adjusting the number of static server instance, system can effectively decreases the waiting time, T_w. That also makes the total cost, T_q, decreases.

$$\rho = \lambda T_s / N \qquad (1)$$

4.2 Caching of Frequently Used Data

The second performance optimization aspect of grid data interoperation is to reduce the impact caused by the increase of logic instance between the two systems. The performance optimization design about this aspect aims at improving the data transfer speed between two grid systems. The main idea of the optimization design is to cache frequently used data in the system. In other words, if a data is frequently used by foreign grid system, it will be cached in the foreign grid system so that it may be not accessed through a long logic distance. In this paper, we use the PQ algorithm [19] to determine when to cache data stored in foreign grid system. Response time (T_{resp}) is the sum of service time (T_s), waiting time (T_w), and communication cost (T_c), that is $T_{resp} = T_s + T_w + T_c$. The response time threshold $T_{threshold}$ and two parameter P and Q ($Q>P$) are set, which control the degree of aggressiveness of cache. The process of cache creation takes the following steps:

(1) if $T_{resp} < T_{threshold}$, aborting cache creation, else go to (2);

(2) $\forall t \in P$, if $T_{resp} > T_{threshold}$ and $\dfrac{dT_{resp}}{dt} > 0$, go to (4), else go to (3);

(3) $\forall t \in Q$, if $T_{resp} > T_{threshold}$, then go to (4), else aborting cache creation;

(4) Caching the data from foreign grid system.

For the process of cache deletion, $\forall t \in P$, such that $T_{resp} < T_{threshold}$ and $\dfrac{dT_{resp}}{dt} < 0$, then the cache is to be deleted.

5 Experiments

The experiment environment includes two grid systems: one is ChinaGrid system, located at Tsinghua University, Beijing, China; and the other is SRB system, located at Huazhong University of Science and Technology, located at Wuhan, China. Two aspects of data interoperation are made: comparison of response time, and performance comparison of data transfer.

5.1 Comparison of Response Time

In this subsection, we compare the response time with different server utilization ratio, which are 0.6, 0.7, and 0.8, under different arrival rate, λ, which is from 1 to 128. As ρ increases, the total cost, T_q, also goes up. Fig. 4 shows the result of the comparison. As shown in the Fig.4, the difference of T_q is not very large with a small arrival rate. The total cost keeps on increasing with the increase of λ. The gap between $\rho=0.8$ and $\rho=0.7$ is much larger than that between $\rho=0.7$ and $\rho=0.6$ when λ arrives at a relative large value. The result shows that it may waste system resource when the value of ρ is smaller than 0.6. It may lead system busy when the value of ρ is larger than 0.8. So 0.7 may be the proper value for ρ.

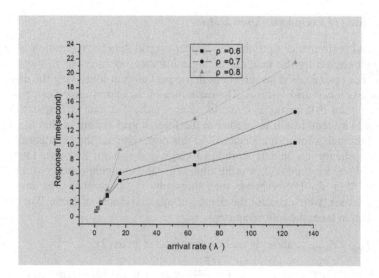

Fig. 4. Comparison of response time between different server utilization ratios

After choosing 0.7 as the default value for the threshold of ρ, we compare it with direct access. The metric of the comparison is response time and we get different response time under different arrival rate, which is from 1 to 128. The result is shown in Fig. 5, which indicates that the average response time of optimized methods with $\rho=0.7$ is 47% faster than direct access.

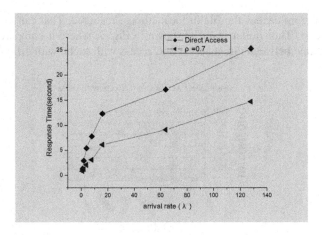

Fig. 5. Comparison of response time between direct access and ρ=0.7

5.2 Performance Comparison of Data Transfer

This subsection compares the cost of data operation when accessing a given piece of data between directly access and access with cache, where the *P/Q* ratio is 0.25. We randomly select a file, with the size of 10MB. The selected file is stored in ChinaGrid located at Tsinghua University, Beijing. We access the file through SRB system located at Huazhong University of Science and Technology, Wuhan. Through the interoperation, we access the file in ChinaGrid system under SRB. Here the cost for data transfer occupies a large part of the total cost and the service cost is just a tiny part. The result is shown in Fig. 6.

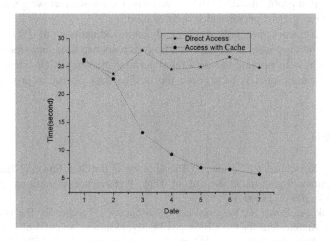

Fig. 6. Comparison of data transfer cost between direct access and access with cache

From it we can see that the file transfer time for directly accessing a remote file is stable, but the cost is expensive. However, to access a remote file with cache, the cost is also expensive at the beginning. However, as time goes on, the cost decreases. This is because system caches the file in local storage resource. That can largely decrease the access cost. The similar result is shown in Fig. 7, where it compares the average data access time between direct access and access with cache with different data size.

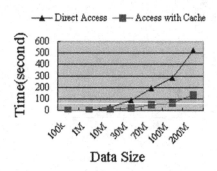

Fig. 7. Comparison of data transfer cost with different data size

6 Conclusion

This paper presents the grid data interoperation between ChinaGrid and SRB. It introduces how to implement transparent data access from ChinaGrid to SRB and from SRB to ChinaGrid, which attains the goal of grid data interoperation between those two grid systems. Performance may be the largest problem in grid data interoperation, and two main reasons leading the performance decrease are expensive service cost and increased logical instance. Two optimization strategies are proposed in order to resolve those two problems. From the experiment it is shown that we get a good result through the strategies of performance optimization.

In our future work, we will work on dynamic adjustment of P/Q ratio, which makes the cache algorithm more efficient both in response time and storage cost. We will work on how to operate the data interoperation between SRB-island and SRM-island. The ultimate goal is to propose the unified data operation protocol for grid computing.

References

1. Foster, I., Kesselman, C., Tuecke, S.: The Anatomy of the Grid: Enabling Scalable Virtual Organizations. International Journal of High Performance Computing and Applications 15(3), 200–222 (2001)
2. Chervenak, A., Foster, I., Kesselman, C., Salisbury, C., Tuecke, S.: The Data Grid: Towards an Architecture for the Distributed Management and Analysis of Large Scientific Data Sets. Journal of Network and Computer Applications 23(3), 187–200 (2001)
3. Rajasekar, A., Wan, M., Moore, R., Kremenek, G., Guptil. T.: Data Grids, Collections, and Grid Bricks. In: Proceedings of the 20th IEEE/NASA Conference on Mass Storage Systems and Technologies, San Diego, California, pp. 2–9 (2003)

4. Barish, B.C., Weiss, R.: LIGO and the Detection of Gravitational Waves. Physics Today 52(10), 44–50 (1999)
5. C.-E. Wulz: CMS – Concept and Physics Potential. In: Proceedings of First Tropical Workshop on Particle Physics and Cosmology, San Juan, Puerto Rico, pp. 467–478 (1998)
6. NVO (2004) http://www.us-vo.org
7. Globus, http://www.globus.org
8. Foster, I.: Globus Toolkit Version 4: Software for Service-Oriented Systems. In: Jin, H., Reed, D., Jiang, W. (eds.) NPC 2005. LNCS, vol. 3779, pp. 2–13. Springer, Heidelberg (2005)
9. Rajasekar, A., Wan, M., Moore, R., Schroeder, W., Kremenek, G., Jagatheesan, A., Cowart, C., Zhu, B., Chen, S., Olschanowsky, R.: Storage Resource Broker – Managing Distributed Data in a Grid. Computer Society of India Journal, Special Issue on SAN 33(4), 42–45 (2003)
10. SRM, http://sdm.lbl.gov/srm-wg
11. Menday, R., Wiede, P.: GRIP: The Evolution of UNICORE towards a Service-Oriented Grid. In: Proceedings of Cracow Grid Workshop, Cracow, Poland, pp. 142–150 (2003)
12. GRIP, http://www.grid-interoperability.org
13. GIN project, https://forge.gridforum.org/projects/mgi
14. Jin, H.: ChinaGrid: Making Grid Computing a Reality. In: Das, N., Sen, A., Das, S.K., Sinha, B.P. (eds.) International Collaboration and Cross-Fertilization. LNCS, vol. 3334, pp. 13–24. Springer, Heidelberg (2004)
15. GIN-Data, https://forge.gridforum.org/sf/wiki/do/viewPage/projects.gin/wiki/GINData
16. The Web Services Resource Framework, http://www.globus.org/wsrf
17. Harrison, P., Patel, N.M.: Performance Modeling of Communication Networks and Computer Architectures. Addison-Wesley Longman Publishing Co., Inc., Boston (1992)
18. SRB Jargon, http://www.sdsc.edu/srb/index.php/Jargon
19. Lee, B.-D., Weissman, J.B.: An Adaptive Service Grid Architecture Using Dynamic Replica Management. In: Goos, G., Hartmanis, J., wan Leeuwen, J. (eds.) GRID 2001. LNCS, vol. 2242, pp. 63–74. Springer, Heidelberg (2001)

Redundant Parallel File Transfer with Anticipative Recursively-Adjusting Scheme in Data Grids*

Chao-Tung Yang[1,**], Yao-Chun Chi[1], Tsu-Fen Han[1], and Ching-Hsien Hsu[2]

[1] High-Performance Computing Laboratory
Department of Computer Science and Information Engineering
Tunghai University, Taichung, 40704, Taiwan R.O.C
{ctyang,g932910,g942813}@thu.edu.tw
[2] Department of Computer Science and Information Engineering
Chung Hua University, Hsinchu 300, Taiwan
chh@chu.edu.tw

Abstract. The co-allocation architecture was developed to enable the parallel download of datasets/servers from selected replica servers, and the bandwidth performance is the main factor that affects the internet transfer between the client and the server. Therefore, it is important to reduce the difference of finished time among replica servers, and manage changeful network performance during the term of transferring as well. In this paper, we proposed an Anticipative Recursively-Adjusting Co-Allocation scheme, to adjust the workload of each selected replica server, which handles unwarned variant network performances of the selected replica servers. The algorithm is based on the previous finished rate of assigned transfer size, to anticipate that bandwidth status on next section for adjusting the workload, and further, to reduce file transfer time in a grid environment. Our approach is usefully in unstable gird environment, which reduces the wasted idle time for waiting the slowest server and decreases file transfer completion time.

1 Introduction

Heretofore, Grid research was mainly focused on the coordination of geographically distributed compute resources for high performance. Presently, the requests of collaborating and sharing huge amounts of widely distributed data are as important as sharing high-performance computes resources [1, 5, 6, 7, 8, 9, 12, 13, 14, 15, 16, 24, 25]. For the purpose of manipulating huge amount of data, which is depended on data file management systems to replicate files, manage files transfer and access distributed data. The Data Grid infrastructure integrates data storage devices and data management services into the grid environment, which consists of scattered computing and storage resources, perhaps located in different countries/regions that

---

* The work is supported in part by National Science Council, Taiwan R.O.C., under grant no. NSC95-2221-E-029-004 and NSC95-2218-E-007-025.
** Corresponding author.

H. Jin et al. (Eds.): ICA3PP 2007, LNCS 4494, pp. 242–253, 2007.

obtainable to users [8]. In Data Grid environment, large data sets are replicated and distributed to multiple datasets/servers. Since datasets/servers are significantly large in size, it leads to the problem of access efficiency.

Replicating popular content in distributing datasets/servers is widely used in practice [10, 12, 13]. Recently, in large-scale, data-sharing scientific communities such as [1, 5] also use the technology to replicate their large datasets over several sites. Downloading large datasets from any replica locations may result in varied performance rates because different replica sites may have different architectures, system load, and network connectivity. The quality of bandwidth is the most important factor that affects the internet transfer between a client and a server. The downloading speed is limited by the bandwidth traffic congestion in connecting the server and the client.

One of the methods uses replica selection techniques to determine the best replica location for improving the downloading speed [13]. This way of downloading datasets from single best server often results in ordinary transfer rates, because of the quality of bandwidth vary unpredictably from the shared nature of internet. Another way uses co-allocation [12] technology to download data. The co-allocation architecture was developed to enable the client to download data from multiple locations by establishing multiple connections in parallel. Therefore, it can improve the performance compared to the single server case and alleviates the internet congestion problem [12].

In previous work [2, 12], several co-allocation strategies are provided. There still exists a drawback of idle time: faster servers must wait for the slowest server to deliver the final block. In [2], may consume the network performance to transfer the same block repeatedly. Hence, it is important to reduce the difference of finished time between each selected replica server, and avert the bandwidth traffic congestion from transfer the same block in the link among the servers and the client.

In this paper, based on the architecture for co-allocation files transfer in Grid environment, we propose a dynamic co-allocation scheme, called Anticipative Recursively-Adjusting Co-Allocation. The algorithm adjusts continuously the workload of each selected replica server, which depends on the previous assigned transfer size finished rate, and further, to anticipate the bandwidth status on next section to adjust the workload. The method reduces the total idle time on awaiting the slowest server, simultaneously; improves the performance on file transfer. Our results demonstrate that the approach is superior to the previous methods.

In the rest part of this paper, we discuss about related work in Section 2. In section 3, we introduce the co-allocation architecture, and propose our approach in Section 4. Furthermore, we analyze the performances in Section 5. Finally, the conclusion is stated in Section 6.

2   Related Work

The co-allocation architecture is able to allow the client to download data from multiple locations in parallel through establishing multiple connections. Thus, it can improve the transference performance and alleviates the internet congestion problem. From the previous work, several co-allocation strategies have been presented.

We describe related work in the following, such as *Multi-Source Data Transfer (MSDT) algorithm* has been provided in [17] that proposes an efficient data replication algorithm for multi-source data transfer, whereby a data replica can be assembled in parallel from multiple distributed data sources and adapted to the variability of network bandwidths.

Tuned Conservative Scheduling technique in [25] is used to predict means and variances for network performance to make a decision of data selection. This stochastic scheduling technique adjusts the amount of data fetched on a link, which is related to the link performance and the expected variance in that performance.

In [12], the authors propose co-allocation architecture for co-allocating Grid data transfer across multiple connections by exploiting the partial copy feature of GridFTP. Some strategies have been supplied by author, such as Brute-Force, History-base and two Dynamic Load balancing techniques, conservative and aggressive for allocating data block.

- *Brute-Force Co-Allocation*: It works by dividing the file size equally among available flows. It does not address the bandwidth differences among the various client-server links.
- *History-based Co-Allocation*: The scheme keeps block sizes per flow proportional to predict transfer rates.
- *Conservative Load Balancing*: It divides requested datasets into k disjoint blocks of equal size. Available servers are allocated single blocks to deliver in parallel. The server is assigned to work in sequential one after another, until the requested files are downloaded completely. The loadings on the co-allocated flows are automatically adjusted because the faster servers will deliver larger portions of the file quickly.
- *Aggressive Load Balancing*: It adds functions that change block size deliveries by:
  1. gradually increasing the amounts of data requested from faster servers, and
  2. reducing the amounts of data requested from slower servers or stopping to request data from them altogether.

The co-allocation strategies described above do not handle the shortcoming of faster servers having to wait for the slowest server to deliver its final block. In most cases, this wastes much time and decreases overall performance. The technique in [2] is to bring up *Dynamic Co-allocation Scheme with Duplicate Assignments (DCDA)*. It neither uses predictions nor heuristics, instead of dynamically co-allocate with duplication assignments and coping up nicely with the changing speed performance of the servers.

The scheme develops an algorithm using circular queue, let D be the dataset, k be the number of blocks of a dataset of fixed block size, D is divided into k disjoint blocks of equal size and the every available server is assigned to deliver in parallel, when the requested block is received from a server, one of the unassigned blocks will be assigned to the server. Co-allocator repeats this process until all the blocks of a dataset are assigned. The schemes tackle even when the link to servers under consideration is broken or becomes idle.

The *Dynamic Co-allocation Scheme with Duplicate Assignments (DCDA)* has the fault in consume the network performance to transfer the same block repeatedly. This wastes much network performance, and easy to cause the bandwidth traffic jam in the link the server and client.

In our previous work [3, 18, 19, 20, 21, 22, 23, 24], we discuss a dynamic co-allocation scheme, namely *Recursively-Adjusting Co-Allocation scheme*, to improve the performance of file transfer in Data Grids. Our approach can reduce the idle time spent waiting for the slowest server and decreases file transfer completion time. Also, it provides an effective scheme for reducing the cost of reassembling data blocks. Considering the potential effect of servers broken/idle status during the transfer, we propose an efficient approach called *Anticipative Recursively-Adjusting Co-Allocation* extended from *Recursively-Adjusting Co-Allocation* scheme [20].

It provides to control of variant network performances of the selected replica servers, which is according to the previous assigned transfer size finished rate, to anticipate the bandwidth status on next section for adjust the workload on next section of each selected replica server. As the result, it improves overall transfer performance by the method of *Anticipative Recursively-Adjusting Co-Allocation* that can monitors the network performances of the selected replica servers, then continuous adjusting the workload of each selected replica server, and reduces wasted idle time for waiting the slowest server, and decreases file transfer completion time.

3   Co-allocation Architecture

In this study we used the grid middleware Globus Toolkit [11] as the data grid infrastructure. The Globus Toolkit provides solutions for such considerations as security, resource management, data management, and information services. One of its primary components is MDS [6, 9, 11, 22], which is designed to offer a standard mechanism for discovering and publishing resource status and configuration information. It supplies a uniform and flexible interface for data collected by lower-level information providers in two modes: static (e.g., OS, CPU types, and system architectures) and dynamic data (e.g., disk availability, memory availability, and loading).

In this research, we use GridFTP [1, 9, 11] to enable parallel file transfers. GridFTP is a high-performance, secure, reliable data transfer protocol optimized for high-bandwidth wide-area networks. Among its many features are security, parallel streams, partial file transfers, third-party transfers, and reusable data channels. Its partial file transfer ability allows files to be retrieved from data datasets/servers by specifying the start and end offsets of file sections.

As datasets are replicated within Grid environments for reliability and performance, clients require the abilities to discover existing data replicas, and create and register new replicas. A Replica Location Service (RLS) [4] provides a mechanism for discovering and registering existing replicas. Several prediction metrics have been developed to help replica selection. For instance, Vazhkudai and Schopf [14, 15, 16] used past file transfer histories to estimate current file transfer throughputs. In our previous work [19, 20], we proposed a replica selection cost model and a replica selection service to perform replica selection. Figure 1 shows the co-allocation of Grid file transfers [12], which extends from the basic template for resource management [7] provided by Globus Toolkit.

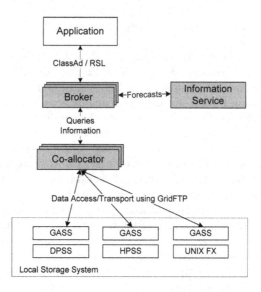

Fig. 1. Co-Allocation architecture in data grid

The co-allocation of Grid file transfers [12], which extends from the basic template for resource management [7] provided by Globus Toolkit. The architecture comprises of three main components: an information service, broker/co-allocator, and local storage systems. An application specifies the characteristics of the desired data and passes this attribute description to a broker. The broker queries the available resource and the replica locations from information services [6] and replica management services [11]. Then it gets a list of physical locations for the desired files. In our work, we pass the candidate replica locations to a replica selection service [11] which we develop in the previous work [5]. Our replica selection service provides estimates of candidate transfer performance based on our cost model and chooses the appropriate amounts of a better location. Then the co-allocator downloads the data in parallel from these selected replica servers.

4 Our Approach

4.1 Assumptions

We outline the assumptions for our system design model and list as following:

1. Replica selection server provides the better replica datasets/servers list to transfer the data file. Once some of the selected replica datasets/servers are taken, they enable to access during the co-allocator downloads the data in parallel.
2. The non-selected replica candidate servers are permitted to use when the co-allocator needs transmission.

3. The process is not obvious in the experiment of performing the co-allocation algorithm (the operation time).
4. The time in transferring processes of stopping or assigning to the selected replica server is negligible.

4.2 Anticipative Recursively-Adjusting Scheme

Anticipative Recursive-Adjustment Co-Allocation by means of continuous adjusting the workload of each selected replica server, which measures the actual bandwidth performance during the term of transferring data file, and according to the previous assigned transfer size finished rate anticipates bandwidth status at next transfer section, to regulate the workload on next section.

The basic idea is to assign less data on selected replica server with performance of a greater variability network link. In other words, for a link with more variable bandwidth, effective bandwidth will be smaller, and the finished rate of the previous assigned transfer size would be smaller as well. The goal is to make the expected finished time of each server to be the same. Our approach provides nicely tactics, even when the link to selected replica servers is broken or become idleness. Besides, it reduces the wasted idle time for waiting the slowest server finished the transfer job.

As an appropriate file section is selected, first step divides it into proper block sizes according to the respective server bandwidths and the previous assigned file size to transfer finished rate. Initially, the finished rate is set 1. Next, the co-allocator assigns the blocks to selected replica servers for transfer. At this moment, it is expected that the transfer finished time will be consistent with $E(t_1)$. However, server bandwidths may fluctuate during segment deliveries, actual completion time may be dissimilar to expected time $E(t_1)$ (solid line, in Figures 2 and 3). Once the quickest server finishes its work at time t_1, the next step is to measure the size of unfinished transfer blocks (italic block, in Figures 2 and 3) to infer the finished rate.

There were two kinds of statuses, one is the quickest server finished time t_1 that is greater than or equal to expected time $E(t_1)$. We could calculate the different transferred size between expected time and actual completion time (italic block in Figure 2). The other status is the quickest server finished time t_1 less than expected time $E(t_1)$. We would reckon up the block size which did not transferred between the earliest and the expected time (italic block in Figure 3).

In status one, the performance of the network link was non-changed or had been poorer during transferring term, so that we measured the difference in transferred size between expected and actual completion time.

In status two, the quickest server finished time t_1 is faster than expected time $E(t_1)$. It is likely on account of the excessively pessimistic anticipated the network performance, or the replica server network links in performance had become better in the course of transfer. After that, we gauged the non-transferred size between the earliest time and the expected time. If we anticipated the network performance that is pessimistic excessively in the previous transferred time, it was adjusted in the next section.

The next section is to assign proper block sizes to the servers along with respective bandwidths and the previous finished rate. It allows each server to finish its assigned workload by the expected time at $E(t_2)$. These adjustments are repeated until the entire file transfer finished.

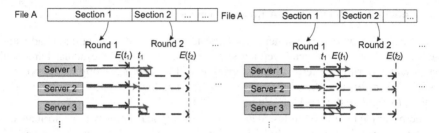

Fig. 2. The adjustment process(later than expected time)

Fig. 3. The adjustment process(earlier than expected time)

When user asked and downloaded the file A in the Data Grid environment, the replica selection server will respond with the subset of all available servers defined by the maximum performance datasets/servers. The datasets/servers are for the co-allocator selected to transfer the file, and then start to transfer the target file from some selected replica datasets/servers.

Assuming n replica servers are selected, Si denotes server i such that $1 \leq i \leq n$. A connection for file downloading is then built to each server. The Anticipative Recursively-Adjusting Co-Allocation process is shown as follows. A new section of a file to be allocated is first defined. The section size,

$$SEj = (UnassignedFileSize + Total UnfinishedFileSize) \times \alpha \,(0 < \alpha < 1) \tag{1}$$

Where SEj denotes the section j such that $1 \leq j \leq k$, assuming we allocate k times for the download process, and there are k sections, while Tj denotes the time section j allocated. *UnassignedFileSize* is the portion of file A not yet distributed for downloading; initially, *UnassignedFileSize* is equal to the total size of file A, and *Total UnfinishedFileSize* is equal to zero in first round. α is the rate that determines how much of the section remains to be assigned.

In the next step, SEj is divided into several blocks and assigned to n servers. Each server has a real-time transfer rate to the selected replica server of Bji. rj_{-1} denotes the server transfer finished rate of previous assigned file size to deliver, which the initial value is 1. The block size per flow from SEj for each server i at time Tj is Sji:

$$Sji = SEji \times (Bji \times rj_{-1}i) \bigg/ \sum_{i=1}^{n}(Bji \times rj_{-1}i)\,(0 \leq rj_{-1}i) \tag{2}$$

$$Bj = \sum_{i=1}^{n}(Bji \times rj_{-1}i) \tag{3}$$

$$ETji = Sji \big/ Bji \tag{4}$$

This fulfills our requirement to minimize the time which faster servers must wait for the slowest server to finish. In some cases, network variations greatly degrade transfer rates, a faster channel finishes its assigned data blocks at real finished time RTj_i may later or earlier than expected time ETj_i, TSj_i denotes the actually transfer size at the real finished time RTj_i is:

$$TSji = Bji \times RTji \tag{5}$$

$$rji = \frac{TSji}{Sji} \tag{6}$$

If the first finished time of $RTji$ is earlier than expected time $ETji$, the reason may be the excessively pessimistic anticipated the network performance, or the network links in performance had become better in the course of transfer. We have compared with the block size transferred between the earliest time and the expected time of each selected server. If the transferred size $TSji$ is greater than expected size Sji at first finished time, the rji is tantamount to 1; else the first finished time of $RTji$ may be the network link in performance that was non-changed or had been poorer during transferring term.

$$rji = \begin{cases} \frac{TSji}{Sji}, & RTji \geq ETji \\ 1, & RTji < ETji, and\ TSji \geq Sji \end{cases} \tag{7}$$

Then the co-allocator measures the bandwidth performance of each server, and anticipates bandwidth status at next transfer section for adjusting the workflow at next session; at the same time, it eliminates the *unfinishedfilesize* at the servers in advance. The *unfinishedfilesize* will be summed up and assigned to the next section. After allocation, all selected replica servers still continue to transfer data blocks. When a faster selected replica server finishes its assigned data blocks, the co-allocator begins allocating an unassigned section of file A again. The process of allocating data blocks is continued to adjust workflow until the entire file has been allocated.

4.3 Algorithm

We list the algorithm in the following:

[Initialization]
  Define new section to be allocated

  $SEj = (UnassignedFileSize + \text{Total } UnfinishedFileSize) \times \alpha \ (0 < \alpha < 1)$

[Allocation of blocks to the selected servers]
Loop when (The *UnassignedFileSize* and Total *UnfinishedFileSize* are greater then zero)
{
  If (The *UnassignedFileSize* and Total *UnfinishedFileSize* are greater then Total Enabled
      Transfer Bandwidth) then

  {

      Define new section to be allocated

      $SEj = (UnassignedFileSize + \text{Total } UnfinishedFileSize) \times \alpha \ (0 < \alpha < 1)$

  }

Else

{

Define final section

SEj = the *UnassignedFileSize* + Total *UnfinishedFileSize*

}

Step 1.Define new section to be allocated SEj

Step 2 Monitor every selection replica server

Step 3 Allocate blocks to each selected replica server,

According to the Bandwidth of the selected replica server Bji, and the Previous Finished Rate rj_{-1} of the selected replica server (Initial $r0 = 1$)

Step 4 Monitor each download flow

When (the fastest flow finishes its assigned data blocks) then

{

If (the first finished time of $RTji$ is earlier than the expected time $ETji$ and the transferred size $TSji$ is greater than the expected size Sji) then

{the $rji = 1$;}

Else

{Measure the finished rate of the previous assigned file size to deliver ($0 \leq rji \leq 1$)}

}

} End Loop;

5   Experimental Results and Analyses

In this section we discuss the performance of our Anticipative Recursive-Adjustment Co-Allocation. We evaluate different co-allocation schemes: (1) Brute-Force (Brute), (2) History-based (History), (3) Conservative Load Balancing (Conservative), (4) Dynamic Co-allocation Scheme with Duplicate Assignments (DCDA) and (5) Anticipative Recursively-Adjusting Co-Allocation (Anticipative). After that, we analyze the performance of each scheme by comparing their finished transfer time that faster servers awaiting slower servers to finish delivering the last block. We defined α to 0.5 and used different file sizes as 500MB, 1GB, 1.5GB, and 2GB. For an objective comparison, we used equal block numbers (the number of blocks is 10) above to calculate the performance of each size when using the Conservative Load Balancing and Dynamic Co-allocation Scheme with Duplicate Assignments. In

In the example, we assume the client can fetch a file from four selected replica servers which the network link performances had broken or become idleness. The network status has shown in Figure 4. We used the same condition for this example. In Figure 5, we show the completion time of each scheme that transfers different file size. And in Figure 6, we evaluate the total waiting idle time based on various file sizes which the network link performances had broken or become idleness. When the Network link performances had broken or become idleness, it would take more idle time. By contrast, there were almost no wasted time to wait for broken or idle servers in the (DCDA) and (Anticipative). Perceptibly, it shows that our approach improves the performance efficiently compared with the other schemes.

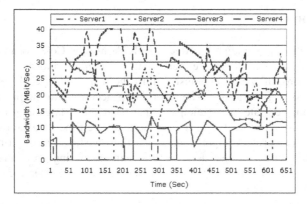

Fig. 4. The network variation (which had broken or become idleness) between client and servers

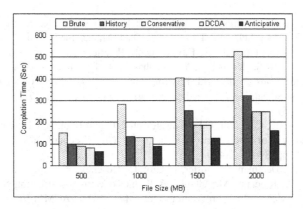

Fig. 5. Completion time of different methods which are the network link performance had broken or idled

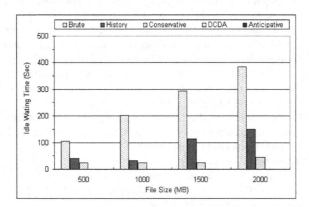

Fig. 6. Idle waiting time of different methods which are the network link performance had broken or idled

6 Conclusion

In this research, the Anticipative Recursively-Adjusting Co-Allocation scheme is proposed to improve the file transfer performances on the co-allocation architecture in [14]. In our approach, we continuously adjust the workload of each selected replica server in process of file transfer. The algorithm is according to the previous assigned transfer size finished rate, and anticipates that bandwidth status adjust the workload on the next section. The goal is to reduce the total idle time on awaiting the slowest server, after that improve the performance on file transfer. The experimental results show the effectiveness of our new technique in improving the transfer time and reduce the total idle time in awaiting the slowest server even when the link to servers are broken or become idle.

References

1. Allcock, B., Bester, J., Bresnahan, J., Chervenak, A., Foster, I., Kesselman, C., Meder, S., Nefedova, V., Quesnel, D., Tuecke, S.: Data Management and Transfer in High-Performance Computational Grid Environments. Parallel Computing 28, 749–771 (2002)
2. Bhuvaneswaran, R.S., Katayama, Y., Takahashi, N.: Dynamic Co-allocation Scheme for Parallel Data Transfer in Grid Environment. In: Proceedings of First International Conference on Semantics, Knowledge, and Grid (SKG 2005), vol. 17, IEEE CS Press, Los Alamitos (2005)
3. Chen, C.H., Yang, C.T., Lai, C.L.: Towards an Efficient Replica Selection for Data Grid, In: Proceedings of the First Workshop on Grid Technologies and Applications (WoGTA'04) pp. 89–94 (2004)
4. Chervenak, A., Deelman, E., Foster, I., Guy, L., Hoschek, W., Iamnitchi, A., Kesselman, C., Kunszt, P., Ripeanu, M.: Giggle: A Framework for Constructing Scalable Replica Location Services. In: Proceedings of the 2002 ACM/IEEE conference on Supercomputing, pp. 1–17 (2002)
5. Chervenak, A., Foster, I., Kesselman, C., Salisbury, C., Tuecke, S.: The Data Grid: Towards an Architecture for the Distributed Management and Analysis of Large Scientific Datasets. Journal of Network and Computer Applications 23, 187–200 (2001)
6. Czajkowski, K., Fitzgerald, S., Foster, I., Kesselman, C.: Grid Information Services for Distributed Resource Sharing. In: Proceedings of the Tenth IEEE International Symposium on High-Performance Distributed Computing (HPDC-10'01), pp. 181–194 (2001)
7. Czajkowski, K., Foster, I., Kesselman, C.: Resource Co-Allocation in Computational Grids. In: Proceedings of the Eighth IEEE International Symposium on High Performance Distributed Computing (HPDC-8'99) (1999)
8. Hoschek, W., Jaen-Martinez, J., Samar, A., Stockinger, H., Stockinger, K.: Data Management in an International Data Grid Project. In: Proceedings of the First IEEE/ACM International Workshop on Grid Computing (2000)
9. Open Grid Forum, http://www.ogf.org
10. Stockinger, H., Samar, H., Allcock, A., Foster, B., Holtman, I., B., T.: File and Object Replication in Data Grids. Journal of Cluster Computing 5, 305–314 (2002)
11. The Globus Alliance, http://www.globus.org
12. Vazhkudai, S.: Enabling the Co-Allocation of Grid Data Transfers. In: Proceedings of Fourth International Workshop on Grid Computing, pp. 44–51(2003)

13. Vazhkudai, S., Tuecke, S., Foster, I.: Replica Selection in the Globus Data Grid. In: Proceedings of the 1st International Symposium on Cluster Computing and the Grid (CCGRID'01) pp. 106–113 (2001)
14. Vazhkudai, S., Schopf, J.M.: Using Regression Techniques to Predict Large Data Transfers. International Journal of High Performance Computing Applications 17, 249–268 (2003)
15. Vazhkudai S., Schopf, J.M.: Predicting Sporadic Grid Data Transfers. In: Proceedings of 11th IEEE International Symposium on High Performance Distributed Computing (HPDC-11'02) pp. 188–196 (2002)
16. Vazhkudai, S., Schopf, J.M., Foster I.: Predicting the Performance of Wide Area Data Transfers. In: Proceedings of the 16th International Parallel and Distributed Processing Symposium (IPDPS'02) pp. 34–43 (2002)
17. Wang, C.M., Hsu, C.C., Chen, H.M., Wu, J.J.: Efficient Multi-Source Data Transfer in Data Grids. In: Proceedings of the Sixth IEEE International Symposium on Cluster Computing and the Grid (CCGRID'06) pp. 421–424 (2006)
18. Yang, C.T., Yang, I.H., Chen, C.H.: Improve Dynamic Adjustment Mechanism in Co-Allocation Data Grid Environments. In: Proceedings of the 11th Workshop on Compiler Techniques for High-Performance Computing (CTHPC-11'05) pp. 189–194 (2005)
19. Yang, C.T., Chen, C.H., Li, K.C., Hsu, C.H.: Performance Analysis of Applying Replica Selection Technology for Data Grid Environments. In: Hurd, J., Melham, T. (eds.) TPHOLs 2005. LNCS, vol. 3603, pp. 278–287. Springer, Berlin Heidelberg New York (2005)
20. Yang, C.T., Yang, I.H., Li, K.C., Hsu, C.H.: A Recursive-Adjustment Co-Allocation Scheme in Data Grid Environments. LNCS, vol. 3719, pp. 40–49. Springer-Verlag, Heidelberg (2005)
21. Yang, C.T., Yang, I.H., Li, K.C., Wang, S.Y.: Improvements on Dynamic Adjustment Mechanism in Co-Allocation Data Grid Environments. The Journal of Supercomputing (2007)
22. Yang, C.T., Yang, I.H., Chen, C.H., Wang, S.Y.: Implementation of a Dynamic Adjustment Mechanism with Efficient Replica Selection in Co-Allocation Data Grid Environments. In: Proceedings of the 21st Annual ACM Symposium on Applied Computing (SAC 2006) - Distributed Systems and Grid Computing (DSGC) Track, 1, pp. 797–804 (2006)
23. Yang, C.T., Wang, S.Y., Lin, C.H., Lee, M.H., Wu, T.Y.: Cyber-Transformer: A Toolkit for Files Transfer with Replica Management in Data Grid Environments. In: Proceedings of the Second Workshop on Grid Technologies and Applications (WoGTA'05) pp. 73–80 (2005)
24. Yang, C.T., Wang, S.Y., Fu, C.P.: A Dynamic Adjustment Mechanism for Data Transfer in Data Grids. In: Proceeding of the third IFIP International Conference on Network and Parallel Computing (NPC2006) pp. 110–120 (2006)
25. Yang, L., Schopf, J.M., Foster, I.: Improving Parallel Data Transfer Times Using Predicted Variances in Shared Networks. In: Proceedings of the fifth IEEE International Symposium on Cluster Computing and the Grid (CCGrid'05) vol. 2, pp. 734–742 (2005)

A Strategy-Proof Combinatorial Auction-Based Grid Resource Allocation System

Yi Liang[1], Jianping Fan[2], Dan Meng[2], and Ruihua Di[1]

[1] Gird and distributed Computing Lab, Beijing University of Technology
National Research Center for Intelligent Computing System
[2] Institute of Computing Technology, Chinese Academy of Sciences
yliang@bjut.edu.cn, fan@ict.ac.cn, md@ncic.ac.cn

Abstract. In this paper, we introduce a strongly strategy-proof combinatorial auction-based grid resource allocation system, called PheonixMarket. The key advantages of PheonixMarket are that it makes the scheduling with the time-varying job value information; guarantees the combinatorial allocation of heterogeneous resources, incents users to reveal true value information of their jobs, encourages users to contribute their redundant resources and avoids exceeding resource use by the baleful users. In the performance experiments, the economic efficiency of PheonixMarket is analyzed. We then measure the price sensitivity of PheonixMarket and make the load balance experiment based on its price 'signal'. Finally, the issue of taking the funding as a form of priority is measured in the experiments.

Keywords: Grid, Resource allocation, Combinatorial Auction, Accounting.

1 Introduction

A key advantage of the grid is its ability to pool together shared computational resources, data storage and computer networks among communities distributed across the world known as virtual organizations [1]. The key challenges for resource allocation in grids are the strategic users who have diverse jobs and objectives, and try to maximize their own interest; and the heterogeneous resources, which are physically and administratively distributed [1, 2]. In grids, diverse jobs have different and time-varying values to their users. For example, a typical pharmacy company has jobs, such as the medical ingredient calculation, image simulations, history data statistic, etc. Some of these are critical to the business and some provide benefits, but are not critical. The medical ingredient calculation may benefit the company more, if it starts sooner. However, the job value information isn't typically known a priori. Traditional resource allocation scheme fails in such environment since it either treats all job values as the same or cannot prevent strategic users from overprizing their jobs, when the contention for resources increases [3]. On the other hand, incentive policies are lacking in the traditional resource allocation to encourage the reluctant organizations to contribute their surplus resources in grids [2,3].

H. Jin et al. (Eds.): ICA3PP 2007, LNCS 4494, pp. 254–266, 2007.
© Springer-Verlag Berlin Heidelberg 2007

The approach taken here is to incorporate economic mechanisms into the resource allocation system. They are better than the traditional resource allocation schemes because they are decentralized in structure, motivate users to reveal the true job value, promote the contribution of surplus resources, and meet the multiple objectives of end users by optimizing the aggregated user job value [1, 2].

Several economic-based resource management systems, such as Contract/Net, Spawn, Nimrod-G, G-Commerce, Popcon and etc, [3,4, 5, 6, 7, 8, 9, 10, 11, 12,18] have provided the effectiveness of economic-based mechanisms in the resource allocation. Due to the limitation of the space, details will not be described. In this paper, we focus on both issues of the combinatorial allocation of heterogeneous resources and incentive for users to reveal the true job value, (that is, in economic terms, strongly strategy-proofness) in an economic-based grid resource allocation system. We consider these two issues as the preconditions of the allocation efficiency in the economic manner since strategic users have multiple resource demand and will maximize their profits in their own interests. Previous works mainly focus the strategy-proofness study on the homogenous resource allocation [11, 12, 13, 14, 19, 20]. The past research on the combinatorial allocation mainly focuses on the expression of resource preference with the static job value information and tries to find the approximate optimization [10, 11, 15, 16, 17].

This paper presents the PhoenixMarket, a market-based resource allocation system for grids. PhoenixMarket can support users to express the time-varying job value information on submitting the requirement for multiple heterogeneous resources, incent users to reveal the true job value information and encourage users to provide their surplus resources.

Contributions of PheonixMarket are the followings:

✓   Propose a resource bidding model with the expression of job value function. With this model, the time-varying job value information can be scheduling-aware, which improves the scheduling efficiency.

✓   Present a combinatorial auction-based resource scheduling strategy, called HtRAA (Heterogeneous Resource Aggregating Allocation). We prove that HtRAA is strongly strategy-proof, that is, revealing the true job value is the only dominant strategy of HtRAA, which guarantees the economic efficiency of the resource scheduling. Experiment results show that HtRAA achieves higher economic efficiency than the introduced strategy-proof economic mechanisms in the previous grid resource scheduling systems.

✓   Propose the close-looped virtual currency use mode and the LOPI (Limited Output Periodic Input) funding and accounting model. The close-looped use of virtual currency encourages users to contribute their surplus resources. The funding can be taken as a form of priority and help the system to control the resource sharing among users. The LOPI funding and accounting model prevents the baleful and exceeding resource use happened in the traditional peer-to-peer system.

The paper is structured as follows. Section 2 presents the related work. Section 3 gives out the architecture of PhoenixMarket, In section 4 to section 6, the new resource requirement model, the HtRAA scheduling strategy and the virtual currency and the LOPI funding and accounting model are discussed in detail. Section 7 presents the experiment and analysis. In section 8, we draw conclusions and present future research directions.

2 The Overview of PheonixMarket

Figure 1 demonstrates the overview of the architecture of PheonixMarket. The main participants in PheonixMarket are: User agents (UA), Grid Resource Allocation Center (GRAC) and Grid Resource Provider Agent (GRPA).

User Agent (UA): Each grid user has a User Agent. The User Agent is responsible for resource and account information query (by ***resource & account discovery agent***), including the resource information, the history prices of resources and the user account information, submitting the resource bidding information to the Market Center(by ***bidding agent***), and job creation, submission and monitoring (by ***job management agent***).

Grid Resource Provider Agent (GRPA): Each grid resource provider has a Grid Resource Provider Agent. The Grid Resource Provider Agent is responsible for posting the GSP's characteristics, including the dynamic and static resource information, on the Resource Information Center (by ***resource posting agent***), executing and monitoring jobs from user agents (by ***local resource scheduler***).

Grid Resource Allocation Center (GRAC): GRAC is the essential part of PheonixMarket. It is responsible for collecting and providing the resource information (by ***resource information center***), market-based resource scheduling (by ***market center***), funding and charging the users for services (by ***account center***).

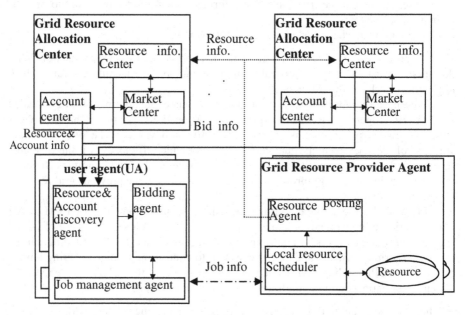

Fig. 1. The overview of the architecture of PheonixMarket

Compared to the traditional grid resource allocation systems, the key issues of a market-based resource allocation system are:

✓ How to support users to bid resource (*bidding agent*).
✓ How to design the scheduling strategy based on the efficient market mechanism (*market center*).
✓ How to design the resource funding and accounting policy (*account center*).

3 Resource Bidding Model in PheonixMarket

3.1 The Time-Dependent Job Value

All users have some notion of value when running jobs on a grid. In a market-based system, such value can be measured with the currency. The job value expresses the importance of a job, and it is time-dependent. The value has both a magnitude, which expresses the importance, and a rate of delay, which reflects users' sensitivity to delay. Thus the job value in grids can be defined as following:

$$V = v\,(I,\,t) \qquad (1)$$

I: the original importance of the job
t: times that a job has been scheduled in the queue

In a market-based system, such value can be viewed as the valuation of resources being contented for. Thus, in grid systems, the resource bidding model needs to express both the original magnitude and the delay rate of a job values, so that the scheduler can resort the job queue and guarantee the higher-valued job to be scheduled in priority.

3.2 The Resource Bidding Model in PhoenixMarket

With the consideration of the time-varying job value, the resource bidding model in PhoenixMarket is constructed as follows:

$b =(\ \{r_1,\ r_2,\ \bullet\ \bullet\ \bullet\ ,r_m\},\ \{q_1,\ q_2,\ \bullet\ \bullet\ \bullet\ ,\ q_m\},\ I,\ td,\ \{(ts_1,\ vu_1(t)),\ (\ ts_2\ ,$
$v_2(t)),\ \bullet\ \bullet\ \bullet\ ,(ts_n, v_n(t))\ \})$

Where we define the variables as follows:
$R = \{R_1, R_2, \bullet\ \bullet\ \bullet, R_n\}$, the global resources set;
t_d is the deadline of the job; I is the original value of the job;
For each r_i in $\{r_1, r_2, \bullet\ \bullet\ \bullet, r_m\}$, $r_i \in R$;
For each q_i in $\{q_1, q_2, \bullet\ \bullet\ \bullet, q_m\}$, $q_i \geq 1$, is the total number of resource r_i required;
for each $(ts_i, v_j(t))$ in $\{(ts_1, v_1(t)), (\ ts_2\ ,\ v_2(t)), \bullet\ \bullet\ \bullet, (ts_n, v_n(t))\ \}$, indicates the time-varying job value information in the time interval $[ts_i, ts_{i+1}]$. $v_i(t)$ is the job value function. The maximal of ts_{i+1} will be t_d.

However, due to the diversity of the job value function ($v_i(t)$), PheonixMarket provides an additional module to support users to transform the value function into a *Taylor polynomial*. With the *Taylor polynomial*, users can transform their job value functions with the desired precisions, and thus the grammar of the job value information surmounts the impediment of the unexpectedly diverse expression of the job valuation function.

4 HtRAA — The Scheduling Strategy in PheonixMarket

In this section, we discuss features that the market-based resource scheduling strategy need to be endowed according to the characteristic of resources and jobs in grids and then present the scheduling strategy based on a strongly strategy-proof combinatorial auction.

4.1 Features of a Market-Based Resource Scheduling Strategy

Ian Foster summary the characteristic of grids [1]: *physically and administratively distributed, dynamic and heterogeneous.* We argue that jobs in grids have the following characteristics:

✓ *The incomplete job value information.* This is due to that users in grids are strategic and come from different virtual organizations.
✓ *The time-dependent job value information.* This is discussed in Section 4.1.
✓ *Need of the combinatorial allocation of the heterogeneous required resources in the scheduling.* This is due to that obtaining partial of the required resources will cause the job lower performance or even not running.

Characteristics of resources and jobs in girds ask for the following features that the market-based scheduling strategy should provide:

✓ *Incentive for the strategic users to reveal their true job value information.* It is the prerequisite for the scheduling efficiency in a market-based grid scheduling system. In economic terms, the mechanism needs to be *strongly strategy-proof,* that is, revealing the true value information is the only dominant strategy of users. With the only dominant strategy, the rational users will reveal their true job value when they pursuing their own objects and thus the global economic efficiency will be guaranteed by scheduling with the true value information.
✓ *The little communication iteration and the low network overload.* This is because of 1) the physically distributed resource buyers / sellers on the wide-area unreliable network, 2) users' sensitivity to the time-dependent job value varying.
✓ *Trade-off between the computationally efficiency and the economic efficiency.* This is also due to the time-decaying job value. Hence, too much time spent in the single scheduling round may cause the long-term revenue of all the jobs reduced in such batch scheduling system.
✓ *The combinatorial allocation of the heterogeneous required resources in the scheduling.* This is due to the heterogeneity of grid resources and the requirement of users in the resource allocation.

4.2 HtRAA Scheduling Strategy

First, we give out the definition in the strategy.

Definition 1: Average resource bidding for each job, the average resource bidding can be defined as following:

$$avg_i = b_i \bigg/ \sum_{j=1}^{n} q_{ij} \qquad (2)$$

b_i: the bidding of user job i in a scheduling round;

q_{ij}: the total number of resources with type j required by user job i;

HtRAA scheduling strategy can be described as follows:

HtRAA scheduling strategy:

1. Sort all bids from user jobs with the highest the first according to the **average resource bidding**; and generate the user job bid list $(U_1, U_2, \cdots, U_k)$,

2. Sort all resources according to resource types and generate the global resource set $(R_1, R_2, \cdots, R_n)$,

3. Set *Alloced* as the set of the bids that are satisfied in the allocation, set *Unalloced* as the set of the bids that are not satisfied in the allocation. Initialize both *Alloced* and *Unalloced* as NULL.

4. Loop on the sorted user job bid list, For each bid U_i, check the following conditions:

   1) $\forall j, \left(Q_j - \sum_{u_k \in Alloced} q_{kj} - q_{ij} \geq 0 \right) \quad 1 \leq j \leq n$

      Q_j: *the total number of resources with type j;*

   2) $avg_i \geq$ reserve price

   If the above conditions satisfied, put U_i into *Alloced*, else put it into *Unalloced*.

5. For each Ui in *Alloced*, do the following:

   i) Find the user job bid in *UnAlloced*, which satisfies the following condition:

   $\exists j, \left(\left(q_{ij} + q_{kj} + \sum_{u_i \in Alloced, l \neq i, l \neq k} q_{lj} \right) > Q_j \right) \wedge$

   $\left(\left(q_{ij} + \sum_{u_i \in Alloced, l \neq i, l \neq j} q_{lj} \right) \leq Q_j \right) \wedge$

   $\left(\left(q_{kj} + \sum_{u_i \in Alloced, l \neq i, l \neq j} q_{lj} \right) \leq Q_j \right), 1 \leq j \leq n$

   ii) For U_i, , if there is no user job bid found in i), set the payment to each of the resources, which has been allocated to it, as the reserve price, or else as the minimum **average resource bidding** of the bid found in i).

---

* *Reserve price is set by system as the minimal charge for users*

4.3 Analysis of HtRAA Strategy

HtRAA introduces the combinatorial auction mechanism designed based on the principle proposed in [20]. However, in [20], it is never proved that revealing the true value is the only dominant strategy of the introduced auction mechanism. Hence, we analyze the dominant strategy- of HtRAA as follows:

For any user job j_i with the value being v_i, the bidding price being b_i and the required resource set being U_i. The expected profit of j_i, under three possible conditions, is analyzed as follows:

1) $b_i = v_i$

Set p_1 as the possibility of j_i winning in the auction in such condition. The expected profit of j_i is

$$ep_1 = p_1 * (v_i - c_i) + (1 - p_1) * 0 \qquad (3)$$

c_i is the payment of j_i.

2) $b_i < v_i$

Set p_2 as the possibility of j_i winning in the auction in such condition. The expected profit of j_i is

$$ep_2 = p_2 * (v_i - c_i) + (1 - p_2) * 0 \qquad (4)$$

However, by lower b_i than v_i, j_i may take more risk to lose in the auction, so that $p_1 > p_2$, and thus, $ep_1 > ep_2$.

3) $b_i > v_i$

We analyze the two possible conditions:

If by reveal the true value, j_i can win in the auction, increasing b_i higher than v_i will be sure for j_i to win. That is, the possibility of j_i winning in such condition is equal to p_1.

If by revealing the true value, j_i loses in the auction, and then by increasing b_i, j_i may win in the auction with the possibility p_3. However, in such condition, there must be at least a job with the resource requirement set ranking ahead of j_i in the sorted user resource requirement set list, which has the resource conflict with j_i. Hence, the payment (c_i'), in such condition, is higher than v_i or equal to v_i. Set ep ($v_i - c_i'$)as the expectation of ($v_i - c_i'$), thus $ep(v_i - c_i')$ must be lower than 0.

In summary, the expected profit of j_i when $b_i > v_i$ is:

$$ep_3 = p_1 * (v_i - c_i) + (1 - p_1) * (p_3 * (ep(v_i - c_i')) + (1 - p_3) * 0) \qquad (5)$$

$\because ep(v_i - c_i') < 0$

$\therefore ep_3 < ep_1$

In summary, when $b_i = v_i$, user can gain the maximum expected profit of j_i. Hence, *revealing the true job value is the only dominant strategy of HtRAA.*

With HtRAA, the user only needs to send his resource requirement to the Market Center once when submitting a job, and hence, minimal the communication cost of the scheduling. The characteristic of the combinatorial auction makes users either win with allocation of his entire resource requirement or fail with nothing in a scheduling round. The partial allocation of the resources required by a job will never occur with HtRAA. The greedy approximate optimization in the resource scheduling of HtRAA, makes the trade-off between the computational efficiency and the economic efficiency. In section 7, we will compare the economic efficiency of HtRAA with the strategy-proof mechanisms used in grid resource scheduling.

5 The Virtual Currency and the LOPI Funding and Accounting Model

Compared to the E-Commerce, the adoption of the economic mechanism in grid scheduling is for the resource aggregation and sharing, instead of just resource exchange. Participators in the grid have both the resource requirements and the surplus resources. The grid market-based scheduling provides assurances to the resource provider that the resource contribution will be returned in the kind of using more resource share. On the other hand, the system administrator in the grid needs to have some control of the resource shares among users from multiple organizations.

5.1 The Virtual Currency

In PheonixMarket, virtual currency is the means for users to obtain resources. Users can obtain the virtual currency in two ways: one is assigned by system; the other is earned from resource contribution. The virtual currency will never be redeemed to the real currency. The advantage of the close-looped use of the virtual currency lies in:

✓ The system administrator can control the resource sharing via the virtual currency assignment among users.
✓ Incenting the user to contribute resources, when the assigned virtual currency is not enough for his/her resource requirement.

5.2 The LOPI Funding and Accounting Model

Based on the use of virtual currency, the issue of how to control the resource sharing among strategic users needs to be resolved. In PheonixMarket, the solution is the LOPI (Limited Output Periodic Input) funding and accounting model.

The principle of LOPI model is somewhat similar to that of a reservoir. In PheonixMarket, each user has an account and system periodically 'injects' the funding currency into user's accounts. The system administrator will set the maximal amount of virtual currency in each account. Users are free to allocate their virtual currency on their jobs in any manner. When a job starts, the accounting center will draw the virtual currency from the job owner's account and inject this virtual currency to the corresponding resource providers' accounts periodically, according to the price settled in the resource scheduling. Once the amount of virtual currency in the user's account is not enough for the payment, the job will be stopped.

The advantage of LOPI model is as follows:

✓ Injecting funding periodically surmounts the defect of providing users a mass of virtual currency once on their participation in the grid, which burdens the user with the difficulty of making the virtual currency allocation plan among the decided and pending jobs.
✓ By bounding the maximal amount of the injected virtual currency and charging users for their running jobs periodically, LOPI can prevent users from accumulating virtual currency in their accounts and taking the baleful and exceeding resource use.

Moreover, the amount of the periodically injected virtual currency can be treated as a form of priority, and LOPI provide more flexibility to users than the traditional priority scheduling policy, which is unaware of the job value and set all jobs from a user as the same priority.

6 Evaluation

The main performances measured for PheonixMarket are: the economic efficiency, the price sensitivity and the feature of prioritizing users.

6.1 Simulation Environment and Workload

We have conducted initial experiments by analyzing data from Shanghai Super Computing Center (the major site of **China Nation Grid**) workload traces and synthesize the workload. The simulation environment is based on Dawning super server [21]. 32 nodes are included in the simulation environment. Half of them are with CPU as Intel XEON 2.8GHZ *2 and 2GB memory, and others are with CPU as AMD OPTERON 1.8GHZ *2 and 1GB memory.

The workload used in this experiment is as follows:

Table 1. Workload in This Experiment

Job type	Node number	Job type	Node number
Big job	16	Small job	4
Medium job	8	Mini job	1

The ratio between mini jobs and other jobs is 1:2; the ratio among big, medium and small jobs is 1:23:86. The total number of jobs is 1980. The workload is called job-1980. The Poisson process governs the arrival of jobs.

6.2 Experiments

6.2.1 Economic Efficiency
We measure the economic efficiency with the metric of *aggregated user job value*. In economic terms, this is known as maximizing *social welfare*. We compare the strategy-proof scheduling strategies used in grid resource allocation systems: HtRAA, the scheduling strategies based on Double Auction (D.A) and commodity market (C.M) mechanism. We also compare HtRAA with the scheduling strategy based on Bargain (Barg.) mechanism or Vickrey auction (V.A).

Figure 2 – 5 shows the economic efficiency improvement with HtRAA under different resource heterogeneities, variation of the user job value (simulated by changing the ratio between the high job value mean and the low job value mean), job delay tolerance and job arrival rate. Overall, we observe efficiency improvement of 1.22-1.69 times in Figure 2, 1.21-1.55 times in Figure 3, 1.1-3.7 times in Figure 4, 1.08 - 1.52 times in Figure 5.

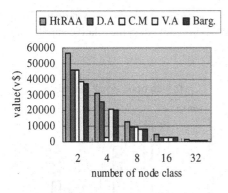

Fig. 2. The economic efficiency under different node heterogeneity

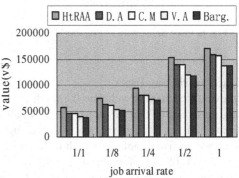

Fig. 3. The economic efficiency under different variation of job value

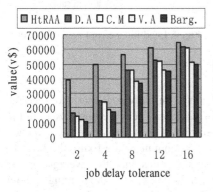

Fig. 4. The economic efficiency under different distribution of the job delay tolerance

Fig. 5. The economic efficiency under different job arrival rate

6.2.2 Price Sensitivity

In this section, we measure the price response to changes in the relative supply and demand, which is called price sensitivity. We change the job arrival rate to simulate the different relative supply and demand and collect the average prices during multiple time intervals after the start of the simulation respectively.

Figure 6 shows the price sensitivity of PheonixMarket. The average price, during the same duration, declines with the arrival rate of jobs dropping. In general, PheonixMarket complies with our intuition in the simulations and have fine price sensitivity. Figure 7 shows that the price information can be used as the 'signal' for load balance among resource pools. We establish two resource pools, each pool is same as we described in 6.1. We simulate the two conditions: one is that users choose the pool with the lower price; the other is that users choose the pool randomly. In all simulations, by using the price 'signal', the job average waiting time is reduced by a range of 10% - 25%. The improvement is more significant when the relative supply and demand becomes intensive.

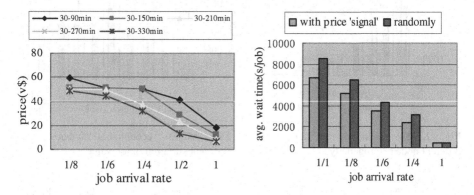

Fig. 6. Price Sensitivity in PheonixMarket   Fig. 7. Load Balance in PheonixMarket

6.2.3 Prioritizing Users

In this experiment, we change the funding amount to an individual user and trace the aggregated value that the user gains from all of his jobs. There are thirty users in the simulation; each job in the workload belongs to one of the users randomly. To each user, we do five simulations with different funding amount, while fixing the funding amount (100$ /s) of other users. Figure 8 demonstrates that the average of the aggregated value from all users increases by up to 4.34 times, when the funding amount change from 100v$/s to 1000v$/s. The reason is that, with the more funding amount, the possibility of job 'blocking' becomes lower. In another word, the system provides more priority to users with more funding amount to avoid the job 'blocking'.

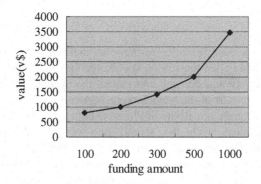

Fig. 8. The variation of the average of the aggregated job value

7 Conclusion

In this paper, we present a strongly strategy-proof combinatorial auction-based grid resource allocation system, called PheonixMarket. Contributions of PheonixMarket are 1) a new resource bidding model with the expression of the time-varying job value information, 2) a strongly strategy-proof auction-based scheduling strategy HtRAA 3) a funding and accounting model LOPI to incent users to contribute their resources and take the funding as a form of priority. Experimental results demonstrate that 1) compared with other strategy-proof market-based scheduling strategies used in grid resource scheduling, PheonixMarket improves the economic efficiency by a maximum of 3.7 times. PheonixMarket achieves the load balance with the price 'signal', and hence, reduces the job waiting time by a factor of up to 25%. The issue of taking funding as a form of the user priority is also tested. In future work, we plan to deploy PheonixMarket on a real grid environment, which will allow real life testing. The scheduling strategy will be improved to be strategy-proof for resource providers, so that resource providers can express their resource cost in a more free and accurate way.

References

1. Foster, I., Kesselman, C.: The grid: a Blueprint for a New Computing Infrastructure, 2nd edn. Morgan Kaufmann, San Francisco (2003)
2. Nabrzyski, J., Schof, J.M., Weglarz, J.: Grid Resource Management, State of the Art and Future Trends. Kluwer Academic Publishers, Boston (2003)
3. Buyya, R., Abramson, D., Giddy, J., Stockinger, H.: Economic models for resource allocation and scheduling in grid computing. Concurrency and Computation: Practice and Experience 14(13-15), 1507–1542 (2003)
4. Grosu, D., Das, A.: Auction-based resource allocation protocols in grids. In: Proc. Of the 16th IASTED International Conference on Parallel and Distributed Computing and Systems, pp. 20–27 (November 2004)
5. Smith, R.G.: The Contract Net Protocol: High-Level Communication and Control in a Distributed Problem Solver. IEEE Transactions on Computers 29, 1104–1113 (1980)
6. Waldspurger, C.A., Hogg, T., Huberman, B.A: Spawn: A Distributed Computational Economy. IEEE Transaction on Software Engineering 18(2), 103–117 (1992)
7. Pindyck, R.S.: Microeconomics. Prentice-Hall, Englewood Cliffs (2004)
8. Buyya, R., Venugopal, S.: The Gridbus toolkit for service oriented grid and utility computing: an overview and status report. In: Proc. Of the 1st IEEE International Workshop on Grid Economics and Business Models, pp. 19–66 (2004)
9. Wolski, R., Plank, J. S., Bryan, T., Brevik, J.: G-commerce: market formulations controlling resource allocation on the computational grid. In: Proc. Of the 15th IEEE International Parallel and Distributed Processing Symposium (April 2001)
10. Wolski, R., Brevilk, J.: Grid Resource Allocation and Control using Computational Economics. Concurrency: Practice and Experience 29, 1–24 (2002)
11. Regev, O., Nisan, N.: The Popcorn market – An online market for computational resources. In: Proc. Of the 1st international conference on Information and Computation economies, pp. 148–157 (1998)
12. Wen, C., Lu, D.: A double auction-based resource allocation strategy in the computational grid. Computer Research and Development 29(6), 1004–1008 (2006)

13. Assuncao, M., Buyya, R.: An evaluation of communication demand of auction Protocols in grid environments. In: Porc. Of the 3rd International Workshop on Grid Economics and Business (GECON 2006), World Scientific Press, Singapore (2006)

14. Wolski, R., Plank, J.S., Brevik, J., Bryan, T.: Analyzing market-based resource allocation strategies for the computational grid. The. international Journal of High. Performance Computing Applications 15(3), 258–281 (2001)

15. Cerquides, J., Endriss, U.: Bidding Languages and winner determination for mixed multi-unit combinatorial auctions, To be appeared In: Proc. Of the 20th International Joint Conference on Artificial Intelligence (2007)

16. Das, A., Grosu, D.: Combinatorial Auction-based Protocols for Resource Allocation in Grids. In: Proc. Of the 19th IEEE Parallel and Distributed Processing Symposium (2005)

17. Nisan, N.: Bidding and allocaton in combinatorial auctions. In: Proc. Of the 2nd ACM Conference on Electronic Commerce, pp. 1–20 (2000)

18. Barrnote, A., Buyya, R.: GridBank: a Grid Accounting Services Architecture (GASA) for distributed systems sharing and integration. In: Proc. Of the IEEE International Parallel and Distributed Processing Symposium (April 2003)

19. Mu'alem, A., Nisan, N.: Truthful Apprximation Mechanisms for Restricted Combinatorial Auctions, In: Proc. Of the Eighteenth national conference on Artificial intelligence, pp. 379–348 (2002)

20. Lehmann, D., O'Callaghan, L.I., Shoham, Y.: Truth Revelation in Rapid, Approximately Efficient Combinatorial Auctions. Journal of the ACM 49(5), 577–602 (2002)

21. Zhang, Z., Meng, D., Zhan, J.: Easy and Reliable Cluster Management: The Self-management Experience of Fire Phoenix. In: Proc. Of IPDPS 2006 SMTPS workshop

Method for Computational Grids Resources Allocate Based on Auction and Utility Analyses*

Dong-E Chen[1,2] and Yang Yang[1]

[1] Information Engineering School, University of Science and Technology Beijing,
Beijing, China, 100083
Chen_donge@126.com
[2] Computer Center, HeBei University of Economics and business,
Shijiazhuang, China 050091

Abstract. Considering dynamic, heterogeneous and autonomous characteristics of computing resources in the computational grid environment and the advantages of economics mechanism applied to solve the problem of resource management, a sealed-bid auction method for resource allocation on computational grids is presented. Firstly, a grid service markets framework for resource allocation in the computational grid environment is described. Secondly, a sealed-bid auction mechanism is presented, where centered on users, and driven by user's needs. Thirdly, Bayes equilibrium point and utility, strategy and efficiency in the Bayes equilibrium state are discussed. Finally, utility function-based resources allocation algorithm is presented.

Keywords: grid service markets, resources allocation, sealed-bid auction, Bayes equilibrium, utility.

1 Introduction

Nowadays, Economic mechanism, which is the flexible and effective management method of grid resources, is the hot issue in grid research, where auction as a kind of economic mechanism is highlighted because it can solve the grid resources allocation problem significantly fast and effectively. There are resource demanders, they compete for the resource at different prices. Finally, the Auctioneer confirms the winner and the price of trade success according to auction classes. Four auction classes in common use are English Auction (ascending price Auction), Dutch Auction (descending price Auction), First-Price Sealed Auction and Second-Price Sealed Auction (Vickrey Auction), the first two kinds are called Open Auction , the last two Sealed Auction .

The rest of the paper is organized as follows: Section 2 mentions related work. Section 3 describes a resource allocation frame based on grid service market. Section 4 proposes computational grid resource allocation model based on sealed-bid auction and analyzes Bayes equilibrium point of this auction mechanism and the efficiency, strategy and utility in equilibrium state. An algorithm for the resource

---

* This work is supported by National Natural Science Foundation of China (No.90412012).

H. Jin et al. (Eds.): ICA3PP 2007, LNCS 4494, pp. 267–277, 2007.
© Springer-Verlag Berlin Heidelberg 2007

allocation based on user utility function is presented in Section 5. Finally, Section 6 concludes our paper and outline further work.

2 Related Work

In different application environments, researchers have developed different economics models for grid resource management, Spawn[1] is a scheduling system based on distributional computation, which applies Vickrey Auction method. A number of jobs compete for the processor time of computer. Jobs can be realized with different compete strategies in terms of users preference. Popcorn[2] is a system for Web browser, Popcorn is realized by Java language. Users divides distributional application into a tasks group, they decide the price of each task according to calculated value, and enter market to search resource seller, the resource owner sells CPU time of own computer and executes user task. Jaws[3] similar to Popcorn, is also based on web browser. The buyer and seller submit order to matchmaker in Jaws system, the trade succeeds once the buyer's order matches the seller's in matchmaker. Order can be updated at any moment. All these three systems use economics mechanism to solve resource allocation issue, however, the systems emphasize on load equilibrium, weaken in quality of service, what is more, the extension and opening capability is not so good because of the fixed system structure. Nimrod/G[4][5] grid resource scheduler can be used in the computational grid management and scheduling, the system applies commodity market model to manage and allocate resources, it is a scheduling strategy for application level, driven by the deadline and budget constraint defined by user. The research of Nimrod/G and the references [6][7][8][9] will be interesting to investigate the realization of resource allocation system, no study has yet been made for the efficiency, strategy and utility on auction mechanism.

3 Resource Allocation Frame Based on Grid Service Markets

In the frame, computational grid is regarded as an economic system that compose of many Grid Service Markets (GSM). In GSM, service is taken for valued economical goods, and the owner of grid resources is regarded as Grid Service Providers (GSP), the grid resource consumer is regarded as grid user, both the grid resource provider and grid user are taken for economic individuals independently. Both GSP and Grid user must register through Information Service Agent (ISA) when they enter or exit Grid service markets. In grid service markets, grid user submit task and description of his own QoS requirement through Application Server Broker (ASB), ASB sorts out tasks according to service categories, and then registers them on ISA, publishes the service and QoS requirement. In ISA, grid user can get useful information about local service resources as well. The above mentioned local resources refer to the service resources in the same GSM as grid user. If grid user wants to get service resources information of other GSM, he has to get the service resources list through the local ISA communications with other one; The grid service provider registers on ISA through Resource Service Agent (RSA), the registered information includes name of service resource, location, hardware configuration. In multi-grid service market, in general, a service resource belongs merely to one market, and only registered in ISA of corresponding GSM. If a service resource belongs to several GSM, at the same time, then it should be registered in ISA of GSM respectively.

4   Auction Model and the Analysis of Utility

4.1   Overview to Auction

Auction is defined economic environment simply and easily. On one hand, auction model just require a little price information. On the other hand, auction model is operated and realized easily. It can make resources reasonable allocated in a very short time, therefore the best solution or preferred solution can be reached among the system. One auction in fact is an obvious market principle, which is based on bidder's bids, and then the price and allocation of service resources are decided. There are three elements on the evaluation of auction model: utility, strategy and efficiency. In view of utility, the maximal overall system utility should be guaranteed, that is to say, the maximal utility of both grid service provider (the Seller) and grid user(the Buyer) is achieved; in view of strategy, the optimal strategy or the preferred should be reached and the rational requirement of the independent economic individual in grid should be lowered as much as possible; in view of efficiency, the time complexity during auction should be as simple as possible, or the auction round number should be as less as possible.

4.2   Sealed-Bid Auction

Here we say reverse auction, reverse auction means the auction sponsored by grid users, a game among service providers. A grid user, as a buyer, submit his service application and QoS requirement, service providers, as the sellers, bidding for the service demand according to QoS requirement, the one bid at the lowest price win the job. There are 3 key players in auction, for instance, Seller, Auctioneer, Buyer, in this model, grid users can describe their QoS requirement thoroughly, this is a model centered on users. In reverse sealed-bid auction, each seller seals bid document according to buyer's requirement, all the bid document should be opened by the auctioneer at the same time, the seller bidden at the lowest price is winner. If there is more than one bidder bidden at the same lowest price, the auctioneer will choose one of them as the winner randomly.

4.2.1   Auction Principle
In view of auction efficiency, we choose single round sealed auction, which can allocate resources reasonably in a short time. In this model, Information Service Agent (ISA) is the auctioneer, ASB set up a reserved price (user's budget) in ISA in advance, if the won price is higher than the reserved price, the auction is aborted. Steps as follow:

(1)   grid users submit tasks application with QoS to ASB.

(2)   ASB classifies tasks according to service categories, then registers in ISA, publishes their service requirement, such as task's length, deadline, budget, and then goes for auction.

(3) Each RSA seals its bid document.

(4) Open the bid document at the same time, the lowest price bidder is winner (auction bid succeeds), the trade is implemented at the bid price. If there are several bidders with the same lowest price, the winner is chosen by lot by ISA; and if the lowest bid price is higher than the budget of the buyer, the auction bid is terminated by ISA(the bid is aborted).

(5) If the bid is not terminated by ISA, then turn to following steps, the RSA which won the job accepts the task and carry out the task.

(6) The winner RSA return back the result to ASB.

(7) ASB pays to RSA according to trade successful bid price

4.2.1 Auction Model

In Sealed-bid auction, each RSA decides its own bid price, since the bid document is submitted respectively and sealed, meanwhile all the bid document is opened at the same time, no one knows the bid prices of other RSA, and it is only a one time choice, therefore, sealed auction bid is a limited information static game.

Definition 1. Sealed-bid auction is a limited information static game:$<A,K,C,P,U>$

Where $A = \{ aj \mid 1 \leq j \leq m \}$,is a set of M Service Resource Agents;

$K = \{ kg \mid 1 \leq g \leq l \}$,is a set of service category l of ASB task application;

$C = \{ cgj \mid 1 \leq g \leq l, 1 \leq j \leq m \}$,is a set of production cost of M service resource, cgj is the cost price that No. j service resource provider takes to finish service category g;

$P = \{ pgj \mid 1 \leq g \leq l, 1 \leq j \leq m \}$,is a set of bid prices of each RSA(bid policy space), pgj is the bid price that the j bidder bids for the service category g;

Obviously, the bid policy of the seller is how to maximize its profit by selecting the bid price, bid price is the function of service category and service resource cost,

$$p_{gj} = p_{gj}(k_g, c_{gj})$$;

$U = \{ ugj \mid 1 \leq g \leq l, 1 \leq j \leq m \}$, is a set of utility of each RSA bidder, ugj is utility that the j bidder carry outs service category g.

4.2.3 Analysis of Utility

Definition 2. In sealed-bid auction, the utility of the seller ,who winner, is the value that the trade successful bid price minus service resources cost, it acts as an agent, the utility of the loser is zero.

- if only the seller j offers the lowest price, then the seller j wins the bid, its utility is:

$$u_{gj} = u_{gj}(p_{gj}, c_{gj}) = \min_g (p_{gj}) - c_{gj}, \ u_{gj} \in U \qquad (1)$$

- if there are h $(1 \leq h \leq n)$ bidders bidden at the same lowest price, the win probability of the seller j is 1/h, its utility is

$$u_{gj} = u_{gj}(p_{gj}, c_{gj}) = (\min_g(p_{gj}) - c_{gj})/h \qquad (2)$$

- if the seller j loses the bid,

$$u_{gj} = u_{gj}(p_{gj}, c_{gj}) = 0 \qquad (3)$$

Obviously, the utility of the winner of the sellers is not only related to trade successful bid price, but also the cost of service resource.

- the total utility of the seller

$$U = \sum_{g=1, j=1}^{l,m} u_{gj} = \sum_{g=1, j=1}^{l,m} u_{gj}(p_{gj}, c_{gj}) \tag{4}$$

- the utility of the buyer

$$u_{gj} = u_{gj}(b_g, p_{gj}) = b_g - p_{gj} \tag{5}$$

b_g is grid user's budgetary price for service need of category g.

- the total utility of the buyer

$$\sum_{g=1, j=1}^{l,m} u_{gj} = \sum_{g=1, j=1}^{l,m} (b_g - p_{gj}) \tag{6}$$

Definition 3. In sealed-bid auction, the total utility of system Us equal to the total utility of the buyer add the total utility of the seller

$$U_s = \sum_{g=1, j=1}^{l,m} u_{gj}(p_{gj}, c_{gj}) + \sum_{g=1, j=1}^{l,m} (b_g - p_{gj}) \tag{7}$$

It is obvious that total utility of the system is maximal only if both the total utility of buyer and the total utility of seller is maximal respectively.

In sealed-bid auction game, the utility of the winner of the sellers is not only related to trade successful bid price, but also the cost of service resource. The strategy of the seller j is a function $p_{gj} = p_{gj}(k_g, c_{gj})$, the strategy space of the seller j is a set of all the function.

Theorem 1. In sealed-bid auction for grid resource allocation, auction is ended with transaction, under this circumstance, there is the exclusive optimal strategy that buyer has $p_{gj}^* = p_{gj}^*(k_g, c_{gj})$,   which maximizes the utility of the buyer.

Proof: first, let's prove trade successful strategy is the best one of the buyer

Auction for buyer is ended by trade success, the price $p_{gj}^* = \min(p_{gj})$

The utility of the buyer:

$$u_{gj}^* = u_{gj}(b_g, p_{gj}^*) = b_g - p_{gj}^* = b_g - \min(p_{gj})$$

For $\forall p_{gj}' = p_{gj}'(k_g, c_{gj}), p_{gj}' \in P$

$$\exists u_{gj}' = u_{gj}(b_g, p_{gj}') = b_g - p_{gj}'$$

$$\leq b_g - \min(p_{gj}) = b_g - p_{gj}^* = u_{gj}^*$$

Trade successful strategy is the best strategy for the buyer since p'_{gj} can be anything

Exclusivity:

As proved above, the utility of the buyer get under any strategy p'_{gj} is less than that under Trade successful strategy p^*_{gj}. According to auction principle, the price during auction is the only element which can decide the auction success or failure, if the seller's cost is fixed, the auction strategy is only decided by bid price, therefore, p^*_{gj} is the exclusive optimal strategy of the buyer.   □

Theorem 2. There is no maximal utility of the seller j in sealed-bid auction for grid resource allocation.

Proof:

(1) if the auction succeeds,

$$\forall p'_{gj}, \exists u'_{gj}(p'_{gj}, c_{gj}) = p'_{gj} - c_{gj}$$

$$\geq \min(p_{gj}) - c_{gj} = p^*_{gj} - c_{gj}$$

$$= u^*_{gj}(p^*_{gj}, c_{gj})$$

It can be seen that the utility $u^*_{gj}(p^*_{gj}, c_{gj})$ is not the maximal under trade successful strategy p^*_{gj}, no matter what p'_{gj} is.

(2) the utility of the seller j is nothing if there is no trade success.

As analyzed above, in sealed-bid auction for grid resource allocation, the lower the bid price is, the better chance to win the bid, the lower utility of winner; on the contrary, the higher the bid price is, the less the chance to win the bid, the higher utility of winner. Thus, there is no maximal utility of sellers in sealed-bid auction.   □

Theorem 3. In sealed-bid auction for grid resource allocation, the seller j (1<=j<=m) wins the auction at bid price p^*_{gj}, under this strategy, the system is in Bayes equilibrium state.

Proof: Functional relationship among game players (sellers) can have many formats and classes, thus, there are a lot of strategies in sellers' strategy spaces, therefore, Bayes equilibrium can have many combinations, it is difficult to find out all the possible Bayes equilibrium in sealed-bid auction, even impossible. For easy analysis, we assume that there are only two sellers(the seller i and the seller j(i,j=1,2;i≠j)), the auction strategy combination for a specific service resource should be $[p_1(c_1), p_2(c_2)]$, the cost of each seller is c_j, assuming c_j is uniform distribution in [0,1], $c_j \in [0,1]$.

Assumption, the optimal bid price Pj of the seller j is the function of the cost of some service, $p_j = p_j(c_j)$, also, assuming $p_j(c_j)$ is a monotony ascending function. Practically, the higher the manufacture cost of the seller is, the higher the bid price. So there is an inverse function $c_j = p_j^{-1}(c_j) = \Phi(p_j)$, it means the cost of the seller is c_j, if the bid price is p_j.

The utility function of the seller j is

$$u_j = u_j(p_1, p_2, c_1, c_2)$$

$$= \begin{cases} p_j - c_j, & if\, p_j < p_i \\ (p_j - c_j)/2, & if\, p_j = p_i \\ 0, & if\, p_j > p_i \end{cases}$$

Where $i, j = 1, 2; i \neq j$

Since c_j is uniform distribution in[0,1], the utility of the seller j is

$$u_j(p_1, p_2, c_1, c_2)$$

$$= (p_j - c_j).prob\{p_j < p_i\} + \frac{1}{2}(p_j - c_j)$$

$$.prob\{p_j = p_i\} + 0.prob\{p_j > p_i\}$$

Where c_j the inverse is function of $p_j(c_j)$, and c_j is a continuous random variable, therefore,

$$prob(p_i = p_j) = prob(\Phi(p_i) = \Phi(p_j)) = 0$$

Due to c_j being a uniform distribution in [0,1], so

$$prob(p_j < p_i)$$

$$= prob(p_j^{-1}(c_j) < p_i^{-1}(c_i))$$

$$= prob(\Phi(p_j) < \Phi(p_i))$$

$$= \Phi(p_j) < c_i = \Phi(p_j)$$

Thus,

$$u_j(p_1, p_2, e_1, e_2)$$

$$= (p_j - c_j).prob(p_j < p_i)$$

$$= (p_j - c_j)\Phi(p_j)$$

The maximal utility of the seller j can be presented as follow:

$$\max_{p_j}(u_j) = \max_{p_j}(p_j - c_j)\Phi(p_j)$$

The optimal condition can be achieved from the derivative of cost c_j :

$$-\Phi(p_j) + (p_j - c_j)\Phi'(p_j) = 0$$

Solving the differential equation:

$$p_j = 2c_j$$

So, the strategy combination $(2c_1, 2c_2)$ is the Bayes equilibrium for the auction.

It can be figured out that the space between the bid price of the seller and its actual cost become smaller as the number of sellers is bigger. If there are m sellers for the bid, and the cost of each seller is independent, and the cost is uniform distribution in [0,1], the seller j (1<j<m>), then the utility function of seller j is

$$u_j = (p_j - c_j)\Phi^{m-1}(p_j)$$

The optimal condition:

$$-\Phi(p_j) + (m-1)(p_j - c_j)\Phi'(p_j) = 0$$

Solving the differential equation

$$p_j = \frac{m}{m-1}c_j$$

So, when m→∞, $p_j \to c_j$, that is to say, , the more sellers are, the less the buyer to pay.   □

Of course, if there is no assumption about the strategy of the seller in the monotony ascending function, Bayes equilibrium will be changed. If the probability distribution of the seller is not uniform distribution in [0,1], Bayes equilibrium will vary in sealed-bid auction as well, which should be investigated according to specific probability distribution.

Theorem 4. In sealed auction for grid resource allocation, if the auction succeeds at bid price p^*_{gj} , namely, the system is under Bayes equilibrium, the utility of grid economic system is maximal, the grid resource is reasonably allocated.

Proof: In equation (7)

$$U_s = \sum_{g=1, j=1}^{l,m} u_{gj}(p_{gj}, c_{gj}) + \sum_{g=1, j=1}^{l,m}(b_g - p_{gj})$$

The total utility of the seller at trade successful price is

$$U = \sum_{g=1,j=1}^{l,m} u_{gj} = \sum_{g=1,j=1}^{l,m} u_{gj}(p_{gj}, c_{gj})$$

It can be drawn from theorem 3, there is a combination of strategies which keep the system in Bayes equilibrium, and the utility of the seller is fixed under certain strategy combination.

And, it can be drawn from theorem 1 that the buyer obtains the optimal utility under the circumstance.

$$\sum_{g=1,j=1}^{l,m} u_{gj} = \sum_{g=1,j=1}^{l,m} (b_g - p_{gj})$$

According to definition 3, the total utility of system Us= the total utility of the buyer + the total utility of the seller, the total system utility is maximal at this point. □

So, in successful auction, the system maximizes its utility while grid users do. Individual optimization and system optimization are achieved at the same time, the reasonable resources allocation is obtained.

5   An Algorithm for Resources Allocation on Computational Grid

Let t_d present the service implementation time that user required, let e stand for the budget that agent need to accomplish the job, in order to better express QoS requirement of users, we adopt the method of weighing both the users budget and service implementation time together to set up formula as follow:

$$u(t_d, e) = a \ln(k t_d) + \beta \ln(e) \qquad (8)$$

Where k is the service category vector which fulfills customer's need, α, β are coefficients given by user, and $\alpha+\beta=1$, which stands for the requirement of service quality, in another word, the user prefers a shorter processing time or a lower expense.

The optimal algorithm based on utility function is given below:

Step 1: buyer announces its service need, ASB sort out service and determine the values of α, β;

Step 2: each seller offers its bid price in sealed-bid auction;

Step 3: determine the bid winner

Step 4: proceed trade. compute the utility value according to utility function, refer to equation (8), then figure out service expense according to trade successful price.

Step 5: Sort resources by the increasing order of $u(t_d, e)$)

Step 6:

```
{For each service_application d_i in services_application D
do
        Until all services_application  in D are scheduled
        {For each t in order  u(t_d,e)
```

if minimum $\alpha < \beta$ and $ETC(d_i,t) < T_{di}$

        `do select` r_j `while` $p_{ij} << e_{ij}$

          `allocate the job to the most cheap` r_j

```
                enddo
            endif
```

if $\alpha > \beta$ and $p_{ij} < e_{ij}$

        `do select` r_j `while` $ETC(d_i,t) << T_{di}$

          `allocate the job to the most shortest time` r_j

```
                enddo
            endif
        endfor}
    endfor}
    (where
```

T_{di} : the deadline to finish service d_i required by client

$ETC(d_i,t)$: service request d_i

e_{ij} : the expense the client would like to pay for service d_i

p_{ij} : the price that service d_i occupies resource r_j)

6 Conclusions and Future Work

It is a very flexible and effective method to implement computational grid resources management by auction mechanism, this paper stresses on the application of sealed-bid auction to grid resource allocation, as service oriented, it sets up a resource allocation frame founded on grid service markets, the frame based on OGSA has a better opening and expansion performance. Under the frame, resource allocation is described as a sealed-bid auction model, the objective is to maximize the total system utility while the QoS requirement of users are fulfilled. In order to better explain the requirement of grid users, we adopt the utility   model by weighing both processing time and customer's budget together, grid service market reach equilibrium point as long as every independent economic unit maximize its utility. The system resources are optimally allocated at equilibrium point of market transaction. The complexity of the calculation is lower, it can dynamically allocate grid service resources according to the QoS requirement of users in an effective and flexible way. The article is based on static game that information is limited, namely, based on the transient course of auction, in the future, the method for computational grid resources allocation all players take part in auction continuously will be researched and investigated.

References

1. Waldspurger, C., Hogg, T., Huberman, B., Kephart, J., Stornetta, W.: Spawn: A distributed computational economy. IEEE Trans. Softw. Eng. 18(2), 103–117 (1992)
2. Nisan, N., London, S., Regev, O., Camiel, N.: Globally distributed computation over the internet: The POPCORN project, presented at the Int. Conf. Distributed Computing Systems (ICDCS'98), Amsterdam, The Netherlands, pp. 26–29 (May 1998)
3. Lalis, S., Karipidis, A.: An open market-based framework for distributed computing over the internet, presented at the 1st IEEE/ACM Int. Workshop Grid Computing (GRID 2000) Bangalore, India (December 17, 2000)
4. Moore, R., Baru, C., Marciano, R., Rajasekar, A., Wan, M.: Nimrod-G: An architecture for a resource management and scheduling system in a global computational grid, presented at the 4th Int. Conf. High Performance Computing in Asia-Pacific Region (HPC Asia 2000), Beijing, China (May 2000)
5. Buyya, R., Murshed, M., Abramson, D.: A Deadline and Budget Constrained Cost-Time Optimization Algorithm for Scheduling Task Farming Applications on Global Grids. In: The 2002 International Conference on Parallel and Distributed Processing Techniques and Applications, Las Vegas, Nevada, USA (June 2002)
6. Wolski, R., Brevik, J., Plank, J., et al.: Grid Resource Allocation and Control Using Computational Economies. In: Grid Computing: Making the Global Infrastructure a Reality, Berman F, Fox G, Hey T. (eds.) pp. 747–772 (2003)
7. Buyya, R.: Economic-Based Distributed Resource Management and Scheduling for Grid Computing. Ph.D.Dissertation (2002)
8. Buyya, R., Abramson, D., Venugopal, S.: The Grid Economy. In: Proceedings of the Ieee, vol. 93(3) (March 2005)
9. Wolski, R., Plank, J.S., Brevik, J., et al.: Analyzing market-based resource allocation strategies for the computational Grid. International Journal of High. Performance Computing Applications 15(3), 258–281 (2001)

Service Dependency Model for Dynamic and Stateful Grid Services*

Li Qi, Hai Jin, Yaqin Luo, Xuanhua Shi, and Chengwei Wang

Service Computing Technology and System Lab
Cluster and Grid Computing Lab
School of Computer Science and Technology
Huazhong University of Science and Technology, Wuhan, 430074, China
hjin@hust.edu.cn

Abstract. Deploying the grid services with complicated dependency and status is a big challenge in service provisioning. A new model, named as *Dependency Steelyard,* is proposed in this paper. By measuring and calculating a set of metrics for dependency, the steelyard can generate the critical path of deployment action (including deploy, undeploy, and redeploy) on demand automatically for any service distributed in specific virtual organization. A practical use case, deployment of ChinaGrid Support Platform, will be demonstrated.

1 Introduction

Recently grid community dedicates to implement the grid technologies into production level. The efforts of *Grid Interoperation Now* (GIN) project and the latest release of Globus Toolkit [2] reflect this trend. However some factors obstructed the grid technologies reaching the production level. The complexity of grid management is one of the challenges. It includes three problems:

First, because the large-scale grid services are usually composed by several remote service components at multiple sites, this loosely coupled architecture lowers down the availability and reliability of grids and brings high costs for management and maintenance. For example, the execution system of grids is often composed of data center and information center. When information center is under the maintenance, the availability of execution system would be affected due to the calling dependencies. Moreover the failure to upgrade information center will drive the execution system unavailable eventually.

Second, the stateful grid services, which are concerned in *Web Service Resource Framework* (WSRF) [5], shift the states frequently and dynamically during the runtime. The calling dependencies among them are also changed due to the shift of states. Hence the dynamic deployment for these grid services becomes more complicated and unpredictable.

---

* This paper is supported by Natural Science Foundation of China under grant 90412010, 60673174, and 60603058.

H. Jin et al. (Eds.): ICA3PP 2007, LNCS 4494, pp. 278–289, 2007.

Finally, the correct deployment of a service in a grid is no more than one unique (atomic) operation due to the dependencies. Instead, the deployment is always a workflow running at multiple sites. Recall the former example, if the administrator deploys the execution service without deploying the data and information center, the execution service will be invalid.

To solve the three above problems, a dependency model is needed to describe the dynamical dependencies among the grid services to help administrators analyze the runtime status of a grid before executing deployment actions. In addition to the model, a self-organizing mechanism should be proposed to generate the maintaining workflow to finish the upgrading or deploying jobs. Although many solutions [12, 17] are investigated to describe the service dependency and try to improve the availability and reliability of distributed system, most of them focus on the analysis on static dependency relationship among the services. They can not handle problem 2 and 3.

This paper recognizes the challenges and proposes a new model, called *dependency steelyard*, which supports dependency analysis for service components with the state in WSRF or other similar specification [6, 7]. By measuring and calculating a set of metrics for dependency, the steelyard can generate the critical path of deployment action (including deploy, undeploy, and redeploy) for any service automatically upon the runtime states of grid on demand.

The proposed model, *dependency steelyard*, and its implementation have the following contributions: (1) investigating the service dependency model and proposing the state matrix with it to adapt the dynamicity of grid; (2) introducing two metrics (i.e. depending degree and depended degree) to help administrator understanding the cost of deploying a specific service. In addition, they are significant on detecting dependency circuits and reducing deployment steps; (3) proposing the optimized algorithm for automatically generating the deployment workflow.

The remainder of this paper is organized as follows: Section 2 introduces the related works. Some concepts and the service dependency model are proposed in section 3. The kernel logic and algorithm will be detailed in Section 4. In Section 5, a use case, deployment of ChinaGrid Support Platform, will be demonstrated. We will have a conclusion and outlook for future works in the last section.

2 Related Work

The investigation on deployment and management for distributed software packages is rather popular recently. W3C releases *Installable Unit Deployment Descriptor* (IUDD) [8] specification to describe the distributed software packages. It describes the static dependencies among software packages. It can not adapt the dynamic changes during the runtime. Moreover, IUDD cannot generate the deploying workflow for distributed nodes.

Configuration, Description, Deployment and Lifecycle Management (CDDLM) specification [4] proposed by GGF also dedicates to provide a set of adaptive solutions for distributed software deployment and configuration management on experienced demand. However, it is a specification of deployment infrastructure. It considers how to combine the deployment infrastructure to run-time execution system and support the dynamical variety of configuration. In addition, it investigates less on the dependency among the services, especially the stateful dependencies.

Kunling et al. [12] proposed a dependency isolation mechanism, named as dependency capsule, to improve the availability of multi-thread based Internet services. They discussed three kinds of service dependency (aggregating, bypass-able, and replication dependencies). Nevertheless they did not explore the application on deployment problem. Their focus is on the runtime to avoid the availability of multi-thread based system when block happens.

Neeraj et al. [16] invented a dependency structure matrix to describe the dependencies among legacy software. It is efficient to explore the software architecture from the view of software engineering. But they did not discuss the stateful dependency and how to generate efficient deploying solutions. The dependency structure matrix is not convenient for dynamic deployment in grid.

Progressive Deployment System (PDS) [10] was developed from the view of virtual machine. Robert [17] defined a dependency markup language for web service. These solutions do not consider the variable dependency and the optimized deployment solutions for stateful grid services either.

3 Service Dependency

3.1 Concepts of Dependency

We classify the dependencies into two categories: (1) *Direct Dependency* means that the correct execution of a grid or web service requires invoking the methods or subscribing the resource properties directly. Specifically, we call the relationship as Inner Direct Dependency when the invocation (subscription) happens in a same local hosting environment. On the contrary, when the invocations are to the remote sites, the related services are in Outer Direct Dependency. (2) *Indirect Dependency* means that the successful execution of a grid service directly depend on some services that also depend on the other services. For instance, Service a directly depends b (marked as $a>b$); furthermore, service b directly depends on c ($b>c$). The relationship between c and a (marked as $a>>c$) is indirect dependency.

The two types are the starting point to investigate the relationships among services. However they are helpless to optimize the deployment solutions. Hence we detail the service dependency into twelve sub types from the view of execution logic based on the practical experience of CGSP [2]. As shown in Fig.1, it includes seven elementary types (a-g) and five advance types (h-l). The XOR-* and AND-* series are conditional dependency. Namely, the dependency would actually happen when execution condition or status is matched. In addition to that, the *-Aggregating series (i.e. b, d, and j in Fig.1) mean that the successful execution of a service depends on the correct execution of the composed services; while *-Dispatching dependencies (i.e. c, e, and i in Fig.1) mean that the correct execution of several services depends on the correct execution of some unique services. They are widely seen in some decision making services.

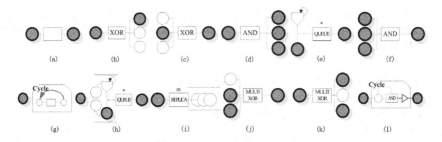

Fig. 1. Dependency Types: (a) Sequent Dependency, (b) XOR-Aggregating Dependency, (c) XOR-Dispatching Dependency, (d) AND-Aggregating Dependency, (e) AND-Dispatching Dependency, (f) Replication Dependency, (g) Cycle Dependency, (h) Queued Dependency, (i) Parallel Queued Dependency, (j) Multiple XOR-Aggregating Dependency, (k) Multiple XOR-Dispatching Dependency, and (l) AND-Cycle Dependency

The detailed taxonomy of service dependency covers most cases. The data and environment dependency can be composed by the Sequent Dependency or AND-Aggregating Dependency. Furthermore, the Queued Dependency and Parallel Queued Dependency are widely implemented in multi-thread based containers such as Apache Tomcat, jBoss. The Cycle Dependency and AND-Cycle Dependency are significant in explaining the periodic or loop invocations among the grid services.

Exploring and differentiating these dependencies before the deployment and upgrades can help optimizing the deploying solutions. For the XOR-Aggregating dependency, if we (re)deploy the depending services in different groups, the breaking down time for the system will be shorter. Similarly, for the AND-Dispatching dependency, if we deploy the depending service first and block all of the requests from the depended services during the deployment, the availability will be promised.

A novel model should be proposed to present these dependencies and their runtime states.

3.2 Service Dependency Model

We define $S = \{s_1, s_2 \ldots s_n\}$ as a set of stateful grid services in a VO.

Definition 1. Service Dependency R is a binary relationship on a collection S. We mark it as si > sj. It has the properties of:

1. For any s_i in S, $s_i > s_i$ does exist. Namely, any service *depends on* itself by default. Hence dependency is reflexive;

2. For any s_i, s_j, s_k in S, if $s_i > s_j$, and $s_j > s_k$, we have $s_i \gg s_k$. This means dependency is transitive. To identify the direct and indirect dependency, we mark the latter relationship as '$\gg$'. Particularly, if $s_k = s_i$, we can get a cycle dependency $s_i \gg s_i$.

$S_{in}(s_i)$ and $S_{out}(s_i)$ are the sets of depended and depending (including direct and indirect) services for s_i, respectively. For any two services in S, if they have the same depending and depended set, we call them *isomorphic*. The isomorphic services can be deployed in parallel or in a same package to target sites.

Definition 2. We define $\sum(s_i)$ as a direct dependency set for a proper service s_i in the whole VO. By exploring $\sum(S)$, we can draw a *Directed Graph* DG<S, $\sum(S)$> with the properties of:

1. Each s_i in S is a vertex in DG;
2. Each dependency in $\sum$ is a directed edge in DG.

In addition, we define $R^k(s_i)$ ($k>0$) as the kth transitive dependency relationship for service s_i. Such as $R^3(s_i)$, it means three steps away from s_i. Furthermore, the symbol $\sum^{closure}(s_i)$ is the transitive closure for service s_i. Simply put, it means all the dependencies (including indirect and direct) for s_i. The operator 'U' in Formula 1 means the combination of the dependency sets.

$$\sum\nolimits^{closure}(s_i) = \bigcup_{k=1}^{n} R^k(s_i) \quad n = |S|, n > 0 \tag{1}$$

Definition 3. Critical Deployment Path is a minimal subset of $\sum(si)$ in which the edges can link all of the vertexes that service si is depending on.

By exploring all the vertexes (services) on this path, we can build a minimal deploying solution to promise correct deployment of service s_i.

Definition 4. Similar to [16], we define a *Service Dependency Matrix* (SDM) as an $n \times n$ mesh. Each element d_{ij} in SDM matrix means the direct dependent relationship between s_i and s_j. As described in formula 2, the value of ith row and jth column will be 1 if s_i depends on s_j, otherwise it will be 0.

$$d_{ij} = \begin{cases} 1 & s_i > s_j \\ 0 & else \end{cases} \tag{2}$$

Furthermore, we define the service *Depending Degree* of a specific service as $DGD(s_i)$ which records how much service s_i depend on the other services. Similarly, we define the *Depended Degree* of a specific service as $DDD(s_j)$ which measures how much the other services depend on s_i. The value of DGD and DDD are defined in formula 3 and 4.

$$DGD(s_i) = \begin{cases} 0 & n=1 \\ \frac{1}{n-1}(\|SDM_i + SDM_i^2 + \cdots + SDM_i^n\| - 1) & n>1 \end{cases} \tag{3}$$

$$DGD(s_i) = \begin{cases} 0 & n=1 \\ \frac{1}{n-1}(\|T_i + T_i^2 + \cdots + T_i^n\| - 1) & n>1 \end{cases} , T = SDM^T \tag{4}$$

In formula 3, the SDM_i is the vector of ith row in mesh SDM. The SDM_i^k denotes the kth transition vector [9]. In addition to that, Operator '+' is defined as Boolean OR for vectors.

In formula 4, SDM^T is the transpose of the matrix SDM. The value of DDD and DGD can be recorded as a reference for deployment purpose. They do make sense to help dependency steelyard to evaluate and simplify the deployment for grids. The Lemma 1, Lemma 2 can prove this.

Lemma 1. A graph DG<S, $\sum(S)$>, and we have the DDD(S) and DGD(S) in Definition 4:

1. If there is no circuit on DG, then for any service s_i in S, the summation of DDD(s_i) and DGD(s_i) SHOULD be less than 1.
2. If there are one or more circuits on DG, we can find at least two services of which the summation of DDD and DGD is greater than 1.
3. More specifically, these service vertexes are on the circuits.

Proof. Item 1 and 2 can be proven easily from the definition of DDD and DGD. A service on the circuit will be the depended vertex and depending vertex at the same time for the other services on the circuit. Naturally it will be counted twice respectively in DDD and DGD. Hence the summation of them will be greater than 1.

For Item 3, we take the counterevidence:

Suppose there is a service s_i which is not on any circuit and the summation of DDD and DGD is greater than 1. From the former discussion, we can find at least a service s_j both in the depended set and depending set of s_i. Namely, we have $s_i >> s_j$ and $s_j >> s_i$. From the Defnition 1, the dependency is transitive, hence we have $s_i >> s_i$. It indicates that s_i is on a circuit. This conflicts with the hypothesis. Hence the conclusion of item 3 is true.

Lemma 2. If there is a circuit in graph DG<S, $\sum(S)$>, for each service vertex on that circuit, the value of DDD (resp. DGD) is equal to each other. Namely, these vertexes are isomorphic.

Proof. With the definition of isomorphic in Definition 1 and DDD, DGD in Definition 4, if any two services (s_i, s_j) in DG are isomorphic then they should have the same DDD and DGD. Hence, we just need proving s_i and s_j are isomorphic.

Because s_i and s_j are in the circuit, we have $s_i >> s_j$ and $s_j >> s_i$. For any s_k in $S_{out}(s_i)$, we have $s_i >> s_k$ and $s_j >> s_k$ easily. Hence for any service in $S_{out}(s_i)$, it should be also in $S_{out}(s_k)$. Vice versa, based on the reflexive feature, any service existing in $S_{out}(s_k)$ should be also in $S_{out}(s_i)$. Then s_i and s_j have the same depending set. Similarly, we can prove that they share the same depended set. So s_i and s_j are isomorphic. The conclusion of Lemma 2 is true.

Definition 5. We define a state matrix (SM) to record the necessary state Boolean value. There are multiple SMs with the transformation of stateful services, e.g. the XOR-Aggregating Dependency, AND-Aggregating Dependency. The result of operations between original SDM and the SM will be a new SDM.

4 Kernel Algorithm

In this section, three kernel algorithms are introduced to describe the core working flow of dependency steelyard. All the algorithms are described in pseudo codes.

Algorithm 1. Calculate Depending Degree

```
function float caculateDGD (int i, int[][] SDM,
  GridRuntimeConf runTime){
  /* Input parameter is the •(s_i) and the global SDM is
  a complete nxn array. And runTime is a status
  collector in charge of collect the necessary
  dependency information */
      int[][] SM = null;      //The runtime states mesh.
      float result = 0.0;     //The DGD variable.
      /* Operate with the state Matrix which is collected
  from the runtime configuration or state resource
  properties.*/
      SM = runtime.collectStateMatrix(SDM); //collect the
  SM for related services.
      SDM = runtime.operateSDM(SDM,SM);   //get new SDM
      int[] sigSi = SDM[i]; //Get the vector of s_i
      int n = sigSi.length(); //Get the size of n:
  ||SDM||.
      /* Get the transitive closure for s_i using Washall
  algorithm[11]*/
      int[] closureSi = Warshall.getClosure(SDM)[i];
      int count =0; //variable to count the depending set
      for (tempIndex=0; tempIndex<n; tempIndex++)
          if (closureSi[tempIndex] == 1) count++;
      result = (count -1)/(n-1);
      return result;
  }
```

DDD value can be calculated in the similar way. The difference is that we input the transpose of SDM instead of SDM itself.

Algorithm 2. Compose Isomorphic Service Packages

```
function int[][] composeIsoService (int[][] SDM){
  /* Input parameter is the direct dependency SDM nxn
  array.*/
      Array result = new LinkArray();
  //LinkArray is designed to combine the linkages and
  generate the mesh.
      int n = SDM[].length(); //get the order of SDM.
  /* Step 1. Calculate the DDD and DGD for each service
  in VO.*/
      float ddd, dgd;
      for (int tempIndex =0; tempIndex< n; tempIndex++){
          ddd = calculateDDD(
                          tempIndex,SDM,Grid.getRuntime());
          dgd = calculateDGD(
                          tempIndex,SDM,Grid.getRuntime());
          Degree.record(tempIndex,ddd,dgd);
  //Class Degree is designed to record the degree values
  for each service.
      }
```

```
/* Step 2. Check the circuit and isomorphic dependency
*/
    Array isoServ = Degree.findEqualServices();
    //findEqualServices will locate the services with
    equal DDD+DGD value and DDD+DGD >1;
    for (int tempIndex=0;
                tempIndex<isoServ.length();tempIndex++){
    if(Degree.hasSameDDDVertex(isoServ.get(tempIndex)&&
        Degree.hasSameDGDVertex(isoServ.get(tempIndex)))){
        result.combineVertex(SDM,Degree.getServIDs());}
    return result.toArray();
}
```

Algorithm 3. Generate Critical Deployment Path

```
function vector genCriticalDeployPath (int I, int[][]
SDM){
/* Input parameter is the service id and the direct
dependency SDM nxn array.*/
    Vector result = new Vector();
    //result is vector type to store the sequence of
deployment.
    int n = SDM[].length(); //get the order of SDM.
/* Step 1. Merging the isomorphic services.
    SDM = composeIsoService(SDM);
/* Step 2. add the s_i as the start point of path.*/
    result.add(i);
/* Step 3. Get all the vertexes directly depend on s_i
and adopt the service vertexes which are directly
depended on.*/
    traverseCriticalPath(i,result);
    return result;
}
function traverseCriticalPath(int i, Vector result){
    if (result.get(i)==null){
        while((int j = findDependency(i,SDM))!=0){
            if (getDependencyType(i,j,SDM)==Type.DIRECT
            &&result.get(j)==null)
                result.add(i->j);
/* Recursively invoke to get all the services depended
by service i*/
            traverseCriticalPath(j,result);
        }
    }
}
```

5 Use Case Study

In this section, a practical use case, *ChinaGrid Support Platform* (CGSP), will be explored to demonstrate the efficiency and usage of dependency steelyard. CGSP [2] is designed purely following *Service Oriented Architecture* (SOA). There are seven critical system services for CGSP. As shown in Fig. 2, they are Portal Service (marked as *S1*), General Running Service (*S2*), Data Management Service (*S3*), Domain Management Service (*S4*), Execution Management Service (*S5*), Information Service (*S6*), and Container Service (*S7*). For the convenience of discussion, some detailed and internal services are cut off or simplified. The functionality of each service has been discussed in [2][13][14].

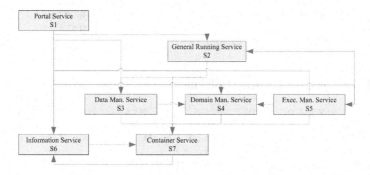

Fig. 2. Service Calling Dependencies in CGSP

From Fig. 2, we can find the dependencies discussed in section 3. Most dependencies (like *S1>S2*, *S1>S6*, *S3>S7*, *S4>S7*, and so on) are all sequent dependencies. There are also many conditional dependencies, such as (i) *S7>S6* would happen only if Status Notification is correctly configured on the grid container and the Information Service has been confirmed OK to receive the status report. If condition is not true, the invocations will be bypassed. It is a typical XOR-Aggregating dependency. (ii) More specifically, if the dependency (*S7>S6*) is true, *S7* and *S6* is a cycle dependency. (iii) *S2>S3* is a replication dependency which means that GRS delivers the staging data to the physical replica of GridFTP resources during executing jobs. (iv) *S5>S2* and *S5>S4* are AND-aggregating dependency, the correct execution of *S5* depends on the success of *S2* and *S4*. In short, these dependencies are decided by the runtime status.

These services are deployed in different ChinaGrid [1] domains. We take two typical provisioning operations as use case: (i) deploy *S1* in a clean environment; (ii) upgrade *S6* fundamentally (including its all depending services) without the configuration of notifications (namely, *S7>S6* is false).

Deployment of *S1*

Dependency steelyard traverses the dependencies stored in the service repository and generates the SDM for the deployment task as shown in Fig. 3. At the same time, a directed graph based on SDM is shown in Fig. 3A. By calculating the depending degree and depended degree, we can collect all of the data as shown in column DGD-F and DDD-F in Table 1. We can conclude easily that the *S6* and *S7* are highly depended by other services – they will cost much to redeploy or undeploy. While the *S1* depends on all of other services in CGSP's system services – it can be re-deployed easily. Furthermore, the summation of DDD and DGD for $S6$ and $S7$ is 1.167 (greater than 1). After checking and composing the circuits and isomorphic services, the steelyard generates SDM_B (in Fig. 3). In addition to the new SDM, the new depending and depended degree are also re-counted. They are listed in column DGD-FS, and DDD-FS in Table 1. More specifically, dependency steelyard will generate the deployment path (as shown in Fig.3B): $S1>S5>S2>S3>S4>\{S6, S7\}$. By deploying these service packages in a stack sequence, $S1$ is successfully deployed in a clean environment.

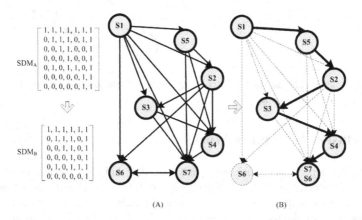

Fig. 3. Deployment of $S1$ (A) is a complete dependency, (B) is the critical deployment path for S1

Table 1. The Variety of DGD and DDD in Different States

Services	DGD			DDD		
	F	FS	US	F	FS	US
S1	1	1	1	1	0	0
S2	0.667	0.6	0.667	0.333	0.4	0.333
S3	0.5	0.4	0.333	0.5	0.6	0.5
S4	0.333	0.2	0.167	0.667	0.8	0.667
S5	0.833	0.8	0.833	0.167	0.2	0.167
S6	0.167	0	0.167	1	1	0.5
S7	0.167	N/A	0	1	N/A	1

Fundamental Upgrade of $S2$

After deploying all of the CGSP services, the administrator finds that a new version of $S2$ has been released. The fundamental upgrading for $S2$ is necessary. Before generating the solution, the SDM of $S3$ and the related DGD and DDD are listed in Table 1 (column DGD-U and DDD-U). Different with the former use case, after operating with SM, the dependency mesh changed. In addition, the cycle dependency disappeared. Based on the new generated SDM_D and algorithm 3, we can get the critical deployment path for upgrading of $S2$: $S2>\{S3>S4, S6\}>S7$.

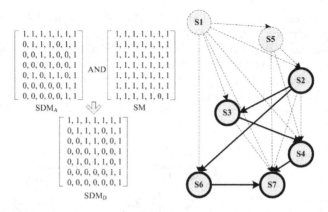

Fig. 4. Fundamental Upgrade of *S2*. After operate with SM, the new directed graph and critical deployment path for *S2* is generated.

6 Conclusion and Future Works

In this paper, dependency steelyard is introduced to help administrators of the grid managing the service deployment work. Some definitions and lemmas are proposed. The metrics (including depending degree and depended degree) are used to evaluate the deploying complexity and dependency for grid services. In addition, the state matrix is invented to handle the dynamical stateful dependencies. Finally, by using steelyard, the critical deployment path for a service can be generated automatically based on the runtime states and degree of the services.

In the near future, we plan to investigate more metrics (e.g. the deployment price, deployment costs) for the deployment of complicated depended services. Furthermore, a runtime monitoring system will be developed to help the administrators enforce the conditional dependencies in runtime.

References

1. ChinaGrid Project. http://chinagrid.hust.edu.cn
2. ChinaGrid Support Platform. http://www.chinagrid.edu.cn/cgsp
3. Globus Toolkit Project. Globus Alliance. http://www.globus.org
4. Configuration, Deployment Description Language and Management, GGF. http://www.gridforum.org/documents/GFD.50.pdf
5. Web Service Resource Framework Specification. OASIS. http://docs.oasis-open.org/wsrf/2004/06/wsrf-WS-ResourceProperties-1.2-draft-04.pdf
6. Web Services Transfer. http://www.w3.org/Submission/WS-Transfer
7. Web Services Events. http://devresource.hp.com/drc/specifications/wsmf/WS-Events.pdf
8. Installable Unit Deployment Descriptor Specification. http://www.w3.org/Submission/InstallableUnit-DD
9. Aho, A., Garey, M.R., Ullman, J.D.: The Transitive Reduction of a Directed Graph. SIAM Journal of Computer 1, 131–137 (1972)

10. Alpern, B., Auerbach, J., Bala, V., Frauenhofer, T., Mummert, T., Pigott, M.: PDS: A Virtual Execution Environment for Software Deployment. In: Proceeding of First ACM/USENIX Conference on Virtual Execution Environments, Chicago, IL, USA, pp. 175–183 (June 11–12, 2005)

11. Henry, S.W.: A Modification of Warshall's Algorithm for the Transitive Closure of Binary Relations. In: Communications of the ACM, vol. 18(8), pp. 218–220. ACM Press, New York (1975)

12. Chu, L., Shen, K., Tang, H., Yang, T., Zhou, J.: Dependency Isolation for Thread-based Multi-tier Internet Services. In: Proceedings of the 24th Annual Joint Conference of the IEEE Computer and Communications Societies, 13-17 March 2005, Miami, FL, USA, pp. 796–806 (2005)

13. Jin, H.: ChinaGrid: Making Grid Computing a Reality. In: Chen, Z., Chen, H., Miao, Q., Fu, Y., Fox, E., Lim, E.-p. (eds.) ICADL 2004. LNCS, vol. 3334, pp. 13–24. Springer, Heidelberg (2004)

14. Jin, H., Gong, W., Wu, S., Xiong, M., Qi, L., Wang, C.: An Efficient Data Management System with High Scalability for ChinaGrid Support Platform. In: Proceedings of the 6th International Workshop on Advanced Parallel Processing Technologies, Hong Kong, China, October 27–28, pp. 282–291(2005)

15. Qi, L., Jin, H., Foster, I., Gawor, J.: HAND: Highly Available Dynamic Deployment Infrastructure for Globus Toolkit 4. In: Proceedings of the 15th Euromicro Conference on Parallel, Distributed and Network-based Processing, Naples, Italy, pp. 155–162 (February 2007)

16. Sangal, N., Jordan, E., Sinha, V., et al.: Using Dependency Models to Manage Complex Software Architecture. In: Proceedings of International Conference on Object Oriented Programming, Systems, Languages and Applications, San Diego, CA, USA, pp.167–176 (October 2005)

17. Tolksdorf, R.: A Dependency Markup Language for Web Services. In: Proceedings of Web and Database-Related Workshops on Web, Web Services, and Database Systems. LNCS, vol. 2593, pp. 129–140. Springer-Verlag, Heidelberg (2002)

Automatic Conceptual Indexing of Web Services and Its Application to Service Retrieval*

Dunlu Peng

College of Computer Engineering,
University of Shanghai for Science and Technology, Shanghai, 200093, China
dlpeng@fudan.edu.cn

Abstract. Web service retrieval is a very important issue for making the paradigm of service-oriented computing more practical. In this paper, we develop an automatic conceptual indexing approach of web services and investigate its application to service retrieval at the operation level. Relevant service operations are grouped into the same service concepts using a new variant k-Means algorithm, and with these service concepts, web services can be indexed conceptually. A service retrieving approach, which is supported by the conceptual indexing of web services, is devised to retrieve web services in an efficient way. Experimental results show that the proposed approach greatly improves the performance of retrieving web services.

Keywords: Web service, SOC, conceptual indexing, k-Means algorithm.

1 Introduction

With the rapid development of *Service-Oriented Architecture*(SOA)[1], many enterprises are moving their core business onto the Web in the form of web services. Currently, at service registry centers, a number of categories are manually assigned to each incoming web service by the providers when they register the services. These categories are chosen from a set of pre-specified categories according to the service provider's business purposes. If a consumer wants to find a service satisfying some special requirements, he/she needs to browse the "right" categories. This category-based service-discovery is quite insufficient, for the consumer has to endure the boring filter of the extreme large number of irrelevant services.

Indexing technique, which has gained great success in improving the performance of retrieving information in structured databases and textual documents, becomes a promising way to address the above problem. However, at least three reasons determine applying traditional database indexing techniques to web services straightforward is infeasible. Firstly, service description files (or WSDL), which describe web services in XML-style documents, are semi-structured and

---

* This work is supported by the National Hitech R&D Program of China under Grant No. 2006AA01Z103, and Scientific Research Foundation of the University of Shanghai for Science and Technology under Grant No.X700.

cannot be stored like traditional structured databases. Secondly, since a WSDL document depicts a web service at different granularity, it is unreasonable to characterize a service with the terms in the document without discrimination. Finally, on one hand, most terms have multiple meanings, many unrelated web services may be also indexed by same terms just because the terms appear in the description of the service; on the other hand, a function can be described by multiple terms, relevant web services will not be indexed with the same terms if their description files do not contain any of the terms.

Unlike the traditional indexing techniques, this work proposes a novel approach to index web services conceptually. The idea underlying it is that a web service is more related to the service concepts, which characterize the functions provided by the service, than the terms used in its description file. With this conceptual index, when retrieving web service, it should match the service concept present in the query to the service concepts present in the index file. The main contributions are as follows:

1. An approach of modeling web services in the vector-space is proposed. This approach vectorizes web services at the operation level, which is more reasonable than at the entire service level. Based on this approach, a web service can be characterized with a set of operation vectors (or an operation vector group), in which each operation vector represents an operation (or function) provided by the service.
2. A conceptual indexing technique is designed to effectively index web services. Each *service concept* represents a set of *relevant* service operations (termed *guiding set*) provided by the web services. If two web services provide a *relevant* function, they will be grouped into the same service concept. By this means, web services are clustered according to their functional relevance rather than the terms contained in their description files.
3. To investigate the application of conceptual indexing to service retrieval, a service retrieving model has been proposed based on the conceptual indexing. Some useful algorithms and definitions are also developed to realized that model. The experimental results show that the proposed approach has better performance on service retrieval than some traditional methods.

The remainder of the paper is organized as follows. Section 2 provides an overview of related work. Section 3 describes the modeling of web services in the vector space. Section 4 describes the algorithms implementing the conceptual indexing. Section 5 shows the retrieving model of web services supported by conceptual indexing. Section 6 presents the experimental evaluation of the performance of retrieving web service using the proposed approach. Finally, Section 7 offers the concluding remarks and discusses some future research.

2 Related Work

Our work touches on two main domains: service matching and service retrieval.

2.1   Service Matching

In this area, the most related work to our study is software component matching. Existing approaches split software component matching process into two steps: signature (data type) matching and specification (program behavior) matching [2]. These methods verified that signature matching is an efficient means for component discovery. But it is infeasible to apply these methods in service matching context, because the required analysis of data type and post-conditions cannot be easily obtained for services [3].

2.2   Service Retrieval

In recent years, service retrieval technology has been studied from several perspectives. For example, in information retrieval community, researchers have focused on retrieval of natural language service description and emphasized the keyword-based approaches [4,7]. These approaches are a poor way to capture the semantics of a query or item which leads to both low precision and imperfect recall. Table-based models [8] typically represent a detailed description of the methods for invoking the service, but do not include what the service actually does. The semantic approaches [5,6]improve the precision and recall very much, but they need to introduce some new standards, such RDF, DAML-S or OWL-S, into the description of services, and it is infeasible for the large deployed traditional services.

3   Modeling Web Services in Vector Space

In this section, firstly, the fundamental of web service are introduced, and then the approach of modeling services in vector space is presented.

3.1   Fundamental of Web Service

According to the previous study, a service can be abstracted as a collection of operations [3]. Each operation represents a function provided by the service. An operation is described by six components, i.e., the input/out messages ($\mathcal{D}_1$ and $\mathcal{D}_2$), the description of its function ($\mathcal{D}_3$), the name of operation($\mathcal{D}_4$), the name of service ($\mathcal{D}_5$) and the description of the entire services($\mathcal{D}_6$). These information can be obtained from WSDL files and UDDI entries. Therefore, a service can be formally defined as follows.

Definition 1. *A **web service** is a set of operations $ws = \{op_1, op_2, \ldots, op_n\}$, where $op_i \in ws$ is a **service operation** representing a function provided by ws. Each operation op_i can be described with a six-tuple $op_i = \langle \mathcal{D}_{i,1}, \mathcal{D}_{i,2}, \mathcal{D}_{i,3}, \mathcal{D}_{i,4}, \mathcal{D}_{i,5}, \mathcal{D}_{i,6} \rangle$, in which $\mathcal{D}_{i,1} \sim \mathcal{D}_{i,6}$ denote respectively the corresponding component described above.*

Definition 1 illustrates that a service may contain more than one operations, and these operations represent different functions provided by the service. It means that to index a service with just a set of terms at the entire service level is quite unreasonable. Because a term could have different meanings in different service description. This determines some unrelated service being probably indexed by the same set of terms, and it will make some negative effects on the result of service retrieval. Therefore, to avoid this disadvantage, in this work, services are indexed at the operation level.

3.2 Modeling Web Services in Vector Space

To generate the concepts more precisely, services are represented using the vector-space model which has been very popular in information retrieval. According to the above discussion, it is reasonable to index services at the operation level. Therefore, for each operation provided by a given service should be represented by an individual vector. Correspondingly, for a specific service, it is modeled as an operation vector group in the vector space.

Definition 2. *In the vector space, a service is represented by a* **operation vector group** $V_{\vec{ws}} = \{\vec{op}_1, \vec{op}_2, \ldots, \vec{op}_n\}$, *each* $\vec{op}_i \in V_{\vec{ws}}$ *stands for an* **operation vector** *representing a specific operation of ws.* $\vec{op}_i$ *can be formulated by the vector*

$$\vec{op}_i = \{\omega_{i,1}, \omega_{i,2}, \ldots, \omega_{i,m}\} \tag{1}$$

where m is the vocabulary size, $\omega_{i,j}$ *is the weight of* t_j *in operation* op_i. $\omega_{i,j}$ *is calculated by tf/idf weighting scheme[9]:*

$$\omega_{t_j} = tf_{i,j} \times idf \tag{2}$$

where $tf_{i,j}$ *is the frequency of term* t_j *in operation* op_i. *idf is the inverse class frequency in the operation collection containing* op_i.

Normally, the length of each operation vector is normalized to a unit length, i.e., $\|\vec{op}_i\| = 1$, which enables us to account for operation of different lengths. This work is accomplished by equation 3 [9].

$$\omega_{i,j} = \frac{tf_{i,j} \times \frac{log|P|}{idf_{i,j}}}{\sqrt{\sum_{j=1}^{m} tf_{i,j}{}^2 [\frac{log|P|}{idf_{i,j}}]^2}} \tag{3}$$

where $|P|$ is the size of operation collection. The rest of this work is based on the assumption that the vector representation $\vec{op}$ of each operation op has been weighted using tf/idf and normalized to a unit length.

4   Conceptual Indexing of Web Services

As discussed in Section 1, unlike the traditional term-based indexing, conceptual indexing technique computes the *service concepts* by finding the groups of relevant operations and using them to generate the concept vectors. In this section, we describe the main ideas and algorithms of conceptual indexing used in the service context.

4.1   Service Concepts and Conceptual Indexing

In the previous section, operations are modeled into the vector space. The relevance between any two operations op_i and op_j can be measured using the well-known cosine function:

$$Relevance(op_i, op_j) = \frac{\vec{op_i} \cdot \vec{op_j}}{||\vec{op_i}|| \times ||\vec{op_j}||} = \frac{\sum_{k=1}^{m} \omega_{i,k}\omega_{j,k}}{\sqrt{\sum_{k=1}^{m} \omega_{i,k}^2 \sum_{k=1}^{m} \omega_{j,k}^2}} \qquad (4)$$

where "$\cdot$" is the dot-product of the two vectors, that is to say, $\vec{op_i} \cdot \vec{op_j} = \sum_{k=1}^{m} \omega_{i,k}\omega_{j,k}$. Since the operation vectors are normalized to a unit length, formula 4 is simplified to $relevance(op_i, op_j) = \vec{op_i} \cdot \vec{op_j}$. Let s be the pre-defined threshold s for the determination of the relevant operations. If $relevance(op_i, op_j) \geq s$ is satisfied, then op_i and op_j are regarded as relevant operations, which means they have the same functionality. Based on Formulae 4, a service concept is defined as follows.

Definition 3. *Given a set P of operations and the corresponding vectors $V_{\vec{P}}$, P is firstly partitioned into k relevant groups $\{C_1, C_2, \ldots, C_n\}$, according to the pairwise relevance among the operations in P. Then, for each group C_i, the centroid vector $\vec{C_i}$ represents a **service concept** present in P. $\vec{C_i}$ is also called the **service concept vector** of C_i.*

Suppose that $G = \{op_1, op_2, \ldots, op_l\}$ is a group of relevant operations in a service concept, and $V_{\vec{G}} = \{\vec{op_1}, \vec{op_2}, \ldots, \vec{op_l}\}$ is the set of the corresponding vectors. The service concept vector of $V_{\vec{G}}$ is computed as:

$$\vec{C_G} = \frac{1}{|G|} \sum_{\vec{op_i} \in V_{\vec{G}}} \vec{op_i} = \{\frac{1}{|G|} \sum_{op_i \in G} \omega_{i,1}, \frac{1}{|G|} \sum_{op_i \in G} \omega_{i,2}, \ldots, \frac{1}{|G|} \sum_{op_i \in G} \omega_{i,m}\} \qquad (5)$$

where $\omega_{i,j}$ is the weight of term j in operation i. Obviously, $\vec{C_G}$ is obtained by averaging the weights of the various terms in the operation set G. G is addressed as the *guiding set* of service concept $\vec{C_G}$. Note that $||\vec{C_G}|| \leq 1$, because all the operations have been normalized to unit length.

Similar to individual operations, the relevance between an operation op_i and a service concept C_G is computed using the following cosine measure, given by:

$$relevance(op_i, C_G) = \frac{\vec{op_i} \cdot \vec{C_G}}{||\vec{op_i}|| \times ||\vec{C_G}||} = \frac{\vec{op_i} \cdot \vec{C_G}}{||\vec{C_G}||} \qquad (6)$$

Equation 6 denotes that the relevance between a service operation op_i and a service concept vector C_G is the proportion of the dot-product between $\vec{op}$ and $\vec{C_G}$ divided by the length of $\vec{C_G}$, that is:

$$\vec{op_i} \cdot \vec{C_G} = \frac{1}{|G|} \sum_{op_j \in G} relevance(\vec{op_i}, \vec{op_j}) \qquad (7)$$

and

$$\|\vec{C_G}\| = \sqrt{\frac{1}{|G|^2} \sum_{op_k \in G} \sum_{op_l \in G} relevance(op_k, op_l)} \tag{8}$$

where G is the guiding set of service concept C_G. The dot-product is the average relevance between op and other operations in G, and the length of the concept vector $\|\vec{C_G}\|$ is the square-root of the average pairwise relevance among the operations in G, including self-relevance. Equation 7 measures the average relevance between op_i and the operations in the guiding set G of C_G, and Equation 8 illustrates that the length of concept vector $\|\vec{C_G}\|$ is scaled with the average pairwise relevance among the operations in guiding set G. Therefore, Formulae 6 evaluates the relevance between a operation and a service concept by considering the relevance between the operation and the guiding set (Equation 7), as well as the pairwise relevance among the operations in the guiding set.

Definition 4. *Given a service collection S, the operations extracted from each service in S form an operation collection S_{OP}. S_{OP} is grouped into k service-concept set $C_{S_{OP}} = \{C_1, C_2, \ldots, C_k\}$, where C_i is an individual service concept. For any C_i ($C_i \in C_{S_{OP}}$, $1 \le i \le k$), let $G_i = \{op_1, op_2, \ldots, op_l\}$ be its guiding set , if for every $op_j \in G_i$, $relevance(op_j, C_{G_i}) \ge \tau$ (τ is the relevant threshold between an operation and a service concept)is satisfied, then, $C_{S_{OP}}$ is the* **conceptual indexing** *of S.*

Definition 4 implies the ideas behind the conceptual indexing. In next section, we will discuss how to capture the service concepts for a specific service collection.

4.2   Capturing Service Concepts

Recall that in Section 3.1, a service is viewed as a set of operations, each of which is represented by an operation vector of terms and weights. Thus, given a collection of services S, its operation collection and the operation vector group (see Definition 1) is denoted as S_{op} and $V_{\vec{S_{op}}}$, respectively. They are computed by

$$S_{op} = \bigcup_{ws_i \in S} ws_i, V_{\vec{S_{op}}} = \bigcup_{\vec{op}_j \in \vec{ws_i}, ws_i \in S} \vec{ws} \tag{9}$$

where $ws = \{op_1, op_2, \ldots, op_n\}$ refers a service in S, and $\vec{ws} = \{\vec{op}_1, \vec{op}_2, \ldots, \vec{op}_n\}$ stands for the operation vector group of ws.

A partition algorithm can be defined to capture the service concepts of a given service collection by clustering the corresponding operations into k clusters. With the relevance functions (see Equation 4 and Equation 6), it seems that a number of existing algorithms can be applied to group the operations from a given service collection. We try to use the already-developed methods, such as k-means, hierarchical clustering, to derive the service concepts from the operation vectors. However, they does not work well for the extreme sparseness of the operation vectors. Therefore, a new variant of k-Means, named as **Capturing-WsConcepts**, is developed to find the service concepts of a specific collection

---

Algorithm 1: CapturingWsConcepts

Data: $V_{\vec{S}}$ -the operation vector group of a given service collection S; τ-the threshold of relevance between a operation and a service concept.

Result: $C = \{C_1, C_2, \ldots, C_k\}, G_C = \{G_{C_1}, G_{C_2}, \ldots, G_{C_k}\}$-the set of result service concepts and their guiding sets.

1 $m \leftarrow 1$;
2 $C_m \leftarrow$ Create a new service concept;
3 $C \leftarrow C \cup C_m$;
4 $G_C \leftarrow G_C \cup G_{C_m}$;
5 **foreach** $C_i \in C_{k=1,2,\ldots,m}$ **do**
6 $\quad \vec{C_i} \leftarrow \vec{op}_i$ where $\vec{op}_i$ is picked from $V_{\vec{S}}$ at random and $op_i \in S$;
7 **end**
8 **repeat**
9 $\quad$ **foreach** $\vec{op}_i \in V_{\vec{S}}$ **do**
10 $\qquad$ **foreach** $C_j \in C_{k=1,2,\ldots,m}$ **do**
11 $\qquad\quad$ $\gamma_{i,j} \leftarrow relevance(op_i, C_j)$;
12 $\qquad$ **end**
13 $\qquad$ $\gamma_l \leftarrow max(\gamma_{i,1}, \gamma_{i,2}, \ldots, \gamma_{i,m})$;
14 $\qquad$ **if** $\gamma_l \geq \tau$ **then**
15 $\qquad\quad$ $G_{C_j} \leftarrow G_{C_j} \cup op_i$;
16 $\qquad\quad$ $\vec{C_i} \leftarrow \{cw_{i1}, cw_{i2}, \ldots, cw_{ih}\}$, where $cw_{il} \leftarrow \frac{1}{|G_{C_i}|} \sum_{n=1}^{|G_{C_i}|} \omega_{nl}$;
17 $\qquad$ **else**
18 $\qquad\quad$ $C_{|C|+1} \leftarrow$ Create a new service concept;
19 $\qquad\quad$ $G_{|C|+1} \leftarrow op_i$;
20 $\qquad\quad$ $C \leftarrow C \cup C_{|C|+1}$;
21 $\qquad\quad$ $m \leftarrow m + 1$;
22 $\qquad$ **end**
23 $\quad$ **end**
24 **until** *concept vectors no longer change*
25 $k \leftarrow |C|$;
26 **return** $C = \{C_1, C_2, \ldots, C_k\}$ *and the corresponding guiding set* $G_C = \{G_{C_1}, G_{C_2}, \ldots, G_{C_k}\}$;

---

of operation vectors. Algorithm 1 describes a sketch of the main idea behind the algorithm **CapturingWsConcepts**.

CapturingWsConcepts initially creates a single service concept and randomly assigns an operation vector to it as the concept vector (lines 1-7). Then, the algorithm groups the operations according to the relevance between the operation and the service concepts (lines 8-23). If the largest relevance threshold is greater than the pre-defined threshold, the operation vector will be assigned to the corresponding service concept (lines 13-15). Otherwise, a new service concept is created, and the operation vector is clustered into it (lines 18-21). The relevance between an operation vector and a service concept is computed by Formula 6 (line 11).When an operation vector is grouped into a service concept, the corresponding operation is appended to the guiding set of that service concept(lines 15,19), and the service concept vector is computed after each operation is grouped (lines 16). Finally, the set of service concepts and their guiding sets are returned. The complexity of **CapturingWsConcepts** is $O(|V_{\vec{s}}|\times|C|\times t)$, where $|V_{\vec{s}}|$ is the size of operation vector group, $|C|$ is the number of service concepts, and t is the times of iteration.

5   Conceptual Indexing Supported Service Retrieval

The conceptual indexing methods described in above sections can support a variety of applications, such as service classification, service filtering, and service retrieval. In this section, we investigate the application of conceptual indexing to service retrieval.

5.1   The Vectorial Representation of Service Retrieval

The purpose of service retrieval is to find the relevant services from a service collection satisfying a given query describing the special requirements of the user. Similar to services, queries in service retrieval are also represented by vectors. The normalized weight of term t_i in a given query q is computed by[9]:

$$\omega_{q,i} = (0.5 + \frac{0.5tf_{q,i}}{max_l tf_{q,l}}) \times log\frac{|S_{op}|}{n_i} \tag{10}$$

where $tf_{q,i}$ is the frequency of term t_i in query q, $|S_{op}|$ is the total number of operations in the service collection, and n_i is the number of queries in which the characterizing terms t_i appears. Therefore, q can be represented by a normalized vector $\vec{q} = \{\omega_{q,1}, \omega_{q,2}, \ldots, \omega_{q,m}\}$, i.e., $||q||=1$, in the vector space using Equation 10.

5.2   Retrieving Services Using Conceptual Indexing

Suppose that S is the service collection, and S_{op} is the set of the operations extracted from the description of services from S. The operations in S_{op} are indexed conceptually by k service concepts, $C_1, C_2, \ldots, C_k$, whose guiding sets are disjoint. Particularly, let M_{op} be an $l \times m$ operation-term matrix, where l is the number of operations, m is the total size of vocabulary. Thus, the ith row of M_{op} represents the vector-space representation of the ith operations, that is to say, $M_{op}[i, *] = \vec{op}_i$.

According to Section 4.2, each concept vector $\vec{C}_i$ can be computed by Algorithm 1, and is denoted as $\vec{C}_i = \{c\omega_1, c\omega_2, \ldots, c\omega_m\}$. Let $\{\vec{C}_1, \vec{C}_2, \ldots, \vec{C}_k\}$ be these concept vectors, M_C be the $m \times k$ matrix whose ith column corresponds to $\vec{C}_i$, $M_{op}M_C$ is an $l \times k$ matrix whose ith row denotes a k-dimensional vector representing $op_i \in S_{op}$. Similarly, given a group of queries Q, the corresponding service vectors form a $n \times m$ query-term matrix M_Q, where q is the number of queries. The jth query vector can be reduced to k dimensions, and represented as the jth row of $M_Q M_C$. When retrieving service, the relevance between an operation and a query in the k-dimensional vector space is computed by cosine

---

Algorithm 2: RetrievingWs

Data: S-the service collection; $C = \{C_1, C_2, \ldots, C_k\}$-the service concepts;
$G = \{G_{C_1}, G_{C_2}, \ldots, G_{C_k}\}$-the guiding set corresponding to C;
$Q = \{q_1, q_2, \ldots, q_n\}$-the set of query descriptions.

Result: $R = \{r_1, r_2, \ldots, r_n\}$-the ranked operations with respect to each query.

1 Let $S_{op} \leftarrow \{op_1, op_2, \ldots, op_l\}$, $V_{S_{op}^{\rightarrow}} \leftarrow \{\vec{op}_1, \vec{op}_2, \ldots, \vec{op}_l\}$ denote the operations extracted from the services contained in S and the corresponding operation vectors, respectively;

2 Let $V_{\vec{Q}} \leftarrow \{\vec{q}_1, \vec{q}_2, \ldots, \vec{q}_n\}$ represent the query vectors calculated by Equation 10;

3 Let M_C, M_{op} and M_Q be the matrices formed by the service concepts from C, the operation vectors from $V_{S_{op}^{\rightarrow}}$ and the query vectors from $V_{\vec{Q}}$;

4 $V_{k\vec{S}} \leftarrow M_{op}M_C$;

5 $V_{k\vec{Q}} \leftarrow M_Q M_C$;

6 **for** $i \leftarrow 0$ **to** n **do**

7 $\quad | \quad r_i \leftarrow \phi$;

8 **end**

9 **foreach** *row* rq_i *in* $V_{k\vec{Q}}$ **do**

10 $\quad$ **foreach** *row* rp_j *in* $V_{k\vec{S}}$ **do**

11 $\quad\quad | \quad \gamma_{i,j} \leftarrow relevance(rq_i, rp_j)$;

12 $\quad\quad | \quad \gamma_i \leftarrow \gamma_i \cup \gamma_{i,j}$;

13 $\quad$ **end**

14 $\quad r_i \leftarrow$ {the ranked operations according to the relevance in γ_i};

15 $\quad R \leftarrow R \cup r_i$;

16 **end**

17 **return** R;

---

function. The operations are ranked with respect to each query according the operation-query pair relevance. By this way, it is convenient to select the top-k operations that are relevant to a specific query. The pseudo-code description of the algorithm is given in Algorithm 2(termed **RetrievingWs**).

6   Performance Evaluation

In this section, we study the performance of conceptual indexing and demonstrate its performance of retrieving services comparing with some existing approaches.

6.1   Service Corpus

We formed a corpus by gathering the services from the main authoritative UDDI repositories, such as IBM, BEA, XMethod and Microsoft etc. This corpus contains 693 service information description(WSDL) files and 2734 operations in total.

In Section 3.2, we mentioned that the information sources for describing each operation include the input/out messages ($\mathcal{D}_1$ and $\mathcal{D}_2$), the description of its function ($\mathcal{D}_3$), the name of operation ($\mathcal{D}_4$), the name of service ($\mathcal{D}_5$) and the description of the entire services ($\mathcal{D}_6$). The above textual information was pre-processed by performing word stemming, removing stopwords and splitting syn-thetical words into individual words (such as "OrderTickets" into "Order" and "Ticket") before representing operations in vector space. The weight $\omega_{i,j}$ of a term t_i in an operation vector $\vec{op}_j$ is computed by

$$\omega_{i,j} = \sum_{k=1}^{6} \beta_k \times \omega_k \tag{11}$$

where ω_k is the weight of t_i in $\mathcal{D}_k$ calculated with tf/idf method, and $\sum_{k=1}^{6} \beta_k = 1$. By setting the value of β_k, we can justify the effects of information obtained from different sources on the operation vector.

6.2   Experimental Results

In our evaluation, we adopted the conventional performance measures in infor-mation retrieval areas, i.e., precision(p), recall (r) and F_1-measure, as the metrics to evaluate the proposed method.

Two groups of experiments were conducted during our evaluation. The first one is to investigate the effect of the relevance threshold τ between operations and service concepts on the performance of capturing service concepts and re-trieving services against different size of service corpus. The second one is to evaluate the effectiveness of the proposed approach by comparing it with some existing ones.

Effect of Different τ. To evaluate the effects of the relevance threshold τ on the performance of finding service concepts using our approach, we conducted the algorithm **CapturingWsConcept** against different size of operation corpus with different value of τ. The experimental result shown in Table 1 illustrates that the number of service concepts increases as τ increases. It is because when τ becomes larger, fewer operations are similar enough to be grouped into the same service concept.

Table 2 demonstrates that the increase of relevance threshold τ will lead to the increase of the average precision of service retrieval. The reason is that the operations appended into the guiding set of a service concept are more similar with a larger value of τ than that with a smaller value of τ. But it does not to say, the larger is τ, the better is the whole performance of the system. If taking the execution time into account, things will be change. Because when τ increases, the number of service concepts also increases. The more time will be needed to evaluate the pairwise relevance between service concepts and the queries. Therefore, in real applications, it is very important to determine the value of τ (generally, 0.5~0.8) which can balance the retrieval precision and the response time according to the user requirements.

Table 1. The effect of relevance threshold (τ) on the size of conceptual index

Number of Operations	Value of relevance threshold (τ)								
	0.1	0.2	0.3	0.4	0.5	0.6	0.7	0.8	0.9
400	70	159	251	277	298	343	339	338	347
800	99	234	344	423	482	530	583	616	634
1200	111	264	437	518	600	681	759	867	936
1600	97	211	345	482	649	836	976	1145	1193
2000	95	228	435	589	807	961	1152	1363	1400
2400	115	267	469	689	911	1086	1325	1569	1683

Table 2. The average precision of retrieving operations under deferent value of relevance threshold τ

Number of Operation	The value of relevance threshold τ								
	0.1	0.2	0.3	0.4	0.5	0.6	0.7	0.8	0.9
400	0.51	0.63	0.68	0.70	0.74	0.79	0.81	0.83	0.88
800	0.53	0.61	0.68	0.69	0.72	0.77	0.76	0.83	0.82
1200	0.49	0.60	0.68	0.71	0.71	0.82	0.81	0.79	0.85
1600	0.55	0.69	0.67	0.70	0.74	0.75	0.81	0.86	0.89
2000	0.56	0.65	0.73	0.70	0.76	0.74	0.79	0.82	0.85
2400	0.50	0.63	0.71	0.77	0.79	0.79	0.84	0.86	0.88

Comparison with Some Existing Service Retrieval Approaches. We examined the performance of the proposed approach by comparing its accuracy with that of the k-NN and Naive Bayes (NB). Figure 1 presents the result for retrieving services based on the mentioned approaches. The figure indicates that the precision is improved as τ increases, see Figure 1(a). Notice that this trend does not apply to *recall*. That is because when τ increases, fewer operations

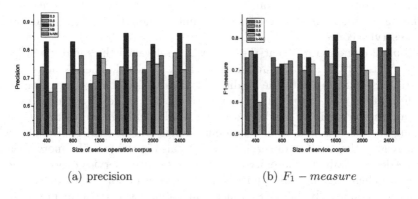

(a) precision   (b) $F_1 - measure$

Fig. 1. Precision and F_1-measure for different retrieving approaches

are appended into the guiding set of the same service concept, which leads the decrease of *recall*. Figure 1(b) illustrates that the F_1-measure of our approach is relative high, which means our approach can better compromise between recall and precision.

7 Conclusion

Service retrieval is a very important issue for making the paradigm of service-oriented computing more practical. In this paper, we have proposed a novel approach for effectively retrieving services based on conceptual indexing of services. Before building the conceptual indexes, each operation is modeled as a vector in the vector space. This representation of services enables us to find services at the operation level which is more accurate than at the entire service level. To capture the service concepts, a new variant k-means algorithm is devised to group the operation into different service concepts. Based on these service concepts, we develop a new service retrieving approach. Experimental results show that the proposed approach offers a good performance if the parameter, i.e., the value of relevance threshold between operations and service concepts, is assigned a reasonable value. For the drastic increase of services on the Web, in our future work, an incremental approach of conceptual indexing of Web services will be developed to support service retrieval more efficiently.

References

1. Organization for the Advancement of Structured Information Systems (OASIS) (2005) www.oasis-open.org/committees/tc_home.php?wg_abbrev=soa-rm
2. Zaremski, A.M., Wing, J.M.: Specification Mathing of Software Components. ACM Transactions on Software Engineering and Methodology (TOSEM) 6(4), 33–369 (1997)
3. Dong, X., Halevy, A., Madhavan, J., Nemes, E., Zhang, J.: Similarity Search for Web Services. In: Proceedings of the 30th Very Large Database Conference (VLDB'04), Toronto, Canada (2004)
4. Wu, J., Wu, Z.: Similarity-based Web Service Matchmaking. In: IEEE Intl Conf. on Service Computing (SCC), Orlando, FL, USA (2005)
5. Bianchini, D., De Antonellis, V., Pernici, B., Plebani, P.: Ontology-based Methodology for E-service Discovery. Information Systems 31(4), 361–380 (2006)
6. Miller, J., et al.: WSDL-S: Adding Semantics to WSDL - White Paper (2004) http://lsdis.cs.uga.edu/library/download/wsdl-s.pdf
7. Wang, Y., Stroulia, E.: Flexible Interface Matching for Web-Service Discovery. In: Proceedings of Fourth International Conference on Web Information Systems Engineering(WISE'03) Roma, Italy (2003)
8. Bernstein, A., Klein, M.: Towards High-Precision Service Retrieval. In: Proceedings First International Semantic Web Conference, Sardinia, Italy (June 9-12, 2002)
9. Baeza-Yates, R.A., Ribeiro-Neto, B.A.: Modern Information Retrieval. ACM Press, New york, Addison-Wesley, London (1999)

Design and Implementation of Computational Bioinformatics Grid Services on GT4 Platforms*

Chao-Tung Yang[1,**], Tsu-Fen Han[1], Ya-Ling Chen[1], Heng-Chuan Kan[2],
and William C. Chu[1]

[1] High-Performance Computing Laboratory
Department of Computer Science and Information Engineering
Tunghai University, Taichung City, 40704, Taiwan
{ctyang,g942814,chu}@thu.edu.tw
[2] Southern Business Unit
National Center for High-Performance Computing
Hsinshi, Tainan, 74147, Taiwan
n00hck00@nchc.org.tw

Abstract. Availability of computer resources is key factor limiting use of bioinformatics analyses as a result of the growing computational demands. Grid computing provides a way to meet these requirements. But it is complicated to build a grid for users. This paper describes an approach to solve this problem using Grid Service technologies. Building the grid based on accepted standards and platforms makes the development and deployment of the grid much easier. A bioinformatics grid computing environment (BioGrid) which consists of the distributed computing application for bioinformatics is presented in this paper. Based on this environment, we propose the architecture of bioinformatics applications which is delivered using Grid Services constructed with the Globus Toolkit 4. We developed a simple program which is defined as the client-server application with grid services. It provides users an approach of grid services to impose grid resources and customize their own grid applications.

1 Introduction

Biology is defined as the study of living things. In the course of that study, biologists collect and interpret data from the interaction of species and populations, to the function of tissues and cells within an individual organism. In the past, using sophisticated laboratory technology allows us to collect data faster than we can interpret it. There are vast volumes of DNA sequence data, and we need to figure out which parts of that DNA control the various chemical processes of life and determine the function of new proteins from the known function and structure of some proteins [1], [2], [6], [7], [9], [10], [11], [15].

---

* The work is supported in part by National Science Council, Taiwan R.O.C., under grant no. NSC95-2221-E-029-004.
** Corresponding author.

H. Jin et al. (Eds.): ICA3PP 2007, LNCS 4494, pp. 302–313, 2007.

Bioinformatics is the science of using information to understand biology. It is the application of information technology and capable of analyzing and managing biological data. Availability of computer resources is key factor limiting use of bioinformatics analyses as a result of the growing computational demands. A bioinformatics grid computing environment called BioGrid [3], [4], [5], [9], [13], [16-19] which consists of the distributed computing application for bioinformatics is presented in this paper. We propose the architecture of biological Grid Services constructed with the Globus toolkit 4.0.1. When the services are connection by producing and using compatible XML documents, the process of orchestrating these services can be automated. It should be concerned about efficiency, throughput, and workflow when considering tools for comparative genomics. Grid Services provide flexible, extensible, and widely adopted XML-based mechanisms for describing, discovering, and invoking network services [12-14]. Services can be deployed on different platform, described by unified standardized Grid Services mechanisms.

It allows the developers to focus their attention on implementing application logic, and provides users an approach of Grid Services to impose grid resources and customize their own grid applications. The approach contributes to the field of parallel performance analysis by enabling users to meaningfully and efficiently compare parallel performance data, regardless of the format of data and system. Finally, we developed a simple portal which is defined as the client-server application with Grid Services. The user portal enables interactions between application and Grid Services obtaining parametric inputs for problems and reporting results upon execution completion.

2   Parallel Bioinformatics Applications

2.1   mpiBLAST

The Basic Local Alignment Search Tool (BLAST) is a sequence database search tool that seeks similarities between two substrings in molecular biology by using score matrices to improve filtration efficiency and to introduce more accurate rules for locating potential matches. BLAST attempts to find all locally maximal segment pairs in query sequences and database sequences with scores above the set threshold value. mpiBLAST is a freely available, open-source parallelization of NCBI BLAST. It contains a pair of programs that replace formatdb and blastall with versions that execute BLAST jobs in parallel on clusters of computers with MPI installed [10].

There are two primary advantages to using mpiBLAST rather than conventional BLAST. First, mpiBLAST segments a target database, and then dispatches the segments to nodes in clusters. Because the database segment in each node is small, it can usually reside in the buffer-cache, yielding a significant speedup due to the elimination of disk I/O. Second, it allows BLAST users to take advantage of efficient, low-cost Beowulf clusters because inter-processor communication demands are low. The main executable programs in the BLAST distribution are:

- [blastall] performs BLAST searches using one of five BLAST programs: blastn, blastp, blastx, tblastn, or tblastx.
- [blastpgp] performs searches in PSI-BLAST or PHI-BLAST mode. blastpgp performs gapped blastp searches and can be used for iterative searches in psi-blast and phi-blast mode.
- [bl2seq] performs a local alignment of two sequences. bl2seq allows the comparison of two known sequences using blastp or blastn. Most of the bl2seq command-line options are similar to those for blastall.
- [formatdb] is used to format protein or nucleotide source databases. It converts a FASTA-format flat file sequence database into a BLAST database.

The mpiBLAST algorithm consists of two primary steps: (i) databases are segmented and put on a shared storage device; (ii) mpiBLAST queries are run on each node. The mpiBLAST partitioning schema is shown in Figure 1. It uses multi-threading to segment databases, assigning distinct portions of the database to each processor. It wraps the standard NCBI formatdb called mpiformatdb to format the database. Command line arguments specify the number of fragments. mpiformatdb formulates command line arguments that force NCBI formatdb to format and divide the database into many fragments of approximately equal size. When mpiformatdb execution is complete, the formatted fragments are placed in shared storage. Alignment of the database is accomplished by the local sequence alignment algorithm implemented in the NCBI [10] development library. If a node does not have fragments needed by a search, the fragments are copied from shared storage. Fragments are assigned to nodes using an algorithm that minimizes the number of fragments copied during each search.

2.2 FASTA

FASTA is another popular tool for searching sequence databases. It compares any two sequences by trying to align them from a database [8]. FASTA is capable of delivering very fast search results from sequence databases. Like BLAST It is available both as a service over the Web and as a downloadable set of programs. In the experimental environment of this paper, MPI versions of the programs that include the libary-vs-library comparison programs are listed below:

- [fasta]: Compares a protein sequence against a protein database (or a DNA sequence against a DNA database) using the FASTA algorithm
- [ssearch]: Compares a protein sequence against a protein database (or DNA sequence against a DNA database) using the Smith-Waterman algorithm
- [fastx /fasty]: Compares a DNA sequence against a protein database, performing translations on the DNA sequence
- [tfastx /tfasty]: Compares a protein sequence against a DNA database, performing translations on the DNA sequence database
- [align]: Computes the global alignment between two DNA or protein sequences
- [lalign]: Computes the local alignment between two DNA or protein sequences

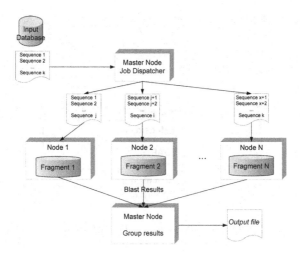

Fig. 1. The mpiBLAST partitioning schema

2.3 Web Services and WSDL

Web Services provide a standard means of interoperating between different software applications, running on a variety of platforms and/or frameworks. The Web Services Architecture (WSA) document is intended to provide a common definition of a Web Services, and defines its place within a larger Web Services framework to guide the community. The WSA provides a conceptual model and a context for understanding Web Services and the relationships between the components of this model.

WSA is interoperability: it identifies those global elements of the global service network to ensure interoperability between Web Services. WSA involves many layered and interrelated technologies. There are many ways to visualize these technologies, just as there are many ways to build and use Web Services. The technologies that we consider here, in relation to the Architecture, are XML, SOAP, and WSDL. However, there are many other technologies that may be useful. Figure 2 provides an illustration of some of these technology families.

WSDL is an XML format. The operations and messages are described abstractly, and then bound to a concrete network protocol and message format to define an endpoint. It describes the network services as a set of endpoints operating on messages containing either document-oriented or procedure-oriented information. WSDL is extensible to allow description of endpoints and their messages no matter what message formats or network protocols are used to communicate. However, the only bindings in this document describe how to use WSDL in conjunction with SOAP 1.1, HTTP GET/POST, and MIME [4].

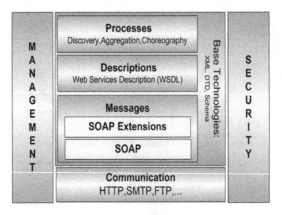

Fig. 2. Web Services architecture stack

2.4 WSRF

The WS-Resource Framework (WSRF) has been proposed as a means of expressing the relationship between stateful resources and Web Services. Web Services specifications define a rendering of the WS-Resource approach in terms of specific message exchanges and related XML definitions. These specifications allow the programmer to declare and implement the association between a Web service and one or more stateful resources. They describe the means by which a view of the state of the resource is defined and associated with a Web Services description, forming the overall type definition of a WS-Resource. They also describe how the state of a WS-Resource is made accessible through a Web Service interface, and define related mechanisms concerned with WS-Resource grouping and addressing. The WSRF has five separate specification documents that provide the normative definition of the framework: WS-ResourceProperties, WS-ResourceLifetime, WS-RenewableReferences, WS-ServiceGroup, and WS-BaseFaults.

3 System Design and Implementation

3.1 System Design

It uses a GT4 core based Grid Services as a thin middleware layer to our application. The implementation language of Grid Services is Java. The user portal enables interactions between the application user and the application, obtaining parametric inputs for problems and reporting results upon application execution completion. Our portal uses Java-based Application as interface for easy control of the parallel bioinformatics software. We have also developed various basic services for the Grid systems.

The Java-based Application uses the grid service to connect to the Grid system. We develop several grid services. The grid services represent a simple gram job and allow for submitting jobs to a gatekeeper. GridFTP can upload DNA sequences to the Grid System. It allows user to compare the specific sequences with the target database.

System architecture is shown in Figure 3. We will describe what would be implemented and tested within a Grid environment. mpiBLAST program allows the user to specify the number of segmentations according to the number of processors. If the performance of one of VOs (Virtual Organizations) is low comparatively, it would lower the whole performance. It depends on the performance of each VO to segment the target database into the different size before we use [mpiformatdb] commands and submit the jobs. Thus, it parallelizes the processes of mpiformatdb and mpiblast. BioGrid user can query and segment the database via the portal. By querying information database, the status information can be noticed. When the computing job is completed, the results will be transferred to the system portal.

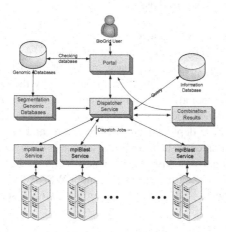

Fig. 3. System architecture of our proposed system

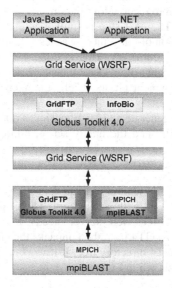

Fig. 4. The software architecture of our proposed system

3.2 Specifications of Grid Services

This section describes the deployment details of our grid services. Our application is a set of grid services that offers standard bioinformatics applications. Figure 4 illustrates the software architecture of Grid Services application. At top layer, the BioGrid users can develop their specific application in Java or .NET application to query the Job_Dispatcher service on infoBio. Through the Job_Dispatcher service, BioGrid users can submit jobs to each node. At bottom layer, MPICH program such as mpiBLAST is wrapped by grid service on each node. It also provides GridFTP service to upload DNA sequences to the Grid System. It allows user to compare the specific sequence with target database.

3.2.1 Deployment and Configuration

The Grid Services is deployed on Linux server with GT4. The resource details are saved in a configuration file to allow easy modification of the computed resources available to the service. The configuration file is read by the service at deploy time. The interesting details include, the domain name of the resource's head node, the number of computed nodes, memory etc. The Grid Services including Job_dispatcher and mpiblast_services are deployed on infoBio server and the master nodes of each VO, which are implemented. When mpiblast_service is deployed, it returns a message to mpiblast_client and delivers a notice that a new VO joined grid environment.

There are five steps for writing and deploying a WSRF Web Service. We describe the details of developing a grid service by using mpiBLAST_service as an example in the following:

1. Define the service's interface: The first step is to define the service interface. It needs to specify what the service provides. In the example, we want our do_mpiBLAST operation to receive four parameters.
2. Implement the service: The next step is implementing that interface. We need to provide the implementation of our remotely accessible methods (do_mpiblast).
3. Define the deployment parameters: This is done with the WSDD language and using a JNDI deployment file. Deployment descriptor is one of the key components of the deployment phase. It tells the Web Services container how it should publish the service.
4. Compile everything and generate a GAR file: This is done with the Ant tool. Using the provided Ant buildfile and the handy script, building a web services as the following:
   ```
   ./globus-build-service.sh -d <service base directory> -s
   <service's WSDL file>
   ```
   If it works fine, the GAR file will be generated.
5. Deploy service: This is done with a GT4 tool. The GAR file contains all the file and information, which the web server needs to deploy the web service. Deployment is done with a GT4 tool, then unpacks the GAR file and copies the file into key location in the GT4 directory tree. If it works fine, we can find the service in the list of services as shown in Figure 5.

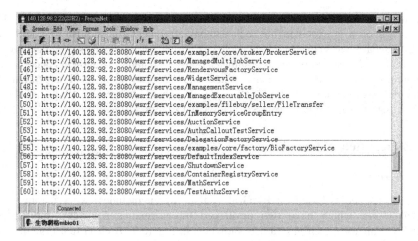

Fig. 5. The BioFactoryService

3.2.2 Job_Dispatcher Service

In this section, we discuss our database segmentation approaches for scheduler. As the scheduler receives the request from end users, it calculates the file ranges for each partition and distributes them to each VO according to the number of available VOs, in terms of (start offset, end offset) pairs. Then the master node uses such file ranges to read, split the target database and generates the mpiBLAST's database fragment files.

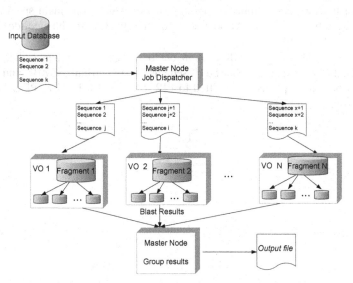

Fig. 6. Schematic of database fragment

We wrapped mpiBlast as the Grid Services, mpiblast_service, which are deployed on master nodes. The scheduler calls the mpiblast_service from remote side and dispatches the job with all arguments including offset files of database fragment as described above. The application provides several common databases such as nr and env_nt. This mechanism is represented in Figure 6. At each VO, the mpiBLAST program chosen is executed for each database fragment file. mpiBLAST splits the target database across each node in each VO. Instead of the database segmentation of functionality immediately, we use stable number of database fragments according to the number of available workers. When all VOs end their local execution, the scheduler has to assemble the partial results at each VO to create a unique result file. The output of program will be saved as temp.dat in user's directory.

4   Experimental Results

4.1   Testbed

Our grid testbed is based on BioGrid system, which includes two separate virtual organizations, which have two developed bioinformatics packages: mpiBLAST, FASTA. Hardware configuration is shown as in Figure 7. Both virtual organizations (VOs) contain four nodes. The Fedora Core 4 Linux distribution has been installed on each node. We assessed the performance of the environment by executing mpiBLAST program using 2, 4, 8, and 16 processors. Table 1 shows the hardware configuration of our experimental environment. The following section describes an introduction of the databases that we adapted for our experimentation.

- Swiss-Port (uniprot_sprot.fasta): Swiss-Prot was set up in 1986 as a kind of protein database with remarks and Swiss Institute of Bioinformatics and EMBL Outstation - The European Bioinformatics Institute, EBI, worked together to launch it in 1987. It consists of a large number of orders, each of which contains a specific format. The formatting is made as identical to that of EMBL Nucleotide Sequence Database as possible.
- NCBI (nr database): The NR Protein database contains sequence data from the translated coding regions from DNA sequences in GenBank, EMBL and DDBJ as well as protein sequences submitted to PIR, SWISSPROT, PRF, PDB (sequences from solved structures).

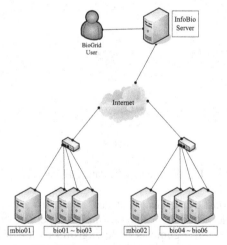

Fig. 7. Experimental environment

Table 1. Hardware configuration of our experimental environment

	InfoBio	mBio01	Bio01	Bio02	Bio03
Host Name	infobio	mbio01	bio01	bio02	bio03
IP Address	140.128.98.1	140.128.98.2	140.128.98.3	140.128.98.26	140.128.98.27
CPU	Intel(R) Pentium(R) D CPU 2.80GHzx2	Pentium III 1GHzx2	AMD Athlon(tm) 64 X2 Dual Core Processor 3800+	AMD Athlon(tm) 64 X2 Dual Core Processor 3800+	AMD Athlon(tm) 64 X2 Dual Core Processor 3800+
RAM	1024MB	1024MB	1024MB	1024MB	1024MB
Hard Disk	80 GB	140GB	160 GB	160 GB	160 GB
Network Interface Card	100Mbps	100Mbps	100Mbps	100Mbps	100Mbps
Switch HUB	100Mbps				
	mBio02	Bio04	Bio05	Bio06	
Host Name	mbio02	bio04	bio05	bio06	
IP Address	140.128.98.3	140.128.98.28	140.128.98.29	140.128.98.230	
CPU	Pentium III 1GHzx2	AMD Athlon(tm) 64 X2 Dual Core Processor 3800+	AMD Athlon(tm) 64 X2 Dual Core Processor 3800+	AMD Athlon(tm) 64 X2 Dual Core Processor 3800+	
RAM	1024MB	1024MB	1024MB	1024MB	
Hard Disk	120 GB	160 GB	160 GB	160 GB	
Network Interface Card	100Mbps	100Mbps	100Mbps	100Mbps	
	100Mbps				

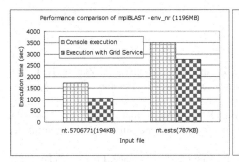

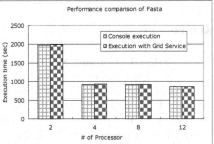

Fig. 8. Performance comparison of mpiBLAST   **Fig. 9.** Performance comparison of FASTA with mwkw.aa

4.2   Experimental Results

In this case, we use mpiBLAST program which allows the user to specify the number of segmentations according to the number of processors. If the performance of one of VOs is low comparatively, it would lower the whole performance. In order to force the completion time of each VO can be closely. It depends on the performance of each VO to segment the target database into the different size before we perform [mpiformatdb] commands and submit the jobs. Thus, it parallelizes the processes of mpiformatdb and mpiblast. Figure 8 shows a comparison between executing from the console end and from the grid service and it uses the env_nr database. The database is about 1.2GB. We can find that there is great different between console execution and execution with grid service. In the experimental environments, the performance of two VOs is the same. The reduction time of mpiformatdb is visible but the reduction time of mpiblast is not. The results clearly show that the system reduced the execution time. The other case, we used FASTA program as an example. Figure 9 shows the performance comparisons of number of processors. The FASTA can reduce the execution time, as indicated from comparison with the number of work nodes.

5 Conclusion

Biologists access to grid environments using the serial command line or other unfriendly way in the past. Web services provide flexible, extensible, and widely adopted XML-based mechanisms for describing, discovering, and invoking network services. Building the basic platform of grid computing environment is attempted in this study. Globus toolkit v.4 which serves as middleware is used for message transfer and communication between various Grid platforms. Results show that the BioGrid indeed saves significant time in sequence alignment problems with increasing number of processors used in the computations. In this paper, we proposed the architecture of bioinformatics applications which is delivered using Grid Services constructed with the Globus Toolkit 4.0.1. It provides users an approach of grid services to impose grid resources and customize their own grid applications. We developed a simple program which is defined as the client-server application with grid services. It provided users an approach of grid services to impose grid resources and customize their own grid applications.

References

1. Alexander, S., Bernhard, M., Roland, P., Johannes, R., Thomas, T., Zlatko, T.: Client-Server Environment for High-Performance Gene Expression Data Analysis. Bioinformatics 19(6), 772–773 (2003)
2. Bala, P., Jaroslaw, P., Miroslaw, N.: BioGRID – An European Grid for Molecular Biology. In: Proceedings of the 11th IEEE International Symposium on High Performance Distributed Computing, p. 412 (2002)
3. Foster, I.: The Grid: A New Infrastructure for 21st Century Science. Physics Today 55(2), 42–47 (2002)
4. Foster, I., Kesselman, C.: The Grid 2: Blueprint for a New Computing Infrastructure (Elsevier Series in Grid Computing), 2nd edn. Morgan Kaufmann, San Francisco (2004)
5. Foster, I., Kesselman, C.: Globus: A metacomputing infrastructure toolkit. The International Journal of Supercomputer Applications and High. Performance Computing 11(2), 115–128 (1997)
6. Gernot, S., Dietmar, R., Zlatko, T.: ClusterControl: A Web Interface for Distributing and Monitoring Bioinformatics Applications on a Linux Cluster. Bioinformatics 20, 805–807 (2004)
7. Fumikazu, K., Tomoyuki, Y., Akinobu, F., Xavier, D., Kenji, S., Akihiko, K.: OBIGrid: A New Computing Platform for Bioinformatics. Genome Informatics 13, 484–485 (2002)
8. FASTA, http://fasta.bioch.virginia.edu
9. Micha, B., Campbell, A., Virdee, D.: A GT3 based. BLAST grid service for biomedical research. In: Proceedings of the UK e-Science All Hands Meeting (2004)
10. mpiBLAST, http://mpiblast.lanl.gov
11. Oswaldo, T., Miguel, A., Alfonso, V., Zapata, E.L., Carazo, J.M.: Computational Space Reduction and Parallelization of a new Clustering Approach for Large Groups of Sequences. Bioinformatics 14, 439–451 (1998)
12. Pierce, M., Fox, G., Youn, C., Mock, S., Mueller, K., Balsoy, O.: Interoperable Web services for computational portals. In: Proceedings of the 2002 ACM/IEEE Conference on Supercomputing, pp. 1–12 (2002)

13. Suzumura, T., Matsuoka, S., Nakada, H., Casanova, H.: GridSpeed: A Web-based Grid Portal Generation Server. High Performance Computing and Grid in Asia Pacific Region. In: Seventh International Conference on (HPCAsia'04) pp. 26–33 (2004)
14. Shui, W.M., Wong, R.K.: Application of XML Schema and Active Rules System in Management and Integration of Heterogeneous Biological Data. In: Proceedings of BIBE, pp. 367–374 (2003)
15. Satish, M.K., Joshi, R.R.: GBTK: A Toolkit for Grid Implementation of BLAST. High Performance Computing and Grid in Asia Pacific Region. Seventh International Conference on (HPCAsia'04) pp. 378–382 (2004)
16. Yang, C.T., Kuo, Y.L., Lai, C.L.: Designing Computing Platform for BioGrid. International Journal of Computer Applications in Technology (IJCAT) 22(1), 3–13 (2005)
17. Yang, C.T., Kuo, Y.L., Li, K.C., Gaudiot, J.L.: On Design of Cluster and Grid Computing Environments for Bioinformatics Applications. In: Sen, A., Das, N., Das, S.K., Sinha, B.P. (eds.) IWDC 2004. LNCS, vol. 3326, pp. 82–87. Springer, Heidelberg (2004)
18. Yang, C.T., Hsiung, Y.C., Kan, H.C.: Implementation and Evaluation of a Java Based Computational Grid for Bioinformatics Applications. In: Proceedings of the International Conference on Advanced Information Networking and Applications (AINA 2005) vol. 1, pp. 298–303 (2005)
19. Yang, C.T., Kuo, Y.L., Lai, C.L.: Design and Implementation of a Computational Grid for Bioinformatics. In: Proceedings of the 2004 IEEE International Conference on e-Technology, e-Commerce and e-Service (EEE 04) pp. 448–451 (2004)

On-Demand Capacity Framework*

Chi-Hung Chi and Chao Wang

School of Software, Tsinghua University
chichihung@mail.tsinghua.edu.cn

Abstract. Web service technology has generated a lot interest, but its adoption
rate has been slow. This paper discusses quality of service issues which is one
of the contributing factors to this slow take up, and argues that nowadays
policy, which requires the service providers to ensure a certain level of QoS, is
not practical and will invoke high business risks. Therefore, we introduce four
innovating concepts to SOA community, and propose an extending framework
to ensure on-demand capacity by decoupling classical service provider into
service logic provider and QoS provider. Moreover, we present a qualitative
comparison in a typical web service scenario between the model proposed,
classical SOA and enhanced SOA models introduced by previous publication.

Keywords: Web Service, SOA, Performance, QoS.

1 Introduction

Web Services become the core application in this Internet era. The well-accepted
framework of web service—Service-Oriented Architecture (SOA) attracts widely
interest of research, and becomes an important research area.

The difference between web service and traditional application includes many
aspects, in which the Quality of Service (QoS) is included. As the important attributes
which describe the service, QoS helps applying SOA in publishing, discovery and
binding steps, and it rises as one of the main concerns.

In order to achieve high QoS, today's policy is burden on the web service
providers—it requires the service providers to ensure a certain level of QoS. This
requirement seems reasonable. However, there are some basic problems involved
which need to be clarified first. Actually this is also some of the reason why SOA is
still in its infant stage and cannot be deployed widely in general Internet services.

It is natural that being a provider, it can provide the function, or better say
functional requirements to the end users. However, it might not be practical for the
provider to ensure non-functional issues (QoS) at the stage of service publishing or
even the stage of service discovery and selection. Because:

- Comparing to functional requirements, QoS requirements are harder to capture
hence to be satisfied. Although market research could smooth this process, until
the moment that a customer submits a request and pays for it, the true QoS
requirements could not be accurately predicted. Therefore today's policy is not
cost-effective.

* This work is supported by the China National Science Foundation Project #90604028.

H. Jin et al. (Eds.): ICA3PP 2007, LNCS 4494, pp. 314–325, 2007.
© Springer-Verlag Berlin Heidelberg 2007

- Wide variation of potential customers' QoS demands makes it a hard problem that providing a "certain" QoS level to all customers. Even if the QoS requirement could be predicted, in order to satisfy all the potential demands, the service provider has to set up an unreasonably high QoS service. However, at this stage, there is still no purchase order yet.
- Moreover, malicious attacks, such as distributed denying of service (DDoS), or unpredictable burst workload, such as sports event in video-broadcasting service, make today's policy on QoS worse.
- Furthermore, there exist some companies, especially the medium or small ones, who produce attractive service, yet cannot set up their own servers and thus cannot grantee a certain QoS level due to the limitation of funding or other business problems. It is obviously that nowadays policy barricades those companies contributing to the whole SOA community.

Therefore, we argue that:

- Service QoS provision should be decoupled from the service function provision. Service function is more focus on the business logic while the QoS is more related with the execution environment.
- A novel mechanism should be established, under which QoS capacities could be outsourcing to (or rent from) the third parties. Therefore, we can image that a new type of provider, which is called "QoS provider" will appear in the SOA framework.

As a result, in this paper we would like to propose a new methodology to provide QoS for services under SOA. It includes four fundamental concepts and a reference model. The basic idea is to build a capacity framework for outsourcing. In this framework, a service's logic once moved, or better say, replicated onto the third party in real time, can make use of the execution environment to provide QoS..

2 New Concepts

2.1 Requirement Engineering Principles

In the past software developing practices, no matter the succeed ones or the failed ones, requirement analysis has been proved to be a critical stage in the whole software life-cycle. A typical scenario is, at the very beginning of a project, the customer provided the initial requirements to describe the target features of the output product. These requirements are either rough or not well-defined, but reflect the problems which customers were facing. Then the software engineers and the customer worked together, to polish the initial requirement into a series of well-organized documents, and at the same time, customer would put down deposit, thus the risk of developer is decreased. Although there would be evolutions and updating of those documents in the following stages, the product, or better say solution, was designed and developed specifically aiming the requirements. In other words, the requirement engineering principles ensures the mapping from problem space to the solution space, thus makes the whole process smooth and cost-effective.

Look back to the workflow of classical SOA. Service providers developed their business logic, and published the description and API of this service to UDDI registry first. And then customers submitted service inquiry to registry with their requirements, hoping that there would be some services matching those requirements. It is obviously that the order of this typical workflow completely conflicts the requirement engineering principle which discussed above—it is the mapping from solution space to problem space. At the very moment that service providers developed and published their service, they got no actual customer yet, and what they own is the "potential" customer and "potentially promising" market share. This introduces a high risk to those providers. Moreover, the design of services is based on the investigation of "potential" requirement which is coarse and sometimes misleading, and such uncertainties are likely to harm the solution's cost-effectiveness.

We observed a very interesting situation in nowadays SOA related industry that many successful SOA applications are deployed on the intranet, such as the private network in an enterprises or a community. This phenomenon inspired us that one of the reasons which contribute to the success is their narrow or implicitly well-defined requirements. For example, under EAI, the very area where SOA works well, the target customers is almost determined before a service is developed. Furthermore, in those small or medium organizations, the smooth and easy communicating also helps a lot in clarifying and mining the true requirements of the customers. We believe that all of those relieve the hazard due to the lack of requirement engineering principles. Unfortunately, the SOA applications which deploy on the public net, or say Internet, are still under the suffering.

2.2 Web Service Decoupling

For a long time, the definition of term "Web Service" is the integration of mainframes, executing web applications and supporting database systems. What is more, the applications are pre-deployed on the mainframes. However, we'd argue that this integration is not necessary, and the web service could be decoupled into three loose-depended parts as follows:

- **Execution Environment.** Execution Environment (EE) is the physical entity which service running on. It includes not only the execution resource, such as CPU, memory and extra storage; but also the networking device, such as router, switcher and firewall; and some unique devices which supports special services such as high-performance graph card, wave table card and vector processing unit. Although those parts mentioned above are mostly the hardware, EE do include supporting software such as virtual machine, middleware platform, web server, etc. In a word, EE is the platform, which is the common part shared by most sorts of web services.
- **Portable Package of Service Logic.** Portable Package of Service Logic (PPSL) is the business logic of a web service, and it includes the business procedure and the implementations of each stages. Due to its executive and portable nature, PPSL is neither a simple document which describes the process, nor the binary package which does not obey the existing standards. Ideally, each PPSL includes a script which helps deploy the corresponding PPSL full-automatically. In a word, PPSL is the implementation of business logic, which reflects the functional difference between services.

- **Supporting Dataset.** Supporting Dataset (SD) includes the data or information which would be accessed in one instance of service. Typically, SD is a perceivable subset in this transaction comparing with the whole dataset which a service may manage or utilize, and the size of SD is much small than the size of whole set. In a word, SD is the unique part among the different instances of same service.

2.3 QoS Provision

Under the decoupling of web service, we notice that the functional and non-functional requirements are fulfilled by separated parts of service—PPSL and SD together implement the business logic thus fulfill the functional requirements, while EE is responsible for the capability issues thus fulfill the non-functional requirements. In particular, we believe that the QoS of a service comes from two parts: the PPSL provides the benchmark in design-time, and the EE enhances the base in run-time by providing the on-demand capacity.

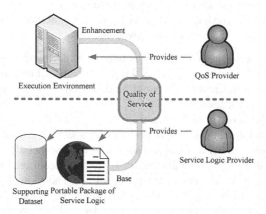

Fig. 1. QoS and its provider. Under the situation that web service could be decoupled into Execution Environment, Portable Package of Service Logic and Supporting Data.

We take the executing time as an example to illustrate the above concept. Executing time is an important QoS attributes which is mainly related to the run-time performance of a service. On one hand, the base performance is determined in the design-time according to the service's architecture and implemented algorithms; on the other hand, the capacity reserved for running this service determines how much the ultimate performance which user will get is enhanced in the run-time. In order to quantify the enhancement which is provided by EE, a package of standard evaluating routine should be established. Under those routines, the user's demand on executing time could be satisfied by selecting the proper EE and its reserved workload.

Therefore, based on the decoupling of web service and their roles, the actor "Web Service Provider" in the classical SOA could be decoupled into "Service Logic Provider" and "QoS Provider", as the Fig. 1 shows. PPSL and SD belong to the service logic provider who designs and implements the solution according to the business problem; and the base performance of this service is also evaluated, described and published by the service logic provider. EE belongs to the QoS provider who evaluates and describes the enhancement comparing to the reference EE. In a word, the service logic provider satisfies functional requirements of customer, while the QoS provider satisfies the non-functional ones.

2.4 Service Function Mobility

In recent years, content mobility or better say content delivery networks (CDN), has been studied and applied widely, and it is proved to be a efficient way to support wide-spread customers in accessing the central-organized web content by replication [2]. The prosperity of nowadays SOA has triggered further research efforts into developing advanced web service replication. However, most of the existed works [3] are more focusing on the replicating and delivering supporting data, which we've mentioned on the above. For example, in a video-broadcasting scenario, the broadcasting service has been pre-installed on the edge server, while the video content is replicated real-timely. Furthermore, although some papers [4] do have discussed the application replicating, they treat the replicating of service logic as no more than a trivial issue, which is not the fact. We believe that, according to the service function mobility, at least below issues and their solutions should be carefully reviewed and designed.

- **Feasibility.** Due to the heterogeneous nature of the Internet, a series of related standards should be established to keep the compatibility of EE and PPSL. Therefore a well-defined PPSL could be deployed on an arbitrary EE smoothly and without modification.
- **Business Relationship.** In the practical business world, it is very common to see such a scenario that service logic provider S_A and S_B are competitors, and each of them build their own alliance chain which may include several EEs. It is obviously that the EE in the alliance of S_A is not encouraged or even forbidden to support the web service from alliance of S_B. Therefore, besides the logical compatibility which fulfilled by technologies or published standards, the relationship between a service logic provider and a QoS provider should be taken into account when making any business decision. It calls for a formal language to describe such relationship, or at least to mark the relationship as discrete variables labeled "partner", "neutral" or "competitor", etc.
- **Re-distributing Management.** When a QoS provider Q_A requires for a PPSL from a service logic provider S_A, it is easy to image that if other QoS provider Q_B which has deployed that PPSL could share its PPSL with Q_A, and the network latency between Q_A and Q_B is short than one between Q_A and S_A, the delay caused by replication and deployment may decrease, thus the customer's experience will be improved. Therefore, considering the protection of intellectual property, the re-distributing management should distinguish the EE by at least three kinds of licenses: executable, re-distributable and modifiable.
- **Activating or Replicating.** The service function on EE could be pre-installed, as the classical web service did, or on-demand deployed. The advantage of pre-installed service is that there is no replicating and deploying delay. Moreover, when pre-installed service has no customer call, it is in hibernation thus cost ignorable computation resource. When a customer request comes in, it only needs to be activated. On the other hand, since the storage of EE is limited and

the on-demand deployment is more oriented thus gains higher cost-effectiveness, it needs to make a trade-off between the policy of activating and replicating.

3 Extending Framework

3.1 Overview

The current proposed SOA model for Web services' publishing and discovery is concise, yet not powerful enough—it lacks for the QoS representing and publishing, nor QoS enhanced service discovery. Recent years, many innovated ideas have been applied to these issues. On the other hand, based on the classical SOA framework, the on-demand capacity framework which we proposed, is not only aiming to integrate QoS information into nowadays SOA, as previous work do, but also considering how the QoS is provided. Furthermore, we believe that the latter issue is as same important as the former one.

The main block diagram of ODCF is shown in the Fig. 2. Comparing with current SOA model, ODCF has three abstract roles, which called customer, registry and provider, too. And the relationship between each abstract role does not change, either. As an extension of SOA, ODCF keeps this similarity to make a smooth migration from classical SOA.

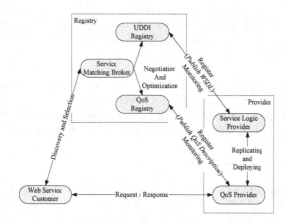

Fig. 2. On-Demand Capacity Framework

According to the new concepts "Web Service Decoupling" and "QoS Provision" introduced in Section 2, we subdivide roles provider and its corresponding registry for fulfilling:

- **Functional Requirements.** The service logic providers maintain the portable package of service logic and supporting data. They describe the API of a web service with WSDL, and publish it to a UDDI registry, as they done in classical SOA model. Besides that, as Section 2.3 discussed, the basement of QoS could be determined in the design-time, and these extra QoS information should be described and published to UDDI registry by the service logic provider, too. Moreover, they set up a FTP-like service to support the replication of service.

- **Non-Functional Requirements.** The counterpart of service logic provider is QoS provider. They describe the EE's capacity and publish it to QoS registry. Due to the high-dynamic nature of QoS attributes, real-time monitoring is very important in providing on-demand QoS, and some attributes' recursively tracking approach [5] could be adopt.

Obviously, selecting optimal service logic provider and QoS provider separately would not yield an optimal pair for the end user. Therefore, a service matching broker is added into ODCF to negotiate and optimize the final output pair. We notice that, for service matching broker, the negotiating process needs many rounds of communicating with UDDI registry and QoS registry, while the communicating with end user is comparatively simple. Consequently the service matching broker is put into the abstract role registry considering about performance issues.

3.2 Publishing and Discovery

As the extending framework, ODCF inherits the publishing stage, especially the publishing of service logic provider, from basic SOA. On the other hand, service logic provider should publish base QoS descriptions together with classical web descriptions. Therefore, these extra QoS information could be included in UDDI by extending "bindingTemplates" block, which locates in "businessService" block, with tag "qualityInfo". Note that in previous works, this technic is used to integrate the whole QoS info into UDDI structure, but we now use it to describe the base of QoS which the end user will get, and the final QoS is determined by QoS provider.

The registering of QoS provider is quite same as the one of service logic provider. Considering that the UDDI is a well-accepted standard for registering, we adopt the technic mentioned above to describe QoS provider's capability. According to the end user, what he needs to do is submitting the web seeking request to service matching block along with QoS constrains, which is almost the same as that published works [1]. Therefore, the practicability and compatibility could be guaranteed.

3.3 Negotiation and Optimization

The negotiation and optimization stage is accomplished by service matching broker. As Fig. 3 will show, different strategies will lead to the variant performance of ODCF. Furthermore, besides of the capability and resource that a QoS provider own and the workload, other issues should be taken into account when designing it.

- **Compatibility.** From the technical view point, some service depends on the special hardware or software environment which is not common through all EEs. Therefore, this issue could be used as a filter to filter out incompatible pairs.
- **Business Relationship.** The relationship between service logic provider and QoS provider is an important issue in selecting the pairs. For example, in current web service, the service logic provider and the QoS provider is the same organization, therefore the PPSL and SD cannot be re-deploy to other EEs.
- **Replicating Overhead.** Web services are called by customers frequently, thus the situation that some candidate pairs have already bind together is very often to happen. If such situation occurs, select these pairs will improve the user experience due to the avoidance of replicating overhead.

Among those non-functional attributes, time is a frequently used one. Therefore, we choose the whole time that a transaction lasting as the non-functional attribute to illustrate three extreme conditions caused by different optimizing strategies.

From the view of customer, a complete transaction of a service starts at asking for binding, and ends at finishing the task and closing the service client. Consequently, it includes three parts: the networking delay due to the service replicating, the execution time and the networking delay due to the server-client communication in run-time. Note that the first one is related to the size of service package and the speed of backbone, and the third one is related to the size of run-time interaction and the speed of public network.

The three extreme conditions are listed bellow, if we only optimize the selection for:

- **Portable Package of Service Logic and Supporting Dataset.** This is the strategy used in current enhanced SOA model. However, the QoS information on the registry is a stable value which is verified in the publishing stage and rarely be updated. Hence the requests are redirect to the same service logic provider regardless of the network bandwidth or congestion situation between customers and provider. It is obviously that the final user experience will quite differ with the QoS which provider declared.
- **Execution Environment.** If the client machine is so strong that better than other QoS providers, then this strategy will leads to such a decision that replicating the PPSL and SD to local host, deploying and running on it. Actually, when using a video broadcasting service, if the server is a hotspot and could not provide a certain playback bit rate, user would better download the video content and necessary codecs through FTP or other protocol, and then play it locally. However, it does not consider the size of PPSL and SD thus the user experience will be poor if the PPSL and SD is too large.
- **Service Matching.** In this situation, the pre-installed service will get the best evaluation because they have "matched" thus have no replicating delay. And ODCF is degenerated to enhanced SOA since there is no replicating at all.

Therefore, the design of service matching broker should take all these issues together in order to find an optimal pair.

4 Evaluation and Comparison

4.1 Simulation Setup

We carefully designed a simulated internet environment. In this typical scenario, the whole network is composed by several sub-networks, or known as autonomy systems in networking area, which would be maintained by different ISPs. Edge servers, which refer to service logic providers and QoS providers in this paper, locate at the entrance of those sub-networks, and connect to each other through high speed backbone. On the other hand, end users are clustered surrounding those edge servers and connect to each other through low speed public network. In order to simplify the discussion, all QoS providers are compatible and all service logic providers publish the service with same function attributes—of course their QoS base is different due to the different implementation.

We choose the whole time that a transaction lasting as the non-functional attribute in the following discuss, and it has been mentioned in Section 3.3.

Table 1. Parameters of Simulation

Parameter Name	Value
Service Logic Provider Number	10
QoS Provider Number	10
Customer Number	40,000
Backbone's speed	10Mbps~100Mbps
Public Net's speed	28.8kbps~2Mbps
Demand of Customer (second)	20~300
Service Size	256MB~1GB
Interaction Size	1MB~5MB

We take the reject rate as the measurement to compare different models. In this typical scenario, rejection occurs at two different situations. First of all, the service request could not be accomplished. It may because of the workload of selected server is so high that it cannot accept a new request, or the storage of selected server is full that cannot replicate a new service. Secondly, the service is completed, but the time exceeds the customer's tolerance. In most of time, customer has a prediction towards the time that completing a certain task will cost, and this evaluation could be seen as a non-functional requirement. The parameters of scenario are shown in the Table. 1.

4.2 Comparison

In this section, we comparing among three kinds of service provision framework, and they have different service selecting strategies:

- **Current SOA.** There's no QoS concept in current SOA, thus the selection of service is barely depends on the functional attributes. Unfortunately, the service which appears in this simulation provides the same function. Therefore the customer will select a service provider from all providers randomly.
- **Enhanced SOA.** It based on the model introduced by Ran [1]. At the publish stage, service provider publish their QoS info to the third party called "Web Service QoS Certifier". Hence the customer will select a service provider who has the highest claimed QoS, or say, static QoS.
- **ODCF.** It will do replicating and deploying real-timely in ``best" service-pair. We here consider two kinds of strategies. The first one, which labeled "ODCF—I", selects the QoS provider which locates in the same sub-net as customer locates in, then choose the service logic provider who matches this QoS provider best. The second one, which labeled "ODCF—II", selects the best pair by exhaustively enumerate all possible pairs.

The simulation result is show in Fig. 3. It is clear that the looser (the longer the time) the customer's demand is, the lower the reject rate is. Moreover, ODCF performs much better than both current SOA and enhanced SOA. It is also very interesting that even in ODCF different strategy causes a tiny difference on reject rate.

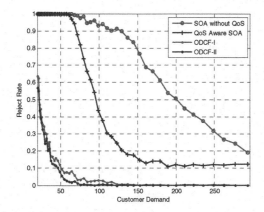

Fig. 3. Comparison among current SOA, enhanced SOA and ODCF we proposed

4.3 Work Characterization

Different characteristic of services derives different performance of ODCF. In this section, we simulate the scenario under variant range of service package size. The larger the package size is, the overhead of replicating delay is more significant, hence the reject rate is higher. From the result in Fig. 4, we can see that, when service package size is too large (in our simulation it is 2Gbytes to 8Gbytes, but it depends on other parameters), the performance of ODCF is almost as same as the performance of enhanced SOA (see Fig. 3)

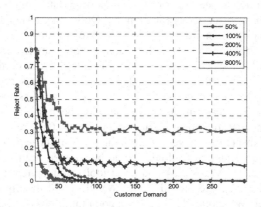

Fig. 4. Package size and ODCF

The size of data in server-client interaction also influences the performance of ODCF and enhanced SOA. Fig. 5 shows that the less the size is, the smaller the difference between ODCF and enhanced SOA is. When the size decreases to zero, the reject rate curves of ODCF and enhanced SOA are almost the same, except the situation that customer's demand is too severe.

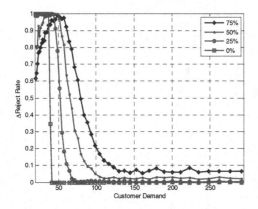

Fig. 5. Interaction size and the performance difference between ODCF and enhanced SOA

5   Related Work

The replication of web service is tightly related to the previous content replication technologies. A typical example of such a system is a Content Delivery Network (CDN) [6, 7]. Accompany with the popular of web service, application replication also attracts the research interests [8, 9]. These systems replicate the code at the replica servers, but either do not replicate the application data or cache them at the replica servers. This limits the system performance as all write accesses need to be forwarded to a single remote location irrespective of their update patterns. In the other words, they haven't developed the concept "supporting data" and haven't discovered the relation between web service replication and QoS issues. Another related area of our work is capacity planning [10] and workload balancing [11] in system engineering. When applying to web environment, a typical application is [12]. It has a central controller which schedules the replication of service according to workload situation. However, they still burden the QoS issues onto the service provider. The "HP Virtual Server Environment" [13] also discussed these issues, but it does not invoke those innovative ideas, either. QoS issues have been the hot topic [14] in SOA community. Current research focuses on two problems: QoS representing [15] and enhancing service discovery stage by utilizing QoS information [16], especially semantic information. These technologies could be adopted in the implementation of ODCF. For example, DAML-S [15] is a good tool to integrate base QoS attributes measured by the service logic provider with WSDL-based description of functional attributes. Moreover, WS-Policy [17] based negotiation process [18] should be a fine template when designing and implementing the service matching broker.

6   Conclusion

Web service technology has generated a lot interest, but its adoption rate has been slow. This paper discusses quality of service issues which is one of the contributing factors to this slow take up, and argues that nowadays policy, which requires the service providers to ensure a certain level of QoS, is not practical and will invoke high business risks. Therefore, the paper introduces four innovating concepts to SOA community, which are "Requirement Engineering Principles", "Web Service Decoupling", "QoS Provision" and "Service Function Mobility". Moreover, we propose an extending framework to ensure on-demand capacity by decoupling classical service provider into service logic provider and QoS provider. Furthermore, a qualitative comparing simulation is designed in a typical web service scenario. The model compared here includes the ODCF proposed, classical SOA model and enhanced SOA model introduced by previous publication [1].

References

1. Ran, S.: A Model for Web Services Discovery with QoS, ACM SIGecom Exchanges, vol. 4(1) (2003)
2. Sivasubramanian, S., Szymaniak, M., Pierre, G., van Steen, M.: Replication for Web Hosting Systems, ACM Computing Surveys, vol. 36(3) (2004)
3. Pierre, G., van Steen, M., Tanenbaum, A.S.: Dynamically Selecting Optimal Distribution Strategies for Web Documents, IEEE Transactions on Computers, vol. 51(6) (2002)
4. Sivasubramanian, S., Pierre, G., van Steen, M.: Replicating Web Applications On-Demand. In: Proceedings of IEEE International Conference on Services Computing (2004)
5. Wang, C., Chi, C.: Quantitative Trust Based on Actions. In: Proceedings of IEEE International Conference on Web Services (2006)
6. Hull, S.: Content Delivery Networks (2002)
7. Verma, D.: Content Distribution Networks: An Engineering Approach (2002)
8. Rabinovich, M., Xiao, Z., Agarwal, A.: Computing on The Edge: A Platform For Replicating Internet Applications. In: Proceedings of International Workshop on Web Content Caching and Distribution (2003)
9. Cao, P., Zhang, j., Beach, K.: Active cache: Caching dynamic contents on the Web. In: Proceedings of the Middleware Conference (1998)
10. Menasce, D.A., Almeida, V.: Capacity Planning for Web Services (2002)
11. Menasce, D.A.: Workload characterization, Internet Computing (2003)
12. Keidl, M., et al.: Reliable Web Service Execution and Deployment in Dynamic Environments, Lecture Notes on Computer Science, Technologies for E-Services (2003)
13. Herington, D., Jacqueot, B.: The HP Virtual Server Environment (2006)
14. Menasce, D.A.: QoS issues in Web services, Internet Computing (2002)
15. Zhou, C., et al.: DAML-QoS Ontology for Web Service. In: Proceedings of International Conference on Web Service (2004)
16. Shaikhali, A., et al.: UDDIe: An Extended Registry for Web Service. SAINT'03 Workshops (2003)
17. Bajaj, S., et al.: WS-Policy.
18. Wohlstadter, E., Tai, S., Mikalsen, T., Rouvellou, I., Devanbu, P.: GlueQoS: middleware to sweeten quality-of-service policy interactions. In: Proceedings of International Conference on Software engineering (2004)

An Interest-Based Intelligent Link Selection Algorithm in Unstructured P2P Environment*

Hao Ren, Nong Xiao, and Zhiying Wang

School of Computer, NUDT, ChangSha, China
Renhao1973@gmail.com

Abstract. Nowadays, most of the running P2P file sharing systems, such as Gnutella, generally adopt an unstructured topology and flooding search algorithms, which facing very serious search efficiency problem. In this paper, we proposed a novel intelligent link selection algorithm to address the search efficiency problem by exploiting the principle of interest-based locality. Specifically, peers continually build new connections with the others peers with same interests, this enables peers find its interest files in the nearby ones. In addition, in order to avoid adding too many connections in the overlay network which may lead the flooding search produce excessive redundant message as a consequence, we adopt a dynamic balance mechanism to delete the connection between peers which brings the least useful message. The simulation study shows our algorithm can significantly cut down the reply path lengths, achieve high search success rate with smaller search scope, and reduce the total communication cost in unstructured P2P systems.

1 Introduction

Today, P2P file sharing is one of the most popular applications on the Internet [13-16], which has been widely used by hundreds of millions of people. Among all the proposed P2P systems, unstructured P2P systems are popular ones for file sharing due to its flexibility on peers joining and leaving and simple search mechanism allowing arbitrary criteria. Flooding is the most popular used searching algorithm in an unstructured P2P environment, specifically, a query peer simply sends a query to all neighbors, and the neighbors will relay the query to their neighbors until time-to-live (TTL) in terms of forwarding steps is exhausted or a loop is detected (queries bear a unique ID for this purpose). Query results are routed back along the query path to the original requester. The main disadvantage of flooding is that there exists extremely high redundancy on broadcast messages which causes excessive traffic overhead.

To address the problems of flooding and improve search efficiency in an unstructured P2P environment, many algorithms have been proposed to optimize the topology by exploiting the *principle of locality*. Generally, there are two different types of locality: temporal locality, which states that recently accessed items are likely to be accessed in the near future and spatial locality which refers that items whose

---

* Support by NSF of China 60573135, 863-2006AA10A118, 863-2006AA10A106.

H. Jin et al. (Eds.): ICA3PP 2007, LNCS 4494, pp. 326–337, 2007.

addresses are near one another tend to be referenced close together at a given time. Previous algorithms often utilize the spatial locality by choosing a proper position for a peer when the peer joins in, and try to achieve high search hit rate in a small search scope. In addition to that, these methods should be able to dynamically adjust peer's position after peers have joined in.

In this paper, we proposed a novel "intelligent" link selection (ILS in short) algorithm, which can significantly improve search efficiency and reduce the traffic overhead by gathering peers with same interests. As the accesses in a file sharing application follow the principle of locality, a peer can find another peer who has the same interests by recording and analyzing all successful searching, and build a direct connection with it which enables each peer find its interest files in its neighbors. At the same time, to avoid adding too many connections in the overlay network and make flooding searching produce less redundant messages, we adopt a token-based dynamic balance mechanism in which peers cut down the connection that bring the least useful message. Our extensive simulation studies have shown that intelligent algorithm can significantly cut down the reply path lengths and achieve high search success rate with less TTL value, and reduce the total communication cost in an unstructured P2P system.

The rest of the paper is organized as follows: we discuss the related works in section 2; in section 3 we proposed the problem background in detail and define link selection model; in section 4 we present the results analyzing and comparison to related works; finally, we conclude in section 5.

2 Related Works

In recent years, many researches have been proposed to improve the efficiency of P2P system. Especially, the method by exploiting principle of locality is effective to improve search efficiency for the P2P file sharing applications [4][5]. Specifically, the principle of interest-based locality refers to the cases if a user is looking for some files, and then he/she will probably look for alike files before long; if the user find his/her interest files in a node, and then he/she will find others interest files from the same node with high possibility.

The general strategy of exploiting interest-based locality is to form interest-based clusters by analyzing the content of peer's sharing and clustering peers based on the same interests. But it is very hard to analyze peer's sharing well and match the query in all kinds of environments as files are different in thousands ways.

Sripanidkulcha et al. [6] design a content location algorithm that explores common interests among peers. Peers that share similar interests create "shortcuts" to one another and use them to locate content. When shortcuts fail, peers resort to use the underlying Gnutella protocol. Experiment results show that it could significantly reduces the search response time and communication cost. However, the management of shortcut list increases peer's load. Furthermore, their algorithm may slow down the search response time when the hit rate of the shortcuts is not high enough. We compare this approach with our proposed approach in the later experiment section.

Barbosa M. W. et al. [8] improve the search efficiency by organizing the peers into communities which share some of the locally stored files. However the method increases the peer's degree and the seed of communities have to send many additional query messages to find the peer with same interests with it.

Similar to [6], Hai Jin [7] analyze peer's sharing content and build shortcut between peers with similar semantic characteristics, however, this method requires semantic knowledge of applications, which is hard to implement.

3   Intelligent Link Selection Algorithm

In this section, we present our intelligent link selection algorithm, which helps reduce the searching cost and response path length by wisely adding or deleting links of the overlay topology. We first briefly review the background related with the proposed method. Then, we propose our algorithm and evaluation model of adding and deleting connection. Finally, we discuss the setting of parameters and the load balance mechanisms.

3.1   Background

As the file sharing in P2P systems is a typical application that follows the principle of interest-based locality, if we build a connection in the overlay network between peers with same interests, this link would satisfy more searches than the others as users will find their interest files though such a link with higher probability, the added links will be more efficient than others. If we add a large amount of such links in P2P systems, the search efficiency can be improved as a whole. However, in an unstructured P2P environment with a flooding search algorithm, continuously adding connections in the overlay network will increase the average degree of peer, which raises up the maintenance cost of connections as a consequence. Furthermore, more links will inevitably make the flooding search produce more redundant query messages and the system will become less scalable.

In fact, for flooding search, not all links are necessary in an unstructured P2P environment. For a peer, if one of its neighbors is reachable from another short path, it is reasonable to delete the link between the peer to this neighbor, as most query message can still be sent to the peer by flooding. In addition, the different links have different values for a peer. If a peer always gets result from some links, it is no doubt these links are very valuable; whereas a link is useless if it seldom returns a query result, and even the query messages it brings can be received from another link. The main function of these useless links is bringing redundant messages. Thus, deleting links in the overlay network reduces peer's burden, moreover, it will reduce the consumption of network bandwidth produced by flooding too. Like adding link, continually deleting link will bring a serious side-effect as well, which would inevitably decrease the search scope and search results, even make the peer be prone to break away from the overlay network, or splitting network into several parts. Thus, we propose some evaluation models to measure the benefits of adding or deleting links in the next section. Fig.1 gives an example showing the effect of adding or deleting links.

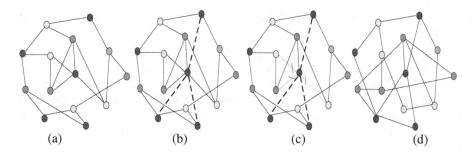

Fig. 1. The effect of link selection

As show in Fig. 1, the nodes have the same color means they have same interests, suppose nodes would always find files in the peers with same interests and seldom success in others. In Fig. 1-a, peers always take a long trip to find its request files. By adding some links between peers with same interests, it will make a peer get its target files in the nearby (Fig. 1-b), but it brings more connections to the network. In order to avoid adding too many links, peer can delete some inefficient links to delete (Fig. 1-c). At last, the topology of network is adjusted by the efforts of all peers, which achieves high search efficiency than initial situation.

Both adding and deleting links change peer's degree, and have some side-effects to the system. Nevertheless, determining the approximate number of neighbors for a peer is another challenge research issue, which is not the focus of this paper. In this paper, we only focus on improving the link efficiency rather than changing link number. We integrate the operations of adding and deleting in the overlay network in order to improve the link's usage. The peers with the same interests would be clustered and most of searches can find the results in the neighbor peers.

3.2   Intelligent Link Selection Model

In this section, we first give the evaluation method for adding link, then deleting link, at last, we propose a load balance mechanism.

3.2.1   Link Selection of Adding Link
It is essential to find an appropriate approach to discover the search efficiency improvement after peers add a link between them. We have designed the following three approaches:

- ILS-FAB (Find and Build): If peer A find its interest file from peer B, immediately build a direct connection with peer B.
- ILS-MB (Most Benefit): every peer evaluates and chooses a peer which will bring maximum benefit for the whole system when building a link with it.
- ILS-MIS (Most Interest Similarity): every peer finds out the peer with the most interest similarity to build connection.

We discuss the detailed steps for the above three algorithms which are listed as follows:

(1) ILS-FAB: A straight forward approach, explanation is omitted.
(2) ILS-MB: Peers record all search results from others and all searches that it has result periodically, forecast access quantity between peers, choose the link with high forecast value (more than a system threshold) as candidate, and then compute the benefit of adding link from candidate set accord to the forecasted value and the distance between peers. Finally, the peers build links with the one has the most benefit.

Formula (1) is the forecasting algorithm: $f_{(x,y)}(t)$ is the actual interaction times between peer x and y in time t, and $F_{(x,y)}(t)$ is the forecast value in time t. α =0.33 here, it is the parameter controls the ratio of contribution of the last statistical data.

$$F_{(x,y)}(t+1) = f_{(x,y)}(t) \times \alpha + F_{(x,y)}(t) \times (1-\alpha) \quad (0 \le \alpha \le 1, F_{(x,y)}(0) = 0) \quad (1)$$

Formula (2) is used to calculate the total benefits of adding a link: $Dis(x,y)$ denote two peer's distance, $F_{(x,y)}(t) \times (Dis(x,y)-1)$ express the direct benefit of adding link, and we also consider the indirect benefit that the added link will reduce the search path length between x's neighbor and y as well as y's neighbor and x.

$$Benefit(x, y) = F_{(x,y)}(t) \times (Dis(x,y)-1) + \sum_{(y' \in Y', y' \ne x, Dis(x,y')>2)} F_{(x,y')}(t) \times (Dis(x,y')-2)$$
$$+ \sum_{(x' \in X', x' \ne y, Dis(x',y)>2)} F_{(x',y)}(t) \times (Dis(x',y)-2) \quad (2)$$

Every time a peer chooses the peer have the most benefit from candidates and send request for building connection, if the other side also considers this peer could bring enough benefit compare to others, then a link can be added between them.

(3) ILS-MIS: Peers use formula (3) to evaluate the interest similarity between peers and choose the peers have most similarity to build links. Because the ILS algorithm builds links between peers with same interests, peers will have many neighbors with same interests, thus it is better for a peer to consider the interest similarity of the other peers and neighbors of that peer too.

$$S(x, y) = \frac{Qs(x,y)}{Qt(x,y)} + \frac{Qs(x,y)}{Qt(x,y)} * P(x) + \frac{Qs(x,y)}{Qt(x,y)} * P(y) \quad (3)$$

Qs is the amount of success query between peers, Qt is the total amount of query between peers. P(x) express the similarity between peer and its neighbor, use the quantity of success query which gets result in one hop divide the quantity of all query it send out. The rest of the steps are the same as those of ILS-MB.

3.2.2 Link Selection Model for Deleting Link

Like adding a link, we need to design an evaluation model to measure benefit after deleting a link. When we delete a link, first, the deletion needs to guarantee that the neighbors will still be accessible through other path after deleting the connection with it; second, we set weigh value for each kinds of message. A peer will lose all messages that come from the deleted link, and different messages have different meanings to the peers. The response message is far more important than query message; For a peer, the response message it received which satisfy its query or the response message it send out which satisfy other's query are more important than the response message just passing through it, we set the weigh value for each kinds of message.

The message received only from a certain connection has its exclusive value of a peer, it is the absolute loss of deleting, and the value could represent the weightiness for the link. We use the following formula to express the ratio that exclusive message takes, m expresses the exclusive message set that a peer received, m' denotes the exclusive message received from a certain link, W_m states the weigh of the message.

$$Part(l_i) = \frac{\sum_{m' \in M} m' \times W_{m'}}{\sum_{m \in M} m \times W_m} \tag{4}$$

$$Value(l_i) = \sqrt{Len(x,y) - 1} \times Part(l_i) \tag{5}$$

Formula (5) is used to calculate the total losing of a link deletion. $Len(x, y)$ expresses the path length between peers after deleting links. Every time a peer chooses the connection which has the least losing value as the candidates and sends a request of deleting connection. If the other side of the connection also considers this link have not enough benefit compare to others, then the connection between them is deleted.

3.2.3 The Balance Mechanism and Other Parameter

In order to stabilize total numbers of links in the overlay network, we propose a dynamic balance mechanism which can make deleting correspond to adding. To add a link, there is a token produced in the network and attach to the peer which actives a request for adding, any peers want to delete a link must have a token first by flooding search with the limited range (TTL<=2). The initial value of TTL has important function to limit the change of overlay network topology. If TTL=0, then a peer can only do deleting after adding link, it has no chance to alter more than one connection. When we set TTL=1 or 2, a peer will have the ability to change its degree, but the change is easier with search have high initial TTL value. Furthermore, a peer is not allowed to have more than one token, and the peer want to add link should have no token, if it has one, it must pass it to one of its neighbor. At last, we make the needs of deleting are always more than adding by choose proper threshold value of deleting and adding.

4   Experiments and Results Analyze

To evaluate ILS, we adapt Peersim[9] simulator and choose three types of network topologies. One is random link topology in which every peer has same degree (express as random (degree)), the other is a kind of Small-World [10] topology proposed by Watt and Strogatz (express as SW(product parameter), and a scale-free topology proposed by Barabasi-Albert [11] (express as BA(product parameter)).

We have built the P2P simulation environment with 5000 (only one with 8000) peers, and settled 40000 unique files as the sharing. We assume that all files are 50 types and each type and file assigned a popular degree value as zipf distribution with parameter $a = 0.4$ and 0.6 separately. There are more unique files with a more popular type and more replicates for more popular file.(The type is more popular, the number of unique files is larger. This situation is same for file and its replicates.) We assign a set of files to every peer as its sharing, and assign another set of files to every peer as its interests, a peer will search files within its interest set. While assigning files to peer as sharing, we assume that each peer only shares files with several types. We also assume that 80% files are shared by 20% peers and 20% files are shard by 80% peers, which expresses the differences of peer's contribution. Files in each peer's interest set also belong to several types, and the file types have the possibility of 70% chosen from peer's sharing as peers usually share its interest files.

We conduct the simulation run in cycles, every peer sends out about from 1 to 20 times flooding search, and afterward every peer orderly executes adding link algorithm and deleting algorithm. Though it is impossible to run link selection like these in the real world, but the simulation results can totally present the effectiveness of link selection algorithm. We set the peer's upper limit degree as 60, floor limit degree as 3, the default initial TTL value of flooding search as 6, and the initial TTL value of token search as 2. The weight value of query and three kinds of response message are set as 1, 50, 200, and 200 separately. The default threshold value of add link for ILS-MIS and ILS-MI are set as 0.48. At last, every cycle, a peer would at most add or delete one link, and we always adopt the data of cycle 8 as the performance data.

4.1 The Effect of Self-parameters

As discussed in Section 3.2, ILS will significantly improve success rate, reduce ARPL (the average reply path length) and communication cost of search. We will show these characteristics as followed:

Experiment 1: what we test is ILS's impact to reduce ARPL, which could improve search quality from a client's perspective. The results are reported in Fig. 2 and Fig. 3. As shown in the figures, the results of many simulations show that ILS could always reduce ARPL more than 45%. In the environment of random(5), about 20% searches fail at the beginning, for the TTL value of flooding limited search scope. The search reply path length distribution of ILS-MIS is presented in Fig. 2 (1-8). At the beginning, there are 35744 successful searches and 8310 failure searches, but the failure searches continually reduces and vanished finally at cycle 5. The fall of ARPL under different algorithm and settlement is presented in Fig. 3. ILS-MIS acquires the best effect of three in the same environment, ARPL reduces from 5.95 to 3.248, and ILS-MI and ILS-FAB also get 100% search success rate, and ARPL reduces to 3.598 and 3.685 separately, the difference is that ILS-FAB works more soon than others. When we change the experiment setup of ILS-MIS, the results are changed. By extending the network scales to 8000 nodes, ARPL reduced from 6.219 to 3.4. With the original network scales, by changing the threshold of adding link to 1.0, ARPL increased from 3.248 to 3.672, which is 19.3% longer compared with the original method. The lowest curve of random(5) in Fig. 3 shows the result of applying two phase search algorithm, in which the first is flooding search with small scope (3 hop), and then flooding with a large scope (6 hop) to locate the target of fail search, which get the best improving of search response time, ARPL reduced to 2.8.

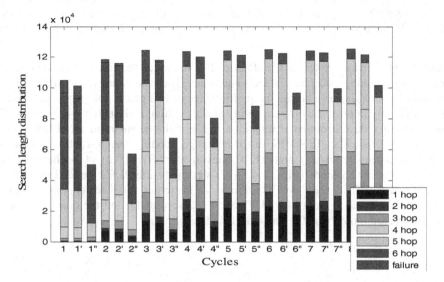

Fig. 2. Search length distribution, 1-8 Exp1-1, 1'-8' Exp2, 1''-8'' Exp4

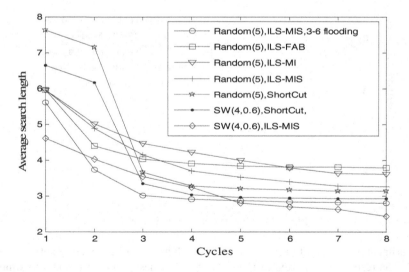

Fig. 3. Average reply path length of search

Experiment 2: what we test is ILS's ability of getting high search success rate within very small search scope. The experimental results listed in Fig. 2(1''-8'') show that ILS could reduce TTL value by two and gain about the same search success rate and results. Because ILS could cluster the peers with same interests, even peers outside the search scope, and the searches could get the result which could not be found before. In the environment of random(5), the search get 98.9% hit rate with TTL=7 flooding and 80% hit rate with TTL=6 flooding while not adopting ILS algorithm. We use flooding search with TTL=4 to simulate the ILS-MIS, shown in Fig. 2 (1"-8"), there are 86.2% searches failed at beginning, and the hit rate increases to 82.1% finally. While adopting 5 hops flooding searches, the hit rate increases from 38.5% to 98.3%.

Experiment 3: what we test is the effect of ILS to reduce the communication cost of search by adopting two phase search algorithm. The results are reported in Fig. 4. Compared with single flooding, the performance of two phase flooding search could be sufficiently improved by the capability of ILS, getting high search success rate and significantly reduced communication cost. In Fig. 4, in the environment of BA(5) and SW(4, 0.6) to simulate ILS-MIS, just using singe flooding search, each search takes 17670 messages in BA(5) and 11707 messages in SW(4,0.6) at beginning, and message number becomes 16152 and 15773 separately after ILS's work. If using first flooding with TTL=3 and then TTL=6 to locate the target of fail search, the messages taken by each search reduced to 3477 and 3282 separately, and the communication cost decreased more than 70% and only 10% loss of results.

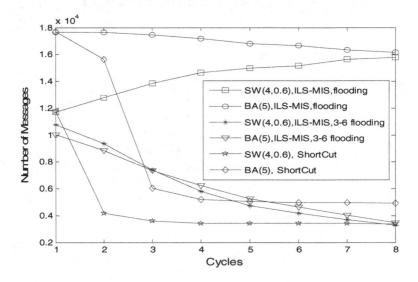

Fig. 4. Communication cost of link selection

Experiment 4: what we test is the influence of dynamic of P2P overlay network to the ILS. The results are reported in Fig. 2 (1'-8'). We design a churn model to simulate such a problem. In every cycle we randomly choose some percent of peers renew to build connections use random link algorithm. The new built links number equals to its degree before churn (not influence network average degree), and the assigned sharing file and interests set are renewed. Adding 5% churn in every cycle in the same simulation settlement of Fig. 2 (1-8), ARPL increases from 3.248 to 3.542.

Experiment 5: what we test is the influence of different file sharing distribution models to the performance of ILS. The results show that ILS would get better performance in more imbalances sharing environment, which making peer easy to choose the target to add or delete links and gain benefit. But it also brings more imbalance of peer degree too. In above experiments, there is not much difference of sharing file number in the peers belong to 20% or 80%, such settlement may be a littlie unreasonable because there should be more imbalance in peer's sharing in real system. We suppose that peer would share files following Zipf law too, thus there are some peers would share far more files than others. The simulation results show that ILS-MIS could get better ARPL compared with Fig. 2 (2.935 vs. 3.24). Furthermore, supposing there are very serious free riding phenomenon and only 30% peer share files, it gets even shorter ARPL (2.868).

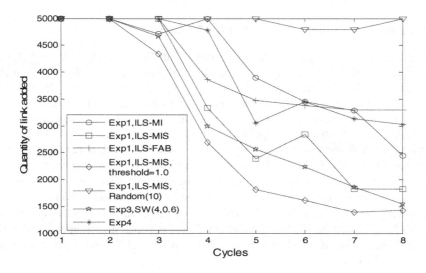

Fig. 5. Adjustment times of link selection

At last, we evaluate the cost of ILS itself under different settlement. The adjustment quantities of some experiments are shown in Fig. 5. For in most situations, the link deleted always equals to link added, so here we only give the number of link added. From the result, we could find that ILS-FAB has much more final cost than ILS-MI and ILS-MIS, because it has the lowest threshold for added link, so it can not guarantee that the efficiency of link added by ILS-FAB is better than the one just deleted, even if peer chooses the link with worst efficiency to delete every time, there would be many links will be added and deleted, deleted and added. ILS-MB and ILS-MIS both could get trade-off of cost and performance by settling the threshold for adding link. There are less and less links which evaluation values exceeding the system threshold along with time, thus adjustment times would be less and less and reach a very low value if only there is no churn in the network. This is the reason that the cost of ILS-MIS in Experiment 1 with threshold equal 1.0 has the least cost of all. In the environment of random(10), in which peers have higher degree, there are more places to hold same interest peers yet, so it needs more adjustments to get stable performance and the highest cost in Fig. 5. At last, the network with churn (Exp4) has obviously more adjustment times compared with static environment. Especially, the adjustment times would not have distinct decrease later and it keeps steady at about 2000 times at last, as it is the situation more close to reality, so we could analyze the cost of ILS algorithm in real systems accordingly.

Deleting a link needs to find another path to reach the neighbor by a flooding search. Finding the token needs a very small scope flooding search too. Adding a link will not take many messages if peer could record the IP address of interacted peers. Otherwise, it also needs a flooding search to lookup the peer with its ID. Because about 5% peers churn would usually take several minutes in real P2P system, thus the cost is totally acceptable for a peer would additionally build a link and delete a link every 2.5 cycle time on average.

4.2 Performance Comparison with Other Methods

In this section, we conduct some comparisons with ShortCut algorithm [6]. When ShortCut algorithm builds an upper overlay network that every peer has 10 shortcuts, it would get 53-54% search success rate in the real KaZaA and Gnutella P2P file sharing system after one hour. If the number of shortcut is not limited, the search success rate would increase 7%-12%. But sometimes the number of shortcut would be more than 300, which is unacceptable. If using flooding search with TTL=2 in the shortcuts network, the hit rate would be improved, and it also get more results.

We implement the ShortCut algorithm with the total same experiment settlement of ILS. Under the environment of random(5), in which every peer has no more than 7 shortcuts. Using flooding search with TTL=6 and look up in shortcuts network with 2 hop, it achieves 68% search hit rate in the shortcuts network, increases the total search hit rate from 81% to 86% (the increase would not happen just look up with 1 hop in shortcuts network), also reduces ARPL from 5.63 to 3.132, and every peer have average 6.04 shortcuts at last.

Fig. 3 presents the comparisons of ShortCut with ILS on ARPL in the environment of random(5) and SW(4,0.6). ARPL got by ShortCut is better than ILS just use flooding in random(5)(3.132 vs. 3.248, 3.598, 3.685), but is worse than that got by ILS-MIS with two phase flooding search (3.132 vs. 2.79). While in SW(4,0.6), ARPL got by Shortcut is obviously worse (2.93 vs. 2.43) than that got by ILS-MIS even not adopting two phase search algorithm. The ARPL of ShortCut is obviously inferior.

Reducing communication cost is the most important effect of ShortCut algorithm. The comparison of ShortCut with ILS which adapts two-phase-flooding-search is presented in Fig. 4. Obviously, ShortCut works fast and the performance is nearly no change after cycle 4. While in the environment of SW(4,0.6), the messages taken by every search of ShortCut are almost the same with ILS at cycle 8 and ILS apparently could continue to decrease the communication cost afterward. And the effect of reducing communication cost of Shortcut is obviously not as good as ILS in BA(5).

Except all the above, ILS could effectively improve the search success rate and ShortCut have little effect of it. Furthermore, ShortCut has additional burden of peer to maintain shortcuts list. Thus, ILS has notable advantages.

5 Conclusion

In this paper, we discussed the problem that improving the search efficiency in unstructured P2P environment, and proposed a intelligent link selection algorithm to optimize the overlay network's topology based on the principle of interest-based locality by adding "high efficiency" connections and deleting "low efficiency" connections in balance. It is proved by the simulation that could gather peers with same interests into incompact communality, and get very high search success rate with very small scope search, it could significantly improve search efficiency both improve the search response time and reduce the communication cost, and it have notable advantage compare to other related work.

References

1. Bittorrent protocol specication. http://bitconjurer.org/BitTorrent/protocol.html
2. http://www.gnutella.co.uk
3. Kazaa media desktop. http://www.kazaa.com/us/index.htm
4. Liu, Y., Zhuang, Z., Xiao, L., Ni, L.M.: A distributed approach to solving overlay mismatching problem. In: Proceedings of IEEE ICDCS (2004)
5. Liu, Y., Xiao, L., Ni, L.M.: Building a scalable bipartite P2P overlay network. In: Proceedings of IEEE IPDPS (2004)
6. Sripanidkulchai, K., Maggs, B., Zhang, H.: Efficient content location using interest-based locality in peer-to-peer system. In: Proceedings of IEEE INFOCOM (2003)
7. Jin, H., Ning, X., Chen, H.: Efficient search for peer-to-peer information retrieval using semantic small world. In: Proceedings of WWW (2006)
8. Barbosa, M.W., Costa, M.M., Almeida, J.M., Almeida, V.A.F.: Using locality of reference to improve performance of peer-to-peer applications. ACM SIGSOFT Software Engineering Notes archive 29(1), 216–227 (2004)
9. http://peersim.sf.net
10. Watts, D.J., Strogztz, S.H.: Collective dynamics of small-world networks. Nature 393, 440–442 (1998)
11. http://arxiv.org/abs/cond-mat/0106096, http://arxiv.org/pdf/cond-mat/0408391
12. Chawathe,Y., Ratnasamy, S., Breslau, L., Lanham, N., Shenker, S.: Making gnutella-like P2P systems scalable. In: Proceeding of the ACM SIGCOMM 2003, Karlsruhe (2003)
13. Liu, Y., Liu, X., Xiao, L., Ni, L.M., Zhang.X.: Location-aware topology matching in P2P systems. In: Proceedings of IEEE INFOCOM (2004)
14. Chawathe, Y., Ramabhadran, S., Ratnasamy, S., LaMarca, A., Shenker, S.: A case study in building layered DHT applications. In: Proceedings of ACM SIGCOMM (2005)
15. Qiu, D., Srikant, R.: Modeling and performance analysis of BitTorrent-Like peer-to-peer networks. In: Proceedings of ACM SIGCOMM (2004)
16. Han, J., Liu, Y.: Rumor Riding: anonymizing unstructured peer-to-peer systems. In: Proceedings of IEEE ICNP (2006)

Keyword Search in DHT-Based Peer-to-Peer Networks

Byungryong Kim[1] and Kichang Kim[2]

[1] Department of Computer and Science Engineering, Inha University,
Incheon, Korea
[2] School of Information and Communication Engineering, Inha University,
Incheon, Korea
{doolyn,kchang}@inha.ac.kr

Abstract. DHT(Distributed Hash Table) provides a very effective and reliable search scheme in P2P networks. However, when the search involves a multiple-keyword query, it suffers heavy network traffic due to the passing around of a large inverted list among P2P nodes. In this paper, we propose Distance-Based Pruning technique to cut down the size of the inverted list considerably. It utilizes the concept of distance between keywords in the query and removes those entries in the inverted list that are going to be dropped sooner or later. We prove this prediction is accurate and effective such that it reduces the size of the inverted list by 29%.

1 Introduction

P2P(Peer-to-Peer) system can be characterized as one with no central server. All participating nodes are potential servers, and finding the location of a target document as fast as possible is one of the most important and difficult problems in this system. In early P2P systems, documents are serviced directly by the servers which own them, and a query asking the location of some document has to be broadcasted to all nodes. This early technique is called Partition-by-Document and is still being used in Gnutella[1], google, Yahoo, KaZaA[2], etc. The query could contain the title of the file or keywords in it. For the latter case, the serving nodes manage a local index table that maps keywords to documents.

It is obvious that we need more structured way of managing files to avoid the expensive query broadcasting. A Distributed Hash Table(DHT) is used to map a keyword to the peer responsible for holding the corresponding reverse index. Partition-by-Keyword uses DHT to store the indices of files, and uses these tables to find the location of a target document. It hashes the keyword of a document and stores the index of the document (that is its actual location such as URL address) in a node which controls the hash table corresponding to the keyword's hash value[1]. Since a document can contain several keywords, the index of this document can be stored in a number of nodes. To find the location of a document that contains a keyword x, the

---

[1] How to find the controlling node for some hash value is explained in Section 2 where various techniques implementing DHT are surveyed.

H. Jin et al. (Eds.): ICA3PP 2007, LNCS 4494, pp. 338–347, 2007.

client peer simply hashes it and send a query to a node which controls the corresponding hash table.

Partition-by-Keyword is much superior to Partition-by-Document in finding a document quickly with given keywords. However it still poses some performance problems, especially when the query contains multiple keywords. Multiple keyword search is common, and it is known that 71.5% of search queries in Internet contains at least two keywords [3]. For multiple keywords, the query should be sent to all nodes that control these keywords. Since the inverted lists (lists mapping the keyword to a list of documents that contain it) from the relevant nodes need to be combined through JOIN operation(intersection), the query is passed around with the inverted list being updated at each node. If the first keyword in the query was a common keyword, the starting inverted list would be huge, and transmitting this huge list to the next node would cause a heavy traffic. Usually the keywords in a particular query consist of a set of common words and another set of specific words that occur only in a limited number of documents. Most of the indices of documents in the starting inverted list, therefore, will most likely be dropped through JOIN operation sooner or later.

It would be beneficial if we can cut down these irrelevant indices from the inverted list before transmitting it to the next node. But how can we know which indices will eventually be dropped? In this paper, we suggest a technique based on the concept of distance between keywords that can remove irrelevant indices from the list. Our technique is explained in detail later in the paper, and the preliminary result shows the technique is very promising. The rest of the paper is organized as follows: Section 2 explains the basic operations of DHT-based P2P system and surveys searching techniques for multiple keywords; Section 3 explains the proposed technique in detail; Section 4 evaluates its performance; and Section 5 gives a conclusion.

2 Related Works

DHT-based P2P system[4, 5,6, 7] stores the document IDs and the addresses of the owner nodes, represented by a 2-tuple, {document ID, URI of node ID}, in a distributed way at each node. The document ID is obtained by hashing some unique information of each document such as URI, while node ID is computed through hashing its IP address. To ensure an even distribution of the identification numbers, a consistent hashing technique is used[8]. Since document IDs and node IDs do not always match one-to-one, we order the node IDs in an increasing order and store a document ID to the first node whose node ID is greater than or equal to the document ID. If we know all the nodes that are participating in the current P2P system, it is simple to compute the location of the controlling node that has the target document ID -- it is simply the first node in the ordered node list. However, a typical P2P system contains a huge number of participating nodes and many of the nodes constantly enter or exit the system. In this large changing network of nodes, it is very hard to keep track of all active nodes correctly. Instead, many DHT-based search techniques adopt a strategy where only some reference nodes are remembered at each node, and use them to hunt down the location of the target document ID. Which nodes are selected as reference nodes varies with the search technique.

CHORD[4] is one of the most popular DHT systems. It is an overlay of so-called Chord Rings. A chord ring is defined as an ID circle where the nodes are ordered in an increasing order in their ID values. As explained above, we can not store the entire circle at each node. Chord first divides the ID space into buckets whose sizes grow with a power of 2, and at each bucket selects a node with the smallest node ID as the reference node. A table, called Finger Table, is used to store all reference nodes. Since the ID space is divided into buckets which is essentially a binary tree representation of the space, the size of Finger Table is less than or equal to $\log(n)$, where n is the size of the ID space. An example is shown in Figure 1.

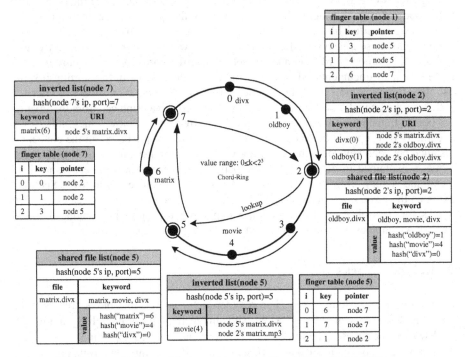

Fig. 1. Finger Tables and Inverted Lists for a Chord-ring with 3-bit ID space

The IDs in this Chord-ring, including both document IDs and node IDs, are represented by 3-bit. Therefore the size of the ID space is $2^3 = 8$. To make the situation simple, we assume node X is one whose IP becomes X when hashed. Node 2, 5, 7 are participating nodes, and node 2 and 5 have files that are shared in this P2P system. For example, Node 5 shares a file "matrix.divx" which contains keywords such as "matrix", "movie", and "divx". The hash values of these keywords are 7, 5, and 2. Consequently the tuple {matrix, URI of node 5}[2] will be stored at node 7, {movie, URI of node 5} at node 5, and {divx, URI of node 5} at node 2. Each node maintains a Finger Table for routing purpose. If we want to find a file containing a keyword

---

[2] For keyword-based DHT, the tuple becomes {keyword, URI of node ID} instead of {document ID, URI of node ID}.

"matrix", whose hash value is 6, and we are at node 2, the query will be sent to node 7 because a key with hash value 6 belongs to the last bucket which covers the half of the ID space starting from ID 6 ending just below ID 2. Node 7 happens to have the {matrix, URI of node 5} tuple, so the URI of node 5 will be sent back to the requesting node 2.

The above scheme can cause heavy network traffic when the query contains multiple keywords. Suppose the query contains two keywords, such as "movie" and "matrix". Again assuming we are at node 2, the query will be sent first to node 5 since "movie" is handled by node 5, and the result will be routed to node 7 for a JOIN operation. The result at node 5 contains two URI's, and only one of them finally turned out to include both keywords. If the first keyword was a very common word, such as "flower", the resulting URI list would have been huge and have caused a heavy traffic while many of the URI's in the initial list were not needed anyway and wouldn't have reached the final destination.

Numerous researches have been performed to reduce the network traffic. Multi-level partitioning (MLP) transmits the query only to some limited number of peers to decrease the traffic. In order to select appropriate peers, the technique divides the node space into k logical groups[9]. [3,10] uses Bloom Filter and previous search results to compress the intermediate URI list. Bhattacharjee proposed another technique to improve efficiency: result caching[11]. Keyword Fusion[12] uses Fusion Dictionary, which contains a set of common keywords, to achieve an efficient searching. SCALLOP[13] utilizes a balanced lookup tree to avoid the hot spot problem. In order to reduce query overhead, KSS(Keyword Set Search) by Gnawali partitions the index by a set of keywords[14]. Hybrid-indexing[15] extracts a set of important keywords from the document and utilizes it together with the inverted URI list. mSearch[16] also employs Hybrid-indexing, but it defines a multicast tree for each keyword in order to multicast the query only to some relevant nodes. pSearch[17] reduces the number of visiting nodes for a given query and still achieves high accuracy.

The above techniques have been successful in reducing the network traffic in some aspect, but either the reduction rate is not enough, or they require another type of system resource such as memory space. MLP introduces additional cost for communication between nodes to maintain the grouping information. Using Bloom Filter can cause the problem of false positive in which the hit rate varies considerably depending on the number of hash functions and the size of the bit vector. The dictionary in Keyword Fusion takes time to build and needs to be updated frequently, which costs additional traffic. SCALLOP requires additional storage for lookup table. KSS also causes increasing storage overhead as the number of keyword combination increases. The multicast tree used in mSearch demands additional space overhead, and Hybrid-indexing requires additional space to store major keywords for each document.

3 Distance-Based Pruning

To resolve a multiple-keyword query in DHT-based structured P2P networks, several nodes have to be visited, and for each visit an inverted list containing the URI list have to be transmitted for the JOIN operation. The problem is that this list may contain a significant number of irrelevant URI's (ones which will not show up in the final result). We focus in reducing the size of the inverted URI list by predicting the irrelevant entries in the list and removing them before sending to the next node. We can predict the irrelevant ones with the concept of distance. We define the distance of a key, k_n, as

$$\text{distance}(k_n) = \text{hash}(k_n) - \text{hash}(k_{n-1}), \text{ for } n > 1$$
$$\text{distance}(k_n) = -1, \text{ for } n = 0$$

where k_1, k_2, ..., k_n are keys sorted in increasing order of hash values, and $\text{hash}(k_n)$ is the hash value of key k_n. According to this definition, the distance of a key in a document shows how far this key is separated from the previous key in the sorted key list. And more importantly it shows that this document does not contain a key whose hash value falls between these two keys.

We utilize this fact to identify and remove the documents that will be dropped eventually from the inverted list. Suppose a query contains three key words, k_a, k_b, and k_c, where $\text{hash}(k_a) > \text{hash}(k_b) > \text{hash}(k_c)$. We collect an inverted list with k_a by sending the query to the controlling node for k_a. The list will be huge (suppose k_a is a common word), and we want to remove irrelevant documents from this list before we sending it to the next controlling node for k_b. Irrelevant documents are ones that do not contain key k_b at all. We can identify those documents by comparing the distance(k_a) of each document with the difference between the hash values of two keys, that is $\text{hash}(k_a) - \text{hash}(k_b)$. If we find a document for which distance(k_a) is greater than the difference between $\text{hash}(k_a)$ and $\text{hash}(k_b)$, it means this document does not have key k_b as explained above, and we can remove it from the inverted list.

Figure 2 shows an example. The Chord-ring in the figure contains 32 documents, Doc_0 to Doc_{31}. Doc_x is located in node x. Each document contains a number of single character keywords. For example, Doc_{31} contains keywords "f", "j", "k", "t", and "x". We assume the hash value of a keyword is its position in the alphabetic order: i.e. hash("a") = 0, hash("b") = 1, etc. In this scheme, the two tuples for Doc_{31}'s keywords, that is {"f", node 31}, {"j", node 31}, {"k", node 31}, {"t", node 31}, and {"x", node 31} are distributed to corresponding controlling nodes. Suppose someone at node 2 requests Lookup(p & t). The hash value of "p" is 15, and the query will first be sent to node 15, the controlling node for key "p". The result contains 9 entries as shown at node 15 in Figure 2. This list then is sent to node 19, the controlling node for key "t". The inverted list for key "t" has again 9 entries. After joining these two lists, we get Doc_{11}. This is the document that contains both keywords, "p" and "t". This example shows that 8 entries in the original list transmitted from node 15 turned out to be all irrelevant ones.

By removing those irrelevant ones from the list, we can cut down the network traffic considerably. To recognize the irrelevant ones, we add "distance" value for each entry in the inverted list making the entry a three tuple as shown in Figure 3. For example, the first entry in node 19's inverted list is {"t", node 31's Doc_{31}, 9}. This means document Doc_{31} located at node 31 contains key "t", and the "distance" of key "t" from the previous key in this document is 9. Since in the current example all keys are single characters and their hash values are their position in the alphabet list, we can safely assume Doc_{31} does not contain any key from "l" to "s". Therefore, if Doc_{31} was in the first resulting list (the first key in the query was "t"), and the second key was a character between "l" to "s", we can remove Doc_{31} from the candidate list to be sent to the next hop.

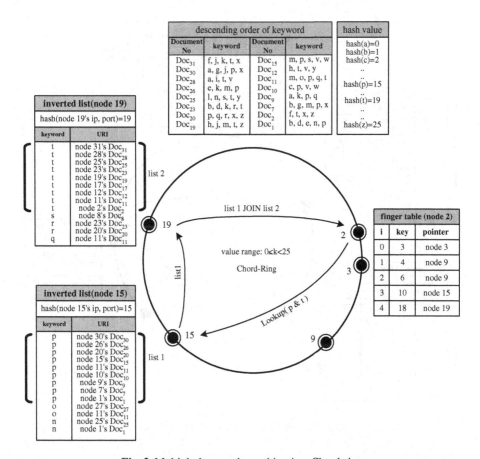

Fig. 2. Multiple-keyword searching in a Chord-ring

Let's consider the same example we have used in the previous section. A user at node 2 issues Lookup(p & t). We first reorder the keys in the query in ascending order in their hash values. The query, therefore, becomes Lookup(t & p), and we send a request to node 19, the controlling node for key "t", first. Node 19 selects 9 entries in the candidate list as before. But this time, node 19 also computes the difference between the hash values of the first and the second key, which is 4 since hash("t")=19 and hash("p")=15, for each entry. Then it remove those in the 9-entry candidate list whose distance value is greater than 4: they are entries for Doc_{31}, Doc_{28}, Doc_{19}, Doc_{17}, Doc_{12}, and Doc_2. The removed documents do not contain key "p" because a distance value for "t" greater than 4 means the document does not have key "p", "q", "r", and "s". Figure 4 shows explicitly the distances among keywords for Doc_{31} and Doc_{25}. Both contains the first key "t", but the distances of keys for Doc_{31} in the figure shows that the nearest key below "t" is "k" meaning this document can not have the second key "p". Doc_{25} is different: the nearest key to "t" is "s", and we can not be sure this document does not have key "p" since we only record distance("t") for Doc_{25} at node 19. Therefore we remove Doc_{31} from the candidate list and 5 other documents for the same reason, but not Doc_{25}, Doc_{23}, and Doc_{11}.

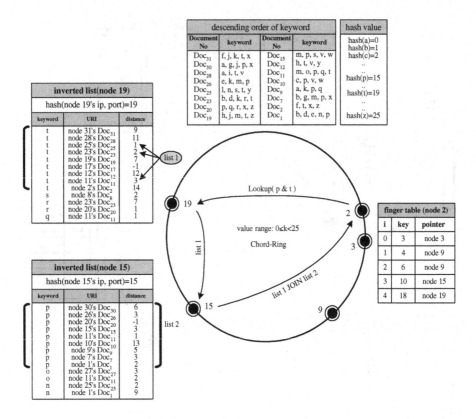

descending order of keyword				hash value
Document No	**keyword**	**Document No**	**keyword**	hash(a)=0 hash(b)=1 hash(c)=2
Doc_{31}	f, j, k, t, x	Doc_{15}	m, p, s, v, w	..
Doc_{30}	a, g, j, p, x	Doc_{12}	h, t, v, y	
Doc_{28}	a, i, t, v	Doc_{11}	m, o, p, q, t	hash(p)=15
Doc_{26}	e, k, m, p	Doc_{10}	c, p, v, w	
Doc_{25}	l, n, s, t, y	Doc_{9}	a, k, p, q	hash(t)=19
Doc_{23}	b, d, k, r, t	Doc_{7}	b, g, m, p, x	
Doc_{20}	p, q, r, x, z	Doc_{2}	f, t, x, z	..
Doc_{19}	h, j, m, t, z	Doc_{1}	b, d, e, n, p	hash(z)=25

inverted list(node 19)

hash(node 19's ip, port)=19

keyword	URI	distance
t	node 31's Doc_{31}	9
t	node 28's Doc_{28}	11
t	node 25's Doc_{25}	1
t	node 23's Doc_{23}	2
t	node 19's Doc_{19}	7
t	node 17's Doc_{17}	-1
t	node 12's Doc_{12}	12
t	node 11's Doc_{11}	3
t	node 2's Doc_2	14
s	node 8's Doc_8	2
r	node 23's Doc_{23}	7
r	node 20's Doc_{20}	1
q	node 11's Doc_{11}	1

inverted list(node 15)

hash(node 15's ip, port)=15

keyword	URI	distance
p	node 30's Doc_{30}	6
p	node 26's Doc_{26}	3
p	node 20's Doc_{20}	-1
p	node 15's Doc_{15}	3
p	node 11's Doc_{11}	1
p	node 10's Doc_{10}	13
p	node 9's Doc_9	5
p	node 7's Doc_7	3
p	node 1's Doc_1	2
o	node 27's Doc_{27}	3
o	node 11's Doc_{11}	2
n	node 25's Doc_{25}	2
n	node 1's Doc_1	9

Lookup(p & t)

value range: 0≤k<25

Chord-Ring

list 1 JOIN list 2

finger table (node 2)

i	key	pointer
0	3	node 3
1	4	node 9
2	6	node 9
3	10	node 15
4	18	node 19

Fig. 3. A Chord-ring with "distance" value added

The length of the candidate list is now 3 reducing the network traffic to one third. We send this list to the next node which controls the second key, "p". 9 entries are selected again as shown in Figure 3, and this list is combined with the transmitted one from node 19 through JOIN operation. The result is Doc_{11}. It turned out that 8 out of 9 entries in the original candidate list were all irrelevant. We were able to filter out 6 of them at the first node with the help of "distance" values.

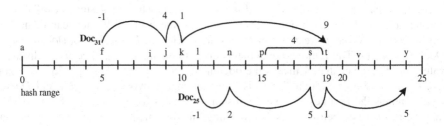

Fig. 4. Distances among keywords for Doc_{31} and Doc_{25}

4 Experiments

Experiments were performed to measure the reduction rate in network traffic. We
have modified Chord Simulator[18] for this purpose. The number of nodes was 1000,
and the average number of keywords per document was 12[19]. A query can contain
maximum 5 keywords. Figure 5 shows the processing flow in Chord Simulator. The
traffic generator generates a traffic file to build a Chord network, and the resulting
traffic is fed into the Chord Simulator.

To implement our technique, we have modified the traffic generator (to generate
multiple-key search traffic), Chord-Simulator (to support multiple key search),
request format, and DocumentList format.

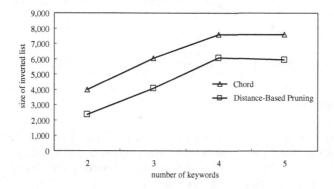

Fig. 5. The size of inverted list transmitted during query processing

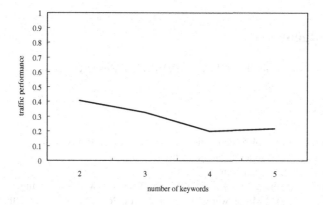

Fig. 6. Reduction of the size of transmitted inverted list with Distance-based Pruning

Figure 5 and 6 show the results of our technique. Figure 5 shows the size of inverted
list generated is much less when our DBP(Distance-Based Pruning) technique is applied : about 1700 entries in average are removed from the list. Figure 6 shows the
reduction rate when compared with the Chord. When the query contains 2 key words,
about 40% decrease can be seen, and this amounts to 29% network traffic decrease.

Figure 7 compares storage overhead between Keyword Fusion and DBP. Keyword Fusion constantly updates the Fusion Dictionary at each node whenever a common-keyword is registered. As time goes on, this dictionary will get larger as shown in the figure.

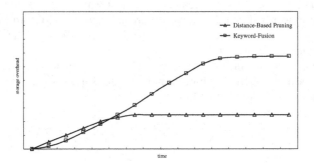

Fig. 7. Storage overhead in Keyword Fusion and DBP

5   Conclusion

DHT is very effective for fast keyword-based-search of a file in P2P network. However multiple-keyword query has been known to cause a heavy traffic due to a large inverted list that has to be passed around. We have proposed a technique based on the concept of distance which can cut down the size of the inverted list considerably and therefore reduce network traffic. The technique has been implemented by modifying Chord-Simulator and shown to reduce the size of inverted list by 29%.

Acknowledgements

This work was supported by INHA UNIVERSITY Research Grant.

References

1. The Gnutella Protocol Specification v0.41 Document Revision 1.2., http://rfc-gnutella. sourceforge.net/developer/stable/index.html
2. Kazza. http://www.kazza.com
3. Reynolds, P., Vahdat, A.: Efficient Peer-to-Peer Keyword Searching. In: Endler, M., Schmidt, D.C. (eds.) Middleware 2003. LNCS, vol. 2672, Springer, Heidelberg (2003)
4. Stoica, I., Morris, R., Karger, D., Kaashoek, M., Balakrishnan, H.: Chord: A scalable peer-to-peer lookup service for internet applications. In: ACM SIGCOMM (2001)
5. Ratnasamy, S., Francis, P., Handley, M., Karp, R., Shenker, S.: A scalable content-addressable network. In: SIGCOMM'01 (2001)
6. Rowstron, A., Druschel, P.: Pastry: Scalable, Decentralized Object Location and Routing for Large-Scale Peer-to-Peer Systems. In: Guerraoui, R. (ed.) Middleware 2001. LNCS, vol. 2218, Springer, Heidelberg (2001)

7. Zhao, B.Y., Kubatowicz, J., Joseph, A.: Tapestry: an infrastructure for fault-tolerant wide-area location and routing, Tech. Rep. UCB/CSD-01-1141, University of California at Berkeley (April 2001)

8. Karger, D., Lehman, E., Leighton, T., Levine, M., Lewin, D., Panigrahy, R.: Consistent Hashing and Random Trees: Tools for Relieving Hot Spots on the World Wide Web. In: Proceedings STOC, pp. 654–663 (May 1997)

9. Shi, S., Yang, G., Wang, D., Yu, J., Qu, S., Chen, M.: Making Peer-to-Peer Keyword Searching Feasible Using Multi-Level Partitioning. In: IPTPS (2004)

10. Bloom, B.: Space/time trade-offs in hash coding with allowable errors. Communications of the ACM 13(7), 422–426 (1970)

11. Bhattacharjee, B., Chawathe, S., Gopalakrishnan, V., Keleher, P., Silaghi, B.: Efficient peer-to-peer searches using result-caching. In: The 2nd International Workshop on Peer-to-Peer Systems(IPTPS'03) (2003)

12. Liu, L., Ryu, K.D., Lee, K-W.: Keyword fusion to support efficient keyword-based search in peer-to-peer file sharing, CCGRID 2004, pp. 269–276 (2004)

13. Jerry, C., Chou, Y., Huang, T.-Y., Huang, K.-L., Chen, T.-Y.: SCALLOP: A Scalable and Load-Balanced Peer-to-Peer Lookup Protocol. IEEE Trans. Parallel Distrib. Syst. 17(5), 419–433 (2006)

14. Gnawali, O.: A Keyword Set Search System for Peer-to-Peer Networks, Master's thesis, Massachusetts Institute of Technology (2002)

15. Tang, C., Dwarkadas, S.: Hybrid Global-Local Indexing for Efficient Peer-to-Peer Information Retrieval. In: Proceedings of the Symposium on Networked Systems Design and Implementation (NSDI) (June 2004)

16. Gulati, A., Ranjan, S.: Efficient Keyword Search using Multicast Trees in Structured p2p Networks submitted to Middleware (2005)

17. Tang, C., Xu, Z., Dwarkadas, S.: Peer-to-Peer Information Retrieval Using Self-organizing Semantic Overlay Networks. In: Proceedings of SIGCOMM (2003)

18. The Chord Simulator, http://pdos.csail.mit.edu/chord/sim.html and http://cvs.pdos.csail. mit.edu/cvs/~checkout~/sfsnet

19. Liu, L., Ryu, K.D., Lee, K.-W.: Keyword fusion to support efficient keyword-based search in peer-to-peer file sharing, CCGRID 2004, p. 274 (2004)

Implementing Digital Right Management in P2P Content Sharing System

Yang Liu, Chun Yuan, and Yu-Zhuo Zhong

Department of Computer Science and Technology,
Tsinghua University, Beijing 100084
liu-y-05@mails.tsinghua.edu.cn
yuanc@sz.tsinghua.edu.cn
zyz-dcs@mail.tsinghua.edu.cn

Abstract. With the enrichment of digital content over the Internet, more
and more people are using software for content sharing especially for multimedia content sharing, and most of these softwares are on the basis of
P2P architecture which makes good use of high scalability and high efficiency. However, most P2P file sharing systems do not have security mechanism to protect intellectual property of authors and issuers. Moreover, it
is difficult to control each peer's behavior due to its self-control principle
and light-weight server. So we propose a new system based on P2P architecture for file sharing, to which we apply new DRM(Digital Right Management) mechanisms. Results have shown that our system outperforms
other systems in features of security, server load and scalability.

1 Introduction

Facing the opportunities and challenges of digital content distribution, authors
and issuers, on one hand, require a system to efficiently and quickly distribute
their works, on the other hand, need mechanisms to protect their intellectual
property and prevent hostile copy and redistribution. P2P file sharing systems
could meet the need of fast delivery, but put weak management and control
on peers, thus increasing the possibilities of spreading pirate and illegal works.
DRM is a technology to distribute digital contents in a secure manner which can
protect and manage the rights of all participants involved. The main focus of
DRM system is to prohibit illegal copy and distribution of digital contents and
to permit only authorized users to access the contents. Thus, DRM is applicable
to P2P content sharing and makes a good complement to P2P system in the
sense of security and management.

However, since most DRM systems are suitable only for conventional client-
server based content sharing, some properties of DRM need to be adapted before
being applied to P2P file sharing system. The principle of applying DRM to P2P
file sharing system is keeping P2P's advantages of high scalability and easiness in
issuing content as well as developing new controlling mechanism for management,
authorization and supervision. Therefore, some researchers have proposed some
P2P based file sharing systems with DRM mechanism[1][2], others emphasized

H. Jin et al. (Eds.): ICA3PP 2007, LNCS 4494, pp. 348–355, 2007.

the importance of license management in P2P systems[3][4][5]. Unfortunately, some of the existing researches implemented most DRM functions in server[7], thus put so much burden on server and reduced overall performance of the system. Others keep server light-weight and distribute responsibility of DRM among peers[8], but system of this kind faces a fatal problems:trusted peers may perform illegal behavior and there are no supervision mechanisms to restrict them. Therefore, we propose our method which not only well performs DRM in P2P file sharing system but also keeps server load in a relative low level.

The rest of this paper is organized as follows: In Section 2, we introduce related researches and work. Section 3 gives a detailed description of the proposed system, while Section 4 provides analysis of our system compared with other systems. Finally, in Section 5, conclusion is drawn and future work is stated.

2   Related Work

In this section, we will introduce existing research related and give a brief comparison among existing systems.

Generally speaking, existing research examples can be divided into two categories. The first category is centralized P2P file sharing system, which has a server to strongly control each peer's activity and only uses P2P network for content delivery. The second category is distributed P2P file sharing system in which there is a light-weight server or even no server at all, in such a system, nearly all of the DRM functions exist on the peer node.

Centralized P2P architecture uses existing server-client DRM architecture for protecting contents. To avoid distributing pirate contents, server has to perform

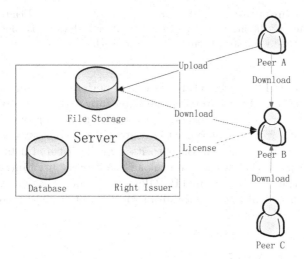

Fig. 1. Architecture of Centralized System: Suppose Peer C has already begun downloading the content. Peer B downloads content from Server, Peer A and Peer C, then requests a license from Server before viewing the content.

the function of content storage. When a peer needs to share a content, he has to upload it to server, after that server will check the copyright of the content, then publish it onto file list to let other peers download if it could pass the check. Therefore, this kind of system includes at least three function modules in the server side, which are file storage module, right issuer module and database module. Right issuer module issues license that contains content decryption key and usage permission or right to the authorized peer. Database module stores peers' information and track each peer's activity. File storage module stores content that uploaded by peers. Since this architecture relies solely on the server in implementing DRM, server could be a bottleneck especially when the number of peers turns large.

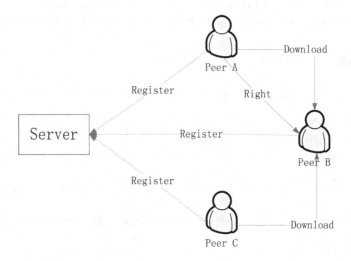

Fig. 2. Architecture of Distributed System(Supposed Peer C has already begun downloading the content. Having registered to server, Peer B downloads content from Peer A and Peer C, then requests a license from Peer A which is the source of content).

In a distributed P2P architecture, each peer performs the function of a client as well as a server. Most systems of this kind are without server or having a light-weight server to process peers' registry, log in and log out. When a peer shares a content, it firstly encrypts the content, then generates its own license and publishes content information onto its own file list and acts as a content source. Other peers that want to download the content first authenticate with the source peer, if passed, a normal P2P download process begins. After finishing downloading, peer will fetch license from source peer to implement decryption in order to view the content.

3   Proposed System

In this section, we will propose a system based on P2P architecture for file sharing. Our system is divided into server side and client side.

Server is a light-weight one, and has only three basic function: (a)processing peers' registry, log in and log out; (b)publishing content information; (c)issuing license to peer who has downloaded the whole content. The first and second function are similar to those in centralized system, which record basic information of peers and keep system in order. However, these two functions do not increase much payload onto servers as content storage and download services do. Therefore, compared to centralized system we eliminate the function of content storage and download services, but compared to distributed system we take rights of issuing licenses and publishing content information back to the server side from peers.

Client in the proposed system is a normal peer with a list of functions in addition: (a)encrypting content; (b)sending content meta data to server; (c)providing download service to other peers.

To keep the advantage of P2P file sharing system, we adopt FastTrack[6] which was applied in the Gnutella to support content searching and downloading among peers. Also, we take advantage of DHT(Distributed Hash Table) which is stored and published in the server side to help accelerate peer discovering and content downloading.

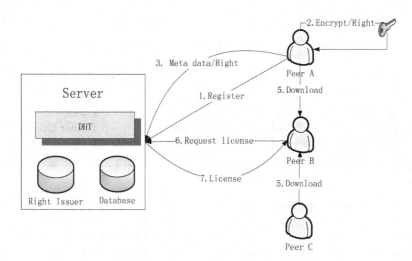

Fig. 3. Architecture of Proposed System(Supposed Peer C has already begun downloading the content)

A normal process of file sharing is as below and shown in Figure.3:

(1)Peer A has a content to share, at first it registers to server

(2)Peer A encrypts content using CEK(Contents Encryption Key). CEK is generated uniquely according to Peer A's private information registered to server. Peer A generates meta data(eg.file name, file type, file length) of content and set access rights to the encrypted content. Access rights consist of (a)period of validity(b)right possessor(eg. peers in the same network segment with peer A)

(3)Peer A sends meta data and access rights to server in the form of XML

(4)Server generates License according to meta data, access rights and Peer A's private information stored in database.A license consists of right object and CEK. Right object is expressed in ODRL. Server publishes content information on DHT to let other peers know that Peer A has issued a content.

(5)Peer B discovers from DHT that a content is being distributed. It searches and obtains encrypted content in normal P2P manner.

(6)Finished downloading encrypted content, Peer B asks server for license.

(7)The proposed system uses asymmetric encryption to distribute licenses.On receiving Peer B's request, server encrypts license using public key and send encrypted license to Peer B.

(8)Peer B decrypts license using its private key, then obtains CEK and right object. After that, Peer B decrypts content with CEK. Peer B should do with the content as what the right object has authorized it to.

4   Comparison Analysis of Proposed System

We will compare proposed system with existing systems and give the result of our analysis in this section.

Table 1. Comparison among three systems in features

Analysis	Centralized system	Distributed system	Proposed System
Server load	High	Low	Fair
Scalability	Poor	Rather Good	Good
Security	Good	Poor	Rather Good
Supervision on peers	Good	Poor	Good
Distributed License	None	Rather Good	Good

In the view point of server load, server in centralized architecture has the highest load, while the one in distributed architecture has the lowest. The proposed system gets a compromise between centralized architecture and distributed architecture in view of this feature.Seen from Fig.4, we can see that with the number of nodes of network goes higher, server in centralized architecture has more cost of CPU usage than the other two, especially when more nodes get involved, while other two kinds distributed one and the proposed one remain almost the same no matter how many nodes are in P2P network. Server in centralized architecture involves in almost all the functions, so it is easy for the server to control each peer's activity and perform functions of DRM. However, it is not wise to gain DRM mechanisms in sacrifice for scalability of P2P network and server load. Since distributed architecture with light-weight server is unsupervised and uncontrolled, it could be a platform for spreading pirate and illegal content. Compared with server in distributed architecture, server in proposed system takes up the responsibility of issuing license which does not increase much burden, since size of license is much trivial compared with multimedia content. Generally speaking, our system has performed DRM mechanisms while increased acceptable server load.

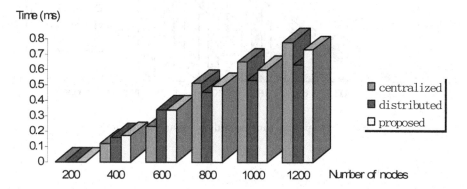

Fig. 4. CPU cost according to number of nodes

In view of security, our system has used asymmetric key for license distribution and PKI for content encryption. Moreover, each peer has to register to server in order to get authentication and send meta data together with right information to server when it shares a content to other peers. Since other peers who require to download the license is also tracked by server, if a peer has shared a pirate content, it will be easy to note which peer has downloaded and spread that content. If a peer has download a pirate content, server will not send it a license, thus making it impossible to decrypt and view the content. The proposed system performs good quality of security as centralized systems.

In view of scalability, the proposed system does not involve and intervene P2P delivery of content, thus well maintains P2P's nature of scalability and efficiency. However, centralized system has reduced efficiency in P2P delivery due to its centralized control and the fact that server is the original source of content. Therefore, bandwidth and processing ability of server will have a strong influence on the efficiency of P2P delivery and can be a bottleneck. Fig.5 shows the time length(in millisecond) between a node's entrance into P2P network and the time point it begins downloading file content, which is called preparing time. It is deduced that the proposed system has achieved almost the same scalability as distributed one while implements security mechanism which is omitted in distributed system.

There are some other originalities in proposed system.Peer has been authorized to grant right to other peers, thus provides authors and producers a platform to spread their works. Moreover, since server participates in critical processes of content spreading, like accepting meta data and sending license, it is undisputable for peers who has generated or distributed pirate content to deny their behaviors.

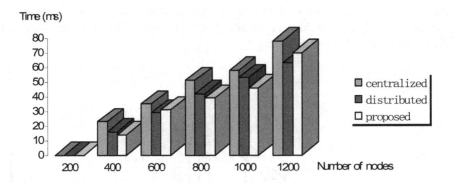

Fig. 5. Preparing time according to number of nodes

5   Conclusion

As a file sharing system, P2P architecture has demonstrated its scalability and efficiency in content delivery, however, to avoid spreading pirate content through P2P systems, DRM mechanism should be added to P2P file sharing systems.In our paper, we have implemented DRM mechanisms to a P2P file sharing system, which outperform other existing system in the feature of server load and scalability. Moreover, the system has gained good quality of security through a series of measures, such as PKI, asymmetric keys and license control.

Our future work will be performing DRM mechanisms in live video streaming system over P2P network to protect intellectual properties of authors and TV stations.

Acknowledgements

This work is supported by the China National Science Foundation committee - Guangdong Province National Science United Foundation U0675001.

References

1. Iwata, T., Abe, T., Ueda, K., Sunaga, H.: A DRM system suitable for P2P content delivery and the study on its implementation, the 9th Asia-Pacific Conference, vol. 2, pp. 806–811 (September 2003)
2. Kalker, T., Epema, D.H.J., Hartel, P.H.: Music2Share-Copyright-Compliant Music Sharing in P2P System. In: Proceeding of the IEEE, vol. 92(6) (June 2004)
3. Kwok, S.H., Lui, S.M.: A License Management Model to Support B2C and C2C Music Sharing, 10th International World Wide Web Conference, Hong Kong, pp. 136–137 (May 2001)
4. Kwok, S.H., Lui, S.M.: A license management model for peer-to-peer music sharing. International Journal of Information Technology and Decision Making 3, 541–558 (2002)

5. Kumar, S., Girimondo, M., Weimerskirch, A.: Embedded End-to-End Wireless Security with ECDH Key Exchange. In: Proceeding of 46th IEEE Midwest International Symposium on Circuits and Systems, vol. 2, pp. 786–789 (December 2003)
6. Barbera, M., Lombardo, A., Schembra, G., Tribastone, M.: A Markov model of a freerider in a BitTorrent P2P network, IEEE Global Telecommunications Conference, vol. 2 (November 2005)
7. Kamvar, S.D., Schlosser, M.T., Garcia-Molina, H.: The Eigentrust algorithm for reputation management in P2P networks. In: Proceedings of the 12th international conference on World Wide Web, pp. 640–651 (2003)
8. Aberer, K., Cudr-Mauroux, P., Datta, A.: P-Grid: A Self-Organizing Access Structure for P2P Information Systems. SPECIAL ISSUE: Special topic section on peer to peer data management 32, 29–33 (2003)

IPBGA: A Hybrid P2P Based Grid Architecture by Using Information Pool Protocol

Deng Li[1], Hui Liu[2], Zhigang Chen[1], Zhiwen Zeng[1], and Jiaqi Liu[1]

[1] School of Information Science and Engineering, Central South University,
Changsha 410083, China
dongxuanlee@gmail.com, czg@csu.edu.cn
[2] Department of Computer Science, Missouri State University, Springfield, MO 65897, USA
huiliu@missouristate.edu

Abstract. Current representatives of Grid systems are Globus and Web Services, however, they have poor scalability and single point failure. It is a hot research topic to build a P2P and grid hybrid framework for resource management and task schedule. We propose Information Pool Based Grid Architecture (IPBGA), which is a real sense hybrid of P2P and grid instead of only introducing P2P methods into grid systems for resource management. The key of IPBGA, information pool protocol, is presented. In our information pool protocol, all of resources and tasks are abstracted into information, and resource requests for tasks and task appeals for resources are viewed as information services, then grid resource management and task schedule are treated as information matching. Therefore, our architecture is very adaptive to heterogeneous, dynamic, and distributed grid systems. We use tri-information centers for collecting information, which strengthens the robustness of our system. Simulation experiments show information pool protocol of IPBGA is more efficient in resource management and task schedule, and has less bandwidth and processing cost compared with other hybrid P2P systems.

Keywords: Information aggregation, information matching, hybrid P2P based grid architecture, information pool protocol.

1 Introduction

The representatives of Grid systems are Globus[11] and Web services[9]. However, these systems are based on client/server (CS) mode. As the services are published and discovered in centralized mode, they have poor scalability and a single point of failure. Thus, many service oriented grid architectures have been proposed, which absorb the advantages of pure P2P and C/S modes. In [4], storage nodes periodically report their states and file lists to a centralized server that is used to maintain whole information. It is not totally decentralized since only nodes request resources in P2P mode. In order to provide large-scale intelligent services in knowledge grid, Zhuge, Sun and etc. [5] propose to incorporate a semantic overlay with an underlying structured P2P network that provides object location and management services, but they mainly discuss searching and location algorithms in P2P. In [7], an interesting

H. Jin et al. (Eds.): ICA3PP 2007, LNCS 4494, pp. 356–367, 2007.

preliminary work is presented to extend P2P computing with a framework that allows Grid computing over the internet. In this five-layer sandglass grid architecture, services layer lies above connectivity layer and management layer. However, the authors build this grid architecture without using concepts of combination of virtual organization and services abstraction, thus the coupling of services and structures is very loose. Aberer and etc. [6] introduces a self-organizing P2P system called P-Grid which is a peer-to-peer lookup system based on a virtual distributed search tree. P-Grid has the advantages of both structure P2P systems and unstructured P2P systems. On the other hand, it is not fault-tolerant because of its index tree structure.

We can see most of the current researches focus on either P2P based algorithms for transferring data to reduce the burden of centralized server [8] or utilize P2P routing algorithms to locate available resources. Thus, they just adopt P2P mode as an improvement to pure grid systems, and introduced P2P mode only into resource management aspect of grid systems.

In our paper, we analyze SOA, P2P, and grid in details, and integrate them together to build a fault tolerant architecture. The new architecture we propose in this paper is called Information Pool Based Grid Architecture (IPBGA) in which virtual organization is separated into information services layer and cooperation layer via service oriented method. Information services layer is responsible for collecting information for all the available resources, and then builds complete view for shared dynamic resources. The structure of information service layer is in P2P mode. Through local optimization of autonomous system, nodes can cooperate with each other to transfer tasks in cooperation services layer based on the complete view provided by information services layer. Therefore, our architecture itself is hybrid P2P based grid mode. It is proved that our architecture is robust, and has less processing cost and bandwidth cost than other grid systems via simulation experiments.

In section 2, our proposed architecture, IPBGA, is introduced, and the integration of IPBGA with SOA and P2P is explained. In section 3, detailed descriptions of fault-tolerant information pool protocol (IPP) and process of information matching are given. The experimental results are presented in section 4. Finally, the conclusion and future work is given in section 5.

2 Overview of IPBGA

Our goal in describing the new grid architecture is to identity fundamental system components, specify the purpose and function of these components, and indicate how these components interact with one another. Our architecture and the subsequent discussion organize components into layers, as shown in Fig. 1. Components within each layer share common characteristics but can build on services and behaviors provided by the lower layers.

Grid available resources are typically described in terms of standard service interfaces. We build complete view about resources and tasks among autonomous systems via abstracting and encapsulating the resources and tasks into information services.

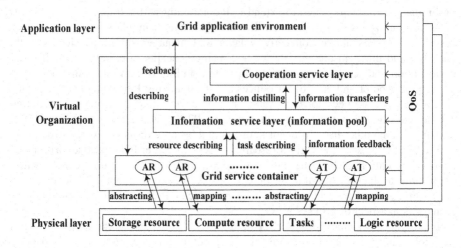

Fig. 1. Overview of information pool based grid architecture (IPBGA)

(1) Physical layer. In our IPBGA mode, physical layer includes both available resources and all of dynamic tasks. Resources typically refer to as physical entities such as computers, networks or storage systems. Here, resources broadly consist of physical resources such as computation capabilities, scientific equipments, and etc., and logical resources such as bandwidth, software, applications, and so on. Some examples of tasks are computing tasks, data storage, and searching.

(2) Virtual organization (VO) layer. Grid technologies and infrastructures are defined to support the sharing and cooperation of diverse, dynamic, and distributed resources in VO. We separate VO into information services layer and cooperation services layer via P2P based hybrid grid method. Then, functionalities of management and searching of resources are divided correspondingly in order to integrate distributed, dynamic, heterogeneous, and autonomic resources and tasks.

Information service layer. Heterogeneous resources are abstracted according to their various capacities for solving problems. Dynamic random tasks are abstracted according to their requirements for resources. Abstract resources (AR) and abstracted tasks (AT) are maintained in grid service container in IPBGA, as shown in Fig. 1. By resource and task describing respectively, the abstracted resources and tasks are encapsulated as information services. Information service layer can effectively manage the status of resources and tasks. Using P2P structure in this layer, many schemes could be provided to guarantee fault-tolerance and QoS. Through grid service container, all information are aggregated in information service layer as a pool, so we also regard information services layer as information pool protocol (IPP). In IPP, their information could be viewed as relative static files after abstraction and encapsulation, even though resources and tasks are dynamic. Therefore, processing cost is reduced, since the sharing cost of relative static files is less than that of dynamic resources and tasks. Nodes exchange information directly without any centralized coordinators. Different applications may require different resources distribution and task schedule. To deal with this, we adopt multi-autonomous systems.

Cooperation services layer. The main responsibility of this layer is to dispatch resources and schedule tasks based on information received from the information service layer. Nodes cooperate with each other directly without any centralized schedulers, which is distinguished from any traditional systems for resources distribution and task schedule widely used in grid computing. Free peers locate tasks via information exchanged between resource information and task information. This layer performs the matching between available resources and task's requirements for resources instead of simply scheduling tasks. As the cost of information transferring is low, our mode effectively avoids the abnormal phenomenon called "pingpong" of tasks transferring and "hungry" of resources scheduling.

We separate information management from resources management. The main advantage of this separation is that the aggregation of resources information can adopt loose and consistent model for resources discovering in grid. The separation also further reduces the cost of searching and collecting distributed resources information. Through virtual organization, we strengthen the dynamic binding between resources and applications. Thus, our mode can support finely granular resources sharing crossing different VOs.

(3) Application layer. In IPBGA, we describe tasks' requirements for resources via abstract description language which is similar with RSL [10, 11] used in Globus. Demands for computational capacity in grid computing or requests for specific file types in file searching systems are two examples of task's requirements for resources. User interfaces are provided by related programming models and human machine interaction schemes. Such grid applications, i.e., e-business and scientific computations, are built on top of our service-oriented architecture.

(4) QoS. QoS is applied to every layer. In grid, "service" broadly involves many concepts such as various computing resources, storage resources, networks, programs, database and etc. In IPBGA, QoS provides quality guarantee for various services in order to satisfy services' requirements for performance, scalability, and manageability.

3   Implementation Details of IPP

3.1 Information Aggregation

Many current researchers present P2P overlay concepts based on semantic-similarity[2], content-similarity[1] or shared interests[3]. But for the heterogeneous and loosely-coupled systems such as P2P, those overlay methods have problems in mapping from logical IDs to physical IP addresses, since it has great possibility that logical neighbors in one group are very far away from each other, and it may suffer long delay in querying and transferring between two peers even though they are logical neighbors. In this paper, we propose an efficient scheme to designate an appropriate group for each peer. The key idea of our scheme is to construct the overlay network by considering the physical underlying infrastructure. Nearby peers join an Autonomous System (AS) according to their physical distances to the AS in the network. We also give high priority to active peers which have high information exchange frequency. For example, consider two peers, A and B, A is closer to an AS compared with B, so A has more chances to join this AS than B. If A and B have the same distances from an AS, and A is more active than B, A also has more chances to join the AS than B. We prefer to select the peer with higher information exchange frequency in order to avoid the problem that a large percentage of clients rely on a small percentage of servers. Each peer must belong to exactly one unique AS.

The idea of the prime meridian or longitude 0 used to describe longitude and latitude inspired us. We propose a normative node called origin node (ON) with which ASs in the overlay calculate its approximate coordinate in the same virtual space. ON is not a permanent node since our overlay is a full self-organising architecture; it is mainly used to form the structured overlay considering the physical situation. Moreover, ON dissapears when the initial overlay becomes a stable overlay in which ASs can keep the structured overlay by themselves.

We assume that the longer time a node remains active in network, the higher successful information exchange ratio is achieved. Thus, we denote the three nodes, which have the top three highest ratios of successful information exchange in each AS, as Information Centers (ICs). Based on the assumption, ICs have high processing power and broad access bandwidth. These three ICs are named as A-node, B-node, and C-node respectively, and they are connected with each other. ICs cooperate with each other to provide the geographical partitioning feature. Therefore the problem of fixed landmarks can be avoided since the unavailability of ICs will affect only that local region. Other nodes in the AS are called Normal Nodes (NNs), whose tasks and resources are abstracted as information. We define the maximum number of NNs in each AS is denoted as d. Each node including ICs and NNs has a status function which has three kinds of status: free, busy, and normal. The information exchange between two nodes called burst trigger mechanism is driven by the node whose status is changed from either busy or normal to free but not periodical updates.

The maximum number of peers in one AS is limited to $d+3$. The AS which has $d+3$ peers is said to full. The threshold is used for AS so that the IC's load will not be too heavy to performance abnormally. ASs are grouped into levels, planar spaces in Fig. 3. Each level has a threshold (A_i), which is the maximum number of ASs allowed in this level. A new level will be created above the previous level to hold more new ASs while the number of ASs in the previous level already reaches the predefined threshold. Each layer also maintains a threshold (L_i) that is the maximum number of levels allowed in this layer. When the number of levels in a layer reaches the predefined threshold L_i, the overlay grows in a three-dimensional space, i.e. a new layer will be created above the previous layer to hold new levels. ASs communicate with each other via ICs across ASs, levels, and layers, as shown in Fig. 2. In this paper, we assume that the overlay has been stable, that is, there is enough ASs for self-organizing.

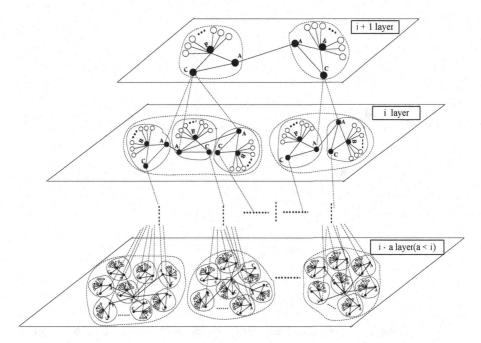

Fig. 2. The multi-layer P2P overlay of IPBGA

As our overlay is formed according to the physical distances among peers, the following properties are satisfied.

○ The distance between any two different peers in the same AS is shorter than that between any two peers belong to different ASs.

○ In one layer, the distance between two different peers in different ASs in the same level is shorter than that between two peers in the different ASs which are in different levels.

○ The distance between two different peers in the same layer is shorter than that between two peers belonging to different layers.

A, B, and C nodes have different functions, but they are backups of each other. We denote $N_{(k)(t)}^{(i)(j)}$ as the tth NN, $t \in \{1 \ldots d\}$, of the kth AS in the jth level of the ith layer. $N_{(k)(A)}^{(i)(j)}$, $N_{(k)(B)}^{(i)(j)}$ and $N_{(k)(C)}^{(i)(j)}$ denotes the A-node, B-node and C-node of the kth AS in the jth level of the ith layer respectively. Our ID naming system is maintained by ASs themselves without any global centric controller or distributor. In our protocol, each node has a unique global ID since it is located in exactly one AS, one level, and one layer. Therefore, it avoids the cheating activity of an AS that may advertise itself a fake ID belonging to others. As we see, peers with near logical IDs also have close distances.

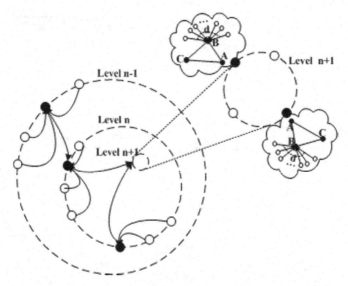

Fig. 3. The hierarchical structure of one layer

Fig. 3 shows a sample hierarchical structure in one layer. B-node aggregates information such as ID, IP, applications, resources, and status from NNs of the same AS. Each A-node is connected by at most d lower neighbor level A-nodes, each lower neighbor level A-node submits the tasks and resource information of its ASs to corresponding A-node in upper neighboring level as $N_{(k)(A)}^{(i)(j)} \rightarrow N_{(k')(A)}^{(i)(j+1)}$. Thus, the A-node not only backup the information from NNs aggregated by B-node in the AS, but also stores NNs' information in lower neighbor level ASs. Node $N_{(k)(C)}^{(i)(j)}$ communicates with d A-nodes in the $(i-1)^{th}$ layer. Each A-node connects with only one C-node in upper neighboring layer. The A-node also submits ID and IP information of its ASs to corresponding C-node in upper neighboring layer as $N_{(k')(A)}^{(i)(j)} \rightarrow N_{(k)(C)}^{(i+1)(j)}$. Since the distance across layers is longer than the distance between levels in the same layer, the possibility of fault in transferring large data increases. However, the amount of ID and IP information is small and it is suitable to be transferred across layers in order to improve the whole protocol's robustness. All ICs in the same layer use information index structure for information aggregation.

3.2 Routing Algorithm

The mainly routing algorithm in IPP is an algorithm termed as a two-direction routing based on the small world characteristic. The peer (e.g. $N_{(k)(t)}^{(i)(j)}$) receiving the query request searches for the information respectively in the upper neighbor level AS (i.e. $N_{(k_m)(A)}^{(i)(j+1)}$) and the upper layer AS (i.e. $N_{(k_u)(C)}^{(i+1)(j)}$). Meanwhile, the peer also queries the information respectively in the nearest lower neighbor level AS and in the nearest lower neighbor layer AS which is closer to the peer. Figure 4 presents the example of the routing algorithm in one layer across several levels. Each black node denotes one AS. To simplify the description of the algorithm, several nodes are denoted with numbers directly and predefined denotations weren't used. For instance, the node labeled 3 means AS 3 which is further denoted as AS_3. A_5 denotes the A-node in the AS_5 (other nodes look similar). AS_3 is the upper neighbor level AS of AS_5; the AS_6 and AS_7 are the two lower neighbor level ASs.

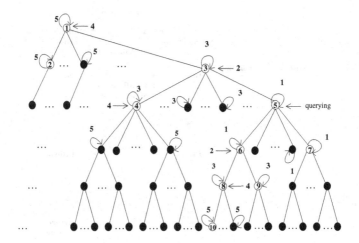

Fig. 4. The process of information matching

The querying begins at node 5, the process of routing is performed as follows: (1) AS_5 searches information stored in B_5 and information of NNs in lower neighbor level ASs stored in A_5 (e.g. information of NNs stored in B_6 and B_7 is copied as backup in A_5); (2) according to the simultaneous up and down directions, querying is sent to AS_5's upper neighbor level AS (AS_3) and to the nearest of the lower neighbor level ASs (e.g. AS_6); (3) AS_3 searches information stored in B_3 and the information of NNs of lower neighbor level ASs stored in A_3 (e.g. in B_4), while AS_6 searches B_6 and its lower neighbor level ASs such as B_8 and B_9; (4) AS_1, AS_4 and AS_8 are new drivers in the routing. This process is repeated until the query is accomplished.

The algorithm is useful as the searching cost is low. It is showed that the expected delivery time of our routing algorithm with more long-range contacts is much less than $\alpha_2 (\log n)^2$, compared with the decentralized algorithm A that there is only one long-range contact and a constant α_2 [13]. Another advantage is that since there are various peers including various resources in each AS, it is very likely that one peer's requirement is satisfied in the same AS or in only several neighbor ASs. The searching diameter is short. Moreover, the overlay combined with the ratios of successful information exchange presented in 3.1 can avoid cheating in routing. In one AS, NNs are supervised by ICs and other NNs, while every IC supervise the others and is also supervised by upper neighbor level ICs. The detailed mechanism for preventing cheating will be discussed in other papers.

3.3 Information Matching

Functionalities of Information matching are performed on cooperation services layer bases on aggregated information provided by IPP. The cost of information matching is low since the cost of transferring is far less than that of task scheduling and node processing. Information matching is implemented via a suit of kernel modules. The process of information matching is illustrated as Fig. 5.

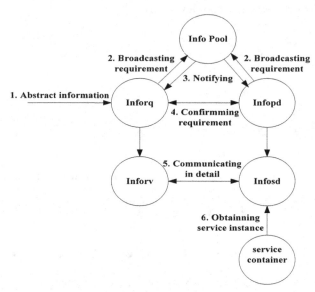

Fig. 5. The process of information matching

Before we give the steps of information matching process, we describe some notations in the process.

Information Requester (Inforq): The responsibilities of Inforqs include submitting requirements for information, querying information, deleting, and so on.

Information Provider (Infopd): Infopd provides information which satisfies the demand of Inforq, and monitors status of peers. If there exist peers that do not satisfy peers capacity requirements, i.e., load and bandwidth, Infopq will terminate the process of information providing.

The steps of information matching processes are as follows:

(1) Requirement information is submitted to Inforq;
(2) Both Inforq and Infopd broadcast their requirements.
(3) If Information matching is found via P2P algorithm, both Inforq and Infopd receive the notification;
(4) Inforq and Infopd handshake and confirm that they satisfy the requirements from each other;
(5) Inforv and Infosd, which are rigid processes respectively for Inforq and Infopd, are created, and communicate with each other for details;
(6) Infosd obtain instances of information services from service container.

In Information pool, there is no centralized controller. Inforq and Infopd directly match each other in pure P2P mode. After matching, Inforv and Infosd communicate each other directly before transferring actual information in order to avoid the invalid information.

4 Experimental Results and Performance Evaluation

We conducted our experiments on the 10000 node transit-stub physical network topologies generated by using the GT-TTM library[12]. Given every specific physical topology, we randomly choose nodes in stub domains from the underlying topology in which to place overlay nodes, and compute the latencies of the shortest paths between all pairs of overlay nodes. We use these as the distances between nodes in the overlay network and as one of the basis of grouping. ICs are selected from transit domains based on the distance and information exchange frequency.

In our experiments we compare the performance of the IPP with a classical hybrid P2P system in which there is one super-node and two redundant nodes in each AS.

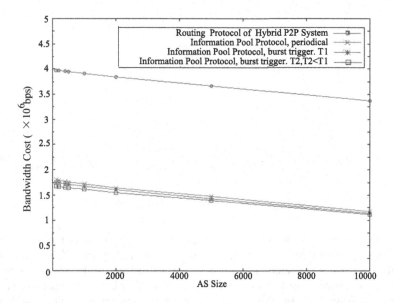

Fig. 6. Comparing protocols about bandwidth cost

Fig. 6 presents the comparison among periodical routing in IPP, periodical hybrid P2P routing protocol mode and burst trigger mechanism IPP about bandwidth costs, where T means times of trigger mechanism performed in one period of time. The y-axis represents the instantaneous bandwidth cost measured at each 2000 AS partition, and the x-axis represents AS size. In Fig. 6, the curve gradually drops because the number of ICs in system decreases by the increased AS size. Therefore, communication between ICs across AS decreases and successful searching probability in one AS increases, which results in low bandwidth cost produced by the low-diameter protocol. Since periodical update has to interrupt peers periodically, trigger mechanism used to drive information exchange should be better than periodical update. As Figure 6 shows, bandwidth cost of trigger mechanism is less than that of periodicity mechanism. And if the less times information exchange is triggered, the less system's bandwidth cost. Hence if node's threshold can be set up reasonably, trigger mechanism of information exchange will be better. The exact threshold will be considered in other papers. We compare the processing cost of our protocol including periodical and burst trigger mechanism with that of hybrid protocol since AS size increases, as shown in Fig. 7.

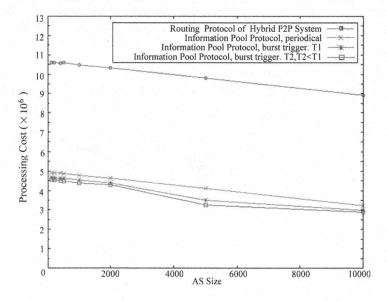

Fig. 7. Comparing protocols about processing cost

It is clear that our protocol has much less processing cost than traditional hybrid P2P routing protocol. Since there are three ICs in our overlay, each IC's load is lighter than the only one super-node in traditional hybrid structure. And each IC has no extra load such as distributing tasks or collecting information but only passively receives information from NNs. In addition, each NN need not maintain a routing table about other nodes in the same AS. Therefore, the processing cost in IPP is lower. And in IPP, information exchange triggered by threshold, has less cost than periodical information exchange.

5   Conclusion and Future Works

In this paper, we propose a new grid architecture named IPBGA based on VO. this is actual hybrid P2P grid architecture. We abstract and encapsulate demands into information services, then aggregate them together. These demands may include tasks requirements of resources in resource distribution and resources requirements of tasks in task schedule. Thus, the complex jobs of resources distribution and tasks schedule are transformed to information matching process in pure P2P mode. We separate VO into information service layer and cooperation service layer. The functionalities of cooperation service are performed in pure P2P mode based on the information provided by information service layer. Simulation experiments show our protocol has better performances than those of classical P2P hybrid systems. In the future, we will give a detailed description about the abstraction and encapsulation of resources and tasks based on RSL-like language. A prototype will be expected to present.

Acknowledgments

This research is supported by the National Natural Science Foundation of China under Grant No. 60573127.

References

1. Rong, L., Burnett, I.: Dynamic resource adaptation in a heterogeneous peer-to-peer environment. Second IEEE Consumer Communications and Networking Conference, pp. 416–420 (2005)
2. Chen, H., Jin, H., Ning, X., Yuan, P., Wu, H., Guo, Z.: SemreX: A semantic similarity based P2P overlay network. Journal of Software 17(5), 1170–1181 (2006)
3. Johnstone, S., Sage, P., Milligan, P.: iXChange – A Self-Organising Super Peer Network Model. In: 10th IEEE Symposium on Computers and Communications(ISCC 2005) pp. 164–169 (2005)
4. Chen, M., Yang, G.W, Wang, D.X.: Large-Capacity media library supporting highly simultaneous access. Journal of Software 17(4), 915–924 (2006)
5. Zhuge, H., Sun, X.P., Liu, J.: A Scalable P2P Platform for the Knowledge Grid. IEEE Transactions on Knowledge and Data Engineering 17(12), 1721–1736 (2005)
6. Aberer, K., Cudre-Mauroux, P., Datta, A., et al.: P-Grid: A Self-organizing Structured P2P System. ACM SIGMOD Record 32(2), 29–33 (2003)
7. Prem, U., Narendranadh, J., Uday, J., Yugyung, L.: P2P Grid: Service Oriented Framework for Distributed Resource Management. IEEE International Conference on Services Computing 1, 347–350 (2005)
8. Sunaga, H., Oka, T., Ueda, K., Matsumura, H.: P2P-based grid architecture for homology searching. Fifth IEEE International Conference on Peer-to-Peer Computing(P2P 2005) pp. 148–149 (2005)
9. W3C, Web Services Architecture (2003) http://www.w3.org/TR/2003/WD-ws-arch-20030808
10. Jovanovic, M. A.: Modeling large scale peer to peer networks and a case study of Gnutella [M. S. dissertation], University of Cincinnati (2001)
11. Foster, I., Kesselman, C.: Globus: A metacomputing infrastructure toolkit. International Journal of Supercomputer Applications 11(2), 115–128 (1997)
12. Zegura, E.W., Calvert, K.L., Bhattacharjee, S.: How to model an internetwork. In: Proceedings of IEEE INFOCOM (1996)
13. Kleinberg, J.: The small-world phenomenon: an algorithmic perspective. Cornell computer science technical report 99-1776 (2000)

Understanding Peer Behavior and Designing Incentive Mechanism in Peer-to-Peer Networks: An Analytical Model Based on Game Theory

Min Xiao and Debao Xiao

Department of Computer Science,
HuaZhong Normal University, Wuhan, China
{minxiao,dbxiao}@mail.ccnu.edu.cn

Abstract. In this paper, we present a game-based model to analyze nodes' behaviors and influence of incentive mechanism on nodes in a peer-to-peer network in which the altruistic and selfish peers coexist. In this model, a mental cost is attached to a peer to describe the level of the peer's altruism and determine the type of the peer. The merit of our model is the relation between the equilibrium and incentive mechanism(i.e. the influence of incentive mechanism on equilibrium) can be denoted by an analytic formula directly. Therefore, we can evaluate and compare the efficiency of diversified incentive mechanisms conveniently, the network operators can choose proper incentive mechanism to achieve certain optimal objective.

1 Introduction

Peer-to-peer (P2P) networks have gained a great deal of exposure recently as a way for a distributed group of users to easily share resources(storage,computing, content etc). However, peer-to-peer systems are self-organizing networks and rely on the willingness of individual user to provide resources to other users. Consuming network resources without providing resources to the network in return is commonly known as free-riding. By various measure techniques for network flow, it has been improved that the free-riding is a prevalent phenomenon in P2P networks regardless of when and where [1] [2]. Our ability to understand the behavior of peer and free-riding phenomenon is critical for well development of the P2P community.

In order to reduce the influence of free-riding behaviors on the performance of network, a plenty of researches are made and methods are advised to restrict the free-riding. Payment mechanism [3] [9] and reputation schemes [13] [14] are two main methods. These incentive or punitive mechanisms follow a common principle, that is, the quality of services that a peer can enjoy from the P2P community is determined by its contributions to the community. The stern penalty for free-rider is to ignore their requests [5] or to charge users for every download and to reward them for every upload (i.e. payment mechanism) [3] [9] in order to achieve the purpose of eliminating free-riding. Nevertheless, too

H. Jin et al. (Eds.): ICA3PP 2007, LNCS 4494, pp. 368–379, 2007.
© Springer-Verlag Berlin Heidelberg 2007

rigorous punishment may force some peers to leave the community and hurt the profits of network operator, because to them, the number of on-line customers in P2P network may be an important index that measures the system's value for the purpose of advertisement. The moderate punishment is to reduce the probability that the requests of free-riders can get response [5] [6] or to decide whether to limit free-riders according to the load of the network [4].

When various incentive mechanisms are introduced into P2P networks, game theory naturally becomes an analysis and mechanism design tool for studying the P2P network [4] [6] [7] [8] [9] [10]. Game theory studies decisions that are made by players in an attempt to maximize their returns and in an environment where various players are interdependent and interactional. In other words, game theory studies choice of optimal behavior when costs and benefits of each option are not fixed, but depend upon the choices of other individuals. The P2P network is just a community that is suitable for game theory. In P2P system, there are games between peer and peer, peer and network. The game between peer and peer is typical public good provision and the main consideration in current literatures. However, most of the models are built based on detailed statistic for each peer contribution and consumption, and the implementation of complete information game model needs a plenty of information exchange and consumes too much network resource to practice eventually. This is also the main problem that game model encounters in P2P network. Therefore, a more practicable model is needed for game theory becoming a decision-making tool in the P2P community. The macro-level and incomplete information game model may be more appropriate selection.

In our paper, by using game theory, we model the behavior of the peer and seek to understand how and when heterogeneous peers will contribute to P2P networks, how behaviors of peers will be influenced by diverse incentive mechanisms, Whether it is optimal that each participant contributes to the network, and if it is uncertain, then how to select proper incentive mechanism and control the appropriate proportion of contributors for certain optimal objective. Our work is more macro-level and more suitable for managerial demand in contrast to those researches paying attention to single peer's decision. And that, in our paper, a intrinsical attribute–the level of altruism of a peer is considered as the type of the peer. In a P2P system without any incentive mechanism and from high level, we see that the system treats equally every peer and provides the same utility to every peer. This angle of view make our model be free of overloading with details and we can only take the number of contributions in total network as parameter under certain assumption about cost distribution. By applying the reduced model, we obtain some results that can not be gotten from micro-level models. The game models with complete and incomplete information are respectively built and the equilibria are discussed. The merit of our model is the relation between the equilibrium and incentive mechanism(i.e. the influence of incentive mechanism on equilibrium) can be denoted by an analytic formula directly. Therefore, we can evaluate and compare the efficiency of diversified incentive mechanisms conveniently, the network operators can choose proper incentive mechanism to achieve certain optimal objective.

1.1   Related Work-The Application of Game Theory in P2P Network

In this section, we briefly introduce game-theoretic approaches in P2P network in related literatures. In [7], a benefit matrix is presented to describe how much the contribution made by every peer is worth to each other, and based on this, the utility function of each peer is constructed and a game model is presented to guide peer decision. [4] models the whole resource request and distribution process as a competition game between the competing nodes who request file download from a node synchronously. In [6], the authors model nodes' activities as a infinitely repeated game in the P2P network where nodes get services based on their reputation. In [8], a Cournot Oligopoly game model with dynamic payoff functions is built and a control-theoretic is proposed for solution to the problem. In [9], authors classify peers into two types: altruistic and non-altruistic nodes. A game theoretic model is built to analyze the nodes' strategies under several payment mechanisms in a centralized P2P system. These models pay attention to single peer's strategy at micro-level and are all complete information game models which need exchange of global information about all peer behaviors. Obviously, this requirement is non-practicable in P2P networks where peers enter and exit at any moment.

In [10], the game model is built from a higher level and slips the leash exchanging information of all peers' activities and only considers the value of content that a peer holds. The values of contents provided by peers are ranked and become the types of peers. The authors prove that the peers with higher value should share and those peers with lower value free-ride in equilibrium, and that all peers that share content provide the same utility to the other peers in the network. In contrast to the literatures purposing to eliminate free-riding, the model demonstrates that it is not necessarily socially optimal to eliminate free-riding and networks can persist in spite of free-riding. In practice, it is difficult to valuate the value of content provided by a peer, especially, value of a content could not be uniform for all other peers and it is not a intrinsical attribute of a peer. Our model is similar to [10], but a more intrinsical attribute is considered as the type of peer and more results are obtained.

1.2   Organization of the Paper

The reminder of this paper is organized as follows. Section 2 introduces a theoretic framework of game model with complete information and incomplete information, with incentive mechanism and without incentive mechanism respectively. The selection for incentive mechanism is also presented. Experimental results are given in Section 3. Section 4 concludes the paper.

2   Theoretic Framework of Game Model

In this section, we first present purely theoretic framework of game model with complete and incomplete information in the P2P network without incentive mechanism and with incentive mechanism respectively.

2.1 Complete Information Game Model Without Incentive Mechanism

In complete information game, the player's preference and type are common knowledge, that is, each player's profits for each profile decided by actions that each player selects are common knowledge[11]. In this section, we depict the behaviors of peers in the P2P network without any incentive mechanism by a complete information game model.

We consider a P2P network in which the altruistic and selfish peers coexist, each peer i has unique cost C_i incurred from contributing and acts as the player of this game. The cost can be explained from following two aspects. On the one hand, contributing consumes the peer's private resources, such as storage space, bandwidth etc., and we call it physical cost. On the other, there are differences of peers' altruism levels, the some are altruistic and the other some could be motivated by self-interest. Obviously, peers with different altruism level suffer from distinctive mental costs for same contribution, the altruists have smaller mental cost than selfish peers. In this paper, we take the two costs into account, under the assumption of the same physical costs for all peers, cost can be considered as a metric of altruism level of peer.

We utilize a static game model of providing public good to describe the decision of peer in the p2p network. Assume that there are N peers acting as players of this game and the cost and utility function of each peer are common knowledge; each player has a set of actions {contribute, not contribute} and S_i denotes the pure strategy of player i; players decide simultaneously whether to contribute to the public good, and contributing is a 0-1 decision. $S_i = 0$ means "not contribute" and 1 means "contribute". In this model, we first do not consider the difference of number of players' contributions and uniform the number of contribution to one unit if a player decides to contribute, and in later section, we will explain its extension to more general situations. In addition, under the above assumption, the physical cost indicates the resource consumption that one unit contribution induces and is also assumed to be the same for all contributors.

For the utility that the system provides to peer, from high level and global perspective, we see that the system treats equally every peer and provides the same utility to every peer in a P2P system without any incentive mechanism. Specifically, the utility of peer is involved in not only absolute number of contributions but also relative proportion of contributors in total network. Obviously, the more contributions there are in the network, the more options peers will have and the better services players can enjoy. At the same time, the high proportion of contributors can balance the load of the network, improve the transmission performance of the network and the response time of peer request. In addition, a weight factor may be needed to balance the influence of the two aspects on peer utility. We denote the utility function as U(m,N,d), where m is the absolute number of contributors, N is the size of the network and d is the weight factor. Following the general assumption in economics, the utility function U(m,N,d) should be a increasing function with decreasing marginal utility of sum m of all contributions in the network. The decreasing marginal utility describes that with the growth of contributions, the satisfactory sense of peer for increase of one unit contribution will decrease.

Strictly speaking, there should be a lower bound m_* of number m of contributors below that the utility U is zero, it is the lowest level of the system survival. Therefore, m should take value in $[m_*, N]$. In existing systems, this condition should hold naturally, i.e. there always are adequate altruists such that the system can survive. In our discussion, this condition can be transformed to estimation for cost distribution of peer.

Based on statement above, we analyze the behavior of peer and equilibria of this game. If a peer i selects action "not contribute", then $S_i = 0$, the payoff is

$$U_i^0 = U(\sum_{j=1, j \neq i}^{N} S_j, N, d) \tag{1}$$

and if the choice of player i is "contribute", then $S_i = 1$ and the payoff is

$$U_i^1 = U((\sum_{j=1, j \neq i}^{N} S_j) + 1, N, d) - C_i \tag{2}$$

Obviously, only if $U_i^0 \leq U_i^1$ is satisfied, the player i will choose to contribute. This condition can be further translated into

$$C_i \leq U((\sum_{j=1, j \neq i}^{N} S_j) + 1, N, d) - U(\sum_{j=1, j \neq i}^{N} S_j, N, d) \tag{3}$$

where $\sum_{j=1, j \neq i}^{N} S_j$ denotes the number of contributions in the network except for player i. And as we can see from above formula, there exists a upper limit of cost C^* with related to sum of contributions in the network, and only for those peers with less cost than C^*, contributing is optimal strategy in order to maximize their benefits. When the cost of peer makes the two sides of Eq.3 be equal, the peer can select two actions discretionarily. For the sake of simplicity, in later content, we assume that the peer always selects "contribute" at this situation. For the equilibrium of this game, naturally we can conclude:

Proposition 1. In this game, there is a pure strategy equilibrium, where the peers with non-larger cost than C^* contribute and the others free-ride, and C^* satisfies following equation

$$C^* = U(N_{C \leq C^*} + 1, N, d) - U(N_{C \leq C^*}, N, d) \tag{4}$$

where $N_{C \leq C^*}$ denotes the number of peers with non-larger cost than C^*.

2.2   Incomplete Information Game Model Without Incentive Mechanism

Complete information game model may not be easily actualized in practice because it is difficult to know the cost of every peer. Therefore in this section it is assumed that individual cost is distributed according to continuous density function f(C) with cumulative distribution function F(C) and support $[\underline{C}, \bar{C}]$. The preference of players and inference F(C) are common knowledge. However, the cost C_i is the player's type and is known only to that player. We will look for a symmetric Bayesian equilibrium.

A pure strategy in this game is a function $S_i(C_i)$ from $[\underline{C}, \bar{C}]$ into $\{0, 1\}$. It is well known that in models of this type, such as Palfrey and Rosenthal (1989), there exists a upper bound C^* such that Bayesian equilibrium strategy is $S_i^* = 1$ if $C_i \leq C^*$ and conversely, $S_i^* = 0$ if $C_i > C^*$ for all $i = 1, 2, \ldots, N$ [12]. In this game, the expected payoff of peer i is

$$E_C[U_i] = E_C[U(\textstyle\sum_{j=1}^N S_j(C_j), N, d) - S_i(C_i)C_i] \tag{5}$$

where $C = (C_1, C_2, \ldots, C_{i-1}, C_{i+1}, \ldots, C_N)$, E_C denotes expectation conditional on C. The equilibrium cutoff level C^* must satisfy following equation

$$\sum_{m=m_*}^{N-1} \binom{N-1}{m} F(C^*)^m (1 - F(C^*))^{N-1-m} U(m, N, d)$$

$$= \sum_{m=m_*}^{N-1} \binom{N-1}{m} F(C^*)^m (1 - F(C^*))^{N-1-m} U(m+1, N, d) - C^*$$

The LHS of above equation is the expected profits when the peer does not contribute and the RHS is the expected profits given contributing. This equation can be further transformed to

$$C^* = \sum_{m=m_*}^{N-1} \binom{N-1}{m} F(C^*)^m (1 - F(C^*))^{N-1-m} \times [U(m+1, N, d) - U(m, N, d)] \tag{6}$$

Proposition 2. In this game, there is a pure strategy equilibrium, where the peers with non-larger cost than C^* contribute and the others free-ride, and C^* satisfies Eq.6.

2.3 Incomplete Information Game Model with Incentive Mechanism

In terms of principle of incentive mechanisms restraining free-riding, the contributors should enjoy high priority service in contrast to the non-contributors (i.e. free-riders) under any incentive mechanisms. At this situation, the system differentially treat contributors and non-contributors and does not provide the same utility to every peer in the network. We introduce a penalty parameter $P \in [0, 1]$ into utility function U(m, N, d) and as a differentiator. For free-riders, the utility that they can get is only PU(m, N, d), at the same time, for contributors, the utility could be $(1 + \alpha(1 - P))U(m, N, d)$, where $\alpha \in [0, 1]$ is a parameter controlling the extent of contributors' utility growth resulting from the restrictions on free-riders. In an overloaded system, the restrictions can bring bigger improvement of contributor's utility in contrast to light-loaded system. Thus, to some degree, the selection of α depends on current performance of the system. The penalty parameter P could be seen as the probability that free-riders obtain their desired services from the system. Note that P=1 corresponds to the situation where there is not any incentive mechanism and P=0 corresponds to the incentive mechanism purposing to eliminate free-riders, such as payment mechanism. Therefore, the approach here is a natural extension of the model without incentive mechanism. In addition, we think the more suitable punishment is to decide whether to limit free-riders according to the load of the network and P can be taken as a function of the network load.

At this scenario, the Eq.5 and Eq.6 become to

$$E_C[U_i] = E_C[r(S(C_i), P)U(\sum_{j=1}^{N} S_j(C_j), N, d) - S_i(C_i)C_i] \tag{7}$$

$$C^* = \sum_{m=m_*}^{N-1} \binom{N-1}{m} F(C^*)^m (1 - F(C^*))^{N-1-m}$$
$$\times [r(1, P)U(m+1, N, d) - r(0, P)U(m, N, d)] \tag{8}$$

where $r(S(C_i), P) = \begin{cases} r(1, P) = 1 + \alpha(1 - P) \text{ if } S(C_i) = 1 \\ r(0, P) = P \qquad\qquad \text{if } S(C_i) = 0 \end{cases}$

Proposition 3. In this game, there is a pure strategy equilibrium, where the peers with non-larger cost than C^* contribute and the others free-ride, and C^* satisfies Eq.8.

2.4   The Selecting of Incentive Mechanism with Certain Optimal Attribute

The appropriate incentive mechanism can improve performance and efficiency of the P2P system. For network operators, they can achieve certain optimal objective by selecting incentive mechanism. In this section, we will discuss the selecting of incentive mechanism under our model. Let certain objective function be $W(P, C^*, N)$, this optimal problem is to decide the equilibrium upper-bound of cost C^* by selecting appropriate penalty parameter P and further maximize the objective function W. This problem is formalized as:

$$\begin{cases} \max_{P} W(P, C^*, N) \\ \text{subject to Eq. (8)} \end{cases} \tag{9}$$

Note that the reason that we design optimal objective $W(P, C^*, N)$ as the function of C^* is the optimal objective must be related to the number of contributors in the network, and the number of contributors is the function of C^*. For instance, under incomplete information model, the expected number $\bar{m}$ of contributors can be denoted as $\bar{m} = \sum_{m=0}^{N} m \binom{N}{m} F(C^*)^m (1 - F(C^*))^{N-m}$

In addition, for network operators, the number of on-line customers N (i.e. the size of network) in P2P network could be an important index that measures the system's value for the purpose of advertisement.

3   Experimental Results

In this section, we give an intuition for our theoretic model by an instance and experimental results.

Firstly, in terms of the requirements for utility function U in Section 2, we take U as:

$$U = \beta \log(\tfrac{1}{N}(\textstyle\sum_{j=1}^{N} S_j)^d + 1) \tag{10}$$

β is a system parameter tuning the units of utility and cost.

The equilibrium condition corresponding to the Eq.4 under complete information and lack of incentive mechanism is

$$C^* = \beta \log \frac{\tfrac{1}{N}(N_{C \le C^*}+1)^d+1}{\tfrac{1}{N}(N_{C \le C^*})^d+1} \tag{11}$$

Assume that the distribution of all peers' cost is uniform in $[0,2]$, we get equilibrium point shown in Fig.1. As it reveals, there are about 0.1% contributors and the proportion may be too low to ensure the network survival. This result also shows our assumption about cost distribution should imply more altruists. Fig.2 shows the equilibrium point under the assumption that the cost of all peers follows normal distribution with mean 1/2 and standard variance 1/5. The probability that the observation from this normal distribution is less than 0.002 is 0.0232, thus at equilibrium point, there are more than 2% contributors in the system. This result is more coincident with investigation in [1].

In terms of the Eq.6, the equilibrium cutoff level C^* under incomplete information and lack of incentive mechanism must satisfy following equation

$$C^* = \textstyle\sum_{m=m_*}^{N-1} \binom{N-1}{m} F(C^*)^m(1 - F(C^*))^{N-1-m}$$
$$\times \beta \log \left((\tfrac{1}{N}(m+1)^d + 1)/(\tfrac{1}{N}(m)^d + 1)\right) \tag{12}$$

We take m_* as $1\% \times N$ and assume that inference $F(C)$ is normal distribution with mean 1/2 and standard variance 100/467. the Fig.3 reveals that there are approximate 1% contributors at equilibrium point. Due to the absence of incentive mechanism, the proportion of contributors is low. Therefore, it may be necessary to offer some incentive mechanisms in P2P network.

Adopting utility function in Eq.10, the Eq.8 becomes to

$$C^* = \textstyle\sum_{m=m_*}^{N-1} \binom{N-1}{m} F(C^*)^m(1 - F(C^*))^{N-1-m}$$
$$\times \beta \left[r(1,P) \log \left(\tfrac{1}{N}(m+1)^d + 1\right) - r(0,P) \log \left(\tfrac{1}{N}(m)^d + 1\right)\right] \tag{13}$$

If we take the inference $F(C)$ is normal distribution like previous section and other conditions remain unchanged, the Fig.4 reveals the equilibrium points under different penalty P. Unfortunately, there are non-unique equilibria. Therefore, further analysis is required to determine which equilibrium will be achieved in practice. The learning theory of game may be a appropriate tool. In addition, a deeper study for choosing function $r(S(C_i), P)$ and cost distribution is also required. These are our future works and beyond this paper.

Similar to [4], whether to penalty free-riders is decided by the performance of the network, then P can be taken as a function of proportion of contributors. We assume that P=1 (so r(0,P)=r(1,P)=1)when the proportion is more than 50%, and conversely, $P \in (0,1)$. Thus, the Eq.13 becomes to

$$
\begin{aligned}
C^* = \sum_{m=m_*}^{N/2} &\binom{N-1}{m} F(C^*)^m (1 - F(C^*))^{N-1-m} \\
&\times \beta \left[r(1,P) \log \left(\tfrac{1}{N}(m+1)^d + 1 \right) - r(0,P) \log \left(\tfrac{1}{N}(m)^d + 1 \right) \right] \\
+ \sum_{m=N/2+1}^{N-1} &\binom{N-1}{m} F(C^*)^m (1 - F(C^*))^{N-1-m} \\
&\times \beta \left[\log \left(\tfrac{1}{N}(m+1)^d + 1 \right) - \log \left(\tfrac{1}{N}(m)^d + 1 \right) \right] \quad (14)
\end{aligned}
$$

The Fig.5 shows the equilibrium points in this situation and we do some comparison of Fig.4 and Fig.5. Since the incentive mechanism corresponding to Fig.4 has nothing to do with the performance of the system and is sterner penalty mechanism than that in the Fig.5, the equilibrium upper bound of cost in Fig.4 is higher than corresponding equilibrium point in Fig.5. For example, when P=0.1 or 0.2, the Fig.4 shows almost all peers must contribute because the inequality (3) always holds. At the same time, the Fig.5 indicates there are only about 60% contributors at the equilibrium points.

In our model, the selecting of incentive mechanism is equivalent to the selecting of P. We solve C^* as the function of P from Eq.13, and subsequently, substitute this function into $W(P, C^*, N)$ and determine the optimal P maximizing W. For the incentive mechanism in Fig.4, the Eq.13 can be transformed to

$$
\begin{aligned}
& p \sum_{m=m_*}^{N-1} \binom{N-1}{m} F(C^*)^m (1 - F(C^*))^{N-1-m} \times \beta log[((m+1)^d/N + 1)(m^d/N + 1)] \\
& = 2 \sum_{m=m_*}^{N-1} \binom{N-1}{m} F(C^*)^m (1 - F(C^*))^{N-1-m} \times \beta log((m+1)^d/N + 1) - C^* \quad (15)
\end{aligned}
$$

The Fig.6 reveals the function relation between C^* and P under the assumption that the inference F(C) is uniform distribution in [0,2]. For incentive mechanism in Fig.5, the similar expression can be obtained from Eq.14 directly.

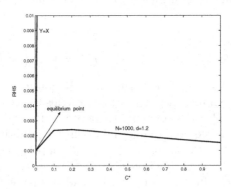

Fig. 1. Nash equilibrium under uniform distribution, complete information and lack of incentive mechanism

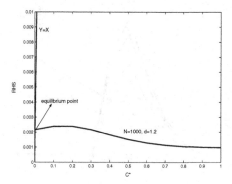

Fig. 2. Nash equilibrium under normal distribution, complete information and lack of incentive mechanism

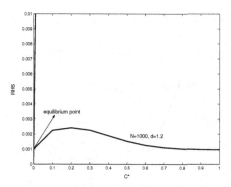

Fig. 3. Bayesian equilibrium under normal distribution, incomplete information and lack of incentive mechanism

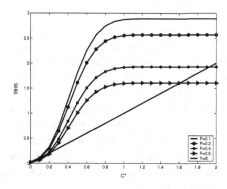

Fig. 4. Bayesian equilibria under constant P, normal distribution

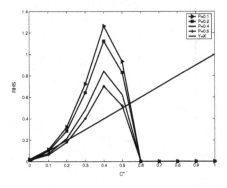

Fig. 5. Bayesian equilibria under variable P and normal distribution

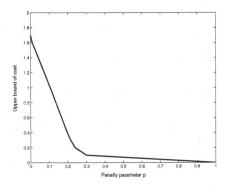

Fig. 6. Equilibrium upper-bound of cost against penalty parameter p

4   Conclusion

In this paper, we present a game theoretic model under complete information and incomplete information respectively in order to analyze and understand the behaviors of peers in P2P networks. The equilibrium of the system without incentive mechanism is contrasted with that of the system with incentive mechanism. The result shows that incentive mechanism can encourage more peers to contribute to the p2P network. In contrast to other literatures that attach full importance to restraining free-riding, the purpose of this paper is to present a model that could be used to analyze and understand the behaviors of peers and effect of incentive mechanism in P2P networks. Especially, our model can help P2P network operators or designers to achieve certain optimal objective by selecting proper incentive mechanism.

In practice, our model can be easy adapted to a variety of network circumstances by tuning the parameters in the model. For the cost distribution of peer, an empirical distribution may be used. In previous analysis, we assume that all peers only contribute one unit to the network. The simplest extension of the model is to decompose the peer who contributes more units into serval virtual peers with one unit contribution and the same cost. Considering the stern punishment could induce some peers to leave the system and alter the size of the network, we think that it is required to design analytic model based on dynamic game theory, and it is our future work.

References

1. Adar, E., Huberman, B. A.: Free-riding on Gnutella. First Monday, vol. 5(10) (2000)
2. Hughes, D., Coulson, G., Walkerdine, J.: Free riding on Gnutella revisited: the bell tolls ? IEEE Distributed Systems Online, vol. 6 (2005)
3. Vishumurthy, V., Chandrakumar, S., Sirer, E. G.: KARMA: A Secure Economic Framework for Peer-to-Peer Resource Sharing. In: Proceedings of the 2003 Workshop on Economics of Peer-to-Peer Systems, Berkeley, CA (2003)
4. Richard, T.B.M., Sam, C.M.L., John, C.S.L., David, K.Y.Y.: A game theoretic approach to provide incentive and service differentiation in P2P networks. SIGMETRICS, pp. 189–198 (2004)
5. Karakaya, M., Korpeouglu, I., Ulusoy, O.: A distributed and measurement-based framework against free riding in peer-to-peer networks. In: Proceedings of the fourth international conference on peer-to-peer computing (P2P'04) pp. 276–277 (2004)
6. Gupta, R., Somani, A. K.: Game theory as a tool to strategize as well as predict nodes' behavior in peer-to-peer network. In: Proceedings of the 2005 11th international conference on parallel and distributed systems (ICPADS'05) pp. 244–249 (2005)
7. Buragohain, C., Divyakant, A., Suri, S.: A Game Theoretic Framework for Incentives in P2P Systems. Peer-to-Peer Computing, pp. 48–56 (2003)
8. Wang, W., Li, B.: To play or to control: a game-based control-theoretic approach to peer-to-peer incentive engineering. In: Proceedings of the Eleventh International Workshop on Quality of Service (IWQoS 2003) pp. 174–194 (2003)
9. Golle, P., Leyton-Brown, K., Mironov, I.: Incentive for sharing in peer-to-peer networks. In: Proceedings of the ACM conference on electronic commerce, pp. 264-267 (2001)
10. Krishnan, R., Smith, M. D., Tang, Z., Telang, R.: The Impact of Free-Riding on Peer-to-Peer Networks. In: Proceeding of the 37th Hawaii International Conference on System Sciences(HICSS-36 2004) pp. 199–208 (2004)
11. Mas-colell, A., Whinston, M.D., Green, J.R.: Microeconomic Theory. Oxford University Press, New York (1995)
12. Tabarrok, A.: The private provision of public goods via dominant assurance contracts. Public Choice 96, 345–362 (1998)
13. Marti, S., Garcia-Molina, H.: Limited reputation sharing in P2P systems. In: Proc. of the 5th ACM conference on Electronic commerce, New York, USA (2004)
14. Gupta, M., Judge, P., Ammar, M.: A reputation system for peer-to-peer networks. In: ACM 13th International Workshop on Network and Operating Systems Support for Digital Audio and Video (2003)

An Efficient Source Peer Selection Algorithm in Hybrid P2P File Sharing Systems

Jingyuan Li[1], Weijia Jia[3], Liusheng Huang[2], Mingjun Xiao[2], and Jun Wang[1]

[1] Joint Research Lab between CityU and USTC in Their Advanced Research
Institute in Suzhou, Jiangsu, China
[2] Department of Computer Science, University of Science and Technology of China,
Anhui, China
[3] Department of Computer Science, City University of Hong Kong, Hong Kong SAR, China
{50008990,50009101}@student.cityu.edu.hk
itjia@cityu.edu.hk
{lshuang,xiaomj}@ustc.edu.cn

Abstract. We propose a source peer selection algorithm which efficiently chooses peers as sources from a set of peers having the requested file in a hybrid P2P file sharing system. Our proposed algorithm considers the energy factors as well as the communication issues and the peers' contribution to the file sharing system. The core idea of our algorithm is to minimize the workload of the wireless peers, and to leave those jobs to cable connected peers which are much stronger than wireless ones. We validate our algorithm through comprehensive simulations, which show that the algorithm works correctly and effectively.

Keywords: Energy Efficient, File Sharing System, Hybrid P2P, Source Selection.

1 Introduction

Peer-to-peer (P2P) file sharing systems are becoming more and more popular throughout the world. It is said that about 30 percent of the internet traffic is peer-to-peer related by the end of the year 2004 [1]. Moreover, Researchers from University of California believe that P2P will continue to develop despite the lawsuits against music and movie sharing systems in recent years [2]. P2P file sharing systems are appealing to many people due to the following reasons [3]. Firstly, by weakening or eliminating dependency on centralized point, scalability is improved. P2P techniques reduce the risk of system failure as compared to centralized systems. Secondly, elimination of the need for a powerful and stable infrastructure on a central point greatly reduces the cost of a system. Workload is assigned evenly amount network connections. Finally, P2P file sharing systems enable the resource aggregation. On the other hand, wireless network techniques, including 3G networks, Wi-Fi, WiMAX and Bluetooth, are developing extraordinarily fast in recent years.

Therefore, it is very attractive to combine cable connected P2P techniques with wireless techniques, in a system we name hybrid P2P. (The definition of hybrid P2P

H. Jin et al. (Eds.): ICA3PP 2007, LNCS 4494, pp. 380–390, 2007.

in this paper is very different from [3], where a hybrid P2P system is defined as a P2P system with some servers.) In fact, the goal of accessing the P2P systems anytime anywhere can be achieved only by adding wireless networks to the existing file sharing systems. However, there are a number of problems to be solved such as the energy problem, the communication problem and the contribution measurement problem. The major problem is the energy of the wireless end devices. It is known to all that P2P file sharing processes are very energy consuming, and in many cases, time consuming as well. This problem may not influence cable connected devices very much. However, it indeed bothers wireless devices, which are energy sensitive. Limit of communication resources, i.e. relatively narrow and expensive air interface, is another factor that limits the use of wireless P2P. The situation will continue for many years according to the level of present wireless techniques and the governments' radio policies.

Trying to solve the above problems, we propose a model that would guarantee communication and data sharing between wired and wireless peers considering energy, communication and contribution issues to hybrid P2P file sharing systems. The main idea of our algorithm is to minimize the workload of the wireless peers in hybrid P2P file sharing systems, leaving as much work as possible to cable connected peers. We design a marking system in our algorithm, in order to successfully implement our core idea. Wired devices have great power in computation abilities and storage capacities, while wireless end hosts have the advantages of entering networks any time anywhere. The ultimate goal of our model is to take advantage of both wired and wireless techniques.

For example, when a peer p requests file f, it asks to its peers in the group, 'who has f? Some peers respond, 'I have'. Traditionally, p checks the energy, communication and contribution conditions of these qualified peers, and then chooses the best peer or a group of peers from the affirmative peers. However, due to the limitation of energy of the wireless devices, special policies should be implemented to protect the weak and precious wireless peers from dying early due to heavy load.

The rest of the paper is organized as follows. Section 2 introduces relevant research in P2P and wireless techniques. In section 3 we propose our source peer selection algorithm in hybrid P2P file sharing system. Some simulations are shown in section 4, and we conclude the paper in the final section.

2 Related Work

A lot of research on P2P applications has been published. A review by Milojicic, and Kalogeraki et al. suggested that P2P applications can be divided into three dimensions: distributed computing, file sharing, and communication and collaboration [3]. They further studied that there are three kinds of P2P algorithms that are commonly used: centralized directory model, flooded requests model, and document routing model.

On wireless techniques aspect, Wireless Grid is a hot spot, where many groups are interested in this topic. Foster et al. believed [4] that Grid is a way of 'flexible, secure, and coordinated resource sharing among dynamic collections of individuals, institutions and resources.' Agarwal, and Gupta et al. defined [5] Wireless Grid to be 'an augmentation of a wired grid that facilitates the exchange of information and the interaction between heterogeneous wireless devices.'

In wireless networks, great improvement has been made. Ohrtman published a detailed introduction to IEEE 802.11 standard on how to transport voice over the standard [6]. Dan O'Shea suggested that IEEE 802.16 and its commercial edition WiMAX are going to rule the wireless networks in future [7], while Wongthavarawat, and Ganz et al. proposed a Quality of Service (or QoS) aware packet scheduling mechanism that satisfies the need of different kinds of data flows [8]. Jia implemented the 3G-324M protocol stack to transmit real-time video, audio and data between the Internet and 3G networks [9].

Some research groups are interested in wireless P2P techniques. Leung and Kwok proposed a decentralized and dynamic topology control protocol called TCP2P to unify the energy efficiency, fairness and incentive factors of the P2P file sharing networks [10]. Bordetsky et al. designed two experiments to the problems in wireless P2P collaborative learning, and gave a solution for improving them [11]. Kang and Mutka et al. proposed an interesting P2P data download structure for 3G networks [12].

3 Our Proposed Algorithm

3.1 Introduction to Hybrid P2P File Sharing Systems and the Position of Our Algorithm

We need to clearly define the terms used in this paper. We define a *wired peer* as a peer in a P2P file sharing system that runs on a wired end device implementing wired network techniques, such as Ethernet. Similarly, we define a *wireless peer* to be a peer in a P2P system that sets up on a wireless device implementing wireless network techniques, such as 3G and Wi-Fi. A hybrid P2P file sharing system is then defined as a P2P application that has both wired peers and wireless peers.

Generally speaking, a P2P file sharing system operates three main protocols: a resource lookup protocol, a source peer selection protocol and a file transport protocol. A resource lookup protocol is used when a peer requests a file from the file sharing system. Then a peer selection protocol is executed to choose a peer or a set of peers from the group of peers that have the requested file. Lastly, the P2P file sharing system implements a file transport protocol to transport the file from the chosen source peers to the requested peer in time.

The selection of the source peer selection protocol is critical to the performance of a P2P file sharing systems. A good source peer selection protocol can dramatically accelerate the speed of file download, and minimize the consumption of networks resources. Our proposed algorithm is located at the source peer selection protocol in hybrid P2P file sharing systems.

We all know that P2P file sharing systems are located at the application layer. Ideally, we do not need to distinguish between wired peers and wireless peers. However, as we have mentioned above, wireless end devices have some intrinsic characteristics, such as finite energy compared to wired ones, shortage in both computation and storage capabilities, and limitations of air interfaces and so on.

Therefore, in a hybrid P2P file sharing system, the peer selection protocol should fully consider the advantages and disadvantages of wireless peers so as to get a better performance of the file sharing system.

In our algorithm, we design a special peer structure. Peers in a hybrid P2P file sharing system are equally treated except that we add a *Classifier* attribute to each peer. The value of the *Classifier* attribute is either *wired* or *wireless*. Thus, at the initialization phase or peer entering phase, each peer is assigned a peer ID and a style value based on the network access mechanism of the end host. The model is depicted in Fig. 1. The goal of our model is to protect wireless peers from heavy workloads and accent the advantages of their mobile characteristics. To achieve the goal, many factors should be considered, including energy issues, communication expenses, and contributions of peers to the system.

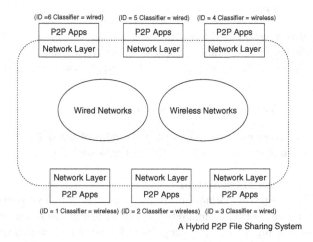

Fig. 1. The proposed structure of hybrid P2P file sharing systems

3.2 Factors to be Considered

3.2.1 Energy Mark System

The energy level of the host is a crucial factor. For wired end devices, we suppose that their energy is infinite. For wireless end devices, however, the energy policies are important. A good source peer selection policy is very likely to postpone the 'death' of precious and expensive wireless peers.

For a file *doc*, we define *destination peer* to be the peer that requests *doc*, and define *source peers* to be the peers that have *doc*. The energy consumption is divided into two categories: the process consumption and the transport consumption.

For a hybrid P2P file sharing system, the process consumption of a peer, i.e. the energy spends to process the resource lookup protocol and the source peer selection protocol, is trivial compared to the transport consumption, i.e. the energy cost of transporting files from the source peers to the destination peer. Therefore, we omit the process consumption.

For transport consumption, we suppose that the energy cost to send a file *doc* from the source peer p_i to the destination peer p_j is proportional to the file size of *doc*. We therefore set an array *Energy[1..N]* to represent current energy level of each peer in the file sharing system, where N is the total number of living peers. Let *MaxEnergy* be a constant. Without losing of generality, the energy space is divided into three sections from $-\infty$ to *MaxEnergy*, named the *dead* section, the *wireless* section and the *wired* section respectively. Let *Energy[i]* be the current energy level of peer p_i. If *Energy[i]* = *MaxEnergy*, then p_i is the *wired peer*; if $0 <$ *Energy[i]* $<$ *MaxEnergy*, then p_i is a living *wireless peer*; if *Energy[i]* $\leqslant 0$, then p_i is a *dead peer*, and we eliminate it from the file sharing system instantly.

Suppose p_i transmits the file *doc* to p_j, which reduces the energy value of *Energy[i]* and *Energy[j]*. *Energy[i]* subtracts a certain value as follows:

$$Energy[i] = Energy[i] - \alpha \cdot size(doc).\tag{1}$$

where *size(doc)* is a function which returns the size of the file *doc* and α is a scale parameter which describes the ratio of the size of the transmitting file to the reduction of the energy level in the source peer p_i. *Energy[j]* subtracts a certain value as follows:

$$Energy[j] = Energy[j] - \beta \cdot size(doc).\tag{2}$$

where β is a scale parameter which describes the ratio of the size of the transmitting file to the reduction of the energy level in the destination peer p_j.

3.2.2 Communication Mark System

Communication is very important for both wired and wireless peers, especially wireless peers, because of the limitations to wireless bandwidth resources. Peers in a hybrid P2P file sharing system are geographically separated, which are connected through wired and wireless networks. Therefore the connection qualities may be extraordinarily different from each other, which is the reason why we take communication issues into consideration. Generally speaking, three factors need to be considered: the size of the file to be transported, the bandwidth of the connection and the lag between the establishment of connection and the start of the file transportation.

The larger the bandwidth of the connection, the less the communication time would be used. And the size of the file *doc* is proportional to the communication time. We can therefore calculate the time needed to deliver *doc* from the source peer p_s to the destination peer p_d as follows:

$$time_{sd} = lag_{sd} + \frac{size(doc)}{bw_{sd}}.\tag{3}$$

where bw_{sd} is the bandwidth between p_s and p_d, and lag_{sd} is the expected time lag between the connection establishment of p_s and p_d and the start of the file transportation.

In a hybrid P2P file sharing system, time is the definitive factor that influences the performance of a connection. Suppose p_d requests *doc*, and there are M peers p_{s1},

$p_{s2},..., p_{sM}$ which have *doc*. Define $time_{sdk}$ as the time needed to successfully transmit *doc* from p_{sk} to p_d, and define *larTime* as follows:

$$larTime = \max(time_{sdk}).$$ (4)

where $k = 1,2,...,M$. We hereby need an array $Commun_{doc}[M]$ to compare the transportation capabilities of the M connections:

$$Commun_{doc}[dk] = \frac{time_{sdk}}{larTime}.$$ (5)

3.2.3 Contribution Mark System

'Why should I help you?' is frequently asked in P2P applications. If a peer contributes to the file sharing system very much but receives nothing in return, it would become 'selfish'. In our approach, we define a contribution mark system that objectively evaluates the contribution of the peers in a hybrid P2P file sharing system. At the beginning, every peer is given an initial score. When the source peer p_s transmits a file *doc* to the destination peer p_d, p_s's score increases by certain points pt based on the size of the file transferred. Meanwhile, p_d's score decreases by pt.

Considering the special situations in hybrid P2P file sharing systems, we should provide some preferential conditions. If p_i is a wireless peer, its score goes up more than a wired peer does for equal workloads. Let Φ ($\Phi>1$) be a constant, for a file *doc*, if pt is the score earned by a wired peer for transporting *doc*, then $pt \cdot \Phi$ is what a wireless peer would gain for transmitting *doc*. Correspondingly, if p_j is a wireless peer, when it receives *doc* from other peers, p_j's score decreases by pt/Φ. We define an array $Contri[N]$, where N is the total number of peers alive in the file sharing system, and $Contri[k]$ is the current contribution score of peer p_k, $k=1,2,3,...,N$.

3.3 The Decision Function

The decision function is a combination of the energy mark system, the communication mark system and the contribution mark system. Suppose the destination peer p_d requests a file *doc*, and there are M peers $p_{s1}, p_{s2},..., p_{sM}$ that have *doc*. Therefore there are M possible connections to transmit *doc* to p_d. Define *peerSet* as:

$$peerSet = \{(p_d, p_{s1}), (p_d, p_{s2}), \cdots (p_d, p_{sM})\}.$$ (6)

where (p_d, p_{sk}) represents the connection between p_d and p_{sk}, $k=0,1,...,M$. We need an array $FinalMark[M]$ as follows:

$$FinalMark[k] = \eta_{energy} \cdot EnergyMark[k] + \eta_{commun} \cdot CommunMark[k] + \eta_{contri} \cdot ContriMark[k].$$ (7)

where η_{energy}, η_{commun} and η_{contri} represent the relative importance of the three factors, and $FinaMarkl[k]$ is the mark of the connection (p_d, p_{sk}). $EnergyMark[M]$, $CommunMark[M]$ and $ContriMark[k]$ are derived from $Energy[N]$, $Commun_{doc}[M]$, $Contri[N]$ respectively, as shown in Fig. 2.

> **Decision Function**
> Input:
> *doc*: the requested file of the destination peer.
> *peerSet*: the set of all the possible connections for file *doc*.
> Output:
> *resultSet*: the set of connections chosen to transport the file *doc*.
>   1: $i = 1$;
>   2: M = the number of possible connections for *doc*;
>   3: while $i \leqslant M$ do
>   4: *con* = the i_{th} connection of *peerSet*;
>   5: *src* = the source peer of *con*;
>   6: *EnergyMark[i]=Energy[src]*;
>   7: *CommunMark[i]=Commun$_{doc}$[i]*;
>   8: *larScore* = the largest contribution score of the source peers
> of *peerSet*;
>   9: *ContriMark[i]=larScore-Contri[src]*;
> $FinalMark[i] = \eta_{energy} \cdot EnergyMark[i] +$
>   10: $\eta_{commun} \cdot CommunMark[i] + \eta_{contri} \cdot ContriMark[i]$;
>   11:i++;
>   12:end while;
>   13: $j = 1$;
>   14:while $j \leqslant M$ do
>   15:if $FinalMark[i] \geqslant threshold$
>   16:add the i_{th} connection to the *resultSet*;
>   17:end if;
>   18:end while;
>   19:if no value in the array *FinalMark[M]* is larger than
> *threshold*
>   20:add the connection with the largest *FinalMark[M]* value to
> *resultSet*;
>   21:end if;

Fig. 2. The pseudo code of the decision function (DF)

We choose the connections from *peerSet* based on *FinalMark[M]*. All the connections of *peerSet* whose corresponding *FinalMark[M]* value are larger than a *threshold* value would be chosen to transport the whole or part of *doc*. If not a single connection meets the requirements of the *threshold*, then we choose the connection with the highest *FinalMark [M]* value. The pseudo code of the decision function is depicted in Fig. 2.

3.4 Our Proposed Source Peer Selection Algorithm

Our source peer selection algorithm is executed after the resource lookup procedure and before the file transportation procedure. Therefore, we know exactly the destination peer p_d that starts the lookup function of the file sharing system. We are also fully aware of the set of peers that have the requested file *doc*, which we name *sourcePeerSet*.

Suppose the size of *sourcePeerSet* is M. Initially, the algorithm establishes connections between p_d and the peers in *sourcePeerSet*. The resulting set of connections is named as *connectionSet*. Within each connection, the algorithm detects the connecting time lag and the bandwidth available to transport the file *doc*. It also records the energy level and the score of the contribution system of the destination peer p_d and the peers in *sourcePeerSet*.

Input:
doc: the requested file of the destination peer;
p_d: the destination peer;
sourcePeerSet: the set of peers which have *doc*;
Output:
resultSet: the set of connections that are chosen to transport doc;
   1: for each peer p_s in *sourcePeerSet*
   2: set up a connection between p_d and p_s;
   3: detect the bandwidth of this connection and the connecting lag;
   4: add this connection to *connectionSet*.
   5: end for
   6: *resultSet* = DecisionFunction (*doc*, *connectionSet*);
   7: change the energy level and contribution score of all the peers taking part in the file transfer procedure according to the regulations described in Section 3.2 of this paper.

Fig. 3. The pseudo code for the proposed source peer selection algorithm

The algorithm then inputs the *connectionSet* and the requested file *doc* into the decision function. The decision function outputs a *resultSet* that contains the connections chosen to transport *doc*. After that, algorithm adjusts the energy level of both p_d and the peers in *sourcePeerSet*: decreases the energy level of wireless peers according to the size of the file it transmits or receives; does not change the energy level of wired peers because their power are considered infinitive. Meanwhile, the algorithm increases the score of the contribution system of the peers in *sourcePeerSet*, and decreases the destination peer p_d's score based on the size of the file transported. Last but not least, the algorithm eliminates the peers whose energy levels are equal to or lower than zero. The pseudo code for the algorithm is shown in Fig. 3.

4   Simulations

4.1   Simulation Establishment and Parameters Selection

In this paper, a Java-code simulator was established to evaluate the performance of the proposed algorithm. The major goal of our algorithm is to minimize the workload of the precious wireless peers. Therefore, the percentage of dead wireless peers by the end of the simulations is what we were concerned about. We aimed at investigating the impact of the decision function defined in our source peer selection algorithm.

In the hybrid P2P file sharing system, the total number of peers in the hybrid P2P file sharing system was set to 500, where all the peers were supposed to be one-hop connected. The bandwidth of a connection was uniformly selected between 0.1 to 1.0Mbps, and the connecting lag was from 0.1 to 5 seconds. The size of the file was randomly selected between 0 and 10M. After executing the decision function, the workload was evenly separated among the source peers that were chosen to transmit the requested file. The ratio of the scale parameters α and β for the source peer and the destination peer was 1:0.7.

For the sake of simplicity, the marks of the arrays *EnergyMark[i]*, *CommunMark[i]*, *ContriMark[i]* and *FinalMark[i]* ranged from 0 to 100, and the sum of the three relative importance factors η_{energy}, η_{commun} and η_{contri} was set to 1, where $0 \leqslant \eta_{energy}, \eta_{commun}, \eta_{contri} \leqslant 1$.

4.2 Simulation Results

Fig. 4 shows the relationship between the number of files transported and the percentage of the dead wireless peers. In Fig. 4 (a), (b), (c) and (d), 80/60/40/20 percent of the peers were wireless peers, and the threshold value was 75. In the four charts, '80%' means that the relative importance factors η_{energy}, η_{commun} and η_{contri} are 0.8, 0.1 and 0.1, respectively; '40%' means that η_{energy}, η_{commun} and η_{contri} are 0.4, 0.3 and 0.3, respectively; "0%" means that η_{energy}, η_{commun} and η_{contri} are 0.0, 0.5 and 0.5, respectively. From Fig. 4, we can see that the precious wireless peers tend to 'die' much more quickly if we do not consider energy issues as a major factor to the performance of the hybrid P2P file sharing system, which proves the ability of our proposed source peer selection algorithm to protect wireless peers.

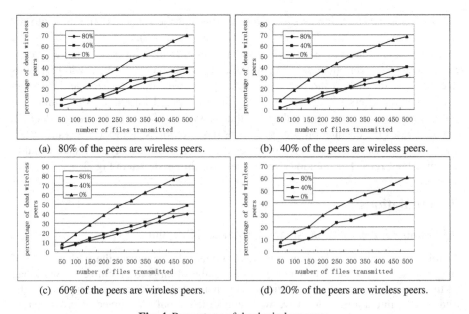

(a) 80% of the peers are wireless peers.   (b) 40% of the peers are wireless peers.

(c) 60% of the peers are wireless peers.   (d) 20% of the peers are wireless peers.

Fig. 4. Percentage of dead wireless peers

Moreover, comparing the four charts of Fig. 4, we discover that the decrease of the proportion of wireless peers leads to a decrease of the percentage of dead wireless peers. This phenomenon is easy to be explained, since the less the number of wireless peers in the file sharing systems, the less the decision function would choose them.

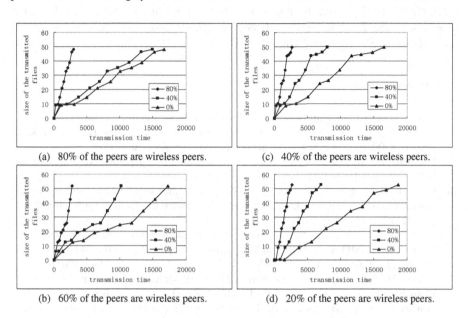

(a) 80% of the peers are wireless peers.   (c) 40% of the peers are wireless peers.

(b) 60% of the peers are wireless peers.   (d) 20% of the peers are wireless peers.

Fig. 5. Velocity of file transmission

Fig. 5 describes the transmission velocity of the hybrid P2P file sharing system. We find from the four charts that the average velocity of file transmission is higher if the value of η_{energy} is larger, i.e. the energy factor are more important than the other two factors in hybrid P2P file sharing systems. The reason is that if we do not seriously consider the limitations of wireless peers, i.e. minimum their workload, they would die out quickly, which in turn tremendously degrades the performance of the hybrid P2P file sharing system.

5 Conclusion

We have proposed an algorithm in hybrid P2P file sharing systems. The algorithm protects wireless peers and prolongs their lives by proposing a decision function which takes into consideration energy issues, communication environments and contributions of peers to the hybrid P2P file sharing system. By simulation, we have proved that the algorithm works correctly and efficiently. The algorithm not only protects the precious wireless peers from heavy workload, but also improves the average velocity of file transmission. Our current work includes investigating the impacts of the differences between P2P overlay networks and the topologies of physical networks, especially in the wireless domain.

Acknowledgment

This work is partially supported by CityU Applied R & D Funding (ARD) No. 9668009 and National Basic Research Fund of China ("973" Program) no.2003CB317003, and has been benefited from various discussions among the group members of the Joint Research Lab between CityU and USTC in their advanced research institute in Suzhou (China).

References

1. Top Tech News (2005) http://www.toptechnews.com/story.xhtml?story_id=38121
2. Karagiannis, T., Faloutsos, M.: P2P Technology Still Going Strong Despite Lawsuits, Fines (2004) http://www.newsroom.ucr.edu/cgi-bin/display.cgi?id=935
3. Milojicic, D., Kalogeraki, V., Lukose, R.: Peer-to-Peer Computing. Technical Report HPL-2002-57. HP Lab (2002)
4. Foster, I., Kesselman, C., Tuecke, S.: The Anatomy of the Grid: Enabling Scalable Virtual Organizations. International Journal of High Performance Computing Applications 15(3), 200–222 (2001)
5. Agarwal, A., Gupta, A., Norman, O.: Self-Configuration and Self-Administration of Wireless Grids. MIT Sloan School of Management, Working Paper 4460-04 (2004)
6. Ohrtman, F.: Voice over 802.11. ISBN: 1-58053-677-8, Artech House, Inc. (2004)
7. O'Shea, D.: A Standard Argument: Why WiMAX Will Rule. Telephony, pp. 4–9 (2004)
8. Wongthavarawat, K., Ganz, A.: IEEE 802.16 Based Last Mile Broadband Wireless Military Networks with Quality of Service Support. In: IEEE Military Communication Conference, Boston, MA, pp. 779–784 (2003)
9. Jia, W., Han, B., Fu, H., Shen, J., Yuen, C.: Efficient Implementation of 3G-324M Protocol Stack for Multimedia Communication. In: IEEE 11th International Conference on Parallel and Distributed Systems, Fukuoka, Japan (2005)
10. Leung, A., Kwok, Y.: On Topology Control of Wireless Peer-to-Peer File Sharing Networks: Energy Efficiency, Fairness and Incentive. In: Sixth IEEE International Symposium on World of Wireless Mobile and Multimedia Networks, pp. 318–323 (2005)
11. Bordetsky, A., Hutchins, S., Kemple, W., Bourakov, E.: Network Awareness for Wireless Peer-to-peer Collaborative Environments. In: Proceedings of the 37th Annual Hawaii International Conference on System Sciences, pp. 89–98 (2004)
12. Kang, S., Mutka, M.: Efficient Mobile Access to Internet Data via a Wireless Peer-to-peer Network. In: Proceedings of the Second IEEE Annual Conference on Pervasive Computing and Communications, pp. 197–205 (2004)

A New k-Graph Partition Algorithm for Distributed P2P Simulation Systems

Chunjiang Wu, Shijie Zhou, Linna Wei, Jiaqing Luo, Yanli Wang,
and Xiaoqian Yang

School of Computer Science and Engineering,
University of Electronic Science and Technology of China,
Chendu, Sichuan 610054, P.R. China
chunjiangwu@126.com, sjzhou@uestc.edu.cn

Abstract. While simulating a P2P system with distributed simulator, it generally requires that one single large network topology should be pre-divided into some small sub-nets, each of which denotes a group of peers in the P2P system. Because of interconnectivity of the simulated network, the sub-nets running on different simulation node must exchange message with each other to complete the simulation task. Based on the knowledge of degree sequence and breadth-first search, this paper proposes a novel approximate algorithm of k-graph partition. By this optimized algorithm, a large P2P network topology can be divided into k sub-nets while not only the traffic among different sub-net is minimized, but also the tasks of simulation are balanced. Through the analysis of time complexity, load balance and edge-cut experimental results for different network topology, it shows our algorithm is a feasible method applied for distributed P2P simulation systems.

Keywords: P2P, Distributed Simulation, Graph Partition, Degree Sequence, Breadth-First Search.

1 Introduction

In recent years, peer-to-peer (P2P) has become one of the most popular issues in computer academia [1]. Since P2P system is a large scale and high dynamic system, it is prohibitively expensive and unpractical to test a new algorithm by deploying it in an existing P2P network. Therefore, assessing the performance of P2P algorithm and the character of P2P network topology needs powerful tool: simulator [2] [3].

For resolving the problem of P2P simulation scale, adopting distributed technology to design P2P network simulator has already become popular. However, before simulation, the topology of the simulated P2P network must be partitioned into k sub-nets and distributed to each simulation node.

The simulation nodes not only control message exchanges, but also manipulate network communication. Because the speed of data communication in network is slower than that between CPU and memory, it is necessary to subtly design a partition algorithm to reduce the communication between any two sub-nets. Additionally, the topology partition algorithm must also satisfy that the number of all sub-nets must be equal as possible.

H. Jin et al. (Eds.): ICA3PP 2007, LNCS 4494, pp. 391–402, 2007.

The network topology k-partition problem in distributed P2P simulation can be defined as: given a complete P2P simulating network topology, and partition it into k simulation nodes which are connected mutually in physical and logical, while the network topology of every simulation node and the logical connection between them should be average, and the sum of logical connection should be minimal. Fig.1 shows the principle of graph division in large scale distributed P2P simulation.

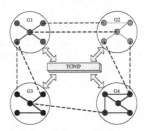

Fig. 1. Distributed P2P Simulation

From the description above, the network topology k-partition problem can be regarded as k-graph partition problem.

Based on the knowledge of degree sequence and breadth-first search, this paper proposes a novel approximate algorithm of k-graph partition. By this optimized algorithm, a large P2P network topology can be divided into k sub-nets while the traffic among different sub-net is minimized.

Generally speaking, the main contributions of this paper are summarized as followings:

- A new k-graph partition algorithm based on degree sequence and breadth-first search. This new algorithm can divide the whole network topology into k sub-nets with the time complexity $O(n^2)$.

- A full experimental study of the new division algorithm. We test our algorithm in different P2P network topology with various scales. Primary experimental result, including load balance, edge-cut balance and time complexity, shows the algorithm can be as a feasible method applied in distributed P2P simulation.

The remainder of this paper is organized as followings. Section 2 briefly introduces the related work. Section 3 proposed our novel division algorithm and described its detail. Section 4 presents our experimental results by using our algorithm in different kinds of P2P network topology. The conclusion and our future research works are addressed in the last section.

2 Related Work

Currently, the distributed simulation researches mainly include the aspects of time synchronization, network communication, load balance and fault tolerance, etc. Due to the random and dynamic in P2P network, the recent distributed P2P simulators can not simulate large scale P2P system. Therefore, a distributed P2P simulation system should be employed to improve the performance and the faithfulness of P2P simulation, which leads to the requirement of graph partition in P2P simulation system.

The k-graph partition problem can be defined as: given an undirected connective graph $G = (V, E)$, $|V| = n$, and find a partition of the vertices V into disjoint sets

$$V_1, V_2, \cdots, V_k \text{ with } \bigcup_{i=1}^{k} V_i = V \text{ , } \forall i \neq j \text{ , } 1 \leq i, j \leq k \text{ , } V_i \cap V_j = \varnothing \text{ and}$$

$|V_i| = \lceil n/k \rceil \pm d$, while minimizing the sum of edges connecting vertices in different sets [4][5].

The graph partition problem is an NP-hard problem which is impossible to find a best solution in limited time and space. Currently, the main graph partition algorithms include geometry-based partition algorithm [6], quadratic-based partition algorithm [7], spectral partition algorithm [8] and multilevel partition algorithm [9] [10] [11] [12], etc. [13] [14].

Geometry-based partition algorithm collapses d dimensions graph into one dimension graph according to the coordinate of nodes, but it does not take the adjacency of nodes into account. Quadratic-based partition algorithm is trying to aggregate the high connective nodes together according to the adjacency. Spectral partition algorithm is related to an eigenvector (Fiedler vector) corresponding to the second smallest value of the graph's Laplacian. The main idea of multilevel partition algorithm is to compress the original graph smaller, and revert to the initial state after partition.

3 Algorithm of k-Graph Partition for Distributed P2P Simulation System

3.1 Algorithm Description

Based on the knowledge of degree sequence and breadth-fires search, this paper proposes a new algorithm of k-graph partition, which can be applied in Distributed P2P simulation. The algorithm is described as follows:

Step 1: Generate the degree sequence of graph $G = (V, E)$:
$$D = (d_1, d_2, \cdots, d_n), 1 \leq i \leq n, n - 1 \geq d_1 \geq d_2 \geq \cdots \geq d_n$$
Step 2: Choose the first k disjoint nodes' degree value in sequence D,
$$D' = (d_1, d_2, \cdots, d_k)$$
and generate the node sequence:
$$V' = (v_1, v_2, \cdots, v_k), 1 \leq i \leq k \text{ , } d(v_i) = d_i$$
Step 3: Partition $V' = (v_1, v_2, \cdots, v_k)$ into disjoint subsets $V_1, V_2, \cdots, V_k$:
$$V_i = \{v_i\}, \quad 1 \leq i \leq k$$
where v_i is the source node of set V_i.
Step 4: Define
$$S_i = \{p \mid p \text{ is } 1 - \text{hop neighbor node of } v_i, 1 \leq i \leq k\}$$
and from set V_1 to set V_k, each set performs the following actions:

IF ($\exists q \in S_i$ **AND** $q \notin V' - V_i$) **THEN**

   $V_i = V_i + q$; $V' = V' + q$; $S_i = S_i - q$

END IF

Step 5: Find the number of 1-hop neighbor nodes of v_i ($1 \le i \le k$) existing in V_i as c_i', and generate the degree sequence D_i' of which the nodes is 1-hop neighbor of v_i existing in V_i, and generated node sequence V_i' :

$$D_i' = (d_1', d_2', \cdots, d_{c_i}')$$

$$V_i' = (v_1', v_2', \cdots, v_{c_i}') , \quad 1 \le j \le c_i' , \quad d(v_j') = d_j$$

Step 6: From V_1 to V_k, each set performs the following functions in turn:

1)   Choose node $p \in V_i'$, with $d(p) = \max(D_i')$, $1 \le i \le k$

2)   Define $S_i = \{q \mid q \ is \ 1 - hop \ neighbor \ node \ of \ p, \ 1 \le i \le k\}$

3)   **IF** ($\exists a \in S$ **AND** $a \notin V' - V_i$) **THEN**

   $V_i += a$; $V' = V' + a$; $D_i' = D_i' - d(p)$; $V_i' = V_i' - p$;

   END IF

4)   **IF** ($\exists D_i' \ne \varnothing$ **AND** $\exists V_i' \ne \varnothing$, $1 \le i \le k$) **THEN**

   GOTO Step 6

   ELSE

   GOTO Step 7

   END IF

Step 7: Repeat above processes method for the n-hops neighbor nodes of v_i until all nodes have been partitioned into one sub-net.

3.2 Algorithm Instance

According to the algorithm proposed in 3.1, we illustrate the whole processed by an example shown in Fig. 2.

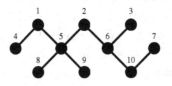

Fig. 2. Topology of Graph For Instance

The partitioning steps are as follows:

Step 1: Generate the degree sequence of graph:

$$D = (4, \ 3, \ 2, \ 2, \ 2, \ 1, \ 1, \ 1, \ 1, \ 1)$$

Step 2: Choose the first 2 disjoint node 5 and node 6, and generate $D' = (4, 3)$ and $V' = (5, 6)$

Step 3: Partition $V' = (5, 6)$ into subsets V_1 and V_2:
$$V_1 = \{5\}, \ V_2 = \{6\}$$
node 5 and node 6 are the source nodes.

Step 4: Partition the 1-hop neighbors of node 5 and node 6, and the results are:
$$V_1 = \{5, 1, 8, 9\}, \ V_2 = \{6, 2, 3, 10\}$$

Step 5: Generate the degree sequence D_1' and node sequence V_1' of node 5's 1-hop neighbors existing in set V_1, and generate the degree sequence D_2' and node sequence V_2' of node 6's 1-hop neighbors existing in set V_2:
$$D_1' = (2, 1, 1), \ V_1' = (1, 8, 9)$$
$$D_2' = (2, 2, 1), \ V_2' = (10, 2, 3)$$

Step 6: Based on D_1', V_1', D_2', V_2', partition the 2-hop neighbors of node 5 and node 6, and the results are:
$$V_1 = \{5, 1, 8, 9, 4\}, \ V_2 = \{6, 2, 3, 10, 7\}$$

Step 7: Finished, and the final result is as following:
$$V_1 = \{5, 1, 8, 9, 4\}, \ V_2 = \{6, 2, 3, 10, 7\}$$

3.3 Algorithm Analysis

In step 1 of algorithm, generating the degree sequence needs sort the nodes. We adopt the quick sort algorithm, and the time complexity is $O(n \log n)$.

Compared with the size of topology, the partition value k usually is too small so that this time of choosing the first k nodes can be ignored.

From step 3 to step 7, the main action is actually the process of breadth-first search, the time complexity of which depends on the data storage architecture. Adopting 2-dimension array as the data storage architecture of graph, the time complexity is $O(n^2)$, while adopting the adjacency list, the time complexity is $O(n+e)$. Therefore, the worst time complexity of graph partition algorithm is $O(n^2)$.

4 Experiments

4.1 Measurement Standards

The usual measurement standards of graph partition include load balance and edge-cut balance. The ratio of maximal number and average number of the nodes in k sets is defined as the load balance. We use λ denote the load balance, so $\lambda = \dfrac{\max(|V_i|)}{aver(|V_i|)}$, $1 \le i \le k$. In general, a good partition algorithm should guarantee that the size of sets be average as possible. Therefore, the value of load balance λ is smaller, the partition result is better. The best result is that the value of λ is 1, and the number of nodes in every set are same.

The number of edges connecting vertices in different sets is defined as edge-cut. The ratio of maximal number and average number of edge-cut is defined as the edge-cut balance. We use E_{ij} denote the set of edges connecting vertices in set i and set j, and β denote the edge-cut balance, so $\beta = \dfrac{\max(|E_{ij}|)}{aver(|E_{ij}|)}$, $1 \le i, j \le k$, $i \ne j$. The edge-cut balance depicts the intercommunication requirement between sets. The value of edge-cut balance is smaller, the connection of nodes in the same set is closer, the partition result is better. The best result is that the value of edge-cut β is 1.

In addition, the time complexity is also an important measurement parameter.

4.2 Experiment Environment and Parameters

In this paper, we use Peersim simulator to run graph partition experiments, and the P2P network topology is created by the topology file generated by BRITE topology generator.

Our experiments aim at graph partition which topology is designed according to Waxman (random) or Barabasi (power-law) model. The parameters of the two type network topology are as table 1 and table 2, and the explanations of parameters are as follows:

Table 1. The Parameters of Random P2P Network Topology

Content	Parameter
Topology Type	ROUTER ONLY
N	1000—50000
Model	Waxman
Node Placement	Random
Growth Type	Incremental
m	2/5

Table 2. The Parameters of Power-law P2P Network Topology

Content	Parameter
Topology Type	ROUTER ONLY
N	1000—50000
Model	Barabasi
Node Placement	Random
Growth Type	Incremental
m	2/5

- **Topology Type:** BRITE provides 4 type network topologies: AS-Level, Router-Level, Top–down and Bottom-up.
- **N:** Number of nodes in the graph
- **Model:** Use one of the models built into BRITE. BRITE provides Waxman for random P2P network topology and Barabasi for power-law P2P network topology.
- **Node Placement:** Dictates how nodes are placed on the plane.
- **Growth Type:** Dictates how edges are created between nodes.
- **m:** Number of links added per new node.

4.3 Experiment Results and Analysis

4.3.1 Load Balance Experiment and Edge-Cut Balance Experiment

In this experiment, we generate different scale power-law network topologies and random network topologies according to the parameters of table 1 and table 2, and define k = 5. The experimental results are as follows:

Table 3. Experimental results of 5-partition for power-law P2P network topology (m = 2)

N	$|E|$	$\max(|V_i|)$	$\mathrm{aver}(|V_i|)$	λ	$\max(|E_{ij}|)$	$\mathrm{aver}(|E_{ij}|)$	β
1000	1997	284.01	200	1.42	137.87	78.81	1.75
2000	3997	572.15	400	1.43	260.77	151.74	1.72
3000	5997	898.23	600	1.49	413.2	232.86	1.77
4000	7997	1207.96	800	1.51	516.87	305.84	1.69
5000	9997	1305.2	1000	1.31	665.0.	392.94	1.71
6000	11997	1791.2	1200	1.49	809.61	463..2	1.74
7000	13997	2054.6	1400	1.47	981.2	549.14	1.79
8000	15997	2462.4	1600	1.54	1066.75	616.62	1.73
9000	17997	2561	1800	1.42	1220	706.42	1.73
10000	19997	2693	2000	1.35	1338	787.2	1.70
aver	10997	1582.98	1100	1.44	749.36	424.62	1.73

Table 4. Experimental results of 5-partition for power-law P2P network topology (m = 5)

N	$|E|$	$\max(|V_i|)$	$\mathrm{aver}(|V_i|)$	λ	$\max(|E_{ij}|)$	$\mathrm{aver}(|E_{ij}|)$	β
1000	4985	273.2	200	1.37	502	315.96	1.59
2000	9985	475.2	400	1.19	826.4	640.08	1.29
3000	14985	820	600	1.37	1508	949.72	1.59
4000	19985	1039.6	800	1.30	1792.8	1270.64	1.41
5000	24985	1242.4	1000	1.24	2350.4	1579.66	1.49
6000	29985	1510	1200	1.26	2557.6	1908.66	1.34
7000	34985	1818.2	1400	1.30	3251	2222.36	1.46
8000	39985	2023.4	1600	1.26	3684.6	2536.36	1.45
9000	44985	2404.4	1800	1.34	4374.6	2848.74	1.54
10000	49985	2672.6	2000	1.34	4663.6	3171.86	1.47
aver	27485	1427.9	1100	1.30	2551.1	1744.404	1.46

From the experimental results above, the value of load balance, λ, and the edge-cut balance, β, are both between 1 and 2, which are considered as acceptable results for graph partition algorithms. The partition results for random network topology are better than that for power-law network topology obviously. And for the same type graph (i.e. the same parameters except for the number of nodes), the partition results are approximately same as the Fig. 3~Fig. 6.

Table 5. Experimental results of 5-partition for random P2P network topology (m = 2)

N	$|E|$	max($|V_i|$)	aver($|V_i|$)	λ	max($|E_{ij}|$)	aver($|E_{ij}|$)	β
1000	2000	226.8	200	1.13	109.6	79.46	1.38
2000	4000	466	400	1.17	219.8	159.98	1.37
3000	6000	740.2	600	1.23	339.6	236.3	1.44
4000	8000	1008.8	800	1.26	444.6	315.8	1.41
5000	10000	1209.4	1000	1.21	539.4	398.82	1.35
6000	12000	1387.2	1200	1.16	631	477.18	1.32
7000	14000	1666.4	1400	1.19	775.8	555.58	1.40
8000	16000	1969	1600	1.23	897	633.1	1.42
9000	18000	2149.8	1800	1.19	974.2	712.32	1.37
10000	20000	2432.4	2000	1.22	1103.6	796.22	1.39
aver	11000	1325.6	1100	1.20	603.46	436.476	1.38

Table 6. Experimental results of 5-partition for random P2P network topology (m = 5)

N	$|E|$	max($|V_i|$)	aver($|V_i|$)	λ	max($|E_{ij}|$)	aver($|E_{ij}|$)	β
1000	2000	229.6	200	1.15	389.4	315.6	1.23
2000	4000	431.6	400	1.08	739.4	636.18	1.16
3000	6000	656	600	1.09	1144.2	955.68	1.20
4000	8000	869	800	1.09	1528	1274.08	1.20
5000	10000	1052	1000	1.05	1785	1589.74	1.12
6000	12000	1259.8	1200	1.05	2130.8	1910.94	1.12
7000	14000	1500.6	1400	1.07	2545.4	2232.46	1.14
8000	16000	1703.8	1600	1.06	2922.6	2551.88	1.15
9000	18000	1962.4	1800	1.09	3285.6	2866.94	1.15
10000	20000	2091.6	2000	1.05	3465	3194.08	1.08
aver	11000	1175.64	1100	1.08	1993.54	1752.758	1.15

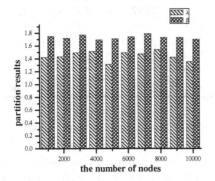
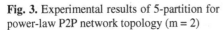
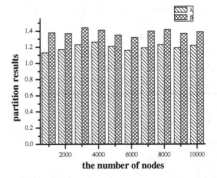

Fig. 3. Experimental results of 5-partition for power-law P2P network topology (m = 2)

Fig. 4. Experimental results of 5-partition for power-law P2P network topology (m = 5)

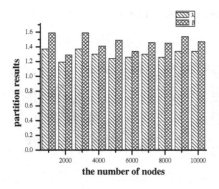

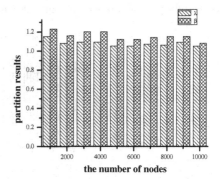

Fig. 5. Experimental results of 5-partition for random P2P network topology (m = 2)

Fig. 6. Experimental results of 5-partition for random P2P network topology (m = 5)

4.3.2 Size of Sets Experiment and Size of Edge-Cut Experiment

We also run some experiments to test the size of sets and the size of edge-cut with the random network topology. The size of network topology is defined as 5000, and the number of edges is changed. The experimental results are as follows:

Table 7. Size of sets experimental results of 5-partition for random P2P network topology

N	m	$|E|$	$|V_1|$	$|V_2|$	$|V_3|$	$|V_4|$	$|V_5|$	λ
5000	2	10000	1067	1075	876	915	1067	1.075
5000	3	15000	1071	1056	952	1063	858	1.071
5000	4	20000	1064	1007	976	1034	919	1.064
5000	5	25000	1014	972	1070	952	992	1.07
5000	6	30000	1027	950	992	1046	985	1.046
5000	7	35000	925	1033	957	1027	1058	1.058
5000	8	40000	1038	925	971	958	1108	1.108
5000	9	45000	1006	1001	1008	994	991	1.008
5000	10	50000	1080	1004	934	931	1051	1.08

Table 8. Size of edge-cut experimental results of 5-partition for random P2P network topology

N	m	$|E|$	$|E_{12}|$	$|E_{13}|$	$|E_{14}|$	$|E_{15}|$	$|E_{23}|$	$|E_{24}|$	$|E_{25}|$	$|E_{34}|$	$|E_{35}|$	$|E_{45}|$	β
5000	2	10000	486	365	415	479	355	403	450	302	369	391	1.21
5000	3	15000	924	836	929	719	792	915	710	801	642	701	1.17
5000	4	20000	1305	1119	1424	1135	1077	1334	1181	1265	981	1149	1.19
5000	5	25000	1596	1649	1450	1625	1681	1415	1648	1631	1731	1503	1.09
5000	6	30000	1830	2092	2251	1948	1920	1998	1680	2203	1932	2108	1.12
5000	7	35000	2219	1889	2311	2301	2360	2686	2642	2217	2465	2709	1.13
5000	8	40000	2633	2839	2573	3044	2513	2203	2858	2697	3245	2989	1.17
5000	9	45000	3084	3234	3116	3145	3192	3060	3308	3300	3273	3168	1.04
5000	10	50000	4099	3385	3581	3836	3099	3221	3629	3120	3656	3698	1.16

And the experimental results are shown in Fig.7 and Fig.8.

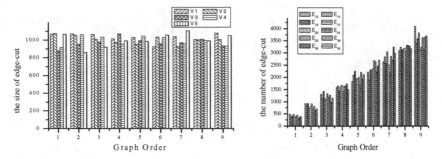

Fig. 7. Size of sets experiment results   **Fig. 8.** Size of edge-cut experiment results

From the experimental results, we can see that the size of sets and the size of edge-cut are approximately same, and the value of load balance and edge-cut balance are close to 1, which are also regarded as the reasonable metrics for graph partition algorithms.

4.3.3 Time Complexity Experiment

In addition, we carry out some experiments for time complexity testing with power-law and random P2P network topology. The experimental results are as follows:

Table 9. Time complexity testing of graph partition

N	Power-law (ms)	Random (ms)	N	Power-law (ms)	Random (ms)
1000	7.7	18.6	8000	700.4	402.9
2000	29.6	17.2	9000	1299.9	607.5
3000	32.9	39.1	10000	1745.2	891.1
4000	73.5	56.8	20000	17551.9	9334.5
5000	123.3	79.7	30000	59710.8	33022
6000	225.8	151.7	40000	144924.8	80334.7
7000	462.2	241.6	50000	245286	162435

Fig.9 and Fig.10 shows the relationship between time and node scale. It is clear that the time increases while the number of nodes is increased. From the experimental results, while the scale of network topology increasing, the time of partition changes according to $O(n^k)$, which is a polynomial and can input division results in limited time. Apparently, their relationship is polynomial and this accords with our analysis of the algorithm as well. Therefore, the experimental results suggest that our new graph partition algorithm is optimal for large scale distributed P2P simulation applications.

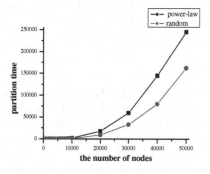
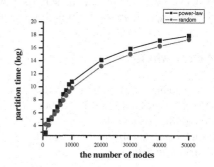

Fig. 9. Time complexity testing   **Fig. 10.** Time complexity testing (log)

4.3.4 Especial Graph Partition Experiment

We also consider the application of our new division algorithm in some special network topology. These topologies include circle, binary tree and completed bipartite graph (see Fig.11, Fig.12, and Fig.13). In this paper, we only discuss the 2-grpah partition problem for these especial topologies. For the 20-node circle, the load balance λ is 1.1 and the value of edge-cut balance β is 1. For the 31-node binary tree, the value of load balance λ is 1.032 and the value of edge-cut balance β is 1. For the 10-node complete bipartite graph, the value of load balance λ is 1 and the value of edge-cut balance β is 1. The results also accords with our experiments for random and power-law topologies and thus can be considered as acceptable results. Therefore, we can conclude that our new graph division algorithm is effective in different kinds of network topology and thus can be used in various distributed P2P simulations.

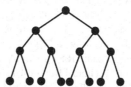

Fig. 11. Circle   **Fig. 12.** Binary Tree   **Fig. 13.** Complete Bipartite Graph

5 Conclusion and Future Work

The proposed k-graph partition algorithm is based on degree sequence and breadth-first search and achieves the time complexity of $O(n^2)$. The primary experimental results, including load balance, edge-cut balance and time complexity, shows our new graph division algorithm is a feasible one for various distributed P2P simulations.

However, we only give a coarsely theoretical analysis for this algorithm. In the future, we will improve this algorithm to make it more efficient and more acceptable.

Acknowledgement

This paper is sponsored by **the** National Natural Science Foundation of China (NSFC), granted No.60473090, and by the Young Science and Technology Foundation of UESTC, granted No.JX04029. This project has been made possible in part by a grant from the Cisco University Research Program Fund at Community Foundation Silicon Valley.

References

1. Stephanos, A.T., Spinellis, D.: A Survey of Peer-to-Peer Content Distribution Technologies. ACM Computing Surveys 36(4), 335–371 (2004)
2. Ingalls, R. G.: Introduction to Simulation. In: Proceedings of the 2002 Winter Simulation Conference (WSC 2002) San Diego, California, USA (2002)
3. Joseph, S.: An Extendible Open Source P2P Simulator. P2P Journal (2003)
4. Sedgewick, R.: Algorithms in Java. Parts 1-4, 3rd edn. vol. 1, Tsinghua University Publisher (2004)
5. Buckly, F., Lewinter, M.: A Friendly Introdution to Graph Theory. 1st edn. Tsinghua University Publisher (2005)
6. Pilkingtong, J., Baden, S.: Partition With Spacefilling Curves. Technical Report CS94-394, Dept.of Computer Science And Engineering, Univ. of California (1994)
7. Hager, W., Krylyuk, Y.: Graph Partition And Continuous Quadratic Programming. SIAM Journal on Discrete Mathematics (1999)
8. Simon, H., Sohn, A., Biswas, R.: HARP: a Fast Spectral Partition. In: Proceedings of 9th ACM Symposium on Parallel Algorithms And Architectures, Newport, Rhode Island(1997)
9. Karypis, G., Kumar, V.: A Fast and High Quality Multilevel Scheme for Partition Irregular Graphs. SIAM Journal on Scientific Computing, pp. 359–392 (1998)
10. Karypis, G., Kumar, V.: Multilevel k-way Partition Scheme for Irregular Graphs. Journal of Parallel and Distributed Computing (1998)
11. Monien, B., Preis, R., Diekmann, R.: Quality Matching And Local Improvement for Multilevel Graph – Partition. Technical Report, University of Paderborn (1999)
12. Walshaw, C., Cross, M.: Parallel Optimization Algorithms for Multilevel Mesh Partitioning. Technical Report 99/IM/44 [A], University of Greenwich, London, UK (1999)
13. Arora, S., Rao, S., Vazirani. U.: Expander Flows, Geometric Embeddings and Graph Partition. ACM Symposium on Theory of Computing (STOC'04) Chicago, Illinois, USA (2004)
14. Ji, X.: Graph Partition Problems With Minimum Size Constraints. Rensselaer Polytechnic Institute, Troy, New York (2004)

A Dominant Input Stream for LUD Incremental Computing on a Contention Network*

Cho-Chin Lin

Department of Electronic Engineering
National Ilan University
Yilan 260, Taiwan
cclin@niu.edu.tw

Abstract. Incremental computing masks the communication latency by overlapping computations with communications. However, a sequence of messages with a large latency variance still makes computations proceed intermittently. It is known that a *dominant* input stream from a data server maximizes the CPU utilization of the networked computation server [7]. Unfortunately, the problem of finding a dominant input stream is $\mathcal{NP}$-hard in the strong sense. In this paper, a dominant input stream for LU decomposition is proposed. It is shown that the dominant input stream outperforms the input stream sending data in traditional order. In addition, the nonexistence of dominant input streams is proved for the case that the compressed format is used for sending input data.

1 Introduction

With the advance in information technology, global network computing systems such as computation grids [3] have been deployed. A global network computing system consists of many computation servers and data servers. The data needed for a compute-intensive application can be stored entirely in a data server beforehand. The resource broker of the system assigns the application to the computation server which cooperates with the data server to complete the application. As the computation server starts to execute the application, the data are replicated from the cooperative data server concurrently. Although the networking technology has improved in the last decades, unpredictable network latency can be experienced by the computation server. To hide the network latency, a possible approach is to overlap computations with communications [12]. It can be achieved by partitioning input data into several data pieces then pipelining the data pieces into the network. Thus, the computation server performs the computations using the partial input to produce the partial results. This type of computation is referred as *incremental* computing. However, network latency cannot be effectively hidden without considering the order of sending data [6].

Consider the job of computing $\frac{d_2}{f(d_0)+d_1}$ at a computation server using data items d_0, d_1 and d_2 sent from a cooperative data server, where $f(x) = x^2 + \frac{1}{x} + \sqrt{x}$.

---

* This research is partially supported by National Science Council under the grant 95-2221-E-197-013.

H. Jin et al. (Eds.): ICA3PP 2007, LNCS 4494, pp. 403–414, 2007.

The basic arithmetic operations for a server to compute $f(x)$ are: one square operation, one square root operation, one reciprocal operation and two addition operations. Assume each basic arithmetic operation takes one clock and the arriving interval of the three data items are g_0 clocks and g_1 clocks. If the input stream is $d_2d_1d_0$ then the time to complete the task is $g_0 + g_1 + 7$. If the input stream is $d_0d_1d_2$ then the time to complete the task is $g_0 + \max\{g_1, \max\{5 - g_0, 0\} + 1\} + 1$. Since $g_0 + g_1 + 7 \geq g_0 + \max\{g_1, \max\{5 - g_0, 0\} + 1\} + 1$, it is obvious that the first input stream is worse than the second input stream. It implies that the computation and communication issues are closely inter-wined in the network-based computing and should be studied together.

LU decomposition (LUD) can be applied to solve systems of linear equations. A best input stream of an application maximizes the CPU utilization for any network traffic pattern at any time. This research studies whether it is possible to find a best input stream for an *existing* LUD algorithm. The steps to build a best input stream for LUD in linear time are given in this paper. The compressed format for sending elements of a sparse matrix is also studied. The nonexistence of dominant input streams is proved for the sparse case. This paper is organized as follows. In Sect. 2, background and related works are discussed. General notations used in this paper are defined in Sect. 3. In Sect. 4, the theorems as the foundation of finding a best input stream are developed and a best input stream is proposed. In Sect. 5, the comparison of the completion times of performing LUD using a dominant input stream and another input stream is conducted. In Sect. 6, the compressed format for sending input data is studied. Finally, concluding remarks are given in Sect. 7.

2   Background and Related Works

Communication has been recognized as the major overhead of executing an application across the network. To minimize the communication overhead, many software-based mechanisms have been developed by optimizing the communication modules [10], [11]. Other techniques based on communication scheduling have also been proposed to improve the efficiency of complicated communication routines [1], [8], [9], [13], [14]. In [1], effective heuristic algorithms called *fastest edge first* and *earliest completing edge first* were proposed to reduce the communication time for distributed heterogeneous systems. The authors showed that their heuristics have achieved significant performance improvement over previous approaches. In [8], an effective heuristic called *fastest nodes first* (FNF) was proposed to reduce the broadcast time for heterogeneous cluster systems. The author also showed that the FNF heuristic guarantees the total communication time to be within twice of the time from an optimal schedule. In [9], [13], a two-phase communication algorithm was proposed to attack the communication delay occurred by messages with large variance in length. In the first phase, each processor evenly distributes the data to be moved to the same destination among the processors. In the second phase, each processor sends the data received from the first phase to their final destinations. In [14], an efficient algorithm was proposed to reduce the overall communication time by partitioning large messages into multiple small messages and scheduling them by using the minimum number of steps without communication contention. In [4], [5], techniques have been proposed for reducing communication cost by minimizing the number of data movement during data redistribution. The main idea of the techniques is to develop mapping functions for computing a new rank for each target processor. Based on the computed ranks, the amount of data need to be exchanged is minimized.

Most of the previous techniques were developed by assuming that there is no other work running on the platform at the same time or the communication of one application will not be disturbed by the communications of the other applications. However, the independent applications running concurrently on a non-dedicated network computing platform tend to compete for the communication channels. The competition leads to the network contention which results in significant network latency. A best input stream for a given application is the data-sending sequence which maximizes the CPU utilization of the computation server for any network traffic pattern at any time. That is, the CPU utilization attainable using a best input stream is always no worse than those attainable using the other input streams. Unfortunately, the problem of finding a best sequence is $\mathcal{NP}$-Hard [7]. Thus, a best sequence of input data cannot be found in reasonable time for the applications of medium scale or above. Theoretical perspective of incremental computing using a well-organized data sequence was discussed in [6]. In the paper, the completion time of executing application $\mathcal{J}$ was shown to be $W_{\mathcal{J}} + \Delta_{\max}$, where $W_{\mathcal{J}}$ is the number of total computations (measured in CPU cycles) needed to complete the application $\mathcal{J}$ and $\Delta_{\max}$ is the delay. The delay is due to the wasted CPU cycles. The analyses on the performance of employing incremental computing using specially tailored data sequences have also been made in the paper. In [7], dominant sequences have been found for the three applications: the product of two polynomials, matrix multiplication and Fast Fourier Transform (FFT). Algorithms have also been developed for the three applications to build best input streams in linear time. The authors also demonstrated that no dominant sequences exist for any of the three applications if a compressed format of sending input is used for the sparse cases of matrix multiplication, polynomial product and FFT computation.

3   Incremental LUD Decomposition

In this section, the general notations used in this paper and the definition of incremental LUD is provided. Let Q be the problem that can be solved by *incremental computing*. In the incremental computing paradigm, the server tries to do as much work as possible using the incoming data items. Let $\mathcal{G}_T$ be the class of algorithms for solving problem Q in time $O(T)$. A *critical step* of an algorithm in $\mathcal{G}_T$ is a computation step that is executed $O(T)$ times. There may be more than one type of critical step in an algorithm. In this paper, two types

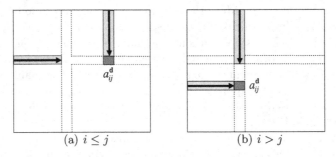

$$\text{(a) } i \leq j \qquad\qquad\qquad \text{(b) } i > j$$

Fig. 1. The data dependency of a_{ij}^{d}

of critical steps are considered for LUD: scalar multiplication/division denoted by mul/div and scalar addition/subtraction denoted by add/sub.

A recurrence relation of LUD computation which decomposes a matrix $\mathcal{A} = [a_{ij}]$, $0 \leq i,j < n$, into an upper triangular matrix $U = [u_{ij}]$ and a lower triangular matrix $L = [l_{ij}]$ is given as follows.

$$\mathcal{A}^{\mathrm{d}} = \mathrm{LUD}(\mathcal{A}) = \begin{pmatrix} 1 & w \\ v/a_{00} & \mathrm{LUD}(\mathcal{A}' - vw/a_{00}) \end{pmatrix} . \qquad (1)$$

where $\mathcal{A}'$ is formed by deleting the first row and first column of $\mathcal{A}$, v is a column vector $(a_{10}, a_{20}, a_{30} \cdots a_{n-1\,0})$ and w is a row vector $(a_{01}, a_{02}, a_{03} \cdots a_{0\,n-1})$. Let $\mathcal{A}^{\mathrm{d}} = [a_{ij}^{\mathrm{d}}]$. The elements of matrices L and U are given as follows: $l_{ij} = a_{ij}^{\mathrm{d}}$ if $i > j$; $l_{ij} = 1$ if $i = j$; $l_{ij} = 0$ if $i < j$ and $u_{ij} = a_{ij}^{\mathrm{d}}$ if $i \leq j$; $u_{ij} = 0$ if $i > j$. The recurrence implies that the elements in $\mathrm{LUD}(\mathcal{A}' - vw/a_{00})$ depends on the values of w and v/a_{00}. The incremental algorithm considered in this paper for performing LUD implements the recurrence given in (1). Interested readers should refer to [2] for detail on the topic of solving systems of linear equations.

Define active matrix $E_{\mathcal{A}} = [e_{ij}]$ as a $(n+1) \times (n+1)$ matrix, where $-1 \leq i,j < n$. In the matrix, $e_{ij} = 1$ or 0. $e_{ij} = 1$ implies that the final value of a_{ij}^{d} has been obtained and can be used to derive other elements of $\mathcal{A}^{\mathrm{d}}$. Based on (1), the value of a_{ij}^{d}, $i \leq j$, depends on the values of $a_{i0}^{\mathrm{d}}, a_{i1}^{\mathrm{d}} \cdots a_{i\,i-1}^{\mathrm{d}}$ and the values of $a_{0j}^{\mathrm{d}}, a_{1j}^{\mathrm{d}} \cdots a_{i-1\,j}^{\mathrm{d}}$ as shown in Figure 1(a). The value of a_{ij}^{d}, $i > j$, depends on the values of $a_{i0}^{\mathrm{d}}, a_{i1}^{\mathrm{d}} \cdots a_{i\,j-1}^{\mathrm{d}}$ and the values of $a_{0j}^{\mathrm{d}}, a_{1j}^{\mathrm{d}} \cdots a_{j\,j}^{\mathrm{d}}$ as shown in Fig. 1(b). To give the recurrence for e_{ij}, some notations are defined first. $\omega(E(i,*), k, \wedge)$ and $\omega(E(*,j), k, \wedge)$ denote $e_{i-1} \wedge e_{i0} \wedge e_{i1} \wedge \cdots \wedge e_{ik}$ and $e_{-1\,j} \wedge e_{0j} \wedge e_{1j} \wedge \cdots \wedge e_{kj}$, respectively. The receipt of data item a_{ij} by the computation server is indicated using the function $\hbar(a_{ij})$. $\hbar(a_{ij}) = 1$ if a_{ij} is received by the computation server; $\hbar(a_{ij}) = 0$, otherwise. Thus, the recurrence for e_{ij} is given as follows.

$$e_{ij} = \begin{cases} 1 & \text{if } i = -1 \text{ or } j = -1 . \\ \omega(E(i,*), i-1, \wedge) \wedge \omega(E(*,j), i-1, \wedge) \wedge \hbar(a_{ij}) & \text{if } 0 \leq i \leq j < n . \\ \omega(E(i,*), j-1, \wedge) \wedge \omega(E(*,j), j, \wedge) \wedge \hbar(a_{ij}) & \text{if } 0 \leq j < i < n . \end{cases}$$
$$(2)$$

4   A Dominant Input Stream

The scenario considered in this paper is as follows: the elements of matrix $\mathcal{A}$ stored at the cooperative data server are sent to the computation server using a sequence of matrix elements and matrix $\mathcal{A}^d$ are computed incrementally at the computation server. Denote $\mathcal{A}_m$ as the set of m data items which have been received by the computation server. The layout of the m data elements is denoted as $P_{\mathcal{A}_m}$. It is characterized by a sequence of 2-tuples $((R_0, C_0), (R_1, C_1) \cdots (R_{n-1}, C_{n-1}))$, where R_i is a subset of $S_{Ri} = \{a_{ii}, a_{i\,i+1} \cdots a_{i\,n-1}\}$ for $0 \le i \le n-1$, C_i is a subset of $S_{Ci} = \{a_{i+1\,i}, a_{i+2\,i} \cdots a_{n-1\,i}\}$ for $0 \le i \le n-2$ and C_{n-1} is a dummy set. $P_{\mathcal{A}_{10}}$ for the matrix $\mathcal{A}$ of 5×5 is given in Figure 2. In the figure, $R_0 = \{a_{00}, a_{02}, a_{04}\}$, $R_2 = \{a_{23}, a_{24}\}$, $C_0 = \{a_{10}, a_{20}, a_{40}\}$, $C_1 = \{a_{41}\}$ and $C_3 = \{a_{43}\}$. The other sets R_1, R_3, R_4 and C_2 are empty sets. $a_{ij} \in R_i$ or $a_{ij} \in C_j$ implies a_{ij} is received by the computation server. The 2-tuple (R_i, C_i) is full if $|R_i| = n-i$ and $|C_i| = n-i-1$, is empty if $|R_i| = |C_i| = 0$; otherwise, is growing. (R_i, C_i) is growing symmetrically if $0 \le |R_i| - |C_i| \le 1$ and $a_{ii} \in R_i$. Based on the above statements, define $P_{\mathcal{A}_m}$ as a compact layout if $(R_0, C_0), (R_1, C_1) \cdots (R_{k-1}, C_{k-1})$ are full, (R_k, C_k) is either growing or empty, and $(R_{k+1}, C_{k+1}) \cdots (R_{n-1}, C_{n-1})$ are all empty. $P_{\mathcal{A}_m}$ is symmetrically compact layout if (R_k, C_k) is symmetrically growing or empty.

Denote $\Im(P_{\mathcal{A}_m}, op)$ as the number of executable operation op based on the data elements in $\mathcal{A}_m$. Layout $P_{\mathcal{A}_m}$ is optimal for op if $\Im(P_{\mathcal{A}_m}, op) \ge \Im(P_{\mathcal{A}'_m}, op)$, where $P_{\mathcal{A}'_m}$ is the layout for any other set of m data items. $P_{\mathcal{A}_1} P_{\mathcal{A}_2} \cdots P_{\mathcal{A}_{n^2}}$ is a dominant layout sequence for op if $\mathcal{A}_m \subset \mathcal{A}_{m+1}$ and $\Im(P_{\mathcal{A}_m}, op) \ge \Im(P_{\mathcal{A}'_m}, op)$ for $1 \le m < n^2$, where $P_{\mathcal{A}'_m}$ is the layout of any other set of m data items. Based on the above, define $d_0 d_1 d_2 \cdots d_{n^2-1}$ as a dominant input stream, where $d_0 d_1 d_2 \cdots d_i \in \mathcal{A}_{i+1}$ for $0 \le i < n^2$. In this section, a dominant input stream for incremental LUD computation is proposed.

The following lemma states that the number of executable mul/div operations using a symmetrically compact layout is no less than that using any compact layout for the same number of received data items.

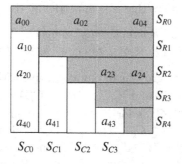

Fig. 2. $P_{\mathcal{A}_{10}}$, where $\mathcal{A}$ is a 5×5 matrix

Lemma 1. *Let $P_{\mathcal{A}_m}$ be symmetrically compact and $P_{\mathcal{A}'_m}$ be compact. Then,* $\Im(P_{\mathcal{A}_m}, mul/div) \geq \Im(P_{\mathcal{A}'_m}, mul/div)$

Proof. Let (R'_k, C'_k) be the growing 2-tuple or the empty 2-tuple with the smallest index k in the compact layout $P_{\mathcal{A}'_m}$. Assume $|R'_k| + |C'_k| = b < 2(n-k) - 1$. The number of executable mul/div operations using the elements in R'_k and C'_k is $|R'_k|(b - |R'_k|)$ or 0. It is equal to 0 if $a_{kk} \notin R'_k$. If b is even and $a_{kk} \in R'_k$ then the maximum value of $|R'_k|(b - |R'_k|)$ is $\frac{b^2}{4}$ when $|R'_k| = |C'_k| = \frac{b}{2}$. If b is odd and $a_{kk} \in R_k$ then the maximum value of $|R'_k|(b - |R'_k|)$ is $\frac{b^2-1}{4}$ when $|R'_k| = \frac{b+1}{2}$ and $|C'_k| = \frac{b-1}{2}$. In either of the cases, a symmetrically compact layout satisfies the requirement to maximize $|R'_k|(b - |R'_k|)$. □

Based on the recurrence in (2), the number of executable mul/div operations $\Im(P_{\mathcal{A}_m}, mul/div)$ can be computed as follows:

$$\Im(P_{\mathcal{A}_m}, mul/div) = \sum_{\ell=0}^{n-2} \sum_{i=\ell+1}^{n-1} \sum_{j=\ell}^{n-1} (e_{i\ell} \wedge e_{\ell j}) . \tag{3}$$

The equivalence of two 2-tuples (R_k, C_k) and (R'_k, C'_k) means $R_k = R'_k$ and $C_k = C'_k$. The following lemma states that two symmetrically compact layouts $P_{\mathcal{A}_m}$ and $P_{\mathcal{A}'_m}$ have the same number of executable mul/div operations even though the growing tuples $(R_k, C_k) \neq (R'_k, C'_k)$.

Lemma 2. *Let $P_{\mathcal{A}_m}$ and $P_{\mathcal{A}'_m}$ be symmetrically compact. Then,* $\Im(P_{\mathcal{A}_m}, mul/div) = \Im(P_{\mathcal{A}'_m}, mul/div)$.

Proof. $P_{\mathcal{A}_m}$ and $P_{\mathcal{A}'_m}$ are symmetrically compact. Assume (R_i, C_i) and (R'_i, C'_i) are full for $0 \leq i < k$, and (R'_k, C'_k) and (R_k, C_k) are growing symmetrically. We have $|R_i| = |R'_i|$ and $|C_i| = |C'_i|$ for $0 \leq i \leq k$. It implies that $\sum_{i=0}^{k} |R_i| \cdot |C_i| = \sum_{i=0}^{k} |R'_i| \cdot |C'_i|$. That is, $\Im(P_{\mathcal{A}_m}, mul/div) = \Im(P_{\mathcal{A}'_m}, mul/div)$. □

The following theorem shows that a symmetrically compact layout is optimal.

Theorem 1. *Let $P_{\mathcal{A}_m}$ be symmetrically compact. Then,* $\Im(P_{\mathcal{A}_m}, mul/div) \geq \Im(P_{\mathcal{A}^*_m}, mul/div)$, *where $P_{\mathcal{A}^*_m}$ is any other not symmetrically compact layout.*

Proof. Let (R^*_k, C^*_k) be the growing or empty 2-tuple with the smallest index k in $P_{\mathcal{A}^*_m}$. Assume $|R^*_k| + |C^*_k| = b$ and $\sum_{i=k+1}^{n-1} (|R^*_i| + |C^*_i|) = b'$. If $b + b' \leq 2(n-k) - 1$, then the elements in (R^*_i, C^*_i)'s for $k < i < n$ are removed and b' elements are added symmetrically to (R^*_k, C^*_k). The new layout denoted as $P_{\mathcal{A}'_m}$ is a symmetrically compact layout. Based on (2), (3) and Lemma 2, it is obvious that $\Im(P_{\mathcal{A}_m}, mul/div) = \Im(P_{\mathcal{A}'_m}, mul/div) \geq \Im(P_{\mathcal{A}^*_m}, mul/div)$. If $b + b' > 2(n-k) - 1$, then delete $2(n-k) - 1 - b$ elements in (R^*_i, C^*_i)'s starting from the 2-tuple with the largest index, where $k < i < n$, and add $2(n-k) - 1 - b$ elements to (R^*_k, C^*_k).

We call the resulting layout $P_{\mathcal{A}_m^1}$ in which (R_k^*, C_k^*) is full. Based on (2) and (3), it is obvious that $\Im(P_{\mathcal{A}_m^1}, \text{mul/div}) \geq \Im(P_{\mathcal{A}_m^*}, \text{mul/div})$. This process repeats until the layout has the following property: $(R_0^*, C_0^*) \cdots (R_{x-1}^*, C_{x-1}^*)$ are full, (R_x^*, C_x^*) is symmetrically growing or empty, and $(R_{x+1}^*, C_{x+1}^*) \cdots (R_{n-1}^*, C_{n-1}^*)$ are empty. The resulting layout $P_{\mathcal{A}_m'}$ becomes a symmetrically compact layout. Based on (2), (3) and Lemma 2, it is obvious that $\Im(P_{\mathcal{A}_m}, \text{mul/div}) = \Im(P_{\mathcal{A}_m'}, \text{mul/div}) \geq \Im(P_{\mathcal{A}_m^*}, \text{mul/div})$. Thus, the theorem is proved. $\quad\square$

Denote $I = I_0 I_1 \cdots I_{n-1}$ as an input stream, where $I_j = a_{jj} \, a_{j+1j} \, a_{jj+1} \, a_{j+2j}$ $a_{jj+2} \cdots a_{n-2j} \, a_{jn-2} \, a_{n-1j} \, a_{jn-1}$ for $0 \leq j < n$. The following theorem shows that I is a dominant input stream for LUD.

Theorem 2. *I is a dominant input stream of LUD regarding mul/div operation.*

Proof. Let $\mathcal{A}_m$ consist of the first m data items of I. Then, $P_{\mathcal{A}_m}$ is symmetrically compact and $\mathcal{A}_m \subseteq \mathcal{A}_{m+1}$ for $1 \leq m < n^2$. Based on Theorem 1, I is a dominant input stream. $\quad\square$

In the LUD computation, one multiplication is followed by one addition if a_{ij}^d has stored a temporary value. Thus, adding k multiplicative terms $(a_{i\ell_0} \times a_{\ell_0 j})$, $(a_{i\ell_1} \times a_{\ell_1 j}), (a_{i\ell_2} \times a_{\ell_2 j}) \cdots (a_{i\ell_{k-1}} \times a_{\ell_{k-1}j})$ to an existing value stored at a_{ij}^d needs k additions. If $a_{i\ell_0} \times a_{\ell_0 j}$ is the first value to be stored at a_{ij}^d, then there is no addition. Thus, Equation (3) needs to be modified for counting the number of executable add/sub.

$$\Im(P_{\mathcal{A}_m}, \text{add/sub}) = \sum_{\ell=0}^{n-2} \sum_{i=\ell+1}^{n-1} \sum_{j=\ell+1}^{n-1} (e_{i\ell} \wedge e_{\ell j})) - \sum_{i=1}^{n-1} \sum_{j=1}^{n-1} \delta_{ij} \;. \tag{4}$$

The term δ_{ij} at the righthand side of (4) is used to adjust the number of add/sub operations which have been performed to generate a_{ij}^d . It is defined as follows:

$$\delta_{ij} = \begin{cases} 1 & \text{if } \hbar(a_{ij}) = 0 \text{ and } \bigvee_{\ell=0}^{\min\{i,j\}} (e_{i\ell} \wedge e_{\ell j}) = 1 \;. \\ 0 & \text{otherwise} \;. \end{cases} \tag{5}$$

The condition for setting δ_{ij} to 1 in (5) consists of two terms: $\hbar(a_{ij}) = 0$ and $\bigvee_{\ell=0}^{\min\{i,j\}} (e_{i\ell} \wedge e_{\ell j}) = 1$. The first term checks whether a_{ij} has been received by the computation server. The second term checks whether any of the pairs $(a_{i\ell}^d, a_{\ell j}^d)$ is ready to generate the temporary value of a_{ij}^d. Thus, Equation (5) states that the number of add/sub operations is one less than the number of multiplication operations, if a_{ij} has not arrived at the computation server and at least one pair of $(a_{i\ell}^d, e_{\ell j}^d)$'s can be used to generate the temporary value of a_{ij}^d.

The following theorem shows that there is no dominant sequence for LUD regarding add/sub operation. The theorem is proved by given a counterexample.

a_{00}	a_{01}	a_{02}			
a_{10}	a_{11}	a_{12}			
a_{20}	a_{21}	a_{22}			

(a) $P_{\mathcal{A}_9}$

a_{00}	a_{01}	a_{02}			
a_{10}	a_{11}	a_{12}			
a_{20}	a_{21}				
a_{30}	a_{31}				

(b) $P_{\mathcal{A}_{10}}$

Fig. 3. The layouts used in the proof of Theorem 3

Theorem 3. *There is no dominant input stream for LUD regarding add/sub operation.*

Proof. Assume $\mathcal{A}$ is a 6×6 matrix. If the computation server receives 9 data items, the maximum value of $\Im(P_{\mathcal{A}_9}, \text{add/sub})$ is 5. It occurs when $R_i = \{a_{ii}, a_{i\,i+1} \cdots a_{i\,2}\}$ and $C_i = \{a_{i+1,i}, a_{i+2\,i} \cdots a_{2\,i}\}$ for $0 \le i \le 2$; $|R_i| = |C_i| = 0$ for $3 \le i \le 5$ as shown in Fig. 3(a). If the computation server receives 10 data items, the maximum value of $\Im(P_{\mathcal{A}_{10}}, \text{add/sub})$ is 6. It occurs when $R_i = \{a_{ii}, a_{i\,i+1} \cdots a_{i\,2}\}$ and $C_i = \{a_{i+1,i}, a_{i+2\,i} \cdots a_{3\,i}\}$ for $0 \le i \le 1$; $|R_i| = |C_i| = 0$ for $2 \le i \le 5$ as shown in Fig. 3(b). Since $\mathcal{A}_9 \not\subseteq \mathcal{A}_{10}$, Thus, there is no dominant input stream. □

5   Performance Evaluation

In this section, the performance of a dominant input stream for mul/div is evaluated by comparing its execution time with that of another input stream which sends the matrix elements in a traditional order.

Let $I = d_0 d_1 d_2 \cdots d_{n^2-1}$ be the dominant input stream as given in Theorem 2. The order of sending matrix elements is expressed by a one-to-one function σ. It maps a pair of integers (i, j) to an integer $\sigma(i, j)$, where $0 \le i, j < n$ and $0 \le \sigma(i, j) < n^2$. That is, $d_{\sigma(i,j)} = a_{ij}$. The function σ is given as follows:

$$
\sigma(i,j) = \begin{cases}
\sum_{\ell=0}^{i-1}(|R_\ell| + |C_\ell|) & \text{if } i = j. \\
\sum_{\ell=0}^{j-1}(|R_\ell| + |C_\ell|) + 2(i-j) - 1 & \text{if } i > j. \\
\sum_{\ell=0}^{i-1}(|R_\ell| + |C_\ell|) + 2(j-i) & \text{if } i < j.
\end{cases}
$$

The function alternately assigns the elements in R_i and C_i to consecutive positions starting at 0 and proceeds to assign the elements in R_{i+1} and C_{i+1} after all the elements in R_i and C_i have been assigned. Since the dominant input stream is a symmetrically compact, the number of executable mul/div operations based on the elements in R_i and C_i is $|R_i| \cdot |C_i|$. Denote $F_{\sigma(i,j)}$ as the total executable

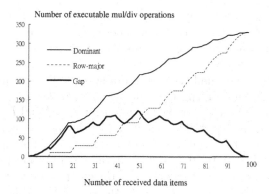

Fig. 4. Decomposition of a matrix of 10×10 using various input streams

mul/div operations after $d_0 d_1 \cdots d_{\sigma(i,j)}$ have been received by the computation server. $F_{\sigma(i,j)}$ can be calculated using the following formula:

$$F_{\sigma(i,j)} = \begin{cases} \sum_{\ell=0}^{i-1}(|R_\ell| \cdot |C_\ell|) & \text{if } i = j \text{ .} \\ \sum_{\ell=0}^{j-1}(|R_\ell| \cdot |C_\ell|) + (i - j)^2 & \text{if } i > j \text{ .} \\ \sum_{\ell=0}^{i-1}(|R_\ell| \cdot |C_\ell|) + (j - i + 1)(j - i) & \text{if } i < j \text{ .} \end{cases}$$

The curve of $F_{\sigma(i,j)}$ for incremental LUD computation on a matrix of 10×10 is illustrated in Fig. 4. The number of total executable mul/div operations is 330 after all the data items arrive at the computation server.

Next, the input stream $I' = d'_0 d'_1 d'_2 \cdots d'_{n^2-1}$ which sends matrix elements in row-major order is studied. The reason that I' is selected for comparing with the dominant input stream is given as follows. In general, the data items need to be placed in consecutive memory addresses before they can be delivered using a sequence of messages. Most of the computers store the matrix elements at consecutive memory locations using row-major order. The order of sending the matrix elements can be expressed by a one-to-one function ρ. It maps a pair of integers (i, j) to an integer $\rho(i, j)$, where $0 \le i, j < n$ and $0 \le \rho(i, j) < n^2$. That is, $d'_{\rho(i,j)} = a_{ij}$. The function ρ is given as follows: $d'_{\rho(i,j)} = a_{ij}$, where $\rho(i, j) = i \times n + j$. Denote $F'_{\rho(i,j)}$ as the total executable mul/div operations after $d'_0 d'_1 \cdots d'_{\rho(i,j)}$ have been received by the computation server. Define the topmost row of the matrix as the 0th row and the leftmost element in each row as the 0th element. It is easy to verify that the executable mul/div operations triggered by the elements in row i are only based on the first $i - 1$ elements in the input stream. The jth element in row i triggers $n - j$ mul/div operations for $0 \le j < i$. $F'_{\rho(i,j)}$ can be calculated using the following formula:

$$F'_{\rho(i,j)} = \begin{cases} \sum_{\ell=0}^{i-1} \frac{(2n-\ell+1)\ell}{2} + \sum_{\ell=0}^{j}(n - \ell) & \text{if } i > j \text{ .} \\ \sum_{\ell=0}^{i} \frac{(2n-\ell+1)\ell}{2} & \text{if } i \le j \text{ .} \end{cases}$$

The curve of $F'_{\rho(i,j)}$ for incremental LUD computation on a matrix of 10×10 is illustrated in Fig. 4. In the figure, the number of executable mul/div operations triggered by input stream I' is always less than that triggered by I for the first k data items, $0 \le k < n^2$.

The difference in the numbers of executable mul/div operations between a pair of input sub-streams of length k is defined as their kth *gap*. That is, the kth gap is $F_{k-1} - F'_{k-1}$. The gaps for the two input streams I and I', for $1 \le k \le n^2$, are also illustrated in Fig. 4. The maximum of the gaps is 121 when the first 50 data items have arrived at the computation server. Let t_0 and t_1 denote the time that the first data item arrives at the computation provider and the time the computation provider complete all the computations, respectively. The execution time is defined as $t_1 - t_0$. In [6], the completion time of executing an application $\mathcal{J}$ was shown to be $W_{\mathcal{J}} + \Delta_{\max}$. Note that $W_{\mathcal{J}}$ is the number of total computations needed to complete the application $\mathcal{J}$. The amount of delay $\Delta_{\max}$ is defined as the maximum of $(\{G_i - F_i | 0 \le i < n^2 - 1\} \cup \{0\})$, where G_i is the number of CPU cycles available for the computation server to execute the task before the $i+1$th data item arrives. Let the completion times of performing LUD using I and I' be $T = W_{\mathcal{J}} + \Delta_{\max}$ and $T' = W'_{\mathcal{J}} + \Delta'_{\max}$, respectively. Since I and I' are used to perform LUD of the same problem size, $W_{\mathcal{J}} = W'_{\mathcal{J}}$. It is known that $\Delta'_{\max} \ge \Delta_{\max}$. Thus, $T' \ge T$. Consider the case: $G_i = F_i$ for $0 \le i < n^2 - 1$ under the assumption that one mul/div operation takes 1 CPU cycle and one add/sub operation takes 0 CPU cycle. The difference in their completion time can be calculated as follows:

$$T' - T = \Delta'_{\max} - \Delta_{\max}$$
$$= \max\{F_i - F'_i | 0 \le i < n^2 - 1\} - 0 \quad \text{because } G_i = F_i$$
$$= 121 \quad \text{cycles} .$$

Thus, performing LUD using the dominant input stream can take up to 121 CPU cycles less than that using the other input stream. The data-sending order in a dominant stream does not meet the traditional order in storing the matrix elements in memory, thus, dynamically reorganizing data is necessary. However, the overhead of reorganizing matrix elements can be eliminated by assigning the elements to their proper addresses once the elements are going to be stored in memory.

6   Sparse Incremental LU Decomposition

In this section, performing LUD on a sparse matrix $\mathcal{A}$ of $n \times n$ is considered, where only non-zero data items are sent, and all unsent data items are assumed to be zero and are known to the computation server. The format of sending data is named as compressed format. The final value of a^d_{ij}, $i \le j$, can be directly computed if $a_{i0} = a_{i1} = \cdots = a_{i\,i-1} = 0$ or $a_{0j} = a_{1j} = \cdots = a_{i-1\,j} = 0$. The final value of a^d_{ij}, $i > j$, can be directly computed if $(a_{i0} = a_{i1} = \cdots = a_{i\,j-1} = 0$ or $a_{0j} = a_{1j} = \cdots = a_{j-1\,j} = 0)$ and $e_{jj} = 1$. Note that in the case of a

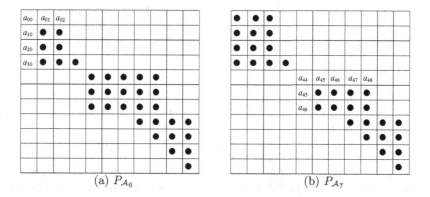

Fig. 5. The layouts used in the proof of Theorem 4

sparse matrix, the number of data items in the columns or rows of a matrix can be different and there are many zero's in the columns and rows. The following theorem shows that there is no dominant input stream if the compressed format is used to send data. The theorem is proved by giving a counterexample.

Theorem 4. *If the compressed format is used to send data, then there is no dominant input stream for LUD regarding mul/div operation.*

Proof. Consider the case as shown in Fig. 5. In the figure, the black dots are the non-zero data items of $\mathcal{A}$ which have not been received by the computation server yet, the a_{ij} 's are the non-zero data items of $\mathcal{A}$ which have been received by the computation server and the blanks represent zero's which will not be sent to the computation server. The elements of R_0 do not appear at the same columns as the elements of R_4 and the elements of C_0 do not appear at the same rows as the elements of C_4. Thus, the maximum of $\Im(P_{\mathcal{A}_6}, \text{mul/div})$ is 9 as shown in Fig. 5(a) and the maximum of $\Im(P_{\mathcal{A}_7}, \text{mul/div})$ is 10 as shown in Fig. 5(b). Since the $\mathcal{A}_6 \not\subseteq \mathcal{A}_7$, Thus, there is no dominant input stream.   □

7 Concluding Remarks

In this paper, a dominant input stream for incremental LUD computation is proposed. It has been shown that the dominant input stream outperforms the input stream which sends data in traditional order. In addition, the nonexistence of dominant input streams is proved for the case that the compressed format is used for sending input data. A dominant input stream maximizes the CPU utilization of the networked computation server which competes the network bandwidth with the others. The proposed sequence for sending data to the computation server can be used to develop an efficient library for performing LUD computation across the network. It is believed that the concept can also be adopted by a mobile computing platform. In the platform, the network connection may be disconnected for a while. A well-organized data sequence can be applied to keep the computation servers as busy as possible. Thus, the computations will not be suspended due to a short term of disconnection.

References

1. Bhat, P.B., Prasanna, V.K., Raghavendra, C.S.: Efficient Collective Communication in Distributed Heterogeneous Systems. J. Parallel and Distributed Computing 63(3), 251–263 (2003)
2. Cormen, T.H., Leiserson, C.E., Rivest, R.E., Stein, C.: Introduction to Algorithms, 2nd edn. MIT Press, Cambridge (2002)
3. Foster, I., Kesselman, C., Tuecke, S.: The Anatomy of the Grid: Enabling Scalable Virtual Organizations. Int'l J. Supercomputer Applications 15(3), 200–222 (2001)
4. Hsu, C.H., Chung, Y.C., Yang, D.L., Dow, C.R.: A Generalized Processor Mapping Technique for Array Redistribution. IEEE Trans. on Parallel and Distributed Systems 12(7), 743–757 (2001)
5. Kalns, E.T., Ni, L.M.: Processor Mapping Techniques Toward Efficient Data Redistribution. IEEE Trans. Parallel Distrib. Systems 6(12), 1234–1247 (1995)
6. Lin, C.C.: Strategies for Achieving High Performance Incremental Computing on a Network Environment. In: Proc. the 17th Int'l Conf. Advanced Information Networking and Applications, pp. 113–118 (2004)
7. Lin, C.C., Hsu, T.S., Wang, D.W.: Bounds on the Client-Server Incremental Computing. IEICE Trans. Fundamentals of Electronics, Communications and Computer Sciences E89-A(5), 1198–1206 (2006)
8. Liu, P.: Broadcast Scheduling Optimization for Heterogeneous Cluster Systems. J. Algorithms 42(1), 135–152 (2002)
9. Ranka, S., Shankar, R. V., Alsabti, K. A.: Many-to-Many Personalized Communication with Bounded Traffic. In: Proc. Symp. the Frontiers of Massively Parallel Computation, pp. 20–27 (1995)
10. Shyamasundar, R.K., Rajan, B., Prasad, M., Jain, A.: LLM A Low Latency Messaging Infrasture for Linux Cluster. In: Sahni, S.K., Prasanna, V.K., Shukla, U. (eds.) HiPC 2002. LNCS, vol. 2552, pp. 112–123. Springer, Heidelberg (2002)
11. Strumpen, V.: Software-Based Communication Latency Hiding for Commodity Workstation Networks. In: Proc. Int'l Conf. Parallel Processing, pp. 12–16 (1996)
12. Strumpen, V., Casavant, T. L.: Exploiting Communication Latency Hiding for Parallel Network Computing: Model and Analysis. In: Proc. Int'l Conf. Parallel and Distributed Systems, pp. 622–627 (1994)
13. Wang, C.L., Prasanna, V.K., Kim, H.J., Khokhar, A.A.: Scalable Data Parallel Implementations of Object Recognition using Geometric Hashing. J. Parallel and Distributed Computing 21(1), 96–109 (1994)
14. Yu, C.W., Hsu, C.H., Yu, K.M., Liang, C.K., Chen, C.I.: Irregular Redistribution Scheduling by Partitioning Messages. In: Srikanthan, T., Xue, J., Chang, C.-H. (eds.) ACSAC 2005. LNCS, vol. 3740, pp. 295–309. Springer, Heidelberg (2005)

A Double-Objective Genetic Algorithm for Parity Declustering Optimization in Networked RAID

Xiaoguang Liu, Gang Wang, and Jing Liu

Department of Computer Science, Nankai University, Tianjin, 300071, China
{liuxg74,wgzwp}@hotmail.com, jingliu@nankai.edu.cn

Abstract. RAID, as a popular technology to improve the performance and reliability of storage system, has been used widely in computer industry. Recently, the technique of designing data layout in order to fit the requirements of networked storage is becoming a new challenge in this field. In this paper, we present a double-objective Genetic Algorithm for parity declustering optimization in networked RAID with a modified NSGA, we also take *Distributed recovery workload* and *Distributed parity* as two objects to find optimal data layout for parity declustering in networked RAID.

1 Introduction

Since RAID (Redundant Array of Independent Disks) [1] was invited in 1980s, it is becoming the most important technology in storage systems. Especially, RAID 5 has been treated as the most reliable storage standard. However, a shortcoming of RAID 5 is that its performance falls obviously in degrade and reconstruction mode. To solve this problem, parity declustering was introduced by Muntz and Lui[2]. Through parity stripe distribution and Reconstruction Load Balance, parity declustering can improve the performance and reduce the time cost of reconstruction. Holland and Gibson also defined six standards to estimate ideal data layout[3]. It includes *Single failure correcting, Distributed recovery workload, Distributed parity, Efficient mapping, Large write optimization* and *Maximal parallelism*. Following the six standards, Alvarez proved that building an ideal data layout was difficult in most cases[4]. So the problem has been converted to how to find a data layout which is as close to ideal data layout as possible. Many data layouts have been studied, such as BIBD, PRIME,PDDL and RELPR[2-5]. All of them emphasized only parts of the six standards for different applications. However, since ideal data layouts are required by the six standards, the multiobjective optimization algorithm is obviously a nature selection to find ideal data layouts.

One way to solve multiobjective problems is transforming the original problem into a single objective problem by weighting the objectives with a weight vector. But the solution obtained in this way depends on the weight vector used in the process. Genetic algorithm works with a population, so we expect that it can find the Pareto optimal front to our problem.

Many Pareto-based multiobjective GAs are developed in recent years. VEGA(vector evaluated genetic algorithm) performs the selection operation for each objective

H. Jin et al. (Eds.): ICA3PP 2007, LNCS 4494, pp. 415–420, 2007.

respectively. The pareto-based ranking GA was proposed by Fonseca and Fleming[6]. An individual's rank equals the number of other individuals in the population by which it is dominated. NPGA (niched pareto genetic algorithm) uses the concept of pareto dominance and tournament selection in solving multiobjective optimization problems[7].NSGA (Non-dominated Sorting Genetic Algorithm) was first implemented by Srinivas and Deb[8]. While it follows the standard genetic algorithm for parent selection and offspring generation, it determines the fitness of the individual using the concept of parato dominance also. To improve the performance, NSGA-2 was proposed in 2000[9], and its source codes also can be download.

In this paper, we use NSGA to find a better data layout for networked RAID systems. Because *Distributed recovery workload* and *Distributed parity* take more weights on the networked RAID systems, we set them as the two objects of our algorithm. To compare the performances of the solution, an experiment based simulated annealing was done simultaneously. The results show that the double-objective Genetic Algorithm can produce better data layout for networked storage. To our knowledge, this work is firstly applied the multiobjective genetic algorithm to solve parity declustering optimization problem.

2 The Double-Objective Genetic Algorithm

2.1 The Design of Algorithm

Among the six standards of ideal data layout, the second, *Distributed recovery workload*, and the third, *Distributed parity*, take the largest influence on the performance of networked storage. So we set these two standards as the objects of NSGA. According to the choice of double-objective optimization function, the partial relation on the target space can be converted to pareto dominance on the decision space. After enough iterations, the partial relation can be converted to pareto dominance on the decision space under the control of the double-objective function. At last, we can get a set of pareto dominated solutions. The optimum data layout can be selected from this set.

2.2 The Detail of Algorithm

2.2.1 Objective Functions
In this section, the detail of objective functions is presented.

(1) Weight
During initial period, we set the weight under the following rules,

Rule 1: To all local connected disk, the value of weight, e_{ij}, is 1;

Rule 2: If there is one controller node in the networked storage system, and all storage management job run only on the controller (supposing the number of controller is 0), then we have,

$$e_{ij} = \begin{cases} 1, & (j \bmod m) = 0 \\ e, & (j \bmod m) \neq 0 \end{cases} \tag{1}$$

Rule 3: To the distributed storage system, such as petal, the storage management job can run on more than one node. If disk i and disk j belong to the same node, then e_{ij} is 1,else e_{ij} is e. Here, m is the number of disks.

$$e_{ij} = \begin{cases} 1, & (j \bmod m) = (i \bmod m) \\ e, & (j \bmod m) \neq (i \bmod m) \end{cases} \tag{2}$$

(2) The function of Reconstruction Load

$$H_{WEIGHTED}(L) = \sum (X_{ij} \bullet e_{ij})^2 \tag{3}$$

Here, X_{ij} means the number of stripes read from disk j while disk i broke down, e_{ij} means the cost of the system which reads a stripe unit from disk j while disk i failed. In order to improve the performance, we should minimize the value of function H.

(3) The function of Parity overhead

$$P_{WEIGHTED}(L) = \sum P_i^2 \tag{4}$$

Here, P_i is the number of parity units on disk i. Obviously, we should also minimize function P.

2.2.2 Parameters of Algorithm

The data layout is used as the chromosome in the algorithm. Every data layout is presented as a $r \times v$ matrix. Here, r is the number of lines in the data layout, v is the number of the disks, k is the length of the stripe. Simply, we only consider the situation that v can be divided exactly by k in this paper. The absolute value of the elements in the matrix is the sequence number of the stripes, and the elements which value less than zero are parity unites in stripes. An example(r=5, v=6, k=3) is shown in figure 1.

The Pareto dominate relation on decision space can be described as follows,

$$\text{A Dominat B} \Leftrightarrow ((H(A) \leq H(B)) \& \&(P(A) \leq P(B)))$$
$$\& \&((H(A) < H(B)) \| (P(A) < P(B))) \tag{5}$$

In order to avoid illegal data layout produced during iterations, we make some restrictions on the intercross and mutation regulars. For example, all lines must be interchanged between two data layouts in intercross, and mutation only interchanges two elements in the same line.

	d1	d2	d3	d4	d5	d6
r1	− 1	2	− 2	1	2	1
r2	4	3	4	− 3	− 4	3
r3	− 5	5	6	6	5	− 6
r4	7	8	− 8	− 7	8	7
r5	9	− 10	9	− 9	10	10

Fig. 1. An example of data layout

2.2.3 The Algorithm

The algorithm can be described as follows,

a. Initially, N data layouts are given randomly.

b. The functions of Reconstruction Load (H) and Parity overhead (P) are computed.

c. According to their pareto relations, all the data layouts are divided into m sets.

d. According to the regulars in niche, we set all sets with the shared fitness values in turn.

e. N better data layouts are selected from all sets.

f. The parents are selected by roulette, and N new data layouts are produced after intercross and mutation.

g. The functions of Reconstruction Load (H) and Parity overhead (P) are calculated again. If the difference between the actual value and ideal value is less than the threshold which is defined initially, then the program ends, else turns to step b.

Here, the population size in the first iteration is N, and it is 2N in the others. However, the population, which used for selection, intercross and mutation, is still N in each generation. Specially, these N individuals are the better ones in the 2N data layouts.

2.2.4 Simulated Annealing Algorithm

In order to compare the performance of the double-objective Genetic Algorithm, we also implement a simulated annealing algorithm for the same problem. The simulated annealing algorithm can be described as follows,

a. Initialization. The default values of parameter are set. Such as *length*, the maximal length of Markov chain, T_0, the temperature in initial state, *ngel*, the maximal number of data layouts which have same value, *gen*, the maximal number of iteration.

b. If the number of iteration exceeds *gen*, end the program, else turns to step c.

c. If the number of same data layouts exceeds *ngel*, turns to step g.

d. If the length of Markov chain exceeds *length*, turns to step g.

e. Generate new data layout, and calculate its value of reconstruction function.

f. The length of Markov chain adds 1. If the probability estimation can be accepted, then the new data layout is legal and turns to step d. Else, the number of same data layouts adds 1 and turns to step c.

g. According to *Distributed parity*, if the new data layout is the best solution until now, then records it. The number of iteration adds 1 and turns to step b.

In our experiments, T_0 is 0.5, *length* is 1000, *ngel* is 10 and *gen* is 10.

3 Experimental Results

There are two groups of test in the experiment. One is the optimum data layout in local disk array. The other is the result in distributed storage system. Simultaneously, the best results in this experiment are compared with the best results in theory.

Table 1. The optimum data layout in local disk array (v = 12,k = 6,N = 50)

Lines	ideal X_{ij}	Actual X_{ij}	Difference	Ideal P_i	Actual P_i	Difference
117	53.18	55	3.309%	19.5	20	2.25%
308	140	142	1.428%	51.333	52	1.346%
1121	509.54	512	0.482%	186.833	187	0.358%
4873	2215	2219	0.18%	812.167	813	0.103%

According to the conclusion in reference 10, any X_{ij} has the same value in local disk arrays[10], and the value should be equal to $r \times (k-1)/(v-1)$. Besides, any P_i also has the same value, it equals to r/k. As shown in table 1, X_{ij} and P_i in actual test have nearly reached the best results in theory.

Table 2. The optimum data layout in distributed storage system(r = 117, k = 10, v = 40)

Nodes	H^a	H^b	Ideal P_i	Actual P_i
2	5805760	2105600	12	12
4	8140350	3766204	12	12
5	8605310	4335244	12	13
8	9306610	5828024	12	13

[a] The value of function H using simulated anneaing.
[b] The value of function H using double-Objective Genetic Algorithm.

Using double-objective Genetic Algorithm, the parity units are distributed more even in storage system. As shown in table 2, the value of function H using double-Objective Genetic Algorithm is much smaller than that using simulated annealing. In a word, the double-objective Genetic Algorithm has selected the most two important standards from six standards of ideal data layout. It can produce better data layouts for networked storage.

4   Conclusion

In this paper, we use the double-objective Genetic Algorithm to design the optimum data layout for networked storage system. To the objective functions in the algorithm, we chose *Distributed recovery workload* and *Distributed parity*, which are more important standards to the performance of storage system. The experimental results show that the double-objective Genetic Algorithm can produce better data layout for networked storage. We can conclude that multi-objective Genetic Algorithm is a feasible and effective optimization algorithm for designing ideal data layout. As far as we know, our paper is the first to use multi-objective Genetic Algorithm in the design of ideal data layout, and this application may become popular to multi-objective Genetic Algorithm in the future.

Acknowledgements

This paper is sponsored by NSF of China (90612001), Science and Technology Development Plan of Tianjin, (043185111-14) and Nankai university science and technology innovation fund and ISC.

References

1. Patterson, D., Gibson, G., Katz, R.: A case for redundant arrays of inexpensive disks(RAID). In: Proceedings of ACM SIGMOD, Seattle, Washington, USA, pp. 109–116 (1998)
2. Muntz, R., Lui, J.: Performance Analysis of Disk Arrays Under Failure. In:Proceedings of the conference on Very Large Data Bases, Brisbane, Queensland, Australia, pp. 162–173 (1990)
3. Holland, M., Gibson, G., Sieworuk, D.: Architectures and Algorithms for On-Line Failure Recovery in Redundant Disk Arrays. Journal of Parallel and Distributed Databases 2, 295–335 (1994)
4. Alvarez, G., Burkhard, W., Stockmeyer, L., Cristian, F.: Declustered Disk Array Architectures with Optimal and Near-Optimal Parallelism. In: Proceedings of the 25th Annual ACM/IEEE International Symposium on Computer Architecture, Barcelona, Spain, pp. 109–120 (1998)
5. Schwarz, T., Steinberg, J., Burkhard, W.: Permutation Development Data Layout (PDDL) Disk Array Declustering. In: Proceedings of the Fifth International Symposium on High-Performance Computer Architecture, Orlando, FL, USA, pp. 214–217 (1999)
6. Fonseca, C., Fleming, P.: Genetic algorithm for multiobjective optimization. In: Proceedings of 5th International conference on Genetic Algorithms, San Mateo, CA, USA, pp. 416–423 (1993)
7. Horn, J., Nafpliotis, N., Goldberg, D.: A niched Pareto genetic algorithm for multiobjective optimization. In: Proceedings of 1st IEEE conference on Evolutionary Computation, Piscataway, NJ, USA, pp. 82–87 (1994)
8. Srinivas, N., Deb, K.: Multiobjective optimization using nondominated sorting in genetic algorithms. Evolutionary Computation 2, 221–248 (1994)
9. Deb, K., Agrawal, S., Pratap, A., Meyarivan, T.: A Fast Elitist Non Dominated Sorting Genetic Algorithm for Multi Objective Optimization: NSGA-2. In: Proceedings of Parallel Problem Solving from Nature (PPSN) 6th International conference, Paris, France, pp. 858–862 (2000)
10. Schwabe, E., Sutherland, I., Holmer, B.: Evaluating Approximately Balanced Parity-Declustered Data Layouts for Disk Arrays. Parallel Computing 23, 501–523 (1997)

Hybrid Diffusion Schemes for Load Balancing on OTIS-Networks

Chenggui Zhao[1], Wenjun Xiao[1], and Yong Qin[1,2]

[1] School of Compuer Science and Engineering, South China University of Technology,
Guangzhou, 510640, China
zhaochenggui@126.com
[2] Information and Network Center, Maoming University, Maoming, 525000, China
mmcqinyong@126.com

Abstract. Several diffusion schemes have been developed for load balancing on general networks. But these schemes are not well adapt to the optical transpose interconnection network (OTIS) because this network usually has high order Laplace matrix such that computing its spectrum becomes complicated. Even if its spectrum is obtained simply, diffusion schemes sometimes are rather difficult to implement because of large scale of network usually.

Corresponding to traditional X schemes, we propose hybrid diffusion schemes called DED-X for load balancing on OTIS network. By DED-X schemes, load flows are scheduled on intragroup and intergroup links on OTIS network separately. The DED-X schemes only compute the Laplace spectrum of the factor graph of the OTIS network. The spectral information of whole OTIS network is not necessary. We also provide some theoretical evidences to show that DED-X schemes are better than those traditional X schemes. Simulation results show that proposed schemes have significant promotion in efficiency and stability.

1 Introduction

When parallel computer system distributes unevenly work loads on all its nodes in runtime, it must equilibrate node loads by moving load items between nodes and their neighbors via communication links, specially, when highly uneven load distribution emerges and system performance degrades evidently. Load balancing algorithm supposes that node loads consist of equally sized items. The goal of load balancing is to design scheduling algorithm to migrate node loads across edges so that all nodes have equal loads finally. In common, load balancing process can be completed by two steps. Firstly, calculate the amount of load that should be migrated between a node and its neighbors for achieving the balanced status. Secondly, select load items to transfer them. A good balancing algorithm means that it has a numerically stable iterative procedure with less steps and a small flow over the edges of the graph for achieving the load balanced sate.

Some diffusion algorithms have been proposed for load balancing on general networks, homogeneous or heterogeneous. For homogeneous networks, Cybenko

H. Jin et al. (Eds.): ICA3PP 2007, LNCS 4494, pp. 421–432, 2007.

[1] presented a local diffusion scheme denoted as first order scheme (FOS) in [2]. To speed up the iteration process in FOS, Ghosh et al. provided the second order scheme (SOS) based on FOS, by using over-relaxation iterative method. R. Diekmann et al. in [3] developed the optimal polynomial scheme (OPS) and illustrated that OPS is optimal. Elsässer in [5] presented other optimal diffusion scheme called OPT with a simpler iteration construction than OPS. Once the Laplace spectrum of the graph become known, OPT balances node loads in finite iterative steps. In [4], the authors generalized several diffusion schemes from homogeneous networks to heterogeneous ones. Their generalized schemes balance node loads to be proportional to their weights. The schemes cited above all determine the l_2-minimal balancing flow. In fact, It has been stated all local diffusion algorithms lead to a minimal flow, independent of the algorithms and parameters used.

General diffusion algorithms are not well suit to load balancing on large, irregular networks, due to their complicated spectrum computation, such as optical transpose interconnection system (OTIS) which was presented recently as a preferable parallel computer architecture. However, most parallel interconnection networks have scalable architectures derived from other networks by cross-product composition, recursive substitution and hierarchical composition. To this class of networks, the general diffusion schemes listed above must be revised for less computational complexity and a better numerical stability.

Our focus of discussion in this paper is to construct new diffusion algorithms based on general diffusion algorithms like FOS, SOS and OPT so that they can complete load balancing issue on OTIS networks in the same level of computational overhead with in their factor networks. Our schemes are efficient when they are applied to a wide array of OTIS networks whose factor networks have regular topologies. After giving some basic definitions about modeling problem of load balancing in section 2, and reviewing several existing general schemes in section 3, we introduce our hybrid diffusion algorithms in section 4. In section 5, we analyze the performance of these schemes. Some simulation results in the last section help to show availability of our work.

2   Definitions

Let $G = (V, E)$ be a connected undirected graph with n nodes and m edges. Node v_i has an initial load $w_i^0 \geq 0$. The goal of the load balancing algorithm is to determine the vector w^l of balanced loads such that $w^l = (1/n\Sigma_{i=1}^n w_i^0)(1, 1, ..., 1)^T$. Let B be the node-edge incidence matrix of G having in each column exactly two non-zero entries 1 and -1 which represent the nodes incident to the corresponding edge. The signs of these non-zero entries decide implicitly directions of the flows produced in the process of load balancing on corresponding edges of the G. Denote the adjacency matrix of G with A and the node degree diagonal matrix of G with D. The Laplacian L of graph G is usually defined as $L = BB^T$. Let $\alpha \in (0, 1)$ be a constant edge weight.The $n \times n$ matrix M defined by $M = I - \alpha L$ is called diffusion matrix. Let x^k and y^k are two flow vectors whose entries corresponding edge e_i represent respectively current flow and total amount of flows in k-th iteration over e_i. The directions of the flows are determined by the directions of the edges in the incidence matrix B of G. The flow x is called a balancing flow on G if and only if $Bx = w^0 - w^l$. Let $\lambda_i (1 \leq i \leq r)$ be r distinct eigenvalues of the Laplacian L of the graph G in increasing order. Then M has the eigenvalues $\mu_i = 1 - \alpha\lambda_i$ and α has to be chosen such that $\mu_1 > \mu_2 > ... > \mu_r > -1$. Denote the second largest eigenvalue of M according to absolute values with $\gamma = \max(|\mu_2|, |\mu_m|)$. For any polynomial based diffusion scheme, γ decides the convergence speed of this scheme, with e^k representing the error after i-th iteration, which was stated in [3].

The OTIS network OTIS-G, derived from the n-node factor graph G, is defined as following, see [11].

Definition 1. *Let $G = (V_G, E_G)$ be an undirected graph. The OTIS-$G = (V, E)$ is an undirected graph given by $V = \{\langle g, p \rangle | g, p \in V_G\}$ and $E = \{(\langle g, p_1 \rangle, \langle g, p_2 \rangle) | g \in V_G, (p_1, p_2) \in E_G\} \cup \{(\langle g, p \rangle, \langle p, g \rangle) | g, p \in V_G, g \neq p\}$.*

The graph G is called the factor network of OTIS-G. If G has N nodes, then OTIS-G is composed of N node-disjoint subnetworks $G_i (i = 1, 2, ...n)$, called groups. Each of these groups is isomorphic to G. Denotes the vertex set of G_i with $V_i = \{v_{ij}, 0 \leq j \leq (n-1)\}$ and edge set $E_i = \{(v_{ik}, v_{il}) | (v_k, v_l) \in E(G)\}$. Now, the vertex set V of OTIS-G satisfies $V = \cup_{i=0}^{n-1} V_i$. The edge set E of OTIS-G can be partitioned into two subsets E_b called intragroup edge set and E_s call intergroup edges set. E_b represents all edges on $G_i, (i = 1, 2, ...n)$ and E_s means other edges among G_i. Clearly, $E_b = \cup_{i=0}^{n-1} E_i$ and $E_s = \{(v_{ij}, v_{ji}) | i \leq j\}$. Let B_b and B be the node-edge incidence matrices of factor graph G and whole network OTIS-G respectively; B_s denote the matrix incident the intergroup edges of E_s to nodes of OTIS-G. For short, let symbol G_s denote the OTIS network OTIS-G. At last, Let e^k denote the error vector resulting from diffusion scheme after k-th iteration.

3   Several Existing Diffusion Schemes for General Networks

Firstly, it is necessary to state several known algorithms, including FOS in [1], OPS in [3] and OPT in [5]. They all service as diffusion schemes for load balancing on general network topology. The FOS scheme can be expressed as local iterative scheme. It changes the work load vector w^k of nodes and schedules the flow vector x of edges according to following procedure.

$$\text{for } k \geq 1, w^k = Mw^{k-1}, x^k = x^{k-1} - \alpha B^T w^{k-1}.$$

About the error estimation e^k, with [3], it holds $\|e^k\|_2 \leq \gamma^k \cdot \|e^0\|_2$. To improve the relatively slow convergence of FOS, another polynomial iterative method called second order scheme (SOS) was presented in [2]. The SOS is based on the second order Richardson method in numerical analysis. The scheme SOS takes the polynomials $p_0(t) = 1, p_1(t) = t, p_k(t) = \beta t p_{k-1}(t) + (1 - \beta)p_{k-2}(t), k > 2$. The iterating process of SOS migrates work loads according

$$w^1 = Mw^0, w^k = \beta M w^{k-1} + (1 - \beta)w^{k-2}, k \geq 2.$$

The authors of [10] have shown that w^k converges to w^l whenever $\beta \in (0, 2)$ and the fastest convergence occurs for $\beta = 2/(1 + \sqrt{1 - \gamma^2})$. Denoting this optimal value of β with β_o, as stated in [3], the iterating error e^k in $k - th$ fulfills

$$\|e^k\|_2 \leq (\beta_o - 1)^{k/2}(1 + k\sqrt{1 - \gamma^2})\|e^0\|_2 \beta_o = 2/(1 + \sqrt{1 - \gamma^2}). \tag{1}$$

After these parameters are computed, SOS algorithm can be expressed a form of algorithm, which appeared in a general frame in [3]. The process of flow scheduling and load updating can be expressed as $y^0 = \beta_o B^T w^0, x^1 = y^0$; for $k > 1, y^{k-1} = \beta_o B^T w^{k-1} - (1 - \beta_o y^{k-2}), x^k = x^{k-1} + y^{k-1}, w^k = w^{k-1} - By^{k-1}$.

The optimal scheme OPT has a more simple iteration process, shown as for $2 \leq k \leq (r - 1), y^{k-1} = \frac{1}{\lambda_{k+1}} B^T w^{k-1}, x^k = x^{k-1} + y^{k-1}, w^k = (I - \frac{1}{\lambda_{k+1}} L)w^{k-1}$.

4   Hybrid Diffusion Schemes for OTIS Networks

For OTIS-network, with n vertices on its factor network, all eigenvalues of a matrix with order n^2 have to be computed before load balancing process starts. We have shown that sometimes it is unpractical. Therefore we will introduce hybrid schemes of diffusion and dimension exchange called DED-X schemes for OTIS networks. The common ideal of DED-X schemes is to divide load balancing process into three stages by a process of diffusion-exchange-diffusion. Now we construct new algorithm DED-FOS, DED-SOS and DED-OPT as follows. Other polynomial based schemes can be obtained easily by a similar way. Let $L \in \mathbb{R}^{n^2}$ and $L_b \in \mathbb{R}^n$ be the Laplacian of OTIS network and its factor; $M = I_{n^2} - \alpha L$ and $M_b = I_n - \alpha_b L_b$ be the corresponding diffusion matrices of diffusion schemes based polynomial. Let A_{ij} denote $n \times n$ matrix with only ij-th entry being 1 and other entries being 0. Let A_s be a matrix with ij-th entry being $A_s(i, j) = A_{ij}$. Then $L = I_n \otimes (L_b + I_n) - A_s$, where $\otimes$ represents the Knonecker product. Let $w_i = (w_{i1}, w_{i2}, ..., w_{in})^T$ be the work load on i-th factor of OTIS network and $w = (w_1, w_2, ..., w_n)^T$ be the work load on OTIS network. The work load w^k in step k for polynomial based diffusion schemes can be commonly expressed as a general form $w^k = p_k(M)w^0$. In the series of DED-X schemes, In the first stage we iteratively diffuse node loads until for all i, the initial loads w_i^0 of i-th factor network achieves the balanced status w_i^l locally on this factor. In this stage, the work load w_k in step k can be decides according to

$$w^k = (I_n \otimes p_k(M_b))w^0. \tag{2}$$

When second stage starts, we perform a dimension exchange strategy over all intergroup links. In this stage, factor networks pairwise interchange their balanced node load by a way of interchanging load of node (u, v) with one of node (v, u). After this stage, the total amount of all node loads on each factor network is common. In succession to the first stage the load of whole network after second stage is

$$w^{l+1} = A_s w^l \tag{3}$$

In the third stage, we proceed diffusion with the same iterative polynomial as in the first stage but we only compute the amount of load migration on one of the factors and have common flow on all other factors, based on the fact that each factor network has same initial load vector. Following theorem show that any polynomial based scheme must converge w^k to the average of node loads on whole network after such diffusion-exchange-diffusion process passes through.

Theorem 1. *For any polynomial based scheme X, if X takes as most l steps to iteratively balance load w_i^0 of i-th factor network to the balanced load $\frac{1}{n} J w_i^0$ then DED-X scheme balances load w^0 to the balanced load $\frac{1}{n^2}(J \otimes J)w^0$ in at most $2l + 1$ steps.*

Proof. By the condition of this proposition it holds that $p_l(M_b) = \frac{1}{n} J$. For DED-X we have

$$w^{2l+1} = [I_n \otimes p_l(M_b)]A_s[I_n \otimes p_l(M_b)]w^0 = \frac{1}{n}(I_n \otimes J)A_s(I_n \otimes J) = \frac{1}{n^2} J \otimes J \tag{4}$$

which shows that w^0 achieves to $\frac{1}{n^2}(J \otimes J)w^0$ within $2l + 1$ steps.

We now describe DED-X schemes as iterative algorithms. Its performance will be discuss in detail in following sections.

Algorithm: DED-X
Input: OTIS-network consists of factors G_i with load vector $w_i, 0 \le i < n$.
Output: Balanced load vector $w^l = 1/n^2 \sum_{i=0}^{n-1} \sum_{j=0}^{n-1} w_{ij}$ and a sequence of flow
   x^k.
1. for all factors G_i of OTIS-G
2. run the procedure X on $G_i, 0 \le i < n$ and input the balanced load vector as
   w_i^l;
3. end for
4. for all intergroup edges $e = ((i, j), (j, i)), i \ne j$
5. $y_e^E = (w_i^l - w_j^l); w_{ij}^E = w_{ij}^l - y_e$;
6. end for
7. $w_0^0 = w^E; y_1^0 = \alpha B_b^T w_0^0$;
8. run the procedure X on $G_i, 0 \le i < n$ and input the balanced load vector as
   w_i^l;

5   Algorithm Analysis

Let $\mathbb{R}^V$ be the set of functions from vertex set V of graph G to $\mathbb{R}$, $\mathbb{R}^V = \{f : V \to \mathbb{R}\}$. Let e denote the all 1 vector of n dimension and e_i denote i-th column vector of the $n \times n$ identity matrix.

Theorem 2. *Let λ_1^b and λ_1 represent the second smallest Laplace eigenvalue of factor network G and G_s respectively. Let λ_{max}^b and λ_{max} denote their largest eigenvalue respectively. Then it is true that*

$$\lambda_1 \leq \lambda_1^b. \tag{5}$$

and

$$\lambda_{max}^b + 1 \leq \lambda_{max}. \tag{6}$$

Proof. Let $f \in \mathbb{R}^{V_G}$ be a function defined by the eigenvector corresponding λ_1^b; then $f \perp e$, $e = (1, 1, ..., 1)^T$. For any $g \in \mathbb{R}^n$ it holds $(g \otimes f)^T (e \otimes e) = 0$ so $(g \otimes f) \perp e$. Now think of the Rayleigh quotient expression of matrix eigenvalue, because $L_b f = \lambda_1^b f$, we have

$$\lambda_1 \leq \frac{\langle L_s(g \otimes f), g \otimes f \rangle}{\langle g \otimes f, g \otimes f \rangle} = \frac{(g \otimes f)^T (I_n \otimes L_b + I_{n^2} - A_s)(g \otimes f)}{(g \otimes f)^T (g \otimes f)}$$
$$= \lambda_1^b + 1 - \frac{(g^T \otimes f^T) A_s (g \otimes f)}{\langle g, g \rangle \langle f, f \rangle}. \tag{7}$$

But we have

$$\frac{(g^T \otimes f^T) A_s (g \otimes f)}{\langle g, g \rangle \langle f, f \rangle} = \frac{1}{\langle g, g \rangle, \langle f, f \rangle} \sum_{i=1}^{n} g_i f^T (\sum_{k=1}^{n} A_{ki} g_k f) \tag{8}$$

together with

$$\sum_{i=1}^{n} g_i f^T (\sum_{k=1}^{n} A_{ki} g_k f) = \sum_{i=1}^{n} g_i f_i f^T g = \langle g, f \rangle^2. \tag{9}$$

Synthesizing equation 7,8 and 9 we have

$$\lambda_1 \leq \lambda_1^b + 1 - \frac{\langle g, f \rangle^2}{\langle g, g \rangle \langle f, f \rangle} \tag{10}$$

By choice of g equal to f, we have $\frac{\langle g, f \rangle^2}{\langle g, g \rangle \langle f, f \rangle} = 1$ and $\lambda_1 \leq \lambda_1^b$. The equation 5 becomes true. Similarly, for any $g \in \mathbb{R}^{V_G}$, choosing f as an eigenvector of the maximal eigenvalue λ_{max}^b of L_b, since $g \otimes f \in \mathbb{R}^V$, so for $h \in \mathbb{R}^V$ the largest eigenvalue λ_{max} satisfies

$$\lambda_{max} = \max_h \frac{\langle L_s h, h \rangle}{\langle h, h \rangle}. \tag{11}$$

Let $h = g \otimes f$, we have

$$\lambda_{max} \geq \max_g \frac{\langle L_s(g \otimes f), g \otimes f \rangle}{\langle g \otimes f, g \otimes f \rangle}. \tag{12}$$

With a similar way of proving the equation 6, it holds that

$$\frac{\langle L_s(g \otimes f), g \otimes f \rangle}{\langle g \otimes f, g \otimes f \rangle} = \lambda_{max}^b + 1 - \frac{\langle g, f \rangle^2}{\langle g, g \rangle \langle f, f \rangle}. \tag{13}$$

Equation 12 together with equation 13 yield

$$\lambda_{max} \geq \max_g \left(\lambda_{max}^b + 1 - \frac{\langle g, f \rangle^2}{\langle g, g \rangle \langle f, f \rangle} \right). \tag{14}$$

Equation 6 holds when take g satisfying $\langle g, f \rangle = 0$.

Next theorem shows that DED-FOS always converges more quickly than FOS.

Theorem 3. *Let γ_b and γ denote the diffusion norm of the factor network G and OTIS-G respectively. Then it holds that $\gamma_b < \gamma$, which means that when apply DED-FOS scheme and FOS scheme to OTIS-G, DED-FOS will has a smaller upper bound of error than FOS in k-th iteration.*

Proof. Let ρ_b and ρ represent the condition number of the Laplace matrix L_b and L apart, by the use of the theorem 2 it follows that

$$\rho = \frac{\lambda_1}{\lambda_{max}} \leq \frac{\lambda_1^b}{\lambda_{max}^b + 1} < \frac{\lambda_1^b}{\lambda_{max}^b} = \rho_b. \tag{15}$$

Therefore

$$\gamma_b = \frac{1 - \rho_b}{1 + \rho_b} < \frac{1 - \rho}{1 + \rho} = \gamma \tag{16}$$

Equation 16 implies that at k-th step, for OTIS network, the iteration error $||e_b^k||_2 \leq \gamma_b^k$ for DED-FOS but error $||e^k||_2 \leq \gamma^k$ for FOS , with $\gamma_b < \gamma$.

Next theorem states the the performance of DED-SOS scheme, which displays better convergency property related to the ordinary SOS scheme for OTIS networks.

Theorem 4. *The upper bound of iteration error $b(e_b^k)$ on G and $b(e^k)$ on OTIS-G by the general SOS scheme satisfies*

$$b(e_b^k) = \tau^{2k-1} b(e^k), \tag{17}$$

where $\tau < 1$ is a real constant decided by the ratio of diffusion norms γ_b and γ.

Proof. In equation 1, let $\sqrt{1 - \gamma_b^2} = \theta$ and $\sqrt{1 - \gamma^2} = \epsilon$. Then it is known that $0 \leq \epsilon, \theta < 1$ and $\epsilon < \theta$ such that it holds that

$$\frac{b(e_b^k)}{b(e^k)} = \left[\frac{(1 - \theta)(1 + \epsilon)}{(1 + \theta)(1 - \epsilon)} \right]^{k/2} \left(\frac{1 + k\theta}{1 + k\epsilon} \right). \tag{18}$$

Let $\frac{1+\epsilon}{1+\theta} = \delta$ then $\delta < 1$ and $\frac{1-\theta}{1-\epsilon} = \frac{\delta \gamma_b^2}{\gamma^2}$. Since $\frac{1+k\theta}{1+k\epsilon} < \frac{\theta}{\epsilon}, k > 0$ we have

$$\frac{b(e_b^k)}{b(e^k)} < \delta^{k-1} (\gamma_b/\gamma)^k. \tag{19}$$

Let $\tau = \max(\delta, \gamma_b/\gamma)$. Then $\tau < 1$ and equation 19 becomes the equation 17

Theorem 4 means that when apply DED-SOS scheme and SOS scheme to OTIS-G, DED-SOS will have a smaller upper bound of error than SOS in k-th iteration. About DED-OPT scheme, let d be the diameter of the factor graph. We have following theorem.

Theorem 5. *In the worst case, to achieve balanced status on OTIS network, DED-OPT has a lower bound $d + 1$ of the number of iteration required. But OPT needs at least $2(d + 1)$ iterations in this case.*

Proof. In the worst case, OPT scheme requires a number of iteration equal to the number of all distinct eigenvalues of Laplace matrix of OTIS topology. But DED-OPT scheme requires iterations equal to all distinct eigenvalues of factor graph. A known fact is that the Laplacian of a graph always has the same number of distinct eigenvalues with its adjacency matrix. The latter has at least $d + 1$ distinct eigenvalues [see[16]]. Another known fact is that OTIS network has diameter $2d + 1$ when factor graph has diameter d [see [11]].

6   Experiments

Here some numerical results help to illustrate the properties of DED-X scheme series and the advantages of these schemes by comparing them with general diffusion schemes. These results are based on some familiar factor network including Hypercube(H_d), Mesh($M_{m \times n}$), Path(P_n), Cycle(C_n) and Complete graph(K_n). Each OTIS-G network constructing from these factor networks consists of 64 nodes. To emphasize on influence of initial load, we experiment with a highly unbalanced as well as a randomly distributed initial load, modeling as following.

- PEAK: One node has a super overweight load of $100 \times n$ and the others are free, with a load 0;
- RAN: $100 \times n$ load items are randomly distributed among n nodes.

We want to compare our new load balancing strategies DED-FOS and DED-OPT with the traditional FOS and OPT methods with respect to speed, stability and flow quality. we did experiments on a mesh network with factor of dimension 3, using initial load distribution PEAK and RAN. The balance process stops when the error $\|w^k - w^l\|_2$ is less than 0.01.

6.1   Convergence Speed

Table 1 shows several diffusion parameters used in X schemes and DED-X schemes, coming from spectral computation of factor network G and corresponding OTIS-G. The symbol G_s is identical with "OTIS-G". All OTIS networks listed have smaller second minimal eigenvalue λ and condition number ρ of Laplacian, larger diffusion norm γ, than their corresponding factor network, which validates the theorems 2 and 3. These results theoretically show that DED-FOS and DED-SOS schemes should converge faster than FOS and SOS because they use the same diffusion parameters with factor network to implement diffusion on OTIS network.

Table 1. Comparison of diffusion parameters of factor networks and corresponding OTIS networks (G_s=OTIS-G)

G	$\lambda_2(G)$	$\lambda_2(G_s)$	$\lambda_m(G)$	$\lambda_m(G_s)$	$\alpha(G)$	$\alpha(G_s)$	$\rho(G)$	$\rho(G_s)$	$\gamma(G)$	$\gamma(G_s)$
H_3	2.0000	0.5857	6.0000	7.4142	0.2500	0.2500	0.3333	0.0790	0.5000	0.8535
$M_{2\times4}$	0.5857	0.2508	5.4142	6.9319	0.3333	0.2874	0.1081	0.0362	0.8047	0.9301
P_8	0.1522	0.0732	3.8478	5.6542	0.5000	0.3492	0.0396	0.0130	0.9239	0.9744
C_8	0.5858	0.2509	4.0000	5.7491	0.4361	0.3333	0.1464	0.0436	0.7445	0.9164
K_8	8.0000	0.8769	8.0000	10.0000	0.1250	0.1839	1.0000	0.0877	0.0000	0.8388

In the following Table 2 we present the results of a number of experiments in order to compare the convergence speed of traditional X schemes and DED-X schemes, started on the PEAK and RAN initial load distribution. As we have proven before, practically, DED-FOS has a evidently smaller number of iterations than traditional FOS scheme. The number of iterations of DED-FOS in the case of PEAK and RAN are almost same. DED-OPT behaves better which almost,compared to existing OPT scheme, halves the number of iterations for both PEAK and RAN, besides in the case of complete graph K_n.

Table 2. Comparison of the number of the iterations of general diffusion schemes X and the hybrid diffusion schemes DED-X, N_X represents the number of iterations

G	load	N_{FOS}	N_{OPT}	OTIS-G	load	N_{FOS}	$N_{DED-FOS}$	N_{OPT}	$N_{DED-OPT}$
H_3	RAN	14	3	OTIS-H_3	RAN	76	37	15	7
	PEAK	16	3		PEAK	77	38	15	7
$M_{2\times4}$	RAN	48	6	OTIS-$M_{2\times4}$	RAN	162	112	42	13
	PEAK	49	6		PEAK	165	114	42	13
P_8	RAN	133	7	OTIS-P_8	RAN	460	306	15	15
	PEAK	134	7		PEAK	462	309	15	15
C_8	RAN	36	4	OTIS-C_8	RAN	134	85	22	9
	PEAK	37	4		PEAK	138	86	22	9
K_8	RAN	1	1	OTIS-K_8	RAN	72	3	4	3
	PEAK	1	1		PEAK	71	3	3	3

6.2   Solution Quality

A known factor (see [3]) is that polynomial based schemes all compute the same flow which is l_2-minimal. This infers that all DED-X schemes have same flows in the first and third stage. Since the second stage, dimension exchange, is based on the initial load of local balanced status, All DED-X schemes product the same flows. So we can conclude that all DED-X schemes compute the same flow, although they are possibly not minimal. Based on this, we only give the flows of DED-OPT on OTIS networks to illustrate the solution quality of DED-X schemes. Table 3 shows that in most cases, the flow of DED-OPT scheme is smaller than the flow of OPT. Sometimes it only a smaller fraction large than

Table 3. Comparison of the flows of general diffusion schemes and the hybrid diffusion schemes

networks	initial load	OPT flows	DED-OPT flows
OTIS-H_3	RAN	3555.3298	3106.9855
	PEAK	4598.9345	4636.0903
OTIS-$M_{2\times4}$	RAN	65804.9817	4970.6308
	PEAK	47213.1788	6279.2174
OTIS-P_8	RAN	263219.98	9064.6780
	PEAK	188852.7152	11299.558
OTIS-C_8	RAN	5394.6648	5648.7938
	PEAK	6127.1514	6437.3907
OTIS-K_8	RAN	2726.9987	2487.1934
	PEAK	3261.9012	3261.9012

the l_2-minimal flow. Specially, the flow of DED-OPT scheme is far smaller than the flow of OPT in the case of OTIS-$M_{2\times4}$ and OTIS-P_8. Therefore, DED-OPT should preferably be applied to practices.

6.3   Stability

As stated in section 1, the criteria of judging the quality of balancing algorithm also includes its numerical stability. However, finding a load balancing scheme with stable iterative procedure and less steps is often not easy. FOS scheme has a good numerical stability but a slow speed. OPT need relatively smaller iterative steps but possible numerical trap. Figure 1 and 2 shows that for OTIS network, DED-FOS schemes are numerically stable and have faster convergence speed than FOS.

Figure 1 shows that DED-FOS is stable in both diffusion stages, with error decreasing monotonously, only a suddenly dropping of error arising in the seconde stage (load exchange) after the error decreasing steadily in the first stage. Due to node loads move over optical links in this stage, this is apparently not

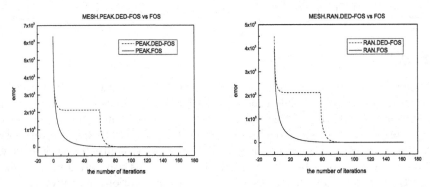

Fig. 1. DED-FOS and FOS on OTIS-$M_{2\times4}$ network, with PEAK and RAN inital load distribution respectively

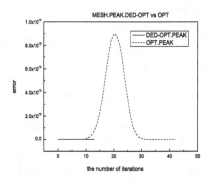 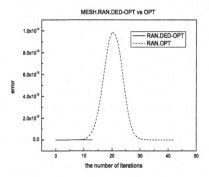

Fig. 2. DED-OPT and OPT on OTIS-$M_{2\times4}$ network, with PEAK and RAN inital load distribution respectively

a problem. The best behavior of DED-X can be observed from Figure 2 where DED-OPT has a much better stability than general OPT. Relative to OPT, numerical problems are almost never observed in DED-OPT and it has the largest error 22294.98367, but OPT with a approximatively error up to 9×10^{13}, which shows that general OPT scheme fails to implement load balancing on OTIS network with large factor network due to numerical problems with the high error number and DED-OPT should be a very proper substitution manner. From Figure 1 and 2, one can discover that distinct initial load distribution RAN and PEAK do not bring forth apparent difference in stability.

7   Conclusion

Although the schemes described in this paper are based on a commonly simple ideal, they should benefit to load balancing on OTIS networks. This work also presents some opportunities for future work. A main focus of ongoing work is to consider if these schemes can be improved to diminish the number of iterations. It is expected that they can be generalized to globally or locally heterogeneous networks since these networks often emerge from many applications in the field of high performance computing.

Acknowledgment. This paper is supported by the Natural Science Foundation of Guangdong Province, China, under Grant No.05011896, and the Natural Science Foundation of Education Department of Guangdong Province, China, under Grant No. Z03080.

References

1. Cybenko, G.: Load balancing for distributed memory multiprocessors. Journal of Parallel and Distributed Computing 7, 279–301 (1989)
2. Muthukrishnan, S., Ghosh, B., Schultz, M.H.: First- and second-order diffusive methods for rapid, coarse, distributed load balancing. Theory of Computing Systems 31, 331–354 (1998)

3. Diekmann, R., Frommer, A., Monien, B.: Efficient schemes for nearest neighbor load balancing. Parallel Computing 25, 789–812 (1999)
4. Elsässer, R., Monien, B., Preis, R.: Diffusion schemes for load balancing on heterogeneous networks. Theory of Computing Systems 35, 305–320 (2002)
5. Elsässer, R., Frommer, A., Monien, B., preis, R.: Optimal and alternating direction load balancing schemes. In: Amestoy, P.R., Berger, P., Daydé, M., Duff, I.S., Frayssé, V., Giraud, L., Ruiz, D. (eds.) Euro-Par 1999. LNCS, vol. 1685, pp. 280–290. Springer, Heidelberg (1999)
6. Elsässer, R., Monien, B., Preis, R., Frommer, A.: Optimal diffusion schemes and load balancing on product graphs. Parallel Processing Letters 14, 61–73 (2004)
7. Elsässer, R., Monien, B., Schamberger, S.: Load Balancing in Dynamic Networks. In: 2004 International Symposium on Parallel Architectures, Algorithms and Networks (ISPAN'04) ispan (2004)
8. Arndt, H.: On finite dimension exchange algorithms. Linear Algebra and its Applications 380, 73–93 (2004)
9. Arndt, H.: Load balancing: Dimension exchange on product graphs. In: Proceedings of IPDPS 2004, IEEE Computer Society Press, Los Alamitos (2004)
10. Golub, G., Varga, R.: Chebyshev semi-iterative methods, successive overrelaxation iterative methods, and second order Richardson iterative methods. In: numer. Math. pp. 147–156 (1961)
11. Day, K., Al-Ayyoub, A.: Topological properties of OTIS-Networks. IEEE Transactions on Parallel and Distributed Systems 13, 359–366 (2002)
12. Parhami, B.: Swapped interconnection networks: Topological, performance, and robustness attributes. Journal of Parallel and Distributed Computing 65, 1443–1452 (2005)
13. Parhami, B.: Introduction to Parallel Processing: Algorithms and Architectures. Plenum Press, New York (1999)
14. Mohar, B.: Some applications of Laplace eigenvalues of graphs. In: Hahn, G., Sabidussi, G. (eds.) Graph Symmetry: Algebraic Methods and Applications. NATO ASI Series C, vol. 497, pp. 225–275. Kluwer, Dordrecht (1997)
15. Chung, F. R. K.: Spectral Graph Theory. In: Regional Conference Series in Mathematics. Vol. 92. American Mathematical Society (1997)
16. Godsil, G.: Algebraic Graph Theory, pp. 279–306. Springer, Heidelberg (2001)

A Dynamic Localized Minimum-Energy Agent Tree-Based Data Dissemination Scheme for Wireless Sensor Networks

Ping Ding and JoAnne Holliday

Computer Engineering Department, Santa Clara University
{pding,jholliday}@scu.edu

Abstract. The problem of efficiently disseminating data from a mobile stimulus (source) to multi-ple mobile users (sinks) in a large-scale sensor network has been challenging. We address this prob-lem by proposing a minimum-energy tree-based data dissemination scheme, *Dynamic Localized Minimum-Energy Agent Tree-Based Scheme* (DLATS). We exploit the fact that sensor nodes are stationary and location-aware. In DLATS, each sensor node finds its *Relative Neighborhood Graph* (RNG) neighbors and a RNG is generated over the whole network. Then, the source broadcasts its position information to all the other nodes using our localized minimum-energy broadcast protocol, *Improved RNG Broadcast Oriented Protocol* (IRBOP). A dynamic agent tree is generated between each source and multiple sinks using our *Shortest Direct Parent First* (SDPF) where the sinks become the agents, e.g., the leaves of the agent tree. Finally, each source uses IRBOP for multicast-ing the stimulus data to the users over the agent tree. We evaluate the performance of DLATS through simulations. Results show DLATS outperforms previously proposed protocols for data dis-semination in large-scale sensor networks.

Keywords: Dynamic Localized, Minimum-Energy, Data Dissemination, Sensor Networks.

1 Introduction and Related Work

Because of the limited power supplies, there are several research issues in such sensor networks: 1) How to efficiently detect stimulus or users; for example, [1] summa-rizes scalable location services and compares their performances. 2) How the sinks collect data from the sources. There are several research issues in this topic: a) How to locate the sources to the sinks or how to locate the sinks to the sources; b) How to report each source's data to multiple sinks; that is, how to do energy-efficient multicast between them; c) How to efficiently reconfigure or regenerate the links between each source and the multiple sinks when either the source or the sinks are reassigned; that is, how to maintain the energy-efficient multicast between them. In this paper, we focus on these three issues. To the best of our knowledge, there has not been any published work that efficiently solves all three problems simultaneously.

H. Jin et al. (Eds.): ICA3PP 2007, LNCS 4494, pp. 433–445, 2007.

To minimize the total energy consumption in broadcasting but still enable a message originating from a source node to reach all the other nodes, the source node can adjust its transmission power. This is called the minimum energy broadcasting problem [2]. Minimum energy broadcasting problem can be solved by topology control protocols which aim to adjust transmission power while preserving strong connectivity of the network. *Relative neighborhood graph* (RNG) has been used in topology control pro-tocol [3]. Cartigny et al. [2] propose a localized minimum-energy broadcasting proto-col, RNG broadcast oriented protocol (RBOP). RBOP broadcasts to one-hop neighbors in a RNG. In this paper, we argue that a less greedy, two-hop broadcast approach where each node is less greedy because it considers the energy expenditure of its neighbors when deciding its own transmit radius. And, we show it save energy.

Li et al. [4] propose a location system to estimate the target position as well as its motion, which takes advantage of the independently calculated time-difference-of-arrival of successive pulses from the targets. In [5], authors give the directed diffusion paradigm to achieve energy saving by selecting paths between the sources and the sinks. In [6], authors propose the two-tier data dissemination (TTDD) scheme where each source needs to generate a grid to tell its position to all other sensors. Sensor nodes located at the grid points work as agents. Then, each sink communicates with the source through the agents. Both of the two algorithms provide multicasting between one source and multiple sinks, however, they do not provide efficient multi-casting and are not efficient when the sources and the sinks are mobile. In [7], authors build a dynamic proxy tree-based data dissemination scheme where it realizes mini-mum-energy multicasting between each source and the sinks based on a centralized algorithm.

Lou et al. [8] perform dominant pruning and partial dominant pruning to reduce broadcast redundancy. Cagalj et al. [9] creates a heuristic, Embedded Wireless Multi-cast Advantage algorithm which realizes a minimum-energy broadcast and takes the advantage of relaying nodes. Wu et al. [10] study how to realize efficient broadcasting using a small set of forwarding nodes. All of the previous algorithms do not guarantee the total consumed energy is within a constant factor of the optimum. Wan et al. [11] have proved that minimum-energy broadcasting based on Euclidean Minimum Span-ning Tree (MST) or MST-based graph consumes energy within a constant factor of the optimum. Since MST cannot be constructed in a localized manner, a localized approx-imation structure of MST, RNG, has been suggested for broadcasting.

The contributions of the paper are: 1) the localized data dissemination scheme from each mobile stimulus to multiple mobile users, *Dynamic Localized Minimum-Energy Agent Tree-Based Scheme*, DLATS; 2) efficient broadcasting via two-hop neighbors, *Improved RBOP*; 3) building an agent tree between each mobile stimulus to multiple mobile users where the energy paths from the agents to the root are the minimum, *Shortest Direct Parent First*, SDPF; 4) fast and low-cost reconfiguration and regenera-tion of the agent tree. The paper is organized as follows: we propose DLATS in Sec-tion 2. We present our performance studies in section 3 and conclude in section 4.

2 Dynamic Localized Minimum-Energy Agent Tree-Based Scheme

2.1 Network Model

We assume that a sensor network has the following properties:
1) Nodes are dispersed in a 2-dimensional space and cannot be recharged after deploy-ment; 2) Nodes are stationary once deployed. Both the stimuli and the users are mobile; 3) Nodes transmit at the same fixed power levels which are dependent on the transmission distance; 4)   Nodes base decisions on local information only; 5) Nodes are location-aware, which can be defined using GPS, signal strength, or direction; 6) The energy consumption among nodes is not constrained to be uniform.

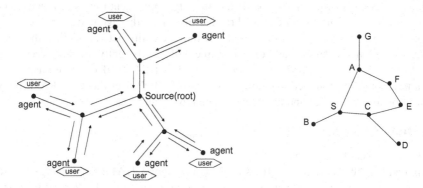

Fig. 1. A dynamic agent tree   **Fig. 2.** A RNG

2.2 Design Objectives

1) The network connectivity is preserved with the use of minimum possible power.This is the most important objective of minimum-energy broadcasting.
2) DLATS is distributed. This is because the network may be composed of thousandsof nodes. It is expensive to know all other node's information. To run DLATS, a nodeonly needs to know its local information.
3) DLATS is not affected by mobility. When either stimuli or users or both of themmove, the minimum-energy broadcasting or multicasting can be guaranteed.
4) All links are bi-directional. For example, there are two nodes u and v in the network.If u can reach v then v can reach u.
5) DLATS expects a node's degree to be small but does not require the node's degreeto be minimal. This is because: a) a small node degree may help to mitigate the hiddennodes problem; b) a small node degree can not guarantee that the graph approximatesthe optimal broadcast structure in terms of the total energy consumption [12].

2.3 DLATS Framework

Due to the dynamic characteristics of the sources and the sinks, it is difficult to maintain a tree that directly connects a source and multiple sinks that are interested in the source, or disseminate data from the source to the sinks. To realize minimum-energy multicasting, we generate a *dynamic agent tree*, which is a subset of RNG, between a source and the sinks. Figure 1 shows a dynamic agent tree between the source and the sinks. The source is the root and the sinks are the leaves in the tree. To generate the tree, a source implements our minimum-energy broadcasting protocol, IRBOP, over the RNG graph. Sink nodes are agents of the mobile users and join the tree to obtain information on behalf of the users. After a sink joins the tree, it becomes an agent. Each node that wants to be part of the tree will find an optimal (minimum-energy) path to the root based on a heuristic algorithm, *Shortest Direct Parent First* (SDPF). After each node finds its optimal path, a dynamic agent tree is generated. The source implements minimum-energy broadcasting over the agent tree. Effectively, this is akin to multicasting to a set of nodes within the entire network. When the users move, the sink nodes change and the agent tree will be efficiently reconfigured based on a localized algorithm, *Inform Direct Parent Only* (IDPO). If the stimulus moves and a new source is assigned, the new source runs IRBOP over the same RNG to tell its position to other nodes and the dynamic agent tree can be easily regenerated.

2.4 DLATS

DLATS consists of five steps.
1) Finding neighbors: each node finds its RNG neighbors; 2) Minimum-energy broad-casting: each source node broadcasts its position information to all other nodes using a minimum-energy broadcast protocol, *Improved RNG broadcast oriented protocol*, IRBOP(A); 3) Dynamic agent tree generating: each agent finds its minimum-energy path to the source using *Shortest Direct Parent First*, SDPF. Only the nodes on the paths are in the agent tree; 4) Minimum-energy Multicasting: each source implements minimum-energy multicasting over the agent tree with a more energy-efficient broad-cast protocol, IRBOP(B); 5) Dynamic agent tree reconfiguration: When the users move so that the sinks change, the dynamic agent tree can be reconfigured using *Inform Direct Parent Only,* IDPO. Once a stimulus moves, a new dynamic agent tree can be efficiently regenerated over the same RNG with a new source.

Notations

Energy Path: It is the cumulative energy consumption from the emitter to the receiver (calculation is in Section 2.4.3).

Energy Consumption (EC): The energy consumed by a node considers the energy consumption from the root to the node along the energy path. The EC of the receiver is equal to the EC of the emitter plus the energy path from the emitter to the receiver. The EC of the root is zero. Assume a node is u, then its EC is EC(u).

Direct Parent: It is a node's one-hop neighbor in the RNG. When a node looks for its direct parent, it treats its one-hop neighbors as the emitters and recalculates its EC. The one which makes the node's EC be the least will be the node's direct parent.

Two-hop Neighbor: Assume a node A has a neighbor B on the RNG, and B has a neighbor C on the RNG which is not A's neighbor. We define C to be A's two-hop neighbor on the RNG if C is inside A's maximum transmission range, R.

Minimum Transmission Range (Rtr_r): This transmission range is the minimum energy range large enough to reach a node's one- or two-hop neighbors in the RNG ($Rtr \leq R$, calculation is in Section 2.4.3).

2.4.1 Finding RNG Neighbors

Since sensor nodes are stationary, the RNG neighbor finding can be implemented by off-line. Once the RNG neighbors have been chosen, they will never be changed. A node can find its RNG neighbors as in [2].

In this paper, if a node v is node u's one-hop RNG neighbor, then the edge uv belongs to RNG. We call the induced RNG over the network RNG and the induced MST over the network MST. After a RNG is generated, a node finds its one-hop neigh-bors in the RNG, exchanges its one-hop neighbor information with its neighbors, and records its two-hop neighbors as in Table 1.   After a node records its one and two hop neighbor information, these will never be updated. In the rest of the paper, a node's neighbors means the neighbors in the RNG.

2.4.2 Minimum-Energy Broadcasting Via IRBOP(A)

In this section, we explain our *improved RNG broadcast oriented protocol,* IRBOP(A), that is used by the sources to broadcast their position information to all other nodes in the network. In Section 2.4.5, we will discuss IRBOP(B) for sending multicast messages to those nodes (sinks) who are interested in subsequent informa-tion that the sources provide.

IRBOP(A) is a minimum-energy broadcasting protocol which is based on the algo-rithm RBOP proposed in [2]. We summarize RBOP as follows. A source node trans-mits a broadcast message with the minimum-energy to reach all of its one-hop neighbors in the RNG. Those neighbors apply neighbor elimination scheme [13] to decide whether their one-hop neighbors in the RNG received the message or not.

Table 1. Node and its Neighbors in a RNG

node name	one-hop neighbor	two-hop neighbor
S	A, C, B	A, B, C, D, E, F
A	G, F, S	G, F, E, S, B, C
B	S	S, A, C
C	D, E, S	D, E, F, S, B, A
D	C	C, S, E
E	C, F	C, D, S, F, A
F	A, E	A, G, S, C, E
G	A	A, F

Those neighbors respectively forward the message using the minimum-energy to reach all their one-hop neighbors which have not received the message previously. In this way, the message from the source is broadcast to all other nodes. RBOP saves energy using only localized information. However, we have noted that additional savings can be realized with the message sent to two-hop neighbors directly without relaying. In IRBOP(A), a broadcast node needs to calculate its R_{tr} and decide whether to reach its one- or two-hop neighbors. A node which we call the emitter should follow the follow ing rules to determine its *Minimum Transmission Range*, R_{tr}:

A) To guarantee connectivity, the emitter transmits the broadcast message using theminimum-energy to reach all its one-hop neighbors which have not received the broad-cast message previously as RBOP does, call this transmission range R_1, and *Rtr=R1*.

B) To save energy, the emitter considers transmission to its two-hop neighbors directly without relaying by its one-hop neighbors. When the emitter finds an one-hop neigh-bor has not received the message, the emitter sends a HELLO message to the one-hop neighbor, say N, and asks for its R_1, here, we call it R_2. N gives both R_2 and the fur-thest node name to the emitter where N calculates R_2 based on Rule A. If N's furthest one-hop neighbor, say M, is not the emitter's two-hop neighbor, then the emitter gives up considering two-hop broadcasting in M. If M is the emitter's two-hop neighbor, then the emitter considers transmission to M directly. Let the distance from the emitter to M be R_3. If $R_3^2 < R_1^2 + R_2^2$, then it is more efficient to let *Rtr* be R_3. So, N does not need to forward the message to its one-hop neighbors where the emitter transmits to them directly. The emitter checks each of its one-hop neighbors which have not received the message previously and chooses the maximum R_3 to be its *Rtr* which should be equal or larger than R_1.

Let us consider a graph shown in Figure 2 (To compare with RBOP [2], Figure 2 is from [2]) which consists of RNG edges. Table 1 shows their relations. S is the emitter. S's one-hop neighbors are A, B, and C. S's two-hop neighbors are A, B, C, D, E and F. S calculates its R_1, $\|SA\|$ based on Rule A. Since C is a neighbor and has not received the message (S has not sent it yet), S asks C what is its R_2. C responds with the length of $\|CD\|$ and D. After S finds D is its two-hop neighbor, S calculates $\|SA\|^2 + \|CD\|^2$ and $\|SD\|^2$. Since $\|SA\|^2 + \|CD\|^2 > \|SD\|^2$, D satisfies two-hop broadcasting. Thus, S sets R_{tr} to be $\|SD\|$

Since B does not have any other neighbors, S skips B. S continues to check with node A. Because G is outside transmission range of S, G is not S's two-hop neighbor. S gives up two-hop broadcasting to G. The reason is as follows: We assume C, D, and E have already received the message. We also assume $\|SF\|^2 < \|SA\|^2 + \|AF\|^2$, and $\|AG\| > \|AF\|$. If S applies two-hop broadcasting to F, then S lets *Rtr* be $\|SF\|$. When A receives the message, A still has to forward it to G with $\|AG\|$ and . F, will AGreceive it also. Thus, the total energy consumption is $\|SF\|^2 + \|AG\|^2$ instead of $\|SA\|^2 + \|AG\|^2$ which is total energy consumption using RBOP (based on the definition of RNG, $\|SF\| > \|AS\|$). Finally, S decides its R_{tr} to be $\|SD\|$.

Let us call the graph induced by R_{tr} on the network to be RNG . Then, RNG is the subgraph of *RNG* where *RNG* consists of RNG plus additional edges added by R_{tr}. Next, we introduce two rules to calculate *Energy Path*: A) When the broadcast message is from a one-hop neighbor, the energy path is the square of the Euclidean distance between them. B) When the broadcast message is from a two-hop neighbor, the receiver needs to cal-culate its energy path from all of the possible energy paths from the emitter to it inside two-hops. The receiver calculates the energy paths from the emitter to the receiver directly which is the square of the Euclidean distance between them, and all of the energy paths from the emitter to its one-hop neighbors plus from the one-hop neigh-bors to the receiver. The energy path of the receiver is equal to the least one.

For example, in Figure 2, when S is the emitter, the energy path from S to C is $\| SC \|^2$. The EC(C) is equal to EC(S) plus $\| SC \|^2$. When F receives broadcast message from S, F calculates $\| SA \|^2 + \| AF \|^2$ and $\| SF \|^2$. Assume $\| SA \|^2 + \| AF \|^2 > \| SF \|^2$. then the energy path from S to F is $\| SF \|^2$. Thus, EC(F) is equal to EC(S) plus $\| SF \|^2$.

Algorithm:

1. The source node emits the message with R_{tr} which is calculated by R_{tr} calculation Rule A or B. The source node also includes its EC in the message, which is zero.

2. When a node receives a new broadcast message either from its one-hop or from its two-hop neighbors, the node accepts the message:

2.1 The node calculates its energy path and EC.

2.2 The node applies neighbor elimination scheme to eliminate neighbors to whom it does not need to forward the message. The message will not be forwarded if the node's one-hop neighbors have all received it.

2.3 The node checks its one-hop neighbors:

a)If there are some one-hop neighbors have not received the message, then the node calculates its R_{tr} and forwards the message with R_{tr}

b)If all of its one-hop neighbors have received the message, the node will not forward it.

3. When a node receives a new broadcast message from its non-neighbors, the node ignores the message.

4. When a node receives an already received message:

4.1 The node ignores the message if it has already forwarded it.

4.2 The node applies neighbor elimination scheme to eliminate neighbors to whom it needs to forward the message; the message is ignored if the node's one-hop neighbors have all received it.

4.3 Otherwise, the node calculates R_{tr} and forwards the message with R_{tr}

Fig. 3. IRBOP(A)

Next, we explain how IRBOP(A) works. The objective of broadcasting from the source is to help the agents find their paths to the source, so, each node can only accept broadcast messages from its one or two hop neighbors. Otherwise, they will not be able to find their direct parent in the next step using SDPF. As in [2], we apply *neigh-bor elimination scheme* to one-hop neighbors in the RNG.

For example, in Figure 2, S is the emitter which broadcasts with R_{tr} equal to $\|SD\|$ and includes its EC in the broadcast message (EC(S) is zero). After B receives the message, it checks R_{tr} against the position of its one-hop neighbors. Since S is the only one and is the emitter, B eliminates S, calculates EC(B), and then it stops. After C receives the message, it calculates EC(C) also. Since C deduces that S, E, and D have already received the message, C eliminates them and stops. F accepts the message because S is its two-hop neighbor via A. Then, it calculates EC(F). Since all of its one-hop neighbors have received the message, F will not forward it. D and E do the same as F. A calculates EC(A) and checks its one-hop neighbors. A finds that G is the only one left. A forwards the message to G with R_{tr} equal to $\|AG\|$ and includes EC(A). After G receives the message, it calculates EC(G), checks its one-hop neighbors, elim-inates A for transmission, and stops. The broadcast is received by all of the nodes and only two transmissions were needed with a total cost of $\|SD^2\| + \|AG^2\|$.

Figure 3 is IRBOP(A). The cost of the broadcasting is the total energy consumption for sending broadcast messages and the HELLO messages. During IRBOP(A), the complexity of the HELLO message exchange for each node is O(1). Compared with RBOP, IRBOP(A) consumes extra energy in broadcast nodes' one-hop neighbors sending HELLO message to their two-hop neighbors. However, compared to the energy consumed in sending broadcast message, the energy consumed in sending HELLO is little.

2.4.3 Generating the Dynamic Agent Tree

After the source broadcasts its information, all other nodes know where it is. The nodes nearest the users become the sinks (agents). Those agents need to find their paths to the source. We propose a heuristic algorithm, *Shortest Direct Parent First (SDPF)*, to find the paths from those agents to the source. When each agent finds its path to the source, a dynamic agent tree is generated where the tree is composed of RNG edges.

Shortest Direct Parent First (SDPF): To save energy, each agent should find the minimum-energy path to the source. SDPF is a heuristic algorithm which works as fol-lows: 1) A node looking for its direct parent broadcasts a HELLO message to its one-hop neighbors and asks for their EC. 2) After receiving EC from any of its one-hop neigh-bors, the node recalculates its EC to the source. The node's updated EC is its neigh-bor's EC plus the square of Euclidean distance between the one-hop neighbor and the node (energy path between them). 3) The node picks a one-hop neighbor as its direct parent which makes the EC of the node be the least among all its one-hop neighbors. Ties are broken by the node ID. Then, the node sends a HELLO message to inform the neighbor. 4) The direct parent records the node in its children list in the tree. If the direct parent does not have a direct parent, then it goes to step 1. The process continues until the source is found. 5) When all agents find their paths to the source, the dynamic agent tree is completed. The tree consists of all of the agents and their paths to the source, and all edges are RNG edges.

Once a node's direct parent is found, the direct parent will not be changed until the source moves. The cost of generating the dynamic agent tree is the total energy consumption for finding all agents' paths to the source.

2.4.4 Minimum-Energy Multicasting Via IRBOP(B)

After the dynamic agent tree has been generated, the source will multicast over the agent tree using the algorithm IRBOP(B). Note that IRBOP(A) is designed to help build the agent tree whereas IRBOP(B) is designed to broadcast efficiently. IRBOP(B) is the same as IRBOP(A) except for the following. In IRBOP(B), a node can accept a message sent from a non-neighbor (i.e., not one- or two-hop neighbor) in the RNG. A node does not need to calculate its EC, and its R_{tr} is calculated as IRBOP(A). When a node receives a broadcast message from a non-neighbor in RNG, as in [2], the node will not forward the message immediately; it will wait until the next time frame (depending on the MAC protocol in use) to decide its R_{tr} and forward the message with R_{tr}. In this way, the source multicasts over the agent tree using IRBOP(B) within the RNG.

2.4.5 Dynamic Agent Tree Reconfiguration

There are two cases in which the agent tree needs to be reconfigured, that is, the users move and the stimulus moves. In the first case, when the users move, some nodes are no longer sinks so they need to leave and be taken off the dynamic agent tree and other nodes become sinks and need to join the tree. We propose an algorithm, *Inform Direct Parent Only* (IDPO), to manage the sinks joining and leaving. In the second case, since the sensor nodes are stationary, the RNG does not need to be regenerated. After a stimulus moves, it broadcasts its position over the same RNG. Thus, a new agent tree can be efficiently regenerated.

Joining (IDPO): When a new user comes, the node nearest to it becomes an agent (sink). The agent does the following to join the existing dynamic agent tree: 1) The sink node looks for its direct parent among its one-hop neighbors in the RNG using SDPF. After finding its direct parent, the node sends a HELLO message to inform it. 2) The direct parent writes down the node in its children list in the tree and looks for its direct parent if it does not have one. 3) The process continues until some direct parent is in the agent tree or the source is reached. Thus, the new path from the new agent to the agent tree is added.

The cost of adding the new sink is the total energy consumption from the time of the new sink sending HELLO messages to find its direct parent to the time of the sink being added to the tree. If a node had been added to the tree, then it can send a HELLO message to its old direct parent directly and inform it of its joining.

Leaving (IDPO): When an user leaves, the sink should be removed from the tree. It does the following: 1) The node sends a HELLO message to its direct parent and informs its leaving; 2) The direct parent (not the root) checks its children list in the tree. If the node is the only one in the children list, the direct parent removes the node from its children list in the agent tree and sends a HELLO message to inform its direct parent. And then, this step is repeated. If the children list is not empty, the direct parent removes the node from its children list but will not inform its direct parent any more.

The cost of deleting an agent (sink) is the energy consumed by nodes sending HELLO messages along the path to be removed from the tree. The complexity of HELLO message exchange for each node is O(1) both in joining and leaving.

3 Performance Evaluation

In this section, we present several simulation results to demonstrate the performance of the minimum-energy tree-based data dissemination scheme, *Dynamic Localized Minimum-Energy Agent Tree-Based Scheme* (DLATS). And, we focus on energy consumption. Our simulations will evaluate three parts: 1) the effectiveness of IRBOP(B); 2) the effectiveness of tree generation with IRBOP(A) and shortest direct parent first (SDPF); 3) the effectiveness of inform direct parent only (IDPO). The simulations are conducted in the following settings: 300 nodes are randomly distributed in a 1000 × 1000m^2 . Each value shown in the following figures is averaged over 50 simula-tions. In our calculations, if the energy consumption includes both broadcast message (data packet) and HELLO message (control packet), we consider both of them.

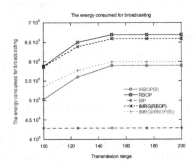
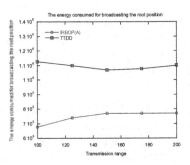

Fig. 4. Energy consumption for broadcasting   **Fig. 5.** Energy for broadcasting root position

3.1 The Effectiveness of IRBOP(B)

We randomly pick a node as a source node and let it broadcast to all other nodes once every second for 20 seconds. We vary a node's transmission range from 100 to 200m. Figure 4 shows energy consumed by different broadcast algorithms. To evaluate the effectiveness of IRBOP(B), we compare the energy consumption in IRBOP(B) with RBOP[2], BIP[14], IMRG(RBOP), and IMRG(IRBOP(B)). With IRBOP(B), a node can accept message from non-neighbors in the RNG. RBOP broadcasts to only one-hop neighbors. IMRG(RBOP) means the graph is generated by IMRG [12] and broadcast algorithm is RBOP. IMRG is a topology control algorithm which is used to generate low-weight approximate MST [12]. IMRG(IRBOP(B)) means the graph is generated by IMRG and broadcast algorithm is IRBOP(B). Since

BIP is a centralized algorithm, it consumes the least energy and is not affected by the change of node's transmission range. IRBOP(B) consumes less energy than RBOP. This is because IRBOP(B) broadcasts to two-hop neighbors directly when doing so will save more energy than relaying. IMRG(IRBOP(B)) consumes more energy than IRBOP(B). This is because the low-weight approximate MST graph can not guarantee the total energy consumption in the broadcasting is less than RNG. IMRG(IRBOP(B)) consumes less energy than IMRG(RBOP). This is because IRBOP(B) considers its two-hop neigh-bors in calculation its minimum broadcasting energy.

3.2 The Effectiveness of IRBOP(A) and SDPF

To evaluate the effectiveness of IRBOP(A) and shortest direct parent first (SDPF), we compare the energy consumption for: 1) broadcasting a source position using IRBOP(A) with generating grid using TTDD [6]; 2) looking for the paths from the sinks to the root using SDPF with using TTDD; and 3) multicasting over the agent tree using IRBOP(B) where each agent has the optimal path to the root (IRBOP(B, with O)), multicasting over the agent tree using IRBOP(B) where each agent doesnot have the optimal path to the root (IRBOP(B, without O)), with multicasting using TTDD.

Figure 5 compares the energy consumed for broadcasting the source position using IRBOP(A) with building the grid using TTDD. In the figure, TTDD consumes much more energy than IRBOP(A) to inform other nodes the source position. This is because IRBOP(A) broadcasts over a RNG. Figure 6 shows the energy consumed for looking for the paths. We change the number of the sinks (agents) from 1, 5, 10 to 15 in the net work. As shown in Figure 6, SDPF saves a lot of energy compared with using TTDD. This is because SDPF is processed in a RNG.

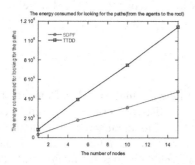
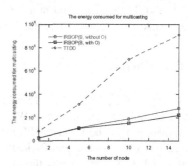

Fig. 6. Energy consumed for finding the paths **Fig. 7.** Energy conumed for multicasting

Figure 7 shows the energy consumed for multicasting over the agent tree using IRBOP(B) with optimal path to the root, IRBOP(B) without optimal path to the root, and with TTDD. The number of the sinks is 1, 5, 10, and 15. TTDD consumed much more energy than the two others in multicasting over the sinks. In IRBOP(B, without O), during the building of the agent tree, each agent treats the one-hop neighbor which sends it the broadcast message as its direct parent; if the broadcast message is sent from a two-hop neighbor, then an one-hop neighbor between them will be the node's direct parent. IRBOP(B, with O) consumes less energy than IRBOP(B, without O). When the number of sinks is 1 or 5, the IRBOP(B, with O) consumes around 5% less energy than IRBOP(B, without O).

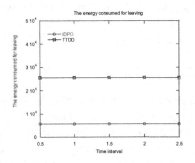

Fig. 8. Energy consumed for leaving

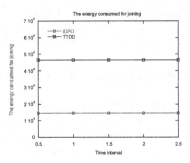

Fig. 9. Energy consumed for joining

3.3 The Effectiveness of Inform Direct Parent Only

To evaluate the effectiveness of IDPO, we compare the energy consumption of IDPO with TTDD in : 1)leaving; 2) joining. Figure 8 compares the energy consumed for leaving using IDPO with TTDD. The x-axis is the time interval, which is 0.5, 1, 1.5, 2, and 2.5 m. The number of total sinks in the network is 15 and there is one mobile sink which is moving at speed of 2.5m/s. As shown in the figure, IDPO con-sumed much less energy than TTDD for leaving. Figure 9 compares the energy con-sumed for joining using IDPO with TTDD. The x-axis is the time interval which is 0.5, 1, 1.5, 2, and 2.5 m. The total number of sinks in the network is 15 and there is one mobile sink which is moving with 2.5m/s.

4 Conclusion

In this paper, we propose DLATS which can efficiently multicast data from a mobile source to multiple mobile sinks. We also propose IRBOP to solve minimum-energy broadcasting over the RNG, SDPF to let a sink find its minimum energy path to the source, and IDPO to energy efficiently reconfigurate the agent tree. Simulations dem-onstrate DLATS outperforms the previous localized solutions for mobile node data dissemination for large-scale sensor networks.

References

[1] Das, S.M., Pucha, H., Hu, Y.C.: Performance Comparison of Scalable Location Services for Geographic Ad Hoc Routing, IEEE Infocom (2005)
[2] Cartigny, J., Simplot, D., Stojmenovic, I.: Localized Minimum-Energy Broadcasting in Ad-Hoc Networks, IEEE Infocom (2003)

[3] Banerjee, S., Misra, A.: Minimum energy paths for reliable communication in multi-hop wireless networks, In: Proc. Annual Workshop on Mobile and Ad Hoc Networking and Computing (MobiHoc'02), Lausane, Switzerland (2002)

[4] Li, T., Ekpenyong, A., Huang, Y.F.: A Location System Using Asynchronous Distributed Sensors, IEEE Infocom (March 2004)

[5] Intanagonwiwat, C., Govindan, R., Estrin, D.: Directed Diffusion: A Scalable and Robust Communication, Mobicom'00 (August 2000)

[6] Ye, F., Luo, H., Cheng, J., Lu, S., Zhang, L.: A Two-Tier Data Dissemination Model for Large-scale Wireless Sensor Networks, ACM International Conference on Mobile Computing and Networking (MOBICOM'02), pp. 148–159 (September 2002)

[7] Zhang, W., Cao, G., La Porta, T.: Dynamic Proxy Tree-Based Data Dissemination Schemes for Wireless Sensor Networks, IEEE International Conference on Mobile Ad-hoc and Sensor Systems (MASS) (2004)

[8] Lou, W., Wu, J.: On Reducing Broadcast Redundancy in Ad Hoc Wireless Networks, IEEE Transactions on Mobile Computing (2002)

[9] Cagalj, M., Hubaux, J.P., Enz, C.: Minimum-Energy Broadcast in All-Wireless Networks: NP-Completeness and Distribution Issues, Mobicom'02, September 23-26, Atlanta, Georgia (2002)

[10] Wu, J., Dai, F.: Mobility Management and Its Applications in Efficient Broadcasting in Mobile Ad Hoc Neworks, IEEE Network (July-August, 2004)

[11] Wan, P.J., Calinescu, G., Frieder, O., Li, X.Y.: Minimum-energy broadcast routing in static ad hoc wireless networks, In: IEEE Infocom 2001, Anchorage, Alaska, (April 2001)

[12] Li, X.Y., Wang, Y., Song, W.Z.: Applications of k-Local MST for Topology Control and Broadcasting in Wireless Ad Hoc Networks. IEEE Transaction on Parallel and Distributed Systems 15(12), 1057–1069 (2004)

[13] Peng, W., Lu, X.: On the Reduction of Broadcast Redundancy in Mobile Ad Hoc Networks,'. In: Proc. Annual Workshop on Mobile and Ad Hoc Networking and Computing (Mobi-Hoc'2000), Boston, Massachusetts, USA (2000)

[14] Banerjee, S., Misra, A., Yeo, J., Agrawala, A.: Energy-Efficient Broadcast and Multicast Trees for Reliable Wireless Communication, Journal of Wireless Networks (WINET) (2002)

THIN: A New Hierarchical Interconnection Network-on-Chip for SOC

Baojun Qiao[1,2], Feng Shi[1], and Weixing Ji[1]

[1] School of Computer Science and Technology, Beijing Institute of Technology,
100081 Beijing, China
[2] Institute of Data and Knowledge Engineering, Henan University,
475001 Kaifeng, Henan, China
{paul2004,bitsf,pass}@bit.edu.cn

Abstract. On-chip communication architectures can have a great influence on the speed and area of System-on-Chip (SOC) designs. A new chip design paradigm called Network-on-Chip (NOC) offers a promising architectural choice for future SOC. Focusing on decreasing node degree, reducing links and shortening diameter, a new NOC, named Triple-based Hierarchical Interconnection Network (THIN), is presented in this paper. The topology of THIN is very simple and it has obviously hierarchical, symmetric and scalable characteristic. The network properties and zero-load latency were studied and compared with 2-D mesh and Hypercube. The results show THIN is superior to 2-D mesh and Hypercube to construct interconnection network for SOC, when the network size is not very large. A new tree-based multicast routing algorithm in THIN is proposed. Thorough analyses and experiments based on different multicast implementation schemes are conducted. The results do confirm the advantage of our scheme over unicast-based and path-based multicast schemes.

Keywords: System-on-Chip, Network-on-Chip, network topology, multicast.

1 Introduction

Continued progress in silicon technology now allows future System-on-Chip (SOC) to integrate from several dozens to hundreds of cores in a single billion-transistor chip [1], [2]. With the trend towards highly integrated SOC designs with many on-chip processing resources, the on-chip communication is soon becoming the bottleneck. Classical on-chip communication architecture uses a traditional Time-Division Multiplexed (TDM) bus, such as IBM Core Connect [3] and ARM AMBA [4]. Bus-based architecture suffers from the clear bottleneck of the share media used for the transmission. The bus allows only one communication at a time, all the cores in the system share its bandwidth, and its operating frequency decreases with the system growth.

Network on Chip (NOC), a new chip design paradigm concurrently proposed by many research groups [2], [5], [6] is expected to be an important architectural choice for future SOC. Using a network to replace global wiring has advantages of structure, performance and modularity [7]. Different network topologies were thoroughly studied

H. Jin et al. (Eds.): ICA3PP 2007, LNCS 4494, pp. 446–457, 2007.
© Springer-Verlag Berlin Heidelberg 2007

by Daniel Wiklund and Dake Liu from a theoretical perspective resulting in the conclusion that the 2-D mesh is most suitable for on-chip networks [8].

In this paper, we propose a new on-chip interconnection architecture: Triple-based Hierarchical Interconnection Network (THIN). THIN is a particular case of the WK-recursive topology [9][10]. The topology of THIN is very simple and it has obviously hierarchical, symmetric and scalable characteristic. The network properties and zero-load latency of THIN are studied and compared with 2-D mesh and Hypercube. The results show that THIN is generally preferable to 2-D mesh and Hypercube to construct interconnection network for SOC, when there are not too many cores. Furthermore, THIN retains the ease of multicast routing for its hierarchy.

The remainder of this paper is organized as follows. Section 2 describes the topology of THIN and nodes addressing scheme. The network properties of THIN are studied and compared with 2-D mesh and Hypercube in section 3. Section 4 compares the zero-load latency of THIN and 2-D mesh. In section 5, we present a new tree-based multicast algorithm in THIN, TRMA (Triple-tree Restricted Multicast Algorithm). Section 6 summarizes the results and concludes the directions for future research.

2   Triple-Based Hierarchical Interconnection Network

2.1   Topology and Construction of THIN

Focus on decreasing node degree, reducing links and shortening diameter, this paper presents a new on-chip network, called Triple-based Hierarchical Interconnection Network, which is a hierarchical, symmetric and scalable interconnection architecture. Figure 1 shows the topology of THIN. As shown in Fig. 1(a), we define a single node as a level 0 THIN. A level 1 THIN can be constructed by connecting three nodes with three communication channels and then forming a triangle, as shown in Fig. 1(b). The level 1 THIN is the base component to form any level THIN.

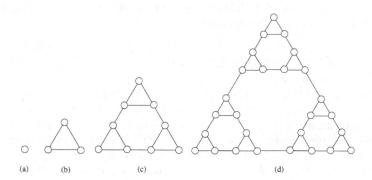

(a)   (b)   (c)   (d)

Fig. 1. The topology of THIN: (a) level 0 THIN; (b) level 1 THIN; (c) level 2 THIN; (d) level 3 THIN

THIN is easily scalable and the constructing process is: replacing the node of level 1 THIN with lower level THIN to structure a higher one, reiterating this process, we can get any higher level THIN, illustrated in Fig. 2.

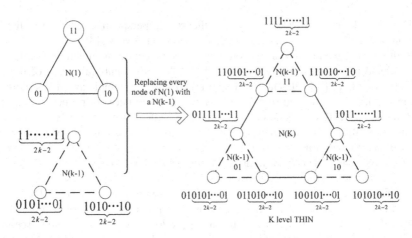

Fig. 2. The construction of level k THIN

The topology of THIN is very simple and the node degree is low. THIN has obviously hierarchical, symmetric and scalable characteristic. The nodes in the lowest hierarchy are fully connected, while other hierarchies have relatively less links and thus the complexity of network is reduced and the silicon cost is decreased.

2.2 Hierarchical Address-Encoding Scheme

In order to quickly and accurately locate a node in THIN, the hierarchical address-encoding scheme is proposed which fully applies the hierarchical characteristic of THIN. The scheme not only describes how to address single node, but also defines the rule to group some nodes in THIN.

Definition 1. The basic addressing set of nodes in THIN is BC, $BC = \{01, 10, 11\}$.

Since the construction of THIN is an iterated process, the node addressing of THIN is also an iterated process. The scheme is:

(i) when $k = 1$, there are only three nodes in $N(k)$ and everyone can be marked with 2 bits symbol b_1b_0, $b_1b_0 \in BC$. 00 can be used as a group-code to denote all nodes of the network, as shown in Fig. 3(a).

(ii) Suppose $N(k-1)$ has been addressed. Then $N(k)$ can be constituted by three $N(k-1)$. Every node of $N(k)$ can be addressed as $2k$ bits by appending the node code of $N(k-1)$ behind the nodes code of $N(1)$ whose nodes are taken place by $N(k-1)$, as illustrated in Fig. 2. Figure 3(b) illustrates a level 3 THIN, which contains 27 nodes.

(iii) Let the code of nodes in $N(k)$ be labeled as $b_{2k-1}b_{2k-2}...b_{2i-1}b_{2i-2}...b_1b_0$. If there exists i ($1 \leq i \leq k$), where $b_{2i-1}b_{2i-2}=00$, then the code is a group-code. This group-code represents a set of nodes composed of whose address can be obtained from $b_{2k-1}b_{2k-2}...b_{2i-1}b_{2i-2}...b_1b_0$ by replacing $b_{2i-1}b_{2i-2}$ with 01, 10 and 11.

Rule (i) and (ii) designate the single node addressing scheme of THIN, and (iii) accounts for how to distinguish between single node and group nodes and how to construct individual code from a group-code.

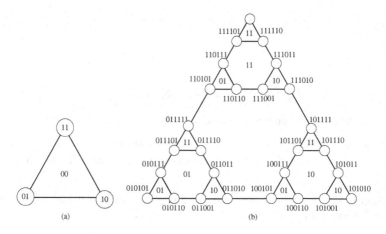

Fig. 3. The address encoding scheme of THIN: (a) level 1 THIN; (b) level 3 THIN

3   Network Properties of THIN

An interconnection network can be mainly characterized by three factors: network degree, number of links and diameter. This section addresses these principle properties of THIN and compares it with 2-D mesh and Hypercube. In the following, we first introduce the definitions and notations of these properties.

Definition 2. An *on-chip interconnection network* I is a strongly connected directed multigraph, $I = G(V, C)$. The vertices of the multigraph V represent the set of cores. The arcs of the multigraph C represent the set of communication channels. We use $n(i)$ to represent the node whose address is i. $P_{i,j}$ is used to represent the path from $n(i)$ to $n(j)$, and $M(i)$ denotes a message which destination address is i.

Let V_k denotes the node set of a level k THIN and N denotes the number of   nodes of the network such that

$$N=|V_k|=3^k .\tag{1}$$

Definition 3. Given a vertex i of a graph G, the number of channels connecting that node to its neighbors is called the degree of i, denoted by d_i. The maximum over the degrees of all nodes of G is called the network degree and is denoted by d. By definition,

$$d = \max(d_i) .\tag{2}$$

Let d_{THIN} denotes the network degree of a level k THIN,

$$d_{THIN} = 3 .\tag{3}$$

Definition 4. L_k is used to denote the number of links in a level k THIN.

According to the constructing process of THIN, the number of links in a level k THIN can be represented by (4):

$$\begin{cases} L_1 = 3 \\ L_k = 3L_{k-1} + 3 \end{cases} \quad (4)$$

From (4) we can know:

$$L_k = 3 \times (3^k - 1)/2 = 3 \times (N-1)/2, \quad (5)$$

where N represents the number of nodes in THIN.

Definition 5. A path $(P_{i,j})$ between two vertices i and j of a graph G is a sequence i_1, i_2, $\cdots$, i_k of vertices such that pairs of consecutive vertices are adjacent while $i_1=i$ and $i_k =j$.

Definition 6. Given two vertices i and j of a graph G, we call the distance between i and j the length of a shortest $P_{i,j}$ and we denote it by $D_{i,j}$.

Definition 7. The diameter of a graph G, denoted by D_G, is the maximum of the distance $D_{i,j}$ over all pairs of vertices of G. By the definition,

$$D_G = \max(D_{i,j}) . \quad (6)$$

Let $D_{THIN(k)}$ denotes the diameter of a level k THIN. Following the constructing process of THIN, $D_{THIN(k)}$ can be represented as equation (7)

$$\begin{cases} D_{THIN(1)} = 1 \\ D_{THIN(k)} = 2D_{THIN(k-1)} + 1 \end{cases} \quad (7)$$

From (7), we can know that:

$$D_{THIN(k)} = 2^k - 1 = 2^{\log_3^N} - 1. \quad (8)$$

Table 1 compares the network properties of the proposed THIN with 2-D mesh and Hypercube, where N denotes the number of nodes in network. It can be seen that the network degrees of THIN and 2-D mesh are constant and furthermore the degree of THIN is lower. Fixed node degree cannot increase the network interface overhead with the network growth and can facilitate the VLSI implementations and network growth. The lower node degree can achieve wider bandwidth than do higher one when the channel is limited by wire density.

Table 1. Comparison of topology properties of three interconnection networks

Type of net-work	Network degree	Number of links	Diameter
THIN	3	$3 \times (N-1)/2$	$2^{\log_3^N} - 1$
2-D mesh	4	$2(N - \sqrt{N})$	$2(\sqrt{N} - 1)$
Hypercube	$\log_2^N$	$\dfrac{N \log_2^N}{2}$	$\log_2^N$

The number of links is used to represent the cost and complexity of a network. When the nodes of a network increase, the links should increase in the linear model in order to minimize the connect cost. Fig. 4 shows the links of THIN, 2-D mesh and Hypercube in different scale. The links of THIN are the fewest when they have the same network size. This is very important for constructing NOC, because the fewer the number of links is, the less the chip resource will be cost.

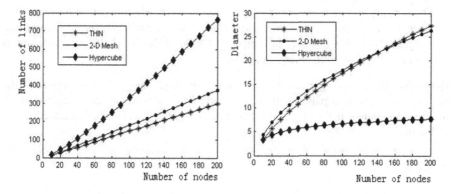

Fig. 4. Comparison of network links   Fig. 5. Comparison of network diameter

The diameter is one of important parameters for interconnection network, and it impacts the communication delay between nodes. In a packet switching network, the diameter is always required to be as short as possible. The diameters of THIN, 2-D mesh and Hypercube in different scale are shown in Fig. 5. The diameter of Hypercube is shortest and the diameter of THIN is shorter than 2-D mesh when the network size is not very large. Though the diameter of Hypercube is the most optimal, the node degree is not fixed, the links is more and the structure is too complex. So Hypercube is seldom used to construct interconnection network for SOC.

The comparison results show that when there are not too many cores, THIN is a better candidate for constructing the interconnection network for SOC, taking into account the node degree, number of links and diameter.

4 Latency of THIN

To evaluate an interconnection network, the network latency must be taken into account. This section mainly compares the zero-load latency between THIN and 2-D mesh.

In [11], a zero-load latency model is presented for wormhole switching networks. Suppose the message contains L-bit data. The phit size and flit size are assumed to be equivalent and equal to the physical data channel width of W bits. The routing header is assumed to be 1 flit; thus the message size is $L+W$ bits. The latency to transfer the message in the network is:

$$T = D_{avg}(t_r + t_s + t_w) + \max(t_s, t_w)\lceil \frac{L}{W} \rceil, \tag{9}$$

where t_r is the time spent by the router to make a routing decision; t_s is the intra-router or switching delay; and t_w is the inter-router delay (the propagation delay across the wires of an external channel). L/W is the packet payload and when addresses and data must be transmitted.

The first expression in (9) computes the latency to transfer the packet header, while the second one determines the time spent by the packet payload to reach the destination node following the header in a pipelined fashion. In this paper, D_{avg} is taken as the average distance of the interconnection network.

Definition 8. The average distance of a interconnection network is the result of the sum of all the minimal path length between any two nodes in the network dividing by the total number of paths [12] and we denote it by D_{avg}. D_{avg} can be calculated as the following equation:

$$D_{avg} = \sum_{i=0}^{D_G} i \times \rho(i), \tag{10}$$

where D_G represents the diameter, and $\rho(i)$ denotes the probability of the message which transmission distance is i over all the messages in the network.

The average distance of a level k THIN, denoted by D_{avg_THIN}, is given by:

$$D_{avg\_THIN} = \frac{1}{3^{k-1}} + \frac{16 \times (6^{k-1} - 1)}{5 \times 3^k} - \frac{1}{3}. \tag{11}$$

In [12], the equation to calculate the average distance of 2-D mesh is given.

$$D_{2\text{-D Mesh}} = \frac{2(N-1)}{3\sqrt{N}} \tag{12}$$

Increasing network degree can reduce the average distance of an interconnection network. So it is very difficult to accurately evaluate the latency of interconnection networks with different degree, if only using the average distance without taking into account the network degree. In this paper, we use the normalized average distance [13] when analyzing the latency.

Definition 9. The normalized average distance of an interconnection network, denoted by μ, is the result of the average distance D_{avg} multiplied by the degree d:

$$\mu = d \cdot D_{avg}. \tag{13}$$

In this paper, when comparing the zero-load latency of different interconnection networks, we use μ to take place D_{avg}. Based on equation (9), (11) and (13), the zero-load latency of level k THIN, denoted by T_{THIN}, is given by

$$T_{THIN} = 3 \times (\frac{1}{3^{k-1}} + \frac{16 \times (6^{k-1} - 1)}{5 \times 3^k} - \frac{1}{3}) \times (t_r + t_s + t_w) + \max(t_s, t_w)\lceil \frac{L}{W} \rceil$$
$$= 3 \times (\frac{3}{N} + \frac{16 \times (6^{\log_3^{N-1}} - 1)}{5 \times N} - \frac{1}{3}) \times (t_r + t_s + t_w) + \max(t_s, t_w)\lceil \frac{L}{W} \rceil \quad , \quad (14)$$

where N represents the number of nodes in the THIN.

The zero-load latency of a 2-D mesh is given by

$$T_{2\text{-D Mesh}} = \frac{8(N-1)}{3\sqrt{N}}(t_r + t_s + t_w) + \max(t_s, t_w)\lceil \frac{L}{W} \rceil. \quad (15)$$

Fig. 6 compares the zero-load latency generated by THIN and 2-D mesh, respectively. The same routing decision, network switching and communication bandwidth are used by both interconnection networks. Suppose the routing decision time (t_r), switching delay (t_s) and channel delay (t_w) all are fixed constant, and we use the normalized average distance to measure the zero-load latency. Fig. 6 indicates that the zero-load latency of THIN is lower than 2-D mesh when the scale of network is not very large.

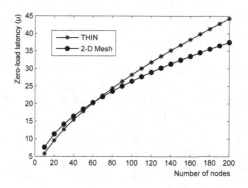

Fig. 6. Comparison of zero-load latency between THIN and 2-D mesh

5 The Restricted Multicast Routing Algorithm

Multicast communication, which delivers the same message from one source node to arbitrary number of destination nodes, is a key issue in almost all applications that run on any parallel architecture. Multicast has many applications, such as barrier synchronization [14], memory update and invalidation, and cache coherence [15].

Three main schemes to implement multicast routing are unicast-based, path-based and tree-based. In this section, we present a new tree-based multicast routing algorithm for THIN. Since the degree of THIN equals 3, the multicast tree is a triple tree, and because the algorithm does not support arbitrary destination nodes but just when the destination is a group-code. So we call the algorithm TRMA (Triple-tree Restricted Multicast Algorithm).

5.1 Triple-Tree Restricted Multicast Algorithm

In TRMA, a multidestination message is delivered along a common path as far as possible, and then replicate the message and forward each copy on a different channel bound for a unique set of destination nodes. The path followed by each copy may further branch in this manner until the message is delivered to every destination node. TRMA has the advantage that no ordering of the destination is required before the message is injected into the network. The shortest path between the source node and all destination nodes can be always taken so the algorithm transmits the message to each destination node using as little time and as few channels as possible. The TRMA which is a distributed multicast algorithm is described as follows.

```
Note:
    b_{2k-1}b_{2k-2}...b_1b_0, the destination of a message.
    b'_{2k-1}b'_{2k-2}...b'_1b'_0, the address of the current node.
Procedure:
if (a message arrived) then
{ extract the destination address, b_{2k-1}b_{2k-2}...b_1b_0,
  from the head of the message;

  for ( i = k; i >= 1; i --)
      if (b_{2i-1}b_{2i-2} ≠ b'_{2i-1}b'_{2i-2}) then break;
  if ( i <= 0) then /*the message arrive at destination*/
      accept the message;
  else /* not arrive destination, route the message  */
      if (b_{2i-1}b_{2i-2} ≠ 00) then
          use unicast routing algorithm to select a
          output port for the message, transmit it
          to the neighbor node;
      else    /* the message should be branched  */
      { replicate the message to get 3 messages,
        each with a new destination:
        b_{2k-1}b_{2k-2}...b_{2i+1}b_{2i} 01b_{2i-3}b_{2i-4}...b_1b_0,
        b_{2k-1}b_{2k-2}...b_{2i+1}b_{2i} 10b_{2i-3}b_{2i-4}...b_1b_0 and
        b_{2k-1}b_{2k-2}...b_{2i+1}b_{2i} 11b_{2i-3}b_{2i-4}...b_1b_0.
        route these 3 messages to the next node;
      }
}
```

In TRMA, the routing decision is fully dependent on the hierarchical characteristic of the destination and the current nodes address. The routing algorithm is simple enough to achieve a low overall message transmission time.

5.2 Performance Comparisons

Two major routing design parameters are time and traffic [16]. For a given multicast communication, the parameter time is the message transmission time or the network latency. The parameter time is measured in time steps, where a time step is the actual time needed to send a message from a node to one of its neighboring nodes. This time is assumed to be constant for all pairs of neighboring nodes. Parameter traffic is quantified in the number of communication links that are used to deliver the source message to all its destinations.

Table 2. Comparison of traffic and time steps in different algorithms

Algorithms	Traffic	Time steps
Unicast-based	54	7
Path-based	12	12
TRMA	14	7

Table 2 compared the traffic and time when n(111111) multicast M(010000) in N(3), using different multicast schemes.

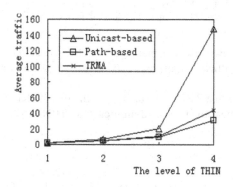

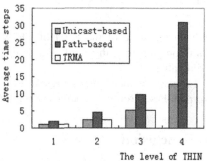

Fig. 7. Comparison of average traffic   **Fig. 8.** Comparison of average time steps

In order to study the performance of the proposed multicast routing algorithm, a simulation program to model restricted multicast communication in different level THIN was written in C. In the simulation, the message queuing model presented in [17] is applied and each full-duplex link is replaced by two half-duplex links, each of which is modeled as a message queuing center. The program measures the average number of channels (i.e. traffic) and average maximum distance between the source and destination nodes (i.e. time steps).

Figure 7 shows the average traffic of these restricted multicast algorithms in different level THIN and Fig. 8 depicts the average time steps. The level of THIN is varied from 1 to 4.

The multicast supported by THIN is restricted multicast and the number of destination nodes in a multicast is not random, it is just determined by the group-code. Figure 9 and 10 compare the average traffic and time steps of 3, 9 and 27 destination nodes in level 4 THIN.

From Fig. 7 and 9, it is observed that the traffic generated by path-based multicast algorithm and TRMA is lower than by unicast-based. However, the conclusion from Fig. 8 and 10 is that the time steps resulting from path-based algorithm is much more than other algorithms. Furthermore the time steps of path-based increase very quickly

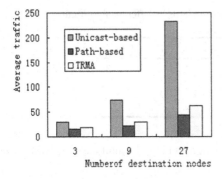 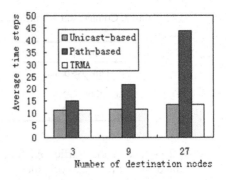

Fig. 9. Average traffic for different number of destination in level 4 THIN

Fig. 10. Average time steps for different number of destination in level 4 THIN

with the increase of the level of THIN. Because the message is delivered along a Hamilton path in path-based restricted multicast algorithm, and the transmission is a serial pattern.

The performance compare results show that TRMA is superior to the unicast-based and path-based routing schemes to implement the restricted multicast in THIN.

6 Conclusion

In this paper, we have proposed a new on-chip interconnection architecture THIN for SOC. Compared the network properties and communication latency with 2-D mesh and hypercube, THIN is preferable to construct interconnection network for SOC when the network size is not very large. A new tree-based multicast routing algorithm in THIN, which named TRMA, is presented. It is observed that TRMA is more suitable for multicast routing in THIN than unicast-based and path-based, taking into account the traffic and time.

In future research, we will base on simulating the routing algorithm in different network load, comparing the performance with other routing algorithms in other interconnection networks, and designing the multicast algorithm that can support arbitrary destination nodes.

References

1. Guerrier, P., Greiner, A.: A Generic Architecture for On-Chip Packet-Switched Interconnections. DATE'2000, pp. 250–256. IEEE Press, Piscataway (2000)
2. Benini, L., De Micheli, G.: Networks on Chips: a New SOC Paradigm. IEEE Computer 6, 70–78 (2002)
3. IBM CoreConnect Bus Architecture. [online]. Accessed:January 20th (2006) http://www-03.ibm.com/chips/products/coreconnect/index.html
4. ARM AMBA. [online]. Accessed, May 13 (2005) http://www.arm.com/products/solutions/AMBAHomePage.html

5. Dally, W. J., Towles, B.: Route Packets, not Wires: On-Chip Interconnection Networks. In: Proc. of the 38th Design Automation Conf., Las Vegas, NV, vol. 6, pp. 681–689 (2001)

6. Kumar, S., Jantsch, A., et al.: A Network on Chip Architecture and Design Methodology. In Proc. of IEEE Computer Society Annual Symposium on VLSI, Pittsburgh, Pennsylvania, USA, vol. 3, pp. 117–124 (2002)

7. Zeferino, C. A., Kreutz, M. E., Carro, L., et al.: A Study of Communication Issues for Systems-on-Chip. In: Proc. of 15th Symposium on Integrated Circuits and Systems Design, Porto Alegre, Brazil, vol. 9, pp. 121–126 (2002)

8. Wiklund, D., Liu, D.: Design of a System-on-Chip Switched Network and its Design Support. In: IEEE 2002 International Conference on Communications, Circuits and Systems and West Sino Expositions, Vol. 2, Chengdu, China, vol. 6, pp. 1279–1283 (2002)

9. Vecchia, G.D., Sanges, C.: A Recursively Scalable Network VLSI Implementation. Future Generation Computer Systems 4(3), 235–243 (1988)

10. Fu, J-S.: Hamiltonian-Connectedness of the WK-Recursive Network. In: Proc. of 7th International Symposium on Parallel, Architectures, Algorithms and Networks, Hong Kong, China, vol. 5, pp. 569–574 (2004)

11. Duato, J., Yalamanchili, S., Ni, L.: Interconnection Networks: an Engineering Approach. Publishing House of Electronics Industry, Beijing (2004)

12. Dong, Y.-f., Wang, D.-x., Zheng, W.-m.: Exact Computation of the Mean Minimal Path Length of N-Mesh and N-Torus. Chinese Journal of Computers 20(4), 376–380 (1997)

13. Gao. P.: Research on Interconnection Networks of Parallel Signal Processor [Ph. D. dissertation], Harbin Engineering University, Harbin China (2004)

14. Xu, H., McKinley, P.K., Ni, L.M.: Efficient Implementation of Barrier Synchronization in Wormhole-Routed Hypercubes Multicomputers. Journal of Parallel and Distributed Computing 16, 172–184 (1992)

15. Li, K., Schaefer, R.: A Hypercube Shared Virtual Memory. In: Proceeding of the 1989 International Conference on Parallel Processing, vol. 1, pp. 125–132 (1989)

16. Lin, X., Ni, L.M.: Multicast Communication in Multicomputer Networks. IEEE Transaction on Parallel and Distributed Systems 4(10), 1105–1117 (1993)

17. Dandamudi, S.P., Eager, D.L.: Hierarchical Interconnection Networks for Multicomputer Systems. IEEE Transactions on Computers 39(6), 786–797 (1990)

Architecture of Adaptive Spam Filtering Based on Machine Learning Algorithms

Md Rafiqul Islam and Wanlei Zhou

School of Engineering and Information Technology
Deakin University, Melbourne, Australia
{rmd,wanlei}@deakin.edu.au

Abstract. Spam is commonly defined as unsolicited email messages and the goal of spam filtering is to distinguish between spam and legitimate email messages. Much work has been done to filter spam from legitimate emails using machine learning algorithm and substantial performance has been achieved with some amount of false positive (FP) tradeoffs. In the case of spam detection FP problem is unacceptable sometimes. In this paper, an adaptive spam filtering model has been proposed based on Machine learning (ML) algorithms which will get better accuracy by reducing FP problems. This model consists of individual and combined filtering approach from existing well known ML algorithms. The proposed model considers both individual and collective output and analyzes them by an analyzer. A dynamic feature selection (DFS) technique also proposed in this paper for getting better accuracy.

Keywords: Machine learning, spam, SVM, NB, FP.

1 Introduction

The Internet is gradually becoming an integral part of everyday life. Internet usage is expected to continue growing and e-mail has become a powerful tool intended for idea and information exchange, as well as for users' commercial and social lives. Along with the growth of the Internet and e-mail, there has been a dramatic growth in spam in recent years. Spam can originate from any location across the globe where Internet access is available. However, it is amazing that despite the increasing development of anti-spam services and technologies, the number of spam messages continues to increase rapidly.

To address the growing problem, each organization must analyze the tools available to determine how best to counter spam in its environment. Tools, such as the corporate e-mail system, e-mail filtering gateways, contracted anti-spam services, and end-user training, provide an important arsenal for any organization.

Spam filtering technique is able to control the problem in a variety of ways. Identification and spam removal from the e-mail delivery system allows end-users to regain a useful means of communication. Many researches on spam filtering have been centered on the more sophisticated classifier-related issues. Currently, ML algorithms for spam filtering are an important research issue. The success of machine learning techniques in text categorization has led researchers to explore learning algorithms in

H. Jin et al. (Eds.): ICA3PP 2007, LNCS 4494, pp. 458–469, 2007.

spam filtering. In particular Bayesian techniques and Support Vector Machine (SVM), effectively used for text categorization (TC) which influences researchers to classify the email, are based on a special case of TC, with the categories being spam and non-spam [1],[2],[4],[6],[8]. Recently boosting algorithm (AdaBoost) is also being used for spam filtering and found to have substantial performance [5]. In this paper we proposed an effective and efficient spam filtering technique by adopting a grey list (GL) analyzer through a multiple classification systems. SVM, Naïve Bayes (NB) and Boosting Algorithm (AdaBoost) have been considered as classifiers in this adaptive model. The main focus of our paper is to analyze the GL emails which are generated by the classifier/(s) and stored in a specific mailbox. The GL is the list of the emails which are not TP or TN. The term GL is related to black-list (BL) and white-list (WL) and considered as the middle of them. In our paper we have also designed a DFS technique which will dynamically collect the features of GL emails and send them to the classifier. This approach reduces the FP problems substantially as well as increasing the overall efficiency of the architecture.

The organization of this paper is as follows: Section 2 will describe the overview of ML algorithms and section 3 will describe the proposed adaptive model and its detail description. Section 4 describes the analysis of the model. Section 5 gives experimental results. Finally, the paper ends with conclusion and references in section 6 and 7 respectively.

2   Overview of ML Algorithms

This section describes the overview of three ML algorithms such as SVM, NB and Boosting, which are used in our proposed model. Each algorithm can be viewed as searching for the most appropriate classifier in a search space that contains all the classifiers it can learn. All machine learning algorithms require the same instance representation. The instances are messages and each message is transformed into a vector $(x_1, \ldots, x_m)$, where $x_1, \ldots, x_m$ are the values of the attributes $X_1, \ldots, X_m$, much as in the vector space model in information retrieval [3]. In the simplest case, each attribute represents a single token (e.g., "money"), of Boolean variables:

$$X_i = \sum \begin{matrix} 1-Contains\_Tokens \\ 0-Otherwise \end{matrix} \tag{1}$$

Instead of Boolean attributes, another two attribute vector representations are considered here [5].

1. **Frequency attributes**- frequency attributes are more informative than Boolean ones. With frequency attributes, the value of X_i in each message d is- $x_i = t_i(d)/l(d)$, where $t_i(d)$ is the number of occurrences in d of the token represented by X_i, and $l(d)$ is the length of d measured in token occurrences.
2. **N-gram attributes**- instead of single tokens the n-grams of tokens with n {1, 2,..,n}, that is sequences of tokens of length 1, 2, or 3, are examined. In that case, $t_i(d)$ is the number of occurrences in message d of the n-gram represented by Xi, while $l(d)$ remains the number of token occurrences in d.

SVM is a new learning algorithm which has some attractive features, such as eliminating the need for feature selections, which makes for easier spam classification.

SVMs are a range of classification and regression algorithms that have been based on the Structural Risk Minimization (SRM) principle from statistical learning theory formulated by Vapnik [2],[6]. The SRM is to find an optimal hyperplane that can guarantee the lowest true error. The key concepts of SVMs are the following: there are two classes, $y_i \in \{-1,1\}$, and there are N labelled training examples : $\{x_1, y_1),....,(x_n, y_n)$, $x \in R^d$, where d is the dimensionality of the vector.

SVM is based on the idea that every solvable classification problem can be transformed into a linearly separable one by mapping the original vector space into a new one, using non-linear mapping functions. More formally, SVMs learn generalized linear discriminant functions of the following form:

$$f(\vec{x}) = \sum_{i=1}^{m'} w_i . h_i(\vec{x}) + w_0 \qquad (2)$$

where m' is the dimensionality of the new vector space, and $h_i(\vec{x})$ are the non-linear functions that map the original attributes to the new ones. The higher the order of the $h_i(\vec{x})$ functions, the less linear the resulting discriminant. The type of $h_i(\vec{x})$ functions that can be used is limited indirectly by the algorithm's search method, but the exact choice is made by the person who configures the learner for a particular application. The function $f(\vec{x})$ is not linear in the original vector space, but it is linear in the transformed one.

The Naive Bayes (NB) learner is the simplest and most widely used algorithm that derives from Bayesian Decision Theory [4],[7]. A Bayesian classifier is simply a Bayesian network applied to a classification task. It contains a node C representing the class variable and a node X_i for each of the features. From Bayes' theorem and the theorem of total probability $P(C = c_k | X = x)$ for each possible class c_k, the probability that a message with vector $\bar{x} = (x_1, \ldots, x_m)$ belongs in category c is:

$$P(C=c|\vec{X}=\vec{x}) = \frac{P(C=c).P(\vec{X}=\vec{x}|C=c)}{\sum_{c' \in \{c_L, c_S\}} P(C=c').P(\vec{X}=\vec{x}|C=c')}. \qquad (3)$$

The boosting algorithms, like SVMs, learn generalized linear discriminates of the form of equation

$$f(\vec{x}) = \sum_{i=1}^{m'} w_i . h_i(\vec{x}) + w_0 \qquad (4)$$

In boosting algorithms, however, the mapping functions $h_i(\vec{x})$ are themselves learnt from data by another learning algorithm, known as weak learner. A common weak learner is decision stump induction [5], which constructs a one-level decision tree that uses a single attribute from the original attribute set to classify the instance $\vec{x}$ to one of the two categories. In the case of continuous attributes, the decision tree is a threshold function on one of the original attributes.

Furthermore, the mapping functions $h_i(\vec{x})$ are learnt by applying iteratively (for $i = 1, \ldots, m'$) the weak learner, in our case regression stump induction, to an enhanced form of the training set, where each training instance $\vec{x}_j$ carries a weight $v_i(\vec{x}_j)$. At each iteration, the weights of the training instances are updated, and, hence, applying the weak learner leads to a different mapping function $h_i(\vec{x})$. This iterative process is common to all boosting methods, where each $h_i(\vec{x})$ can be thought of as a weak classifier that specializes in classifying correctly training instances that the combination of the previous weak classifiers $h_i(\vec{x}_k)(k = 1, \ldots, i{-}1)$ either misclassifies or places close to the classification boundary. This is similar to the behavior of SVMs, which focus on instances that are misclassified or support the tangential hyper planes [5].

3   Proposed Adaptive Model

In this section, the architecture of the adaptive spam filtering model has been proposed, based on ML algorithms. Graphically this architecture is illustrated in Fig.1.

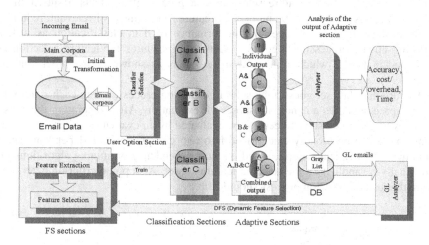

Fig. 1. The block diagram of our proposed architecture of adaptive spam filtering

3.1   Descriptions of the Model

The architecture of our adaptive spam filtering model is shown in Fig. 1. Firstly, the model will collect individual user emails that are considered as both spam and legitimate. Then the email corpus is transformed or indexed using learning algorithms, which is considered as an initial transformation. This model also includes the user interface, feature extraction & selection, email data classification, adaptive section and analyzer section. Finally the evaluation section which will evaluate the classification result. The detail of this model follows the following basic sections

Initial Transformation of an Incoming Email. The email corpus is initially transformed or indexed using learning algorithms, which is considered as an initial transformation. The initial transformation is often a null step that has the output text as just the input text. Sometimes character-set-folding, case-folding and MIME normalization are used for initial transformation. It should be noted that some systems work perfectly without using any initial transformation.

User Interface. In this section, a GUI is used to give options to the user for choosing an individual or combined classifier. The user interface (UI) will give the flexibility and feedback to the user and the system for getting better accuracy and reducing FP tradeoffs. Basically the user interface provides two things; allowing the users to manipulate a system and allowing the system to produce the effects of the users' manipulation. The design of a user interface affects the amount of effort the user must expend to provide input for the system and to interpret the output of the system, and how much effort it takes to learn how to do this. We have designed our user interface as a power interface so that both technical and non-technical user(s) can select the appropriate option for their email classification.

Email Feature Extraction & Selection. Feature extraction is also an important part for spam classification. Feature selection is a process that selects a subset of the original features. It reduces the number of features and removes irrelevant, redundant or noisy data. It also improves the performance of data classification as well as speeding up the processing algorithm. General procedures for feature selection are explained in Fig. 2 which follows four key steps as shown in the block diagram [1],[9].

The original data set goes to the subset generation process, where each state in the search space specifies a candidate subset for evaluation. After generating the subset, each newly generated subset needs to be evaluated by an evaluation criterion. Evaluation criteria can be broadly categorized into two groups, one is independent criteria and other is dependent criteria, based on their dependency on mining algorithms that will finally be applied on the selected feature subset. A stopping criterion determines when the feature selection process should stop.

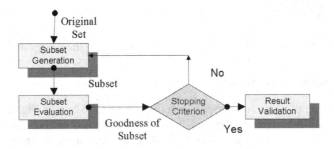

Fig. 2. Basic feature selection algorithm

The Feature selection (FS) and feature extraction (FE) are other domains of our UI. In our UI, there is a option for the user to choose appropriate kernel functions for some classification algorithms like SVM. Here we have used the following four types of kernel functions, which are frequently used in learning algorithms like SVM [1],[5]:

$$\text{Linear: } k\ (\ x_i\ ,\ x_j\ )\ =\ x_i^{\ T}\ x_j \tag{5}$$

$$\text{Polynomial: } K\ (x_i, x_j) = (\gamma x_i^{\ T} x_j + r)^d, \gamma > 0 \tag{6}$$

$$\text{RBF: } K(x_i, x_j) = \exp(-\gamma \parallel x_i - x_j \parallel^2), \gamma > 0 \tag{7}$$

$$\text{Sigmoid: } K\ (\ x_i\ ,\ x_j\ )\ =\ \tanh(\ \ \gamma x_i^{\ T} x_j\ +\ r\ ) \tag{8}$$

Here, γ, r, and d are kernel parameters.

Email Data Classification. In this model, SVM, NB and AdaBoost are considered in the classification algorithm. The basic algorithm of classification is shown in the following Fig. 3. The classifier algorithm /(s) is/are trained using training data sets. The training data set can be spam data or legitimate data. Based on the information of the training data set, the test data will be classified accordingly.

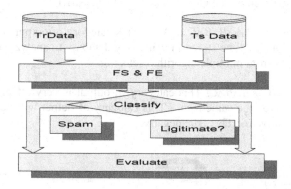

Fig. 3. The block diagram of basic email classification algorithm

Adaptive Section. The output of classifier comes into the adaptive section according to the user selection through UI. In this architecture we have chosen three most popular spam filtering algorithms such as SVM (A), NB (B) and Boosting (C). The main activity of this adaptive section is shown in Fig. 4. As we have described in our model, the user has the option to select an individual algorithm or combined algorithms in the input section of UI. In the case of an individual selection, the adaptive section will send the individual output of the classifier to the analyzer section. But in the case of a multiple classifier selection, the outputs of the classifiers can be represents as follows:

$$O_{(A,B,C)} = \sum_{(A \cap B),(B \cap C),(C \cap A)}^{A \cap B \cap C} \tag{9}$$

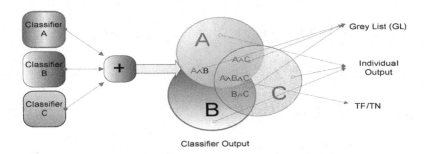

Fig. 4. The adaptive section, where outputs are categories in three different categories

So, it is obvious that the output of the adaptive section will be considered in the following three different categories.

Category 1: output of A, B & C. This category will be considered as an individual output of each classifier. This is a simplest one to analyze because there is no option to compare with other classifier outputs. The output will be sent to the spam or legitimate database based on the identification of the classifier.

Category 2: outputs of A∧B, B∧C & A∧C. This category of outputs is considered as GL of our model and will be stored in a different database to analyze by the analyzer. This output comes from multiple algorithm selection.

Category 3: output of A∧B∧C. This category of output is very effective because all classifiers have given the same result. This category of output will be considered either TP (True positive) or TN (True negative).

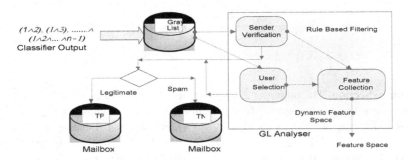

Fig. 5. The flow diagram of analyzer section for analyzing GL emails

Analyzer Section. This section describes the analysis of the GL emails generated by adaptive section. The GL is the list of the emails which are not TP or TN. The term GL is related to blacklist and white list and considered as the middle of them. This is not exactly the white-list or black-list because the unique result has not came from the classifiers. So, the analyzer can not make a final conclusion whether it is spam or legitimate. Fig. 5 shows the main flow diagram of the analyzer section of our proposed architecture. For analyzing GL, we have adopted two techniques in our proposed model. One is user selection technique and the other is sender verification technique.

User Feedback. In the first option, the analyzer will send this output to the user for getting feedback from the user. The user will identify the email and make decision whether it is spam or legitimate. After user feedback it will be sent to the spam or legitimate database. The classifier will also consider the feature of this output which will be considered for further classification. This process is quite simple but more effective in terms of accuracy.

Sender Verification. The second option is quite complicated. This process is based on what we call a C/R technique. In this technique, the analyser will automatically send a message to the sender for verification; until the sender responds with the correct answer within a certain timeframe the e-mail will be remain as GL. If the sender responds with correct answer then the email is considers as TP, otherwise TN. The system will wait for a predefined time and, if the time expires, it is also considered as TN.

Evaluation. The last stage of this adaptive model is evaluating the classification effectiveness, a function of how many correct classification decisions the classifier made. To do this we will consider here the total cost in terms of time, overhead and algorithmic complexity and well as the accuracy of the output in terms of reducing FP problems.

3.2 DFS Algorithm

DFS is an important focus of our proposed adaptive model of spam filtering.. This technique is more effective for getting more accuracy in terms of reducing FP. In this technique, the feature will collect from the analyzer by analyzing the GL emails after making a final conclusion whether it is true positive (*TP*) or true negative (*TN*). The email contents send to the input of a classifier and train the classifier in a dynamic fashion.

The technique of DFS is to train the classifier periodically for a certain time interval. To train the classifier at time t with messages M_t received at time t, contributes more to classifying email received at t-1; and same happens for message received at t+1 compared to t. For example, let $M_t=\{m_{t1},m_{t2},.....,m_{tn}\}$ be a set of training sets available at time t, in which m_{tk} is an additional message supplied for training at time k, for $k=1,....,t$. In a conventional approach, every message in $\bigcup_{k-1}^{t} m_{tk}$ will be used to build a classification model for user at t+1. The framework of our DFS technique is shown in Fig. 6.

However, in the case of changing some feature, earlier messages could pose a negative impact on the reliability of the classification model [9]. In that case, our approach is to generate a term frequency map table (TF-MT) to rank values of training messages. If the new messages come after time t then the rank of the TF-MT will be increased every time. For example, if a message $M_t \in m_{tk}(k<t)$ is selected for training time t, we use its rank value computed at time k.

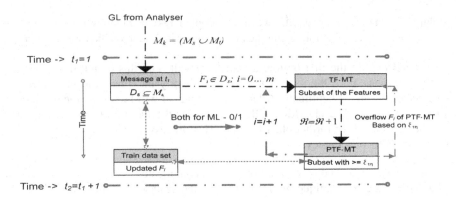

Fig. 6. The framework of DFS Algorithm

However, there is a drawback of memory consumption for incorporating all the ranking values of feature sets. To overcome this limitation we have used priority TF-MT (PTF-MT). The PTF-MT maintains a threshold rank value δ_{rn} and limits the feature set based on the lower range of threshold value from the PTF-MT. Every time the rank value is updating in the PTF-MT, which influence the changing of the feature dynamically.

4   Analysis of the Model

In our proposed adaptive model, emphasis has been given on the following basic research challenges, based on different aspects of anti-spam filtering, especially the learning-based anti-spam filter.

Reduction of FP Problems. Many machine learning techniques for spam filtering can achieve very high accuracy with some amount of FP tradeoffs which are generally expensive in the real world. One misclassified legitimate email can cause a huge problem for the user. Keeping this in mind, the analyzer section of our architecture is producing the GL from outputs of the classifiers. It takes the output of "Out-A∧B, Out-A∧C, Out-B∧C" and analyze them using user selection and sender verification techniques to find out the exact TP and TN. In that case every single output of GL will be analyzed and given the final decision by analyzer, which will increase the reduction of FP problems. Our preliminary experimental result shows that the percentage of FP is minimum compared to individual classification techniques [Table 1]. The emails considered as GL's are sent to the different database for analyzing. After analyzing it would be considered either TP or TN and the feature will be generated from these sorts of emails using DFS technique.

Achieving Greater Accuracy. Accuracy is very important for spam filtering. It has been shown that, sometimes the individual algorithms show better performance for particular data sets and do not show in other data sets and vice versa. This is because the spam data is dynamic. The spammers are always changing their strategy for sending email. So, the combined output will give better accuracy in that case, because in our architecture, the analyzer section will analyze both individual, combined and the grey list. In the existing techniques, there is no option to consider the grey list after classification, which is an innovation of our architecture.

5 Experimental Results

In this section some experimental results have been presented. We are now simulating the proposed architecture, therefore the initial result so far we found is convincing. In our initial result, we have used two of the classifier, SVM and AdaBoost. We are now developing the analyzer section for analyzing the GL. In our experiment, we have used the public data sets PUA [5] for our experiments and converted the data sets based on our experimental design and environment. Firstly we have encoded the whole data sets (both train and test sets), then indexed every email for test data sets and finally recorded the output individually based on the index value.

Table 1. The comparison of FP and FN with A, B and proposed A+B

Data	FP & FN					
	A		B		Proposed (A+B)	
	FP	FN	FP	FN	FP	FN
PUD1	0.0	0.09091	0.0	0.091	0.0	0.091
PUD2	0.091	0.0	0.091	0.0	0.0	0.0
PUD3	0.181	0.0	0.091	0.272	0.091	0.091
PUD4	0.181	0.091	0.0	0.0	0.0	0.0
PUD5	0.181	0.181	0.091	0.0	0.091	0.0
PUD6	0.181	0.181	0.091	0.0	0.091	0.0
AVG	*0.136*	*0.09065*	*0.061*	*0.061*	*0.046*	*0.03*

[Terminology: FP=False Positive; FN=False Negative; TP=True Positive; TN=True Negative; MC=Misclassification; A=SVM; B=AdaBoost; GL=Grey List]

Table 1 shows the comparative result of FP and FN for A, B and both A+B. It has been shown that the average output of FP for our proposed technique is much lower for any individual output and the same thing happened for FN as well. It has also been shown that the FP is zero for some data sets in our proposed system and the average FP is close to zero.

Table 2 shows the percentage of misclassification cost and the classification accuracy of A, B and the proposed A+B. It has been shown that the combined misclassification cost is much lower (almost zero except PUD3) than the individual one. In the case of classification accuracy, the combined output is much higher (93%) compared to any individual one, which is more significant for getting better performance in email classification. The table also shows the GL which are somehow misclassified by any of the classifier. So the analyzer will further analyze it, which will increase the performance of our whole spam filtering architecture.

Table 2. The comparison of MC cost and classification accuracy

Data	MC Cost			GL	Classification Accuracy		
	A	B	Proposed (A+B)		A	B	Proposed (A+B)
PUD1	0.091	0.09	0	0	0.91	0.901	0.91
PUD2	0.090	0.091	0	0.182	0.91	0.91	1.0
PUD3	0.181	0.363	0.091	0.182	0.82	0.636	0.82
PUD4	0.272	0	0	0.273	0.727	1.0	1.0
PUD5	0.363	0.091	0	0.273	0.64	0.91	0.91
PUD6	0.364	0.09	0	0.273	0.636	0.90	0.91
AVG	*0.227*	*0.121*	*0.015*	*0.197*	*0.774*	*0.876*	*0.93*

Fig. 7 shows the final accuracy of our experiment. The accuracy of our proposed technique is higher than any individual one. For some data sets like PUD2 and PUD4 the accuracy is 100%. From the graph it is shown that the average accuracy is almost 96%, which is higher than any individual existing spam filtering technique.

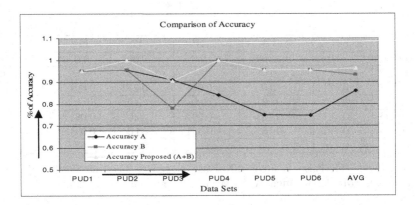

Fig. 7. The comparison of accuracy of proposed technique with individual techniques

6   Concluding Remarks

In this paper, the architecture of an adaptive spam filtering model, based on machine learning algorithms has been proposed. Emphasis has been given to this model based on different aspects of learning based anti-spam filtering for reducing FP problems and getting better performance compared to any of the existing techniques [5],[7]. The simulation of this model has being developed; therefore only preliminary results have been given, not the final result of our architecture. It has been shown from the result that the efficiency of this architecture is higher than any individual classifier technique. Our preliminary result also shows that the adaptive output reduces the FP problems substantially and increases the accuracy. Furthermore, the total cost of this architecture is higher than the individual classifier due to the analyzer section and there is no added algorithmic complexity in adaptive part of this architecture except the DFS algorithm. However, in the case of whole system we have given emphasis on accuracy rather than the added cost and complexity because in the case of spam filtering, getting better accuracy with reduced FP tradeoffs is more important. In our future research we will give more emphasis to reduce the cost as well as the complexity.

References

1. Islam, R., Chowdhury, M., Zhou, W.: An Innovative Spam Filtering Model Based on Support Vector Machine. In: Proceedings of the IEEE International Conference on Intelligent Agents, Web Technologies and Internet Commerce 2, 348–353 (2005)
2. Cristianini, N., Shawe-Taylor, J.: An introduction to Support Vector Machines and other kernel-based learning methods. Cambridge University Press, Cambridge (2000)
3. Cohen, W., Singer, Y.: Context-sensitive learning methods for text categorization. ACM Transactions on Information Systems 17(2), 141–173 (1999)
4. Kaitarai, H.: Filtering Junk e-mail: A performance comparison between genetic programming and naïve bayes. Tech. Report, Department of Electrical and Computer Engineering, University of Waterloo (November 1999)
5. Androutsopoulos, I., et al.: Learning to filter spam e-mail: A comparison of a Naive Bayesian and a memory-based approach. In: Proceedings of the Workshop on Machine Learning and Textual Information Access, 4th European Conference on Principles and Practice of Knowledge Discovery in Databases. Lyon, France, pp. 1–13 (2000)
6. Zhang, J., et al.: A Modified logistic regression: An approximation to SVM and its applications in large-scale text categorization. In: Proceedings of the 20th International Conference on Machine Learning, pp. 888–895. AAAI Press, California (2003)
7. Sahami, M., Dumais, S., Heckerman, D., Horvitz, E.: A bayesian approach to filtering junk e-mail. In Learning for Text Categorization. Papers from the Workshop, Madison, Wisconsin, AAAI Technical Report WS, pp. 98–105 (1998)
8. Drucker, H., Shahrary, B., Gibbon, D.C.: Support vector machines: relevance feedback and information retrieval. Inform. Process. Manag. 38(3), 305–323 (2003)
9. Huan, L., Lei, Y.: Toward Integrating Feature Selection Algorithms for Classification and Clustering. IEEE Transaction on Knowledge and Data Engg. 17(4), 491–502 (2005)

On the Power-Law of the Internet and the Hierarchy of BGP Convergence

Peidong Zhu, Jinjing Zhao, Yan Wen, and Kaiyu Cai

School of Computer, National University of Defense Technology, Changsha 410073, China
{pdzhu,zhaojinjing,wenyan,kycai}@nudt.edu.cn

Abstract. Border Gateway Protocol (BGP) is the de facto inter-domain routing protocol. With the rapid development of the Internet, the convergence problem of BGP attracts more attention. This paper analyzes the relationship between BGP convergence and the characteristics of the Internet. The Internet is classified into three hierarchies based on the power-law and commercial relations of autonomous systems. The relation of network topology and BGP convergence performance is presented for all sorts of convergence events in different layers. The result shows that the power-law nature of network influences the BGP convergence greatly. So we present a new proposal to improve BGP convergence based on power-law, called "best up", which behaves better than normal convergence mode in the experiments.

Keywords: Inter-domain Routing, BGP, power-law, hierarchy, convergence.

1 Introduction

BGP is the *de facto* inter-domain routing protocol; it is a path vector routing algorithm. Although the adoption of the AS_PATH eliminates the count-to-infinity, the slow convergence has not been worked out drastically yet. The path vector algorithm needs the information of whole path to destination in update packets, so it has to select another path in all backups until the route rebuild when the topology is failed.

This paper tries to improving BGP convergence from the characteristics of the Internet. In our work, we analyze the relationship between BGP convergence and the characteristics of hierarchy and power-law of inter-domain system. The Internet is classified into three hierarchies—core layer, forwarding layer and stub layer based on the power-law and commercial relations of autonomous systems (ASs). Based on this, a BGP convergence model, named PH_SPVP[21], is presented. Three convergence parameters—convergence time T, affected ASs set Nc and affected paths factor μ, are analyzed for all sorts of convergence events in different layers. The result shows that the convergence time of core layer is smaller than forwarding layer, but the affected ASs set Nc and affected paths factorμ are larger. And because the power-law nature of network influences the BGP convergence greatly, we present a new proposal to improve BGP convergence, called "best up", which behaves better than normal convergence mode in the experiments.

H. Jin et al. (Eds.): ICA3PP 2007, LNCS 4494, pp. 470–481, 2007.

The remainder of this paper is organized as follows: The section 2 presents an algorithm for hierarchy model of the Internet based on the power-law and relationships between ASs. Based on section 2, section 3 builds a BGP convergence model named PH_SPVP. We analyze all the convergence parameters in ten kinds of convergence events happened in different layers and conclude the maximum and minimum values of the convergence time, the boundaries of affected ASs and the affected paths factor are given. Based on the analysis, a mechanism, named "best up", is present to improve BGP slow convergence problem. After these analyses, the simulations on the real topology of the Internet by SSFNet are taken in section 4.The last section concludes the whole paper.

2   Power Law-Hierarchy Model of the Internet

The main consideration of the power law-hierarchy model is to distinguish the performance of different layer nodes in the BGP convergence process. We build our model according to the hierarchy of the inter-domain system, and then, we testify it with the power-law rules. If the result is right, then the hierarchical model is also a power law-hierarchy model.

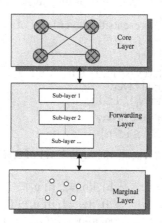

Fig. 1. Three-Hierarchy Model of the Internet

Paper[5] presents a hierarchical formalization method for Internet. In [8], a five-hierarchy model of the Internet is presented based on the commercial relation between ASs. These models are too complex to analyze for BGP convergence. In [4], we build a three-hierarchy model of the Internet and give an efficient algorism for it. The model is organized as follows:

a)   The set of nodes who have no providers forms a clique (interconnection structure), which is the core layer.
b)   If the nodes don't forward data for others, then it belongs to the marginal layer.
c)   The node that does not belong to the core layer or the marginal layer is classified into the forwarding layer. And the forwarding layer has several sub-layers.

In this way, we build the power law-hierarchy model of the inter-domain system based on the commercial relations between ASs, which also obey the heavy-tailed rule of power-law. In the next section, we analyze the BGP convergence on this model.

3 BGP Convergence Model—PH_SPVP

3.1 Model Establishment

Based on the power law-hierarchy model of the inter-domain system, we present a BGP convergence model named PH_SPVP (Power Law - Hierarchy Simple Path Vector Protocol), which is a simple path vector protocol. That is to say, the source AS only selects one path to the destination, and announces the path to its neighbors. The selected path must be valley-free and have no loops.

We model the Internet as a directed graph G= (V, E), nodes V represent the set of ASs in the Internet, links E are connections between them; a link e= (u, v) exists if node u will send update packets to v (but not vice versa). $r = \{ v_1, \ldots, v_k \}$ is a simple path in G, for $\forall\, 1 \leqq i, j \leqq k$ and if i≠j, then $v_i \neq v_j$ and e=$(v_i, v_j) \in E$, the length of r is |r|=k. G is classified into three hierarchies according to the power law-hierarchy model in section 3, the core layer C, forwarding layer T and the marginal layer S.

Definition 1. Function h (v_i) presents the layer level of v_i, $1 \leq h(v_i) \leq 3 (1 \leq i \leq n)$, n is the number of nodes.
a) v_i belongs to the core layer,
iff $\{h(v_i) = 1 \,|\, \forall v_j \notin provider(v_i), \ 1 \leq i,j \leq n\}$
b) v_i belongs to the marginal layer,
iff $\{h(v_i) = 3 \,|\, \forall v_j \notin custom(v_i), \ 1 \leq i,j \leq n\}$
c) v_i belongs to the forwarding layer,
iff $\{h(v_i)=2 \,|\, v_i \notin C, \exists v_i \notin S, 1 \leq i \leq n\}$

Definition 2. Function $l(e_j)$ presents the layer level of $e_j=(u_k, u_m)$, $1 \leq l(e_j) \leq 6 \ (1 \leq j \leq m)$, m is the number of edges.
a) $l(e_j)=1$, iff $u_k \in C, \exists u_m \in C$.   b) $l(e_j)=2$, iff $u_k \in C, \exists u_m \in T$.
c) $l(e_j)=3$, iff $u_k \in C, \exists u_m \in S$.   d) $l(e_j)=4$, iff $u_k \in T, \exists u_m \in T$.
e) $l(e_j)=5$, iff $u_k \in T, \exists u_m \in S$.   f) $l(e_j)=6$, iff $u_k \in S, \exists u_m \in S$.

Definition 3. Convergence Time T: If the convergence Event X happens at t_0 and network converges at t_1, then the convergence time $T = t_1 - t_0$.

Definition 4. Set of the affected nodes Nc: The set of nodes whose convergence states are changing because of the happening convergence event X.

Definition 5. Affected paths factorμ: The percentage of the paths changed because of the happening convergence event X.

For analysis and description, the convergence events are classified into two kinds, the event of edges Te and the event of nodes Tn, both including the down type and up type. Suppose the sum of the transition delay through an edge and the processing time in a node is D.

3.2 Analysis of BGP Convergence

Now, we can analyze the BGP convergence in different layers and convergence events.
1.   e=1, convergence event happens in core layer
    a)   the type of convergence event is Tn

Analysis: If node *a* downs, all the nodes in the core layer would get this change. They will delete the corresponding routes containing *a* in their route table and send withdrawals to their customers. When the customers receiving the messages, they will update their route table and send withdrawals to their customers and so on, until the bottom nodes of the network who has the routes containing *a*.

Parameters:
$Nc=\{v_i \cup customer(v_i) \cup customer(...customer \quad (v_i)) \cup customer(a) \cup \quad customer (...customer(a)) | v_i \in peer(a) \text{ and } h(v_i)=1\} = \{T_i \cup T_j | Root(T_i) \in peer(a) \text{ and } Root(T_j)=a\}$.
Nc composes of two trees, one is the tree rooted at peer(*a*), the other has the root *a*. Then maximum number of elements in set Nc is max|Nc|=N, N is the number of the nodes in G.

Suppose the longest convergence path is $R_{max}=\{v_1,...,v_k \mid v_1 \in peer(a)\}$, then $|R_{max}| \leq H$, H is depth of G. Then the upper bound of the convergence time T is H×D and the lower bound is 2×D.

The affected paths factorμ can be presented by an important parameter in graph theory, the **betweenness centrality** (BC) of a node.

Definition 6. The BC of node v in the network is defined as: $g(v) = \sum_{s \neq t} \dfrac{\sigma_{st}(v)}{\sigma_{st}}$.

Where σ_{st} is the number of shortest paths going from s to t and $\sigma_{st}(v)$ is the number of shortest paths going from s to t and passing through v. BC gives in transport networks an estimate of the traffic handled by the vertices.

In the power-law network, the average BC for nodes of the same degree is defined as:

$$g(k) = \frac{1}{N_k} \sum_{v,k_v=k} g(v)$$

Where N_k denotes the number of nodes with degree k, For power-law networks it has been shown that the centrality scales with k as $g(k) \sim k^\phi$, where ϕ depends on the network.

So the affected paths factor $\mu_1 = \sum_{s \neq t} \dfrac{\sigma_{st}(a)}{\sigma_{st}} \approx g(Degree(a)) = (Degree(a))^\phi$. The

up case is the same to the down case, so we don't discuss it further more.
    b)   the type of convergence event is Te

Analysis: Suppose the link between nodes *a* and *b* is broken, then *a* and *b* will delete the routes to each other, and select another reachable route, as a->c->b or b->c ->a. Whereafter, *a* and *b* will announce the new route to their peers and customers.

Because the topology of the core layer is a complete-graph, the peers of a and b would not change their routes and send updates to their customers.

Parameters:

$Nc=\{a \cup b \cup customer(a) \cup customer(...customer(a)) \cup customer(b) \cup$ customer $(...customer(b))\}= \{T_a \cup T_b | Root(T_a)=a, Root(T_b)=b\}$.

Suppose the longest convergence path is $R_{max}=\{v_1,...,v_k \mid v_1=a$ or $v_i=b\}$, then $|R_{max}| \leqq H$. Then the upper bound of the convergence time T is H×D and the lower bound is 2×D.

The affected paths factorµ is the BC of edge (a,b).

Definition 7. The BC of edge e in the network is defined as: $g(e) = \sum_{s \neq t} \frac{\sigma_{st}(e)}{\sigma_{st}}$.

Where $\sigma_{st}(e)$ is the number of shortest paths going from s to t and passing through e. In the power-law network, g (e) is decreasing with the increasing of the level.

So the affected paths factor $\mu_2 = \sum_{s \neq t} \frac{\sigma_{st}(ab)}{\sigma_{st}}$, edge (a,b) is in the core layer, so μ_2 is lager than other edge's.

2. e=2, convergence event happens between core layer and forwarding layer

Because node a is a core layer node, the degree(a) is high, μ_1 is lager.

Analysis: The convergence event must be Te. Suppose the link between nodes a and b is broken, then a and b will delete the routes to each other, and select another reachable route. Node b will send updates to its customers and node a will send to its peers and customers. The nodes received updates would announce to their customers sequentially.

Parameters:

$Nc=\{T_a | Root(T_a)=a\} \cup \{T_i | Root(T_i) \in peer(a)\} \cup \{T_b | Root(T_b)=b\}$, Then the maximum number of elements in set Nc is max|Nc|=N.

$R_{max} =max (H(T_i) +1, H(Tb)) \leqq H+1$, so the upper bound of the convergence time T is (H+1)×D, the lower bound is 2×D.

The affected paths factor $\mu_3 = \sum_{s \neq t} \frac{\sigma_{st}(ab)}{\sigma_{st}} \in [\mu_{10}, \mu_2]$.

3. e=3, convergence event happens between core layer and marginal layer

Analysis: The convergence event must be Te. Suppose the link between nodes a and b is broken, then a and b will delete the routes to each other, and select another reachable route. Node b needn't notify to any nodes, and node a would send updates to its peers and customers. The nodes received updates would announce to their customers sequentially.

Parameter:

$Nc=\{T_a \cup T_b | Root(T_a)=a, Root(T_b)=peer(a)\}$, Then the maximum number of elements in set Nc is max|Nc|=N.

$R_{max} = \{v_1, \ldots, v_k \mid v_1 \in C\}$, then $|R_{max}| \leq H$. Then the upper bound of the convergence time T is H×D and the lower bound is 2×D.

The affected paths factor $\mu_4 = \sum_{s \neq t} \dfrac{\sigma_{st}(ab)}{\sigma_{st}} \in [\mu_3, \mu_2]$.

4. e=4, convergence event happens in forwarding layer
    a) the type of convergence event is Tn

Analysis: If node *a* downs, its peers, providers and customers will all feel this change. They will update their route table and announce it to their customers and customers' customers. Furthermore, the providers will also announce it to their peers and providers.

Parameter:

$Nc = \{T_i \mid Root(T_i) \in customer(a)\} \cup \{T_n \mid Root(T_n) \in$

$\underbrace{provider...(a)}_{0...n} \} \cup \{T_m \mid Root(T_m) \in peer(\underbrace{provider...(a)}_{0...n})\}$

$R_{max} = max(|H(T_i)|, |H(T_j)|, |H(T_m)|, |H(T_n)|) \leq 2H-1$. Then the upper bound of the convergence time T is (2H-1)×D, the lower bound is 2×D.

The affected paths factor $\mu_5 = \sum_{s \neq t} \dfrac{\sigma_{st}(a)}{\sigma_{st}} \in [\mu_9, \mu_1]$.

5. e=5, convergence event happens between forwarding layer and marginal layer

Analysis: The convergence event must be Te. Suppose the link between nodes *a* and b is broken, then *a* and b will delete the routes to each other, and select another reachable route. Node b needn't send updates to other nodes and node *a* will send to its providers, peers and customers. The providers will also send messages to their providers and peers. And the nodes received updates would announce to their customers sequentially.

Parameter:

$Nc = \{T_i \mid Root(T_i) \in peer(a)\} \cup \{T_j \mid Root(T_j) \in customer(a)\} \cup \{T_m \mid Root(T_m)$

$\in \underbrace{provider(a)}_{0 \sim n} \} \cup \{T_n \mid Root(T_n) \in peer(\underbrace{provider(a)}_{0 \sim n})\}$

$\mid R_{max} \mid = max(H(T_i), H(T_j), H(T_m), H(T_n)) \leq 2H-1$. Then the upper bound of the convergence time T is (2H-1)×D and the lower bound is 3×D.

The affected paths factor $\mu_8 = \sum_{s \neq t} \dfrac{\sigma_{st}(ab)}{\sigma_{st}} \in [\mu_{10}, \mu_6]$.

6. e=6, convergence event happens in the marginal layer
    a) the type of convergence event is Tn

Analysis: If node *a* downs, its peers will delete their routes to a. Because the connected information in marginal layers would not be spread to the upper layers, the peers of *a* need not send updates to others.

Parameters:

Nc={peer(a)}.

The convergence Time T=D.

The affected paths factor $\mu_9 = \sum_{s \neq t} \frac{\sigma_{st}(a)}{\sigma_{st}} \approx 0$.

  b) the type of convergence event is Te

Analysis: Suppose the link between nodes a and b is broken, then they will only delete the routes to each other.

Parameters:
Nc={a, b}.
The convergence Time T=D.

The affected paths factor $\mu_{10} = \sum_{s \neq t} \frac{\sigma_{st}(ab)}{\sigma_{st}} \approx 0$.

   Through the analysis above, we can see that the convergence time T has no severe relation of the hierarchy, but the convergence event happening in the forwarding layer has longer delay than in core layer. The set of affected nodes Nc is smaller with the increasing hierarchy, that is, it's largest in the core layer and tiniest in the marginal layer. But this rule is not obeyed firmly in the forwarding layer. The affected paths factorμ is the influence of the convergence event to the network flow, which has severe relation with the hierarchy. It is ensured by the characteristics of the power-law network. Table 1 compares the maximum and minimum values of these three parameters.

Table 1. Maximum and Minimum of Parameters

• parameters	• value	• hierarchy	• type
• Max (Nc)	N	C	Tn
• Min (Nc)	2	S	Te
• Max (T)	$(2H-1) \times D$	T or T- S	Tn or Te
• Min (T)	D	S	Tn or Te
• Max (μ)	μ_1	C	Tn
• Min (μ)	μ_{10}	S	Te

3.3 "Best Up" Mechanism

According to the analysis to the PH_SPVP model, we can see that the "hub nodes" has rich connections and high BC value. So they are very important in the BGP convergence process. Through them, the update messages can spread more quickly and the convergence time can be reduced. In this section, we present a new mechanism named "best up", which uses the special ability of the "hub nodes" to improve the BGP convergence.

   The "best up" mechanism is very simple to implement. When ASs receiving updates from themselves or their customers, they send the updates to their providers as fast as they can. So the "hub nodes" in the core layer would notice the convergence events and diffuse updates to the network through their rich connections sooner.

In "best up" mechanism, we let the ASs forward BGP updates to their providers as soon as possible, without the effect of MRAI. The algorithm of the mechanism is introduced as follows.

```
Algorithm "Best Up"
/* Function: Node a deals with update packet U which
received from neighbor b */
Begin
/*Update its own route table for the corresponding
routes in U*/
UpdateList* p_update;
p_update = Update (RouteTable* p_routetable, U)
/*Create the update packets to its neighbor except b*/
UpdatePacket[] list_updatepack;
updatepack = CreateUpdate (NeighborList* p_neighbor);
    forecach u∈ updatepack do
{
Node D= GetDestination(u);
/*If u will be sent to one of a' providers, then send
it immediately */
If (D ∈ provider(a)) then
        send (u);
    else
        /*To justify whether the MRAI Timer of
destination of u is expired. */
{
Check: Bool b_time = Check(MRAIList* p_MRAI,D);
      /*If MRAI=0, send u to D immediately, else wait
for 1s and check again*/
 If (b_time = 0) then
{
send (u);
                break;
}
 else
            {
  wait();
                goto Check;
                }
            }
}
End
```

4 Simulation

In this section, we will verify the results drawn in the previous section.

For the authenticity of the test, the real BGP data is samples for the topology of inter-domain system. According to the sampling rules in [20], a network with 110 ASs is built, and the commercial relations are reserved. The network is also be

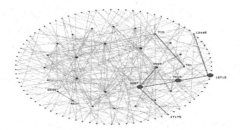

Fig. 2. Topology Graph of Simulation

classified into layers by the hierarchizing algorithm in section 3. Fig. 2 is the topology graph of the network. The distribution of node degree obeys the heavy-tailed rule of power-law. Few nodes have degree above 20, and the degrees of most of the nodes are smaller than 5, the average degree of the network is about 3.3. The total period is 200 seconds. At 100s, the selected AS and link have stopped for 1s and restart.

4.1 General Description of the Simulation

The simulation is completed by SSFNet[14]. We select a random AS or link in the specific layer to stop its BGP process in one second and restart again, and observe the values of the three parameters mentioned above in the down and up convergence processes.

4.2 Analysis and Results

1.   Simulation Setup

All *MinRouteAdver* timers (MRAI) are configured with 30 seconds, and the link delays to be 0.01 second. The CPU processing time of each message was randomly generated during simulation to be between 0.01 and 0.05 second. The withdrawal packets aren't restricted by MRAI timers. After simulation beginning, the BGP sessions set up by 70s, and the network is stability. At 100s, the selected ASs and links are down (down event), and restart (up event) at 101s.

2.   Down Event

Because the withdrawal packets need not be sent after MRAI timers, the convergence process of down events can end in 0.01 second. There are still some distinguish between the 10 cases of different layers. In the marginal layer, changes of connections shouldn't spread to outer layer, so the convergence time T can be limited in e^{-5}. The value T of the forwarding layer is larger than the core layer about 10%.

The set of affected nodes Nc can be used to evaluate the influence of convergence events. Form Fig.3 b), we can see Tn is much lager than Te, i.e., the effect of events on ASs is much more serious than on links. But Nc has no linear relation with the level of layers. The affected ASs are abundant in the core layer, but in the forwarding layer, the number can also be large.

In the simulation network, the depth of topology is 5. But the longest withdrawal path length is 7, happening in forwarding layer or between forwarding layer and marginal layer, which can be seen in Fig.3 c).

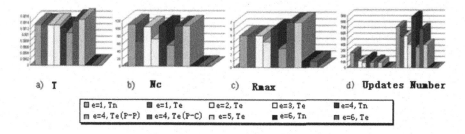

Fig. 3. Parameters of Ten Cases in Down Event

The statistics of withdrawal number and announcement number are printed in Fig.3 d), the left part is the statistics of the withdrawal number of 10 cases and the right part is the statistics of the announcement numbers. In the case e=1,Tn, the number of withdrawal packets is264, the largest one in all cases. Because AS3257 is a hub node in network, there are lots of the paths through it. And the number of the announcements is 892 in the case of e=4,Tn, it is because that there are lots of backup paths to AS7018 in other ASs. So the number of backup paths is also an important factor for BGP convergence.

3.   Up Event

At 101s, the selected AS or links restart, and an up event is produced. The statistics of the parameters in up event is shown in Fig.4. The convergence time T of up event is much longer than down event because of the MRAI timers. The other parameters are much similar with them in down event.

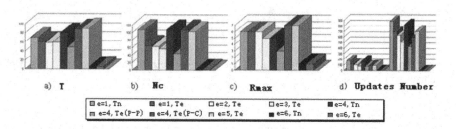

Fig. 4. Parameters of Ten Cases in Up Event

4.   "Best Up" Mechanism

Fig.5 and 6 show the convergence time of the two mechanisms with different node number N in both up and down events, N is from 100 to 500. We can see that the convergence time of the "best up" method is smaller than the normal one's and this phenomenon is more obvious with the increase of N. And we also testified that in the route damping environments, the MRAI mechanism can still be efficient and not be interrupted by "best up" mechanism.

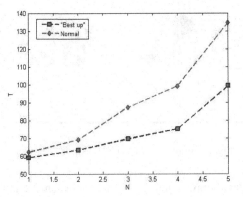

Fig. 5. The Comparison of Convergence Time between Normal Mechanism and "Best Up" Mechanism in Up Events

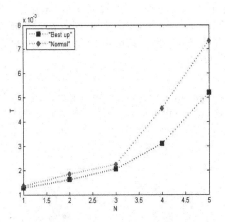

Fig. 6. The Comparison of Convergence Time between Normal Mechanism and "Best Up" Mechanism in Down Events

5.   *Discussion*

The result shows that the convergence time T of core layer is smaller than forwarding layer, but the affected ASs set Nc and affected paths factorμ are larger. The events in marginal layer have little effect on the network. So ASs in the core layer, which can also be called as "hub nodes", are very important to the convergence process. The rules of power-law influence the BGP convergence greatly. So the "best up" mechanism that uses these rules to improve BGP convergence problem gets very good results in the simulation especially in the large scale network environment.

5   Conclusion

We analyze the power-law and hierarchy of the inter-domain system and find that they are consistent with each other. Based on a three-hierarchy model of Internet, routing convergence model PH_SPVP is presented. The relations of network characteristics and three convergence parameters are analyzed for all sorts of convergence events in different layers. In the end, we present a new proposal based on the self-organization nature of the Internet to improve BGP convergence.

Acknowledgement

The work is supported by National Natural Science Foundation of China (Grant No. 60673169) and National High-Tech Research and Development Program (Grant No. 2006AA01Z213).

References

1. Labovitz, C., Ahuja, A., Bose, A., Jahanian, F.: Delayed Internet routing convergence. In: Proceedings of ACM SIGCOMM (2000)
2. Labovitz, C., Ahuja, A., Wattenhofer, R., Venkatachary, S.: The Impact of Internet Policy and Topology on Delayed Routing Convergence. In: Proceedings of INFOCOMM (2001)
3. Griffin, T., Wilfong, G.: An Analysis of BGP Convergence Properties. In: Proceedings of the ACM SIGCOMM (August 1999)
4. Zhu, P., Liu, X.: An efficient Algorithm on Internet Hierarchy Induction. High Technology Communication 14, 358–361 (2004)
5. Govindan, R., Reddy, A.: An Analysis of Internet Inter-Domain Topology and Route Stability. In: Proc. IEEE INFOCOM '97 (March 1997)
6. Chang, H., Govindan, R., Jamin, S., et al.: On Inferring AS-Level Connectivity from BGP Routing Tables[R]. Tech. Rep. UM-CSE-TR-454-02, University of Michigan (2002)
7. Pei, D., Zhang, B., Massey, D., Zhang, L.: An Analysis of Path-Vector Routing Protocol, Technical Report TR040009, March 22nd (2004)
8. Ge, Z., Figueiredo, D., Jaiwal, S. et al.: On the hierarchical structure of the logical Internet graph [A]. In: Proceedings of SPIE ITCOM[C]. USA (August, 2001)
9. Siganos, G., Faloutsos, M., Faloutsos, P., Faloutsos, C.: Power-laws and the AS-level Internet topology. IEEE/ACM Trans. on Networking 11, 514–524 (2003)
10. Faloutsos, M., Faloutsos, P., Faloutsos, C.: On Power-Law Relationships of the Internet Topology (1999)
11. Mao, Z.: Solving the Interdomain Routing Puzzle –Understanding Interdomain Routing Dynamics. PhD thesis, the UNIVERSITY of CALIFORNIA at BERKELEY, Fall (2003)
12. OlafMaennel.: BGP convergence analysis. PhD thesis, Universität des Saarlandes (June 2003)
13. Obradovic, D.: Real-time Model and Convergence Time of BGP, In: Proceedings of the IEEE INFOCOM (June 2002)
14. The SSFNet Project, http://www.ssfnet.org

GDED-X Schemes for Load Balancing on Heterogeneous OTIS-Networks

Yong Qin[1,2], Wenjun Xiao[2], and Chenggui Zhao[2]

[1] Information and Network Center, Maoming University, Maoming, 525000, China
mmcqinyong@126.com
[2] School of Computer Science and Engineering, South China
University of Technology, Guangzhou, 510640, China
zhaochenggui@126.com

Abstract. In this paper, several diffusion schemes, designed for load balancing on optical transpose interconnection system (OTIS), have been generalized to heterogeneous OTIS-networks,based on an ideal of divide and conquer. These generalized schemes are called GDED-X and they schedule the load flow on intragroup links and intergroup links separately. Contrasted with other existing schemes available to heterogeneous networks, GDED-X schemes have a prominent promotion in efficiency and stability of iteration. Some theoretical evidences and experimental results are also be given to show that GDED-X schemes are better than those traditional X schemes for heterogeneous OTIS-networks, which shows the usability of our proposed schemes.

1 Introduction

Load balancing must be implemented on parallel computer network during runtime to prevent system from low performance due to highly uneven load distribution. Load balancing algorithms suppose that node loads consist of equally sized items. The goal of load balancing is to design scheduling algorithm to migrate loads across edges so that all nodes achieve the balanced state after load migration is completed. For homogeneous networks, the balanced state is achieved when all nodes of network have an equal load; but for heterogeneous networks, with different processing capability on nodes, the balanced state of whole network means that each of nodes takes a load proportional to its capability described by a weight. Some significant diffusion algorithms, like the first order scheme (FOS), second order scheme (SOS), optimal polynomial scheme (OPS) and OPT, had been developed for generally homogeneous networks. These traditional diffusion schemes for homogeneous networks have also been generalized to heterogeneous ones for load balancing, by Elsässer et al. in [6]. The kernel of generalization is to replace the Laplacian matrix in diffusion matrix with a generalized Laplacian. The generalized Laplacian is the product of ordinary Laplacian and a diagonal matrix whose diagonal entries are node's weights. Before the beginning of load balancing,all eigenvalues of the generalized Laplacian are required which is rather uneasy to some irregular, large scale networks.Thinking of this, the

H. Jin et al. (Eds.): ICA3PP 2007, LNCS 4494, pp. 482–492, 2007.

authors of the paper [1] provided other generalization of listed above, which has a simple spectral computing and better numerical stability. Details of this work are included in latter section. All schemes listed before determine l_2-minimal balancing flow. In fact, It has been stated that all local diffusion algorithms lead to a minimal flow, independent of the algorithms and parameters used.

General diffusion algorithms cited are not well suit to load balancing on large scale and irregular networks due to their complicated spectrum computation, such as the optical transpose interconnection system (OTIS) which has been proposed recently as a preferable parallel computer architecture. OTIS network has been presented as swapped interconnection networks by Parhami in [10]. Different from other scalable network of large scale like product graph on which the spectrum of network can be obtained directly from its factor graph, OTIS-network is irregular and it often need a rather complicated spectral computing. So load balancing schemes for regular networks including product graph are not available to OTIS- networks.

The authors in [2] have developed several DED-X schemes for load balancing on homogeneous OTIS-network. DED-X schemes combine diffusion and dimension exchange so they are hybrid diffusion schemes. The kernel of these new schemes is to divide load balancing process into three stages by a process of diffusion-exchange-diffusion. In the first stage DED-X schemes iteratively diffuse node loads on all factor network simultaneously until the initial loads on each of them achieve balanced status of this factor locally. In the second stage, they perform a dimension exchange strategy over all intergroup links. In this stage, factor networks pairwise interchange their balanced node load by a way of interchanging load of node (u, v) with one of node (v, u). After this stage, the total amount of node loads on each factor network is common. In the third stage, continue a process of diffusion with the same iterative polynomial as in the first stage but only compute the amount of load migration on one of the factors and have common flow on all other factors, based on the fact that each factor network has same initial load vector. theoretical results show that their schemes must converge work load to the average of node loads on whole network after diffusion-exchange-diffusion process passes through. However, to heterogeneous networks, these DED-X schemes are not possible to achieve to the balanced state by only local balancing on factors after load transposition is implemented in the seconde stage. To generalize DED-X schemes to adapt for heterogeneous OTIS networks, it is necessary to revise the strategy of load exchange and flow schedule of DED-X schemes.

In this paper, we plan to generalize several DED-X schemes for homogeneous OTIS networks as some corresponding schemes, called GDED-X schemes, such that they can complete load balancing task on heterogeneous OTIS-networks. We have theoretical results to show that these generalized GDED-X schemes also have a apparent improvement in efficiency and stability of iteration than general schemes for heterogeneous networks, same as the case of homogeneous networks.

2   Definitions

The OTIS network OTIS-G which is also denoted with G_s in this paper, derived from the n-node factor graph G, is defined as following, see [9].

Definition 1. *Let* $G = (V_G, E_G)$ *be an undirected graph. The OTIS-G = (V, E) is an undirected graph given by* $V = \{\langle g, p \rangle | g, p \in V_G\}$ *and* $E = \{(\langle g, p_1 \rangle, \langle g, p_2 \rangle) | g \in V_G, (p_1, p_2) \in E_G\} \cup \{(\langle g, p \rangle, \langle p, g \rangle) | g, p \in V_G, g \neq p\}$.

The graph G is called the factor network of OTIS-G or base graph. If G has N nodes, then OTIS-G is composed of N node-disjoint subnetworks $G_i (i = 0, 2, ...(n - 1))$, called groups. Each of these groups is isomorphic to G. Denotes the vertex set of G_i with $V_i = \{v_{ij}, 0 \leq j \leq (n - 1)\}$ and edge set $E_i = \{(v_{ik}, v_{il}) | (v_k, v_l) \in E(G)\}$. Now, the vertex set V of OTIS-G satisfies $V = \cup_{i=0}^{n-1} V_i$. The edge set E of OTIS-G can be partitioned into two subsets E_b called intragroup edge set and E_s call intergroup edges set. E_b represents all edges on G_i and E_s means other edges among G_i. Clearly,$E_b = \cup_{i=0}^{n-1} E_i$ and $E_s = \{(v_{ij}, v_{ji}) | i < j\}$.

Let vector $w_i = (w_{i1}, w_{i2}, ..., w_{in})^T$ and $c_i = (c_{i1}, c_{i2}, ..., c_{in})^T$ represent the load and weight on i-th group of OTIS-G. The j-th node v_{ij} of i-th group has an initial load $w_{ij}^0 \geq 0$ and a weight $c_{ij} > 0$. Let vector w and c denote the load and weight of OTIS-G. Then the i-th subvector of w and c are w_i and c_i. Notation C and C_i be the diagonal matrix with c and c_i as their diagonal entries respectively.

Let B_b and B be the node-edge incidence matrices of factor graph G and whole network OTIS-G respectively; B_s denotes the matrix incident the intergroup edges of E_s to nodes of OTIS-G. B_b, B_s and B have in each column exactly two non-zero entries 1 and -1 which represent the nodes incident to the corresponding edge. The signs of these non-zero entries decide implicitly directions of the flows produced in the process of load balancing on corresponding edges. The Laplacian L of graph is usually defined as $L = BB^T$. Let L and L_b the the Laplacian of OTIS-G and its factor network G respectively. Denote m distinct eigenvalues of L and m_b distinct eigenvalues of L_b with $\lambda_i, (0 \leq i \leq m)$ and $\lambda_i^b, (0 \leq i \leq m_b)$ in increasing order. Let $\alpha \in (0, 1)$ be a constant edge weight for OTIS-G and α_b for G. The matrix M defined by $M = I - \alpha L$ is called diffusion matrix. $M = I_{n^2} - \alpha L$ and $M_b = I_n - \alpha_b L_b$ be the corresponding diffusion matrices of polynomial based diffusion schemes. Then M and M_b have the eigenvalues $\mu_i = 1 - \alpha \lambda_i$ and $\mu_i^b = 1 - \alpha_b \lambda_i^b$. Denote the second largest eigenvalue of M and M_b according to absolute values with $\gamma = \max(|\mu_2|, |\mu_m|), \gamma^b = \max(|\mu_2^b|, |\mu_m^b|)$. The work load w^k in step k for polynomial based diffusion schemes can be commonly expressed as a general iteration form $w^k = p_k(M)w^0$. The convergence of a polynomial based scheme depends on whether error $e^k = w^k - w^l$ after iteration k, where w^l is the node load vector when the network achieves the balanced status, tends to zero. For any polynomial based diffusion scheme it holds that [5]

$$\|e^k\|_2 \le \max\{|p_k(\mu_i)| \cdot \|e^0\|_2, i = 2...m\}. \tag{1}$$

Especially, the first order scheme (FOS) satisfies $w^k = Mw^{k-1}$ and with 1 results in $\|e^k\|_2 \le \gamma^k \cdot \|e^0\|_2$. Since $\gamma(M) = \max(|1 - \alpha\lambda_2(L)|, |1 - \alpha\lambda_m(L)|)$, the minimum of γ is achieved for $1 - \alpha\lambda_2(L) = -1 + \alpha\lambda_m(L)$. By this the optimal value of α is $\alpha = 2/(\lambda_2 + \lambda_m)$. Then we have $\gamma = (1-\rho)/(1+\rho)$ with $\rho = \lambda_2(L)/\lambda_m(L)$ being called the condition number of L.

For OTIS-G, let y^k and x^k are two flow vectors whose entry corresponding edge e represents respectively the amount of load migrated along e in step k and the total amount of load until step k. For G, let y_b^k and x_b^k represent corresponding concepts. The directions of the flows are determined by the directions of the edges in the incidence matrix. The flow x is called a balancing flow if and only if $Bx = w^0 - w^l$.

3   Diffusion Schemes for General Heterogeneous Networks

Elsässer in [6] generalized several existing diffusion schemes for homogeneous networks, include FOS, SOS, CHEBY and OPT, to heterogeneous ones. In general, by previous schemes, for FOS and SOS, the work load w^k in step k can be expressed as form $w^k = p_k(M)w^0$, where $p_k(t)$ is a polynomial with degree less or equal to k and satisfying $p(1) = 1$. The FOS takes $p_k(t) = t^k$; SOS takes $p_0(t) = 1, p_1(t) = t, p_k(t) = \beta t p_{k-1}(t) + (1 - \beta)p_{k-2}(t), k > 2$. The fastest convergence occurs when $\beta = 2/(1 + \sqrt{1 - \gamma^2}), \gamma = (\lambda_2 - \lambda_m)/(\lambda_2 + \lambda_m)$. CHEBY has a similar iteration polynomial to SOS. By OPT, the work load w^k in step k can be described as $w^k = (I - \frac{1}{\lambda_{k+1}}L)w^{k-1}$. For applying FOS and SOS to heterogeneous networks, the diffusion matrix $M = I - \alpha L$ is replaced in [6] with $M = I - \alpha LC^{-1}$ and all original eigenvalues of L are replaced with ones of LC^{-1}. if let z_i be the eigenvectors of M with eigenvalues μ_i and with e^k representing the error after i-th iteration, which was stated in [5], the error e^k of their generalized scheme satisfies $\|e^k\|_2 \le \|C^{1/2}\|_2\|C^{-1/2}\|_2 p_k(\gamma)\|e^0\|_2$.

Zhao et al. in [1] presented another generation of these diffusion schemes to heterogeneous networks in which the diffusion matrix is $M = I - \alpha LR$, where $R = (I + 1/n(I - C^*)J)$ with $C^* = n/(\sum_{i=1}^n c_i)C$. The parameter α is independent of the matrix R and only decided by L, which leads to a lower iterative times and better numerical stability because α will not change with different node weight distribution. Following theorem shows that schemes generalized in [1] do not increase iteration error to original those schemes of homogeneous network for the heterogeneity of network.

Theorem 1. *For fixed network and initial load distribution, any polynomial iterative method using diffusion matrix $M = I - \alpha LR$ produces an error e^k at step k equal to one produced by iteration diffusion matrix $M = I - \alpha L$.*

For more details about the theorem 1 please see [1].

4   Hybrid Diffusion Schemes for Heterogeneous OTIS Networks

In common, all diffusion schemes, in [1] or in [6], for heterogeneous networks require the knowledge of eigenvalues of the matrix LC^{-1} or ones of L. For an OTIS-network, with n vertices on its factor network, all eigenvalues of a matrix with order n^2 have to be computed before load balancing process starts, which is unpractical to those large OTIS-networks. Therefore we will develop the work in [2] and generalize its DED-X schemes as GDED-X for load balancing on heterogenous OTIS networks. Being the same with original DED-X, GDED-X schemes combine diffusion and dimension exchange so they are hybrid diffusion schemes. GDED-X still divides load balancing process into three stages by a process of diffusion-exchange-diffusion. In the first stage GDED-X scheme diffuses node loads iteratively until for all i, the initial load vector w_i^0 of i-th group achieves balanced status w_i^l locally on this group. In this stage, the work load w_i^k in step k of nodes on i-th factor can be decided according to

$$w_i^k = p_k(M_b^i)w^0, \text{with } M_b^i = (I_n - \alpha_b L_b R_i), R_i = (I + 1/n(I - n/(\sum_{j=1}^{n} c_{ij})C_i)J).$$
(2)

In the following, we perform a dimension exchange strategy over all intergroup links. In this stage, loads are migrated only via the links between groups. Let $L_s = L - L_b = B_s B_s^T$. Denoting by $f = (l_{01}, \ldots, l_{ij}(i < j), \ldots, l_{(n-2)(n-1)})$ the vector of edge weights and by $F = diag(f)$ the diagonal matrix containing the edge weights on its diagonal, where l_{ij} represents the edge weight on the edge linking the group i and j. Now, assign a value to l_{ij} according to

$$l_{ij} = \frac{(\sum_{k=1}^{n-1} c_{ik})(\sum_{k=1}^{n-1} c_{jk})}{\sum_{i=1}^{n-1}\sum_{j=1}^{n-1} c_{ij}}.$$
(3)

It assumes that GDED-X takes k_1 steps to achieve the local balanced status w^{k_1}. The process of dimension exchange here can be expressed as following.

$$w^{k_1+1} = M_s w^l, M_s = I_{n^2} - B_s F B_s^T C^{-1}$$
(4)

In the third stage, we proceed diffusion on each of groups with the same iterative polynomial as in the first stage, by flow scheduling on intragroup edges of each group. Following theorem shows that any polynomial based scheme must converge w^k to the balanced status of whole network after such diffusion-exchange-diffusion process passes through.

Theorem 2. *For any polynomial based scheme X, if X takes as most k_1 and k_2 steps to iterate the initial load w_i^0 and w_i^l of each of groups to achieve corresponding balanced status respectively, then GDED-X scheme iterates load w^0 to the balanced status in at most $k_1 + k_2 + 1$ steps.*

Proof. For any polynomial based scheme X, for any $0 \leq i \leq (n-1)$, scheme X leads group i to the local balanced status after first stage, by the use of 2 which follows

$$w_{ij}^{k_1} = \frac{c_{ij}}{\sum_{k=1}^{n-1} c_{ik}} \sum_{k=1}^{n-1} w_{ik}^0 \tag{5}$$

After second stage, exchanging loads on intergroup links, by equation 3 and 5 it follows

$$w_{ij}^{k_1+1} = w_{ij}^{k_1} - \frac{(\sum_{k=1}^{n-1} c_{ik})(\sum_{k=1}^{n-1} c_{jk})}{\sum_{i=1}^{n-1} \sum_{j=1}^{n-1} c_{ij}} \left(\frac{w_{ij}^{k_1}}{c_{ij}} - \frac{w_{ji}^{k_1}}{c_{ji}} \right)$$

$$= \left(\frac{c_{ij}}{\sum_{k=1}^{n-1} c_{ik}} - \frac{\sum_{k=1}^{n-1} c_{jk}}{\sum_{i=1}^{n-1} \sum_{j=1}^{n-1} c_{ij}} \right) \sum_{k=1}^{n-1} w_{ik}^0 - \frac{\sum_{k=1}^{n-1} c_{ik}}{\sum_{i=1}^{n-1} \sum_{j=1}^{n-1} c_{ij}} \sum_{k=1}^{n-1} w_{jk}^0$$

After the third stage, because of the same iterative polynomial only different initial load on nodes, it holds that

$$w_{ij}^{k_1+k_2+1} = \frac{c_{ij}}{\sum_{k=1}^{n-1} c_{ik}} \sum_{j=1}^{n-1} w_{ij}^{k_1+1}$$

$$= \frac{c_{ij}}{\sum_{k=1}^{n-1} c_{ik}} \sum_{j=1}^{n-1} \left[\frac{\sum_{k=1}^{n-1} c_{ik}}{\sum_{i=1}^{n-1} \sum_{j=1}^{n-1} c_{ij}} \sum_{k=1}^{n-1} w_{jk}^0 \right]$$

$$= \frac{c_{ij}}{\sum_{i=1}^{n-1} \sum_{j=1}^{n-1} c_{ij}} \sum_{j=1}^{n-1} \sum_{k=1}^{n-1} w_{jk}^0$$

$$= w_{ij}^l$$

which shows that w^0 achieves to w^l within $k_1 + k_2 + 1$ steps.

We now describe GDED-X scheme as local iterative algorithm. One can select a practical scheme, for example, FOS or SOS or OPT, to replace X. The performance of GDED-X will be discuss in detail in following sections.

Algorithm: GDED-X
Input: OTIS-network consists of groups G_i with load vector w_i and node weights vector $c_i, 0 \leq i < n$.
Output: Balanced load vector w^l and a sequence of flow x^k.
1. for all groups G_i of OTIS-G
2. run the procedure X on $G_i, 0 \leq i < n$ and input the balanced load vector as w_i^l;
3. end for
4. for all intergroup edges $e = (i, j), (j, i), i \neq j$
5. $y_e^E = \frac{(\sum_{k=1}^{n-1} c_{ik})(\sum_{k=1}^{n-1} c_{jk})}{\sum_{i=1}^{n-1} \sum_{j=1}^{n-1} c_{ij}} \left(\frac{w_{ij}^{k_1}}{c_{ij}} - \frac{w_{ji}^{k_1}}{c_{ji}} \right)$;
6. $w_{ij}^E = w_{ij}^l - y_e^E$;

7. end for
8. for all factors G_i of OTIS-G
9. $w_i^0 = w_i^E$;
10. run the procedure X on $G_i, 0 \le i < n$ and input the balanced load vector
   as w_i^g
11. end for

5 Algorithm Analysis

Firstly,by theorem 1 we know, in the case of X being FOS, SOS and CHEBY, the convergence speed of GDED-X is decided by the diffusion norm of corresponding factor network, not depended on the distribution of node weights. By theorem 2, it is clear that if scheme X takes $O(n)$ complexity to balance node loads on factor network then GDED-X has the same complexity on the OTIS network of this factor. Following theorem [2] shows that general scheme X has a significant promotion in the number of iteration on OTIS network than on its factor network which displays that GDED-X behaves better in the iterative efficiency than X. When GDED-X begins, each of groups implements load balancing algorithm in parallel. The speed of convergence only depends on the maximal iterative error of groups.It assumes that the maximal number of iterations are required to i-th group.

Theorem 3. *Let λ_1^b and λ_1 represent the second smallest Laplace eigenvalue of factor network G and OTIS-G respectively. Let λ_{max}^b and λ_{max} denote their largest eigenvalue respectively. Then it is true that*

$$\lambda_1 \le \lambda_1^b. \tag{6}$$

and

$$\lambda_{max}^b + 1 \le \lambda_{max} \tag{7}$$

Theorem 4. *Let γ_b and γ denote the diffusion norm of the factor network G and OTIS-G respectively. Then it holds that $\gamma_b < \gamma$, which means that when apply GDED-FOS scheme and FOS scheme to OTIS-G, GDED-FOS will has a smaller upper bound of error than FOS in k-th iteration.*

Theorem 3 and 4 can be applied to the known SOS scheme and the Chebyshev scheme (CHEBY)(see [5]). In both cases, better convergence speed can be expected when using the GDED-FOS or GDED-CHEBY. In fact, experiments validate that the largest improvement is obtain for large scale networks with regular factor networks. In the case of arbitrary factor networks, significant improvements have also be observed in numerical simulation. Denote the diameter of the factor graph with d. Following theorem shows that GDED-OPT scheme often exhibits better performance than the OPT scheme.

Theorem 5. *In the worst case, to achieve balanced status on OTIS network, GDED-OPT has a lower bound $d + 1$ of the number of iteration required. But OPT needs as least $2(d + 1)$ iterations in this case.*

6   Experiments

Here some numerical results help to illustrate the properties of GDED-X scheme and the advantages of these schemes. All results here are completed on two familiar factor networks, including Hypercube(H_3) and Mesh($M_{2\times4}$). In order to test the stability of GDED-X schemes, node initial load are set as highly unbalanced PEAK and random RAN. We also distribute node weights as homogeneous HOMO, semi-heterogeneous SEMI and sharply heterogenous CS to both OTIS networks constructed from H_3 and $M_{2\times4}$.

Node initial load distribution:
PEAK:One node has a super overweight load of $100 \times n$ and the others are free, with a load 0;
RAN: $100 \times n$ load items are randomly distributed among n nodes.

Node weight assignment:
HOMO: All nodes have the identical capability, indicated by $C = I$. This simulates a homogeneous network.
SEMI:The half nodes have a weight of 1 and others 2. This simulates a heterogeneous network with relatively regular weight distribution, like some networks consisting of two subnetworks.
CS:This simulates a heterogeneous network according to the traditional client-server model in which the sever node has a high weight of $n + 1$ and others 1.

We want to compare our new load balancing strategies GDED-FOS and GDED-OPT with the traditional FOS and OPT methods with respect to speed, stability and flow quality. we did experiments on both networks, using every possible combination of initial load and weight distribution listed above. The balance process stops when the error $\| w^k - w^l \|_2$ is less than 0.01.

6.1   Flow Analysis

Firsly, we perform GDED-OPT and OPT schemes on both OTIS-H_3 and OTIS-$M_{2\times4}$ networks to compare the quality of resulted flows. Thinking of the known fact that polynomial based schemes all compute the same flow which is l_2-minimal (see [5]), we only experiment with GDED-OPT and OPT scheme, ignoring other schemes. Table 1 shows that in most cases, GDED-OPT scheme produces a flow smaller than one of the OPT. Specially, the flow of GDED-OPT scheme is far smaller than the flow of OPT in the case of OTIS-$M_{2\times4}$. Therefore, GDED-OPT should preferably be applied to practices. Though the flow calculated by GDED-OPT scheme is not minimal in the l_2 norm, it can seen from table 1 that there is only little difference between the flow resulting from GDED-OPT and the l_2-minimal flow produced by general OPT.

Table 1. Comparison of the flows produced by OPT and the GDED-OPT

networks	initial load	node weight	OPT flows	GDED-OPT flows
OTIS-H_3	PEAK	HOMO	4598.9345	4636.0903
		SEMIHOMO	4517.0283	4947.1279
		CS	2299.4718	2103.6124
	RAN	HOMO	2884.8685	3106.9855
		SEMIHOMO	2760.2311	3497.4927
		CS	2104.6756	1546.6774
OTIS-$M_{2\times4}$	PEAK	HOMO	47213.1788	6279.2174
		SEMIHOMO	53661.5383	6608.8925
		CS	37794.3732	2984.7939
	RAN	HOMO	70986.4104	4970.6308
		SEMIHOMO	134686.730	5311.5263
		CS	85719.2920	2075.4244

6.2   Convergence Speed and Stability

We also list some results in the following Table 2 in order to compare the convergence speed of traditional FOS, OPT schemes and our GDED-FOS and GDED-OPT schemes, with each of possibly initial conditions. As we have proven before, practically, GDED-FOS has a evidently smaller number of iterations than traditional FOS scheme. GDED-OPT behaves better which almost,compared to existing OPT scheme, halves the number of iterations for each of combination of node load and weight. Noticeably, no matter GDED-X or X, the number of iteration does not vary with different load and weight distribution. In the following we want to compare new GDED-FOS and GDED-OPT schemes with original FOS and OPT schemes more intensively. We did experiments on OTIS-H_3 and OTIS-$M_{2\times4}$, using GDED-FOS and FOS (Figure 1), GDED-OPT and OPT (Figure 2)

Table 2. Comparison of the number of the iterations using general diffusion schemes X and GDED-X, N_X represents the number of iterations

networks	load	node weight	N_{FOS}	$N_{GDED-FOS}$	N_{OPT}	$N_{GDED-OPT}$
OTIS-H_3	PEAK	HOMO	77	38	15	7
		SEMIHOMO	77	38	15	7
		CS	73	35	15	7
	RAN	HOMO	76	37	15	7
		SEMIHOMO	76	37	15	7
		CS	71	38	15	7
OTIS-M_{2*4}	PEAK	HOMO	165	114	42	13
		SEMIHOMO	165	114	42	13
		CS	155	105	42	13
	RAN	HOMO	157	112	42	13
		SEMIHOMO	157	112	42	13
		CS	144	112	42	13

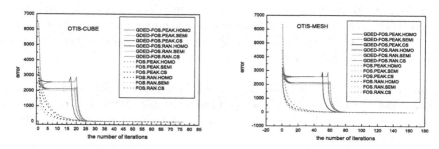

Fig. 1. GDED-FOS and FOS on OTIS-H_3 (left) and OTIS-$M_{2\times4}$ (right) networks

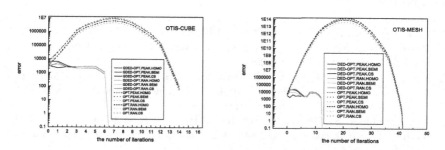

Fig. 2. GDED-OPT and OPT on OTIS-H_3 (left) and OTIS-$M_{2\times4}$ (right) networks

The results show that both GDED-FOS and GDED-OPT behave better numerically stability and faster convergence speed. Figure 1 shows that GDED-FOS is stable in both diffusion stages, with error decreasing steadily, only a suddenly drop down to 0 arising after the seconde stage (load exchange). But this is apparently not a problem because in this stage loads only migrate along optical links which are capable of standing under large scale of load movement. From Figure 1, one can observe that GDED-FOS behaves better on OTIS-Hypercube than OTIS-Mesh because it displays more apparent advantage related to FOS scheme. The best behavior of GDED-X schemes can be observed from Figure 2 where GDED-OPT has a much better stability than general OPT. Related to OPT, numerical problems are almost never observed in GDED-OPT. It can be seen from Figure 2 that OPT scheme leads to high error of iteration which will fail to implement load balancing on large OTIS network due to numerical problem. In this case, GDED-OPT should be a proper substitution manner. Furthermore, Figure 1 and 2 show that distinct node initial load and weight distributions do not bring forth apparent difference in stability.

7   Conclusion

The diffusion schemes described in this paper are closely related to corresponding those in paper [2] and both are based on a common ideal of hybrid diffusion-exchange-diffusion. However, the schemes in this paper still have particular details development based on paper [2]. In essence, GDED-X schemes are several generalizations of DED-X. This work should benefit to load balancing on heterogeneous OTIS networks and it also presents some opportunities for future work. We are going to try to generalize this ideal to general networks, not limited to OTIS networks, for a larger scope of applications.

Acknowledgment. This paper is supported by the Natural Science Foundation of Guangdong Province, China, under Grant No. 05011896, and the Natural Science Foundation of Education Department of Guangdong Province, China, under Grant No. Z03080.

References

1. Zhao, C., Xiao, W., Qing, Y.: Efficient Diffusion Schemes for Load Balancing on Heterogeneous Networks. Dynamics of Continuous, Discrete and Impulsive Systems, Series B S1 1, 147–152 (2006)
2. Zhao, C., Xiao, W., Qing, Y.: Hybrid Diffusion Schemes for Load Balancing on OTIS-Networks. In: The 7th International Conference on Algorithms and Architectures for Parallel Processing, accepted (2007)
3. Muthukrishnan, S., Ghosh, B., Schultz, M.H.: First- and second-order diffusive methods for rapid, coarse, distributed load balancing. Theory of Computing Systems 31, 331–354 (1998)
4. Elsässer, R., Frommer, A., Monien, B., preis, R.: Optimal and alternating direction load balancing schemes. In: Amestoy, P.R., Berger, P., Daydé, M., Duff, I.S., Frayssé, V., Giraud, L., Ruiz, D. (eds.) Euro-Par 1999. LNCS, vol. 1685, pp. 280–290. Springer, Heidelberg (1999)
5. Diekmann, R., Frommer, A., Monien, B.: Efficient schemes for nearest neighbor load balancing. Parallel Computing 25, 789–812 (1999)
6. Elsässer, R., Monien, B., Preis, R.: Diffusion schemes for load balancing on heterogeneous networks. Theory of Computing Systems 35, 305–320 (2002)
7. Elsässer, R., Monien, B., Preis, R., Frommer, A.: Optimal diffusion schemes and load balancing on product graphs. Parallel Processing Letters. 14, 61–73 (2004)
8. Arndt, H.: On finite dimension exchange algorithms. Linear Algebra and its Applications 380, 73–93 (2004)
9. Day, K., Al-Ayyoub, A.: Topological properties of OTIS-Networks. IEEE Transactions on Parallel and Distributed Systems 13, 359–366 (2002)
10. Parhami, B.: Swapped interconnection networks: Topological, performance, and robustness attributes. Journal of Parallel and Distributed Computing 65, 1443–1452 (2005)
11. Godsil, G.: Algebraic Graph Theory, pp. 279–306. Springer, Heidelberg (2001)

A Generalized Critical Task Anticipation Technique for DAG Scheduling

Ching-Hsien Hsu[1], Chih-Wei Hsieh[1], and Chao-Tung Yang[2]

[1] Department of Computer Science and Information Engineering
Chung Hua University, Hsinchu, Taiwan 300, R.O.C.
chh@chu.edu.tw
[2] High-Performance Computing Laboratory
Department of Computer Science and Information Engineering
Tunghai University, Taichung City, 40704, Taiwan R.O.C.
ctyang@thu.edu.tw

Abstract. The problem of scheduling a weighted directed acyclic graph (DAG) representing an application to a set of heterogeneous processors to minimize the completion time has been recently studied. The NP-completeness of the problem has instigated researchers to propose different heuristic algorithms. In this paper, we present a Generalized Critical-task Anticipation (*GCA*) algorithm for DAG scheduling in heterogeneous computing environment. The *GCA* scheduling algorithm employs task prioritizing technique based on *CA* algorithm and introduces a new processor selection scheme by considering heterogeneous communication costs among processors for adapting grid and scalable computing. To evaluate the performance of the proposed technique, we have developed a simulator that contains a parametric graph generator for generating weighted directed acyclic graphs with various characteristics. We have implemented the *GCA* algorithm along with the *CA* and *HEFT* scheduling algorithms on the simulator. The *GCA* algorithm is shown to be effective in terms of speedup and low scheduling costs.

1 Introduction

The purpose of heterogeneous computing system is to drive processors cooperation to get the application done quickly. Because of diverse quality among processors or some special requirements, like exclusive function, memory access speed, or the customize I/O devices, etc.; tasks might have distinct execution time on different resources. Therefore, efficient task scheduling is important for achieving good performance in heterogeneous systems.

   The primary scheduling methods can be classified into three categories, dynamic scheduling, static scheduling and hybrid scheduling according to the time at which the scheduling decision is made. In dynamic approach, the system performs redistribution of tasks between processors during run-time, expect to balance computational load, and reduce processor's idle time. On the contrary, in static approach, information of applications, such as tasks execution time, message size of communications among tasks, and tasks dependences are known a priori at compile-time; tasks are assigned to

H. Jin et al. (Eds.): ICA3PP 2007, LNCS 4494, pp. 493–505, 2007.

processors accordingly in order to minimize the entire application completion time and satisfy the precedence of tasks. Hybrid scheduling techniques are mix of dynamic and static methods, where some preprocessing is done statically to guide the dynamic scheduler [8].

A Direct Acyclic Graph (DAG) [2] is usually used for modeling parallel applications that consists a number of tasks. The nodes of DAG correspond to tasks and the edges of which indicate the precedence constraints between tasks. In addition, the weight of an edge represents communication cost between tasks. Each node is given a computation cost to be performed on a processor and is represented by a computation costs matrix. Fig. 1 shows an example of the model of DAG scheduling. In Fig. 1(a), it is assumed that task n_j is a successor (predecessor) of task n_i if there exists an edge from n_i to n_j (from n_j to n_i) in the graph. Upon task precedence constraint, only if the predecessor n_i completes its execution and then its successor n_j receives the *messages* from n_i, the successor n_j can start its execution. Fig. 1(b) demonstrates different computation costs of task that performed on heterogeneous processors. It is also assumed that tasks can be executed only on single processor with non-preemptable style. A simple fully connected processor network with asymmetrical data transfer rate is shown in Fig. 1(c) and 1(d).

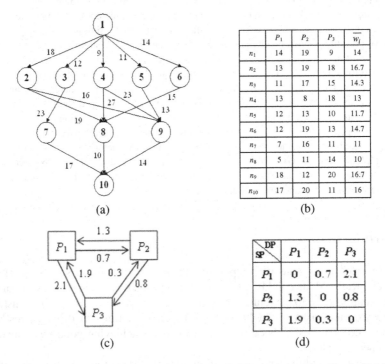

Fig. 1. An example of DAG scheduling problem (a) Directed Acyclic Graph (DAG-1) (b) computation cost matrix (W) (c) processor topology (d) communication weight

The scheduling problem has been widely studied in heterogeneous systems where the computational ability of processors is different and the processors communicate over an underlying network. Many researches have been proposed in the literature.

The scheduling problem has been shown to be NP-complete [3] in general cases as well as in several restricted cases; so the desire of optimal scheduling shall lead to higher scheduling overhead. The negative result motivates the requirement for heuristic approaches to solve the scheduling problem. A comprehensive survey about static scheduling algorithms is given in [9]. The authors of have shown that the heuristic-based algorithms can be classified into a variety of categories, such as clustering algorithms, duplication-based algorithms, and list-scheduling algorithms. Due to page limitation, we omit the description for related works.

In this paper, we present a Generalized Critical task Anticipation (*GCA*) algorithm, which is an approach of list scheduling for DAG task scheduling problem. The main contribution of this paper is proposing a novel heuristic for DAG scheduling on heterogeneous machines and networks. A significant improvement is that inter-processor communication costs are considered into processor selection phase such that tasks can be mapped to more suitable processors. The *GCA* heuristic is compared favorable with previous *CA* [5] and *HEFT* heuristics in terms of schedule length and speedup under different parameters.

The rest of this paper is organized as follows: Section 2 provides some background, describes preliminaries regarding heterogeneous scheduling system in DAG model and formalizes the research problem. Section 3 defines notations and terminologies used in this paper. Section 4 forms the main body of the paper, presents the Generalized Critical task Anticipation (*GCA*) scheduling algorithm and illustrating it with an example. Section 5 discusses performance of the proposed heuristic and its simulation results. Finally, Section 6 briefly concludes this paper.

2 DAG Scheduling on Heterogeneous Systems

The DAG scheduling problem studied in this paper is formalized as follows. Given a parallel application represented by a DAG, in which nodes represent tasks and edges represent dependence between these tasks. The target computing architecture of DAG scheduling problem is a set of heterogeneous processors, $M = \{P_k: k = 1: P\}$ and $P = |M|$, communicate over an underlying network which is assumed fully connected. We have the following assumptions:

- Inter-processor communications are performed without network contention between arbitrary processors.
- Computation of tasks is in non-preemptive style. Namely, once a task is assigned to a processor and starts its execution, it will not be interrupted until its completion.
- Computation and communication can be worked simultaneously because of the separated I/0.
- If two tasks are assigned to the same processor, the communication cost between the two tasks can be discarded.
- A processor is assumed to send the computational results of tasks to their immediate successor as soon as it completes the computation.

Given a DAG scheduling system, W is an $n \times P$ matrix in which $w_{i,j}$ indicates estimated computation time of processor P_j to execute task n_i. The mean execution time of task n_i can be calculated by the following equation:

$$\overline{w_i} = \sum_{j=1}^{P} \frac{w_{i,j}}{P} \tag{1}$$

Example of the mean execution time can be referred to Fig. 1(b).

For communication part, a $P \times P$ matrix T is structured to represent different data transfer rate among processors (Fig. 1(d) demonstrates the example). The communication cost of transferring data from task n_i (execute on processor p_x) to task n_j (execute on processor p_y) is denoted by $c_{i,j}$ and can be calculated by the following equation,

$$c_{i,j} = V_m + Msg_{i,j} \times t_{x,y}, \tag{2}$$

Where:

V_m is the communication latency of processor P_m,

$Msg_{i,j}$ is the size of message from task n_i to task n_j,

$t_{x,y}$ is data transfer rate from processor p_x to processor p_y, $1 \le x, y \le P$.

In static DAG scheduling problem, it was usually to consider processors' latency together with its data transfer rate. Therefore, equation (2) can be simplified as follows,

$$c_{i,j} = Msg_{i,j} \times t_{x,y}, \tag{3}$$

Given an application represented by Directed Acyclic Graph (DAG), $G = (V, E)$, where $V = \{n_j : j = 1 : v\}$ is the set of nodes and $v = |V|$; $E = \{e_{i,j} = <n_i, n_j>\}$ is the set of communication edges and $e = |E|$. In this model, each node indicates least indivisible task. Namely, each node must be executed on a processor from the start to its completion. Edge $<n_i, n_j>$ denotes precedence of tasks n_i and n_j. In other words, task n_i is the immediate predecessor of task n_j and task n_j is the immediate successor of task n_i. Such precedence represents that task n_j can be start for execution only upon the completion of task n_i. Meanwhile, task n_j should receive essential message from n_i for its execution. Weight of edge $<n_i, n_j>$ indicates the average communication cost between n_i and n_j.

Node without any inward edge is called *entry node*, denoted by n_{entry}; while node without any outward edge is called *exit node*, denoted by n_{exit}. In general, it is supposed that the application has only one *entry node* and one *exit node*. If the actual application claims more than one *entry* (*exit*) node, we can insert a dummy *entry* (*exit*) node with zero-cost edge.

3   Preliminaries

This study concentrates on list scheduling approaches in DAG model. List scheduling was usually distinguished into list phase and processor selection phase. Therefore, priori to discuss the main content, we first define some notations and terminologies used in both phases in this section.

3.1   Parameters for List Phase

Definition 1: Given a DAG scheduling system on $G = (V, E)$, the *Critical Score* of task n_i denoted by $CS(n_i)$ is an accumulative value that are computed recursively traverses along the graph upward, starting from the exit node. $CS(n_i)$ is computed by the following equations,

$$CS(n_i) = \begin{cases} \overline{w_{exit}} & \text{if } n_i \text{ is the exit ndoe (i.e. } n_i = n_{exit}) \\ \overline{w_i} + \underset{n_j \in suc(n_i)}{Max}(\overline{c_{i,j}} + CS(n_j)) & \text{otherwise} \end{cases} \quad (4)$$

where $\overline{w_{exit}}$ is the average computation cost of task n_{exit}, $\overline{w_i}$ is the average computation cost of task n_i, $suc(n_i)$ is the set of immediate successors of task n_i,

$\overline{c_{i,j}}$ is the average communication cost of edge $<n_i, n_j>$ which is defined as follows,

$$\overline{c_{i,j}} = \frac{Msg_{i,j} \times \sum\limits_{1 \le x,y \le P} t_{x,y}}{(P^2 - P)}, \quad (5)$$

3.2 Parameters for Processor Selection Phase

Most algorithms in processor selection phase employ a partial schedule scheme to minimize overall schedule length of an application. To achieve the partial optimization, an intuitional method is to evaluate the *finish time (FT)* of task n_i executed on different processors. According to the calculated results, one can select the processor who has minimum finish time as target processor to execute the task n_i. In such approach, each processor P_k will maintain a list of tasks, *task-list(P_k)*, keeps the latest status of tasks correspond to the $EFT(n_i, P_k)$, the earliest finish time of task n_i that is assigned on processor P_k.

Recall having been mentioned above that the application represented by DAG must satisfy the precedence relationship. Taking into account the precedence of tasks in DAG, a task n_j can start to execute on a processor P_k only if its all immediate predecessors send the essential messages to n_j and n_j successful receives all these messages. Thus, the latest message arrive time of node n_j on processor P_k, denoted by $LMAT(n_j, P_k)$, is calculated by the following equation,

$$LMAT(n_j, P_k) = \underset{n_i \in pred(n_j)}{Max}(EFT(n_i) + c_{u,k}, \text{ for task } n_i \text{ executed on processor } P_u) \quad (6)$$

where $pred(n_j)$ is the set of immediate predecessors of task n_j. Note that if tasks n_i and n_j are assigned to the same processor, $c_{u,k}$ is assumed to be zero because it is negligible.

Because the entry task n_{entry} has no inward edge, thus we have

$$LMAT(n_{entry}, P_k) = 0 \quad (7)$$

for all $k = 1$ to P.

Definition 2: Given a DAG scheduling system on $G = (V, E)$, the *Start Time* of task n_j executed on processor P_k is denoted as $ST(n_j, P_k)$.

Estimating task's start time (for example, task n_j) will facilitate search of available time slot on target processors that is large enough to execute that task (i.e., length of time slot > $w_{j,k}$). Note that the search of available time slot is started from $LMAT(n_j, P_k)$.

<u>Definition 3</u>: Given a DAG scheduling system on $G = (V, E)$, the *finish time* of task n_j denoted by $FT(n_j, P_k)$, represents the completion time of task n_j executed on processor P_k. $FT(n_j, P_k)$ is defined as follows,

$$FT(n_j, P_k) = ST(n_j, P_k) + w_{j,k} \tag{8}$$

<u>Definition 4</u>: Given a DAG scheduling system on $G = (V, E)$, the *earliest finish time* of task n_j denoted by $EFT(n_j)$, is formulated as follows,

$$EFT(n_j) = \underset{p_k \in P}{Min} \{FT(n_j, P_k)\} \tag{9}$$

<u>Definition 5</u>: Based on the determination of $EFT(n_j)$ in equation (9), if the earliest finish time of task n_j is obtained upon task n_j executed on processor p_t, then the target processor of task n_j is denoted by $TP(n_j)$, and $TP(n_j) = p_t$.

4   The Generalized Critical-Task Anticipation Scheduling Algorithm

Our approach takes advantages of list scheduling in lower algorithmic complexity and superior scheduling performance and furthermore came up with a novel heuristic algorithm, the generalized critical task anticipation (*GCA*) scheduling algorithm to improve the schedule length as well as speedup of applications. The proposed scheduling algorithm will be verified beneficial for the readers while we delineate a sequence of the algorithm and show some example scenarios in three phases, prioritizing phase, listing phase and processor selection phase.

In prioritizing phase, the $CS(n_i)$ is known as the maximal summation of scores including the average computation cost and communication cost from task n_i to the exit task. Therefore, the magnitude of the task's critical score is regarded as the decisive factor when determining the priority of a task. In listing phase, an ordered list of tasks should be determined for the subsequent phase of processor selection. The proposed *GCA* scheduling technique arranges tasks into a list L, not only according to critical scores but also considers tasks' importance.

Several observations bring the idea of *GCA* scheduling method. Because of processor heterogeneity, there exist variations in execution cost from processor to processor for same task. In such circumstance, tasks with larger computational cost should be assigned higher priority. This observation aids some critical tasks to be executed earlier and enhances probability of tasks reduce its finish time. Furthermore, each task has to receive the essential messages from its immediate predecessors. In other words, a task will be in waiting state when it does not collect complete message yet. For this reason, we emphasize the importance of the last arrival message such that the succeeding task can start its execution earlier. Therefore, it is imperative to give the predecessor who sends the last arrival message higher priority. This can aid the succeeding task to get chance to advance the start time. On the other hand, if a task n_i is inserted into the front of a scheduling list, it occupies vantage position. Namely, n_i has higher probability to accelerate its execution and consequently the start time of $suc(n_i)$ can be advanced as well.

In most list scheduling approaches, it was usually to demonstrate the algorithms in two phases, the list phase and the processor selection phase. The list phase of proposed *GCA* scheduling algorithm consists of two steps, the *CS* (critical score) calculation step and task prioritization step.

Let's take examples for the demonstration of *CS* calculation, which is performed in level order and started from the deepest level, i.e., the level of exit task. For example, according to equation (4), we have $CS(n_{10}) = \overline{w_{10}} = 16$. For the upper level tasks, n_7, n_8 and n_9, $CS(n_7) = \overline{w_7 + (c_{7,10} + CS(n_{10}))} = 47.12$, $CS(n_8) = \overline{w_8 + (c_{8,10} + CS(n_{10}))} = 37.83$, $CS(n_9) = \overline{w_9 + (c_{9,10} + CS(n_{10}))} = 49.23$. The other tasks can be calculated by the same methods. Table 1 shows complete calculated critical scores of all tasks for DAG-1.

Table 1. Critical Scores of tasks in DAG-1 using *GCA* algorithm

\multicolumn{10}{c}{*Critical Scores* of tasks in *GCA* algorithm}									
n_1	n_2	n_3	n_4	n_5	n_6	n_7	n_8	n_9	n_{10}
120.13	84.83	88.67	89.45	76.28	70.25	47.12	37.83	49.23	16.00

Follows the critical score calculation, the *GCA* scheduling method considers both tasks' importance (i.e., critical score) and its relative urgency for prioritizing tasks. Based on the results obtained previously, we use the same example to demonstrate task prioritization in *GCA*. Let's start at the exit task n_{10}, which has the lowest critical score. Assume that tasks will be arranged into an ordered list L, therefore, we have $L = \{n_{10}\}$ initially. Because task n_{10} has three immediate predecessors, with the order $CS(n_9) > CS(n_7) > CS(n_8)$, the list L will be updated to $L=\{n_9, n_7, n_8, n_{10}\}$. Applying the same prioritizing method by taking the front element of L, task n_9; because task n_9 has three immediate predecessors, with the order $CS(n_4) > CS(n_2) > CS(n_5)$, we have the updated list $L = \{n_4, n_2, n_5, n_9, n_7, n_8, n_{10}\}$. Taking the same operations, insert task n_1 in front of task n_4, insert task n_3 in front of task n_7, insert tasks n_4, n_2, n_6 (because $CS(n_4) > CS(n_2) > CS(n_6)$) in front of task n_8; we have the list $L = \{n_1, n_4, n_2, n_5, n_9, n_3, n_7, n_6, n_4, n_2, n_6, n_8, n_{10}\}$. The final list $L = \{n_1, n_4, n_2, n_5, n_9, n_3, n_7, n_6, n_8, n_{10}\}$ can be derived by removing duplicated tasks.

In listing phases, the *GCA* scheduling algorithm proposes two enhancements from the majority of literatures. First, *GCA* scheduling technique considers various transmission costs of messages among processors into the calculation of critical scores. Second, the *GCA* algorithm prioritizes tasks according to the influence on its successors and devotes to lead an accelerated chain while other techniques simply schedule high critical score tasks with higher priority. In other words, the *GCA* algorithm is not only prioritizing tasks by its importance but also by the urgency among task. The prioritizing scheme of *GCA* scheduling technique can be accomplished by using simple stack operations, push and pop, which are outlined in *GCA_List_Phase* procedure as follows.

Begin_GCA_List_Phase
1.   Initially, construct an array of Boolean QV and a stack S.
2. $QV[n_j] = false, \forall\ n_j \in V$.
3.   Push n_{exit} on top of S.
4.   **While** S is not empty **do**
5.   Peek task n_j on the top of S;
6.   **If**(all $QV[n_i]$ are *true*, for all $n_i \in pred(n_j)$ or task n_j is n_{entry}) {
7.   Pop task n_j from top of S and put n_j into scheduling list L;
8. $QV[\ n_j] = true;$ }
9.   **Else**   /* search the $CT(n_j)$ */
10.   **For** each task n_i, where $n_i \in pred(n_j)$ **do**
11.   **If**($QV[n_i] = false$)
12.   Put $CS(n_i)$ into container C;
13.   **Endif**
14.   Push tasks $pred(n_j)$ from C into S by non-decreasing order according to their critical scores;
15.   Reset C to empty;
16.   /* if there are 2+ tasks with same $CS(n_i)$, task n_i is randomly pushed into S.
17.   **EndWhile**
End_GCA_List_Phase

Table 2. Earliest Finish Time of tasks in DAG-1 using *GCA* algorithm

Earliest Finish Time of tasks in GCA algorithm									
n_1	n_2	n_3	n_4	n_5	n_6	n_7	n_8	n_9	n_{10}
9	27	42	19.7	32.7	47.6	53	65.7	54.7	84.7

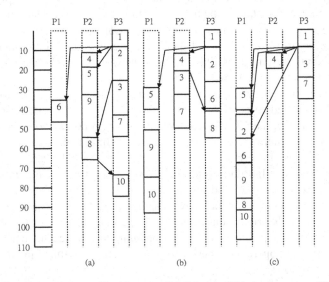

Fig. 2. Schedule results of three algorithms on DAG-1 (a) *GCA* (makespan = 84.7) (b) *CA* (makespan = 92.4) (c) *HEFT* (makespan = 108.2)

In processor-selection phase, tasks will be deployed from list L that obtained in listing phase to suitable processor in FIFO manner. According to the ordered list $L = \{n_1, n_4, n_2, n_5, n_9, n_3, n_7, n_6, n_8, n_{10}\}$, we have the complete calculated $EFTs$ of tasks in DAG-1 and the schedule results of GCA algorithm are listed in Table 2 and Fig. 2(a), respectively.

In order to profile significance of the GCA scheduling technique, the schedule results of other algorithms, CA and $HEFT$ are depicted in Fig. 2(b) and 2(c), respectively. The GCA scheduling techniques incorporates the consideration of heterogeneous communication costs among processors in processor selection phase. Such enhancement facilitates the selection of best candidate of processors to execute specific tasks.

5 Performance Evaluation

5.1 Random Graph Generator

We implemented a Random Graph Generator (RGG) to simulate application graphs with various characteristics. RGG uses the following input parameters to produce diverse graphs.

- Weight of graph (*weight*), which is a constant = {32, 128, 512, 1024}.
- Number of tasks in the graph (n), where n = {20, 40, 60, 80, 100}.
- Graph parallelism (p), the graph parallelism determines shape of a graph. p is assigned for 0.5, 1.0 and 2.0. The level of graph is defined as $\lfloor \sqrt{v} / p \rfloor$. For example, graph with $p = 2.0$ has higher parallelism than graph with $p = 1.0$.
- Out degree of a task (d), where d = {1, 2, 3, 4, 5}. The out degree of a task indicates relationship with other tasks, the larger degree of a task the higher task dependence.
- Heterogeneity (h), determines computational cost of task n_i executed on processor P_k, i.e., $w_{i,k}$, which is randomly generated by the following formula.

$$w_i \times \left(1 - \frac{h}{2}\right) \leq w_{i,k} \leq w_i \times \left(1 + \frac{h}{2}\right). \tag{10}$$

RGG randomizes w_i from the interval [1, *weight*]. Note that larger value of *weight* represents the estimation is with higher precision. In our simulation, h was assigned by 0.1, 0.25, 0.5, 0.75 and 1.0.

- Communication to Computation Ratio (CCR), where CCR = {0.1, 0.5, 1, 2, 10}.

5.2 Comparison Metrics

As mentioned earlier, the objective of DAG scheduling problem is to minimize the completion time of an application. To verify the performance of a scheduling algorithm, several comparative metrics are given below for comparison:

- *Makespan*, also known as schedule length, which is defined as follows,

$$Makespan = \max(EFT(n_{exit})) \tag{11}$$

- *Speedup*, defined as following equation,

$$Speedup = \frac{\min_{P_j \in M}\{\sum_{n_i \in V} w_{i,j}\}}{makespan}, \text{ where } M \text{ is the set of processors} \quad (12)$$

The numerator is the minimal accumulated sum of computation cost of tasks which are assigned on one processor. Equation (12) represents the ratio of sequential execution time to parallel execution time.

- Percentage of Quality of Schedules (PQS)

The percentage of the *GCA* algorithm produces better, equal and worse quality of schedules compared to other algorithms.

5.3 Simulation Results

The first evaluation aims to demonstrate the merit of the *GCA* algorithm by showing quality of schedules using RGG. Simulation results were obtained upon different parameters with totally 1875 DAGs. Fig. 3 reports the comparison by setting different *weight* = {32, 128, 512, 1024}. The term "Better" represents percentage of testing samples the *GCA* algorithm outperforms the *CA* algorithm. The term "Equal" represents both algorithm have same makespan in a given DAG. The tem "Worse" represents opposite results to the "Better" cases. Fig. 4 gives the PQS results by setting different number of processors. Overall, the *GCA* scheduling algorithm presents superior performance for 65% test samples.

Speedup of the *GCA*, *CA* and *HEFT* algorithms to execute 1875 DAGs with fix processor number (*P*=16) under different number of task (*n*) are shown in Fig. 5. The speedup of these algorithms show placid when number of task is small and increased significantly when number of tasks becomes large. In general, the *GCA* algorithm has better speedup than the other two algorithms. Improvement rate of the *GCA* algorithm in terms of average speedup is about 7% to the *CA* algorithm and 34% to the *HEFT* algorithm. The improvement rate (IR$_{GCA}$) is estimated by the following equation:

$$IR_{GCA} = \frac{\sum Speedup(GCA) - \sum Speedup(HEFT \text{ or } CA)}{\sum Speedup(HEFT \text{ or } CA)} \quad (13)$$

weight	32	128	512	1024
Better	65.33%	61.13%	67.07%	67.47%
Equal	34.40%	38.87%	32.93%	32.53%
Worse	0.27%	0%	0%	0%

processor	5	6	7	8
Better	61.13%	72.33%	63.27%	66.60%
Equal	38.87%	27.67%	36.73%	33.40%
Worse	0%	0%	0%	0%

Fig. 3. PQS: *GCA* compared with CA (3 processors)

Fig. 4. PQS: *GCA* compared with *CA* (*weight* = 128)

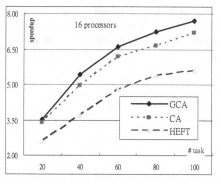
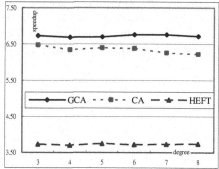

Fig. 5. Speedup of *GCA*, *CA* and *HEFT* with different number of tasks (*n*)

Fig. 6. Speedup of *GCA*, *CA* and *HEFT* with different out-degree of tasks (*d*)

Speedup of the *GCA*, *CA* and *HEFT* algorithms to execute different DAGs with fix processor number (P=16) and task number (n=60) under different out-degree of tasks (*d*) are shown in Fig. 6. The results of Fig. 6 demonstrate the speedup influence by task dependence. We observe that speedups of scheduling algorithms are less dependent on tasks' dependence. Although the speedups of three algorithms are stable, the *GCA* algorithm outperforms the other two algorithms in most cases. Improvement rate of the *GCA* algorithm in terms of average speedup is about 5% to the *CA* algorithm and 80% to the *HEFT* algorithm.

Fig. 7 shows simulation results of three algorithms upon different processor number and degree of parallelization. It is noticed that, graphs with larger value of *p* tends to with higher parallelism. As shown in Fig. 7(a) and (b), the *GCA* algorithm performs well in linear graphs (p=0.5) and general graphs (p=1.0). On the contrary, Fig. 7(c) shows that the *HEFT* scheduling algorithm has superior performance when degree of parallelism is high. In general, for graphs with low parallelism (e.g., $p = 0.5$), the *GCA* algorithm has 33% improvement rate in terms of average speedup compare to the *HEFT* algorithm; for graphs with normal parallelism (e.g., $p = 1$), the *GCA* algorithm has 20% improvement rate. For graphs with high parallelism (e.g., $p = 2$), the *GCA* algorithm performs worse than the *HEFT* by 3% performance.

Speedup of the *GCA*, *CA* and *HEFT* algorithms to execute different DAGs with fix processor number (P=16) and task number (n=60) under different out-degree of tasks (*d*) are shown in Fig. 6. The results of Fig. 6 demonstrate the speedup influence by task dependence. We observe that speedups of scheduling algorithms are less dependent on tasks' dependence. Although the speedups of three algorithms are stable, the *GCA* algorithm outperforms the other two algorithms in most cases. Improvement rate of the *GCA* algorithm in terms of average speedup is about 5% to the *CA* algorithm and 80% to the *HEFT* algorithm.

The impact of communication overheads on speedup are plotted in Fig. 8 by setting different value of *CCR*. It is noticed that increase of *CCR* will downgrade the speedup we can obtained. For example, speedup offered by $CCR = 0.1$ has maximal value 8.3 in *GCA* with 12 processors; for $CCR = 1.0$, the *GCA* algorithm has maximal speedup 6.1

when processor number is 12; and the same algorithm, *GCA*, has maximal speedup 3.1 for *CCR* = 5 with 12 processors. This is due to the fact that when communication overheads higher than computational overheads, costs for tasks migration will offset the benefit of moving tasks to faster processors.

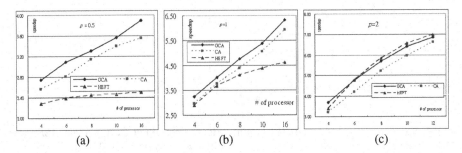

Fig. 7. Speedup with different degree of parallelism (*p*) (a) *p* = 0.5 (b) *p* = 1 (c) *p* = 2

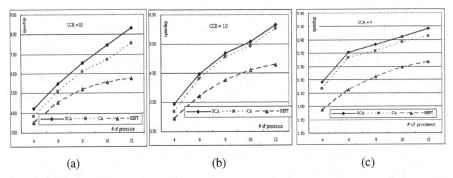

Fig. 8. Speedup results with different *CCR* (a) *CCR*=0.5 (b) *CCR* = 1 (c) *CCR* = 5

6 Conclusion

The problem of scheduling a weighted directed acyclic graph (DAG) to a set of heterogeneous processors to minimize the completion time has been recently studied. Several techniques have been presented in the literature to improve performance. This paper presented a general Critical-task Anticipation (*GCA*) algorithm for DAG scheduling system. The *GCA* scheduling algorithm employs task prioritizing technique based on *CA* algorithm and introduces a new processor selection scheme by considering heterogeneous communication costs among processors. *GCA* scheduling algorithm is a list scheduling approach with simple data structure and profitable for grid and scalable computing. Experimental results show that *GCA* has superior performance compare to the well known *HEFT* scheduling heuristic algorithm and our previous proposed *CA* algorithm which did not incorporate the consideration of heterogeneous communication costs into processor selection phase. Experimental results show that *GCA* is equal or superior to *HEFT* and *CA* scheduling algorithms in most cases and it enhances to fit more real grid system.

Acknowledgements

This paper is based upon work supported by National Science Council (NSC), Taiwan, under grants no. NSC95-2213-E-216-006. Any opinions, findings, and conclusions or recommendations expressed in this material are those of the authors and do not necessarily reflect the views of the NSC.

References

[1] Bajaj, R., Agrawal, D.P.: Improving Scheduling of Tasks in a Heterogeneous Environment. IEEE Trans. on PDS 15(2), 107–118 (2004)

[2] Behrooz, S., Wang, M., Pathak, G.: Analysis and Evaluation of Heuristic Methods for Static Task Scheduling. Jounal of Parallel and Distributed Computing 10, 222–232 (1990)

[3] Gary, M.R., Johnson, D.S.: Computers and Interactability: A guide to the Theory of NP-Completeness. W.H. Freeman and Co (1979)

[4] Hagras, T., Janecek, J.: A High Performance, Low Complexity Algorithm for Compile-Time Task Scheduling in Heterogeneous Systems. Parallel Computing 31(7), 653–670 (2005)

[5] Hsu, C.-H., Weng, M.-Y.: An Improving Critical-Task Anticipation Scheduling Algorithm for Heterogeneous Computing Systems. In: Jesshope, C., Egan, C. (eds.) ACSAC 2006. LNCS, vol. 4186, pp. 97–110. Springer, Heidelberg (2006)

[6] Ilavarasan, E., Thambidurai, P., Mahilmannan, R.: Performance Effective Task Scheduling Algorithm for Heterogeneous Computing System. In: IEEE Proceedings of IPDPS, pp. 28–38 (2005)

[7] Ranaweera, S., Agrawal, D.P.: A Task Duplication Based Scheduling Algorithm for Heterogeneous Systems. In: IEEE Proceedings of IPDPS, pp. 445–450 (2000)

[8] Sakellariou, R., Zhao, H.: A Hybrid Heuristic for DAG Scheduling on Heterogeneous Systems. In: Proc. of the IEEE IPDPS Workshop 1 (2004)

[9] Topcuoglu, H., Hariri, S., Min-You, W.: Performance-Effective and Low-Complexity Task Scheduling for Heterogeneous Computing. IEEE Transactions on PDS 13(3), 260–274 (2002)

Author Index

Lecture Notes in Computer Science

For information about Vols. 1–4430

please contact your bookseller or Springer

Vol. 4488: Y. Shi, G.D. van Albada, J. Dongarra, P.M.A. Sloot (Eds.), Computational Science – ICCS 2007, Part II. XXXV, 1251 pages. 2007.

Vol. 4487: Y. Shi, G.D. van Albada, J. Dongarra, P.M.A. Sloot (Eds.), Computational Science – ICCS 2007, Part I. LXXXI, 1275 pages. 2007.

Vol. 4486: M. Bernardo, J. Hillston (Eds.), Formal Methods for Performance Evaluation. VII, 469 pages. 2007.

Vol. 4485: F. Sgallari, A. Murli, N. Paragios (Eds.), Scale Space and Variational Methods in Computer Vision. XV, 931 pages. 2007.

Vol. 4484: J.-Y. Cai, S.B. Cooper, H. Zhu (Eds.), Theory and Applications of Models of Computation. XIII, 772 pages. 2007.

Vol. 4483: C. Baral, G. Brewka, J. Schlipf (Eds.), Logic Programming and Nonmonotonic Reasoning. IX, 327 pages. 2007. (Sublibrary LNAI).

Vol. 4482: A. An, J. Stefanowski, S. Ramanna, C.J. Butz, W. Pedrycz, G. Wang (Eds.), Rough Sets, Fuzzy Sets, Data Mining and Granular Computing. XIV, 585 pages. 2007. (Sublibrary LNAI).

Vol. 4481: J. Yao, P. Lingras, W.-Z. Wu, M. Szczuka, N.J. Cercone, D. Ślęzak (Eds.), Rough Sets and Knowledge Technology. XIV, 576 pages. 2007. (Sublibrary LNAI).

Vol. 4480: A. LaMarca, M. Langheinrich, K.N. Truong (Eds.), Pervasive Computing. XIII, 369 pages. 2007.

Vol. 4479: I.F. Akyildiz, R. Sivakumar, E. Ekici, J.C.d. Oliveira, J. McNair (Eds.), NETWORKING 2007. Ad Hoc and Sensor Networks, Wireless Networks, Next Generation Internet. XXVII, 1252 pages. 2007.

Vol. 4478: J. Martí, J.M. Benedí, A.M. Mendonça, J. Serrat (Eds.), Pattern Recognition and Image Analysis, Part II. XXVII, 657 pages. 2007.

Vol. 4477: J. Martí, J.M. Benedí, A.M. Mendonça, J. Serrat (Eds.), Pattern Recognition and Image Analysis, Part I. XXVII, 625 pages. 2007.

Vol. 4476: V. Gorodetsky, C. Zhang, V.A. Skormin, L. Cao (Eds.), Autonomous Intelligent Systems: Multi-Agents and Data Mining. XIII, 323 pages. 2007. (Sublibrary LNAI).

Vol. 4475: P. Crescenzi, G. Prencipe, G. Pucci (Eds.), Fun with Algorithms. X, 273 pages. 2007.

Vol. 4474: G. Prencipe, S. Zaks (Eds.), Structural Information and Communication Complexity. XI, 342 pages. 2007.

Vol. 4472: M. Haindl, J. Kittler, F. Roli (Eds.), Multiple Classifier Systems. XI, 524 pages. 2007.

Vol. 4471: P. Cesar, K. Chorianopoulos, J.F. Jensen (Eds.), Interactive TV: a Shared Experience. XIII, 236 pages. 2007.

Vol. 4470: Q. Wang, D. Pfahl, D.M. Raffo (Eds.), Software Process Dynamics and Agility. XI, 346 pages. 2007.

Vol. 4468: M.M. Bonsangue, E.B. Johnsen (Eds.), Formal Methods for Open Object-Based Distributed Systems. X, 317 pages. 2007.

Vol. 4467: A.L. Murphy, J. Vitek (Eds.), Coordination Models and Languages. X, 325 pages. 2007.

Vol. 4466: F.B. Sachse, G. Seemann (Eds.), Functional Imaging and Modeling of the Heart. XV, 486 pages. 2007.

Vol. 4465: T. Chahed, B. Tuffin (Eds.), Network Control and Optimization. XIII, 305 pages. 2007.

Vol. 4464: E. Dawson, D.S. Wong (Eds.), Information Security Practice and Experience. XIII, 361 pages. 2007.

Vol. 4463: I. Măndoiu, A. Zelikovsky (Eds.), Bioinformatics Research and Applications. XV, 653 pages. 2007. (Sublibrary LNBI).

Vol. 4462: D. Sauveron, K. Markantonakis, A. Bilas, J.-J. Quisquater (Eds.), Information Security Theory and Practices. XII, 255 pages. 2007.

Vol. 4459: C. Cérin, K.-C. Li (Eds.), Advances in Grid and Pervasive Computing. XVI, 759 pages. 2007.

Vol. 4453: T. Speed, H. Huang (Eds.), Research in Computational Molecular Biology. XVI, 550 pages. 2007. (Sublibrary LNBI).

Vol. 4452: M. Fasli, O. Shehory (Eds.), Agent-Mediated Electronic Commerce. VIII, 249 pages. 2007. (Sublibrary LNAI).

Vol. 4451: T.S. Huang, A. Nijholt, M. Pantic, A. Pentland (Eds.), Artifical Intelligence for Human Computing. XVI, 359 pages. 2007. (Sublibrary LNAI).

Vol. 4450: T. Okamoto, X. Wang (Eds.), Public Key Cryptography – PKC 2007. XIII, 491 pages. 2007.

Vol. 4448: M. Giacobini et al. (Ed.), Applications of Evolutionary Computing. XXIII, 755 pages. 2007.

Vol. 4447: E. Marchiori, J.H. Moore, J.C. Rajapakse (Eds.), Evolutionary Computation, Machine Learning and Data Mining in Bioinformatics. XI, 302 pages. 2007.

Vol. 4446: C. Cotta, J. van Hemert (Eds.), Evolutionary Computation in Combinatorial Optimization. XII, 241 pages. 2007.

Vol. 4445: M. Ebner, M. O'Neill, A. Ekárt, L. Vanneschi, A.I. Esparcia-Alcázar (Eds.), Genetic Programming. XI, 382 pages. 2007.

Vol. 4444: T. Reps, M. Sagiv, J. Bauer (Eds.), Program Analysis and Compilation, Theory and Practice. X, 361 pages. 2007.

Vol. 4443: R. Kotagiri, P.R. Krishna, M. Mohania, E. Nantajeewarawat (Eds.), Advances in Databases: Concepts, Systems and Applications. XXI, 1126 pages. 2007.

Vol. 4440: B. Liblit, Cooperative Bug Isolation. XV, 101 pages. 2007.

Vol. 4439: W. Abramowicz (Ed.), Business Information Systems. XV, 654 pages. 2007.

Vol. 4438: L. Maicher, A. Sigel, L.M. Garshol (Eds.), Leveraging the Semantics of Topic Maps. X, 257 pages. 2007. (Sublibrary LNAI).

Vol. 4433: E. Şahin, W.M. Spears, A.F.T. Winfield (Eds.), Swarm Robotics. XII, 221 pages. 2007.

Vol. 4432: B. Beliczynski, A. Dzielinski, M. Iwanowski, B. Ribeiro (Eds.), Adaptive and Natural Computing Algorithms, Part II. XXVI, 761 pages. 2007.

Vol. 4431: B. Beliczynski, A. Dzielinski, M. Iwanowski, B. Ribeiro (Eds.), Adaptive and Natural Computing Algorithms, Part I. XXV, 851 pages. 2007.